M

As

Co

P.O. Box 35077

Greensboro, NC 27425–5077

ISBN 1–56109-099-9

This publication is funded in part by the U.S. Department of Education, Office of Educational Research and Improvement, Contract No. ED-99-CO-0014. Opinions expressed in this publication do not necessarily reflect the positions of the U.S. Department of Education, OERI, or ERIC/CASS.

CASS

ERIC

Educational Resources Information Center

Contents

Section B. Assessment Issues for Special Populations and Audiences

Section C. Special Topics and Issues in Assessment

Section E. Resources On Assessment

Preface

Measuring Up: Assessment Issues for Teachers, Counselors, and Administrators was created especially for K-12 educators. Testing and assessment and their use in education, accountability, and educational reform are not new issues to educators, but the associated pressures and politics surrounding those issues are escalating, not diminishing. Educators are being called upon to clearly establish their effectiveness. Employers, disappointed with the products of the educational system, are demanding more performance and higher skills. The public expects schools to document that they are delivering quality programs to ***all*** students.

Tests are routinely called upon to provide the necessary information to address those expectations. In fact, the passing the recent landmark national legislation on education and testing, referred to as the *No Child Left Behind Act*, is intensifying pressure on the educational community to use tests in the documentation of student progress and establishment of school quality and productivity. Similarly, students are expected to show adequate progress and the assimilation of skills through tests and other assessments. Along with this increase in pressure is the general concern, being voiced ever so loudly, over acceptable and responsible test use, the negative and counterproductive effects of testing and standards on the behavior of students and teachers, and the potential of over-reliance on tests for accountability with a disregard for the special and individual attributes of children. So far the opposing forces have made little meaningful noise in the dialogue. Once the consequences of the testing programs become clear, the quiet will dissipate to make room for criticism, consternation, and legal actions.

Despite the vibrations of a backlash, a recent survey indicates broad public support for the standards movement and associated assessments. Among the findings from a survey of students parents, and teachers include:

- Even as students nationwide face more testing and higher hurdles for promotion and graduation, very few seem apprehensive about school or unnerved by what is currently being asked of them.
- Even as standards are being raised nationwide, many students say they could work harder in school, and many classmates often get diplomas without having learned what was expected.
- Broad agreement exists that local schools are moving in the

right direction on standards, and that testing has genuine benefits. No evidence points to a broad backlash against higher academic standards among any of the groups surveyed.

- Employers and professors still say that too many of today's high school graduates lack basic skills, although both groups continue to give young people high marks on computer skills.

Education Week, March 6, 2002, Public Agenda, Reality Check 2002.

The reported backlash is apparently, at least at this point, feeble and ineffectual. Given the importance and pivotal role of assessment in the practice of education, it is surprising that only 14 states require competence in assessment for teacher certification and only three require it to become a principal. Generally, assessment concepts are not given a high priority in the components and requirements of educator preparation programs. It is difficult to fathom that educator preparation programs are not more responsive to the needs of their clients.

Assessment and testing will not go away no matter how passionately one wishes it to because tests are inextricably intertwined with accountability and the implementation of high standards intimately associated with education reform. Since assessment will continue to play a prominent role in shaping the practices of educators and in the lives of students and parents, it is incumbent upon educators to understand testing concepts, how tests should and should not be used, how test results should be used and interpreted, and the issues related to conditions and situations in which tests are used and with whom they are used.

Measuring Up: Assessment Issues for Teachers, Counselors, and Administrators attempts to promote improved understanding of assessment concepts by addressing the broad expanse of issues facing educators as they go about their duties and fulfill their responsibilities in schools and classrooms.

This book can be used as the primary textbook in educational assessment classes or as a supplement to more technical course in assessment in educator preparation programs. Educators can also use the book as a self-help resource to learn about basic concepts and special challenges in educational assessment and testing. This book could also help school board members and state legislators better understand the complexities of assessment issues in education. In any case, the chapters in this book address some of the "hot button" issues related to testing and assessment in our nation's schools, as well as providing a basic understanding of testing concepts. The chapters are non-technical and issue oriented.

Our Authors

The strength and effectiveness of this book emanates from the chapter authors. Readers of this volume are indeed fortunate that so many capable and talented assessment professionals have contributed to this compendium. Reviewing the brief biographies presented in the next section quickly demonstrates that the authors have extensive experience in dealing with assessment on both practical and theoretical levels. As a group they represent hundreds of years of work in researching assessment topics and/or applying good testing practices in their work setting. Authors include university professors, researchers, school and school district testing professionals, individuals in private practice, test developers, individuals associated with test preparation companies, government representatives, and representatives of professional associations. They write about topics as diverse as early childhood assessment through college course placement and admission, from individual test taker rights to large-scale national assessment programs, and from using assessment with special populations to envisioning the future of assessment. We, as editors, are grateful for their willingness to share their expertise in this book and are humbled by their contributions. It is clear that the authors have made purposeful and methodical efforts to convey the information in a clear, understandable, and comprehensive way. We are immensely excited, honored, and proud to include their contributions and hope that the authors are equally pleased to be associated with this compendium and the contributions of their colleagues.

Organization

The book is organized as follows:

A. The Basics of Testing
B. Assessment Issues for Special Populations and Audiences
C. Special Topics and Issues in Assessment
D. Musing Philosophical and Looking Toward the Future
E. Resources on Assessment

As part of the resource section, a special CD is enclosed as a supplement to this book. It includes a comprehensive set of professional ethics statements and standards and major publications on testing concepts and test use.

Section A: The Basics of Testing

This section provides a grounding or refresher in basic testing concepts in a non-technical way. **Fremer** and **Wall** outline the reasons assessments are used in the education community motivated by the many information needs that can be satisfied by tests.

Vansickle addresses the various types of tests that can be useful to the education community and the information that can be gained from them while **McDivitt and Gibson** provide guidelines for selecting tests appropriate to the needs of the student population and requirements of the school. **Harris** highlights important concepts involved in understanding, reporting, and interpreting various types of test scores. Concluding the first section, **Schafer** outlines aspects important to test taker rights and responsibilities.

The format for the first section closely parallels the new *Code of Fair Testing Practices in Education* (JCTP, 2002). This publication, based upon a more technical work, *Standards for Educational and Psychological Testing* (American Educational Research Association, American Psychological Association, National Council on Measurement in Education, 1999), provides guidelines for educators and test developers as they make decisions about tests and assessments as they are developed and selected for use in the school setting. The *Code* attempts to provide testing guidelines in user-friendly language that can be understood easily by educators, parents, and test takers. The *Code* specifies those guidelines for two audiences – test developers and test users and it can be found in its entirety on the supplementary CD.

Section B: Assessment Issues for Special Populations and Audiences

The second section of the book deals with testing fairness, test bias, and the assessment of specific populations of students including students with disabilities, students from various cultural backgrounds, and specific needs of various audiences such as young children and the college bound.

Helms opens this section with a discourse on fair and valid uses of assessment in the K-12 environment. **Ellis and Raju** provide a definition of test bias and mechanisms for its detection and elimination. **Hartmann, McDaniel, and Whetzel** offer a comprehensive summary of group level results when looking at test result outcomes by race, gender, and ethnic group on assessment of interests and cognitive ability. By way of expanding on the concept of assessment differences, **Lundberg and Kirk** caution educators to consider the variety of issues involved in using and interpreting assessment results in view of our increasingly diverse, multicultural society. **Goldsmith** describes the variety of considerations and cautions relating to the translation of tests from one language to another, while **Geisinger** discusses the special assessment concepts that must be considered for students with limited English proficiency, an increasingly important issue given the increase in diversity in the school population.

As it relates to students with disabilities, **Thurlow and Thompson** discuss the broad issue of including special needs students in state and district large-scale assessment programs while **Elliott** describes the conditions and challenges of assessing special needs students from a practitioner point of view. In these chapters, the use of test accommodations and modifications are addressed within the context of assuring educational progress toward standards for all students.

Hansen and Conlon offer comprehensive information in two areas: clinical assessment and counseling assessment. They review the various issues involved in working with students with mental health, behavioral, and counseling issues and offer assessment instruments that could be of assistance to educators.

Cashwell and Watts continue the theme of assisting students with academic, behavioral, and/or emotional problems through data collection techniques involving the family and other than family relationships. **Juhnke and Hagedorn** provide a specific tool that educators can use to determine the severity of alcohol and other drug abuse and the problems that can result. Possible interventions can be identified by scoring the instrument according to a suggested rubric. Tackling the issue of test anxiety, **Goonan** provides descriptions, outcomes, and interventions that can be implemented to help students perform their best on educational assessments, especially those with important, high-stakes outcomes.

Assessment of very young children is the topic of **Guddemi's** chapter. She outlines the special nature of assessment for children in the very early grades and the variety of ways that educators can assess children's learning progress.

Noble and Camera reflect on various issues relating to the use of tests for college entrance to include the use of multiple factors in the college admissions process. They raise issues about the recent call by some educators to use statewide achievement tests for college admissions. Continuing with the theme of assessment in preparation for higher education, **Noble, Scheil, and Sawyer** describe the important issues involved in testing in one specialized area: college course placement. They discuss the need for students to have access to assessments that place them appropriately in remedial, regular, and honors courses. They close by outlining some technical issues related to course placement, and the availability and evaluation of course placement systems.

This section is completed by **Laurence** who discusses a program that has the dual purpose of assisting students with career exploration and assisting the military in identifying youth with the aptitudinal qualities necessary for selection into the military.

Section C: Special Topics and Issues in Assessment

Testing and assessment has a long history of involvement in the educational process. Through various educational reform movements, testing has played a key role. As a result, tests and assessment are replete with side issues, challenges, and pressures. Topics including ethics, test preparation, cheating, the qualifications of test users, proper test use, and reporting test information to particular audiences are noteworthy issues discussed in this section.

Kean opens this section by discussing accountability and the role that politics plays in educational reform and assessment. **Behuniak** expands on educational reform issues by discussing the historical progress of school accountability and the changing emphasis on achievement testing. He provides advice to educators in conducting useful and constructive testing situations.

Nellor Wickwire admonishes educators to be cognizant of the various ethics statements, codes and guidelines of professional organizations with respect to assessment practices. This chapter is followed by **Cizek's** account of cheating on tests and what might be done to prevent inappropriate behavior and practices. **Perlman** tackles the issue of ethical test preparation practices by educators from a school district and practitioner's perspective, while **Rubenstein** outlines issues surrounding test preparation courses and their effectiveness.

Camera discusses the *Standards for Educational and Psychological Testing* by extracting those portions of the standards that are pertinent to good testing practices by educators and offering those standards as an important framework for test evaluation, proper use of tests results, and the testing process as a whole.

As educators become more involved in test development of high stakes tests, **McDivitt** outlines issues involved in working with educators to construct tests that meet particular standards and objectives. She specifies the kinds of skills needed by educators to create solid tests that measure what is desired. Though her chapter focuses on larger-scale assessment programs, the guidelines offered are useful for classroom assessment as well. The theme of improving educator skills is further expanded by **Elmore and Ekstrom** who address specific assessment competencies expected of counselors. **Clawsen and Schweiger** deal with the issues of fair access to tests by school personnel, basing their comments on the needed competencies of test users.

Several authors address the issue of using assessment information in support of instruction and the curriculum. **Arter** addresses the important tie between assessment and classroom learning. She makes a distinction between assessment of learning (summative evaluation) and assessment for learning (formative evaluation). **Krug** supports the use of tests as an objective verification of the learning process and attainment of educational standards indicating that without tests we can only presume learning occurs. **Perlman** specifically address the concepts and issues surrounding performance assessment, the scoring rubrics surrounding this type of test, and the utility of this assessment technique for determining student attainment of skills. **Carlson** ponders the relationship of assessment and grading and suggests various techniques that can be utilized by educators in the evaluation of student progress. The chapter prepared by **Erford and Moore-Thomas** suggests that program and outcomes evaluations are additional and alternative ways in which educators can determine program quality and accountability.

Gibson writes of the importance of working with students and parents in helping them understand their test results and what the results mean to them on a personal level. She claims that interpreting test results can be thought of as part of the educational intervention process. **Erford and Moore-Thomas** discuss what parents want to know and should know about testing while **Roeber** takes a broader view by outlining the importance of reporting test results to the variety of target audiences including students, parents, school boards, teachers, and the general public, why it is important to attended to the needs of each of these stakeholder groups, and how it could be done.

Focusing on the theme of assessment in for the world of work, **Harrington and Feller** engage in a discourse on the use of various assessments in promoting career development by youth. They discuss the place of interest and cognitive assessment in career exploration, computerized career development systems, and the use of videos. Following on that theme, **Lewis and Rivkin** discuss the use of three new assessment instruments that have been created for use in career exploration and workforce development. These instruments have been designed to promote whole person assessment and involve interests, abilities and workplace values. **Hansen and Sullivan** tackle the issue of workplace stress in education occupations, its causes, and instruments that can assist in identifying it. Identifying the causes of stress can suggest procedures and practices to alleviate or cope with the stressful conditions.

Section D: Musing Philosophical and Looking Toward the Future

Harris opens this section by discussing the future of educational assessment, its promises and criticisms, through the specification of the critical role that test publishers will play in educational reform and school accountability. His chapter highlights many of the "hot button" issues in educational assessment, including high-stakes testing, standards-based reform, closing the achievement gap among groups of students, and the use of new technologies in testing. **Hansen** ponders the future of assessment in the education and counseling settings from the broad brush and philosophical perspective, while **Elman** provides a vision on similar issues from the school district and practitioner perspective. Recognizing the increased use of technology in educational assessment, **Wall** offers an overview of issues related to technology-delivered assessment and provides guidelines to educators on using technology in appropriate ways to enhance the testing/learning process. Describing one of the most important uses of technology, **Sireci** provides a primer on computer adaptive testing issues and its utility in educational testing. Using computer adaptive testing is a growing trend in educational measurement. Remaining with the theme of technology **Ciavarelli** outlines critical issues related to the accessibility and assessment of the quality of online learning, a practice that is growing in popularity even in K-12 education.

Moore-Thomas and Erford suggest frequent and focused needs assessment in judging educational programs. They propose that educators can use needs assessment techniques to help plan school improvement initiatives based on data collected from students and other stakeholders. **Wise** reviews the specifics of the National Assessment of Educational Progress (NAEP) and how that information can assist educators in school and curriculum improvements. He describes the various NAEP programs, the contributions that NAEP has made in testing activities and curriculum frameworks, and describes some future modifications and additions to the program that will influence how NAEP could be called upon to document educational gains.

Section E: Resources on Assessment

Because of the importance of testing and assessment in the lives of educators, they must be dogged in the pursuit of new information on testing issues and continuing professional development. This next section provides some practical and useful resources that can help educators take responsibility for their own education in areas relating to educational assessment.

Frumkin discusses the work of the Joint Committee on Testing Practices (JCTP) in creating materials for the education community to assist in the understanding of testing concepts and in promoting appropriate testing practices. Most of the materials produced by this group are available at no or low cost. The JCTP is a group with membership of various professional associations with an interest in proper test understanding and use. **Wall** documents a collection of various websites with information that includes policy statements, primers, white papers, standards, guidelines, and general descriptive information on tests and assessments. The websites include professional associations, test publishers, general organizations, groups, and services, and selected federal resources.

Supplementary CD-ROM

A unique contribution to this book is the supplementary CD, *Measuring Up: An Anthology of Assessment Resources*. The CD includes nearly 100 documents that provide information and guidance on testing issues. Among the documents are various testing guidelines such as the *Code of Fair Testing Practices in Education*, ethics statements such as those from the National Council on Measurement in Education, and documents such as those on the use of tests and assessments in career development produced by the US Departments of Labor and Education. White papers, guidelines, primers, and position statement from a variety of organizations and individuals are included for use by the reader.

The CD was developed as a data base and is searchable by topic and author. Most of the resources are referenced by the authors, but some are not. It is probable that the Anthology will continue to be developed with new editions offered as justified by the number of new resources added.

Our Invitation

We invite you to read the perspectives on testing and assessment provided in this book. It is a treasure trove of ideas, points of view, and reflections on what assessment is and can be. The contents can serve to educate and provide the basis for discussion and debate. What matters most to us is that those closest to the educational process—teachers, counselors and administrators—understand the various facets involved in educational assessment so that they can better serve the mission before them – to provide an outstanding educational program to all students so that they may excel in life and contribute to society in meaningful and productive ways.

Janet Wall and Garry Walz
January 2003

Introduction

When editors Janet Wall and Garry Walz invited NBCC to be part of a project which would culminate in a book on assessment, we were interested. Then, when we saw the outline and author list, there was no doubt that we wanted to be part of this comprehensive approach to testing in education and counseling.

This edited work of original manuscripts has melded the current thinking of testing into a well-planned array of topics. Moreover, those topics are discussed, explained, and elaborated upon by experts who live the issues and have so much to offer us from their knowledge and experience.

Testing Basics as a book section walks a novice or professional through the process of testing. From discussion of reasons to use a test through selection and administration, the user will understand beneficial reasons, appropriate use and, finally, information on reporting, interpreting and informing the test taker and other stakeholders.

Special Audiences have become a major concern of the testing industry. Design of testing to help identify special needs or distinguish within specialized populations is a broad task to write about. Here we find over twenty chapters devoted to special audiences that are crafted by professionals who are uniquely qualified to speak to us on so many topics.

Special Issues have been arising for decades. Though the breadth is great, again our editors have selected another impressive set of authors who give us current information about very pressing issues of testing. From accountability to computers in testing, the authors fill the pages with today's information.

And tomorrow? Looking Forward allows us prediction on what to expect, what to ask for and what to do with the changes we see. By the end of this section, we should feel grounding in testing, its uses and its issues.

However, the editors didn't stop. They supply us with resources that are simply unparalleled to date. If the appendix is not enough, the CD included with the book is an expansive volume of materials not included in this printed edition. The thoroughness of the edited topics is matched by this one-of-a-kind CD appendix.

NBCC involves itself in projects that promote the profession and continue the education of our 34,000 National Certified Counselors (calculated spring 2003). We continue to advocate for counselors in issues of practice, legislation and education. Since 1996, NBCC has housed the National Fair Access Coalition on Testing (FACT) and has been its primary sponsor. FACT represents over half a million testing practitioners in over twenty professional associations. NBCC's intricate association with the practice of testing, the use of testing, and development of more than ten credentialing examinations has positioned it as a leader in testing. We test counselors, and we advocate for the rights of counselors and other professionals to use tests.

NBCC salutes Janet Wall and Garry Walz for their insight. The vision to create this book, the knowledge of what it should hold for us, and the intricate web of professionals to speak to us on to many topics.

Thomas W. Clawson, Ed.D., NCC
Executive Director, National Board for Certified Counselors, Inc. and Affiliates

About the Editors

Janet E. Wall, EdD, has worked at the federal, state, and school district levels in the areas of assessment, evaluation, and career development. Her work has spanned the public and private sectors, focusing on using assessment results for curricular and instructional improvement and career development. Currently, she is president of the Association for Assessment in Counseling and Education (AACE) and co-chair of the Joint Committee on Testing Practices (JCTP), an organization with representation from seven professional associations. She was an active member of or co-chaired several JCTP working groups, including those that produced the *Code of Fair Testing Practices in Education*, the *ABC's of School Testing* video and leaders guide, *Rights and Responsibilities of Test Takers: Guidelines and Expectations*, and a book on assessment of individuals with disabilities. She chaired the group that revised the *Responsibilities of Users of Standardized Tests* (RUST) and was part of a panel that created the policy statement of the American Counseling Association (ACA) on assessment competencies for counselors. Over her career she has delivered hundreds of assessment-related training sessions and web seminars; made several conference presentations; and written many articles, reports, and monographs, including one for parents on understanding school testing. She can be reached at sagesolutions@earthlink.net.

Garry R. Walz, PhD, NCC, is Co-Director of the ERIC Counseling and Student Services Clearinghouse at the University of North Carolina at Greensboro, North Carolina and professor emeritus of the University of Michigan. He is a past president of the American Counseling Association (ACA) and the Association for Counselor Education and Supervision (ACES) and past chair of the Counseling and Human Development Foundation. He is a recipient of the ACA Gilbert and Kathleen Wrenn Humanitarian Award and the National Career Development Association Eminent Professional Career Award. His numerous books, professional articles, and R & D programs cover a broad array of topics, but in particular focus on counselor education, counselor development, cybercounseling, and knowledge dissemination and utilization. Correspondence should be sent to CAPS, Inc at PO Box 35077, Greensboro, NC 27425.

About the Contributors

Judith A. Arter, PhD, has done everything from developing high school graduation tests to professional development on assessment *for* learning. Her newest book is *Scoring Rubrics in the Classroom: Performance Criteria for Assessing and Improving Student Achievement,* with Jay McTighe (Corwin, 2001). Judy is currently director of program development for the Assessment Training Institute (ATI) in Portland, Oregon. Dr. Arter's background is in mathematics, special education, assessment, and Title 1. She spent two years as a district office staff member in Arizona and 21 years at the Northwest Regional Education Laboratory (NWREL) before coming to ATI. She has held teaching certificates in both elementary education and special education. But, mostly, she has had the privilege to work with many dedicated educators working hard to create a vision of success for students through improved classroom assessment. She can be reached at judyar@assessmentinst.com.

Peter Behuniak, PhD, is an educator and measurement specialist. He has more than 20 years of experience in designing, developing, and implementing large-scale educational assessments. He has been an adviser on assessment programs to 12 states, the U.S. Department of Education, and many other public and private organizations. He has presented to many audiences and published articles in 10 professional journals regarding issues related to educational assessment. Currently on leave from the position he has held for more than 10 years as the director of student assessment and testing for the Connecticut State Department of Education, Behuniak is providing support to organizations involved in large-scale assessment projects as the proprietor of Criterion Consulting. Behuniak earned his doctorate in educational psychology with a specialty in evaluation and measurement from the University of Connecticut. He can be reached at PeterBehuniak@cox.com.

Wayne J. Camara, PhD, is vice president for research and development at the College Board. He is responsible for coordinating and conducting all research and product development associated with the SAT, AP, CLEP, and other tests. Previously, he has served as the assistant executive director of science at the American Psychological Association (APA) and as project director of the revision of the *Standards for Educational and Psychological Testing.* A fellow of the

APA and the Society of Industrial and Organizational Psychology, Camara is past president of the APA Divisions of Evaluation, Measurement, and Statistics. He has appeared frequently in the media and testified before Congress on assessment issues. He can be reached at wcamara@collegeboard.org.

Laurie A. Carlson, PhD, is an assistant professor in the counseling and career development program at Colorado State University. Having earned her doctorate from the University of Arkansas, Carlson is both a national certified counselor and national certified school counselor. A member of Kappa Delta Pi and Chi Sigma Iota International, Carlson serves as faculty advisor for the Chi Sigma chapter at CSU. She has ten years of experience in public schools, five years as an English teacher, one year as a long-term substitute in urban high schools, and four years as a K–12 school counselor in Minnesota. She can be reached at lacarlson@cahs.colostate.edu.

Craig S. Cashwell, PhD, received his doctorate from the University of North Carolina at Greensboro. Having worked as a counselor educator at Mississippi State University for six years, he currently works as a counselor educator at the University of North Carolina at Greensboro. He can be reached at cscashwe@uncg.edu.

Anthony Ciavarelli, EdD, served as associate provost for instruction at the Naval Postgraduate School from 1999 to 2001, where he was responsible for supervising curriculum updates, faculty development, and student academic services. During this time, he spearheaded the school's entry into web-based instruction, preparing a strategic plan and faculty development program for distance learning. Having joined the School of Aviation Safety at the Naval Postgraduate School in June 1989, Ciavarelli is a tenured full professor of psychology. Prior to joining the Naval Postgraduate School, he held senior technical and management positions in the defense industry, where he gained considerable experience as a human factors engineer and research psychologist. He is best known for his research on measuring human performance and organizational safety effectiveness. He holds a doctorate from the University of Southern California, and has a master's of science in experimental psychology from California State University at Los Angeles. He can be reached at aciavarelli@nps.navy.mil.

Gregory J. Cizek, PhD, is professor of educational measurement and evaluation at the University of North Carolina at Chapel Hill. His research interests include standard setting, testing policy, and classroom assessment. He is the author of more than 100 journal articles, book chapters, conference papers, and other publications. His work has been published in *Educational Researcher, Educational Assessment, Review of Educational Research, Journal of Educational Measurement, Educational Measurement: Issues and Practice, Educational Policy, Phi Delta Kappan, Education Week,* and elsewhere. Cizek is a contributor to the *Handbook of Classroom Assessment* (Academic Press, 1998); an editor and a contributor to the *Handbook of Educational Policy* (Academic Press, 1999) and *Setting Performance Standards: Concepts, Methods, and Perspectives* (Lawrence Erlbaum Associates, 2001); and author of *Filling in the Blanks* (Fordham Foundation, 1999) and *Cheating on Tests: How to Do It, Detect It, and Prevent It* (Lawrence Erlbaum Associates, 1999). Cizek received his doctorate in measurement, evaluation, and research design from Michigan State University. He can be reached at cizek@unc.edu.

Thomas Warren Clawson, EdD, NCC, is the executive director of the National Board for Certified Counselors (NBCC) and its affiliates, the Center for Credentialing and Education (CCE) and the Research and Assessment Corporation for Counseling (RACC), located in Greensboro, North Carolina. Clawson recently completed two years as chairman of the National Commission for Certifying Agencies. Prior to joining NBCC in 1989, Clawson held the position of associate professor and department chair with the Boston University Overseas Counseling Program in Heidelberg, Germany. He holds a bachelor of science degree from West Virginia University and three advanced degrees, including an EdD in counseling from the College of William and Mary in Williamsburg, Virginia. He can be reached at nbcc@nbcc.org.

Amy L. Conlon, PhD, recently received her doctorate in counseling psychology from the Department of Psychology at the University of Minnesota. She currently works as a counselor at University Counseling and Consulting Services at the University of Minnesota, where she assists undergraduate and graduate students with personal, career, and academic skills issues. Previously she was coordinator of the University's Vocational Assessment Clinic in the Department of Psychology. She can be reached at ACONLON@mn.rr.com.

Ruth B. Ekstrom, PhD, recently retired as a senior associate in the Center for Higher Education Research at Educational Testing Service. She holds a bachelor's degree in psychology from Brown University, a master's degree in educational research and measurement from Boston University, and a doctorate in educational psychology from Rutgers University. Ekstrom has served as co-chair of the Joint Committee on Testing Practices (JCTP), as a member of the APA Committee on Psychological Tests and Assessment, and as a member of the AERA Publications Committee. In addition, she has served on the editorial boards of the *Psychology of Women Quarterly* and the *Journal of Counseling and Development,* and currently serves on the editorial board of *Measurement and Evaluation in Counseling and Development.* In 1994 she was the recipient, with Patricia B. Elmore and Esther E. Diamond, of the ACA Research Award; in 1996 she received the ACA Extended Research Award for her career accomplishments. The author or coauthor of more than 18 book chapters and more than 25 articles in professional journals, Ekstrom is coeditor, with Douglas Smith, of *Assessing Individuals with Disabilities* (APA, 2002) and coauthor, with Margaret Goertz and Donald Rock, of *Education and American Youth* (Falmer Press, 1998). She can be reached at rekstrom@ets.org.

Judy Elliott, PhD, is currently the assistant superintendent of special education in the Long Beach Unified School District, Long Beach, California. Formerly a senior researcher at the National Center on Educational Outcomes (NCEO), she assisted and continues to assist districts and state departments of education in their efforts to update and realign curriculum frameworks, instruction, and assessments to include all students. Her research interests focus on effective instruction; IEP development and its alignment with standards and assessments; decision making for accountability, accommodation, and assessment; and translating information on standards and assessments for various audiences, including parents, teachers, school boards, and other community groups. Dr. Elliott continues to serve as a national consultant and staff development professional to school districts and organizations. Some of her most recent copublished books are *Improving the Test Performance of Students with Disabilities* (Corwin, 2000); *Testing Students with Disabilities: Practical Strategies for Complying with State* *and District Requirements* (Corwin, 2003); *Strategies and Tactics for Effective Instruction* (Sopris West, 1997); and *Timesavers for Educators* (Sopris West, 1997). She can be reached at jelliott@lbusd.k12.ca.us.

Barbara B. Ellis, PhD, is an associate professor of industrial and organizational psychology at the University of Houston. Her research interests are in psychometrics and test development, especially in the application of item response theory to assess the measurement equivalence of translated tests. A member of APA's Division 5 (Evaluation, Measurement, and Statistics) and Division 14 (Society for Industrial and Organizational Psychology), Ellis also belongs to NCME and the Academy of Management. She is a consulting editor for the *International Journal of Testing,* and her work has appeared in journals such as the *Journal of Applied Psychology*, *Educational and Psychological Measurement*, and the *Journal of Cross-Cultural Psychology*. She can be reached at bellis@un.edu.

Linda Elman, PhD, is the director of research and evaluation in the Central Kitsap School District in Silverdale, Washington. Prior to her job in Central Kitsap she spent 12 years as a coordinator of research and evaluation in the Tacoma Public Schools in Tacoma, Washington. She has been active in state and national organizations and serves on the state-level Technical Advisory Committee for Assessment. She has been president of the Washington Educational Research Association, the National Association of Test Directors (NATD), and is active on committees for Division H of the American Educational Research Association (AERA) and the National Council for Measurement in Education (NCME). Elman attended Stanford University and graduated,with a bachelor's degree in history, from Barnard College. She earned a master's degree in teaching social studies from Teachers College. In 1990 she received her doctorate in evaluation and measurement from Kent State University. She can be reached at LindaE@cksd@wednet.edu.

Patricia B. Elmore, PhD, is associate dean in the College of Education and Human Services and professor in the Department of Educational Psychology and Special Education at Southern Illinois University Carbondale (SIUC). She is a past president of the Association for Assessment in Counseling (AAC) and the 1994 recipient, with Ruth B. Ekstrom and Esther E. Diamond, of the American Counseling Association Research Award. In addition to being editor of *Measurement* *and Evaluation in Counseling and Development*, she serves on the editorial boards of *Applied Measurement in Education* and *Educational and Psychological Measurement* and chairs the American Educational Research Association (AERA) Professional Development and Training Committee. Elmore has published in *Educational and Psychological Measurement*, *Educational Researcher*, *Journal of Educational Psychology*, *Journal of Educational Measurement*, *Measurement and Evaluation in Counseling and Development*, *Journal for Research in Mathematics Education*, and *School Counselor,* among other journals. Her book *Basic Statistics* with Paula L. Woehlke was published by Addison Wesley Longman in 1997. She can be reached at pbelmore@siu.edu.

Bradley T. Erford, PhD, president of Counseling Innovations, Inc., is an associate professor of education in the School Counseling Program at Loyola College in Maryland and the 2001 recipient of the Maryland Counselor of the Year and MACD Counselor Advocacy Award. His research specialization falls in development and technical analysis of psychoeducational tests and has resulted in numerous journal articles and six published tests to his credit. He is chair of the American Counseling Association–Southern (U.S.) Region, as well as past president of the Maryland ACD, Maryland ACES, and Maryland AMHC. He was recently elected as president-elect of the Association for Assessment in Counseling. He can be reached at berford@loyola.edu.

Richard W. Feller, PhD, is professor of counseling and career development at Colorado State University, where he directs the Career Development Institute. He is coauthor of *Career Transitions in Turbulent Times* (CLS, 1996) and the *CDM Career Video Series: Tour of Your Tomorrow* (AGS, 2001), and contributing author to *DISCOVER* (ACT, Inc., 2001) and *GIS* (Riverside Publishing, 1998) computerized career planning systems. He has consulted in 49 states, Thailand, Japan, Sudan, China, Switzerland, and Canada. A nationally recognized speaker, he serves on the board of the National Career Development Association. He can be reached at feller@cahs.colostate.edu.

John Fremer, PhD, has 30 years of experience in the field of test publishing at the Psychological Corporation/Harcourt General and Educational Testing Service (ETS). In his career at ETS, Fremer led the team that revised the SAT, served as director of exercise development for the National Assessment of Educational Progress, and was director of test development for school and higher education programs. In recent years, Fremer has designed and delivered measurement training programs for the ETS Global Institute. Fremer served as the ETS representative to the testing-industry-wide Association of Test Publishers (ATP) and is a past president and member of that organization's board of directors. Fremer is also a past president of the National Council on Measurement in Education (NCME) and of the Association for Assessment in Counseling (AAC). He can be reached at jfremer@aol.com.

Lara Frumkin, PhD, currently works at the U.S. Department of Justice. Previously, she worked in the Science Directorate of the American Psychological Association as the testing and assessment officer. In that capacity, she spent three years working with the Joint Committee on Testing Practices (JCTP) and its working groups. Frumkin received her doctorate in social and community psychology in 2000 from the University of Maryland, Baltimore County. She can be reached at laraab@directvinternet.com.

Kurt F. Geisinger, PhD, is vice president for academic affairs and professor of psychology at the University of St. Thomas, Houston. He has been a faculty member and administrator at Fordham University, SUNY-Oswego, and Le Moyne College. He is a coauthor of *Test Interpretation and Diversity* (1998) and *Psychological Testing of Hispanics* (1992), published by the American Psychological Association (APA). He is a former member of the APA's Committee of Psychological Testing and Assessment, the Middle States Regional Council for the College Board, and the Central New York Educational Consortium. Currently, he chairs the Technical Advisory Committee for the Graduate Record Examination (GRE) at Educational Testing Service (ETS), serves *ex officio* on the Board for the Graduate Record Examination and on the College Board's SAT Committee. He presently serves as a consulting editor for *Practical Assessment Research and Evaluation*, the *International Journal of Testing*, *ITEMS*, and *Educational Research Quarterly*. He can be reached at geis@stthom.edu.

Donna M. Gibson, PhD, is a nationally certified counselor and school psychologist. She began her career as a school psychologist, working in schools and clinics to provide multidisciplinary assessments for children from birth through 21 years of age. Gibson currently is an assistant professor of counselor education at the Citadel. She is the membership coordinator for the Association for Assessment in Counseling (AAC) and secretary of the South Carolina Counseling Association. She can be reached at 3gibsond@citadel.edu.

Sharon M. Goldsmith, PhD, an internationally recognized expert on standards, testing, and related policy issues, has held several academic appointments and authored numerous articles and papers. Goldsmith serves on national boards including the American National Standards Institute (ANSI) Personnel Certification Accreditation Committee, the International Commission on Healthcare Professions (ICHP) Standards Committee, and the Joint Committee on Testing Practices (JCTP). Previously Goldsmith was director of professional affairs and senior advisor for Standards and Credentialing for the American Speech-Language-Hearing Association (ASHA). She has worked with governmental and private agencies in the United States, United Kingdom, Canada, Japan, Australia, Israel, Mexico, and Columbia. Goldsmith is currently consulting on a federally funded project for the National Skills Standards Board. Goldsmith earned her doctorate from the Graduate School and University Center of the City University of New York. She can be reached at goldsmith99@msn.com.

Brian Goonan, PhD, is a licensed psychologist and licensed specialist in school psychology in private practice in Houston, Texas. He received his doctorate from Emory University, specializing in interpersonal theory and social and relationship development. Goonan develops individualized treatments for attention problems, emotional regulation, social skills, stress management, performance enhancement, self-improvement, and relationship satisfaction. He routinely presents to special interest groups on these topics. In addition to his extensive experience with children and adolescents in a variety of clinical and academic settings, Goonan has also taught SAT, GRE, GMAT, and LSAT preparation courses for the Princeton Review. He can be reached at goonan@less-stress.net.

Marcy Priess Guddemi, PhD, secretary of the International Play Association, is a nationally recognized expert in early childhood education. She has published numerous articles and books and presents frequently at national and international conferences on literacy development, cognitive development, and play environments. She is the senior product manager of early learner products for CTB/McGraw-

Hill. Most recently she served eight years as the vice president of KinderCare Learning Centers. She also has held faculty positions at the University of South Florida, the University of South Carolina, and Southwest Texas State University. Having begun her career in education in the classroom, Guddemi later became education director for Richland/Morrow Counties Head Start in Ohio. She received her bachelor's and master's degrees from the Ohio State University and her doctorate from the University of Texas at Austin. Marcy can be reached at mguddemi@ctb.com.

William Bryce Hagedorn is a licensed professional counselor in North Carolina whose clinical work has been with individuals suffering from chemical and process addictions. He has worked in several capacities, including crisis assessment, substance abuse inpatient treatment, intensive outpatient treatment, and private practice. Currently he is a doctoral student at the University of North Carolina at Greensboro, where he is working toward developing counselor competencies for those interested in working with clients suffering from sexual addiction. He maintains a small local private practice in the area, continuing to work with individuals battling addictive disorders. He can be reached at brycehagedorn@yahoo.com.

Jo-Ida C. Hansen, PhD, is a professor in the Department of Psychology at the University of Minnesota. She directs the doctoral program in Counseling Psychology, the Occupational Health Psychology Program, the Vocational Assessment Clinic, and the Center for Interest Measurement Research. Currently the editor of the *Journal of Counseling Psychology,* Hansen is past editor of *Measurement and Evaluation in Counseling and Development*. She served on the APA, NCME, and AERA joint committee to revise the *Standards of Educational and Psychological Testing*, and is past president of the Association for Assessment in Counseling and the American Psychological Association's Division of Counseling Psychology. She can be reached at hanse004@maroon.tc.umn.edu.

Thomas F. Harrington, PhD, teaches at Northeastern University in Boston in the Department of Counseling and Applied Educational Psychology. He is coauthor of the *Harrington-O'Shea Career Decision Making System* (AGS, 2000), the *Ability Explorer* (Riverside Publishing, 1996), and the *Handbook of Career Planning for Students with Special Needs* (Pro-ed, 1997). He has served as a researcher for a World Bank project and as visiting scholar or professor at seven overseas universities. He has produced and authored or coauthored four films, two software packages, four books, and many publications, in addition to presenting at numerous international and national meetings. He can be reached at harrington@mediaone.net.

Deborah J. Harris, PhD, is director of measurement research at ACT, Inc., and an adjunct assistant professor at the University of Iowa. She is responsible for overseeing equating, scaling, and other psychometric analyses for various achievement and certification programs. Harris has published or presented numerous journal articles, convention papers, and workshop presentations, primarily in the area of equating. An active member of AERA and NCME, Harris is currently editor for the National Council on Measurement in Education (NCME) Instructional Topics in Educational Measurement Series (ITEMS). Harris received her doctorate from the University of Wisconsin–Madison, and her master's and undergraduate degrees from Central Michigan University. She can be reached at harris@act.org.

William G. Harris, PhD, serves as the executive director of the Association of Test Publishers (ATP). He frequently provides expert testimony on testing and assessment initiatives at the federal, state, and provincial levels. Harris holds a doctorate in psychology from the University of Massachusetts at Amherst and a master's degree in business administration from Duke University. His areas of interest are e-testing, test security, digital copyright, and the effect of the Internet on the economics and future of testing. The co-executive director of the IT Certification Security Council, Harris is also a member of the Secretary of Veterans Affairs' Professional Certification and Licensure Advisory Committee. In addition, Harris is a member of both the Code of Fair Testing Practices in Education Task Force for the Joint Committee on Testing Practices (JCTP) and the Steering Committee of the Fair Access Coalition on Testing (FACT). He can be reached at wgh.atp@att.net.

Nathan S. Hartman is a doctoral student in organizational behavior at Virginia Commonwealth University. He received his master's in business administration from Averett University and his bachelor of science in mechanical engineering from Western Michigan University. He worked as an engineer at Newport News Shipbuilding prior to pursuing his PhD. His research interests include employee selection, situational judgment tests, knowledge workers, and social capital. He can be reached at s2nshart@mail2.vcu.edu

Janet E. Helms, PhD, is professor of counseling psychology and founding director of the Institute for the Study and Promotion of Race and Culture at Boston College. Helms is a fellow in Divisions 17 (Counseling Psychology) and 45 (Ethnic Diversity) of the American Psychological Association (APA), in addition to co-chairing the Joint Committee on Testing Practices (JCTP). Helms has authored or coauthored more than 50 articles, chapters, and books focused on the treatment and assessment of racial and ethnic cultural populations. These include *Black and White Racial Identity: Theory, Research, and Practice*(Greenwood Press, 1990), in which she developed the most widely used measures of racial identity development, and *Using Race and Culture in Counseling and Psychotherapy* (Allyn and Bacon, 1999), with Donelda Cook, in which she offers racially and culturally responsive treatment strategies. She can be reached at helmsja@bc.edu.

Gerald A. Juhnke, EdD, LPC, NCC, MAC, ACS, CCAS, is an associate professor in the Department of Counseling and Educational Development at the University of North Carolina at Greensboro and director of the department's research and training clinic, which provides addictions, mental health, and family counseling to the greater Greensboro community. Juhnke is a past president of the Association for Assessment in Counseling (AAC), past editor and current editorial review board member of the *Journal of Addictions and Offender Counseling,* and past co-chair of the American Counseling Association (ACA) Council of Journal Editors. He has authored more than 30 refereed articles, books, and book chapters. He can be reached at gajuhnke@uncg.edu.

Michael H. Kean, PhD, is vice president for public and governmental affairs at McGraw-Hill Education in Monterey, California, and also serves as chair of the Test Committee of the Association of American Publishers (AAP). Over his career, Kean joined the School District of Philadelphia as assistant to the superintendent and served as executive director of the Philadelphia Office of Research and Evaluation. He directed the Midwest regional office of the Educational Testing Service (ETS) before joining CTB as its publisher in 1983. He served as vice president of marketing before moving into his current position. He is active in numerous professional organizations and was elected vice president of the School Evaluation Division of the American Educational Research Association (AERA). The author of more than 150 articles and papers, Kean holds a doctorate in educational development and planning from the Ohio State University. He can be reached at mkean@ctb.com.

Wyatt Kirk, EdD, is a professor and chair of the counseling program at North Carolina A&T State University. He holds a doctorate in counselor education from Western Michigan University and is a licensed professional counselor. His primary areas of specialization are counseling minorities, racism research, and sports psychology. His most recent book is *Student Athletes: Shattering the Myths and Sharing the Realities* (ACA, 1993). He is a past member of the board of directors of the National Board of Certified Counselors (NBCC). He can be reached at kirkw@ncat.edu.

Samuel E. Krug, PhD, is the author or coauthor of more than 100 articles, books, tests, and computer-based assessment products. His research and publications focus on issues in applied educational and psychological measurement. After completing his advanced degrees at the University of Illinois at Urbana–Champaign, Krug was employed in a variety of roles by IPAT, Inc., eventually as the director of the Test Services Division. Currently, he is president of MetriTech, Inc., an educational and psychological test publisher he founded, and president of Industrial Psychology International, Ltd., which has published a series of employee selection and evaluation tests since 1948. He can be reached at skrug@metritech.com.

Janice H. Laurence, PhD, is a research professor in the Graduate School of Business and Public Policy of the Naval Postgraduate School (NPS) Washington, DC, satellite office. She also teaches in NPS's master's program at the Naval Academy. For more than 20 years, Laurence has conducted personnel policy studies and applied research, particularly in the military setting. She has served on advisory panels and has testified before the U.S. Congress. Editor of the journal *Military Psychology,* Laurence is a fellow of the American Psychological Association's Division of Military Psychology and is also a member of APA's Society for Industrial and Organizational Psychology and Evaluation, Measurement, and Statistics Division. Laurence earned her doctoral degree in industrial and organizational psychology from George Mason University. She can be reached at N130A1@bupers.navy.mil.

Phil Lewis serves as a technical officer for the National O*NET Consortium, a U.S. Department of Labor–funded entity consisting of the North Carolina Employment Security Commission, the Ohio Bureau of Employment Services, and the Center for Employment Security Education and Research. He has served as a consultant for a variety of organizations, including Bridges.com, Sage Solutions, United Way of America, and Healthy Companies U.S. He can be reached at phlewis@doleta.gov.

David Lundberg, PhD, is an assistant professor of counseling at North Carolina A&T State University. He holds a doctorate in counselor education from the University of North Carolina–Greensboro and is a nationally certified counselor. His primary research interests are in multicultural counseling and technology in counseling, and he has published articles in the *Journal of Career Development,* the *Journal of Humanistic Education and Development,* and the *Journal of Technology in Counseling*. He currently serves on the executive council of the Association for Assessment in Counseling. He can be reached at lundberg@ncat.edu.

Michael A. McDaniel, PhD, received his doctorate in industrial and organizational psychology at George Washington University in 1986. He is an associate professor at Virginia Commonwealth University in the School of Business and president of Work Skills First, Inc., a human resources consulting firm. McDaniel is nationally recognized for his research and practice in personnel selection. His 1999 article concerning Holland's vocational theory and occupational databases appears in the *Journal of Vocational Behavior.* In 2000, he was made a fellow of the Society of Industrial and Organizational Psychology, the American Psychological Society, and the American Psychological Association (APA). He can be reached at MikeMcDaniel@WorkSkillsFirst.com.

Patricia Jo McDivitt has more than 17 years of test development experience, including overseeing the item development of multiple and complex assessments for various statewide standards-based programs. She is currently vice president of test development for Data Recognition Corporation (DRC). McDivitt began her career as an educator, serving as a classroom teacher and guidance counselor for 12 years. She is a current member of the Executive Committee of the Joint Committee on Standards for Educational Evaluation (JCSEE) and a past president of the Association for Assessment in Counseling (AAC). She can be reached at pmcdivitt@datarecognitioncorp.com

Cheryl Moore-Thomas, PhD, received her doctorate in counselor education from the University of Maryland. She is currently an assistant professor of education in the school counseling program at Loyola College in Maryland. Former positions include public school educator, counselor, student services specialist, consultant, and trainer. Moore-Thomas's research and scholarly interests include racial identity development of children and adolescents, and accountability in school counseling programs. She can be reached at cmthomas@juno.com.

Julie P. Noble, PhD, is principal research associate in the Research Division at ACT. Her primary responsibilities involve helping secondary and postsecondary personnel make appropriate uses and interpretations of test results. Her research interests include differential achievement by race, ethnicity, and gender; college admissions; course placement; and student outcomes. A member of AERA, NCME, the Association for Institutional Research, and Phi Delta Kappa, Noble is immediate past co-chair of the Joint Committee on Testing Practices (JCTP). She is currently co-chair of a student outcomes working group to develop a sourcebook on student outcomes for the National Postsecondary Educational Cooperative. She can be reached at noblej@act.org.

Carole L. Perlman, PhD, is director of student assessment for the Chicago Public Schools. Perlman holds a doctorate in public policy analysis from the University of Illinois at Chicago. A past president of the National Association of Test Directors (NATD) and past member of the National Council on Measurement in Education (NCME) board of directors, Perlman has also served on many state and federal advisory panels, the National Advisory Board of CRESST, and the Joint Committee on Testing Practices (JCTP). She is the recipient of an AERA Division D Research Report Award and the UIC College of Education Distinguished Alumna Award. She can be reached at cperlman@acct.multi1.cps.il.us.

Nambury S. Raju, PhD, is a distinguished professor in the Institute of Psychology at the Illinois Institute of Technology. He has strong interests in test development, item and test bias, and meta-analysis. He served on the Department of Defense Advisory Committee on Military Personnel Testing, on a National Academy of Science

Committee to evaluate the National Assessment of Educational Progress (NAEP), and on the APA Council of Representatives. He currently serves on the APA Committee on Psychological Tests and Assessments (CPTA) and JCTP. A fellow of APA and SIOP, Raju serves on seven editorial boards including those for *Educational and Psychological Measurement*, *Applied Psychological Measurement*, *Journal of Applied Psychology*, and *Journal of Educational Measurement*. He can be reached at nambury.raju@iit.edu.

David Rivkin is one of the two technical officers for the National Center for O*NET Development, responsible for ensuring the technical quality of O*NET products. He currently codirects projects associated with development and implementation of O*NET career exploration tools and assessment technical assistance guides. Additionally, he manages many of the projects related to developing the O*NET database, O*NET OnLine, and O*NET outreach efforts. He can be reached at drivkin@doleta.gov.

Edward Roeber, PhD, is currently the vice president of External Relations for Measured Progress. In this position, he works with state policy leaders and staff of state and local education agencies to help design, develop, and implement quality assessment programs that lead to long-term student achievement and school improvement. Currently, he is directing the company's efforts to develop alternate assessments for students with severe disabilities. From 1991 to 1998, he was director of student assessment programs for the Council of Chief State School Officers (CCSSO), where he was responsible for assisting states in the development of their statewide student assessment programs. Prior to joining CCSSO in 1991, he was director of the Michigan Educational Assessment Program and a consultant with the Education Commission of the States, working on the National Assessment of Educational Progress (NAEP) in the areas of music and visual arts from 1969 to 1972. Roeber received his doctorate in measurement and evaluation from the University of Michigan in 1970. He can be reached at EdRoeber@aol.com.

Jeff Rubenstein is assistant vice president at the Princeton Review. He has written numerous articles and books on testing and test preparation. He can be reached at JeffR@review.com.

Richard L. Sawyer, PhD, is assistant vice president for measurement and statistical research at ACT, Inc., where he oversees psychometric and statistical work supporting ACT's testing programs. His research interests include validity issues related to college admissions and course placement, effectiveness of remedial instruction, and retention. He is a member of AERA, NCME, and the Association for Institutional Research. He can be reached at sawyer@act.org.

William D. Schafer, EdD, is affiliated professor (emeritus) at the Maryland Assessment Research Center for Education Success, Department of Measurement, Statistics, and Evaluation, University of Maryland, College Park.. A member of the department faculty for 31 years, he typically taught courses in applied statistics through experimental design and multiple regression, classroom assessment, and advanced research methods. He is former editor of *Measurement and Evaluation in Counseling and Development* and is currently on the editorial boards of *Applied Measurement in Education*, *Educational and Psychological Measurement*, and *Measurement and Evaluation in Counseling and Development*. He is coeditor of *Practical Assessment: Research & Evaluation,* an electronic journal sponsored by ERIC and available at http://ericae.net/pare/. For several years, Schafer served as director of student assessment with the Maryland State Department of Education. He can be reached at ws7@umail.umd.edu.

Jeff L. Schiel, PhD, is assistant director of institutional analysis at the University of Colorado, Boulder. He was formerly senior research associate at ACT, Inc. His interests include applied statistics and data analysis. He is a member of the American Educational Research Association (AERA), the Association for Institutional Research, and the National Council on Measurement in Education (NCME). Schiel's doctorate is in educational psychology, with an emphasis in statistics and measurement. He can be reached at Jeff.Schiel@colorado.edu.

Wendi K. Schweiger, MS/EdS, NCC, is currently a doctoral student in the Department of Counselor Education at the University of North Carolina at Greensboro. Since August 2000, she has worked as the national coordinator of the Fair Access Coalition for Testing (FACT). She has approximately four years of clinical experience in counseling and specializes in working with young children and their families. She can be reached at WendiS@nbcc.org.

Stephen G. Sireci, PhD, is associate professor in the Research and Evaluation Methods program and codirector of the Center for Educational Assessment at the University of Massachusetts, Amherst. He earned his doctorate in psychometrics from Fordham University in 1993, and his master's and bachelor's degrees in psychology from Loyola College in Maryland. He is known for his research in evaluating test fairness, particularly issues related to content validity, test bias, cross-lingual assessment, and sensitivity review, and for his applications of multidimensional scaling and cluster analysis to the evaluation of test validity. His research has been published in *Applied Measurement in Education*, *Applied Psychological Measurement*, *Journal of Educational Measurement*, *Educational Assessment*, *Educational Measurement: Issues and Practice*, *Multivariate Behavioral Research*, and several other educational research journals. A reviewer for numerous research journals, Sireci is on the editorial boards of *Applied Measurement in Education* and *Educational Measurement: Issues and Practice*, and is the coeditor of the *Journal of Applied Testing Technology.* He can be reached at sireci@acad.umass.edu.

Brandon A. Sullivan is a coordinator of the Vocational Assessment Clinic in the Department of Psychology at the University of Minnesota–Twin Cities, where he also teaches a course in occupational health psychology and is pursuing a doctorate in counseling psychology and social psychology. Previous positions include teaching at the Center for Learning and Teaching at Cornell University and a research position in organizational behavior at Cornell's Johnson Graduate School of Management. He holds a BA from Carleton College and an MA in counseling and student personnel psychology from the University of Minnesota. He can be reached at sulli078@unm.edu.

Sandra Thompson, PhD, serves as a research associate at the National Center on Educational Outcomes (NCEO) at the University of Minnesota, where she is responsible for a number of research activities that document the participation and performance of students with disabilities in state and district standards and assessments. Thompson has an extensive background in preparing students with disabilities for successful adult lives, spending 10 years with Minnesota's Department of Education as a transition specialist and 10 years as a high school special education teacher. She can be reached at thomp178@tc.umn.edu.

Martha Thurlow, PhD, is director of the National Center on Educational Outcomes (NCEO) at the University of Minnesota. In this position, she addresses the implications of contemporary U.S. policy and practice for students with disabilities, including national and statewide assessment policies and practices, standards-setting efforts, and graduation requirements. Dr. Thurlow has conducted research involving special education for the past 30 years in a variety of areas, including assessment and decision making, learning disabilities, early childhood education, dropout prevention, effective classroom instruction, and integration of students with disabilities in general education settings. She can be reached at thur1001@umn.edu.

Timothy Vansickle, PhD, has worked in educational and psychological testing for more than 15 years, most recently as a senior psychometrician with Data Recognition Corporation (DRC). Prior to joining DRC he was vice president of research and development at Riverside Publishing. He has held several association offices and is currently a member of the American Psychological Association (APA), National Council on Measurement in Education (NCME), American Educational Research Association (AERA), and the American Counseling Association (ACA). Vansickle regularly writes and presents on topics related to testing, assessment, computer-based testing, and education. He can be reached at tvansickle@aol.com.

Randolph H. Watts Jr., received his master's degree from the University of Virginia. He has worked as director of counseling for Episcopal High School in Alexandria, Virginia, and currently is a doctoral student at the University of North Carolina at Greensboro. He can be reached at rhwatts@nc.rr.com.

Pat Nellor Wickwire, PhD, earned her doctorate at the University of Texas at Austin and her master of arts degree at the University of Iowa. She has professional credentials in public school and community college educational administration, instruction, and student services. The American Counseling Association (ACA) representative on the Joint Committee on Testing Practices (JCTP), Wickwire is also president of the American Association for Career Education, and past president of the California Association for Counseling and Development (CACD) and CACD Education Foundation. She is a licensed educational psychologist, licensed marriage family therapist, national certified counselor, and the recipient of awards from the Association for

Multicultural Counseling and Development, California Association for Counseling and Development, and National Career Development Association. Wickwire may be contacted at the Nellor Wickwire Group, 2900 Amby Place, Hermosa Beach, CA 90254-2216.

Lauress Wise, PhD, is currently president of the Human Resources Research Organization (HumRRO), a nonprofit organization conducting research and development on testing, training, and related issues. He also serves as vice-chair of the National Academy of Sciences Board on Testing and Assessment. With research interests focused on testing and test use policy, Wise remains active in research and is currently directing an evaluation of California's high school exit examination. Previously, he served as director of the Personnel Testing Division of the Defense Manpower Data Center. In that capacity, he was responsible for overseeing research and development of the Armed Services Vocational Aptitude Battery (ASVAB) and the ASVAB Career Exploration Program. He can be reached at lwise@humrro.org.

Abbreviations

AAC	Association for Assessment in Counseling
AACC	American Association of Community Colleges
AACE	Association for Assessment in Counseling and Education
AAP	Association of American Publishers
ACA	American Counseling Association
ADA	Americans With Disabilities Act
ADDES	Attention Deficit Disorders Evaluation Scale
ADDIE	analysis, design, development, implementation, and evaluation model
ADHD	attention deficit/hyperactivity disorder
ADHDRS-IV	ADHD Rating Scale-IV
ADHD-SRS	ADHD Symptoms Rating Scale
AE	Ability Explorer
AERA	American Educational Research Association
AFT	American Federation of Teachers
AOD	alcohol and other drugs
AP	Advanced Placement
APA	American Psychological Association
API	accountability performance index
ASCA	American School Counselor Association
ASHA	American Speech-Language-Hearing Association
ASI	Adolescent Symptom Inventory
ASVAB	Armed Services Vocational Aptitude Battery
ASWB	Association of Social Work Boards
ATA	American Translators Association
ATP	Association of Test Publishers
BADDS	Brown Attention Deficit Disorder Scales
BASC	Behavior Assessment System for Children
BASC-PRS	Behavior Assessment System for Children Parent Rating Scale
BASC-TRS	Behavior Assessment System for Children Teacher Rating Scale
BASE	Behavior Academic Self-Esteem
BDHI	Buss-Durkee Hostility Inventory
BDI-II	Beck Depression Inventory II
BULIT	Bulimia Test

CAI	Career Assessment Inventory
CAS	Child Assessment Schedule
CASS	Conners-Wells' Adolescent Self-Report Scale
CAT	computerized adaptive test
CBCL	Child Behavior Checklist
CBT	computer-based testing
CCPT	Conners' Continuous Performance Test
CD	conduct disorder
CDI	Children's Depression Inventory
CDM	Career Decision Making System
CDT	component display theory (also called component design theory)
CEP	Career Exploration Program
CIDS	Career Information Delivery Systems
CLEP	College-Level Examination Program
COPS	Career Occupational Preference System
CPRS-R	Conners' Parent Rating Scale-Revised
CSI	Child Symptom Inventory
CTRS-R	Conners' Teacher Rating Scale-Revised
DICS	Diagnostic Interview Schedule for Children and Adolescents
DIF	differential item functioning
DISC	Diagnostic Interview Schedule for Children
DoD	Department of Defense
DOL	Department of Labor
DRA	Disability Rights Advocates
DSM-IV	Diagnostic and Statistical Manual of Mental Disorders, Fourth Edition
DTF	differential test functioning
DUI	driving while under the influence
EAT	Eating Attitudes Test
ECBI	Eyberg Child Behavior Inventory
ECI	Early Childhood Inventories
EDI-2	Eating Disorder Inventory-2
ELS	English Language Assessment
ESEA	Elementary and Secondary Education Act
ESL	English as a Second Language
ETS	Educational Testing Service
FACES III	Family Adaptability and Cohesion Evaluation Scales III
FACT	Fair Access Coalition for Testing
FCAT	Florida Comprehensive Assessment

FGPA	freshman grade point average
FTC	Federal Trade Commission
GED	General Educational Development
GPA	grade point average
GRE	Graduate Record Exam
HCI	human-computer interaction
HSQ	Home Situations Questionnaire
IBLCE	International Board of Lactation Consultant Examiners
IDEA	Individuals With Disabilities Education Act
IEA	Intelligent Essay Assessor
IEP	Individualized Education Program/Plan
IRA	International Reading Association
IRT	item response theory
ISD	instructional systems development
ISO-30	Inventory of Suicide-30
JCTP	Joint Committee on Testing Practices
JSS	Job Stress Survey
KCSS	KUDER Career Search Schedule with Person-Match
K-FTDS	Kiddie Formal Thought Disorder Rating Scale
K-SADS	Kiddie Schedule for Affective Disorders and Schizophrenia for School-Aged Children
LEP	limited English proficient
MAPI	Millon Adolescent Personality Inventory
MASC	Multidimensional Anxiety Scale for Children
MBI	Maslach Burnout Inventory
MBTI	Myers-Briggs Type Indicator
MCAT	Medical College Admission Test
MEPS	Means-End Problem Solving Procedure
MESSY	Matson Evaluation of Social Skills with Youngsters
MMPI	Minnesota Multiphasic Personality Inventory
MMPI-A	Minnesota Multiphasic Personality Inventory for Adolescents
MSCS	Multidimensional Self-Concept Scale
NAECS/SDE	National Association of Early Childhood Specialists in State Departments of Education

NAEP	National Assessment of Educational Progress
NAEYC	National Association for the Education of Young Children
NAGB	National Assessment Governing Board
NASP	National Association of School Psychologists
NATD	National Association of Test Directors
NBCC	National Board for Certified Counselors
NCE	normal curve equivalent
NCEO	National Center on Educational Outcomes
NCES	National Center for Education Statistics
NCLB	No Child Left Behind Act of 2001
NAEP	National Assessment for Educational Progress
NCME	National Council on Measurement in Education
NEA	National Education Association
NGA	National Governors Association
NRC	National Research Council
OCHS	Ontario Child Health Study
OCR	Office of Civil Rights
OES	Occupational Employment Statistics
O*NET	Occupational Information Network
OSI-R	Occupational Stress Inventory–Revised
PAC	Parent-Adolescent Communication Scale
PEG	Project Essay Grade
PHCSCS	Piers-Harris Children's Self-Concept Scale
PIC	Personality Inventory for Children
PIY	Personality Inventory for Youth
PTSD	post-traumatic stress disorder
QED	Quality Education Data
RADS	Reynolds Adolescent Depression Scales
RCDS	Reynolds Child Depression Scales
RCMAS	Revised Children's Manifest Anxiety Scale
RFP	request for proposals
RIASEC	Realistic, Investigative, Artistic, Social, Enterprising, and Conventional
SAT	Scholastic Aptitude Test
SCANS	Labor Secretary's Commission on Acquiring Necessary Skills
SCL-90-R	Symptom Checklist-90-Revised
SDS	Holland's Self-Directed Search

SEI	Coopersmith Self-Esteem Inventories
SEM	standard error of measurement
SES	socioeconomic status
SII	Strong Interest Inventory
SL-90-R	Symptom Checklist-90-Revised
SOC	Standard Occupational Classification
SOS	Structured Observation System
SRP	Self-Report of Personality
SSBS	School Social Behavior Scales
SSQ	School Situations Questionnaire
SSRS-S	Social Skills Rating System-Student Form
STAIC	State-Trait Anxiety Inventory for Children
STP	Student Testing Program
TAAS	Texas Assessment of Academic Skills
TAI	Test Anxiety Inventory
TASP	Texas Academic Skills Program
TOVA	Test of Variables of Attention
TRF	Teacher's Report Form
TSCC	Trauma Symptom Checklist for Children
USOeC	U.S. Open e-Learning Consortium
VNT	Voluntary National Tests
WASC	Western Association of Schools and Colleges
WBAT	Well-Based Assessment Tool
YSR	Youth Self-Report

l

Section A

The Basics of Testing

Chapter 1
Why Use Tests and Assessments?
Questions and Answers

John Fremer & Janet E. Wall

The terms *assessment, measurement,* and *testing* will be used heavily in this book. Although the terms are often used interchangeably, there are some distinctions between them. *Testing,* generally considered to be the most narrow or specific of the terms, tends to refer to a set of questions that has been compiled to measure a specific concept such as achievement or aptitude. *Assessment* is broader in scope; it encompasses testing, but can also include measurement via observations, interviews, checklists, and other data gathering instruments. The term assessment is used more often in the clinical setting or for determining preferences, interests, and personality types. The term *measurement* generally refers to the attempt at quantifying the results of tests and assessments. This chapter will outline the purpose of testing and assessment, focus on uses, and highlight some of the limitations of all forms of testing.

The concept of testing is one of the major contributions of the field of psychology to society. Carefully developed tests, when used wisely, provide valuable information for decision makers in educational, employment, and clinical settings. It is because of their often-demonstrated utility that tests and other standardized assessments are so widely used in educational settings. In order to gain the potential benefits that tests offer, it is essential to be aware of their strengths and their limitations. In this chapter, we review these key aspects of high-quality testing:

- What is a test or assessment?
- What are the major uses of tests?
- What are the key benefits of systematic, high-quality testing?
- What are the frequent criticisms of testing?
- How can we promote high-quality testing?

What Is a Standardized Test or Assessment?

During the medieval period in Europe, skilled craftsmen who were members of a guild carried with them symbols of their trade. We do not have many examples of that practice now, but the stethoscope around a doctor's neck, the chalk in the hands of a teacher, or the tool belt of a carpenter or telephone line worker all bring to mind that person's line of work. What might a tester carry to signal his or her professional role? It could be a copy of the Iowa Test of Basic Skills or the Florida Comprehensive Assessment (FCAT). Perhaps the Myers-Briggs Type Indicator (MBTI) or the Minnesota Multiphasic Personality Inventory (MMPI). What about a driver's test or a military entrance exam? Yet other options could be an SAT-I, advanced placement test, or a copy of an ACT Assessment.

Basically, testing is a special way of collecting information used to help make decisions about individuals, programs, or institutions. Tests and assessments are generally made up of items or questions that elicit responses from an individual. It is important to note that merely administering some set of questions or performance tasks is only one part of the testing process. If the tests are never scored and the results never used, we have done only part of what is needed. Yet there are instances ranging from the individual classroom level to nationwide assessment where tests are given and little use is ever made of the information. In order for actual measurement to take place as part of testing, one or more of the following steps must take place:

- An individual or group must receive a score along with some guide to interpreting that score.
- The individual or group must be ranked against others who have been tested.
- The individual or group must be classified into some meaningful category; for example, "gifted," "shows some evidence of obsessive behavior," "merits a personal interview," or "needs further evaluation."
- The performance of the individual or group must be compared against some explicit standard.

Most instances of testing very clearly meet one or more of these criteria: An individual who takes a required test receives a score on a well-defined scale and also receives a good deal of comparison information and an interpretive guide. In other instances the situation is not so straightforward. For example, a teacher asks the class to answer a set of questions and to send in electronic or paper responses. The teacher reads all the responses and makes a judgment as to how well the group as a whole has learned the material covered by the questions. Has measurement taken place? Yes, for the class as a unit, but no for the individuals, if the teacher has not classified their responses in any way. In real life, of course, the teacher may recall the specific responses of some students and either confirm or change his or her perception of their level of understanding. For that subset of students the testing process has actually led to measurement. The issue, "What is measurement?" is reviewed by Jones (1971), who notes that although "unanimity concerning the meaning of measurement may appear unlikely . . . each measurement is purposive . . . and the purpose is always . . . to acquire information" (p. 335).

What Are the Major Uses of Tests?

We have maintained that the basic purpose of tests is to provide information for decision makers. In the last section we made the case that the process must also include assigning a score, rank, or classification of some type. We now want to describe five major uses of test results, as follows:

- selection or placement
- diagnosis
- accountability evaluations
- judging progress and following trends
- self-discovery

Selection or Placement

The use of tests to help select individuals for admissions to an institution or special program is so widespread that it is perhaps best described as a standard feature of U.S. society. Entrance examinations are used as early as entrance into kindergarten and with increased frequency as the student moves up the grades and into college and a profession. Usually test information is combined with grades to make decisions; tests are also frequently used at the college level to grant exemption from or credit for college courses taken while a student is still attending high school (Willingham, Lewis, Morgan, & Ramist, 1990).

When using a test to help make selection or placement decisions, it is essential that the decisions made be of higher quality when the tests are used than when they are not. If students are being accepted for admission to a college, for example, the group that is admitted should perform better than the group that would have been chosen without the use of tests.

How might we determine whether tests had improved our process for selecting college students? We could look at overall grade point average, grades in specific courses, record of successful completion of the freshman year, or persistence to graduation of the students who were admitted. Each of these criteria has been employed to evaluate the value of college admissions tests. Most often, though, it is freshman grade point average (FGPA) that is employed in studies of the value of the SAT I and SAT II and of the ACT Assessment. FGPA is routinely determined by virtually all colleges, so it is an easy bit of criterion information to obtain. The results from many thousands of studies of the value of college admissions have yielded consistent results. For most colleges, high school grades are the best predictor of college grades (Donlon, 1984). For many colleges, though, admissions test scores are the best single predictors. The most common practice is to use both test scores and high school grades. Increasingly, colleges are looking at all available information about students, including recommendations, personal essays, past accomplishments, community service record, and other evidence of a student's potential for college achievement and for subsequent contributions to society. In a classic work on this topic, Willingham & Breland (1982) point out that although "some personal qualities are related to success, some have intrinsic merit in their own right and some are demonstrably related to important institutional objectives" (p. 3).

Whereas a great deal of study has been devoted to evaluating the strengths and limitations of college admissions tests, much less attention has been given to other uses for tests in educational selection and placement settings. It is very common for one or more tests to be used to select students for gifted and talented or special education programs. Ideally the managers of such programs would first define the student characteristics that each program is designed to nurture and develop. Then they would develop selection procedures to choose the most appropriate students for the program. Some combination of prior academic work, teacher recommendations, and test results will typically be most effective in the selection process. Whatever approach is used, the results should be carefully evaluated to make sure that all the information used is having the desired contribution to picking the group of students for whom the program will be most effective.

Diagnosis

Tests are also used extensively to evaluate students' special needs. Test results help educators, counselors, and other professionals plan individualized education programs for students or point out specific misconceptions or problem areas that are hindering progress. Often tests help determine the need for counseling services, especially when students are experiencing high personal stress or engaging in substance abuse or other harmful and dangerous behaviors. The home and workplace are other contexts where physical and psychological problems occur for which tests are often part of the solution.

Some of the tests used in diagnostic settings in education measure basic academic skills and knowledge. Has a child mastered basic linguistic and mathematical content? If not, what are the child's areas of strength and weakness? Often a classroom teacher will ask for special diagnostic testing for a child who is not keeping up with other students or not responding to the teaching methods being employed. The goal of diagnostic educational testing of this type is to add information that can be used to plan the child's future educational program. The closer the test content is to the skills that are the goals for instruction, the more useful the results will be to those doing such planning. Another consideration in evaluating the results of diagnostic educational tests is the extent to which parents and other family members can readily understand the test results.

In addition to skills-oriented diagnostic educational tests, trained professionals frequently use a number of other tests, surveys, and inventories in educational and employment settings. Successful performance in school, work, or other settings is not merely a question of having the necessary skills. Grief, anxiety, anger, and other debilitating states of mind can have strong effects on children and adults of all ages and in many different life situations. Tests and related tools can help focus attention on the nature and extent of the difficulty that is interfering with the individual's ability to perform effectively.

The interpretation of nonacademic tests requires specialized training in areas such as counseling, school psychology, or clinical psychology. The trained professional takes into account many factors of a person's situation in order to evaluate test results in a proper context and to make useful recommendations (Bracken, 1991).

Accountability Evaluations

Some testing in education is carried out for the express purpose of holding students, educators, and schools accountable for their performance. Such testing programs set explicit standards and require adherence to these standards, often with some form of reward for those who achieve them and sanctions for those who do not. For students, a requirement to attend summer school is one possible consequence of failing to meet a grade promotion standard. Retention in the current grade or failure to graduate from high school are other possible results of failing to meet the standard.

For teachers, a possible positive outcome is a cash bonus based on high student performance. A possible negative consequence for a school or school system is loss of autonomy, a takeover by a higher administrative unit. In each instance, the goal is to ensure adequate and predefined levels of student performance, as measured by a particular set of tests designed or selected for that purpose. A basic assumption of accountability testing programs is that the identification of performance targets, with testing and consequences for results, will lead to more focused instruction and higher performance.

A major milestone in the growth of accountability testing programs occurred in 2002, when Congress passed the No Child Left Behind (NCLB) act. This legislation requires regular accountability testing as a prerequisite for receiving federal funds. The legislation puts pressure on states to identify poorly performing schools and seek remedies to the situation. The legislation requires testing of higher-order skills and the alignment of assessment to state standards.

Advocates of this dramatic expansion characterize it as an essential step in obtaining systematic information on the effectiveness of educational programs for all students. Critics of the new federal requirement for testing object to what they characterize as a one-size-fits-all overemphasis on testing of basics to the detriment of other important aspects of school programs.

All a testing program can do is collect information and summarize it for those who can use it. In order to evaluate the merits of arguments for and against educational accountability testing programs of various types, one needs to ask incisive questions about the purposes, procedures, and outcomes of these programs: What information is being collected and at what stage in a child's education or a school's program? Is there a good match between what is being taught and what is being tested? Is understandable information being provided to appropriate people, including students and parents, in a timely fashion?

When an accountability program is soundly designed and executed, it can be a valuable component of the educational process. In many ways such a regular checkup on the effectiveness of an educational program is as valuable as the health exams that we seek periodically and the independent financial audits that companies should receive regularly. In every instance we want to see the proper tests employed, but the real payoff comes from skilled interpretation and proper follow-up based on the results.

Judging Progress and Following Trends

In addition to providing information about the group that is currently being tested, an ongoing testing program permits comparisons over time. An important example in American education is the National Assessment of Educational Progress. The word *progress* in the official name of this program is no accident. The intention of American educators is to ensure that students develop their skills as they proceed through school and that improvement from year to year occurs in the overall performance of students and schools. Testing provides a way of describing the current status of education and of tracking trends over time.

One of the significant developments in testing during the later years of the twentieth century was the increase in public attention to the results of international studies of education. These cross-national projects have tended to focus on basic subjects such as reading or language arts and mathematics. There have been significant controversies within the United States as to what the results tell us. It seems quite clear, though, that our students are a far step from being "first in the world in mathematics and science," a national educational goal for the year 2000. Part of the difficulty in evaluating cross-national comparisons is that the vast majority of our elementary and secondary students remain in school until at least age 16. In many countries, most students end their formal education before that time. Very different results are found if we compare the mathematics performance of all our high school students, versus only those in advanced placement mathematics courses, with the performance of students from other countries. The outcomes could be called either very worrisome or exemplary, depending on the U.S. comparison group.

As with any type of trend data, the real benefits accrue as data are collected over several years. Longitudinal data allow us to answer questions such as, Are we doing a better job now than we were the last time we checked? How well are we meeting the needs of the many subgroups that make up our society? Part of the substantial value of well-crafted standardized tests is that they can help us answer questions of this type (Ekstrom & Smith, 2002; Willingham & Cole, 1997; Zwick, 2002). Progress on the individual student level is critical as well. School educators and parents expect to see students making yearly progress due to the provision of an excellent education program offered at the schools.

Self-Discovery

There are many important aspects of people beyond the domains of skills and competencies. It should not be surprising, then, that there are a wide variety of tests in areas such as attitudes, motivation, personality, and other psychological characteristics. With the assistance of a trained testing professional—such as a counselor, psychologist, social worker, or member of some other relevant helping profession—individuals can gain information to help them make more informed career and life decisions as well as deal with troublesome life circumstances. We need only scan the tables of contents of general interest magazines or browse the Internet to find tests that purport to help us find a mate, choose an ideal line of work, or achieve a deeper understanding of "who we really are." Since these tests may not meet high professional standards, they should not be taken too seriously. They may indeed help us reflect on aspects of who we are and how we view the world. If we are facing critical decisions, though, or dealing with some problem that is interfering with our relationships, work, or ability to lead the life we want to live, a test alone is not likely to meet our needs. A skilled professional can combine test results with other information about us and our situation, and work with us to help us improve our quality of life.

When evaluating the results of tests that are designed to help someone gain self-understanding, it is important to take into account the issues of honesty and consistency. Turning first to honesty, keep in mind that the test outcomes will depend in good part on how accurately the person describes himself or herself. If one always chooses the answer that describes an ideal person's choice, rather than one's own, there is no reason to expect an accurate result and interpretation. If someone responds as though he or she never had a selfish thought in their life, and would always choose to visit a sick friend over meeting a favorite athlete, singer, or movie star, don't be surprised if the resulting profile seems a lot nobler than the person really is.

It is also important to consider whether the results from testing are consistent with other available information. This is especially important when making important life decisions. Weigh the results of testing along with the many other pieces of information already available. Be open to new insights, surely, but wonder and seek advice about any guidance that seems contradictory to everything else known. For a true "city" person with little interest in the natural world, perhaps a job as a forest ranger or a gardener may not be as ideal as for someone who finds cities a noisy irritant to life.

What Are the Key Benefits of Systematic, High-Quality Testing?

Given that decision makers are seeking information to help them make decisions of the type we reviewed in the last section, what are the benefits of using the results of high-quality testing? We will discuss each of these valuable qualities:

- objective results
- cost-effectiveness
- technical quality and standards
- fairness
- evolutionary improvement

Objective Results

High-quality testing produces objective results, that is to say results that are consistent from occasion to occasion. This outcome is very clear when you use multiple-choice or other machine scored tests. You can score a test twice and get the same result. High levels of objectivity can also be obtained with assessment exercises that require professional scoring. It is essential to use exercises that well-trained and monitored scorers can grade with the necessary level of consistency, but this is a challenging, albeit attainable, goal. Whatever the type of test to be developed and used, issues such as the following need to be carefully addressed:

- What is the purpose of the test, and how will the results be used?
- What are the characteristics of the people who will take the test?
- What areas of content and skill will be measured?
- What scoring rules will be followed and how will accuracy be checked?

Cost-Effectiveness

High-quality tests are among the most cost-effective means available to obtain high-quality information. To obtain consistent measures of a student's or worker's performance outside of a specially designated testing situation requires several observations and two or more judges or observers. Such observations in real-life situations frequently involve 10 to 100 times the cost to achieve the same level of exactitude as a standardized test.

Technical Quality and Standards

The growth of the standardized movement in the United States has been accompanied by the development and refinement of professional standards for testing. Major testing companies and professional associations whose members make frequent use of tests have endorsed the *Standards for Educational and Psychological Testing* (AERA, APA, & NCME, 1999) as well as the *Code of Fair Testing Practices in Education* (Joint Committee on Testing Practices, 2002). Users of test results need to ascertain whether the tests being reported have been prepared in accordance with these standards. If so, it is possible to place considerable confidence in the technical quality of the results.

Fairness

Test makers strive to develop tests that primarily reflect the skill, knowledge, or other characteristics the test is intended to measure. If individuals or groups differ with respect to what is being measured, then test results should reveal those differences. Unfairness occurs, for example, when factors extraneous to the skill being evaluated have a significant influence on test scores. A test of mathematical skill that uses complex language or sets problems in contexts unfamiliar to test takers would not be a fair measure of this particular skill. Helms (1997) looks at the interaction of race, culture, and social class in cognitive ability testing and concludes that advisories should be included when reporting test scores of test takers with experiences and backgrounds different from advantaged students.

It is important to note that a fair test result, in the sense that it accurately portrays the competence of an individual or group, may well be perceived as unfair. For example, a parent who very much wants to see his or her child admitted to a highly selective program, school, or college will tend to reject any indicator that does not contribute to this objective (Zwick 2002).

Evolutionary Improvement

One of the great strengths of standardized testing as it is typically carried out in the United States by professional test developers is that the basic approaches employed support evolutionary improvement in the quality of the tests. Whereas we may say that we are going to review our work at the close of any important project in our work or home life, all too often we move on to the next task without systematically re-examining the extent to which we attained our goals. Life seems to bring us one string of demands after another and finding the time to review carefully the job just completed loses out to the need to go forward to the next challenge.

In standardized testing, reviewing how we did with this year's test is an essential part of the craft and science of test making. No credible testing professional fails to carry out thorough analyses of a test once it is administered, scored, and reported or interpreted. Indeed the professional standards governing the work of test developers and test users require this type of systematic review. Test developers aim for a test at a certain level of difficulty and one that has scores meeting a particular level of *reliability,* the test makers' term for consistency of results. Text makers explore questions appropriate to the test and how it is used through analyses of data collected at the time of testing and, where necessary, through additional data collection steps. For example, did we achieve our difficulty-level and reliability goals? Moreover, if the test is being used to select people for academic programs or for hiring or promotion, what is the evidence that the test provides information to support such decisions?

This practice of collecting and analyzing data over the years to evaluate the effectiveness of tests and test use is called *validation,* and it provides a regular means for improving the quality of a test over the period of its use. It is this phenomenon that we refer to as evolutionary improvement, and it is a quite important feature of standardized tests when wisely planned and used for test and test program improvement.

What Are the Frequent Criticisms of Testing?

A clear pattern to test criticism emerges if one takes the time to read through the many years of discussions of testing in popular news magazines, leading newspapers, and other major publications. Each time there is a substantial increase in the use of standardized testing or a new application of the approach, a wave of criticism follows. If the application is well planned and implemented, the intensity and duration of the criticism may be lessened, but the critics will still insist on being heard. When a new testing application has been introduced with insufficient notice to those affected or in a manner that violates professional testing standards and good sense, there can be prolonged and very strong criticism that on occasion stalls or derails the proposed testing application. Haney, Madaus, & Lyons (1993) include a chapter, "Test Quality and the Fractured Marketplace for Testing," that provides one perspective on the influence of market factors on test quality.

In this section we are going to look at four main classes of test criticism. A large percentage of all the concerns that are voiced about testing can be classified into one of these four categories:

- bias versus fairness
- coachability
- appropriateness of use
- technical quality

Bias Versus Fairness

The issue of whether standardized tests are fair or promote fairness in decision making is one of the most persistent and, on occasion, hotly debated areas of criticism of testing (Leman, 1999; Willingham & Cole, 1997; Zwick, 2002). One of the reasons for the heat and emotion that frequently characterize discussions of this issue is that the debate has a personal component. Those involved may begin with academic and dispassionate statements about the results of a particular testing program, but they often end up addressing the impact of testing on their own lives or those of their children or other family members.

Communication on the issue of bias or lack of it in testing is also complicated by the fact that participants in the discussion typically bring different definitions of bias to the situation. As we noted in our earlier discussion of test fairness, testing professionals examine the possibility that a test may be biased by checking to see if the results from that test are consistent with other information about the group being tested. If we look at the types of individuals earning high or low scores, does this result make sense in light of other information about the competencies measured by the test? For example, we would expect students who excel in their math classes, have joined the math club, and work on math puzzles for recreation to score high on a math test. Similarly, we would expect those students who take the absolute minimum number of math courses and ignore or fail to deliver math homework not to perform well.

Coachability

Groups reflecting a variety of perspectives would likely view evidence that scores could be readily affected by short-term coaching as a troublesome feature of any test. Thoughtful observers would also worry if a test were much better at predicting the future success of some groups of students than of others. Our expectation and requirement for tests is that they will be effective for all citizens, not only for a subset. Another issue in evaluating coaching are the definitions of coaching and short-term test preparation. In some areas, such as mathematics, there are effective short-term seminars that build both test-taking and other content skills. Finding that scores go up as the underlying skills being tested improve is a good feature of a test, not a source for concern.

In studies of the SAT I and the ACT Assessment, the tests for which perhaps the largest number of studies of the effectiveness of coaching have been carried out, only a small contribution to future test scores can be attributed to coaching courses (Messick, 1980). Whereas individuals trained in testing are inclined to be persuaded by these research results, the coaching companies report gains that are far greater than these average results. Often they present glowing testimonials to the effectiveness of coaching for an individual student, usually without much detail about the circumstances under which the reported gains were obtained. One of our speculations is that coaching companies look only at the gains made by those who earn higher scores, leaving out of their calculations those whose scores stay the same or decrease. So the "average gain" they report is actually the average gain of those who gained, not the average gain across all those who were taught.

As to advice for those who face standardized tests or are working with students or others who take them, by all means prepare carefully for any important test. Read the available material about the test, especially that produced by the test makers. Become very familiar with the types of questions you will encounter. Don't waste time figuring out what you need to do on the day of the test when others have done this task weeks or months ago. If everyone who comes to a test has done this type of preparation, the force of a criticism on the grounds of coachability is substantially undermined.

Appropriateness of Use

One of the criticisms of standardized testing that seems to us to be well supported in many instances deals with the use to which a test is put. Professional test developers are charged by their standards to be explicit about what the intended uses of their tests are. Agencies that choose to employ a test for a different purpose than that for which the test was developed have a responsibility to document the appropriateness of the test for the new use. For example, as we noted earlier in this chapter, a test designed to measure the mathematics competence of a native-speaking group may be completely inappropriate for judging the level of mathematical knowledge of many non-native speakers of English. They could have the skill that is intended to be measured but be unable to show their competence because of their inability to understand the problems that were set for them.

Technical Quality

Criticisms about the technical quality of tests sometimes focus on individual test questions, asserting that they are inadequate for the purpose of testing. Particular items may be judged too easy or too difficult, or perhaps described as too low-level or too ambiguous. The critic may assert that the coverage of the test is too shallow or is unbalanced in some way, giving too much weight to one or more areas and slighting another topic or topics. The format may be dismissed as wrong for the test in question; this happens especially with multiple-choice questions, although sometimes with essay or other question types. Another type of criticism regards the number of questions and the stability of the resultant score.

Those involved in the selection and use of tests should take the concerns of critics seriously, either evaluating the criticisms for themselves or bringing other trained professionals into the process. In some instances we stand to learn more by listening to critics than we would gain by proceeding to enjoy the support of friends, who may give us the benefit of the doubt and fail to give needed criticism.

How Can We Promote High-Quality Testing?

One of the most important ways to promote high-quality testing is to become familiar with the types of testing that are going on. How are tests being used? Are the purposes clearly stated, and do the kinds of tests being employed seem consistent with those purposes? What issues are being raised by individuals who find fault with the testing? Do the criticisms seem warranted?

One of the many benefits of our Internet-linked world is that it is now quite easy to look up what is being said about any test or testing program. We urge looking at both sides of any testing issue. Just as the maker of a test is predisposed to see the virtues of the product that is produced, some critics reflexively reject virtually any standardized test, no matter how carefully it is crafted and how educationally or occupationally sound the use to which it is being put.

For many people being an effective evaluator and user of tests and test results will require learning more about tests and test making. This book is one way for individuals to expand their knowledge. Chapter

53 provides guidance on accessing many types of resources. The following list provides some additional sources of information about tests and test quality.

Sources of Information

One of the best sources of information about any test or testing program is the test developer. Descriptive material, registration bulletins, score reports, and other test-related documents are often available from the test publisher. Be sure to take advantage of any information that you can obtain directly from the publisher; it is usually accurate and up-to-date, and it is often free.

Even if you have no printed materials in your possession, a systematic search of the Internet will often be very productive. Look for test descriptions, sample questions, and media coverage of the tests. There are two major trade associations of test publishers and one professional association, all of whose websites are resources both for general information and for locating specific test publishers and other testing agencies.

Association of Test Publishers (ATP; www.testpublishers.org). This association has well more than 100 member companies, representing clinical, educational, employment, and licensing/certification areas. This association is particularly active in the area of computer-based testing.

Association of American Publishers (AAP; www.publishers.org). This association represents all or virtually all the publishers of textbooks, tests, and related material for U.S. schools and colleges. The AAP Test Committee plays an active role in monitoring legislation and regulations related to testing. It has produced several fine publications about testing.

Joint Committee on Testing Practices (JCTP; www.apa.org/science/jctpweb.html). JCTP is a collaboration among professional associations whose members make extensive use of tests and testing companies. The organization's goal is to work "together to advance in the public interest the quality of testing practices" (JCTP home page, accessed 1/23/03). The JCTP has produced a number of helpful publications and other materials covering areas such as testing standards, test-purchaser qualifications, teaching about testing, the rights and responsibilities of test takers, and the testing of individuals with disabilities.

Collecting Specific Documents

If you are in a position to serve as a resource for others in the area of testing, you might find it useful to build a collection of materials that you could send to interested parties. Chapter 53 contains many references to organizations that might be helpful in obtaining information about tests. The supplementary compact disc also contains many documents that provide varying perspectives and additional information about tests and their uses in education.

References

AERA, APA, & NCME. (1999). *Standards for educational and psychological testing.* Washington, DC: American Educational Research Association.

Bracken, B. A. (Ed.). (1991). *The psychoeducational assessment of preschool children.* Needham Heights, MA: Allyn & Bacon.

Donlon, T. F. (Ed.). (1984). *The College Board technical handbook for the Scholastic Aptitude Test and Achievement Tests.* New York: College Board.

Ekstrom, R. B., & Smith, D. K. (2002). *Assessing individuals with disabilities.* Washington, DC: American Psychological Association.

Haney, W. M., Madaus, G. F., & Lyons, R. (1993). *The fractured marketplace for standardized testing.* Norwell, MA: Kluwer Academic Publishers.

Helms, J. E. (1997). The triple quandary of race, culture, and social class in standardized cognitive ability testing. In D. P. Flanagan, J. L. Genshaft, & P. L. Harrison (Eds.), *Contemporary intellectual assessment.* New York: Guilford Press.

✦Joint Committee on Testing Practices. (2002). *Code of fair testing practices in education.* Retrievable on AAC website at http://aac.ncat.edu.

Jones, L. V. (1971). The nature of measurement. In R. L. Thorndike (Ed.), *Educational measurement* (2d ed.). Washington, DC: American Council on Education.

Leman, N. (1999). *The big test.* New York: Farrar, Straus, & Giroux.

Messick, S. (1980). *The effectiveness of coaching for the SAT.* Princeton, NJ: Educational Testing Service.

Willingham, W. W., & Breland, H. M. (1982). *Personal qualities and college admissions.* New York: College Board.

Willingham, W. W., & Cole, N. S. (1997). *Gender and fair assessment.* Mahwah, NJ: Lawrence Erlbaum Associates.

Willingham, W. W., Lewis, C., Morgan, R., & Ramist, L. (1990). *Predicting college grades.* Princeton, NJ: Educational Testing Service.

Zwick, R. (2002). *Fair game.* New York: Routledge Falmer.

✦ Document is included in the Anthology of Assessment Resources CD

Chapter 2
Types and Uses of Tests

Timothy Vansickle

Describing the types and uses of tests may seem to be an easy task, but it is not as straightforward as it may first appear. Tests vary on many different characteristics, are used in many different ways, cross the typical assessment categories, and in some cases are so unique as to form a category unto themselves. This chapter explores many possible classification schemes and describes how tests may be used in several common settings.

Types of Tests

If you open almost any textbook on psychological assessments, tests, and measurements, or any compendium of test reviews, you will find the author's classification of tests or types of tests. This classification is usually implicit in the table of contents for the book. Anastasi (1982) provides chapters or sections for individual, group, aptitude, achievement, personality, intelligence, and ability testing. Global categories include educational, occupational, and clinical, with more specific categories of self-reports, inventories, projective techniques, and so on. Janda (1998) groups tests into individual tests of intelligence, group ability tests, interests, values, structured measures of personality, projective tests and clinical assessment, neuropsychological assessment of special populations, and alternate approaches to assessment. Hopkins (1998) takes a somewhat simpler approach, with divisions into scholastic aptitude, achievement, personality, and social measures, and standardized versus instructor-made tests.

Murphy, Conoley, and Impara (1994) in the fourth edition of *Tests in Print* chose a much more linear approach to test classification, as illustrated in the following list:

- achievement
- behavior assessment
- developmental

- education
- English
- fine arts
- foreign language
- intelligence and scholastic aptitude
- math
- miscellaneous
- multi-aptitude
- neuropsychological
- personality
- reading
- science
- sensory-motor
- social studies
- speech and hearing
- vocations

As can be seen from this brief sampling, test classification is not straightforward. This confusion may result from the fact that the word *test* can be used in various ways. The new *Standards for Educational and Psychological Testing* (AERA, APA, & NCME, 1999) defines *tests* as "all evaluative devices such as inventories [and] scales." Typical textbooks, manuscripts, and discussions use *test, assessment,* and *measure,* as well as other words, and use these interchangeably. It is, therefore, a good idea to define some of these words with a goal of enabling a classification scheme.

Allen and Yen (1979) define a test as a device for obtaining a sample of an individual's behavior. Anastasi (1982) provides a little more detail in that a test is essentially an objective and standardized measure of a sample of behavior. Hopkins (1998) suggests that a test is a technique for obtaining information. The AERA, APA, and NCME standards define a test as follows: "A test is an evaluation device or procedure in which a sample of an examinee's behavior in a specified domain is obtained and subsequently evaluated and scored using a standardized process" (p. 3).

"*Measurement* is the assigning of numbers to individuals in a systematic way as a means of representing properties of the individuals" (Allen & Yen, 1979, p. 2). Hopkins (1998) suggests that measurement is a process by which things are differentiated and described. Hence, measurement is a furthering of the testing process.

Assessment is typically the larger umbrella under which judgments, actions, or decisions are made based on the tests and measurements used in a given situation. Assessment, therefore, includes testing and measurement, and in many contexts is used in place of either or both terms. For our discussion, we will use *test* to indicate any assessment device that might yield a score, category, or classification, or where the results could be used to make some decision about people, programs, status, or acceptance/admission.

Classifying Tests by Setting

How then do we classify tests into types or categories? Tests differ on many characteristics, such as mode of administration, stimulus materials, response mode, content, construct, level of standardization, and historical context. Test use and classification may vary with the setting in which the test is used. In clinical settings some personality tests may be classified as diagnostic while others are referred to as screening inventories. In personnel settings, tests can have a different classification system that involves selection, progression, and promotion classifications. In this setting, personality tests, aptitude tests, and achievement tests may lose their individual classifications in favor of a more global categorization such as selection battery.

Classifying Tests by Scope

One way of classifying tests may be to look at the nature of the test instrument. That is, does it have specific objectives or a narrow content domain as the target of interest? Instructor-made tests are examples of a narrowly focused type of test having specific objectives. On the other end of the continuum would be tests that measure a broad set of objectives or a large construct; for example, individually administered IQ tests. Certainly, one could argue about where on the continuum a certain type of test may fall; Figure 1 depicts one possible placement of the more general types of tests in use today.

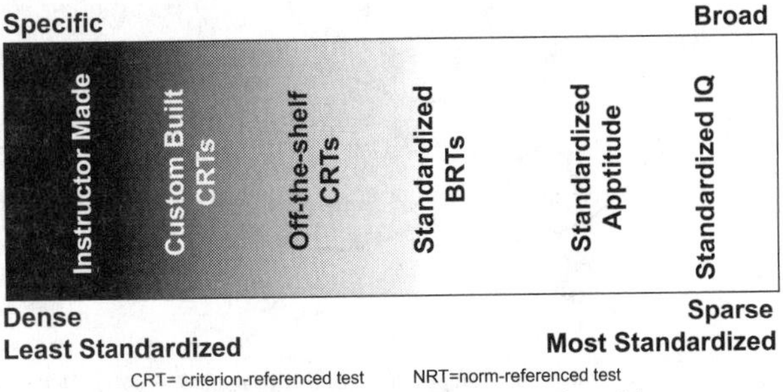

Figure 1. A test classification based on scope, number and rigor

In Figure 1, the number of tests also decreases as we move from left to right. Undoubtedly, there are more instructor-made tests than standardized IQ tests. Although one may argue with the placement of certain categories in Figure 1, it does provide a general sense of how tests might be classified. Additionally, Figure 1 reflects the different degrees of rigor with which tests are developed. In this regard, many instructors will argue that they standardize their tests as well as any commercial publisher, and many publishers would argue that a particular test they sell is the more rigorously developed. Some of those claims will be market driven while others are fairly subjective. Most of the broad-based intelligence tests are based on decades of research on the constructs, methods, item types, and administration procedures used. Newer, group-administered aptitude, achievement, and personality tests cannot match that history. They may however employ newer and more refined research and psychometric methods that may offset the lack of history. In presenting Figure 1, my intention is not to imply a value judgment regarding the various degrees of standardization but merely to illustrate one way of classifying tests.

It is very difficult to determine where to place cognitive tests as a group on Figure 1. For example, where does achievement end and aptitude begin? Figure 2 depicts the different overlapping possibilities in the various types of cognitive tests. Such interrelationships surely also occur in tests of personality or career interests, and in those designed for special populations. Exactly how much overlap exists is a matter of viewpoint or focus rather than a value that can be quantified empirically.

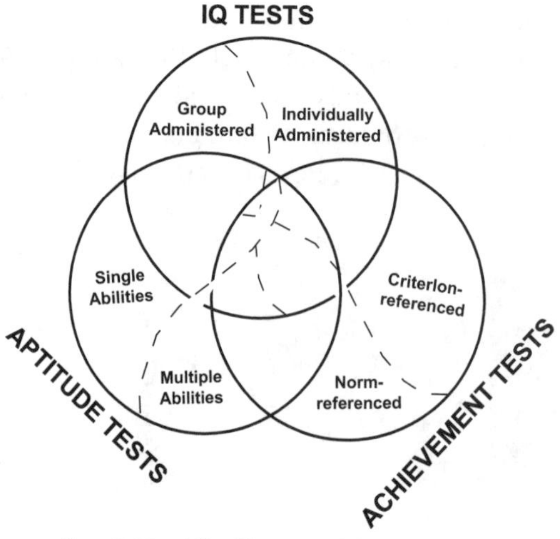

Figure 2. Interrelationships among Cognitive Tests

Classifying Tests Using a Traditional Matrix

A general classification scheme might use traditional perspectives, methodological approaches, and issues presented earlier to produce a means of classifying tests in a way useful for practitioners. Table 1 provides an example of such a matrix, including for some of the cells examples of relevant tests. Thousands of tests, inventories, and assessments are available from commercial publishers, researchers, and other practitioners. Most of these assessments are labeled as to the type of test (e.g., personality), type of administration (e.g., individual), and other characteristics and features. Although the publisher or test developer recommends certain parameters, common practice or usage may extend or restrict how an assessment is utilized, with the result that tests may overlap across cells. In addition, the practitioner could easily extend the table to include test types found most often in specific settings.

Table 1. Example Classification by Major Category, Specific Type, and Type of Administration

		Type of Administration	
Major Category/Specific Type		Group	Individual
Cognitive	Achievement	Iowa Tests of Basic Skills (1)	
		TerraNova (2)	
		Stanford9 (3)	
		The ACT Assessment (ACT) (5)	
		WorkKeys (5)	WorkKeys (5)
		Scholastic Assessment Test (SAT)(4)	
	Aptitude		Differential Aptitude Test (3)
		Cognitive Abilities Test (1)	OLSAT (3)
			Woodcock-Johnson III Tests of Cognitive Abilities (1)
	Intelligence		Stanford-Binet Intelligence Test (1)
			Wechsler Intelligence Test (3)
			Kaufman Assessment Battery for Children (K-ABC) (6)
Personality	Normal	Myers-Brigs Type Indicator (7)	16PF Fifth Edition Questionnaire (8)
		16PF Fifth Edition Questionnaire (8)	MMPI-2 (9)
			Myers-Brigs Type Indicator (7)
	Clinical	MMPI (9)	MMPI (9)
Career	Interests	Self-Directed Search (10)	Self-Directed Search (10)
		Career Decision-Making System (6)	Career Decision-Making System (6)
		Campbell Interest and Skill Survey(9)	Campbell Interest and Skill Survey(9)
	Values	Values Scale (7)	Values Scale (7)
		Career Beliefs Inventory (7)	Career Beliefs Inventory (7)
		Values Preference Indicator (11)	Values Preference Indicator (11)

(1) Riverside Publishing
(2) CTB McGraw Hill
(3) Harcourt
(4) Educational Testing Service
(5) ACT, Inc.
(6) American Guidance Service
(7) Consulting Psychologists Press
(8) Institute for Personality and Ability Testing
(9) NCS
(10) Psychological Assessment Resources
(11) Consulting Resources Group International

Classifying Tests by Measurement Model

A more traditional way of classifying tests is to place each test into one of several bins, including but not limited to norm-referenced versus criterion-referenced. Norm-referenced tests are those that report scores or profiles based on reference to a standard group (i.e., the norm group). People typically think of group achievement tests (e.g., Iowa Tests of Basic Skills) as belonging to this category. In addition, many personality, diagnostic, and intelligence tests also use a reference group in order to place a person into a category or to provide a score. For example, the determination of whether a client is depressed may be made in relation to a standardization group that was not depressed. In these types of tests, a normative sample of individuals is used to determine the distributional characteristics of the responses for that group (e.g., mean and standard deviation). The test is scaled so that various scores can be reported to test takers based on the typical response patterns of the standardization group. The score or scores a test taker receives are a reflection of how the person performed compared to the normative sample.

Criterion-referenced tests use a different technique to provide scores or classifications. In this case, an individual's responses are compared to some predetermined standard (i.e., criterion). The standard may be a cut-off score expressed as a raw score, a percentage, a standard score, or some other value. If the test taker reaches or exceeds the specified standard or criterion, he or she is classified as having learned the material, achieved a specific level of mastery, or falling into some group or category (e.g., addictive behavior problem).

Uses of Tests

So what have learned so far? Classification of tests can and does vary based on the classification scheme and its particular focus. Is one classification model better than another? Not necessarily. The answer depends on the purpose of the testing and the decisions one wishes to make.

Regardless of the category or classification of a test, test usage is something all practitioners must address in their work. Questions of validity, reliability, fairness, and purpose all play a part in determining the use of any instrument. Some tests may be used in multiple situations or contexts, while others may be restricted to a single situation. One key principle to remember is that a test is but a sample of an individual's behavior, learning, cognition, or other characteristic being measured.

As such, a test score should not be the sole determiner in high-stakes decisions.

What then are practitioners to do when deciding which test to use in a specific situation? First, they need to acquire training in test measurements and the specific test instrument, if required. Then, they must ask themselves a series of questions about the testing situation:

- What is the purpose of the testing?
- What decisions will be made about the person or group based on the test results?
- What tests are available for this purpose?
- Is a home-grown or a custom-built test the better option given the purpose and decisions to be made?
- What special training is required to administer and interpret the results of the test?
- What security procedures are required by either the publisher or the testing situation?
- Will the test or tests selected provide the information needed?
- Are there additional stakeholders who need different information than the test will provide?

In some cases the test user will also have to justify the cost of the testing program, in which case additional questions need to be asked:

- What is the initial purchase cost?
- What is the per-examinee cost?
- What discounts are available from the publisher (e.g., for purchasing in quantity)?
- What are the costs associated with the examinee's time (e.g., lost production time, lost instruction time)?
- What alternatives are available that might cost less?

For each context in which testing occurs, there may be additional questions that the practitioner must answer prior to selecting, administering, scoring, and interpreting a test. In the following sections, let's examine some of these particular contexts.

Testing in Schools

By far the most common situation where tests are used is in the academic setting. Whether in the K–12 or postsecondary arena, testing is a ubiquitous event in the lives of teachers, students, and administrators. Teacher-made tests to measure students' learning is by far the most prevalent form of testing. Designed well, instructor-made tests can provide enormous amounts of information for both the teacher and the student.

In addition to teacher-made tests, many large schools and districts develop or purchase tests that they use to make decisions about the effectiveness of programs, teachers, schools, and curriculum. With the advent of the standards-based education movement, many states now incorporate statewide testing to evaluate the effectiveness of instruction and the achievement of state-established curriculum goals or targets. This typically had been done via norm-referenced tests, but standards-based initiatives have replaced or augmented the norm-referenced tests with custom-built, criterion-referenced tests designed specifically to measure the state curriculum and the success of students, teachers, programs, schools, and districts in meeting established academic targets.

Within the academic testing world, new tests are being developed to assess special populations. This is especially true with regard to statewide curriculum standards. The term *alternate assessment* is typically used to describe a test or assessment that is administered when a student's Individualized Education Program (IEP) indicates that he or she cannot be tested using the statewide test in a standard or accommodated format.

Admissions Testing

Another major area is admissions testing. The two most notable and best known of such tests are the ACT Assessment and the Scholastic Aptitude Test (SAT). The region of the country in which a student resides sometimes determines which of these two college entrance exams he or she will take. There are, of course, other admissions tests, such as the Graduate Record Exam (GRE). Most professional degree programs, such as medicine, have specialized admissions tests (e.g., the MCAT).

The goal of admissions testing is to determine who would best be served by further education in a particular field and at a particular university or college. In this respect, each school determines its own test score requirements. In the case of the ACT Assessment and SAT, the goal is to predict a particular student will be successful in the postsecondary institution to which he or she is applying. Today, however, some institutions are downplaying the importance of, or even eliminating the requirement for, a standardized college admissions test.

Tests Used in Clinical and Counseling Settings

The number and range of instruments available for use in counseling is, to say the least, staggering. Instruments exist to measure normal personality, vocational interests, academic ability, depressive tendency, susceptibility to addictive behaviors, self-efficacy, and the need for control or dominance, to name a few. Add to these tests of intelligence or abnormal personality, plus screening and diagnostic instruments, and the practitioner in this area can quickly be inundated to the point of information overload.

Uses range from a high school counselor administering the Armed Services Vocational Aptitude Battery (ASVAB) to a clinician administering a screening instrument for depression. In these settings, the purpose of testing is to gain information about the client's characteristics or behavior. In this regard, the information may be shared with the individual for a variety of reasons, including but not limited to helping individuals make decisions about career or life changes, or understand how others relate to them. The practitioner may be the only person to view the test results; for example, in the case of making a decision as to a client's status or state. That decision may be used to help make a decision to admit a person for treatment or to refer that person to another agency or practice.

Tests Used in Industry

One of the more fascinating areas of testing is that of selection, progression, and promotion in industry. In this setting, there are many different stakeholders, as well as federal, state, and sometimes local regulations and requirements that compete with psychometric characteristics of the test.

In the workplace setting, the purpose of testing is to determine the best candidate for a specific position or job. The goal is to determine the specific knowledge, skills, and abilities needed to be successful in that position and to measure as many of these as is possible prior to hiring, training, or promoting an individual. In industry, hiring a worker is associated with enormous costs, including wages, relocation, training, and benefits. Making a poor choice may have devastating effects on an organization and can develop into a health or safety issue, depending on the industry and specific job.

Many of the tests used in industry are specific to the company, plant site, and job. Developed by outside consultants or in-house personnel, these tests utilize job and task analysis to develop the content of the test and determine the appropriate level of knowledge, skill, and ability needed. This process can be very costly. Hence, firms must engage in a cost analysis to determine whether building or buying a test will benefit the company. Typically, this cost analysis looks for savings in training time, error rates, employee turnover, and other factors in determining the benefit to the company.

Conclusion

Any given test may be classified and used in many ways. The practitioner has a responsibility to look at the testing situation, the decisions to be made by each of the stakeholders in that situation, and the available test instruments in order to determine the best course of action. *Measuring Up* provides insights into many of the issues encountered in the testing arena and provides practitioners with guidance and resources to help them do their work. Many other books are available that review or critique commercially available tests. In addition, several professional organizations address issues of testing, measurement, and assessment. The newsletters and journals of these organizations can provide information beneficial in understanding how a test can be used. You can find specific resources and references to these in chapter 53.

It is important to understand the nature of tests and how they may be used and classified. It is more important, however, to use the best tools available, acquire the training necessary to use these tools correctly, then make good conservative use of the test results in light of the setting and the individuals involved.

References

AERA, APA, & NCME. (1999). *Standards for educational and psychological testing.* Washington, DC: American Educational Research Association.

Allen, M. J., & Yen, W. M. (1979). *Introduction to measurement theory.* Belmont CA: Wadsworth.

Anastasi, A. (1982). *Psychological testing* (5th ed.). New York: Macmillan.

DuBois, P. H. (1970). *A history of psychological testing.* Boston, MA: Allyn & Bacon.

Hood, A. B., & Johnson R. W. (1997). *Assessment in counseling: A guide to the use of psychological assessment procedures.* Alexandria, VA: American Counseling Association.

Hopkins, K. D. (1998). *Educational and psychological measurement and evaluation* (8th ed.). Needham Heights, MA: Allyn & Bacon.

Janda, L. H. (1998). *Psychological testing: Theory and applications.* Needham Heights, MA: Allyn & Bacon.

Murphy, L. L., Conoley, J. C., & Impara, J. C. 1994 . *Tests in print IV.* Lincoln: University of Nebraska Press.

Chapter 3
Guidelines for Selecting Appropriate Tests

Patricia Jo McDivitt & Donna Gibson

In 1990 the American Federation of Teachers (AFT), the National Council on Measurement in Education (NCME), and the National Education Association (NEA) published *Standards for Teacher Competence in Educational Assessment of Students*. Standard 1 of this document states, "Teachers should be skilled in choosing assessment methods appropriate for instructional decisions." (p. 3) Teachers and all educators involved in the selection and use of tests follow several guidelines when seeking to gain this competence. These guidelines include understanding the purpose of the assessment and determining the quality of the assessment. This chapter reviews these guidelines and provides educators with important information to help them select appropriate tests.

Understanding the Purpose of a Test

The first step in attaining competency in selecting appropriate tests involves understanding the purpose or purposes for which an assessment is given. According to Mehrens (2001), in its broadest sense, the purpose of any assessment is to gather data to facilitate decision making. However, many kinds of decisions and many different types of information may be gained from the use of tests and may serve to facilitate decision making. For example, the decision made may involve helping an individual select courses for high school or make wise, realistic career decisions; other decisions might be made to help an individual improve upon his or her strengths and weaknesses in a given subject area; and still others might be made to help an individual build toward mastery of a particular set of content curriculum standards or learning targets. In today's high-stakes arena, still other tests may be used to make important decisions such as whether a particular student should be promoted to the next grade in school or should receive a high school diploma.

Most tests used in modern educational settings can be categorized into two major types: norm-referenced tests and criterion-referenced tests. These two types of tests differ in purpose, content, and the information gained from their use. The main purpose of a *norm-referenced test* is to compare students' performance and to determine relative strengths and weaknesses of students based upon the generalized skills being measured by the test.

In contrast, *criterion-referenced tests* determine "what test takers can do and what they know, not how they compare to others" (Anastasi, 1988, p. 102). Criterion-referenced tests report how well students are doing relative to a predetermined performance level on a specified set of educational goals or outcomes included in the school, district, or state curriculum. Educators may choose to use a criterion-referenced test when they want to determine how well students have learned the knowledge and skills they are expected to have mastered (Bond, 1996).

When deciding whether to use a norm-referenced or a criterion-referenced test, it is important to know about the content differences between the two. The content of a norm-referenced test is selected according to how well it ranks students from high achievers to low. The content of a criterion-referenced test is determined by how well it matches the learning outcomes deemed most important. Although no test can measure everything of importance, the content of a criterion-referenced test is selected based on its significance in the curriculum, whereas that of a norm-referenced test is chosen by how well it discriminates among students (Bond, 1996). Because the purpose of many norm-referenced tests currently used in the classroom is to measure the academic foundation skills that students need, the test questions are usually designed to measure a generalized set of objectives that are common across the country for a given content area.

> When standardized tests are norm-referenced, it means that national samples of students have been used as the norming group for interpreting relative standing. Because these tests are designed to be used in different schools throughout the country, they tend to provide broad coverage of each content area to maximize potential usefulness in as many schools as possible. Thus, close inspection of the objectives and types of test questions is needed to determine how well the test matches the emphasis in the local curriculum. (McMillan, 1997, pp. 79–80)

Evaluating Test Quality

The second step in selecting an appropriate test is to evaluate its quality. Evaluating the quality of a test involves a careful analysis of the characteristics of the population to be tested; the knowledge, skills, abilities, or attitudes to be assessed; and the eventual use and interpretation of the test scores (ACA & AAC, 1987). The following list outlines major quality criteria that teachers, counselors, and other test users should consider when selecting a test. These criteria are relevant for many kinds of tests not strictly those used in educational settings or classrooms. This information is based upon Klein and Hamilton (1999, Table 1), the *Code of Fair Testing Practices in Education* (JCTP, 2002), and *Responsibilities of Users of Standardized Tests* (ACA & AAC, 1987).

Purpose. Compare the purpose and recommended use of the assessment against your assessment goals.

Validity. Check for evidence of validity, that is, the degree to which an assessment measures what it is intended to measure.

Reliability. Check the consistency and dependability of the assessment results. Select only tests that have documented evidence of reliability, that is, consistency.

Alignment with curriculum. For tests intended to measure students' mastery of learning targets, check for instructional validity, or the degree to which the test questions measure what is actually taught in the classroom.

Equity and fairness. Check to be sure that the test meets appropriate standards for bias, fairness, and cultural sensitivity, and is fair and equitable for all test takers in your setting.

Technical standards. If the assessment is norm-referenced, check for norming procedures that are relevant to the local population and intended use of the data; also check for the types and quality of norms.

Costs and feasibility. Check for practical constraints due to cost, conditions, and time required for administration.

Consequences. Check what inferences and actions might result from the use of the test scores.

Timeliness of score reports. Check on the length of time between the test administration and the receipt of score reports.

Motivation. Check for the degree to which examinees will be motivated to do their best.

Quality of the administrative, interpretative, and technical manuals. Check to see that supportive materials are high in quality, user friendly, and readily available.

Each of these issues will be described in more detail in the remainder of this chapter. The selection of a test should be guided by established criteria for technical quality recommended by measurement professionals, including validity and reliability. Therefore, we begin with a discussion of technical qualities, including validity and reliability.

Validity

Assessments need to be fair, reliable, defensible, and free of bias. They also need to be valid. In fact, validity is at the core of the test development process for any assessment. One common definition of validity is contained in Cronbach (1971): Test validation is a process in which evidence is collected by the developer of a test to support the types of inferences that may appropriately be drawn from test scores. A more recent definition of validity is cited in the 1999 version of the *Standards for Educational and Psychological Testing:*

> Validity refers to the degree to which evidence and theory support the interpretations of test scores entailed by proposed uses of tests. Validity is, therefore, the most fundamental consideration in developing and evaluating tests. The process of validation involves accumulating evidence to provide a sound scientific basis for the proposed score interpretations. It is the interpretations of test scores required by proposed uses that are evaluated, not the test itself. When test scores are used or interpreted in more than one way, each intended interpretation must be validated. (AERA, APA, & NCME, 1999, p. 9)

When gathering and examining evidence of validity, the first question to ask is, Validity for what purpose? For example, career interest inventories have been in use for a number of years, and many of these instruments have well-documented validity. The validity of such interest inventories has commonly been determined by comparing individuals' interests with their occupational choices and then determining the rate of correct predictions over a specified period of time (Seligman, 1980). When predicting the occupation that a person is likely to enter in the future, an interest inventory may be valid because the person's answers to the questions will probably relate to career interests. When it comes to predicting whether this person will be successful in the given occupation, however, a career interest inventory may lack validity. Persons who enter an occupation for which they receive a low score on a given career interest inventory may well not stay in the occupation, whereas people who score high are much more likely to stay in the occupation. The low scorers who stay in that field are just as likely to be successful as the high scorers, however. Therefore, a score on a given interest inventory may have some validity for predicting whether people will enter an occupation, and how long they will stay in it, but may have little validity when predicting success in the occupation (Hood & Johnson, 1991).

As a result, determining whether or not a test is valid involves a process of gathering evidence to support a specific interpretation of the test scores. Many different methods for gathering evidence exist, and the evidence gathered establishes what kinds of inferences are appropriate to make (Osterlind, 1989). In looking at validity, educators must keep in mind what specific inferences will be drawn from the scores, then look for and gather evidence to support such inferences. Mehrens (2001) identifies two general types of inferences: (1) inferences about performance other than that measured, and (2) inferences about a characteristic (construct) of the person measured.

When gathering evidence, it is important to note that there are several types of validity. These are discussed in the sections that follow.

Face Validity

Face validity asks the question, Based upon a surface examination, does the test look like it measures what it is intended to measure, with test questions that appear to provide an adequate measure of what the test as a whole is intended to measure? Face validity is simply a matter of whether or not the test questions on the surface seem to be relevant to the person taking the test (Hood & Johnson, 1991). Some would argue that face validity is really not valid at all, especially if the process of examining an assessment is haphazard or not very systematic. For example, when examining a mathematics test consisting of word problems, teachers might ask themselves whether the test items do in fact appear to measure the defined mathematics objectives, or instead measure reading comprehension ability. A quick look at the test may lead them to conclude that the test does not have face validity because it appears to measure reading comprehension more than the mathematics skills or objectives it purports to measure.

Content Validity

Although it is important that an assessment does have some face validity, it is more important that the evidence of validity be documented, or have content validity.

Content validity indicates whether the material in the test is related to what is being measured and reflects the level of learning or development of that skill (Seligman, 1980). Content validity asks the fundamental question, How well does the assessment measure what it is intended to measure? For example, if a high school end-of-course biology test purports to measure the curriculum standards and core skills outlined for the course, then each test item or question must show a close correspondence to those curriculum standards and core skills. This close correspondence must be documented through a content validation study, which seeks to establish a consensus of informed opinions about the degree of congruence between particular test items and specific descriptions of the content domain to be assessed by those items. A content validation study requires convening a panel of expert judges who rate the item-to-content congruence according to established criteria (Osterlind, 1989).

In the development of current criterion-referenced statewide assessment programs, the content validation study often involves educators, including curriculum experts, subject-area teachers, and others. These educators, who are experts in the subject area, are asked to use their professional judgment to determine whether or not the test questions on a given criterion-referenced test do in fact measure the designated curriculum content standards or learning targets. This process depends on the development of clear learning targets. Based upon the learning targets for a given program or subject area, a test blueprint for the assessment is developed. The blueprint outlines the number of items a given test will include, mapped directly to the learning targets. The blueprint also provides information concerning the relative emphasis assigned to particular learning targets.

Instructional Validity

For many criterion-referenced tests used in the schools today, one aspect of content validity is the extent to which the test has instructional validity.

Instructional validity relates to the match between what is taught in the classroom and what is actually assessed. When examining instructional validity, the major questions to ask are, How closely do the test questions correspond to what has actually been taught in the classroom? Have students had the opportunity to learn what is being assessed? Instructional validity is also determined by teachers' professional judgments (McMillan, 1997).

Criterion-Related Validity

Validity also refers to the extent to which the test is related to defined criterion measures. Establishing criterion-related validity involves accumulating various types of evidence: "Evidence of the relation of test scores to a relevant criterion may be expressed in various ways, but the fundamental question is always: How accurately do test scores predict criterion performance? The degree of accuracy deemed necessary depends on the purpose for which the test is used" (AERA et al., 1999, p. 14).

Test developers and researchers seek to establish criterion-related evidence that a test is measuring the same trait, knowledge, or attitude by calculating a correlation coefficient, which measures the relationship between the test and the criterion. Unlike in content-validation studies, teachers and subject-area experts typically do not conduct formal studies to obtain correlation coefficients that will provide evidence of criterion-related validity. However, understanding the principles of establishing criterion-related validity is important. Where there are two or more measures of the same thing, and these measures provide similar results, criterion-related evidence can be established informally (McMillan, 1997). For example, consider the development of a test of computer word processing skills that measures speed and accuracy of key entry. The test might be given to a student who is taking a word processing course. The classroom teacher might then be asked to observe the student's word processing skills and rate the student using a rating sheet. The teacher's rating sheet would be compared with the student's test results, to determine how closely related the two are. If the teacher's observational ratings coincide with the student's score on the test, then criterion-related validity has been established. This type of validity is also called *concurrent validity.* Measures of concurrent validity are usually obtained when the test is going to be used in the future to estimate some type of behavior—such as the ability to do the work of a key-entry word processor.

Another type of criterion-related validity is called *predictive validity.* For example, if a classroom teacher is interested in the extent to which students' test preparation, as indicated by scores on a final examination in mathematics, predicts how well those students will do next year, he or she might examine the grades of students who took the class previously, then determine informally if students who scored high on the final examination are getting high grades, and students who scored low on the final examination are getting low grades, in the current year's math class. If a correlation is found, then an inference predicting how the students in the class will perform, based on the final exam, might be valid (McMillan, 1997).

Construct Validity

Construct validity is determined by gathering evidence that there is a relationship between the content of a test and the construct it is intended to measure. Construct validity demonstrates two points: (1) that the construct measured by the test is required for success on the criterion of interest, and (2) that the specific test under consideration is a good measure of the theoretical construct or trait (Bennett, Seashore, & Wesman, 1991).

> Test content refers to the themes, wording, and format of the items, tasks, or questions on a test, as well as the guidelines for procedures regarding administration and scoring. Test developers often work from a specification of the content domain. The content specification carefully describes the content in detail, often with a classification of areas of content and types of items. Evidence based on test content can include logical or empirical analyses of the adequacy with which the test content represents the content domain and of the relevance of the content domain to the proposed interpretation of test scores. (AERA et al., 1999, p. 13)

Construct validity evidence relies on both logical and statistical means to justify the use of a test. Evidence of construct validity is usually gathered by collecting criterion-related validity evidence, content validity evidence, and information about the test development process.

Guidelines for Selecting

Construct validity also involves gathering evidence or information about the test's overlap with other tests. Convergent validity and divergent validity also provide evidence of construct validity. *Convergent validity* means that an assessment shows a substantial correlation with other tests and assessments that measure similar characteristics. For example, students ought to score similarly on measures of mathematical aptitude and on the mathematics section of an achievement test. *Divergent validity,* on the other hand, is shown when an assessment does not correlate highly with a test or a variable that measures different constructs. For example, a student's score on a test of perceptual speed and accuracy in all likelihood would not show a strong correlation with a test of academic achievement.

According to Hood and Johnson (1991, p. 37), construct validity is a complex concept that encompasses several questions:

- Do the test results make psychological sense?
- Are the test results related to things that they ought to be related to and unrelated to things that they ought not to be related to?
- Do the results on the test change according to what we know about developmental changes?
- Do older students do better on the test than younger students; for example, on an arithmetic test, do sixth graders score higher than third graders do?
- Does the test pick up the kinds of changes known to occur as people develop?

Validity Checklist

The validity checklist in Figure 1 is designed to help test users determine whether or not a given test is valid. Because test selection should be guided by established criteria for technical quality recommended by measurement professionals, including validity, the items on the checklist address what types of validity information are available and whether or not the validity information provided is relevant to the purposes of the test. For example, content validity and instructional validity are important if you are using a criterion-referenced test to determine whether students have mastered specific learning targets. On the other hand, criterion-related validity is important if you are using the test for employee selection purposes.

Figure 1. Validity checklist

Type of Validity	Ask Yourself	Yes/No
Face validity	Does the assessment appear to measure what it is intended to measure?	Y N
Content validity	Is there documentation that the assessment measures what it is intended to measure?	Y N
Instructional validity	Do the assessment questions correspond to what has actually been taught in the classroom?	Y N
Criterion-related validity	Do the test scores predict future performance on a specific criterion?	Y N
Predictive validity	Is there evidence showing that the test accurately predicts future performance?	Y N
Concurrent validity	Is there evidence showing that the test measures performance on the relevant behaviors?	Y N
Construct validity	Does the assessment represent the theoretical entity it is intended to represent?	Y N
Convergent validity	Is there evidence showing that the test results are similar to results on other measures that should be related?	Y N
Divergent validity	Is there evidence showing that the test results are unlike those obtained on other, unrelated measures?	Y N

Reliability

In order to have good validity, a test must be reliable (Lyman, 1998). In general terms *reliability* refers to how consistently a test measures what it is purported to measure (Hood & Johnson, 1997). In fact, a test can be highly reliable (i.e., give consistent results) and not measure what it is purported to measure (i.e., not be valid). Therefore, a good understanding of reliability is required for appropriate testing.

In essence, a reliable test can be depended on to measure the same trait or variable each time it is used.

When a test is reliable, the results can be generalized in several different ways. First, the test user can assume that items that are similar but not identical to those on the original test would produce similar results (called alternate-form reliability). For example, a teacher may test students on their recognition of single-digit numerals by testing recognition of five different single-digit numerals. Because this measure is highly reliable, the teacher may assume that students would receive the same score if they were tested on other single-digit numerals. Hence, the teacher can generalize from one sample of items from the single-digit numeral domain to any other samples from the single-digit numeral domain (Salvia & Ysseldyke, 2001).

Second, results can be generalized from one time to another; that is, the same testing behavior or results will occur again if the students are tested with the same test at a different time (called test-retest reliability). For example, if the teacher gave the single-digit numeral test to students in the morning, he or she should see the same results upon administering the test in the afternoon (provided that no teaching of numerals has occurred in the interim).

Third, there should be consistency in results among testers (called inter-rater or interscorer reliability). If one teacher scores students on their recognition of single-digit numerals, then a second teacher scores the same students on the same measure, the two teachers' results should be similar. If they are, the assumption is made that scorers are consistent and results are reproducible among the scorers. These three types of reliability are discussed in more detail in the following sections.

Alternate-Form Reliability and Internal Consistency

Alternate-form reliability is determined by comparing the consistency of one individual's testing behavior on two equivalent forms of the same test (Hood & Johnson, 1997). Both forms of the test must be constructed to measure the same trait or construct and look similar in terms of format, number of items, and directions (Ponterotto, 1996). If necessary, the individual being assessed can be given both forms of the test without concern that results will reflect being exposed to the same test items. Often school systems will use two forms (e.g., Form A and Form B) of a standardized achievement test to accommodate students being served in special education programs. Alternate-form reliability is particularly important when the test users will need to test individuals or groups several times on the same content or trait, as might occur in research, in examining the effectiveness of teaching methods, or in examining student achievement.

Internal consistency is calculated on only one form of a test and is used to estimate the generalizability of results to different test items (Salvia & Ysseldyke, 2001). Specifically, the *reliability coefficients* obtained through this process indicate the consistency with which the items sample the trait being measured (Hood & Johnson, 1997). This type of reliability is important for tests that are not timed and are not completed under time pressure (Lyman, 1998).

Stability or Test-Retest Reliability

Stability and *test-retest reliability* are often used synonymously because test-retest reliability is an index of stability (Salvia & Ysseldyke, 2001). This method of evaluating reliability involves administering the same test instrument to one group or sample at two points in time (Ponterotto, 1996). Calculating test-retest reliability allows the user to know if the test produces the same results over time.

There are several considerations when evaluating the test-retest reliability of a particular measure. The first is to determine the interval between the two administrations of the test. Reliability coefficients can be expected to decrease as the length of the interval increases. If the interval is too long, maturation of the test takers and events they have experienced (learning) may influence the results. Conversely, test-retest coefficients can be inflated if the interval is too short. When the interval is brief, memory and practice may influence the test takers' results.

Inter-rater or Interscorer Reliability

When establishing *inter-rater* or *interscorer reliability,* two or more scorers score a set of tests independently and their scores are correlated to establish the reliability coefficient (Salvia & Ysseldyke, 2001), or degree to which the two scorers agree. This type of reliability is important when there is an element of subjectivity in scoring tests or rating behaviors (Lyman, 1998). A test that can be scored objectively has perfect interscorer reliability; however, many tests include items that are scored by subjective criteria. For example, individually administered achievement and aptitude tests require the test administrator to evaluate responses for score assignment. Additionally, behavior often must be rated on a subjective basis. With subjective evaluations, there is more variation in how items are rated among the raters (e.g., a student self-report of specific behaviors versus ratings of those behaviors by a parent, a teacher, and an administrator). This is the source of error or error variance in reliability coefficient calculations. Steps should be taken to minimize the error variance for these tests to increase reliability.

When evaluating the reliability of tests, it is important to understand the meaning of the reliability coefficients that are reported. Both validity and reliability coefficients are reported as a correlation coefficient with a range from 0.00 to ±1.00. Reliability coefficients of +1.00 or 1.00 indicate a perfect relationship. A reliability coefficient of 0.00 indicates no relationship or no reliability. Additionally, reliability coefficients provide the cap for validity coefficients, meaning that validity coefficients for a particular test cannot be higher than the reliability coefficients for that test.

What is an acceptable level of reliability? Ponterotto (1996, p. 80) states that there "is no absolute answer to this question." When selecting a test, you need to determine the purpose of the test and implications of the test results. If the results will have significant, life-altering consequences (e.g., decisions about educational placement, admissions, or medical interventions), then high levels of reliability are necessary (Walsh & Betz, 1995). On the other hand, midlevel coefficients may be appropriate for research purposes with large samples. Lyman (1998) has proposed that the following factors affect reliability:

How long is the test? A test with many items that assess a construct or trait is more reliable than one with only a few items, unless the test is so long as to induce fatigue in the test taker.

Who made up the group of people studied in the test construction process? Review the test publisher's description of the groups that were tested and for whom reliability coefficients were calculated. In general, the more group members vary in ability or behavior, the higher the reliability coefficients are likely to be.

How much time elapsed between test and retest sessions? The more time that elapses between sessions, the more likely reliability coefficients are to be low. A two-week time period is considered preferable (Salvia & Ysseldyke, 2001) because the period is long enough that test takers are unlikely to remember specific items from the previous administration but not long enough for significant maturation to have occurred.

What types of reliability are reported? A test publisher may provide coefficients for all the different types of reliability or only certain ones, and the coefficients for the various types of reliability will differ. Remember, consider the purpose of the testing to evaluate which types of reliability are most essential for your purposes.

The validity and reliability of a test are the essential psychometric properties you should review when selecting the appropriate assessment instrument for your needs. Practical considerations related to the usability of a test instrument also factor in to the decision, however.

Usability of the Test Instrument

What happens when the most reliable and valid test instrument is too expensive for an organization to use? What should the test users do when a valid and reliable test is affordable but the test publisher requires six months to score it? What should a principal do if the school district is using a group-administered test that was developed with Caucasian children only, but his or her school is 80 percent African American?

These are a few of the dilemmas that surface when evaluating the usability of a test. Many test publishers facilitate the process of evaluating test usability by including information about the test construction process in the test manual. For norm-referenced tests, characteristics about the norming sample are usually provided. Here are some questions to consider when evaluating the usability of a test for a specific population of test takers. In general the answers to these questions will be found in the test manual or information provided by the publisher.

What is the age group of the test takers? Test publishers provide information about the age range of the group on whom the test was normed. Look for a match between the age range of the normative sample and of your test takers. If a test taker's age falls outside of the normed age range for the test, then the results will not be reliable or valid for that individual.

Is the test designed for both genders? In general, males and females are represented in the norming group for most tests. Certain tests, however, may be designed for males or females exclusively. If a male is given a test created for and normed on females only, then his results will not be valid or reliable.

Where do the test takers reside? In what part of the United States (or what country outside the United States) do your test takers live? In recruiting norm groups, test developers attempt to include a cross section of individuals from various regions of the country. Before choosing a test, you should ensure that your region is represented in the norming sample.

What racial and ethnic groups are represented in the norming sample of the test? For a variety of reasons, different races and ethnic groups perform differently on tests of achievement and intelligence (Salvia & Ysseldyke, 2001). Under-representation or over-representation of specific groups can reflect bias in the construction of the test. Therefore, you need to determine that the norming sample is representative of your population of test takers, in order for the results to be comparable.

There are several additional practical criteria to consider. First, expense is a concern for many test users. If the most valid and reliable test is desired but is too expensive to be practical, then compromise may be the answer. The test user may have to compromise on the standards for choosing the test and seek a more cost-effective one with acceptable levels of reliability and validity.

Second, ease of use is an important criterion to consider when many different people will be administering or scoring the test. Particularly if the test will be administered to large groups, another consideration is the clarity of the administration instructions and directions for the test taker. Finally, scoring procedures need to be clear, and you will need to determine whether the test can be scored on-site or requires off-site scoring, and how much time is required for the scoring process. If you need immediate results, a test that does not require a lengthy off-site scoring process is the best choice.

Third, the amount of time allotted for administration and completion of the test is an important factor to consider, especially for large groups of test takers. For example, most school districts schedule a set number of days for group test administrations. In addition, counselors and psychologists may need to consider when and where students can complete individually administered tests or behavior checklists in order to achieve the maximum level of effort and performance.

Overall, choosing an appropriate assessment instrument can be a complex process. Validity and reliability criteria are essential in determining that a test has been constructed properly. In addition, there are many practical criteria to consider, such as the norming group and logistical issues. Test publishers often provide this information, but other references are available that compare various tests on key parameters. In the next section, we provide several resources to help prospective test users choose appropriate assessment instruments.

Resources for Test Information

The following resources are but a few of the tools available for selecting and evaluating tests. This list is not inclusive and we encourage you also to review test publishers' brochures and Internet resources.

Nonevaluative Descriptive Resources

Several resources assist test users in finding assessment instruments that measure specific traits. These resources provide information only about the test instrument itself, without any reviews or critiques. Hence, these resources are often used in conjunction with evaluative descriptive resources.

The newest edition of *Tests: A Comprehensive Reference for Assessments in Psychology, Education, and Business* (Maddox, 1996) is available from Pro-Ed, Inc. (website: www.proedinc.com). Currently in its fourth edition, this reference provides updated information on approximately 2,000 assessment instruments in the fields of psychology, education, and business. The following information is provided for each test: purpose, a concise description, scoring procedures, cost, and publisher contact information. A second nonevaluative resource is *Tests in Print,* a bibliography of all commercially available tests currently in print and available to users. The current edition, *Tests in Print VI* (Murphy, Plake, Impara, & Spies, 2002), is available through the Buros Institute of Mental Measurements at the University of Nebraska in Lincoln (website: www.unl.edu/buros/).

Evaluative Descriptive Resources

Once you have located specific tests that may fit your needs, we recommend you locate critiques of the tests. The nonevaluative descriptive resources provide information about psychometric properties (i.e., reliability and validity) of the test, but reviews and critiques provide information about the pros and cons of the use of the test. There are several convenient test-review resources available, two of which were mentioned previously.

As a joint project, the ERIC Clearinghouse on Assessment and Evaluation, the Library and Reference Services Division of the Educational Testing Service, the Buros Institute, the Region III Comprehensive Center at George Washington University, and Pro-Ed test publishers have created the Test Locator (available from www.ericae.net/testcol.htm). It contains descriptions of more than 10,000 tests and research instruments that are available through test publishers, and in journal articles or book chapters, as well as reviews and critiques. (A test review search is also offered at the Buros Institute website.)

Another resource available from the Buros Institute (www.unl.edu/buros/) is the *Mental Measurements Yearbook* (Plake, Impara, & Spies, 2003), which is available in hardback, on CD-ROM, and as Silver Platter services for libraries. This resource is a compilation of reviews and critiques for current assessment instruments.

Additionally, several publishing companies publish reviews of test instruments. For example, Pro-Ed, Inc. (www.proedinc.com) publishes *A User's Guide to Tests in Print,* currently in its second edition (Hammill, Brown, and Bryant, 1992). This book includes objective test evaluations with recommendation ratings based on accepted psychometric principles. It lists more than 250 tests, with more than 2,000 test scores reviewed. Another resource from the same publisher is *Test Critiques* (Keyser and Sweetland, 1994). This compilation contains reviews and in-depth studies of more than 800 of the most widely used assessment instruments. Each entry provides the reader with information on the practical applications and uses of the test; settings in which the test is used; appropriate and inappropriate subjects for the test; and guidelines for administration, scoring, and interpretation. Additional resources and references for information about test and testing issues can be found in chapter 53.

Summary

In the current educational environment, teachers are not only being challenged to become more knowledgeable about tests and test interpretation, but also being required to gain the knowledge and skills to select tests appropriately. Competency in test selection depends upon understanding the test's purpose, as well as knowing how to evaluate its quality. It is also important to research the usability of the instrument and its applicability in the particular setting where it will be used.

References

ACA & AAC. [American Counseling Association & the Association for Assessment in Counseling]. (1987). *Responsibilities of users of standardized tests: RUST statement revised.* Alexandria, VA: Authors.

AERA, APA, & NCME [American Educational Research Association, American Psychological Association, & National Council on Measurement in Education]. (1999). *Standards for educational and psychological testing.* Washington, DC: AERA.

▼AFT, NCME, & NEA [American Federation of Teachers, National Council on Measurement in Education, & National Education Association]. (1990) *Standards for teacher competence in educational assessment of students.* Washington, DC: Authors.

Anastasi, A. (1988). *Psychological testing.* New York: Macmillan.

Bennett, H. G., Seashore, H. G., & Wesman, A. G. (1991). *Differential Aptitude Tests for Personnel and Career Assessment technical manual.* San Antonio: The Psychological Corporation.

Bond, L. (1996). Norm- and criterion-referenced testing. In *Practical assessment research and evaluation.* College Park, MD: ERIC Clearinghouse on Assessment and Evaluation.

Cronbach, L. J. (1971). Test validation. In R. L. Thorndike (Ed.), *Educational measurement* (2nd ed.). Washington, DC: American Council on Education.

Hammill, D., Brown, L., & Bryant, B. (1992). *A user's guide to tests in print* (2nd ed.). Austin, TX: Pro-Ed.

Hood, A .B., and Johnson, R. W. (1991). *Assessment in counseling: A guide to the use of psychological assessment procedures.* Alexandria, VA: American Association for Counseling and Development.

Hood, A. B., & Johnson, R. W. (1997). *Assessment in counseling: A guide to the use of psychological assessment procedures* (2nd ed.). Alexandria, VA: American Counseling Association.

✦JCTP [Joint Committee on Testing Practices]. (2002). *Code of fair testing practices in education.* Washington, DC: American Psychological Association.

Keyser, D., & Sweetland, R. (1994). *Test critiques* (Vols. 1–10). Austin, TX: Pro-Ed.

Klein, S. P., & Hamilton, L. (1999). *Large-scale testing: Current practices and new directions.* Santa Monica, CA: RAND.

Lyman, H. B. (1998). *Test scores and what they mean* (6th ed.). Boston: Allyn and Bacon.

Maddox, T. (1996). *Tests: A comprehensive reference for assessments in psychology, education, and business* (4th ed.). Austin, TX: Pro-Ed.

McMillan, J. H. (1997). *Classroom assessment: Principles and practice for effective instruction.* Needham Heights, MA: Allyn & Bacon.

Mehrens, W. A. (2001). Selecting a career assessment instrument. In J. T. Kapes and E. A. Whitfield (Eds.), *A counselor's guide to career assessment instruments* (4th ed.). Alexandria, VA: National Career Development Association.

Murphy, L. L., Plake, B. S., Impara, J. C., & Spies, R. A. (Eds.) (2002). *Tests in print VI.* Lincoln, NE: Buros Institute of Mental Measurements.

Osterlind, S. J. (1989). *Constructing test questions.* Dordrecht, The Netherlands: Kluwer Academic.

Plake, B. S., Impara, J. C., & Spies, R. A. (Eds.). (2003). *The fifteenth mental measurements yearbook.* Lincoln, NE: Buros Institute of Mental Measurements.

Ponterotto, J. G. (1996). Evaluating and selecting research instruments. In F. T. L. Leongs & J. T. Austin (Eds.), *The psychology research handbook: A guide for graduate students and research assistants* (pp. 72–82). Thousand Oaks, CA: Sage Publications.

Salvia, J., & Ysseldyke, J. E. (2001). *Assessment* (8th ed.). New York: Houghton Mifflin.

Seligman, L. (1980). *Assessment in developmental career counseling.* Cranston, RI: The Carroll Press.

Walsh, W. B., & Betz, N. E. (1995). *Tests and assessment* (3rd ed.). Englewood Cliffs, NJ: Prentice Hall.

✦ Document is included in the Anthology of Assessment Resources CD
▼ Document is available on a website

Chapter 4
Reporting and Interpreting Test Results

Deborah J. Harris

Tests and assessments are generally administered to gather data to aid in decision making, either at an individual student level ("What math class should Kyra be placed in next year?" "Is Heru showing improvement in science this year?" "Should Jae apply for early admission to State University?") or at an aggregated level ("Has our school shown enough improvement since we adopted the new curriculum to warrant continuing it?" "What percentage of our students is meeting the new state standards, and how do we increase it?"). In order to incorporate assessment data in informed decision making, test users need to understand the test results.

Types of Test Scores

Test results are typically reported as scores, both scores for individuals and scores aggregated over individuals to obtain group averages. Just as there are many types of assessments, numerous types of scores can be reported. For most tests, the raw score is the fundamental score. Ironically, the raw score is seldom the score on which decisions are based; for many tests, it may not even be reported.

Raw scores are generally derived by counting the number of points a student obtained on the test administered. For a multiple-choice achievement test, this might be either the number of questions answered correctly or the number answered correctly adjusted for guessing. Raw scores can be useful when all students are administered the same test—as in a situation where a teacher administers a classroom test to determine whether to go on to the next science unit or spend more time on the current one—but they are generally inadequate when students take different forms of a test. Test developers try to build multiple test forms to be equivalent, but they are unlikely to be able to make the forms exactly equal in difficulty; thus, using raw scores would advantage those students receiving the easier form. (The statistical process of equating is used to adjust for these differences when scale or derived scores are reported; see Angoff, 1971; Petersen, Kolen, & Hoover, 1989).

Although raw scores generally do not appear on score reports, sometimes percentage correct scores do. For example, the report might show the number of items answered correctly in a particular content category or skill area divided by the total number of questions in that area, to give an idea of whether the student mastered that content or skill, or needs more instruction in it. Scores typically reported include normative scores, such as percentile ranks, stanines, and normal curve equivalents. *Percentile ranks* provide an indication of how an individual's score compares to other scores by reporting the percentage of examinees in some well-defined group who earned the same or a lower score. *Stanines* are integer scores ranging from 1 to 9, with a mean of 5 and a standard deviation of 1; they are a legacy from the punch-card days, when it was desirable to have a single-digit standard score that required only one column of a punch card to record. *Normal curve equivalents* are integers ranging from 1 to 99, with a mean of 50 and a standard deviation of 21.06; they are most commonly used for Chapter 1 evaluation.

In addition to these normative scores, other derived scores may be reported. *Level, category,* or *proficiency* scores are sometimes reported, as is the case with the National Assessment for Educational Progress (NAEP), where a student may be categorized as belonging in one of four categories, such as Proficient. These scores generally have descriptors associated with them that describe what a student receiving a particular classification is likely able to do. *Developmental scores* show a student's position on a developmental continuum; an illustration is grade equivalents, which try to establish a score scale that ranges across multiple grade levels, thus facilitating the tracking of a student over time. Grade equivalents appeal to teachers and parents, who seem to have an intuitive understanding of what they mean. There are potential problems with interpreting grade equivalents, especially extreme scores, such as when a third grader receives a grade equivalent of 8.2, but parents and educators seem pretty savvy about not over-interpreting these results in practice.

Often a test developer creates an original score scale for an assessment, either building in some normative meaning at the time the scale is developed or building it to have particular properties. For example, SAT scores are reported on a scale from 200 to 800, originally scaled to have a mean of 500 and a standard deviation of 100 on a particular sample of examinees. ACT Assessment scores are reported on a scale of 1 to 36, which was developed to try to equalize error variability along the score scale. Both of these scales have developed additional interpretations over time, such as what scores may indicate a student is ready for initial placement into a standard English composition course at a particular college.

Many tests report multiple scores. For example, the Iowa Tests of Basic Skills provides a raw score; a developmental standard score, intended to indicate the student's location on an achievement continuum; a grade equivalent, which also indicates the student's location on an achievement continuum, but one with equal rates of yearly growth between each pair of grades; national and local percentile ranks; stanines; and a normal curve equivalent score (See Hoover et al, 2001, pp. 13–14).

Petersen, Kolen, and Hoover (1989), and Angoff (1971) provide extensive discussions of creating and maintaining score scales including primary and auxiliary score scales, linear and nonlinear transformations of raw to scale scores, and methods of incorporating additional information into a score scale when developing it. For example, Petersen, Kolen and Hoover provide an example of creating a score scale to provide content meaning (where a particular score is interpreted as an indication of what a student knows or can do) or normative meaning (an example might be a grade equivalent, where a score is interpreted relative to what a typical student at that grade can do), and of incorporating score precision information into scores. The increased use and capabilities of computers in recent years has led to many technical and sophisticated types of scores, particularly those based on item response theory and computer-based testing (see Thissen & Wainer, 2001). Mehrens and Lehmann (1991) also provide examples and discussion of several types of reported scores.

Types of Test Score Interpretations

There are two basic types of score interpretations: norm-referenced and criterion-referenced.

Norm-referenced interpretations provide meaning by comparing a student's performance to that of a well-defined group of examinees, such as a nationally representative sample of fifth graders from public and private schools in the United States. How informative the comparison is depends in part on how representative the norm group is, how relevant it is to the comparison one is interested in making, and how recently the data were gathered. Other issues also come into play, such as how motivated the examinees in the norm group were, whether the data were gathered under standardized conditions, and whether the norms are empirical, versus interpolated or extrapolated from other data. For example, if one is interested in being selected for a special program for which there are limited slots, one is probably most interested in comparing one's score to the scores of other applicants. A comparison with the general public may be of less interest and relevance. Percentile ranks are easy to identify as norm-referenced scores. The nature of other scores, such as grade equivalents, may be harder to identify. For example, is a particular grade equivalent established using empirical data or using judgmental methods? It is important to remember that norm-referenced interpretations indicate how students actually performed, not how they *should* perform. A student's norm-referenced scores indicate simply how the student scored compared to other students, not whether the student is functioning at an acceptable level.

To address the issue of performance quality, *criterion-referenced* interpretations provide score information based on a set of criteria, generally skills or knowledge. Such a score represents what a student knows or can do. An example would be a score from a writing assessment that is linked to a rubric detailing what skills a student receiving that score has demonstrated and failed to demonstrate (e.g., "Used strong voice"; "Lack of subject-verb agreement").

The difficulty in developing criterion-referenced interpretations is to define clearly the domain or skill. If the ability to add two single-digit non-negative integers is the skill of interest, one could write out all the possible problems (i.e., 0 + 0; 0 + 1; 1 + 0 . . . 9 + 9), randomly select some to be placed on a test, and use the percentage correct on the test as an estimate of the percentage of the entire domain the student knows. Other skills and content areas are much more difficult to define accurately, however; consider "appreciates literature," "demonstrates appropriate grammar," or "understands Shakespeare's tragedies."

Rarely is a test score interpretation purely norm-referenced or purely criterion- referenced. That is, generally one is not interested in a normative comparison without addressing content, nor is one interested in criterion-referenced interpretations without knowing what reasonable expectations are. For example, a parent of a young child is interested in assessing both whether the child can read successfully (criterion-referenced) and whether the child is progressing in line with his or her peers (norm-referenced).

Information Needed to Interpret Test Results

A test developer has the responsibility to inform a test user of the characteristics of the test, such as content specifications, reliability, validity for particular score uses, and how score scales are developed. The onus is also on the test developer to describe how the test user should use the scores. The test user is responsible for adhering to the cautions, qualifiers, and limitations provided by the test developer. The test user is also responsible for following the administration conditions and for maintaining the integrity of the test. For example, if a test user ignores instructions not to allow calculators, does not time the test as instructed, or allows students to work collaboratively when the directions forbid it, the scores reported for the user's students will not be comparable to scores obtained when the instructions were followed. This will affect both norm-referenced and criterion-referenced interpretations.

The test developer needs to provide good descriptions of the norm group for any normative scores, so the test user will be able to determine if the normative comparison is appropriate for his or her test takers. The test developer also needs to describe how domains and skills were defined, how levels were established (if level scores are reported), and how score scales were developed for scale scores. The test developer should also provide information regarding how accurate scores are likely to be, either as classification consistencies or conditional standard errors of measurement, as well as reliabilities.

The test developer and the test user share responsibility for providing validity evidence for particular score uses. Whereas the test developer is responsible for providing evidence for any uses he or she recommends, the test user is responsible either for ensuring that his or her specific use of the test is encompassed by the test developer's recommendations or for providing additional validity evidence for the specific use. Test developers are also responsible for cautioning test users against likely misinterpretations of test results—such as taking a percentile rank table developed for use with individual student scores and using it to try to find a percentile rank for an entire school, based on an aggregated school mean score.

Test scores should never be interpreted in a vacuum, but instead considered in light of pertinent factors: how the scores are computed, who the norm groups consist of, the test content, whether the test is speeded, the administration conditions, the standard error of measurement, and so on. The type of decision to be made also influences how the test score is interpreted: The same score earned by two very disparate students might be interpreted differently; for example, as exceptional progress for one and average progress for the other.

Interpreting Results from a Modified Test

There are excellent reasons for modifying an existing test to accommodate practical considerations of assessment or for a particular goal, as in the following examples:

- changing the administration conditions to allow a student with visual impairment the use of a reader;
- extending the time limits for a student who works unusually slowly (for example, a student with a hand in a cast);
- changing the mode of delivery by allowing a test to be delivered on a computer or permitting the use of calculators on a mathematical reasoning test;
- eliminating some items to decrease the amount of time spent away from classroom instruction; or
- translating the test into a different language to allow students with limited English proficiency to take it in their native language.

Any or all of these modifications may improve the validity of the assessment scores for the particular use the test user has in mind. That is, a math test given in Spanish may be a more valid measure of math ability for a particular student than a math test given in English. However, test scores that have been derived based on standard conditions must be interpreted with caution when those conditions have been altered. This applies to normative scores when the standardized conditions under which the norms were obtained are altered, and to derived scores when the raw-to-scale-score conversions were obtained under standardized conditions. Context effects have been found to affect test scores in ways that appear unpredictable, and therefore caution must be exercised in interpreting scores from a test that has been altered in any way. For example, switching the order of the tests in a battery to accommodate a school lunch schedule may or may not affect the test scores. Small differences—such as changing the order of administration of the tests, or deleting some items and modifying the time limits accordingly—have been shown to have unanticipated effects. It is wise to err on the side of caution when using data from modified tests for decision making. As the *Standards for Educational and Psychological*

Testing (AERA, APA, & NCME, 1999, p. 61) state, "Although accommodations are made with the intent of maintaining score comparability, the extent to which that is possible may not be known."

Rationale and Procedures for Setting Performance Standards

Numerous procedures exist for setting performance standards (see, e.g., Cizek, 2001), but the Angoff method is perhaps the most widely used (Angoff, 1971). This method requires a group of trained panelists to estimate the probability that a "minimally acceptable person" would answer items on the test correctly. Generally, the first step in an educational setting is to develop narrative descriptors of what content a student at each level should know and what skills the student should possess. The second step is to select panelists to participate in the process. Next, the panelists are trained in internalizing the descriptors. This is an extremely important step, as panelists cannot be expected to determine how a Basic-level student would perform on a given item if they do not really understand what "Basic" means.

Once panelists understand what skills or knowledge is typical of a category, they are asked to picture a student who minimally meets that category of requirements and to judge how this student would respond to items on a test. For example, what is the probability that a minimally Basic student would get a particular item correct? These probabilities are then averaged across panelists and across items to arrive at a cutoff score for the Basic category.

The setting of performance standards is generally an iterative process in which panelists receive feedback data, which might include other panelists' ratings; empirical data on how students actually performed on the test items; and impact data, or what percentage of students in a particular group would be classified in each category based on the proposed cutoff scores. Setting performance levels is a very complicated procedure calling for a great deal of judgment. Decisions regarding the selection and training of the panelists, the number of rounds of ratings to hold, how to derive the ratings themselves, what feedback to provide to panelists, and others all require human judgment. Cizek (2001), Green (1996), and Hansche (1998) provide a great deal of additional detail for the interested reader.

Information Needed to Interpret Test Scores Correctly

To use test scores as one piece of data in making a well-informed decision, the test user must be clear on what the test scores mean. The most important consideration is the test content: what knowledge and skills are being tested, and how they are being tested. For example, does a reading comprehension test use novel material or material a student would likely have seen before? Is the test administered under somewhat hurried conditions, or would almost all students have enough time to complete the assessment? For a math test, are calculators allowed or prohibited?

Knowing what is tested is the most important aspect of interpreting test scores, but it is by no means the only consideration. Many scores (such as percentile ranks) are derived using a norm group. In order to interpret these scores accurately, one must be knowledgeable regarding the conditions under which the data were collected. Was it an operational administration or a special study where the examinees were unlikely to be motivated? How were the data edited? Other important information concerns score precision: how accurate a score is likely to be. For example, if an examinee is reported as being Proficient, how likely is the examinee to be classified as Proficient again, if the same test, or an alternate form of the test, were administered a second time? Most tests are accompanied by some type of reliability or score precision information, but the user must discern whether the information provided is relevant to his or her needs. For example, knowing the internal consistency of a test may not be of as much interest as knowing the classification consistency for a particular score use. Some test score scales, such as the ACT Assessment 1 to 36 scale, have tried to incorporate score precision information into the actual score scale, or to report scores as bands instead of single points, to illustrate measurement error.

Test users need continually to remember that the norms provided with test results are not standards that students must achieve. Not all students will score above the median for a test; not all students will show one year's growth in 12 months' time on a particular score scale. Many scores do not have equal units, meaning that progressing from one score point to another will indicate different amounts of change in different parts of the score scale.

A final point to remember is that scores from one test are not necessarily comparable to scores on another test, even if both scores are termed "grade equivalents" or "national percentile ranks." Different test developers use different norming samples and calculate grade equivalents using different methodologies. Different tests also generally cover different content, have different administration conditions, and are scored and scaled in different ways. One must be cautious when trying to compare scores from different tests.

Timely Provision of Test Results

Tests are administered to obtain data to inform decision making. Therefore, it is important to obtain those data in a timely manner, before the decisions need to be implemented or the data become so dated they are no longer of value. If a student takes a college entrance exam, the results are needed quickly enough to allow the student time to consider the results, in conjunction with other information, and decide whether or not to apply to a particular college prior to the application deadline. How quickly results are needed will depend on particular circumstances, but sooner is better than later. Faster scanners, electronic scoring, computerized score reports, and electronic delivery of score reports all have the potential to speed up the delivery of test results without sacrificing quality.

An additional consideration is who receives test result information. For many educational decisions, there are numerous stakeholders: students, parents, teachers, counselors, administrators, and the public in general. Who receives test score information, and of what type, depends on legal, confidentiality, practical, and situational factors. For example, a young child may not be capable of understanding what a particular derived score means so need not be given that information; a school board may receive aggregate score information for the district but not the particular score information for Pat Smith.

Basing Decisions on Multiple Sources of Information

Because no single test is likely to be comprehensive enough to encompass all the content one is interested in assessing, or to be reliable enough to measure a student's true ability without error, it is important to rely on multiple measures when making decisions, particularly if the decisions are virtually irreversible, long term, or high stakes. The *Standards for Educational and Psychological Testing* (AERA et al., 1999, p. 146) makes this explicit, stating in Standard 13.7: "In educational settings, a decision or characterization that will have major impact on a student should not be made on the basis of a single test score."

Most test developers appear to be in agreement with the standards on this point, also cautioning test users not to rely on a single measure when making a decision. For example, the interpretive guide for the *Iowa Tests of Educational Development* (University of Iowa, 1994, p. 95) cautions, "Throughout this *Guide,* stress has been placed on the necessity of interpreting test results in relation to other available information about students. Any profile of test scores either for an individual student or for a group of students can be misleading if considered without regard to other factors such as classroom performance, interests, expectations, and aspirations." Teachers, counselors, administrators, parents, and the students themselves have knowledge that cannot be obtained from a test score. Likewise, test scores provide information not readily obtainable from other sources. Pieces of knowledge pooled from multiple sources augment each other, and the result is more complete information on which to base a decision.

Some Final Aspects of Test Score Interpretation

For some uses, one is not interested just in the scores from a particular test, but instead wishes to compare scores across different forms of the test. For example, one may wish to compare scores for this year's fourth graders with those from last year, or one may wish to test students before and after they receive an intervention. In order to make these types of comparisons, it is necessary that the scores on the different forms be comparable, usually through a statistical adjustment called *equating.* Test developers who offer different forms of a test should discuss how they ensure that scores from the different forms may be used interchangeably.

In addition to investigating the technical characteristics of the test scores that are reported, the test user needs to ensure the integrity of the scores obtained by the students. This requires adhering to the administration conditions prescribed by the test developer (e.g., regarding timing or use of calculators and dictionaries), and preventing examinees from obtaining inappropriate scores through fraudulent means (such as copying). It also means attempting to motivate students to try their best on the test.

Tests are given to obtain data to inform educational decisions. To the extent that the test user understands the scores from those tests, and the scores are appropriate for the decisions he or she is attempting to make, the decisions will be well informed. By relying on test scores in conjunction with additional information; by ensuring that the test developer has provided complete information regarding how the tests were constructed, how the score scales and norms were developed, and how the scores should be used; and by becoming familiar with all this information, the test user becomes able to make better educational decisions using test results.

References

AERA, APA, & NCME [American Educational Research Association, American Psychological Association, & National Council on Measurement in Education]. (1999). *Standards for educational and psychological testing.* Washington, DC: AERA.

Angoff, W. H. (1971). Scales, norms, and equivalent scores. In R. I. Thorndike (Ed.), *Educational measurement* (2nd ed., pp. 508–600). Washington, DC: American Council on Education.

Cizek, G. J. (Ed.). (2001). *Setting performance standards: Concepts, methods, and perspectives.* Mahwah, NJ: Lawrence Erlbaum Associates.

Green, B. F. (1996, Nov. 6). *Setting performance standards: Content, goals, and individual differences.* Paper presented at the second annual William H. Angoff Memorial Lecture, Princeton, NJ, Educational Testing Service.

Hansche, L. N. (with Hambleton, R. K., Mills, C. N., Jaeger, R. M., & Redfield, D.). (1998). *Handbook for the development of performance standards: Meeting the requirements of Title I.* Washington, DC: U.S. Department of Education and the Council of Chief State School Officers.

Hoover, H. D., Dunbar, S. B., Frisbie, D. A., Oberley, K. R., Bray, G. B., Naylor, R. J., et al. (2001). *Iowa Tests of Basic Skills Complete/ Core Battery: Spring norms and score conversions with technical information.* Form A, Levels 5–14. Itaska, IL: Riverside Publishing.

Mehrens, W. A., & Lehmann, I. J. (1991). *Measurement and evaluation in education and psychology* (4th ed.). Fort Worth, TX: Holt, Rinehart and Winston.

Petersen, N. S., Kolen, M. J., & Hoover, H. D. (1989). Scaling, norming, and equating. In R. L. Linn (Ed.), *Educational measurement* (3rd ed., p. 262). New York: Macmillan.

Thissen, D., & Wainer, H. (Eds.). (2001). *Test scoring.* Mahwah, NJ: Lawrence Erlbaum Associates.

University of Iowa. (1994). *Iowa Tests of Educational Development: Interpretive guide for school administrators.* Forms K and L, Levels 15, 16, and 17/18. Chicago, IL: Riverside.

Chapter 5
Informing Test Takers

William D. Schafer

Three groups of persons are involved in the testing enterprise: test producers, test users, and test takers. A wide literature is available to guide the first two groups, but only recently have measurement professionals considered the interests of test takers in any careful way. Yet there is a real advantage in a conscientious attempt to meet the information needs of test takers. Examinees who understand the nature of an upcoming assessment are likely to be more motivated to do well on it, be able to prepare themselves better, and make better use of the test results than examinees who are confronted with an ill-defined event. Moreover, if the mechanical details of preparing for and completing an assessment are explained to test takers, there will probably be less error in their scores caused by factors other than the construct being assessed, which enhances the reliability and validity of the assessment. Finally, informing test takers is simply the responsible thing to do.

This chapter will draw material from four statements from professional groups that are relevant to our topic:

Standards for Educational and Psychological Testing (3rd ed.). A joint statement of the American Educational Research Association (AERA), the American Psychological Association (APA), and the National Council on Measurement in Education (NCME) issued in 1999, these standards are recognized as the most authoritative source of psychometric best practice. A committee of accomplished association representatives developed each edition, and their work has been the result of much deliberation and public review. If any other source or set of guidelines conflicts with it, these standards should take precedence. (For more information on the application of these standards to educatonal testing, see chapter 35.)

Code of Fair Testing Practices in Education. The *Code of Fair Testing Practices* was developed by the Joint Committee on Testing Practices (JCTP, 2002). A distillation of key concepts from the *Standards for Educational and Psychological Testing, the Code of Fair Testing*

Practices offers less technical guidance to test users and policymakers. The current version is a revision of the original code developed by the same group in 1988. The statement has been endorsed by virtually all major test publishers.

Code of Professional Responsibilities in Educational Measurement. The *Code of Professional Responsibilities* was developed in 1995 by the NCME, a body of educational practitioners working in the schools. Several of the statements in this guide to professionally responsible practice are directly relevant to informing test takers.

Rights and Responsibilities of Test Takers: Guidelines and Expectations. The final source is another statement of the JCTP (2000). The first description that applies broadly and directly to test takers, it has been endorsed by several measurement-related organizations.

Organization of This Chapter

There are phases of test development and use: development, administration, scoring, and interpretation. This chapter is divided into sections corresponding to these phases. Individuals involved in all four phases—both producers and users of tests—share the responsibility to inform test takers; no assessment professional should assume someone else will attend to any of this important task without satisfying himself or herself that it will be done. To do otherwise would contradict the clear statements of several respected organizations of measurement professionals and thus would constitute irresponsible practice.

This volume is intended for educational practitioners. Because classroom assessments developed by their teachers constitute the great majority of testing in education, these sorts of tests will be emphasized. Yet other sorts of tests are also important, including standardized tests. More effort is expended in their development, and they are typically less prone to misuse. When misuse does occur, however, it is commonly the result of poorly trained administrators or poorly informed test takers.

Finally, a clear purpose of informing test takers is to make sure the assessment is fair and is used fairly. Some of the statements in the sources used here are directly aimed at ensuring fairness through informing test takers. Other statements of the testing profession also address enhancing fairness but are only tangentially related to information flow. Nevertheless, those statements are included here because only when a test is fair can it be presented as such to test takers, who certainly have a fundamental expectation that they are neither advantaged nor disadvantaged by irrelevant assessment characteristics, an excellent definition of fairness.

The content of this chapter is presented as a set of 26 recommendations. These are intended as positive statements or guidelines for test users to consider as they develop, administer, score, and interpret assessments. The 26 guidelines will be grouped according the four assessment functions: development, administration, scoring, and interpretation. These are fairly well-defined activities, and it is usually clear which role a professional is engaged in at any given time. This should help a reader focus on the appropriate material so as to make use of the chapter to enhance fairness in his or her future assessment efforts.

Development of Assessments

The *Code of Fair Testing Practices in Education* asks test producers to define what each test measures and what purposes it should be used for. They are also asked to describe the process of test development and to explain how the content and skills to be tested were selected. Certain steps in writing an assessment enable that to happen:

1. Base assessments on a clearly defined domain. Examinees expect a test to conform to what they understand it should cover. For example, an achievement test should cover a certain domain of knowledge and skills. Students should expect a test that does not mislead them into giving wrong answers nor reward them with an artificially high score for guessing or bluffing, because these skills are not part of the domain of the assessment. Finally, a test that is face valid looks to examinees like it measures when they think it should, which enhances their motivation to succeed.
2. Cover the full range of psychological components, such as thinking skills and processes for cognitive tests. Assuming you have included higher-order thinking skills in your instruction, your assessments should prompt students to use the material intellectually, not merely echo memorized material. If tests cover only memorization, the students will merely memorize facts in their test

preparation.

3. Test content that is important for students to know or be able to do as opposed to isolated trivia. Ask yourself what students need to come away with from the course. Tests should focus on what educators who teach that course would agree is important.
4. Cover content in proportion to its coverage in instruction. The test should be representative of what students are supposed to be studying. The best guide for both teacher and student to the appropriate proportions of content is the relative amounts of time spent on those topics during instruction.
5. Make sure all contexts and expressions are equally familiar and interesting to all students. A challenge in developing assessments is to make sure no student is advantaged or disadvantaged because of his or her background. Avoid topics or language that are better known or more intriguing to some students than to others. For example, an item that asks students to plot points on a grid in the context of the job of an air-traffic controller would probably be more easily understood by affluent students who live near cities than by economically disadvantaged students in rural settings. Traditional gender interests (e.g., child rearing, sports) are better avoided too. If creating neutral contexts is impossible, then at least try to make sure the questions that favor some students are balanced with other questions that favor the rest.
6. Avoid topics that are sensitive and may elicit emotional reactions in some students, possibly interfering with their best test performance. For example, an item dealing with death may be difficult to respond to for a student who has experienced a recent death in the family. Similarly, items that are based on stereotypes of minority groups or that assume certain positions on controversial topics—like religion, gun control, or abortion—can cause reactions in students that make it difficult for them to show what they can do. Unless course objectives relate to such topics, including them on an assessment may result in invalidity due to discrimination against these students.

Administration of Assessments

Assessment administration has two phases: before the assessment and during the assessment. In each case, fairness requires that certain information be shared with all examinees.

Before the Assessment

7. Provide examinees with a statement of test-takers' rights and responsibilities well in advance of the test. According to the *Rights and Responsibilities of Test Takers,* all examinees have a right to be informed of their rights and responsibilities as test takers. The *Rights and Responsibilities* document is a clear and concise statement designed for all examinees. It should be a routine handout whenever assessments are administered under the guidelines of an institution such as a school. A copy of this document is found on the supplementary compact disc that accompanies this book.
8. Ensure that all students have had equivalent and adequate opportunities to prepare for the assessment. Whether or not each student has learned as much as he or she can, at least each should have an equal chance to do so. If a student is given extra practice time or materials that are not given to others, the others likely will not feel that they have been treated fairly. With respect to professional statements, this principle can be related to a decision about whether or not to take an assessment. The *Rights and Responsibilities of Test Takers* states that an examinee has a right to know if a test is optional and to know the consequences of taking or not taking the test, fully completing the test, or canceling the scores. The examinee may need to ask questions to learn these consequences. Similarly, a statement in the *Code of Fair Testing Practices* indicates that when a test is optional, the test user should provide test takers or their parents or guardians with sufficient information to help them make a judgment about whether the student should take the test or an available alternative assessment. Although these statements do not speak directly to opportunity to learn, they indicate the importance of providing examinees with

the information they need to decide on their own whether an assessment is appropriate for them. Clearly, that decision will be affected by whether students have been or should have been adequately prepared.

9. Announce assessments in plenty of time for students to prepare for them. There are three fundamental reasons for this. First, students need to know what will be covered and how they will be asked to show their achievement in order to make decisions about how to prepare themselves. Second, students need to know when and where to appear for the assessment and what to bring with them. This requires their being informed about the logistics of the assessment. Finally, an unannounced assessment is a surprise assessment. Students' learning styles differ: Some will stay up to date with the information whereas others will put in extra effort when they need it most. A surprise assessment rewards the former and punishes the latter. Yet these learning styles are not part of the material to be learned. Thus, it is fairer to announce assessments in advance, in order to motivate students to study.

Numerous statements in the professional positions cited here support the need for advance preparation for testing. For example, according to the *Rights and Responsibilities of Test Takers,* students are responsible for knowing, in advance of testing, when the test will be given, if and when the results will be available to them, and whether they are expected to pay any fees for testing services.

The *Code of Professional Responsibilities in Educational Measurement* contains a statement intended to enable students to satisfy this responsibility; the statement indicates the test user should inform examinees about the assessment prior to its administration, including the purposes, uses, and consequences of the assessment; how it will be judged or scored; how results will be kept on file; who will have access to results; how results will be distributed; and what rights examinees have before, during, and after the assessment. Further, the *Code of Professional Responsibilities* indicates test users should (a) provide appropriate opportunities for individuals to ask questions about assessment procedures or directions before administration, (b) inform persons involved in the assessment process how test results may affect them, (c) disclose whether and how long the results will be kept on file, (d) outline the procedures for appeal and rescoring, and (e) state the rights examinees and others have to the test information, and how long these rights may be exercised.

According to the *Rights and Responsibilities of Test Takers,* examinees have a right to receive a brief explanation prior to testing about the purpose or purposes for the assessment, the kinds of tests that will be used, whether and to whom the results will be reported, and planned uses of the results. Individual examinees also have the right to present any concerns about the testing process or their results and to receive information about procedures that will be used to address their concerns.

If a student has a disability, the *Rights and Responsibilities of Test Takers* specifies that he or she has the right to ask about and receive information regarding testing accommodations. If the student has difficulty in understanding the language of the test, he or she has the right to learn in advance of testing whether language accommodations are available. Thus, students who may be challenged by their status as learners of the language of the test or by physical limitations such as blindness may learn about available accommodations such as bilingual dictionaries or brailled versions of the test.

According to the *Rights and Responsibilities of Test Takers,* with these rights come certain responsibilities. It is the examinee's responsibility to know what his or her rights and responsibilities are. The examinee also has the responsibility to read or listen to the descriptive information provided in advance of testing and to listen carefully to all test instructions. He or she should inform an examiner prior to testing if an assessment accommodation is desired or if a physical condition or illness exists that might interfere with best performance on the assessment. If an examinee has difficulty understanding the language of the test, it is his or her responsibility to inform an examiner of this.

Finally, the *Code of Professional Responsibilities in Educational Measurement* specifies that test producers must communicate to potential users, before any purchase or use, of all the applicable fees associated with the assessment products and services. Similarly, the *Rights and Responsibilities of Test Takers* specifies that examinees have the responsibility to know when and where the assessment will be given, to pay for the test if required, to appear on time with required materials, and to be ready to be tested.

10. Make sure examinees are familiar with the response formats on the assessment. If some students are

uncomfortable with the types of items on an assessment, they will not have a fair chance to show their achievement. In such a case, practice with the formats beforehand would likely help them succeed. According to the *Code of Fair Testing Practices,* test producers should provide to qualified users either representative samples or complete sets of test directions, questions, answer sheets, manuals, and score reports. The *Code of Fair Testing Practices* goes on to state that test users should provide test takers with the information they need to familiarize themselves with the question formats, the directions, and appropriate strategies for test taking. Further, test users should strive to make this information equally available to all test takers. Accordingly, examinees have the responsibility, according to the *Rights and Responsibilities of Test Takers,* to ask questions before testing if they have uncertainties about why the assessment is being used, how it is to be given, what they are to be asked to do, and what is to be done with the results.

During the Assessment

11. Administer the assessment exactly as specified in the manual, if there is one. Test administration must conform to standard conditions if scores from different administration sessions, including those from the norm group, are to be compared. Accordingly, the *Code of Professional Responsibilities in Educational Measurement* specifies that users should administer standardized assessments exactly according to the prescribed procedures and conditions. Further, they should notify appropriate persons should any nonstandard conditions occur during testing. As all standardized administration procedures allow, the *Code of Professional Responsibilities* specifies that users should provide examinees with appropriate opportunities to ask questions about the test procedures or directions at identified times during the administration of the test. Should variations to standardized conditions exist, however, the *Rights and Responsibilities of Test Takers* assigns to test takers the responsibility to inform appropriate persons, specified by

the agency responsible for testing, if they believe that these unusual testing conditions may have affected their performance.

12. Administer allowable accommodations as specified. Appropriate accommodations for standardized tests should be identified in the manual. For nonstandardized tests, provide administration accommodations when specified for an individual student according to school and district procedures. The *Code of Professional Responsibilities in Educational Measurement* states that test users should provide and document all reasonable, allowable accommodations when administering a test to people with disabilities or special needs.
13. If the test is nonstandardized, then allow students enough time to complete it. Most tests in education will not assess content that is to be used under time pressure or in a rushed manner. Therefore, most assessments should reward quality over speed. Only by allowing sufficient time that virtually all students have the opportunity to answer all questions will the effects of speed of response be eliminated as a barrier to student performance.

Scoring of Assessments

14. Score each student's responses in isolation, without considering other information about the student. Assign a score to a student's answer based strictly on what the student has done on the assessment, not on other factors. Were other information (e.g., how the student interacts in class discussions) to affect the score, all students would not have an equal chance to do well on the assessment and therefore the results of the scoring would not be fair.
15. Score using a rubric that awards full credit to a response that answers the question, as opposed to demanding more information than asked for to receive full credit. If the question does not prompt an answer that receives full credit, then change the question. It is unfair to give students higher scores for doing more than has been requested; not all of the students will realize that there are different (and hidden) directions besides the ones they

have been told to use.

16. Score using a rubric that does not reward expressions more typical of one group of students than another. High scores should be available to all students, regardless of background, unless they do not possess high levels of the skill or knowledge being measured. This principle is commonly violated on items that ask students to take and defend a position on some issue. The teacher may have a belief about which position is more tenable and thus reward students who choose it by more readily agreeing with their arguments. The highest score should not depend on which position the student takes.
17. Honor all commitments and return assessments in a timely manner. The *Code of Professional Responsibilities in Educational Measurement* specifies that those who score tests should provide complete and accurate information to test users about how the assessment will be scored, including the schedule, scoring process, rationale for the approach to scoring, technical characteristics, procedures for quality control, reporting formats, and fees, if any, for their services. The *Code of Professional Responsibilities* further specifies that scorers should inform users promptly if there is any deviation in the planned scoring and reporting schedule or service and negotiate with users to reach a solution.
18. Allow test takers a reasonable way to challenge how their work was scored. The *Code of Professional Responsibilities in Educational Measurement* states that scorers should establish, if feasible, a reasonable and fair process for appeal and possible rescoring of the assessment.

Interpretation of Assessments

In order to be fair, tests must be used and interpreted accurately. Further, they must be used with an eye to their limitations. Several recommendations in the professional statements revolve around these themes. In addition, I provide some particular recommendations for teachers who use test scores as bases for grading students.

19. Explain to those who receive test information the advantages and limitations of tests in clear and accurate

terms. Especially for naïve users, tests seem to yield more accurate data then they actually can. The *Code of Professional Responsibilities in Educational Measurement* notes that users should provide to those who receive assessment results details about the assessment, its purposes, its limitations, and what is necessary for proper interpretation of the results. Regarding individual score reports, the *Code of Professional Responsibilities* goes on to recommend that recipients receive a report containing an understandable, written description of any reported scores, including proper interpretations and likely misinterpretations.

The *Code of Fair Testing Practices* asks test users to avoid misuses of test results. For example, providing impoverished educational opportunities for students who score low on an intelligence test would constitute a misuse of the test but is nevertheless a not unlikely result. Similarly, the *Code of Professional Responsibilities* recommends that test users interpret, use, and communicate scores in an informed, objective, and fair manner, in the context of the test's limitations and in the light of the potential consequences of use.

20. Accurately represent the nature of norms. When norms are a factor in interpretation, the adequacy of the norms should become part of the interpretation of test scores. Thus, the *Code of Professional Responsibilities* recommends that users evaluate and explain the adequacy and appropriateness of any norms or standards that are used in interpreting assessment results. Similarly, the *Code of Fair Testing Practices* asks users to take into account whatever major differences may exist between the norm groups and the actual test takers, and any differences in test administration, as they interpret scores. The *Code of Fair Testing Practices* goes on to recommend interpreting results carefully if modifications have been made for individuals with disabilities.
21. Communicate scores to appropriate audiences in an accurate and timely way, taking into account the limitations of the scores. There are three components to this recommendation. First, information about how individual examinees scored on a test should be released

only to appropriate persons, usually the test taker if age appropriate, the parents or guardians, and institutional representatives. The *Code of Professional Responsibilities* states that test users should release results of the assessment only to those persons entitled to them by law (i.e., the examinee or his or her parent or guardian) or to those designated by the agency contracting for the testing services.

The second issue is that test information should be released in understandable and timely reports. The *Rights and Responsibilities of Test Takers* indicates that examinees have a right to receive an explanation of their test results within a reasonable time period after testing and in terms that are commonly understood. The *Code of Fair Testing Practices* indicates that test takers should be provided with easily understood and timely score reports that describe test performance accurately and clearly. Test takers should also receive an explanation of the meaning and limitations of reported scores. The *Code of Professional Responsibilities* indicates that test users should communicate the results of the assessment to appropriate audiences in a timely and understandable manner; the communication should include proper interpretations as well as likely misinterpretations.

The third issue is that test users have a responsibility to ensure that others use test results in responsible ways. Thus, the *Code of Professional Responsibilities in Educational Measurement* indicates that users should avoid providing reports that are inaccurate, claims that are unsubstantiated, or interpretations that are inappropriate, false, or misleading about assessment results, and should also actively discourage others from doing so. The *Code of Professional Responsibilities* asks users to develop test score reports and other support materials that promote understanding of test results, and to correct substantive inaccuracies in assessments or supporting materials as soon as is feasible.

22. Allow test takers (or their representatives) reasonable opportunities to challenge or otherwise correct their results. The *Code of Fair Testing Practices* asks users to provide test takers or their parents or guardians with information about any rights they have to obtain a copy of the test and answer sheets, to retake the test, to have the test rescored, or to cancel the scores. The *Code of*

Fair Testing Practices also specifies that users should describe how test takers or their parents or guardians may register complaints and have problems resolved, should explain to test takers or their parents or guardians how long the scores will be kept on file, and should specify when and to whom test scores will and will not be released. Finally, the *Code of Professional Responsibilities in Educational Measurement* asks users to provide corrected assessment results to the examinee as quickly as practicable if errors are found that could affect inferences drawn from the scores.

Because assigning grades is a common use of test scores in schools, several recommendations are oriented toward how tests should be represented in teachers' grading.

23. Base grades on end-of-unit (summative) assessments rather than formative assessment used to make decisions about learning in progress. The latter are diagnostic and are intended to help teachers and students accomplish learning. Because grades are supposed to certify attainment, they should be based on assessments administered after learning has taken place.
24. Base grades on a variety of assessment formats. Students are likely to have different preferred assessment formats. Some students may be advantaged by essay tests, others by selected-response tests, still others by performance assessments, and others by papers and projects. Basing grades on a variety of formats minimizes the chance that some students receive an unfair advantage.
25. Base grades on multiple assessments over time. As with test formats, grades should depend on several assessments taken at different times. The *Code of Professional Responsibilities in Educational Measurement* states that whenever possible those who interpret assessments should use multiple types and sources of information about persons in making educational decisions. Ideally, grades should be based on multiple types of information gathered throughout a marking period instead of information from one single test at the end.
26. If factors existed that may have made a student's

performance atypical on an assessment, the importance of the student's score on that assessment should be minimized in grading. If a student has not had the chance to do his or her best, then basing a grade (or other important decision) on that score is not only inaccurate, it is unfair. It misinforms anyone who interprets it.

Conclusion

Educational professions have a great deal of control over the assessments they use. It is rare that anyone questions how a teacher tests students or what a counselor infers and communicates about a student from his or her responses on a test. Nevertheless, developing and using tests fairly, with an open and honest sharing of relevant information between the test user and the test taker, is an ideal toward which we all should strive. Not only is it simply the ethical thing to do, it promotes more effective use of better information from assessments. I hope that this chapter can promote that goal by presenting positive recommendations within an efficient organization.

References

AERA, APA, & NCME [American Educational Research Association, American Psychological Association, National Council on Measurement in Education]. (1999). *Standards for educational and psychological testing* (3rd ed.). Washington, DC: American Educational Research Association.

✦Joint Committee on Testing Practices. (2000). *Rights and responsibilities of test takers: Guidelines and expectations.* Washington, DC: American Psychological Association.

✦Joint Committee on Testing Practices. (2002). *Code of fair testing practices in education.* Available on *Measuring Up: An Anthology of Assessment Resources* [CD]. Also retrievable online: http://aac.ncat.edu.

✦National Council on Measurement in Education. (1995). *Code of professional responsibilities in educational measurement.* Washington, DC: Author.

✦ Document is included in the Anthology of Assessment Resources CD

Section B

Assessment Issues for Special Populations and Audiences

Chapter 6
Fair and Valid Use of Educational Testing in Grades K-12

Janet E. Helms

In the United States, standardized educational tests have been used for assessment purposes (e.g., classification and diagnosis) in grades K through 12 almost since the inception of the testing movement in the early 1900s (Domino, 2000).

Assessment refers in part to the process of using test scores to make decisions that affect the educational conditions of individual students. Although the assessment process may involve making use of information obtained from the testing process (e.g., test development, administration, scoring, and interpretation), its focus is the individual rather than the group.

Test scores are used for assessment purposes in the following situations: (a) determining whether a student needs to be placed in a remedial or an accelerated educational environment, (b) permitting a student to advance to the next grade or to graduate, and (c) evaluating the student's mastery of academic content or skills. Because test-based assessment can have wide-ranging positive or negative effects on K–12 students, the test user must ensure that the tests used for assessment purposes are used fairly and yield valid scores for each student.

Fair and valid use of educational testing is most problematic when the student being evaluated differs from the test developer's validation (i.e., norm) group on critical dimensions (e.g., ethnicity, social class, racial socialization, physical abilities) that might affect the student's responses and reactions to the testing situation or the test user's interpretations of the student's test results. On a national level, the K–12 population is characterized by children and adolescents whose home environments reflect a diversity of spoken languages, ethnic and cultural customs and traditions, economic resources, and racial socialization experiences (Helms, 1997). Any of these factors might result in individual test scores measuring constructs that are irrelevant for the intended use of the test. Fair and valid use of tests requires recognition of such construct-irrelevant factors and compensatory efforts to exclude these factors from the assessment process.

In this chapter, I discuss some of the issues related to fair and valid use of testing for assessment purposes when construct-irrelevant variance is a potential influence on the quality of students' test performance. Although the current *Standards for Educational and Psychological Testing* (AERA, APA, & NCME, 1999) addresses issues of validity and fair testing throughout, chapters 1 ("Validity"), 7 ("Fairness in Testing"), 9 ("Testing Individuals of Diverse Linguistic Backgrounds"), and 10 ("Testing Individuals With Disabilities") are the focus of this chapter.

Valid Use of Testing

Validity is defined as "the degree to which evidence and theory support the interpretations of test scores entailed by proposed uses of tests" (AERA, APA, & NCME, 1999, p. 9). In other words, if the test developer intends a test to be used for particular assessment purposes (e.g., diagnosis, classification), then the test developer must provide the theoretical rationale as to why such usage is appropriate, as well as empirical information that supports such usage. The test user, in turn, must determine whether the focus of the test seems to match her or his assessment needs.

Empirical validity evidence may be obtained in a variety of ways, including correlations between test scores and intended criteria, criterion-group comparisons, and psychometric investigations of the internal structure of the test. Validation methods typically occur at the group level. Validation studies will ordinarily help clarify what cognitive abilities or skills the test under consideration actually seems to measure. It is on the basis of this group-level validity evidence that the test user or educational assessor must make an initial decision with respect to the appropriateness or validity of the test for assessing the individual student.

Decision making on the part of the test user requires specification of the types of criteria that are relevant to the assessment process (i.e., that the test is intended to describe or predict). The assessor should have in mind multiple (ideally nontest) measures of the relevant construct. So, for example, if test scores are being used to assess academic achievement in a particular domain, then alternatives to test scores might be grades or teacher evaluations in that domain. One can have greater faith in the validity of the assessment process when multiple sources present the same picture of the test taker.

A test may be inappropriate for making decisions with respect to a particular student even though validity evidence suggests that the test may be validly used for the typical student. The testing standards or guidelines of most professional assessment organizations advise that test developers describe relevant background characteristics of their norming population as well as the characteristics of the intended test takers (JCTP, 2002). This type of descriptive information should be compared with the characteristics of the student who will be assessed as a means of determining whether there are any obvious differences in background between the student and the test-development sample or the test developer's population specifications. Such discrepancies potentially make the testing process meaningless (i.e., invalid) for the assessed student.

With respect to cultural, racial, physical ability status, and socioeconomic background diversity, the validity of using a test to make decisions about a student from a background different from the test development sample in any of these dimensions may be challenged if the test appears to assess constructs related to background diversity (i.e., construct-irrelevant variance) rather than the construct defined as the stated purpose of the test. For example, if a test written in English is intended to assess students' reading comprehension, but English is a student's second language, then this bilingual student might obtain a low test score because he or she uses the language structures of his or her first language as the model for communicating in English rather than because he or she does not comprehend English text. A test user unfamiliar with this possibility might automatically interpret the low score as a need for remediation in reading skills without examining additional criteria.

When students' irrelevant background information (e.g., social class) influences their test scores, this unintended outcome of the testing process is a source of systematic variance that is irrelevant to assessment of the intended construct (e.g., students' mastery of a mandated curriculum; Helms, 1997). When the test user or assessor has reason to believe that measurement of construct-irrelevant variance in the testing process may have artificially depressed or enhanced a student's performance, he or she should seek confirmation of this hypothesis by examining the a priori alternative criteria. Multiple administrations of the problematic test, however, do not constitute alternative criteria because if assessment of irrelevant constructs is problematic on the first testing occasion, it is likely to be problematic on subsequent testing occasions for the same reasons.

Fair Use of Testing

Whereas validity generally refers to characteristics of the testing process, fair use of tests ultimately refers to the quality of outcomes or decisions resulting from the testing and assessment processes. In general, fairness with respect to testing can be defined as impartial use of tests and interpretation of test results. The current *Standards* (AERA et al., 1999) applies the term *fairness* in the following four ways: (a) tests that are free from bias, (b) equitable treatment of test takers, (c) equality of testing outcomes, and (d) equal opportunity to learn. It might be useful to consider briefly each of these conceptualizations of fair assessment. For an extended examination beyond what I can present here, I refer the reader to specific standards by number (shown in parentheses) as appropriate.

Bias-Free Tests

Deficiencies in a test itself or in the manner in which the test is used in combination with atypical test taker characteristics may result in test scores that differ in meaning across groups of test takers as well as for individual test takers. The existence of bias or lack of bias is ordinarily inferred from comparisons across demographic (e.g., racial or ethnic) groups of the internal structure of tests (e.g., test takers' differential responses to items) or validity evidence. Demographic groups or categories are usually defined according to societal custom and are crude proxies for test-relevant psychological processes (e.g., different response styles) or socialization experiences (e.g., exposure to tested material). Consequently, these demographic categories can be used to describe differences between groups, but not to explain them. If demographic groups differ, the test user must still be able to search for likely explanations of the differences in the student's familial and school socialization experiences.

Differences between groups in average test scores do not necessarily signal the presence of demographic test bias. If empirical studies demonstrate differences in demographic group responses to test content, in response processes used to answer test items, or in empirical validity evidence, then the test developer should collect separate validity data for the counter-normative as well as the normative examinee population (Standards 7.1, 7.2, 7.6, 7.11, 9.2). Moreover, to rule out demographic group bias, local test users should collect validity information in their own settings to make sure that test scores are not misrepresenting the abilities, knowledge, or skills of the affected students—particularly if the local student population is known to differ from the larger examinee population with respect to demographic background characteristics.

Haney (1993) reported that the College Board (an affiliation of 2,500 schools and colleges) has offered to help colleges perform local validity studies. Presumably, assessors who use tests to make decisions about students in grades K through 12 could also require such services from test developers as a condition for using their tests. Nevertheless, data relevant to demographic test bias as it pertains to individual students may not be available to aid the assessor in interpreting students' test scores. In such cases, common sense will have to prevail. If bias cannot be ruled out as a factor, then the test user should consider the appropriateness of using within-group scoring criteria (e.g., local cutoff scores) as the basis of assessment decisions.

Equitable Treatment

The concept of equitable treatment in the testing process means impartial treatment at every phase of the process. All test takers should be tested under equivalent as opposed to the same testing conditions. For example, unless the stated or intended rationale for test use is assessment of proficiency in the language of the test, then all test takers should have the opportunity to be tested in the language in which they are most proficient (Standards 9.3, 9.4). Test developers may include in their test manuals information about appropriate test accommodations for ensuring equivalence of testing conditions with respect to various demographic groups (Standards 10.1, 10.4), but in case they do not, test users should familiarize themselves with available empirical information as well as relevant testing law to help inform their assessment decision making.

Equitable treatment also involves ensuring that test takers have comparable opportunities to become familiar with the structure of the testing process. A fair testing structure includes appropriate testing conditions and equal opportunities for test takers to familiarize themselves with the test format, practice materials, and related material properties of the testing situation that might be expected to interfere unfairly with a student's test performance. Moreover, if the test user is aware that the student's performance may be enhanced by special preparation routinely available to other students (e.g., coaching), then the test taker or the test taker's guardian should be so advised.

Equality in Testing Outcomes

In the testing literature, fairness of testing outcomes generally refers to whether the use of test scores unfairly penalizes demographic group members with respect to selected outcomes (e.g., selection, promotion, or graduation). As previously mentioned, differences between groups in test-based outcomes do not necessarily mean that the testing process is biased against certain groups or individual members of such groups. Limitations in testing methodology (e.g., less-than-perfect correlations between criteria and test scores), however, make it impossible to rule out test bias or unfair use of tests as possible explanations for between-group differences in outcomes. Common practice among testing professionals is to use such observed differences as inspiration for further study of the tests or to infer fairness from relevant validity evidence, assuming that such evidence has been obtained under equitable testing conditions for all groups.

Although some professional testing standards require that test users and developers remove test score variance that is unrelated to the skills or abilities that are the focus of the assessment, objective techniques for doing so are not commonly used (Helms, in press). If test users or assessors can identify appropriate outcome-relevant validity evidence, they may use inductive reasoning to form hypotheses about whether outcome decisions affecting individual students from atypical backgrounds are fair. Multiple criteria related to the intended outcome will be useful for this purpose.

Opportunity to Learn

Fairness also refers to the extent to which test takers have had comparable opportunities to learn the material covered by the test. This use of fairness, which is typically of concern when achievement tests are used as the basis for decision making, is perhaps the most controversial. Fair use of tests with respect to this definition requires that the test user differentiate the test taker's access to specific resources (e.g., tested material) from her or his relevant intellectual skills or abilities.

For example, a student might receive a low score on a mathematics achievement test because the test covered material to which he or she had not been exposed. If the student's grades in mathematics courses suggest superior skills, then the student's low test score might reflect a difference in opportunity rather than a lack of relevant skills. In such situations, the testing process has assessed construct-irrelevant variance (i.e., deficient curriculum content). Consequently, assessment decisions that penalize the student (e.g., grade retention) are unfair under this definition of fairness. The test user has a responsibility to review test content in combination with relevant factors in the test taker's school environment to help prevent this type of unfair use of tests (JTCP, 2002).

Conclusion

As the role of tests in students' lives grows in significance, test users must acknowledge the diversity of the school-age population as an important aspect of test development and test use. Many student characteristics and environmental conditions and practices may interact and contribute to systematic variance that is irrelevant to measurement of the construct of interest to the test user or assessor. Fair and valid use of tests for making high-stakes decisions affecting children and adolescents requires attention to the racial, cultural, physical ability, and other background factors that may differentially influence individual students' performance on such measures relative to the comparison groups on which the tests were developed. Moreover, fair and valid use of tests for assessment purposes means that the test user sometimes must base high-stakes decisions on the characteristics of the students and schools in which the student functions rather than on national norms or comparison groups.

References

AERA, APA, & NCME [American Educational Research Association, American Psychological Association, & National Council on Measurement in Education]. (1999). *Standards for educational and psychological testing.* Washington, DC: AERA.

Domino, G. (2000). *Psychological testing: An introduction.* Upper Saddle River, NJ: Prentice Hall.

Haney, W. (1993). Testing and minorities. In L. Weis & M. Fine (Eds.), *Beyond silence: Class, race, and gender in United States schools* (pp. 45–73). Albany, NY: State University of New York Press.

Helms, J. E. (1997). The triple quandary of race, culture, and social class. In D. Flanaghan, J. L. Genshaft, & P. L. Harrison (Eds.), *Contemporary intellectual assessment: Theories, tests, and issues* (pp. 517–532). New York: Guilford Press.

Helms, J. E. (in press). A remedy for the Black-White test-score disparity. *American Psychologist.*

✦JCTP [Joint Committee on Testing Practices]. (2002). *Code of fair testing practices in education.* Available on *Measuring Up: An Anthology of Assessment Resources* [CD]. Also retrievable on-line: http://aac.ncat.edu.

✦ Document is included in the Anthology of Assessment Resources CD

Chapter 7
Test and Item Bias
What They Are, What They Aren't, and How to Detect Them

Barbara B. Ellis & Nambury S. Raju

When laypersons refer to a test as biased, they usually think of the test as measuring different test takers in different ways. For example, when someone says that a test of cognitive ability is biased against a group of test takers, the assumption is that the test systematically assesses something other than cognitive ability. Laypersons commonly assume that because there are consistent differences in obtained cognitive ability for Asians versus Whites, and for Whites versus Blacks, on tests of cognitive ability, the tests must be biased. The implication is that these tests are more difficult for some test takers because the test is composed of items written in a manner that does not account for cultural differences between these groups of test takers.

In contrast, no one would argue that a yardstick is a biased measure of the construct we refer to as height. We do not question that a yardstick measures height for everyone in the same manner. As a measurement instrument, we do not suspect that a yardstick is influenced by factors other than the construct it is intended to measure— height. Thus, when a yardstick is used to measure two individuals who are equal in height but who differ in gender or ethnicity, they can be expected to have the same "score" in terms of inches of height. We feel comfortable saying the yardstick is an unbiased measurement instrument. Just because the yardstick is unbiased, however, does not mean that, on average, one group will be the same in height as another. On average, women are likely to be somewhat shorter than men, and Hispanics and Asians are likely to be somewhat shorter than Caucasian Americans or African Americans. In other words, an unbiased measurement instrument does not necessarily imply that different groups will have the same average scores on the construct assessed—groups do differ in average cognitive ability just as they differ in height. (Chapter 10 addresses socioeconomic and cultural factors that may interfere with test performance.)

Likewise, when we assess a psychological construct (e.g., cognitive ability), we would like to obtain test scores that are not influenced by factors that are irrelevant to the construct that the test intends to measure (AERA, APA, & NCME, 1999). For example, scores should not be influenced by factors such as the test takers' group membership but should measure individuals from different groups in the same manner.

Imagine a test designed to measure the construct of mechanical reasoning. If test takers are equal in mechanical reasoning ability, even if they come from different groups, we would expect them to have the same probability of answering an item correctly. A question with these characteristics would be considered unbiased. If, on the other hand, two test takers are equal in mechanical reasoning ability but do not have the same chance of answering a particular mechanical reasoning item correctly, we would question whether this item is measuring mechanical reasoning in the same manner for both examinees. The test takers in this example are, by definition, equal in mechanical reasoning and should have the same probability of a correct response. In that case, we may conclude that the test question is not measuring mechanical ability in the same fashion for these two test takers, that is, the item is biased. If the test were composed of many items like those just described, and if these items always functioned such that one test taker had a higher probability, and the other a lower probability, of answering correctly, we would consider the test to be biased as well. On the other hand, if our test were composed of items like those first described (i.e., test takers who are equal in mechanical reasoning, regardless of group membership, have the same probability of answering correctly), we would consider the test unbiased. Like the yardstick, the latter test is functioning in the same fashion for all test takers; however, this does not preclude there being differences in average mechanical reasoning scores at the group level.

For test developers and psychometricians, the problem becomes one of developing methods that can be used to support the assumption that test takers are equal in the construct being assessed. Once that is accomplished, we can look at the likelihood that examinees who are equivalent in the psychological construct assessed, but who come from different groups, have the same probability of answering a test item correctly (i.e., have the same expected score). If that is the case, we can conclude that the item is measuring in an equivalent fashion for both groups, that is, the item is unbiased. At the test level, we may conclude that a test is unbiased in two ways. Obviously, if a test does not contain any biased items, we would conclude that the test is unbiased. In addition, if we find some items that function against a particular group, but other items function in favor of that group such that the effects of the biased items cancel each other out, the test may be unbiased at the test level (not the item level).

In the remainder of this chapter we briefly describe some of the methods that test developers and psychometricians have devised to identify item and test bias and some of the challenges they still face. Although it may not be reasonable for classroom teachers to use these methods on a day-to-day basis in constructing tests, it is important for readers to know that these methods are widely used by researchers, professional test developers, and state agencies that develop standardized tests of student achievement. Finally, we would like readers to know and understand that if groups differ in test scores, this does not necessarily mean that a test is biased. If we can determine that a test is composed of unbiased items (or that biased items balance out at the test level), we may conclude that the test is unbiased. As in our yardstick example, groups may differ in their test scores, even if the test is unbiased. It is, however, necessary to identify item and test bias prior to comparing group test scores. Without this assessment, we cannot be sure if scores at the group level differ due to item bias or real group differences. Prior to describing and illustrating some of the methods for assessing item and test bias, we provide a few words about the terminology used for describing item and test bias.

Current Terminology

These days, item bias is typically referred to as differential item functioning (DIF) and test bias as differential test functioning (DTF). Early studies of item bias were stimulated by U.S. civil rights legislation in the 1960s. Test professionals wanted to identify test questions that minority groups (e.g., Blacks and Hispanics) responded to differently compared with the White majority group (Angoff, 1993; Cole, 1993). Angoff (1993) noted the following:

> These studies were designed to develop methods for studying cultural differences and for investigating the assertion that the principal, if not the sole, reason for the great disparity in test performance between Black and Hispanic students and White students on tests of cognitive ability is that the tests contain items that are outside the realms of the minority cultures. (p. 3)

Many assumed that biased items functioned against the minority group, that these items would be answered incorrectly more often by the minority (or focal) group than by the majority (or reference) group. Presumably, if these "biased" items could be identified and eliminated, test score differences between minority and majority groups would no longer occur.

In the late 1980s, the term *DIF* began to replace *item bias* in psychometric and professional testing circles. The reasons for this change probably had more to do with linguistics and politics than with psychometrics. The term *item bias* carried with it a negative connotation and was commonly associated with the notion of unfair, discriminatory testing practices rather than with its psychometric definition. Testing professionals felt it would be useful to separate technical, psychometric terms from those that may be politically and socially charged. Hambleton, Swaminathan, and Rogers (1991) write:

> Investigations of bias involve gathering *empirical* evidence concerning the relative performances on the test item of members of the minority group of interest and members of the group that represents the majority. Empirical evidence of differential performance is necessary, but not sufficient, to draw the conclusion that bias is present; this conclusion involves an inference that goes beyond the data. To distinguish the empirical evidence from the conclusion, the term *differential item functioning* (DIF) rather than bias is used commonly to describe the empirical evidence obtained in investigations of bias. (p. 109)

The examinations of DIF have been expanded beyond the early comparisons of groups that differ in terms of race and ethnicity. Nowadays, DIF analyses are frequently used to compare the performance on test items of groups that differ in terms of language, gender, disability status, and age. Researchers have also proposed that DIF analyses may help us understand the psychological processes involved in testing and "the subtle differences in content of a stimulus to which individuals react differently" (Cole, 1981, p. 1076).

Definition of DIF

An item *without* DIF may be defined as follows (Millsap & Everson, 1993):

$$\left\{\begin{array}{l}\textit{Probability of getting an item}\\ \textit{right, given a person's ability}\\ \textit{and group membership}\end{array}\right\} = \left\{\begin{array}{l}\textit{Probability of getting an item}\\ \textit{right, given a person's ability}\end{array}\right\}$$

(1)

In Equation 1, the lefthand side refers to the probability of answering an item correctly given a person's ability*and* his or her group membership, whereas the righthand side refers to the probability of answering the item correctly given a person's ability level *irrespective* of group membership. In essence, the equality in this equation means that the probability of answering an item correctly depends only on the person's ability. The fact that the test taker is a member of one group or another plays no role in the test taker's chances of answering the item correctly. If the equation holds true for an item at all ability (test score) levels, such an item is said to be functioning equally across groups. In other words, the item is said to have no DIF or bias and the item is considered invariant across groups that are examined. On the other hand, if the equality in Equation 1 does not hold, meaning that group membership increases or decreases the test taker's probability of answering correctly, then such an item is said to function differentially across groups and hence is designated as a biased item.

As mentioned previously, an analysis of bias at the item or test level usually involves two groups defined by demographic variables such as race or age (e.g., Blacks vs. Whites or old vs. young, etc.). Recent developments, however, have made it possible to examine bias or DIF across more than two groups simultaneously. In addition, the groups examined are not necessarily limited to subpopulations defined by physical characteristics. For example, the two groups considered could be employees and their immediate supervisors or peers, where ratings of employees by their supervisors and peers may be evaluated for DIF. In such an analysis, one would be interested in knowing whether supervisors and peers are giving the same performance ratings to employees with similar or identical work performance records. An analysis of this sort may help researchers identify rating bias by rater source. Another practical application of a DIF analysis is to establish the equivalence of translated tests. In this case, the language in which the test is administered (e.g., English vs. Spanish) would define the groups examined. This type of an analysis would provide practitioners with information about the quality of the translation beyond what a back translation would reveal (Ellis & Mead, 2000). Thus, for a DIF or bias analysis, the number of groups examined and the way groups are defined should depend on the test at hand and its intended use.

Techniques for Assessing DIF

There are many methods for assessing item bias or DIF. Some of these methods are based on classical test theory (e.g., the Mantel-Haenszel technique, logistic regression method, or SIBTEST), while others are based on item response theory (IRT; e.g., Lord's chi-square test, Raju's area measures, and the likelihood ratio test). Most of these methods provide similar information about DIF, but it is beyond the scope of this chapter to offer a description of these methods. Information about these methods may be found in Camilli and Shepard (1994), Holland and Wainer (1993), Millsap and Everson (1993), and Raju and Ellis (2002). We will, however, illustrate one of the IRT-based methods.

The method based on area measures is illustrated with two items, one with significant DIF, or bias, and the other with no DIF. Figure 1 shows separately for males and females the probability of getting an item right for a given ability or test score on a biased vocabulary item. The x-axis in this figure refers to the ability, or total test score, and the y-axis to the probability of answering the item correctly. When there is no bias, the probability graphs should be identical (or close to identical) for both males and females. The fact that these two graphs are different in Figure 1 implies that the item is biased, or has significant DIF. The graphs in this figure cross at an average ability score of 0.0 on a scale metric ranging from -5 to +5. Above and below this ability level, two persons with identical abilities will have different probabilities of success on the item. At the ability level of 1.00, the probability of success on this item is 0.82 for a member of the male group and 0.62 for a member of the female group. Even though two test takers have the same ability (i.e., 1.00), the individual from the female group has a lower probability of success than the individual from the male group; that is, the item under consideration favors the male group at this ability level. At the ability level of -1.00, the probability of success on the item also varies as a function of group membership, but this time the male group member has a lower probability of success (.18) than the female group member (.38), thus the item favors the female group. An item of this type is said to have significant DIF, and the kind of DIF displayed in Figure 1 is called non-uniform DIF; that is, the type of DIF does not favor the same group across all levels of ability. In Figure 2, graphs for the focal and reference groups, although not identical, are very similar, indicating that the probability of getting an item right varies only as a function of an examinee's ability, not his or her group membership. These types of graphs are helpful in assessing not only the magnitude of DIF, but also where the significant DIF occurs. These graphs are also useful in exploring the reasons for significant DIF.

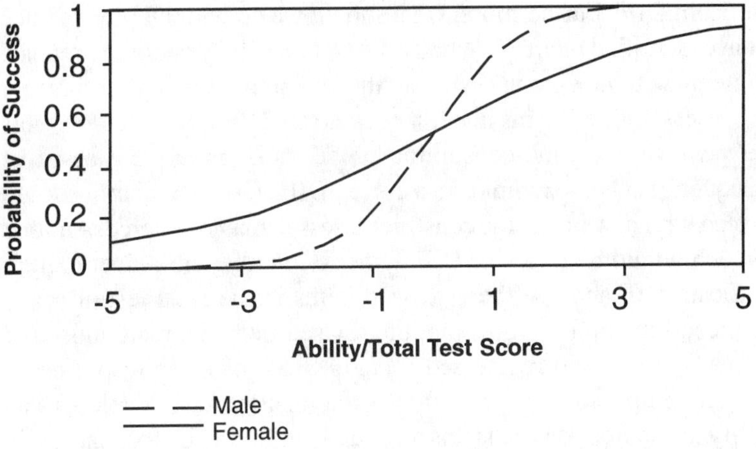

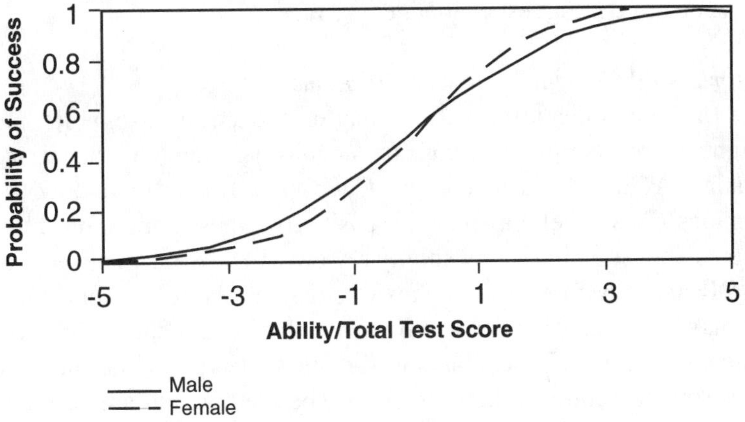

Challenges Ahead for DIF and DTF Analysis

During the last 20 years, we have made great strides in perfecting the methods, mathematical algorithms, and computer software required for assessing differential item and test functioning. However, many interesting and challenging questions remain unanswered. Some of these challenges are described in the following sections.

Understanding and Resolving DIF

Being able to identify DIF items represents a tremendous step forward for test developers, but the ability to identify DIF items raises new and challenging questions. Exactly why do some items have significant DIF? Furthermore, what should we do with DIF items once we have identified them as such? Test developers may choose to replace DIF items with new items, evaluate the new items for DIF, and repeat this process until all items in a test or scale are DIF (bias) free. But this an expensive and time-consuming process that may have negative consequences. For example, if a lot of DIF items are removed and replaced with new items, the construct assessed may be altered. Another approach would be to revise DIF items so that they no longer exhibit significant DIF and use these revised items in the final test or scale. The second method requires that the revised items be readministered to a new sample and reassessed for DIF. Both of these responses to DIF items implicitly or explicitly assume that the test developer can identify the source of DIF. Is this a valid assumption? Unfortunately, in most cases, the reasons for DIF or item bias are not evident. Thus, developing objective, testable methods for identifying the sources of DIF is one of the biggest challenges we face.

Editorial and Content Review of DIF Items

In developing tests, subject matter and editorial experts and members representing the groups under consideration (e.g., males and females, African Americans and Caucasians) usually review the questions. This panel may include sensitivity experts, but in most test development situations, a sensitivity review will have taken place prior to a DIF analysis. In a sensitivity review, items are examined for content that may be offensive or demeaning to members of a focal group. Most commercial test publishers have well-documented guidelines in place for use by their editorial staff members. These guidelines are designed to eliminate sexist and racist language and to avoid stereotypes about women and minorities. But, as Clauser and Mazor (1998) note,

"Sensitivity reviews are separate and distinct from DIF analyses—both are important, and neither can substitute for the other" (p. 32). Research indicates that it is very unlikely that experts will flag the same items that are statistically identified as having significant DIF (Engelhard, Hansche, & Gabrielson, 1990).

Following a statistical analysis for DIF, a committee of experts may be asked to develop hypotheses regarding the sources of DIF. Again, researchers have been disappointed to find that it is difficult or impossible to develop plausible explanations for the sources of DIF. At best, this exercise offers only a post hoc explanation of DIF that must be evaluated in future studies. Needless to say, more work is definitely needed to carefully articulate reasons for DIF in different content areas. Interested readers are referred to Camilli and Shepard (1994) and Holland and Wainer (1993) for further discussion on this topic.

Conclusion

Differential item functioning, or item bias, the assessment of how well two individuals with identical ability but different group membership perform on an item, is an important component of test and scale development. This definition of DIF does not imply nor does it require that the two *groups* under consideration be equal with respect to the construct being assessed (e.g., ability). The definition of non-DIF, or lack of bias, requires only that examinees with equal ability (or equal total test score) have the same probability of answering the item correctly irrespective of their group membership. There is a similar definition of differential functioning at the test level, called DTF. Assessing DTF is obviously important because decisions about examinees are usually based on their performance at the test level rather than at the item level. Although there are several known procedures for assessing DIF and DTF (i.e., item and test bias), many challenges still lie ahead for item bias research, especially in understanding the factors that contribute to item and test bias.

References

AERA, APA, & NCME [American Educational Research Association, American Psychological Association, & National Council on Measurement in Education]. (1999). *Standards for educational and psychological testing.* Washington, DC: AERA.

Angoff, W. H. (1993). Perspectives on differential item functioning methodology. In P. W. Holland & H. Wainer (Eds.), *Differential item functioning* (pp. 3–23). Hillsdale, NJ: Lawrence Erlbaum Associates.

Camilli, G., & Shepard, L. A. (1994). *Methods for identifying biased test items.* Thousand Oaks, CA: Sage.

Clauser, B. E., & Mazor, K. M. (1998). Using statistical procedures to identify differentially functioning test items. *Educational Measurement: Issues and Practice, 17*(1), 31–44.

Cole, N. S. (1981). Bias in testing. *American Psychologist, 36*, 1067–1077.

Cole, N. S. (1993). History and development of DIF. In P. W. Holland & H. Wainer (Eds.), *Differential item functioning* (pp. 25–33). Hillsdale, NJ: Lawrence Erlbaum Associates.

Ellis, B. B., & Mead, A. D. (2000). Assessment of the measurement equivalence of a Spanish translation of the 16PF Questionnaire. *Educational and Psychological Measurement, 60,* 787–807

Engelhard, G., Hansche, D., & Gabrielson, S. (1990). Accuracy of bias review judges in identifying differential item functioning on teacher certification tests. *Applied Measurement in Education, 3,* 347–360.

Hambleton, R. K., Swaminathan, H., & Rogers, H. J. (1991). *Fundamentals of item response theory.* Newbury Park, CA: Sage.

Holland, P. W., & Wainer, H. (Eds.) (1993). *Differential item functioning.* Hillsdale, NJ: Lawrence Erlbaum Associates.

Millsap, R. E., & Everson, H. T. (1993). Methodology review: Statistical approaches for assessing measurement bias. *Applied Psychological Measurement, 17,* 297–334.

Raju, N. S., & Ellis, B. B. (2002). Differential item and test functioning. In F. Drasgow & N. Schmitt (Eds.), *Measuring and analyzing behavior in organizations: Advances in measurement and data analysis* (pp. 156–188). San Francisco, CA: Jossey-Bass.

Chapter 8
Racial and Ethnic Difference in Performance

Nathan S. Hartman, Michael A. McDaniel & Deborah L. Whetzel

Gender, racial, and ethnic differences occur in vocational and cognitive ability assessments when the average scores of various groups are not equal. Results of such assessments indicate that not all groups are equally represented at all points of the assessment continuum. Many attempts to reduce or minimize existing group differences have been unsuccessful, and current research has failed to account fully for the sources of these differences. This chapter provides a summary of group differences on vocational assessments. The information is intended to provide a broad understanding of the core issues in the assessment process and provide accurate information concerning the magnitude of existing group differences.

Goals of Assessment

The goals of assessment in career guidance and counseling are to provide information that objectively describes a client's interests, characteristics, and abilities. Assessment is a systematic procedure for observing behavior and describing it using empirical data. This understanding provides reliable information about vocational interests and abilities that is useful for identifying educational opportunities. Such assessments are especially useful for understanding how one's interests and skills fit with available career choices.

Assessments allow counselors to learn much about their clients in a short amount of time. Assessments describe current functioning, and confirm, refute, or modify the hypotheses a counselor has formed through less structured exchanges with clients, thereby allowing for the systematic identification of therapeutic needs and necessary guidance (Meyer et al., 2001). The counselor can then use the results to help clients become more self-aware of their personal characteristics. Counselors often use assessments when a client's introspection has not led to specific answers to his or her vocational or ability dilemmas. Individuals taking assessments use the results to identify their strengths so that they may take advantage of opportunities in school and in the workforce. An understanding of their weaknesses can also lead to the type of personal development that will allow clients to develop the skills needed to reach their goals. The benefits of using assessments as a tool for identifying individual strengths and weaknesses have been well researched. In addition, these assessments compare in validity and accuracy to assessments used in the medical profession (Meyer et al., 2001).

Types of Assessment Measures

Although assessments are a valued part of counseling, counselors need to have a basic understanding of different types of assessments and the basic skills needed to properly interpret the data. In addition to these basic requirements, they should also know the limitations of tests and understand the history of testing. This knowledge would include a basic understanding of the types of tests available.

Vocational Interest Assessments

Vocational interest assessments are useful in helping clients understand their occupational interests. Assessments in this area include the Strong Interest Inventory, the Career Assessment Inventory, the Kuder Occupational Interest Survey, and the Self-Directed Search (SDS). Vocational interest assessments aid individuals in developing a systematic way of thinking about their interests and how they relate to the working world. An individual's vocational interest can be summarized with reference to six vocational career interest types: Realistic, Investigative, Conventional, Artistic, Enterprising, and Social. Our discussion of gender and racial differences in vocational interest measures will focus on these six vocational interest types because they are reported in most interest inventories.

Realistic people tend to prefer working with their hands or with tools, and they prefer limited social interaction. Often they work outdoors. Their jobs include automobile mechanic, farmer, and electrician. *Investigative* individuals tend to be most comfortable solving problems. Science, math, and research professions are prevalent among these people. Typical investigative occupations include chemist, engineer, and medical technician. *Conventional* individuals tend to be interested in occupations involving bookkeeping and computation.

They prefer tasks requiring an attention to detail, and of the vocational interest types, they are the least interested in artistic tasks. *Artistic* individuals openly seek opportunities to use their talents in art, music, and literature. Typical occupations include photographer, musician, or poet. *Enterprising* individuals are leaders and prefer to be in positions of power. Skills include management and communication, particularly public speaking. Typical careers are financial manager or hotel manager. *Social* individuals desire interaction with others. They have strong preferences for helping others, particularly through teaching. They have careers such as psychologist, counselor, teacher, or occupational therapist (Defense Manpower Data Center,1992).

Cognitive Ability Assessments

Spearman (1927) argued that a single general factor was highly correlated with a variety of cognitive ability tests containing many different kinds of categories (such as verbal, mathematical, and reasoning). Several theories suggest that there are additional specific abilities, such as fluid ability, crystallized ability, and memory ability (Carroll, 1993). Jensen (1980) found that a general aptitude test (such as the SAT), designed to measure how much knowledge a student has acquired, is highly correlated with learning ability and general cognitive ability. Cognitive ability and aptitude tests predict future intellectual achievements. This idea is supported by data showing that academic achievement tests, such as the ACT, GRE, SAT, and MCAT, strongly correlate with most cognitive ability assessments (Neisser et al., 1996).

Group differences in general cognitive ability assessments provide the greatest challenge for counseling applications. These tests are often used in selection for college and job placement; therefore, group differences result in differences in selection rates across groups. Tests designed to measure general cognitive ability show larger differences among races than do tests designed to measure verbal and mathematical ability. This is due to the less than perfect correlation between achievement and general cognitive ability assessments (Roth, Bevier, Bobko, Switzer, & Tyler, 2001).

What Are Group Differences?

You may wonder what procedure is used to determine if test bias or group differences account for the difference in assessment scores. Assessments focusing on cognitive ability and vocational interest were not intended to obtain group differences. Rather, they were constructed to measure abilities or preferences. Obtaining different mean scores from two different groups on the same assessment by itself will not constitute a biased measurement. Group differences typically reflect true differences in ability or preference. The presence of test bias and magnitude of bias is most accurately determined using statistical tools. The following section describes how group differences are identified and the implications of these differences.

Score Differences

Research on test score differences generally begins with comparisons of group performance. A group consists of individuals with similar physical characteristics (such as age, race, or gender). Their performance as a group on a test is represented by the group's mean score. The standard deviation measures the dispersion of scores around the mean. If everyone gets nearly the same test score, and the scores are clustered tightly around the mean, then the standard deviation is small. If the scores vary widely, and are widely dispersed around the mean, then the standard deviation is large. Group differences are summarized by calculating a *d* statistic that expresses the difference between the groups in standard deviation units. A *d* of 0 indicates no difference between two groups. A *d* of 1 indicates one standard deviation difference between the groups.

Assessments used by education professionals often show mean score differences in vocational assessment measures between minorities and non-minorities and between males and females. The persistent question remains whether these differences are illusionary due to some problem or bias in the assessment tool, or whether the differences are real.

Test Bias

It is possible to create an assessment in which the content is biased for some individuals and not for others (Williams, 1972). Bias in terms of assessments has often concentrated on the content validity and whether the items are representative of content that is universally understood. An achievement test would be biased only if it resulted in a lower or higher mean for the group due to inclusion or exclusion of items with content appropriate only to particular segments of the test-taking population. However, professionally developed assessments used in career guidance and counseling are largely absent of these types of biases.

Prediction bias refers to differences in the predictive accuracy of a test. For example, research shows that cognitive ability tends to predict school and work performance (Jensen, 1980; Neisser et al., 1996). Therefore, if tests were biased against African Americans, they would underpredict performance of African Americans relative to Whites. This has not been found to be the case, and it is clear that assessments are not biased against African Americans (Neisser et al., 1996). Therefore assessments can, and often do, show group differences but are not biased. The group differences reflect true differences among groups in the abilities or interests being assessed.

An example of a statistical evaluation of test bias is shown in Figure 1. The bold (center) line in the figure is the common regression line for both Blacks and Whites. One can use this common regression line to make predictions concerning performance (in this example, school performance). When Blacks, on average, score lower than Whites on the variable to be predicted, the common regression line will overpredict the performance of Blacks and underpredict the performance of Whites. This prediction bias is due to the mean score differences in the variable being predicted. To predict performance more accurately, one could use separate regression lines for Blacks and Whites. In Figure 1, the separate regression lines have the same slope. This is evidence that the test is not biased. The situation presented in Figure 1 is typical for those performance domains that show mean differences where Blacks, on average, perform worse than Whites. These domains would include school performance (Roth & Bobko, 2000) and job performance (DuBois, Sackett, Zedeck, & Fogli, 1993; Sackett & DuBois, 1991).

Figure 1. Example of a Prediction Bias Analysis

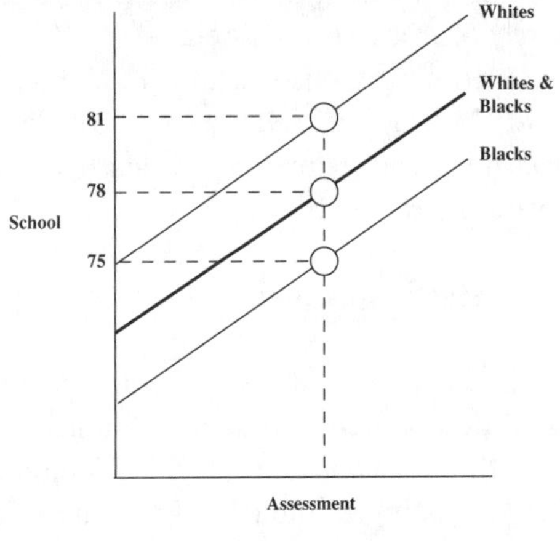

Interest Assessments and Gender

Mean differences between males and females have been found consistently in inventories based on Holland's RIASEC theory. Data from the Holland (1985) SDS manual inventories show that females score substantially higher than males on the Social theme ($d = 1.1$) and moderately higher on Artistic ($d = 0.60$) and Conventional ($d = 0.58$); males tend to have dramatically higher scores on the Realistic ($d = 1.79$) and moderately higher scores on the Investigative ($d = 0.41$) themes.[1] The gender differences found with the SDS are also found for the RIASEC scales from the Strong Interest Inventory (Fouad, Harmon, & Borgen, 1997; Harmon, Hansen, & Hammer, 1994),[2] although they are of a smaller magnitude (R = 0.70, I = 0.20, A = 0.54, C = 0.12, S = 0.26). These gender differences are consistent with the decreased likelihood that females will explore occupations in the skilled trades, medicine, science, engineering, or law and an increased likelihood that males will not explore occupations such as teaching or office assistance. Other interesting gender differences show that women working in traditionally male occupations scored higher in Investigative and women in traditionally female occupations scored higher on the Social scale (Godin, 1975; Rezler, 1967, cited in Holland, 1985).

It is likely that these gender differences have been shaped largely by the social role expectations of men and women. Changes in these expectations may result in a redistribution of these gender score differences, but as of now these differences remain stable. Because men and women show different score distributions in most interest areas, interest measures have often been charged with being biased. Unlike cognitive ability tests in which the causes of mean differences are subject to continual debate, most research shows that gender mean differences on vocational interest tests are strongly related to role expectations of the culture. However, interests also have a moderate genetic basis (Lykken, Bouchard, McGue, & Tellegen, 1993), and whether the differences between men and women are at least in part genetically based is a topic for future research.

Interest Assessments and Race

Unlike the case of gender differences in vocational interest measures, there is little research on racial differences. However, the technical guide to the Strong Interest Inventory has identified differences by gender, race, and ethnicity for the RIASEC scales. For a complete listing of these differences, see Table 1. Here we discuss differences of *d* greater than or equal to 0.20 (thereby eliminating Hispanics from the discussion). African American males score higher than White males in Social, Enterprising, and Conventional dimensions (*d* = 0.43, 0.29, 0.32, respectively), and White males score higher on Realistic interests (*d* = 0.24). White females score higher than African American females on Realistic and Investigative (*d* = 0.27, 0.26), whereas African American females score higher on Social and Enterprising interests (*d* = 0.33, 0.26). White males outscore Native American males on the Investigative measure (*d* = 0.22), but Asian American males score higher than White males (*d* = 0.35). White females score higher than Native American females on Investigative (*d* = 0.27), and Asian American females score higher than White females on Investigative and Realistic interests (*d* = 0.32, 0.20) (Fouad et al., 1997; Harmon et al., 1994). Other evidence has confirmed the finding that African Americans and Whites differed on Social scores, with African Americans being higher, and Whites scoring higher on Realistic and Investigative (Kaufman, Ford-Richards, & McLean, 1998; Kimball, Sedlacek, & Brooks, 1973).

Table 1. Racial and Ethnic Occupational Interest Comparison by Standard Deviation

Compared Groups		Realistic	Investigative	Artistic	Social	Enterprising	Conventional
White females	Hispanic American females	-.13	-.13	.19	.02	.02	-.15
White females	Asian American females	.20	.32	.13	-.08	.18	.13
White females	Native American females	-.02	-.27	-.40	-.10	-.12	.3
White females	African American females	-.27	-.26	-.07	.33	.26	.17
White males	Hispanic American males	-.06	-.06	.19	.13	.05	.021
White males	Asian American males	0.00	.35	.19	.15	.16	.17
White males	Native American males	. 02	-.22	-.11	.16	.17	.02
White males	African American males	-.24	-.10	.13	.43	.29	.32

We calculated these d statistics based on data presented in Table 15.4 in Fouad et al. (1997) and data in Harmon et al. (1994). Positive values indicate that people of color score higher than Whites. Negative values indicate that Whites score higher than people of color.

Some researchers believe that people of different races hold their own distinct values, thereby requiring race-specific vocational interest tests. Day and Rounds (1998) conducted a review of this research and found that the basic structure of vocational interest is invariant across racial groups (African Americans, Hispanic Americans, Asian Americans, Native Americans, and Whites). In addition, counselors and school psychologists continue to indicate that it is plausible that African Americans' interests might reflect economic constraints that might not be present for economically stable youth. Occupations selected by African Americans allow for greater expression of social and interpersonal influence, and are less dependent on higher educational or intellectual attainment than are traditional occupations (Kaufman et al., 1998).

Interest Assessments and Sexual Orientation

Research has also focused on determining if differences exist between heterosexuals and homosexuals in the career selection process. The environmental and personal factors relating to being a member of a minority group may create different decision-making processes. These altered processes potentially create differences in the types of career selections made by homosexuals. A study by Chung and Harmon (1994) provided evidence that such differences are present. This study found that homosexual males' career interests were atypical compared to careers identified as traditional male preferences. Homosexual men scored lower on the Realistic and Investigative scales, and higher on the Artistic and Social scales. The research in this area is still ongoing, and researchers are attempting to reach a consensus on the impact of homosexuality and the development of personality.

Cognitive Ability Assessments

Cognitive ability has multiple definitions with largely similar connotations to the layperson's conception of cognitive ability as mental power—the ability to understand complex ideas, to adapt effectively to the environment, to learn from experience, and to take part in mental reasoning (Neisser et al., 1996). Cognitive ability "is a general mental capability that, among other things, involves the ability to reason, plan, solve problems, think abstractly, comprehend complex ideas, learn quickly and learn from experience. It is not merely 'book learning,' a narrow academic skill, or test-taking smarts. Rather, it reflects a broader and deeper capability for comprehending—'catching on' 'making sense' of things, or 'figuring out what to do'" (Mainstream Science on Intelligence, 1994).

Properties of Cognitive Ability Assessments

Cognitive ability assessments measure constructs on a continuum of high and low scores. With enough data, a normal distribution is found in which the vast majority of scores are near the midpoint of the range. For historical reasons, the term *IQ* (intelligence quotient) is often used to describe scores on tests of cognitive ability (Neisser et al., 1996).

Individuals rarely perform equally well on all items included in a test of cognitive ability. One person may do better on verbal than on spatial items, whereas another person may score equally well on both kinds of items. However, individuals scoring above average on a measure of verbal ability in one cognitive ability test likely will be above average on verbal ability on a different cognitive ability measure as well.

Group Differences in Cognitive Ability

The study of group differences in cognitive ability typically shows that within-race variance is greater than between-race variance. The same is true of gender-group variance. This broad variance places members of every race and gender at every intellectual level, thereby making stereotyping of individuals based on group membership inappropriate. If general mental ability is normally distributed, the practical amount of variance within a racial or ethnic group is approximately six to eight standard deviations. This strongly supports the notion that there are exceptionally intelligent individuals from all racial and ethnic groups (Roth et al., 2001).

Gender Differences in Cognitive Ability

Research shows that on most standard tests of intelligence, there are no overall group score differences between females and males. Cognitive ability differences between the sexes have been reported; however, the direction of the correlation is variable and the effect sizes are small (Held, Alderton, Foley, & Segall, 1993; Lynn, 1994). Differences favoring males do appear on visual-spatial tasks, such as mental rotation and spatiotemporal tasks (Neisser et al., 1996; Maters & Sanders, 1993).

Adolescent females in grade school perform better on quantitative tasks than do their male counterparts (Hyde, Fennema, & Lamon, 1990).

These differences reverse prior to puberty, and males maintain a higher performance level on quantitative tasks throughout the remaining age categories. Strong evidence of this advantage can be found in the math section of the SAT, where many more males score in the highest ranges (Benbow, 1988; Halpern, 1992). The male advantage is between d = 0.33 and d = 0.50. Females tend to score higher on verbal tasks, and their advantage tends to range from d = 0.5 to 1.2. Data on college achievement tests indicate that females score higher in literature, English composition, and Spanish (Neisser et al., 1996; Stanley, 1993). In measures of general mental ability, gender differences are of a very small magnitude. On more specific cognitive abilities, some differences do appear and do represent true score differences between the sexes.

Racial Differences in Cognitive Ability

African Americans. The effect size for cognitive ability measures used in industrial and educational settings records the differences between Whites and Blacks at one standard deviation, with African Americans tending to score one standard deviation below Whites (Jensen, 1980; Neisser et al., 1996; Roth et al., 2001). The difference is largest on those tests that best represent a general cognitive ability factor (Jensen, 1985).

Hispanic Americans. In the United States, the mean cognitive ability scores of Hispanics typically lie between those of Blacks and Whites. Roth et al. (2001) reported Hispanics to have lower cognitive ability scores than Whites had (d = 0.72). The diverse cultural and ethnic divisions of the Hispanic group—which includes Mexican Americans, Puerto Ricans, Central and South Americans, and Cubans—along with linguistic factors may play an important role in these score differences. For Hispanic American high school students with moderate to high English proficiency, standard aptitude tests predicted first-year college grades to be equal to those of non-Hispanic Whites (Pennock-Roman, 1992).

Native Americans. Too little research in this area has been conducted to determine if group differences truly exist. Native Americans as a group speak upwards of 200 different languages and often live on reservations, which are only a couple of the major cultural and ethnic differences making it difficult to identify Native Americans as a single group (Leap, 1981; Neisser et al., 1996). Neisser et al. (1996) presented some information indicating that Inuit and other groups living in Arctic regions tend to have high visual-spatial skills, which do not diverge by gender. In addition, Native American children tend to obtain relatively low scores on tests of verbal intelligence. This information has led to the contention that Native Americans as a group tend to score lower on verbal scales compared to performance scales (Neisser et al., 1996).

Asian Americans. General agreement on the performance of Asian American groups has not been reached. It does seem that Asian Americans perform better than Whites in school achievement and occupational success. It is often perceived that these achievements reflect correspondingly high intelligence test scores; evidence has not yet proved this correlation. Studies have reported Asian Americans to have scores ranging from no difference to $d = 0.75$ above Whites in measures of cognitive ability (Flynn, 1991; Lynn, 1993).

Racial Issues and Cognitive Ability

Controlled studies have shown that racial group differences in cognitive ability scores are not attributable to the characteristics of the tests (Helms, 1992; Jensen, 1980). Efforts to create reliable and valid assessments of cognitive ability that would eliminate or reduce racial and ethnic group differences have been ineffective (Neisser et al., 1996). The study of Whites and African Americans has had far more prominence in research than the comparison of other groups (Roth et al., 2001). It is clear that mean differences between African Americans and Whites reflect large and real group differences in cognitive ability. (Chapter 10 addresses socioeconomic and cultural factors that interfere with good test performance.)

Ethical Issues in Assessment

The role of educator is continually becoming more complicated, and the reliance upon assessment tools is growing beyond the field of education. Assessments are popular because they are standardized to a quality level equal in most environments, thereby guaranteeing that students anywhere using the same assessment will receive similar career advisement. Similarly, counselors and administrators will be able to make some universal judgments based on assessment scores for most students from most backgrounds. It is important to remember that assessments are psychological in nature, and their misuse can have damaging outcomes for students. Even the simple use of test scores for educational development (not including student selection for advanced programs) can have an impact on the students. Students may use their assessment profiles as predictors of their potential for success, resulting in their self-selection to specific programs and prematurely and incorrectly biasing them to specific success levels or professional possibilities without a full understanding of the meaning behind the results.

Teachers will have added administrative duties for providing adequate interpretation of each assessment's theory, assumptions, and the implications resulting from its use. Interpretation has been complicated by the debates concerning the meaning of group differences in cognitive ability and vocational interest assessments. Therefore, opinions formed by students, administrators, community members, and parents about these assessments will require teachers to have technical knowledge for formal and informal discussions with students, parents, and administrators. This information is complex because it must be translated into real-world settings with real implications for students. As a result, teachers have an ethical responsibility to provide precise and complete information about assessments and their meaning.

Teachers who administer assessments need to treat assessment information with sensitivity. Evidence can be found to indicate how college selection practices relying heavily on measures of academic potential result in lost talent. Universities that would select only the high school students with the top grades, for example, would exclude about 86 percent of high school class presidents. Selecting only *A* students results in the exclusion of about 95 percent of national science award winners (Gottfredson, 1999). The true value and goal of assessment is to provide students with information about themselves. Psychometricians are still unable to predict without error the future performance of all individuals or groups based upon assessment scores. The treatment of individuals and groups based solely on their scores is unethical. Misuse of data and technical ineptness are not valid excuses.

Conclusion

This chapter has provided an overview of racial, ethnic, and gender group differences on traditional interest inventories and cognitive ability assessments. Results show that African Americans tend to obtain slightly higher Social scores than do Whites, who tend to score slightly higher on Realistic and Investigative dimensions. Research on the SDS inventory shows that females score substantially higher on the Social, and somewhat higher on the Artistic and Conventional themes than do males, but males tend to have dramatically higher scores on the Realistic and somewhat higher scores on the Investigative themes (Holland, 1985).

Studies of racial and ethnic differences on cognitive ability tests have predominantly focused on differences between African Americans and Whites. Research indicates that cognitive ability assessments show a one standard deviation difference that favors Whites over African Americans. On average, Hispanics' scores are higher than African Americans' scores, but lower than Whites' scores. Scores of Asian Americans and Whites have not shown large differences, but Asian Americans' scores tend to be slightly higher. Gender differences in cognitive ability favor males on visual-spatial tasks, such as mental rotation and spatiotemporal tasks, such as tracking a moving object through space. Females have a clear advantage on quantitative tasks in the early years of school, but these differences reverse prior to puberty, and males score higher on such tasks throughout the remaining age categories. Males also have an advantage in math achievement tests, and females have an advantage in verbal tasks, enabling them to score higher in English and vocabulary.

Assessments used in educational or clinical environments are not typically designed to be the sole information source used to evaluate a particular client's needs. Group score differences are an interesting phenomenon that results from the unique social and biological environments people live in and should not affect the high level of respect due to all racial, ethnic, and gender groups. It should be noted that differences within a group are more numerous and varied than differences across groups. Therefore, we cannot use group data to make definitive statements or predictions about how a particular individual will perform on particular measures. Future research will likely provide more thorough explanations of the environmental and genetic determinants of group differences.

References

Benbow, C. P. (1988). Sex differences in mathematical reasoning ability in intellectually talented preadolescents: Their nature, effects, and possible causes. *Behavioral and Brain Sciences, 11,* 169–232.

Carroll, J. B. (1993). *Human cognitive abilities: A survey of factor analytic studies.* New York: Cambridge University Press.

Chung, Y. B., & Harmon, L. W. (1994). The career interests and aspirations of gay men: How sex-role orientation is related. *Journal of Vocational Behavior, 45,* 223–239.

Day, S. X., & Rounds, J. (1998). Universality of vocational interest structure among racial and ethnic minorities. *American Psychologist, 53,* 7728–7736.

Defense Manpower Data Center. (1992) *Counselor Manual for the Armed Services Vocational Aptitude Battery Forms 18/19.* Washington, DC: Department of Defense.

DuBois, C. L., Sackett, P. R., Zedeck, S., & Fogli, L. (1993). Further exploration of typical and maximum performance criteria: Definitional issues, prediction, and White sub-differences. *Journal of Applied Psychology, 78,* 205–211.

Flynn, J. R. (1991). *Asian-Americans: Achievement beyond IQ.* Hillsdale, NJ: Erlbaum.

Fouad, N. A., Harmon, L. W., & Borgen, F. H. (1997). Structure of interests in employed male and female members of U.S. racial-ethnic minority and nonminority groups. *Journal of Counseling Psychology, 44,* 339–345.

Godin, T. J. (1975). *An application of Holland's theory to the career orientations and job satisfaction of college alumnae.* Unpublished doctoral dissertation, Boston College.

Gottfredson, G. D. (1999). John L. Holland's contribution to vocational psychology: A review and evaluation. *Journal of Vocational Behavior, 55,* 15–40.

Halpern, D. (1992). *Sex differences in cognitive abilities* (2nd ed.). Hillsdale, NJ: Erlbaum.

Harmon, L. W., Hansen, J. C., & Hammer, A. L. (1994). *Strong Interest Inventory: Applications and technical guide.* Palo Alto, CA: Consulting Psychologists Press, Inc.

Held, J. D., Alderton, D. E., Foley, P. P., & Segall, D. O. (1993). Arithmetic reasoning gender differences: Explanations found in the Armed Services Vocational Aptitude Battery (ASVAB). *Learning and Individual Differences, 5,* 171–186.

Helms, J. E. (1992). Why is there no study of cultural equivalence in standardized cognitive ability testing? *American Psychologist, 47,* 1083–1101.

Holland, J. L. (1985). *The Self-Directed Search (SDS) technical manual* (1985 ed.). Odessa, FL: Psychological Assessment Resources.

Hyde, J., Fennema, E., & Lamon, S. J. (1990). Gender differences in mathematics performance: A meta-analysis. *Psychological Bulletin, 107,* 139–155.

Jensen, A. R. (1980). *Bias in Mental Testing.* New York: Free Press.

Jensen, A. R. (1985). The nature of the Black-White difference on various psychometric tests: Spearman's hypothesis. *Behavioral and Brain Sciences, 8,* 193–263.

Kaufman, A. S., Ford-Richards, J. M., & McLean, J. E. (1998). Black-White differences on the Strong Interest Inventory General Occupational Themes and Basic Interest Scales at ages 16 to 65. *Journal of Clinical Psychology, 54*(1), 19–33.

Kimball, R. L., Sedlacek, W. E., & Brooks, G. C., Jr. (1973). Black and White vocational interests in Holland's Self-Directed Search (SDS). *Journal of Negro Education, 42,* 1–4.

Leap, W. L. (1981). American Indian languages. In C. Ferguson & S. B. Heath (Eds.), *Language in the USA.* Cambridge: Cambridge University Press.

Lykken, D. T., Bouchard, T. J., McGue, M., & Tellegen, A. (1993). Heritability of interest: A twin study. *Journal of Applied Psychology, 78,* 649–661.

Lynn, R. (1993). Oriental Americans: Their IQ, educational attainment, and socio-economic status. *Personality and Individual Differences, 15,* 237–242.

Lynn, R. (1994). Sex differences in intelligence and brain size: A paradox resolved. *Personality and Individual Differences, 17,* 273–285.

Mainstream science on intelligence. (1994, December 15). *Wall Street Journal.*

Maters, M. S., & Sanders, B. (1993). Is the gender difference in mental rotation disappearing? *Behavior Genetics, 23,* 337–341.

Meyer, G. J., Finn, S. E., Eyde, L. D., Kay, G. G., Moreland, K. L., Dies, R. R., Eisman, E. J., Kubiszyn, T. W., & Reed, G. M. (2001). Psychological testing and psychological assessment: A review of evidence and issues. *American Psychologist, 56*(2), 128–165.

Neisser, U., Boodoo, G., Bouchard, T. J., Boykin, A. W., Brody, N., Ceci, S. J., Halpern, D. F., Loehlin, J. C., Perloff, R., Sternberg, R. J., & Urbina, S. (1996). Intelligence: Knowns and unknowns. *American Psychologist, 51*(2), 77–101.

Pennock-Roman, M. (1992). Interpreting test performance in selective admissions for Hispanic students. In K. F. Geisinger (Ed.), *Psychological testing of Hispanics.* Washington, DC: American Psychological Association.

Roth, P. L., Bevier, C. A., Bobko, P., Switzer, F. S., & Tyler, P. (2001). Ethnic group differences in cognitive ability in employment and educational settings: A meta-analysis. *Personnel Psychology, 54*(2), 297.

Roth, P. L. & Bobko, P. (2000). College grade point average as a personnel selection device: Ethnic group differences and potential adverse impact. *Journal of Applied Psychology, 85,* 399–406.

Sackett, P. R., & DuBois, C. L. (1991) Rater-ratee race effects on performance evaluation: Challenging meta-analytic conclusions. *Journal of Applied Psychology, 76,* 873–877.

Spearman, C. (1927). *The abilities of man.* New York: Macmillan.

Spokane, A. R., & Calano, M. (2000). A theory-driven array of self-guiding career inventories. In V. L. Campbell (Ed.), *Testing and assessment in counseling practice* (2nd ed.). Mahwah, NJ: Erlbaum.

Stanley, J. (1993). Boys and girls who reason well mathematically. Paper presented at the 1991 Henry B. and Jocelyn Wallace National Research Symposium on Talent Development, Unionville, NY.

U.S. Department of Defense. (1992) *Counselor Manual for the Armed Services Vocational Aptitude Battery Forms 18/19.* Washington, DC: Government Printing Office.

Williams, R. L. (1972). *The BITCH-100: A culture-specific test.* Paper presented at the Annual Convention of the American Psychological Association, Honolulu, Hawaii.

Notes

1. We calculated these *d* statistics based on data presented in Table B1 in Holland (1985).

2. We calculated these *d* statistics based on data presented in Table 15.4 in Fouad et al. (1997) and data in Harmon et al. (1994).

Chapter 9
A Test User's Guide to Serving a Multicultural Community

David Lundberg & Wyatt Kirk

Testing is one means of viewing differences among individuals. Culture is another means. When we mix testing and culture together, the results are fascinating and often confusing. Generally, we test individuals in an attempt either to serve them or to reward them, and if we want to reward people, there is a strong desire and need to be fair. However, fairness is not easy to define or implement in the volatile arena of testing and culture.

One way to pursue fairness in testing is to assess students in a standardized manner, using the same methods, content, administration, scoring, and interpretation for everyone. A major problem with this "equality" approach is that if certain groups differ on irrelevant knowledge or skills that affect their ultimate performance on the test, then bias exists (Lam, 2001). The question arises, "Can identical assessment really be fair to different cultural groups?"

Another way to pursue fairness is to tailor the testing process to each individual's special background (i.e., his or her culture). The major problem with this approach is in ensuring that the results of different testing processes are truly comparable across groups (Lam, 2001). Differing assessments may seem more equitable, but are they really more fair? This is the dilemma of the test administrator or user who serves a multicultural community.

Culture and Assessment

What is culture really? When we view and define culture broadly, the factors involved seem almost endless. Age, sex, place of residence, social status, educational level, income, nationality, ethnicity, language, religion, and a host of affiliations from family of origin to social cliques to professional grouping are all variables in the broad definition of culture (Pedersen, 1991). When we define culture more narrowly, with respect to just a few variables, then group people according to those variables, differences become noticeable. For example, if we compare 14-year-old White females to 14-year-old Hispanic males, some common characteristics will obviously differ between the two groups. In the best sense, making generalizations and intelligent judgments about these cultural differences can provide a background for understanding each person's uniqueness. When judgments about groups become rigid, however, and that picture of a unique human being is lost, stereotyping and its negative effects creep in (Sue & Sue, 1990).

Another means of comparison is testing, and comparisons seen through test results can be valuable. Some tests are interpreted in either a bipolar or a neutral manner, meaning that any individual score is not considered better or worse than any other score. Personality tests and interest inventories given by counselors fall into this category. Examples of these neutral or bipolar tests are the Myers-Briggs Type Indicator (MBTI) and the Strong Interest Inventory (SII). The MBTI is a test that assesses individual personality on four bipolar scales. Whether an individual's score on the first MBTI scale is more Introverted or more Extroverted is considered as neither superior nor inferior. It simply forms a basis for comparison. Likewise, the SII gauges a person's interest in a wide range of occupational areas. Whether a person expresses strong interest or little interest in any particular vocational area is, again, of no inherent value positively or negatively, but it can be valuable as a comparison to that person's interest in the other occupational areas.

In contrast, many educational tests *are* high-low in their interpretation. This high-low orientation generally results in a benefit for the best scoring individuals. They often receive higher grades or better treatment as a result of testing.

Within school systems, most tests are produced locally by teachers who seek to measure the achievement or learning of their students. It is assumed that each student in the teacher's class was exposed to the same instruction and that the test is the same for each student. The teacher compares individual scores on locally produced tests to evaluate the progress of the various students. These locally produced tests are obviously high-low in their orientation.

Standardized tests are generally developed by large companies and often distributed nationally. They are used with broad audiences and given with the assumption that testing conditions and the test itself are the same for all students. The purpose of standardized tests is to compare the scores of a single student or a group of students to the scores of a national sample of students or to a chosen reference score.

Just like the locally produced tests, standardized tests are generally high-low in their purpose and interpretation.

The assumption of sameness for any test, whether locally produced or standardized, is problematic. Although an identical test can be given to different students, no two students are identical. Therefore, the test can never be the same for all individuals. The problem with testing is not that we don't have standardized students, however. Tests are meant to discriminate among individuals. The problem is that we don't have standardized cultures, so differences in culture interfere with the simple comparison of students. Tests may be somewhat similar for people of similar culture, but those tests can be markedly different for people of different cultural groups.

Standardized tests are developed and normed using a particular sample, and historically in our society that sample has been predominantly white and middle class. Today, many test publishers make an effort to include students of all types in their test development process so that the norm group is representative of the target population. When this is not feasible, efforts are made to "prove" that standardized tests are suitable for groups that were not represented or were little represented in the original test development and norming process. In either case, every test user should carefully screen the technical background information of any test to determine its applicability to people of color. Large amounts of time and resources are expended developing efficient, relatively short tests with questions that result in a predictable pattern of correct responses. But there has always been, and there continues to be, great controversy over applicability of standardized tests to all cultures.

Recommended Actions and Strategies

The purpose and use of the comparative results of tests are the real issues in all testing, but particularly in standardized testing. The burning question is, "What comparisons are being made and for what purpose?" Tests are best used when they serve the test taker. The test user should look upon a test as a tool to further the development of the person being assessed. It is very common to see the results of standardized tests being used to categorize individuals rather than to serve them. In addition, the results of standardized tests are now being extended to categorize schools and school systems.

We live a world of incredible diversity, limited resources, and strong desires for quick, efficient answers. Given the variety that exists among human beings and the desire to compare individuals by using tests, how can test users better utilize those tests for the benefit of the various populations they serve? There are a number of crucial multicultural factors in testing. Understanding these factors is the first step in using tests constructively to help diverse populations.

Differences in Communication and Learning Styles

No one prescribed method or model of teaching or learning fits all people. Many teachers and counselors use vary their styles of communication and instruction in an effort to evoke the best results from their students and clients. Skillfully alternating and integrating teaching styles allow material to be presented in several ways with the hope that one of the styles may engage the student in the learning process. Additionally, there is great benefit in not boring students with the same repetitive method.

Just as people think and learn differently from each other, we need to assess their resulting competencies in various ways. Too often we are tempted to assume automatically that a person with a lower score on a given test is less advanced in general than his or her counterpart who achieved a higher score. What we know for sure in such a situation is that the higher scoring student has succeeded in answering the particular questions on that particular test in the particular way they were communicated. If test content is well aligned with curriculum standards, this is also an indication that the higher scoring individuals are more closely approximating those standards. However, the generalization that the lower scoring individuals are less advanced is often fallacious.

We just don't know enough about the learning styles prevalent in many cultural groups and how those learning styles are best assessed. There has been far too little research in these areas. We tend to use communication patterns and teaching methods developed over many years that basically work with the majority population. We implicitly expect minorities to adapt to the majority style. If they do, they are competitive. If they don't, they are low performing. If certain minority members excel, we tend to think of them as superior, but we lose sight of the fact that they are also operating extremely effectively outside their normal culture, a skill that majority members are seldom asked to develop.

Long-Term Poverty

There is a somewhat hidden minority in America. This group contains Whites, Blacks, Hispanics, Native Americans, and many other subgroups. It is spread across all geographical areas, and it is both urban and rural. This minority is the long-term poor. There are disproportionate percentages of Blacks, Hispanics, and Native Americans in this group, which seriously distorts an examination of group performance in testing.

When studies of low test performance by minorities are corrected by statistically controlling for the effect of socioeconomic status (SES), the low performance is just as evident (and often more evident) with those who are poor as it is for minorities. In other words, the primary issue is often one of income, not more visible factors like race or ethnicity (Abbott & Joireman, 2001; Betts, Reuben, & Danenberg, 2000).

Unfortunately, it is much easier to correlate low scores with those more visible factors, and this is constantly done. We continually read that Black students or Hispanic students or Native American students score differently (usually lower) on tests than the majority group. Students do not walk around with signs proclaiming their gross household income, and however silly that statement appears, household income is often a more accurate predictor of test scores than are ethnicity or race (Dixon-Floyd & Johnson, 1997; Fergusson, Lloyd, & Horwood, 1991). Test users should favor tests that are developed or normed with consideration specifically for low-income students.

Expectations, Confidence, and Motivation

Because of the long-term conditions of poverty, many people of color suffer from chronically low expectations, confidence, and motivation. These problems cannot be overemphasized, and they certainly have no quick, effective solutions. Many members of minority groups wage lifelong battles to overcome these limitations. In our society, low SES corresponds with fewer resources for schools, less qualified teachers, and fewer advanced course offerings (Betts, et al., 2000).

Viewing each test taker as an important individual with a unique combination of characteristics and undeveloped potential should be the first step in any test user's approach. The characteristics vary among students, and a student's potential may lie in surprising areas, but seeing that person's uniqueness can be the first crucial step in providing expectations, confidence, and motivation to any student who doesn't fit the mold.

Differing Dialects

In the United States, we tend to think of dialects as something found in Europe or among tribes in third world countries, but differing languages are a reality in this country. This reality goes beyond varying communication styles, and it goes beyond having a different mother tongue. In many inner city environments, for example, the English words and phrases minority members use to communicate on a day-to-day basis nearly comprise a different language.

When students from these other cultures, such as inner city children, take standardized tests that are written in the language of middle- and upper-class students, those children are reading a somewhat foreign language. The resultant test scores are almost always lower than those of the majority.

Test Readiness and Hidden Talent

Few people love tests. But as a matter of survival and advancement, many learn how to prepare for and take tests, and they view testing as important for their future. Many students from low income brackets are not socialized to view tests as important. Other factors are more crucial to their success in school or the everyday world than getting a good grade on a test. Social prowess, leadership, nonverbal communication, and a host of other factors may be more important to many members of minority groups. It is incumbent upon test users and administrators to communicate effectively the importance of testing in today's society. The need for equitable access to test preparation programs should be continually stressed.

Tests don't do a very good job of evaluating creativity or imagination. They have difficulty measuring entrepreneurial drive or initiative. There aren't any tests that are very effective at assessing imagery, the ability to visualize a solution to a problem. Tests are good at demonstrating which students are able to take in, hold, and repeat information presented in certain ways. Tests are good at rewarding certain cognitive processes.

Speed in answering is a prime factor in scoring well on tests. Most tests favor those students who are skilled at memorization and can respond rapidly to the specific test format. A lack of tests that adequately identify important skills along with a lack of test readiness among youth of color (Castenell & Castenell, 1988) limit identification of certain talented individuals.

Other Forms of Assessment

Most standardized testing is in a multiple-choice, matching, or true-false format. There are some advantages to these formats in terms of flexibility in addressing broad areas of content and in measuring specific, sometimes very complex, thinking processes. An overwhelming advantage of the multiple-choice format is that it is inexpensive to score.

Other forms of assessment add more information and a broader picture in evaluating individual performance (Supovitz, 1997). Examples of these alternative instruments are essay questions and performance assessments. These forms are more expensive, and they are prone to criticisms of subjectivity. Individual evaluators have considerable leeway in grading performance when looking at an essay or performance assessment. Biased evaluations or favoritism can be problems; however, standardized multiple-choice tests have inherent bias and favoritism because of the factors mentioned previously. Research with alternative assessment modes has indicated some potential to decrease inequities seen with standardized tests. However, care must be taken in the development of these assessments (Supovitz & Brennan, 1997).

Conclusion

As test users, recognizing that we live in an imperfect world does little to help the individual student who stands before us looking for education and training that will equip him or her for a successful life. Our challenge is immediate, society changes very slowly, and that young man or woman is maturing rapidly.

Our first step is to recognize each individual as a person of great value and undeveloped, unknown talents. No single test or battery of tests of similar format can ever explain a person. No test can level the field or compensate for all the diversity present in a single school, much less in our society. And no evaluation instrument can replace the importance of one human being interacting with another.

Tests provide us with information, not answers. They provide the substance of conversation, not decisions. Answers and decisions about people or groups of people are not what education is about. Our educational system should produce motivated, capable, and confident graduates who are able to satisfy themselves and contribute to our world.

The encouragement and intelligent explanations a test user provides to a test taker form the basis for that student's personal development long after the results of all tests are forgotten. No test can stand alone. Use assessment that is based upon multiple tests with multiple formats. Use other forms of assessment that are realistic, even if they are more labor intensive. If you use standardized tests, choose those that have been developed and normed with full consideration for low-income and minority students. Explore or develop tests that are suitable for members of minority groups, and invite test makers to develop standardized tests that are specific to minority cultures. Don't elevate the results of any one assessment to a supreme degree. Use tests to serve the test taker. Never allow the student to become a servant to the test. In the end, your support of the test taker can be the most important element in assessment, and that support can produce a lasting effect in a student's life.

References

Abbott, M. L., & Joireman, J. (2001). *The relationships among achievement, low income, and ethnicity across six groups of Washington state students.* (Report No. WSRC-TR-1). Lynnwood, WA: Washington School Research Center. (ERIC Document Reproduction Service No. ED454346)

Betts, J. R., Reuben, K. S., & Danenberg, A. (2000). *Equal resources, equal outcomes? The distribution of school resources and student achievement in California.* San Francisco, CA: Public Policy Institute of California. (ERIC Document Reproduction Service No. ED 451291)

Castenell, L. A., Jr., & Castenell, M. E. (1988). Norm-referenced testing and low-income Blacks. *Journal of Counseling and Development, 67,* 205–206.

Dixon-Floyd, I., & Johnson, S. W. (1997). Variables associated with assigning students to behavioral classrooms. *Journal of Educational Research, 91*(2), 123–126.

Fergusson, D. M., Lloyd, M., & Horwood, L. J. (1991). Family ethnicity, social background and scholastic achievement: An eleven year longitudinal study. *New Zealand Journal of Educational Studies, 26*(1), 49–63.

Lam, T. C. M. (2001). Fairness in performance assessment. In G. R. Walz & J. C. Bleuer (Eds.), *Assessment: Issues and challenges for the millennium.* Greensboro, NC: ERIC-CASS.

Pedersen, P. B. (1991). Multiculturalism as a generic approach to counseling. *Journal of Counseling and Development, 70,* 6–12.

Sue, D. W., & Sue, D. (1990). *Counseling the culturally different.* New York: John Wiley and Sons.

Supovitz, J. A. (1997, November 5). From multiple choice to multiple choices: A diverse society deserves a more diverse assessment system. *Education Week,* p. 34.

Supovitz, J. A., & Brennan, R. T. (1997). Mirror, mirror on the wall, which is the fairest test of all? An examination of the equitability of portfolio assessment relative to standardized tests. *Harvard Educational Review, 67*(3), 472–506.

Chapter 10
Lost in Translation
Issues in Translating Tests for Non-English-Speaking, Limited English Proficient, and Bilingual Students

Sharon M. Goldsmith

The need to conduct assessments in languages other than English is growing rapidly. According to Geisinger and Carlson (1992), 15 to 20 percent of school-age children speak a foreign language at home and do not speak English as their primary language. In addition to the rising number of children who do not speak English as their primary language at home, the number of different languages spoken by children in public schools is also increasing rapidly. Bracken and McCallum (1999) conducted a meta-analysis of the studies examining the languages used in U.S. public schools. They reported that children enrolled in the Chicago public schools alone speak one or more of 200 languages; 1.4 million children in the California public schools speak one or more of 150 languages. Several school districts, including Scottsdale, Arizona, Palm Beach, Florida, and Prince William County, Maryland, report between 40 and 80 different languages spoken by children attending their schools. Even in small communities, students speak a large number of languages. Bracken and McCallum (1999) reference a study that reported 30 languages being spoken in a single small high school in the Washington state rural community of Tukwila.

The Case for Test Translation

Shifting demographics strongly support the need to increase the number of assessments that are available in languages other than English. There are several additional reasons to provide test translations, including the increased emphasis on assessment, particularly large-scale, high-stakes assessments, in public schools.

The Council of Chief State School Officers' (2001) survey on public school assessments reports that in 1999, 48 states required statewide assessments in math and language arts, 33 required statewide assessments in science, and 29 required assessments in social studies. These assessments can take a variety of forms. Although the majority of statewide assessments rely on multiple-choice responses, other formats, such as extended response, short-answer, portfolio, and performance, are also common.

These assessments are high stakes for the student in that decisions regarding promotion to a higher grade or graduation from high school may be dependent on the student's performance on these tests. These assessments are also high stakes for the teachers and school administrators because student performance may affect decisions regarding tenure, compensation, and eligibility for state and federal funding. There is pressure on both students and schools to perform well on these assessments.

The majority of assessment procedures are highly language dependent. Demonstrating knowledge of almost any subject matter is dependent on the ability to read and answer questions in English. Even alternative assessment procedures require the ability to follow directions provided in English. The impact of language skill on success in schools cannot be overemphasized. The low performance on high-stakes assessments of students with limited English proficiency (LEP) is well documented.

The *Standards for Educational and Psychological Testing* (1999), issued by the American Educational Research Association, the American Psychological Association, and the National Council for Measurement in Education, provides guidance regarding the construction, evaluation, and use of tests. Standard 11.22 states:

> When circumstances require that a test be administered in the same language to all examinees in a linguistically diverse population, the test user should investigate the validity of the score interpretations for test takers believed to have limited proficiency in the language of the test. The achievement, abilities and traits of examinees who do not speak the language of the test as their primary language may be seriously mismeasured by the test. (p. 118)

Historically, many school districts have addressed the low performance of students with limited English by simply exempting them from participating in these assessment programs. These exemptions were designed to maintain high average test results for districts by not having the mean scores influenced by the scores of those students who statistically do not do as well, particularly students with special needs and those who are in the linguistic minority. Federal legislation now prohibits schools from simply exempting students and requires schools to provide appropriate test accommodations instead. The Individuals With Disabilities Act (IDEA) requires that assessments be administered in the student's native language or in the language used in the student's home.

The need to provide appropriate accommodations to linguistic minority students is also being driven by new legislation such as the No Child Left Behind Act (NCLB) signed by President Bush as part of the reauthorization of the Elementary and Secondary Education Act (ESEA). ESEA will increase the accountability of states for the academic performance of public school students. Among other requirements, states will be required to establish performance standards against which students will be measured. The NCLB also requires states to include more students in assessment programs by creating appropriate accommodations for them. The act will consolidate funding for bilingual education and will require states to test those students with limited English proficiency who have had at least three years of schooling in the United States.

Several professional societies that are concerned with assessment issues have taken the position that assessments are to be conducted in the student's primary language. For example, the American Speech-Language-Hearing Association (ASHA, 1985), in a technical report on the clinical management of communicatively handicapped minority populations, states that assessment should be conducted in the client's primary language.

Therefore, the question for many states and school districts is not whether to provide accommodations for students in the linguistic minority but how. Several researchers, including Figueroa (1990) and others, have suggested that the best accommodation is to assess linguistic minorities in their native language. Several states do offer translations of tests in several languages. For example, New York state offers its high school graduation test, the Regents Competency Examination, in 20 languages. Even small states offer different language versions of statewide tests. Rhode Island, for example, offers its state test for grades 4, 8, and 10 in four languages: Spanish, Laotian, Portuguese, and Cambodian.

Guidelines for Test Translation

Translating tests is a complicated process. Several guidelines should be followed to achieve a quality translation, such as those put forth by the International Test Commission's *International Guidelines for Test Use* (1999):

> When testing in more than one language (within or across countries), competent test users will make all reasonable efforts to ensure that:
>
> - Each language or dialect version has been developed using a rigorous methodology meeting the requirements of best practice;
> - The developers have been sensitive to issues of content, culture and language;
> - Test administrators can communicate clearly in the language in which the test is to be administered;
> - The test taker's level of proficiency in the language in which the test will be administered is determined systematically and the appropriate language version is administered or bilingual assessment is performed, if appropriate. (p. 13)

Standard 9.7 of the *Standards for Educational and Psychological Testing* (AERA, APA, & NCME, 1999) provides additional guidance:

> When a test is translated from one language to another, the methods used in establishing the adequacy of the translation should be described, and empirical and logical evidence should be provided for score reliability and the validity of the translated test's score inference for the uses intended in the linguistic groups to be tested.
>
> For example, if a test is translated into Spanish for use with Mexican, Puerto Rican, Cuban, Central American, and Spanish populations, score reliability and the validity of test score inferences should be established with members of each of these groups separately where feasible. In addition, the test translation methods used need to be described in detail. (p. 99)

Standard 9.6 states:

> When a test is recommended for use with linguistically diverse test takers, test developers and publishers should provide the information necessary for appropriate test use and interpretation.
> Test developers should include in test manuals and in instruction for score interpretation explicit statements about the applicability of the test with individuals who are not native speakers of the original language of the test. However, it should be recognized that test developers and publishers seldom will find it feasible to conduct studies specific to the large number of linguistic groups found in certain countries. (p. 99)

Standard 9.4 states:

> Linguistic modifications recommended by test publishers, as well as the rationale for the modifications, should be described in detail in the test manual.
> Linguistic modifications may be recommended for the original test in the primary language or for an adapted version in a secondary language, or both. In any case, the test manual should provide appropriate information regarding the recommended modifications, their rationales, and the appropriate use of scores obtained using these linguistic modifications. (p. 98)

Test translation requires much more than translating the words on a test from one language to another. It requires constructing an entirely new test. It requires making sure that the semantic content of the test and the concepts used are culturally appropriate and likely to be understood by the test taker. For example, in the widely used Peabody Picture Vocabulary Test that is used to assess language understanding (i.e., receptive vocabulary skills), the test taker is shown a page with four pictures and asked to point to the correct picture as it is named. Several of the pictures are of items or scenes that are familiar in U.S. middle-class culture but would not be familiar in other cultures or environments. Simply translating the verbal stimulus (the word to be identified) into the child's language is not sufficient to measure language understanding accurately. The pictures themselves as well as the vocabulary being tested would need to be appropriate for both the cultural and the linguistic environment.

Additionally, the translated test, even with appropriate linguistic and cultural modifications to the content, would need to be subjected to new analyses of reliability, validity, and scoring norms against the population for which the test has been translated. Standard 9.1 of the *Standards for Educational and Psychological Testing* (AERA et al., 1999) emphasizes the need to establish reliability and validity for a translated test:

> Testing practice should be designed to reduce threats to the reliability and validity of test score inferences that may arise from language differences. (p. 97)

Standard 9.2 states:

> When credible research evidence reports that test scores differ in meaning across subgroups of linguistically diverse test takers, then to the extent feasible, test developers should collect for each linguistic subgroup studied the same form of validity evidence collected for the examinee population as a whole. (p. 97)
>
> Linguistic subgroups may be found to differ with respect to what test content is appropriate, how their test responses are internally structured, how their test scores relate to other variables, and what response processes individual examinees employ. Any such findings need to receive due consideration in the interpretation and use of scores as well as in test revisions. There may also be legal or regulatory requirements to collect subgroup validity evidence. Not all forms of evidence can be examined separately for members of all linguistic groups. The validity argument may rely on existing research literature, for example, and such literature may not be available for some populations. For some kinds of evidence, separate linguistic subgroup analyses may not be feasible due to the limited number of cases available. Data may sometimes be accumulated so that these analyses can be performed after the test has been in use for a period of time. It is important to note that this standard calls for more than representativeness in the selection of samples used for validation or norming studies.

> Rather, it calls for separate, parallel analyses of data for members of different linguistic groups, sample sizes permitting. If a test is being used while such data are being collected, then cautionary statements are in order regarding limitations on the interpretations based on test scores.

Standard 9.9 discusses establishing and interpreting test scores in translated tests:

> When multiple language versions of a test are intended to be comparable, test developers should report evidence of test comparability.
> Evidence of test comparability may include, but is not limited to, evidence that the different language versions measure equivalent or similar constructs, and that score reliability and the validity of inferences from scores from the two versions are comparable. (p. 99)

Although the guidelines previously outlined address the philosophical principles of what is required in quality test translation, other guidelines focus on specific procedures that should be followed in test translation. Many of these guidelines are issued by test developers who expect their tests to be translated into other languages, often for use in other countries. The developers are interested in making sure that the content and format of the test remain true to the original version, even though the scores from the translated tests will not be combined with the scores from the original version, nor will the performance of those taking the different versions be compared. Despite the different intent for the use of scores, these guidelines represent good practice and can be helpful for schools in establishing test translation procedures.

Gross (1986) prepared a manual enumerating the ideal procedures for translating the lactation consultant licensing exam. Gross and Scott (1989) provide an overview of these guidelines in an article in *Evaluation and the Health Professions,* in which they analyze the translation of the exam administered by the International Board of Lactation Consultant Examiners (IBLCE):

> Because of IBLCE's international scope and the probability of testing in languages other than English, the English version should avoid jargon and vernacular and idiomatic phraseology. . . . Traditional item writing guidelines were strictly followed. . . . Translators were directed

to maintain the format of the item stem in the translated version. For example, if the English stem was in the form of an incomplete sentence, the translated stem had to be in the form of an incomplete sentence rather than forming a question. Other issues such as grammatical relationships and verb tense and selection were emphasized also in order to avoid subtle changes in meaning (e.g., "will" versus "would" versus "should"). Finally, translators were asked to avoid making the translated item "more interesting." As an example, the use of synonymous terms (e.g., baby, infant, neonate) interchangeably within the same item was to be avoided because of subtle changes in meaning.

Upon completion of the translation, standard operating procedures required that a different bilingual subject matter expert translate the translated version back to English. This individual received the same guidelines as the initial translator. The retranslated version of the test was then forwarded to a third subject matter expert who was not necessarily bilingual. The responsibility of this third expert was to compare the translated English version with the original English version for corroboration. Any item for which a substantive discrepancy was noted would be flagged for subsequent linguistic review. (p. 66)

Back translation is a common practice in test translation. The back translation process involves checking every word against the original and requires three different translators. It is particularly important that these translators be native language speakers of the language in which the test is translated in order to pick up the cultural nuances as well as nuances in syntax and semantics. Back translation is the accepted procedure of the American Translators Association (ATA). The ATA *Code of Professional Conduct and Business Practices* (1997) recommends that translators have up-to-date knowledge of the subject material and its terminology and mastery of the target language equivalent to that of an educated native speaker.

Auchter and Stansfield (1997) report on a project to translate five forms of the General Educational Development (GED) test into Spanish. The GED is a widely used test designed to enable people who did not graduate from high school to earn the equivalent of a high school diploma. Most colleges and universities, the military, and many employers recognize the validity of the GED. Auchter and Stansfield cite several guidelines that in their view represent best practices in test translation:

- Select those tests and versions of a test most amenable to test translation. The criteria include recency of the test specifications, relevancy of content to Hispanic examinees, and ease with which the language used in the test could be translated into Spanish.

- Select certified trained translators who are native language speakers.
- Educate translators to use all variants of words or phrases; to be sensitive to issues of dialect and syntax; and to conduct initial forward translation, including compiling a list of items that are difficult to translate or words that reflect cultural bias.
- Examine the translated version against the original to judge the congruity of the translation with the English-language version.
- Conduct additional review of the tests using a contractor who has specific expertise in test construction.
- Conduct yet another review using two additional reviewers selected because of their special expertise in understanding variations in dialect that might influence how the test questions are interpreted by various Spanish language speakers.
- Conduct key verification in Spanish to identify the correct answers.
- Document the process that was used to translate each test.

Auchter and Stansfield also describe issues that arise in translating subject matter content. In their study, subject matter experts were called in to review each of the subject-specific tests. Not surprisingly, the mathematics test provided the fewest translation issues. These authors do not support the use of back translation as does Gross (1986) but rather, as evidenced by their guidelines, they recommend multiple variations of front review.

Another translation procedure is *side-by-side translation.* In this model, the translated version of the test is provided with the English-language version (Anderson, Liu, Swierzbin, Thurlow, & Bielinski, 2002). Anderson and colleagues describe a pilot study in which LEP students received versions of the Minnesota Basic Standards Reading Test in both English and Spanish, on audiocassette and in writing. The scores of students receiving the test in both languages were compared to scores of students who received only the English version. Most of the students reported that they did not use the taped version of the test at all and used the Spanish version to translate specific words from English. The scores of students assigned different versions of the test were not significantly different; however, the pilot study involved a small sample size, and the methodology seems promising enough to warrant further study.

Some states and large school districts employ the use of professional translation services. These organizations specialize in translating documents, including tests, into different languages. For example, the Center for Applied Linguistics website (www.cal.org/services) indicates that the company can provide translation into and from all the major world languages.

Using Interpreters

Many school districts, individual teachers, and other school professionals rely on informal means to accomplish translations. A common practice is to ask someone already affiliated with the school, such as a parent, a family friend, another professional, or a school staff member to provide translation services (Dale, 1986). Although standardized tests are no longer valid after translation into another language, other kinds of assessments are more amenable to these kinds of informal translation procedures. These assessments may include case histories, oral interviews, and informal teacher-made assessments. Informal translation procedures are also appropriate for interpreting the directions on nonverbal performance tests.

Wyatt (1998) writes that using a family member or family friend as an interpreter has several advantages. The student may be more comfortable with someone familiar, and the interpreter is more likely to speak the same dialect as the student. Wyatt reports disadvantages as well, however, such as the friend or family member trying to help too much. He or she may misrepresent the student's answers in order to present the student in the best possible light or may inappropriately coach the student to perform better.

In addition, regardless of the relationship between the interpreter and the student, untrained interpreters may be prone to mistranslate, not keep up with the student's rate of speaking, forget to include words, or editorialize or elaborate on the student's actual responses. It is critical, therefore, that the interpreter be educated regarding the teacher's expectations and the proper way to administer instructions and collect information (Wyatt, 1998). McCann, Napoli, and Wyatt (1996) found that 40 percent of California school speech-language pathologists who use interpreters are concerned about adequate interpreter training. Wyatt (1998) reports studies that suggest that optimally the interpreter and the test administrator should meet three times: once to review the client's background and the assessments that will be conducted; next to conduct the actual assessment; and a third time to discuss the interpreter's perceptions of what occurred during the assessment. Test administrators using interpreters can contribute to the accuracy of the translation by speaking slowly and clearly, and by avoiding jargon.

Standard 9.5 of the *Standards for Educational and Psychological Testing* (AERA et al., 1999) addresses the use of interpreters in testing situations:

> When an interpreter is used in testing, the interpreter should be fluent in both the language of the test and the examinee's native language, should have expertise in translating, and should have basic understanding of the assessment process. Although individuals with limited proficiency in the language of the test should ideally be tested by professionally trained bilingual examiners, the use of an interpreter may be necessary in some situations. If an interpreter is required, the professional examiner is responsible for ensuring that the interpreter has the appropriate qualifications, experience, and preparation to assist appropriately in the administration of the test. It is necessary for the interpreter to understand the importance of following standardized procedures, how testing is conducted typically, the importance of accurately conveying to the examiner an examinee's actual responses, and the role and responsibilities of the interpreter in testing. (p. 98)

Problems in Test Translation

Regardless of the quality of a translation, whether performed formally by a professional translation service or informally using an interpreter, there are several other potential problems that can influence the usefulness of translations.

One major variable that influences the utility of translated tests are student characteristics, including attitude. In a National Center on Educational Outcomes (NCEO) study on the impact of bilingual accommodations for LEP students on statewide reading tests, Anderson and colleagues (2002) reported the following findings:

- Accommodations and modifications are not a guaranteed formula for helping LEP students pass a standardized test.
- Translations are not appropriate for every speaker of a particular language.
- Not every student wants, or will use, an accommodation involving translation on a high-stakes test.
- A standardized means of determining which students are likely to benefit from translations should be created.
- English language proficiency, native language proficiency, level of test anxiety, and level of peer pressure to use an English version of a test contribute to determining which students may benefit from a translated test.
- Even within a single language group, the ability to benefit from test translation varies from student to student; generalizations based only on linguistic background should not be made.

The number of different languages spoken by schoolchildren in many states and school districts makes the concept of complete translations fiscally and pragmatically unfeasible even if the psychometric challenges regarding test validity, reliability, cultural bias, and population norming can be overcome.

Additionally, there are insufficient numbers of teachers and other school personnel who are trained to administer, score, and interpret tests in other languages. This is a particular problem for individualized assessment procedures such as those performed by school psychologists, speech-language pathologists, or learning disability specialists because these procedures require a great deal of interaction between the test administrator and the student.

Alternatives to Test Translation

Test translation problems have, in fact, made test translation an unpopular accommodation. In a survey of accommodations employed by states for linguistic minority students, test translation ranked low (Liu, Thurlow, Spicuzza, & Heinze, 1997). Several other methods of accommodating students who are bilingual or who have limited English proficiency exist: performance rating scales, nonverbal measures (particularly of intelligence), tape-recorded test instructions in the student's native language, and allowing additional time to complete the assessment. These accommodations also have advantages and disadvantages. In fact, they are subject to the same issues regarding reliability, validity, and norming as are accommodations using test translation. Standard 11.9 of the *Standards for Educational and Psychological Tests* (AERA et al., 1999) addresses the issue of using accommodations that do not compromise the reliability, validity, or norms of a test:

> When a test user contemplates an approved change in test format, mode of administration, instructions or language used in administrating the test, the user should have a strong rationale for concluding that the validity, reliability and appropriateness of norms will not be compromised. (p. 115)

Alternatives to test translation are often difficult to implement because they require subjective interpretations by the examiner. As a result they are more time-consuming to score and harder to norm. Additionally, teachers are most familiar and comfortable with paper-and-pencil tests because these tests are the mode of assessment that teachers themselves probably experienced in their own educational careers.

Regardless of what accommodations are available, the issue of whether to provide accommodations at all and, specifically, when is it appropriate to translate a test versus using some the accommodations noted previously is often a difficult decision. Standard 9.10 of the *Standards for Educational and Psychological Testing* (AERA et al., 1999) provides guidelines for testing language proficiency:

> Inferences about test takers' general language proficiency should be based on tests that measure a range of language features, and not on a single linguistic skill.
> For example, a multiple-choice, pencil-and-paper test of vocabulary does not indicate how well a person understands the language when spoken or how well the person speaks the language. (p. 99)

Furthermore, Standard 9.3 states:

> When testing an examinee proficient in two or more languages for which the test is available, the examinee's relative language proficiencies should be determined. The test generally should be administered in the test taker's most proficient language, unless proficiency in the less

proficient language is part of the assessment.

Unless the purpose of the testing is to determine proficiency in a particular language or the level of language proficiency required for the test is a work requirement, test users need to take into account the linguistic characteristics of examinees who are bilingual or use multiple languages. This may require the sole use of one language or use of multiple languages in order to minimize the introduction of construct-irrelevant components to the measurement process. For example, in educational settings, testing in both the language used in school and the native language of the examinee may be necessary in order to determine the optimal kind of instruction required by the examinee. Professional judgment needs to be used to determine the most appropriate procedures for establishing relative language proficiencies. Such procedures may range from self-identification by examinees through formal proficiency testing. (p. 98)

Determining Eligibility for a Translated Test

Large-scale testing programs used by states and school districts generally have specific guidelines to determine which students should be assessed in a language other than English. Sometimes these guidelines are based on practical matters such as cost or feasibility of obtaining alternative language tests.

For example, one major testing company that investigated creating licensing exams in a variety of languages determined that it was not fiscally feasible to do so. The agencies using the licensing exams, the test takers, and the testing company were none of them in a position to support the translation costs. Additionally, there were concerns that offering translated versions in some languages but not others might appear to be discriminatory. Instead, the testing company created a policy that permits individuals whose primary language is not English to apply for an accommodation that allows them time and a half to complete the exam. Preliminary research by the testing company has shown that this accommodation doesn't statistically improve performance on the exam. Other research, reported by Anderson and colleagues (2002) and by Ascher (1990), demonstrates that limited English speakers often need more time to take tests because of the additional time they require for language processing—that is, internally interpreting test items from one language to another.

Policies on who may use a translated test are often based on the number of years of English instruction a person has received, rather than on an individualized assessment of English language proficiency. An example of this kind of policy is illustrated by the language in the recent ESEA reauthorization mentioned earlier that requires inclusion of all students in large-scale testing programs if they have been instructed in English for more than three years.

Indeed there appears to be no normative definition of what constitutes limited English language proficiency, much less what proficiency level, or lack of proficiency, provides the student with the right to receive appropriate test translations and related accommodations. Several terms, including linguistic or language minority, limited English proficient, and bilingual, are generally used to describe students whose primary language is not English, but no universal normative definitions are used by all the states. (Liu et al., 1997). Liu and colleagues report in their review of the literature on LEP students and assessment that each state has a definition but that the state definitions contain different components, generally variants of the federal definition.

The federal definition from Title VII of the Improving Schools Act of 1994 (PL 103-382, Part E, Section 7501: Definitions, Regulations) defines a student as LEP if he or she meets the following criteria:

> A student that has sufficient difficulty speaking, reading or understanding the English language and whose difficulties may deny such individual the opportunity to learn successfully in classrooms where the language of instruction is English or to participate in society due to one or more of the following reasons:
>
> - Was not born in the United States or whose native language is a language other than English and comes from an environment where a language other than English is dominant;
> - Is a native American or Alaskan native . . . and comes from an environment where a language other than English has had a significant impact on such individual's level of English proficiency; or
> - Is migratory and whose native language is other than English and comes from an environment where a language other than English is dominant.

Special Considerations in Test Translation

Other considerations in test translation involve distinguishing a language issue from an education issue or learning disability and understanding that one translation does not suit every speaker of a particular language.

Language or education deficiency? Some students with LEP may have come from backgrounds where formal education was limited. This may be particularly true for political refugees from nations whose schools were closed due to military or civil unrest. It may also be true of immigrants arriving from nations where certain groups are denied access to education because of their ethnicity or their sex. For individuals with limited schooling, translating tests into their native language will not help them perform comparably to other students. Translation can provide a better gauge of their educational level, however, and a sense of how much of the difficulties they may be experiencing are due to language differences versus educational differences.

Language difference or disability? Some students with LEP also have a language or learning disability. It is important, therefore, to test the student in his or her native language to determine any special education needs (ASHA, 1985). Federal special education laws (e.g., IDEA) mandate testing in the student's native language; however, disproportionately large numbers of linguistic minority students are mistakenly labeled as having a disability and are assigned to special education programs. Special care must be taken to assess students appropriately so that they are neither inappropriately denied nor inappropriately placed in special education programs. Again, the proper use of test translations, especially the use of skilled interpreters who also have knowledge of appropriate linguistic and behavioral norms, can be invaluable in ensuring that students are properly diagnosed and educated.

The fallacy of the "one translation fits all" model. Much has been written about variations in test performance among English-language speakers due to linguistic differences. Differences in geographic, social, ethnic, and racial background as well as other demographic variables contribute to differences in language use. Differences in language use can include differences in vocabulary, syntax (word order in a sentence), morphology (use of word endings), grammar, pronunciation, and cultural referents. Large-scale testing programs commonly use techniques such as differential item functioning analysis (DIF) to control for any bias in the content of a question that may be a result of these linguistic and cultural differences. Similar variations in language use among speakers of the same language occur in most languages. Test translations must be sensitive to dialectal and other variations that may occur among common language speakers. One approach is to use words that are expected to be understood by all; another is to identify and incorporate several variants of words in the translations. For oral translations, identifying interpreters from the same geographic region and social and cultural background as the student is very important in contributing to accurate and appropriate translations.

Summary

Test translations can be useful for many students who are LEP and determined to be eligible for testing accommodations. Several factors, however, influence the utility of test translations.

One set of factors relates to individual student characteristics and needs. These include the students' native language proficiency, dialect, and culture, as well as the student's interest in using a translated test. Not all students will benefit from test translation. Nor will all translations in a particular language be appropriate for every student who speaks that language.

Another set of factors relates to the technical features of the test, including item bias, validity, and norming. Test users must be sure not only that the test items represent an accurate linguistic translation but also that the cultural referents are appropriate for the individual student's background. Appropriate methods of translation, including back translations or multiple forward translations, must be used. Additionally, the test must be validated and normed on a linguistically and culturally appropriate population, that is, a population similar in demographics to that of the student's. Lastly, teachers, translators, and others involved in the testing process must be educated on how to select, administer, score, and interpret translated tests.

References

AERA, APA, & NCME. (1999). *Standards for educational and psychological testing.* Washington, DC: American Educational Research Association.

AHSA [American Speech-Language-Hearing Association]. (1985, June). Clinical management of communicatively handicapped minority language populations. *Asha, 27*(6), 29–32.

Anderson, M., Liu, K., Swierzbin, B., Thurlow, M., & Bielinski, J. (2002, August). *Bilingual accommodations for limited English proficient students on statewide reading tests, phase 2* (National Center for Educational Outcomes, Minnesota Report 31). Retrieved March 11, 2002, from http://education.umn.edu/nceo/OnlinePubs/MnReport31.html.

Ascher, C. (1990). *Assessing Bilingual Children for Placement and Instruction* (ERIC/CUE Digest No. 65). New York, NY: ERIC Clearinghouse on Urban Education. (ERIC Document Reproduction Service No. ED322273)

ATA [American Translators Association]. (1997, November). *Code of professional conduct and business practices.* Retrieved February 21, 2003, from www.atanet.org/codeofprof.htm.

Auchter, J. & Stansfield, C. (1997). *Developing parallel tests across languages: Focus on the translation and adaptation process.* Paper presented at the annual Large Scale Assessment Conference, Colorado Springs, CO. (ERIC Document Reproduction Center No. ED414320)

Battle, D. E. (1998). *Communication disorders in multicultural populations* (2nd ed.). Boston, MA: Butterworth-Heinemann.

Bracken, B. A., & McCallum R. S. (1999). International testing: The universal nonverbal intelligence test. *The International Test Commission Newsletter* 9(1), 7–11.

Council of Chief State School Officers. (2001). *Annual survey of state student assessment programs for 1998–99 school year*. Washington, DC: Author.

Dale T. C. (1986). *Limited-English-proficient students in the schools: Helping the newcomer.* Washington, DC: ERIC Clearinghouse on Languages and Linguistics. (ERIC Document Reproduction Center No. ED279206)

Figueroa, R. A. (1990). Best practices in the assessment of bilingual children. In A. Thomas & J. Grimes (Eds.), *Best practices in school psychology* (vol. 11). Washington, DC: National Association of School Psychologists.

Geisinger, K. F., & Carlson, J. F. (1992). Assessing language-minority students. *Practical Assessment, Research & Evaluation, 3*(2).

Gross, L. J. (1986). *Examination translation guidelines* (monograph). Memphis, TN: International Board of Lactation Consultant Examiners.

Gross, L. J., & Scott, J. W. (1989). Translating a health professional certification test to another language: A pilot analysis. *Evaluation and the Health Professions, 12*(1).

International Test Commission. (1999). *International guidelines for test use: Version 2000.* Stockholm: Author.

Liu, K., Thurlow M., Spicuzza, R., & Heinze, K. (1997). *A review of the literature on students with limited English proficiency and assessment* (National Center on Educational Outcomes, Minnesota Report 11). Retrieved February 21, 2003, from http://education.umn.edu/nceo/OnlinePubs/MnReport11.html.

McCann, M., Napoli, M., &Wyatt, T. (1996). *Use of paraprofessionals with low-incidence language populations: A survey.* Presentation at the California Speech and Hearing Association conference, Monterrey, CA.

National Academy of Sciences. (2002). *Report on minority students in special and gifted education.* Washington, DC: Author.

Stansfield, C. W. (1996). Content assessment in the native language. *Practical Assessment, Research & Evaluation, 5*(9). Available online at http://ericae.net/pare/getvn.asp?v=5&n=9.

Wyatt, T. (1998). Assessment issues with multicultural populations. In D. Battle (Ed.),*Communication disorders in multicultural populations* (2nd ed.). Boston, MA: Butterworth-Heinemann.

Chapter 11
Testing of Students with Limited English Proficiency

Kurt F. Geisinger

Considerable testing occurs in the schools and in related educational settings. Schools are microcosms of society, and changes that affect society are also likely to affect the schools in similar ways. The composition of American society has been changing dramatically in recent years, and this particular change is one that has influenced schools considerably; its effect on testing is dramatic. This chapter describes some of the ways that testing needs to be considered in light of the population shifts that are occurring, beginning with a description of the extent of these changes, then a consideration of three areas of test use (as described in Geisinger, 2002) from the perspective of dealing with individuals whose native language is not English.

Population Shifts in American Society

Many (e.g., Eyde, 1992) have noted changes in American society. The predominant change is an increase in groups that do not speak English. As discussed in the following section, this change is due to both immigration and increasing birth rates.

Changes in the Population as a Whole

According to the U.S. Census Bureau, the population of the United States was 275 million in 1995 and is expected to grow to 300 million by 2010, and to 338 million by 2025. From July 1, 1995, until July 1, 2000, the United States population grew by 12 million people, approximately 12.5 percent. This growth comes from two primary sources: immigration and increasing birth rates. Both of these factors are leading to increases in the numbers of language minorities in the United States, and this group is growing at rates faster than the rest of the population. Approximately 2.8 million of the increase from 1995 to 2000 emerged from immigration and of these, approximately 43 percent were Hispanic; 25 percent were White, not Hispanic; 24.5

percent were from Asia; and some 7 percent were Black, not Hispanic. The majority of the White, not Hispanic group came from Eastern Europe and the majority of the Asian group came from Southeast Asia. Thus, virtually all these immigrants are coming from countries where English is not spoken, or is not a primary language. The majority of the increases over this five-year period, however, occurred due to differential birth rates, that is, rates that differ by ethnic group membership.

On July 1, 2000, the U.S. Census Bureau estimated the ethnic breakdown of the United States population (rounded to the nearest whole percentage) as follows (Geisinger, 2002):

70 percent White, not Hispanic
12 percent Hispanic American
13 percent African American
4 percent Asian American
1 percent Native American

The U. S. Census Bureau estimates the ethnic breakdown of the United States population by the year 2025 (again rounded to the nearest whole percentage) will be as follows (Geisinger, 2002):

62 percent White (a decline of 8 percent)
18 percent Hispanic-American (an increase of 6 percent)
14 percent African-American (an increase of 1 percent)
6 percent Asian-American (an increase of 2 percent)
1 percent Native American (no change)

Several types of population changes are occurring. Numbers of Hispanic Americans are increasing relative to the population as a whole, and it is estimated that by 2025, they will account for 66 percent more of the United States population, relative to their current status. Asian Americans too are growing rapidly in number and will increase by 50 percent. African Americans are growing by a more modest 8 percent. These gains are offset by a more than 11 percent decrease in the relative proportion of the largest group: Whites who are not Hispanics. Therefore, the three largest minority groups are all increasing, with Hispanic Americans and Asian Americans increasing most rapidly. Whether schools are ready or will be ready to accommodate this large and increasing number of language minorities is not yet clear.

Changes in the Schools

A large and increasing group in United States schools is composed of those students whose native language is not English. This group is frequently known as limited English proficient students, or LEP students. Determinations must be made as to whether these individuals should be educated in English, their home language, or a combination of the two, as is often found in bilingual education. From a psychometric perspective, the testing of these individuals represents a thorny problem. If they are tested in English, they may not be able to show optimally what they know and can do. On the other hand, it is pragmatically difficult to build tests that can assess these students in their home languages—impossible in many school districts and states where more than 100 different languages may be spoken in homes.

LEP students currently comprise some 14 percent of the total test-taking population in our nation's schools, with approximately 75 percent of these students being Hispanic. Of the remaining 25 percent of LEP students, approximately 50 percent are Asian American, primarily Chinese, Vietnamese, and Korean.

Of the Hispanic students, more than 50 percent speak English at home, some 25 percent speak mostly Spanish at home, and 17 percent report speaking English and Spanish equally often at home (National Center for Education Statistics, 2002). The mother's place of birth is the strongest predictor of the Hispanic student's primary language. The language that is spoken in the home of Hispanic students is also closely related to their educational level. For example, "49 percent of the Hispanic students who spoke mostly Spanish at home had parents with a high school education, compared with 83 percent who spoke mostly English at home" (National Center for Education Statistics: Condition of Education, Indicator 6, pp. 1–2). Over the 27 years from 1972 to 1999, the percentage of Hispanic students in the schools has risen dramatically, paralleling the growth in the population as a whole, and there are large geographical differences reflected in the percentage of Hispanics enrolled in schools across the regions of our country. Throughout the entire country, the percentage of Hispanics in public education has risen from 6 percent in 1972 to 16.2 percent in 1999, an increase of 170 percent. At their most numerous, in the western part of the country, however, Hispanics made up 31 percent of the public school population in 1999, up from 15 percent in 1972. At the other extreme is the Midwest, where the percentage of Hispanic students was 6 percent in 1999, up from only 1.5 percent in 1972. Across the country, in 1993–94, 31 percent of Hispanic, Asian, or Native American children were classified as LEP students. Overall, the LEP population in American schools has experienced a 300 percent increase from the early 1990s into the beginning of the twenty-first century. Clearly, the schools are facing the challenges of teaching students whose English is at best generally below that of the majority group, and at worst, very poor (U.S. Department of Education, 1997). These increasing numbers of LEP students demand changes to many aspects of the educational process, including testing.

Critical Psychometric Factors in Testing LEP Students: Culture and Language

The kind of increasingly diverse society that the American melting pot is places demands upon the professional testing community: companies, testing professionals (especially those who develop tests), and those who use the tests that are developed. A number of critical factors must always be considered in making all testing decisions. These include the regularly found differences among cultural and ethnic groups in test performance, especially on cognitive tests of ability and on measures of school achievement. Second, because tests, whether cognitive or of other types, are inherently behavioral samples, and because culture affects behavior, culture too affects test performance. In fact, if culture affects behavior relevant to the domain covered by a test, it must also affect test performance or the test itself would not be validly sampling the behaviors underlying the test. A third factor to consider is that most tests are language specific. Language is considered by many anthropologists to be one major factor inherent in culture, but only a single factor among others.

Determining the composition of the group to be tested is a preliminary consideration for anyone involved in the testing of groups of students or other individuals. Those who make decisions about testing must be aware of the number and size of varying cultural, language, and ethnic groups present in the targeted population. Such data may be acquired from local sources or from national groups, such as the U.S. Census Bureau. Researching the demographics of a group is time well spent.

Three Decisions in Testing

There are three decision areas related to testing that are greatly affected by the composition of the group to be tested. These three are the selection of the testing instrument, the administration of the test, and the use of the test. The last of these, test use, also subsumes test interpretation, as the proper use of test data first involves the appropriate interpretation of test results. Each of these three testing concerns is addressed in turn below.

Test Selection

All individuals who decide what test to use are faced first with a simple question: whether to buy an existing measure or to build one. A variety of factors influence one or the other possibility. An argument for purchasing an existing measure is the fact that a test publisher, at least if the publisher is a major test publisher or a test publisher who specializes in the area covered by the test, generally can bring more research and other resources to the test development process. Included in the test development process is being up to date on the latest strategies of testing and current content. Similarly, such a publisher can also likely gather more extensive validation and normative data. Normative and validation information should be in the test manual, and potential test users are encouraged to contact the test publisher or even the test author if they need answers to specific questions. Normative and validation data are critical for proper test score interpretation and use. If the test has been available for a reasonable period of time, then potential test users can also read evaluations of the measure in sources such as the Buros *Mental Measurements Yearbook*; the Test Critiques series; and assessment-related journals, or in some cases, textbooks, such as Anastasi and Urbina (1997). Of particular interest to the thrust of this chapter is the necessity of considering not only the validity of the test, but also its validity when used with the language minority populations present in a particular setting. In the United States, a finding that validity data are consistent across groups means that a measure is valid for the Hispanic population as well as for the majority population. In specific settings, of course, other language groups may need to be considered.

When one chooses to develop one's own test, the standard factors involved in any test construction demand consideration. If the test is to be administered to and used with a linguistically diverse population, the questions one must ask about the test become much more complex. The ultimate questions that must be asked in any decision-making process relating to test selection and development are (a) is this measure valid for the use that is planned, and (b) is the test appropriate for all the groups involved? The former question requires the potential test user to decide whether there is evidence that the test can provide the kind of useful information that can enlighten decision-making in a particular context. (In the case of an admissions decision, for example, a valid test would provide information on which potential students are most likely to succeed in the ensuing educational program and which are not. In the case of an achievement mastery test, a valid test would provide strong indications of the extent to which different students have in fact learned the material provided in the program.) While data supporting such a contention may emerge from a single study, it is more likely to come from a series of studies, which may or may not have been performed in sequence by the test developer or another test researcher. Such information is most commonly available either for the entire population or for the majority group within that population. Of considerable interest to those testing diverse populations, however, is how well the test works when used with subgroups of the population.

The second question is therefore somewhat more difficult. It relates to whether the kind of validation information called for is available for the varying subgroups within the population. Critical to the present discussion, of course, is whether this information is available for language minorities, in particular, the kinds of language minorities found in the setting of most interest to the potential test user. Simply put, the kinds of validation evidence that are employed to justify the use of a test with the entire population (or with the majority population) must also be present for all of the language minority groups.

Let us consider a few examples. Does a college admissions measure that predicts collegiate grades reasonably for students across the country also work when applied to Hispanics? Does it also work for recent immigrants whose English is quite weak? Does a measure of knowledge in history work for students across the country who have had college-preparatory courses in history throughout their high school education? That is, does it represent the information provided in the curriculum in a representative and fair manner? Does the same measure also fairly and accurately represent the curriculum of students who have been exposed to a bilingual curriculum, which includes some learning in English and some in their home language so that these students do not fall behind their peers as they "catch up" in English? Does it represent the courses taught in an inner-city school where multiple languages and cultures are present? For both of these types of tests, are they valid for individuals whose knowledge of English makes it difficult for them to read and comprehend the test questions as they are presented? Are they valid for individuals whose English mastery does not permit them to read the questions and the choices of answers and to respond to them as quickly as the majority group in our population? Test publishers who wish their tests to be used with linguistically diverse candidates should provide information supportive of positive responses to the preceding questions. To be sure, however, such research is expensive, and only the largest of test publishers are frequently able to perform this research, regardless of its appropriateness and import.

A number of issues must be considered about an instrument that will potentially be used with language minority, or LEP, children. The issue of differential validity is paramount. The issue of whether the test is fair and unbiased is closely aligned with the validity issue. A third issue relates to norms; this topic is discussed in the treatment of test score interpretation and use. The final questions relate to whether there are forms of the measure more appropriate to LEP students (either in their home language or in an English-language reduced version) or whether there is interpretative information so that test users working with LEP children can effectively understand the meaning of these students' scores. (This last type of information is also closely related to the question of validity.)

The question of differential validity is most typically seen in the case of a test that is justified on the basis that it predicts a criterion. Differential validity is established if the test does not predict comparably for a minority group as it does for the majority group. Differential validity can extend to other forms of validity, however. If two groups (the majority group and a minority group) receive very different instruction in schools, for example, a test that covers only the content presented to the majority group could be seen as having differential content validity. Ultimately, the question of differential validity relates to whether the results of testing are equally meaningful for all groups. In the case of LEP students, such questions are critical, for international students have almost assuredly been exposed to different content in their instruction, and even those in the United States may have experienced somewhat different instruction, as for example, if they are in bilingual or remedial instruction.

One type of fairness is actually an assessment of differential validity. Such analyses normally consider the test as a whole. If a test is differentially valid but is used as if it is not, then at least one group will likely receive inappropriate results. It is also possible to consider discrete components of tests, especially individual test questions, to determine if they contribute to the biased nature of a test. Such analyses are called *differential item functioning analyses,* or *dif analyses*. (See Berk, 1982; Embretson & Reise, 2000; or Wasserman & Bracken, 2002, for in-depth treatments of this topic.) Essentially, what dif analyses do is consider whether individual test items are differentially more difficult relative to other items on the test for specific, identifiable subgroups in the population. Such analyses are best performed during the test construction process so that items that do not function equivalently for all groups may be removed from draft versions of an examination. Those involved in the selection of a test are well advised to review the procedures used in the development of tests to see if dif procedures were employed and, in particular, if they were employed using the language minority subgroups to be tested.

Some tests are available in more than one language version, for example, in English and Spanish. Ideally, in such a case, the different forms have been developed and studied in ways to ensure their comparability. (See Geisinger, 1994, or Sireci, 1997, for considerations of some of the issues involved.) If, as is most commonly the case, a test is developed in one language and translated to a second, the term *adaptation* is used rather than *translation.* The reasoning behind this nomenclature is that changes in tests are not related only to language; culture too requires the original language form of a test to be changed to make sure that any references to aspects of culture are equivalent across the two forms. Such a process inevitably involves committee processes in which individuals who know about the content and constructs measured by the test, who are fluent in both languages, and who are knowledgeable about both cultures consider the test item by item to ensure that the two forms are indeed equivalent. A test that is available in more than one language obviously has advantages over one that is not. Nevertheless, the technical considerations that are involved in adapting a test from one language and culture to another are extensive and are infrequently performed in a superlative manner. A prospective test user must become familiar with the requirements involved in test translation and adaptation and inspect the procedures carefully before deciding to use a second language version of a test.

Test Administration

A few test administration issues are particularly relevant to the testing of LEP students. These include the use of second language forms, testing in English, and the sociocultural context of testing.

Before assessing Hispanic students with a test in either English or Spanish, one should make an assessment of each individual's relative language abilities. Although there may be circumstances in which one language needs be used instead of the other, there are also circumstances where the most valid assessment of what a student knows or can do is simply of more critical importance. In such a case, assessments of language competence are needed first. The level of language skill typically required to respond to written test questions in English is quite high, and it is likely that many children whose home language differs from English, but who appear orally to be quite conversant in English (and even bilingual), cannot respond to the level of academic English required by a written examination. The timing of an examination may also be a concern, because their speed of functioning in their second language is likely to be much reduced. An assessment of relative language skills permits a determination of the language in which to test the LEP student using the proper language form of the examination.

If a language test indicates that a LEP child should be tested in English, or if no second language version of the test (or a comparable test) is available, then the child may need to be assessed in English. In such a case, it is possible that interpretations specific to those whose home language is not English may be needed. Such interpretations will likely be based on validation research using students with similar language skills and normative data using comparable groups. It is possible, for example, that a test score may have a different meaning for a student whose native language is English than for one whose native language is Spanish. This demarcation may be especially true if English has significant weight on the test, even if that is not what is intended to be measured by the test (as in the case of a master test of mathematics using many word problems, an essay test of American history, or a scale measuring test anxiety). In such an instance, the impact of language ability on the resultant scales is actually a source of test invalidity, because it reflects something other than what the test was intended to measure.

A test user should determine whether it is appropriate in a given context to use norms for an entire group (that is, the whole population tested) or for the specific group, of which the individual is a member (such as Hispanic children of a given age). Differing rationales argue for each in given contexts, and no general rules are advanced here for making this determination. One does need to determine the extent to which children with backgrounds and language skills similar to those being assessed were included in the reference or norm group. One should also determine whether norms for language minority children are also available, and if they are, whether the child or children being assessed are comparable to those in that specific norm group. Such information can greatly aid in the interpretation of a child's performance. In the same sense that a good test administrator should first assess an LEP child's language skills, the test administrator should also consider assessing the child's acculturation. (A brief discussion of acculturation and its impact on test scores follows in the section on test interpretation and use.)

Anastasi and Urbina (1997) describe the transcultural context that sometimes occurs in testing situations. An example of a transcultural context is when a middle-aged White psychologist administers an individual test to a Hispanic youngster who has not had significant exposure to such individuals. Novelty, fear, and cultural factors can influence the child's performance; although such factors have generally not been found in investigations, they have occasionally been noted, and test administrators should be alert for such possibilities.

Test Interpretation and Use

Most professional test users determine the meaning of scores using validity and norms. Norms help us to interpret where an individual's performance places him or her relative to that person's particular reference group. Sandoval (1998) has called for what he terms "critical thinking in test interpretation." As such, Sandoval calls for those interpreting the test performance of students to examine carefully their preconceptions and the factors they use in explaining performance. Stereotypes are one such possible explanation of behavior against which testing professionals need to guard. Sandoval recommends using the factors that have been properly shown to aid in test score interpretations—such as test validity, norms, base rates, looking at extra-test behavior in addition to test scores and performance—and considering a longer time period than just the testing itself in making proper interpretations of test results.

Test users can follow general principles for permitting culture and cultural differences to influence interpretations of test performance (see Geisinger, 2002). It is particularly important that those using tests understand how members of specific groups tend to perform on given assessments in specific domains. The Office of Ethnic Minority Affairs of the American Psychological Association (1993) has provided guidelines for test interpretation. One is especially relevant. Guideline 2d states, "Psychologists consider the validity of a given instrument or procedure and interpret resulting data, keeping in mind the cultural and linguistic characteristics of the person being assessed. Psychologists are aware of the test's reference population and possible limitations of the instrument with other populations" (p. 46).

The acculturation of culturally diverse individuals being tested should be assessed, just as their language skills should be. CuÈllar (2000) portrays culture as mediating relationships between personality and behavior. That is, one needs to consider the culture from which an individual comes as part of an interpretation and attribution of his or her behavior, including behavior on tests. Acculturation occurs as one learns about and changes in conformance to a new culture. One's learning English after coming to the United States, for example, is one type of acculturation. Test results should be considered in light of the degree to which an individual who has come to this country has become acculturated. (See Geisinger, 2002, for a brief overview of acculturation issues in testing and MarÌn, 1992, and CuÈllar, 2000, for good summaries of issues involved in the assessment of acculturation.)

Conclusion

Our society is changing rapidly. These changes include dramatic changes in the numbers of LEP children in the schools. This influx affects testing. If the acculturation and English proficiency of linguistic minorities are high, tests are likely to be used effectively. To the extent that these factors are not high, however, difficulties often arise. This chapter has presented some information that should help test users in deciding whether to build or select a test to be used with this population, to decide which test to select, to administer the test properly, and to interpret scores accurately. Because these issues are so complex, only high points of the issues involved were mentioned. Test users who work with linguistically diverse populations need to be most concerned with validity, and they need to study test manuals and validation reports carefully to determine whether the tests are appropriate for the populations with which they work. They also need to consider normative information and research on the use of the instruments with the appropriate populations. Caution is, however, the overarching order of the day.

References

Anastasi, A., & Urbina, S. (1997). *Psychological testing* (7th ed.). Upper Saddle River, NJ: Prentice Hall.

Berk, R. A. (Ed.) (1982). *Handbook of methods for detecting test bias.* Baltimore, MD: Johns Hopkins University Press.

Cuellar, I. (2000). Acculturation as a moderator of personality and psychological assessment. In R. H. Dana (Ed.), *Handbook of cross-cultural and multicultural personality assessment* (pp. 113–130). Mahwah, NJ: Erlbaum.

Embretson, S. E., & Reise, S. P. (2000). *Item response theory for psychologists.* Mahwah, NJ: Erlbaum.

Eyde, L. D. (1992). Introduction to the testing of Hispanics in industry and research. In K. F. Geisinger (Ed.), *Psychological testing of Hispanics* (pp. 167–172). Washington, DC: APA Books.

Geisinger, K. F. (1994). Cross-cultural normative assessment: Translation and adaptation issues influencing the normative interpretation of assessment instruments. *Psychological Assessment, 6,* 304–312.

Geisinger, K. F. (2002). Testing the members of an increasingly diverse society. In J. F. Carlson & B. B. Waterman (Eds.), *Social and personality assessment of school-aged children: Developing interventions for educational and clinical use* (pp. 346–364). Boston: Allyn and Bacon.

Marin, G. (1992). Issues in the measurement of acculturation among Hispanics. In K. F. Geisinger (Ed.), *Psychological testing of Hispanics* (pp. 235–252). Washington, DC: APA Books.

National Center for Education Statistics, Office of Educational Research and Improvement. (2000). Condition of Education: Indicator 6. Retrieved January 18, 2003, from nces.ed.gov/programs/coe/2000/section1/indicator06.asp

Office of Ethnic Minority Affairs of the American Psychological Association. (1993). Guidelines for providers of psychological services to ethnic, linguistic and culturally diverse populations. *American Psychologist, 48,* 45–48.

Sandoval, J. (1998). Critical thinking in test interpretation. In J. Sandoval, C. L. Frisby, K. F. Geisinger, J. C. Scheuneman, & J. Ramos Grenier (Eds.), *Test interpretation and diversity: Achieving equity in assessment* (pp. 387–402). Washington, DC: APA Books.

Sireci, S. G. (1997). Problems and issues in linking tests across languages. *Educational Measurement: Issues and Practice, 16* (1), 12–19.

U.S. Department of Education, National Center for Education Statistics. (1997). *A profile of policies and practices for limited English proficient students: Screening methods, program support, and teaching training.* (SASS 1993–94). NCES 97–472, by M. Han, D. Bakers, & C. Rodriguez. Washington, DC: Author.

Wasserman, J. D., & Bracken, B. A. (2002). Selecting appropriate tests: Psychometric and pragmatic considerations. In J. F. Carlson & B. B. Waterman (Eds.), *Social and personality assessment of school-aged children: Developing interventions for educational and clinical use* (pp. 18–43). Boston: Allyn and Bacon.

Chapter 12
Inclusion of Students With Disabilities in State and District Assessments

Martha L. Thurlow & Sandra J. Thompson

The inclusion of students with disabilities in state and district assessments rests on a fundamental belief: *All children can learn.* This belief is not about *almost* all children, or all children *except* the ones in the special education classroom. It is about every single child who receives educational services, even those whose teachers and therapists work with them at home or in the hospital.

A statement directly related to the belief that all children can learn is *All children have the right to work toward challenging educational standards.* Think about the children with whom you have worked. It may be easy to think about Tanya, the girl who just won the state geography contest. It is also possible to assume that the statement applies to Eric, who does not read very well because of a learning disability; we can recognize that by using a scanner and books on tape, he is also working toward standards at grade level. What about Mary, an eighth grader who is nonverbal, requires extensive physical care, and never leaves the special education room?

It is possible to have challenging expectations for Mary, just as for Tanya and Eric. And they all can work toward the same standards. These premises form the basic assumptions of two important federal laws: Title I of the No Child Left Behind Act of 2001 (NCLB), and the 1997 reauthorization of the Individuals with Disabilities Education Act (IDEA). The purpose of this chapter is to clarify the rationale for holding schools accountable for the progress of every student toward challenging educational standards and to describe the assessment options for measuring this progress through state and district assessment systems.

To measure how well children are making progress toward standards, it makes sense to measure that progress through an assessment system that is aligned with the standards. According to Title I, all students in every school must be held to these standards, and the progress of all students must be measured and reported to the public. Students with disabilities are specifically included in the definition of *all* in Title I. Based on assessment reports, schools need to make instructional and structural changes so that the expectations for all students are raised, and all children have opportunities to work toward challenging standards.

No Child Left Behind Act of 2001, P.L.107–110 (2001)

"Such assessments shall . . . provide for the reasonable adaptations and accommodations for students with disabilities (as defined under section 602[3] of the Individuals with Disabilities Education Act), necessary to measure the achievement of such students relative to State academic content and State academic achievement standards." (Sec. 1111 [3] [C][ix][II]).

The amendments to the Individuals with Disabilities Education Act of 1997 also focus state and district attention on full participation of students with disabilities in assessment systems.

Amendments to the Individuals with Disabilities Education Act, P.L. 105-17 (1997)

"Children with disabilities are included in general State and district-wide assessment programs, with appropriate accommodations, where necessary. As appropriate, the State or local educational agency develops guidelines for the participation of children with disabilities in alternate assessments for those children who cannot participate in State and district-wide assessment programs." (Sec. 612 [a] [18] [A] [i]).

State Response to Federal Requirements

For the past 10 years, the National Center on Educational Outcomes (NCEO) has been surveying state directors of special education about the participation of students with disabilities in education reform, with a focus on participation in state assessments and accountability systems. We completed our most recent survey in 2001 (Thompson & Thurlow, 2001). In our survey of all 50 states, we found that more than half of them reported an increase over previous years in the state test participation rates of students with disabilities. Several state directors indicated that this increase was due to the following factors:

- directions given to professionals in the field
- increased awareness of and compliance with the law
- public awareness of new statewide alternate assessments
- provision of more flexible testing accommodations

Directors from about one fourth of the states reported that the performance levels of students with disabilities on state tests had increased. For example, in the state of New York, more students with disabilities passed the regents exams in 2001 than had even participated in the exams in previous years (New York State Education Department, 2001).

Assessment Options

Even though all students are expected to participate in a state's assessment system, it is not possible to assess all students in exactly the same way. Sometimes individual students need individual approaches to assessment in order to show what they know and are able to do. Most states and districts have defined the following options for students to participate in the assessment system:

- in the same way as the majority of students
- with accommodations
- in an alternate assessment

Variations of these three approaches are used in some states. Most of these, like taking tests with nonapproved accommodations (Thurlow & Wiener, 2000) or taking tests designed for lower grade levels out-of-level testing (Thurlow, Elliott, … Ysseldyke, 1999) are controversial.

Estimates of the percentages of students expected to participate in assessments in these different ways have been fairly consistent. About 85 percent of students with disabilities have relatively mild or moderate disabilities and can participate in state and district large-scale assessments, either with or without accommodations (Ysseldyke, Thurlow, McGrew, & Shriner, 1994). These percentages are provided to give state and district administrators an idea about the rates they might expect; they are not meant to be caps or cutoff points. It has been suggested that decision makers start from the premise that most students with disabilities will participate in general assessments, with or without accommodations, rather than in alternate assessments (Thurlow, Elliott, & Ysseldyke, 1998).

Accommodated Assessments

Assessment accommodations are alterations in the way a test is administered; they should not change the content of the test or the performance standard. The purpose of accommodations is to ensure that the student's knowledge and skills are assessed, rather than the student's disability. Researchers argue that accommodations should boost the performance of students who need them and not affect the performance of students who do not need them (Fuchs, Fuchs, Eaton, Hamlett, & Karns, 2000; Tindal, Helwig, & Hollenbeck, 1999). Thus, assessment accommodations are provided to level the playing field for students who need them, not to give those students an advantage over other students.

Currently, every state has a policy governing the use of accommodations on large-scale assessments. These policies vary widely across states, with a great range in both the number of students using accommodations and the variety of accommodations selected (Thurlow, Lazarus, Thompson, & Robey, 2002). Nearly 60 percent of all states now keep track of accommodation use during state assessments (Thompson & Thurlow, 2001). It appears that the use of accommodations is either increasing or remaining stable about half of the states reported an increase in use, and the other half reported stable use. Some directors attributed growth in use to increased awareness and understanding by educators, parents, and students. (To find out more about how students across the United States are using assessment accommodations, go to the NCEO website: www.education.umn.edu/nceo.)

There are six types of assessment accommodations: setting, presentation, timing, response, scheduling, and other. Here is a brief description of each of these categories as they are described in several NCEO publications:

Setting accommodations change the location in which an assessment is given or the conditions of the assessment setting. For example, if a student has a hard time focusing attention in a group setting, or needs to take frequent breaks, he or she could request to take a test in a different room, either alone or in a small group. A student may also need an individualized setting if he or she uses special equipment, such as a tape recorder. Changes in setting could include special lighting, altered acoustics, or adapted furniture.

Timing accommodations change the allowable length of testing time and may also change the way that time is organized. This type of accommodation is most helpful if a student needs extra time to process written text, extra time to write, or time to use certain equipment. Students may also need frequent or extended breaks.

Scheduling accommodations change the particular time of day, day of the week, or number of days over which a test is administered. A student's medication or ability to stay alert for a test may require a request for these changes.

Presentation accommodations change the way a student takes a test and include changes in test format or procedures and the use of assistive devices. Some of these accommodations are controversial, especially in the area of having tests read aloud.

Response accommodations change how a student might respond to an assessment. As with presentation accommodations, these changes may include format alterations (such as marking responses in the test booklet rather than on a separate page), procedural changes (such as giving a response in a different mode pointing, oral response, or sign language, for example), and the use of assistive devices (such as use of a scribe to write student responses or a calculator, a brailler, or other communication device).

Other accommodations include things like reminding students to stay on task or offering incentives to encourage students to do their best.

Table 1 shows several examples of accommodations and decision making questions to ask students. A good resource for specific strategies for selecting and using assessment accommodations is the Council for Exceptional Children's toolkit for educators, called *Making Assessment Accommodations* (ASPIIRE/ILIAD IDEA Partnership Projects, 2000).

Table 1. Examples of Accommodations and Decision-Making Questions

Examples of Accommodation	Questions to Ask a Student
Setting	
• Administer the test in a small group or individually in a separate location with minimal distractions. • Provide special lighting. • Provide special furniture or acoustics.	• Can you focus on your own work in a room with other students? • Do you distract other students? • Can you take a test in the same way as it is given to other students?
Timing	
• Allow a flexible schedule. • Extend the time allotted to take the test. • Allow frequent breaks during testing.	• Can you work continuously for the entire length of a typically administered portion of the test (e.g., 20 to 30 minutes)? • Do you use accommodations that require more time to complete test items?
Scheduling	
• Administer the test in several sessions, possibly over several days, specifying the duration of each session. • Allow subtests to be taken in a different order. • Administer the test at different times of day.	• Do you take medication that slows you down, with optimal performance at a certain time of day? • Does your anxiety level increase dramatically when working in certain content areas, so that these should be taken after other content areas?
Presentation	
• Provide the test on audiotape. • Increase spacing between items or reduce items per page or line. • Highlight key words or phrases in directions. • Provide cues (e.g., arrows and stop signs) on answer form.	• Can you listen to and follow oral directions? • Can you see and hear? • Can you read printed text?
Response	
• Allow marking of answers in booklet. • Tape record responses for later translation. • Allow use of scribe. • Provide copying assistance between drafts.	• Can you track from a test booklet to a test response form? • Can you use a pencil or other writing tool?
Other	
• Allow special test preparation. • Use on-task/focusing prompts. • Allow any accommodation that a student needs that does not fit under the existing categories.	• Is this the first time that you will be taking a district or state assessment? • Do you have the necessary test-taking skills?

Adapted from Elliott, J., Thurlow, M., Ysseldyke, J., & Erickson, R. (1997). Providing assessment accommodations for students with disabilities in state and district assessments (Policy Directions No. 7). Minneapolis, MN: University of Minnesota, National Center on Educational Outcomes, Retrieved September 2001, from the World Wide Web: http://education.umn.edu/NCEO/OnlinePubs/Policy7.html.

Everyone on a student's IEP team needs enough information about assessment participation and accommodations to help a student make good decisions. Some IEP team members may encourage a student to use too many accommodations, while keeping their fingers crossed that *something* will help. Students should try out a variety of accommodations in the classroom and, with the teacher, figure out what works best before the IEP team makes decisions about which ones the student should use on high-stakes tests.

Some students have had limited experience expressing personal preferences and advocating for themselves. Speaking out about their preferences, particularly in the presence of authority figures, may be a new role for students, one for which they need guidance and feedback. Winnelle Carpenter, an educational consultant who prepares students with learning disabilities for high-stakes graduation tests, describes the process of self-advocacy as follows:

> For students with disabilities to self advocate effectively, they must understand their specific disability; learn their strengths and challenges; identify factors that are interfering with their performance, learning, and employment; and develop compensations, accommodations, and coping skills to help them succeed. In addition, through careful guidance, these same students must learn how to apply this knowledge effectively when making decisions, negotiating and speaking up on their own behalf. (Carpenter, 1995, p. iv)

The goal is for students to assume control, with appropriate levels of support, over their assessment participation and to select and use accommodations that are most helpful to them on assessments, throughout their daily lives, and in their plans for a successful transition to adult life.

NCEO interviewed nearly 100 high school students with disabilities about their participation in a large-scale state test that they must pass in order to graduate from high school (Thompson, Thurlow, & Walz, 2001). We wanted to know whether the students had participated in the statewide assessments and whether they knew their success on the tests. We also asked the students what accommodations they used on the state test and in their daily classes, and what accommodations they thought might be most helpful to them in their adult lives. We found that most students knew whether they had participated in testing and how well they did on the tests. About 75 percent of the students said that they had used accommodations on the tests. Older students were more likely to use assessment accommodations than younger students, and the majority of students used three or fewer accommodations. Extended time, testing in a separate room in a small group, having directions repeated, and reviewing test directions in advance were the accommodations used most often.

Alternate Assessment Participation

IDEA 1997 now requires all states to have alternate assessments in place, meaning they are developed and implemented, and the data are reported. An alternate assessment is a way to measure the performance of students who are unable to participate in general large-scale assessments used by a district or state. Alternate assessments provide a mechanism for students with significant disabilities to be included in the assessment system.

Our survey results from all 50 states tell us that nearly all state alternate assessments assess the same standards as general assessments either by expanding state academic content standards, linking a set of functional skills back to standards, or assessing standards plus an additional set of functional skills (Thompson ... Thurlow, 2001). We have seen the alignment of alternate assessments with standards evolve a great deal, especially over the past four years. Several states that in 1999 indicated they were developing alternate assessments based on a special education curriculum are now making a connection between their alternate assessments and state academic content standards. Several strategies have been used to show progress toward academic content standards through alternate assessments. More than half of the 50 states organize the data collected for a student's alternate assessment into some type of portfolio, while others summarize the results on a checklist or rating scale.

Many states have expanded their academic content standards to include functional skills, known in different states as basic, access, essential, or fundamental skills. Selecting performance indicators that are clearly aligned with standards is critical to the inclusion of alternate assessment participants in standards-based reform. For example, one state has this geometry standard: "The student will apply the properties of geometric shapes and spatial sense to connect geometry with problem-solving situations." There are several skills or performance indicators an alternate assessment participant could master to show progress toward this standard. Here are a few:

- Touch a switch to turn on a stereo.
- Open a can using an electric can opener.
- Stock shelves at a grocery store.
- Determine if personal wheelchair will fit through a space.
- Recognize or identify safety symbols.

In their book *Alternate Assessments for Students with Disabilities* (2001), Thompson, Quenemoen, Thurlow, and Ysseldyke acknowledge that some educators question whether these skills sufficiently represent "properties of geometric shapes and spatial sense," and some may see these connections as quite a stretch. The bottom line, however, is that all students gain from an understanding of geometric shapes and spatial sense to solve problems, achieve independence, and make contributions in their home, workplace, and community. Here are examples of two students we might expect to participate in alternate assessments:

> Travis is a nine-year-old student who is cognitively impaired and uses a wheelchair. He has an intro talker that hasn't been used much. His communication is very limited. He is using a small amount of sign language. He sometimes recognizes the letter *T* for his first name but doesn't do this consistently. Due to his nonverbal communication, it is difficult to tell what he knows in math. He can bang on the keyboard of a computer but is currently working on matching the letters from the monitor screen to the keyboard.
>
> Mandy is currently tube fed; suction is required periodically during the day, and oxygen is kept close by with an emergency medical plan in place. She has a regressive genetic disorder and attends school three days per week. Mandy uses a wheelchair. Her goals include maintaining a level of alertness (that is, awake versus sleep, seizure, or semi-responsive) maintaining her weight, and increasing her level of tolerance for range of motion.

Are some students too low functioning to participate in alternate assessments? Think back to the beginning of this chapter when we talked about the students in the "special" classroom—the students who are still learning to chew and swallow food. How could eating be related to an academic standard? Clearly, there are choices involved in eating a meal. Making choices requires communication skills, whether to request a particular drink, choose between two vegetables, or spit out an undesired item. Is the student learning to use any assistive technology for eating? Many states have standards in tools and technology that a student might be working toward. By thinking through what *success* means for each student, the connection between content standards and the learning that students need in order to be successful is clarified. The laws and guidance previously presented make it clear that the educational progress of every child who receives educational services must be assessed.

Assessment Decisions

All members of a student's IEP team need to be clear about the fact that they are not to consider whether a student will participate in assessments, but how that participation might take place. The IEP team must determine whether a student with disabilities receiving special education services will participate in assessments under standardized conditions, with or without accommodations, or will participate in alternate assessments. This is an important responsibility and involves more than just a simple checkmark on an IEP form. Each IEP team member needs enough information about assessment participation options to be able to make informed decisions with a student.

In the past, assessment participation guidelines in several states maintained that students who were not working toward district or state standards should not participate in general district or state assessments; these students were likely candidates for alternate assessments. As we learn more about how *all* students can work toward the same standards, participation decisions in many states are no longer based on such statements as, "Student is not working toward state standards," or "Student has a different curriculum." Students may be showing what they have learned in different ways, and they may be working on different skills at different levels of competence, but the standards should provide the target toward which all students progress.

The question IEP teams need to ask is, "Can this student show what he or she knows on paper-and-pencil tests when given accommodations?" If the answer is no, even with the accommodations the student is accustomed to using, then participation in alternate assessments would be a likely choice. Notice that the question is not, "Can the student do well on the test?" There are students who may not perform well, even with accommodations that they are accustomed to using. When this concern arises (and it will), go back to the purpose of the test. The purpose of this type of assessment is to see how all the students at a particular grade level are progressing toward standards. It is important to see who is doing well and who is not, so that programmatic and budgetary adjustments can be made. Figure 1 shows a practical assessment participation decision process. Decisions about the accommodations a student will need are also a challenge for many IEP teams. The challenge is due, in part, to not having considered accommodations in the classroom. Thus, asking questions like those presented in Figure 1 is a helpful first step. As decisions in the classroom improve, this aspect of assessment decision making should also improve.

Figure 1. Participation Decision-Making Process

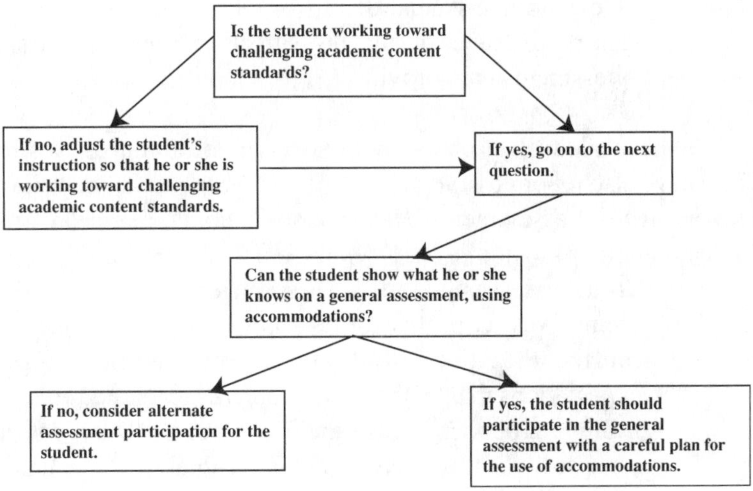

Consequences of Including Students With Disabilities in State and District Assessments

When NCEO asked state directors to tell us about the consequences of including students with disabilities in standards, assessments, and accountability systems, they were overwhelmingly positive in their responses (Thompson & Thurlow, 2001). Here are some of the positive consequences identified by state special education directors:

- "Teachers of students with disabilities report becoming more involved in local general education initiatives to improve instruction in the standards."
- "Some students with disabilities report feeling more involved in general education activities."
- "Parents and special educators support raising the level of expectations for students with disabilities."
- "Students in special education are getting more rigorous curriculum and the standards are effecting change in instruction."
- "Many people have expressed that they are pleased that 'all means all.'"
- "Students are being taught more challenging material based on state standards, since teachers have been given resources to 'extend' the standards."
- "The performance of students with disabilities on some state assessments is improving."

At the local level, teachers, counselors, school administrators, and others have also reported several positive consequences of inclusion in state and district assessments. Here are some comments heard from IEP team members (Thompson, Quenemoen, et al., 2001):

- "Teachers of students with significant disabilities see themselves as professionals—not babysitters once they realize that their students can reach much higher expectations than in the past. Standards are good for kids!"
- "I think in our school, for the first time, these students are seen as who they really are, individuals with a unique personality. This happened as soon as more of the staff and community became involved with them through standards-based instruction and assessment."
- "Standards and assessments bring together the best skills of both general and special educators."
- "Alignment between instruction and assessment is increased with alternate assessment."
- "Assessment ensures that students are represented in the school accountability system, and that's important to getting noticed on our improvement committee."

Nothing new comes without cost, however, and there have been plenty of challenges as students with disabilities are included in standards, assessments, and accountability systems. Here are some of the challenges identified by state directors (Thompson & Thurlow, 2001):

- "Some school district administrators are concerned that including scores of students with disabilities will lower their overall district scores, and consequently, their district ratings."
- "Some schools that have a disproportionate number of students with disabilities attending their school building feel the accountability system that considers the performance of all students enrolled is not fair."
- "Some people question how students with disabilities can access or reach the state learning standards."
- "Some teachers have observed a negative effect to the self-esteem of students with disabilities who were not able to respond to many questions on the state assessment."
- "Some administrators are not abiding by the requirements regarding accommodations and modifications because of the time and paperwork required. It's hard to set up so many testing circumstances."
- "Parents are concerned that their children won't graduate."

The last comment is a concern expressed by parents, students, and educators nationwide. Currently, at least 20 states use their large-scale assessments as a requirement for graduation from high school (Guy, Shin, Lee, & Thurlow, 1999). Students who do not reach a certain score or performance level, or who participate in alternate assessments, may not be eligible for a regular high school diploma. In some states, these students would receive a special education diploma, or some type of certificate of attendance or completion. This may have implications for college entrance or potential employment. In the elementary and middle school grades, not reaching a certain score on grade-level benchmark assessments may require students to repeat a grade or attend summer school (Quenemoen, Lehr, Thurlow, Thompson, & Bolt, 2000). Each state's requirements are different, but generally the stakes for receipt of a high school diploma are increasing. It is important for students to understand the purpose of each assessment they take and the consequences of the scores.

Summary

The shift to standards-based reform is challenging for everyone. Development of inclusive assessment systems to measure progress toward standards is part of that challenge. Overall, state data show a trend toward more inclusive participation and improved performance on state assessments by students with disabilities. As you work with IEP teams on the participation of students with disabilities in state and district assessments, become familiar with the standards, assessment guidelines, accommodations, and alternate assessments in your own state. Most state education agency websites contain basic information about the state standards and assessments, and most states and districts provide ongoing training. It is important to understand your state's approach thoroughly to be able to include effectively in state and district assessments all the students you serve.

References

ASPIIRE/ILIAD IDEA Partnership Projects. (2000). *Making assessment accommodations: A toolkit for educators.* Arlington VA: The Council for Exceptional Children.

Carpenter, W. D. (1995). *Become your own expert: Self-advocacy curriculum for individuals with learning disabilities.* Minneapolis, MN: Cognitive Learning Consultants.

Elliott, J., Thurlow, M., Ysseldyke, J., & Erickson, R. (1997). *Providing assessment accommodations for students with disabilities in state and district assessments* (Policy Directions No. 7). Minneapolis, MN: University of Minnesota, National Center on Educational Outcomes. Retrieved September 2001, from the World Wide Web: education.umn.edu/NCEO/OnlinePubs/Policy7.html

Fuchs, L. S., Fuchs, D., Eaton, S. B., Hamlett, C., & Karns, K. (2000). Supplementing teacher judgments about test accommodations with objective data sources. *School Psychology Review, 29*(1), 65–85.

Guy, B., Shin, H., Lee, S. Y., & Thurlow M. L. (1999). *State graduation requirements for students with and without disabilities* (Technical Report No. 24). Minneapolis, MN: University of Minnesota, National Center on Educational Outcomes. Retrieved September 2001, from the World Wide Web: education.umn.edu/NCEO/OnlinePubs/Technical24.html

New York State Education Department. (2001). *Report to the Board of Regents on special education data.* Albany, NY: Office of Vocational and Educational Services for Individuals with Disabilities.

Quenemoen, R. F., Lehr, C. A., Thurlow, M. L., Thompson, S. J., & Bolt, S. (2000). *Social promotion and students with disabilities: Issues and challenges in developing state policies* (Synthesis Report No. 34). Minneapolis, MN: University of Minnesota, National Center on Educational Outcomes. Retrieved September 2001, from the World Wide Web: education.umn.edu/NCEO/OnlinePubs/Synthesis34.html

Thompson, S. J., Quenemoen, R. F., Thurlow, M. L., & Ysseldyke, J. E. (2001). *Alternate assessments for students with disabilities.* Thousand Oaks, CA: Corwin Press.

Thompson, S., & Thurlow, M. (2001). *2001 State special education outcomes: A report on state activities at the beginning of a new decade*. Minneapolis, MN: University of Minnesota, National Center on Educational Outcomes. Retrieved September 2001, from the World Wide Web: education.umn.edu/NCEO/OnlinePubs/2001StateReport.html

Thompson, S., Thurlow, M., & Walz, L. (2000). *Student perspectives on the use of accommodations on large-scale assessments* (Minnesota Report No. 35). Minneapolis, MN: University of Minnesota, National Center on Educational Outcomes. Retrieved September 2001, from the World Wide Web: education.umn.edu/NCEO/OnlinePubs/MnReport35.html

Thurlow, M., Elliott, J., & Ysseldyke, J. (1998). *Testing students with disabilities.* Thousand Oaks, CA: Corwin Press.

✦Thurlow, M., Elliott, J., & Ysseldyke, J. (1999). *Out-of-level testing: Pros and cons* (Policy Directions No. 9). Minneapolis, MN: University of Minnesota, National Center on Educational Outcomes. Retrieved September 2001, from the World Wide Web: education.umn.edu/NCEO/OnlinePubs/Policy9.htm

Thurlow, M., Lazarus, S., Thompson, S., & Robey, J. (2002). *2001 state policies on assessment participation and accommodations* (Synthesis Report 46). Minneapolis, MN: University of Minnesota, National Center on Educational Outcomes. Retrieved August 2002, from the World Wide Web: education.umn.edu/nceo/OnlinePubs/Synthesis46.html

Thurlow, M., & Wiener, D. (2000). Non-approved accommodations: Recommendations for use and reporting (NCEO Policy Directions 11). Minneapolis, MN: University of Minnesota, National Center on Educational Outcomes.

Tindal, G., Helwig, R., & Hollenbeck, K. (1999). An update on test accommodations: Perspectives of practice to policy. *Journal of Special Education Leadership, 12*(2), 11–20.

Ysseldyke, J., Thurlow, M., McGrew, K., & Shriner, J. (1994). *Recommendations for making decisions about the participation of students with disabilities in statewide assessment programs: A report on a working conference to develop guidelines for statewide assessments and students with disabilities* (Synthesis Report 15). Minneapolis, MN: University of Minnesota, National Center on Educational Outcomes.

Notes

The National Center on Educational Outcomes is supported through a Cooperative Agreement (#H326G000001) with the Research to Practice Division, Office of Special Education Programs, U.S. Department of Education. Opinions expressed herein do not necessarily reflect those of the U.S. Department of Education or offices within it.

✦ Document is included in the Anthology of Assessment Resources CD

Chapter 13
Assessment of and Accountability for Students With Disabilities
Putting Theory Into Practice

Judy Elliott

By now you have a thorough awareness and understanding of IDEA 1997 and the impact of its regulations on assessment and accountability programs for students with disabilities; however, the implementation from state to state and district to district, even in the same state, varies to an amazing degree. As we head into another reauthorization of IDEA, it is accurate to say that we, as a nation, have not fully implemented what we were legislated to do six years ago, but we have accomplished a great deal to better the education of students with disabilities.

In this chapter we will look briefly at some of the realities of the implementation of inclusive assessment and accountability from the school district perspective. The issues may vary from those in your district, or they may be similar or identical. Let this discussion be your guide to what is possible when you keep your eyes, energies, and passion on the target—inclusive assessment and accountability.

Inclusive assessment and accountability for all students with disabilities has been a significant focus of educators for the past six years. Yet only 35 states reported 1999–2000 test results for students with disabilities on some of their state assessments (Bielinski, Thurlow, Callendar & Bolt, 2001). Sixteen of these states reported participation and performance results for students with disabilities on all of their 1999–2000 assessments. To date most states report only the number of students with disabilities taking tests, without indicating what percentage of the total that number is; that practice is better known as drifting denominators and nimble numerators. Only nine states report participation rates, which not only include the number of students taking tests but also compare this number to the whole population of students with disabilities to illuminate how many are not taking tests. So we still do not really know how well students with disabilities are performing according to what the law intended.

What we do know is that the spirit and integrity of IDEA implementation start in our own backyard—at the local level. It is up to local directors and assistant superintendents of special education, working with superintendents and boards of education, to ensure that all students are included in accountability and assessment. This effort to ensure inclusion is critical because the reality is that in many states, accountability and assessment policies do not always focus on all students, including students with disabilities. Loopholes abound. For example, peruse the following short list of critical knowledge for inclusive accountability and assessment and reflect on how much you and your administrators, counselors, teachers, and boards of education know about them:

- Teachers, counselors, and administrators know and understand what is required in terms of district and state assessments.
- Teachers, counselors, and administrators know who actually participates in what assessment, when they participate, and with what accommodations.
- Teachers, counselors, and administrators know how students with disabilities are included in published score reports and accountability reports.
- Teachers, counselors, and administrators know the subtleties of accommodation use and how those scores are reported. (For example, consider the automatic disaggregation or deletion of scores from accountability reports of the students who use certain accommodations.)
- Teachers, counselors, and administrators understand the reporting requirements of IDEA 1997 and its reflection of state assessment policies.

Indeed the areas of assessment and accountability are just one focus of IDEA 1997 and the recently passed No Child Left Behind Act, but they still are an important foundation for providing equal access and opportunity to learn for all students, including students with disabilities. Most important, these areas provide the foundation on which improved curriculum and instruction can be built.

The Rough Realities of Implementation

Let's explore some realities of implementing inclusive accountability and assessment practices at both the district and classroom levels. Do any of the following questions and comments from teachers, counselors, and site administrators ring true with your experiences in the trenches?

- "What happens if I allow one of my students a needed but nonstandard accommodation on the state test?"
- "No student in my classroom gets an accommodation or extended time in or out of my classroom on tests or assignments!"
- "Just how many days does 'extended time' encompass?"
- "You should have planned better for the graduation test administration. It is too late to give your students the accommodations written on their IEPs. We don't have the space, time, or personnel to provide them."
- "Sure, give your students any and all the accommodations they need for the state test!"
- "You know, if we get the parents to say they want to exempt their kids from the testing, we won't have to worry how they perform, and better yet, their scores won't be included."

The good, the bad, and the ugly, as the saying goes, and these are definitely the ugly but also the reality of what school districts and other sites deal with when trying to implement inclusive accountability. Now comes the hard part—effecting change.

Opportunity and Access

This is where it all begins—the opportunity to learn and the access to curriculum and quality instruction. There are a number of questions to ask yourself as you explore this area. For example, what standards are students in your school building and district working toward? How are these reflected in the curriculum? Are the two aligned? What curriculum are students with disabilities learning—same, different, or modified? If "modified" is your answer, then reflect on what exactly modified means and who makes the decisions about what is modified and to what degree. Is this left to teacher discretion? If it is, what aspects of the general education curriculum are allowed to be modified according to teacher discretion? The process and integrity of standards and curriculum implementation should be the same for all students, including students with disabilities.

Education as a field has aggressively entered the arena of high-stakes testing where, in most states, students "do not pass go" if they do not pass the state test. This issue has grown to involve 22 states where graduation exams exist, a figure that changes daily. In other states and districts, benchmarks have been set whereby students may not be promoted to the next grade level unless they meet the requirement. The critical importance of opportunity to learn for all students is part of the focus of a current class-action lawsuit against the California Department of Education.

Legal Repercussions of Denying Opportunity and Access

In May 2001, Disability Rights Advocates (DRA) filed a class-action lawsuit *(Juleus Chapman et al. v. California Department of Education)* against the California Department of Education, challenging the state's high school exit exam (see Figure 1). Issues raised in this suit are (a) the failure to implement effective standards and procedures for ensuring that students with disabilities obtain reasonable accommodations they need on the exam; (b) the failure to align the subject matter tested with what students with disabilities are actually taught; and (c) the lack of an alternate assessment, as required by law, for students with disabilities who cannot demonstrate their skills on the high school exit exam, even with accommodations.

In spring 2002, the first administration of the California High School Exit Exam (CAHSEE) took place. Although the accommodation issue is, for the most part, resolved by allowing students to use any and all accommodations listed on their IEP plans or 504 plans for the CAHSEE, access to the same material tested and equal opportunity to learn is not. Let's face it: There are some folks who say it is hard enough to get the test scores up for the general population without worrying about students with disabilities. On the other hand, there are others who argue that we treasure what and whom we measure.

Figure 1. Notice Regarding Testing Accommodations and Modifications on the California High School Exit Exam

Notice to All Parents and Guardians of Children With an Individualized Education Program (IEP) or a Section 504 Plan

The case *Juleus Chapman et al. v. California Department of Education et al.*, No. C01–1780 CRB, is currently pending in the United States District Court for the Northern District of California. Plaintiffs in the case, a group of learning disabled students, claim that the California High School Exit Exam (CASHEE), to be given to tenth graders on March 5, 6, and 7, 2002, violates rights guaranteed to learning disabled students under federal law. The Court has issued an Order that requires the March CAHSEE to be administered in accordance with the following procedures:

(1) Students shall be permitted to take the CAHSEE with any accommodation or modifications[1] their IEP or Section 504 plan specifically provides for the CAHSEE. If a student's IEP or Section 504 plan does not address the CAHSEE specifically, the student shall be permitted to take the CAHSEE with any accommodation or modifications their IEP or Section 504 plan provides for standardized testing. If a student's IEP or Section 504 plan does not address either the CAHSEE specially or standardized testing generally, the student shall be permitted to take the CAHSEE with any accommodation or modifications their IEP or Section 504 plan provides for general classroom testing.

(2) Some of the accommodations and modifications to which the students are entitled under this Order, pursuant to (1) above, have already been approved by the State. With regard to others, the State has determined that they will "invalidate" the test score and a waiver will be required before a diploma is granted. While this Order requires that students be permitted to take the CAHSEE with any accommodation or modifications defined in (1) above, the Court has not yet decided how taking the CAHSEE with a modification not approved by the State will affect the receipt of a diploma. A student may choose to forego

(Figure 1 cont.)

any accommodation or modification to which he or she is entitled under this Order.

(3) If a student's IEP or Section 504 plan specially provides for an alternate assessment in lieu of the CAHSEE, an alternate assessment shall be provided. If a student's IEP or Section 504 plan does not specifically address the CAHSEE but provides for an alternate assessment in lieu of generalized standardized testing, an alternate assessment to the CAHSEE shall be provided. If a student's IEP or Section 504 plan does not specifically address the CAHSEE or standardized testing but provides for an alternate assessment in lieu of general classroom testing, an alternate assessment to the CAHSEE shall be provided. Students entitled to an alternate assessment shall not be required to take the CAHSEE, but may do so if they choose.

(4) While this Order requires that an alternate assessment be provided to certain students, the Court has not yet decided how an alternate assessment will affect the receipt of a diploma.

(5) In order for a student covered by this Order to avail himself of any rights under this Order, no additional IEP or Section 504 plan meeting shall be necessary.

1. California has defined an *accommodation* as a change in the CAHSEE (in format, student response, timing, or other attribute) that does not invalidate the score achieved. California has defined a *modification* as a change in the CAHSEE that invalidates the test score because it fundamentally alters what the test measures.

What Educators Know

A good place to start in our effort to provide opportunity and access is in finding out what teachers, counselors, administrators, and others do and do not know about standards, instruction, and curriculum adaptation. We cannot assume that all teachers know how to adapt curriculum while maintaining the integrity of the standards. Research has shown that there are essential elements of effective instruction known to improve the academic achievement of students, including students with disabilities. In other words, good instruction is good instruction, regardless of the student. However, for many years, students with special needs have been placed in a separate environment, with different curriculum and slower paced instruction than in the regular classrooms, when in fact these students needed the opposite—fast-paced instruction with precision teaching geared toward what all students should know and be able to do.

Indeed teachers and other educators know about good instruction and standards, but does that knowledge apply to teaching students with disabilities? Too often educators, including special education educators, believe that students with disabilities are not able to work toward the same standards and curriculum as students without disabilities. Too often educators are unaware of the exact nature of a disability, particularly how and when it may or may not affect learning.

Variation in interpretation of the law abounds. In one district, as the administration of the high-stakes exit exam came upon them, teachers of students with disabilities were unaware of accommodations or the need for them to be on the students' written IEPs. This occurred after hours of staff development, inservices, and topical forums on the requirements of IDEA, the state's graduation exam, and the essential elements of effective instruction. Amazingly enough, in some cases, teachers were still unaware that students with disabilities were required by law to be included in some assessment—either district and state or alternate assessments. In randomly perusing written IEPs, one administrator found the words "exempt for district/state testing" written into a student's IEP. This was five years after IDEA 1997.

The third largest urban school district in California, the Long Beach Unified School District (LBUSD), with approximately 97,000 students, uses checklists created for teachers and administrators that are directly related to district initiatives of literacy and effective instruction (see Figure 2). These checklists reflect the elements of effective instruction as well as content-relevant indicators that have been taught through professional development training. In effect, these checklists allow both teachers and administrators to monitor the integrity and implementation of what has been provided through staff development programs and what is expected in the classroom.

Figure 2. Long Beach Unified School District's Components of Effective Instruction and Corresponding Checklist

Components of Effective Instruction

Planning Instruction

- The degree to which goals and expectations for performance and success are stated clearly and understood by the student

Managing Instruction

- The degree to which classroom management is effective and efficient
- The degree to which there is a sense of positiveness in the school environment

Delivering Instruction

- The degree to which there is an appropriate instructional match
- The degree to which lessons are presented clearly and follow specific instructional procedures
- The degree to which instructional support is provided for the individual student
- The degree to which sufficient time is allocated to academics and instructional time is used efficiently
- The degree to which the students' opportunity to respond is high

Evaluating Instruction

- The degree to which the teacher actively monitors student progress and understanding
- The degree to which student performance is evaluated appropriately and frequently

Reprinted from Algozzine, B., Ysseldyke, J., & Elliott, J. (1997). *Strategies and tactics for effective instruction.* Longmont, CO: Sopris West.

(Fig.2 cont.)

Checklist of Critical Factors for Effective Instruction

Planning: The degree to which goals and expectations for performance and success are stated clearly and understood by the student

Effective teachers:

_____ Set clear goals
_____ Set high expectations
_____ Demand high success rates
_____ Check for student understanding
_____ Provide direct and frequent feedback

Managing: The degree to which classroom management is effective and efficient

Effective teachers:

_____ Select 5–7 classroom expectations and procedures, and explicitly communicate expectations about classroom behavior
_____ Handle behavioral disruptions promptly
_____ Have an ongoing surveillance system
_____ Develop a sense of accountability and responsibility in their students

Effective classrooms are those in which:

_____ Well-established instruction routines are used
_____ Transitions are brief
_____ Considerable time is allocated to instruction
_____ Classroom interruptions are held to a minimum

Managing: The degree to which there is sense of positiveness in the school environment

Effective school environments are those in which there is:

_____ An academic focus with a humanistic orientation
_____ A cooperative rather than competitive learning structure
_____ Strong administrative leadership

(Fig.2 cont.)

_____ Parent-teacher contact and collaboration
_____ A belief among teachers that students can learn
_____ A set of realistic, high expectations

Delivering: The degree to which there is an appropriate instructional match

Effective teachers:

_____ Identify the student's level of skill development
_____ Analyze the demands of classroom tasks
_____ Match tasks to student aptitudes
_____ Analyze learning conditions in the classroom
_____ Assign tasks that are relevant to instructional goals
_____ Ensure high student success rates
_____ Check for student understanding

Delivering: The degree to which lessons are presented clearly and follow specific instructional procedures

Effective teachers:

_____ Use a demonstration-prompt-practice sequence
_____ Make instruction explicit
_____ Check for student understanding
_____ Systematically apply principles of learning

Delivering: The degree to which instructional support is provided for the individual student

Effective teachers:

_____ Monitor and adjust instruction
_____ Model thinking skills
_____ Teach learning strategies
_____ Provide time needed to learn
_____ Provide considerable guided practice

(Fig.2 cont.)

Delivering: The degree to which sufficient time is allocated to academics and instructional time is used efficiently

Effective teachers:

_____ Allocate sufficient time to instruction
_____ Get students actively engaged
_____ Engage in frequent, high-intensity student-teacher interaction

Delivering: The degree to which the students' opportunity to respond is high

Effective teachers:

_____Provide many opportunities to respond
_____ Provide specific error correction
_____ Alternate teaching strategies

Evaluating:The degree to which the teacher actively monitors student progress and understanding

Monitoring must be

_____ Active
_____ Frequent

Evaluating: The degree to which student performance is evaluated appropriately and frequently

Evaluation must be:

_____ Frequent
_____ Congruent with what is taught

Reprinted from Algozzine, B, Ysseldyke, J., & J. Elliott (1997). *Strategies and tactics for effective instruction.* Longmont, CO: Sopris West.

Staff Development and Training

What does training in your district or building look and sound like? In LBUSD, all staff development is offered and conducted for both general and special educators together as one group. Staff development is often collaborative and conducted by the general education curriculum coaches and special education personnel. Teachers at all grade levels are trained in content areas, including literacy, and monitored for their implementation of what they learned. There is no separate curriculum or way to teach students with disabilities except that which is highly specialized for specific populations (such as picture exchange communication systems for autistic students). Although the content for students who are learning life skills may be different, the instructional strategies and the essential elements of instruction remain the same. The result is that teachers are now collaborating and conversing more than ever before and are able to share ideas and successful teaching methodologies.

Instruction and Assessment Accommodations: Who Gets Them? Who Decides?

One of the biggest challenges facing schools in the area of assessment is whether and how to accommodate students with disabilities for instruction and for classroom, district, and state assessments. Once again, the interpretation and application of accommodations vary widely.

As you know, an *accommodation* is a change in the way a test is administered. There are six basic areas of accommodations: the way the test is presented, the setting in which it is taken, the manner in which students respond, the timing of the test, the schedule of test administration, and other, which is a category for accommodations that don't not fit neatly into the first five areas. (See chapter 7 for a more complete discussion of accommodation categories.)

The variation in interpretation of accommodations is evident in several court cases, including one recently decided by the federal district court of Oregon. In February 1999, a class-action lawsuit was filed on behalf of students with learning disabilities who attend Oregon public schools (*Advocates for Special Kids [ASK] v. Oregon State Board of Education*). Among the many allegations, the one that clearly stood out the most addressed the accommodations allowed for the state assessment. (*Modifications* is the term for not allowed, or nonstandard, accommodations in Oregon.) At the time of the lawsuit, Oregon used a list of accommodations and modifications. Accommodations were allowed, whereas modifications were said to change the test construct, or what the test was measuring, and therefore were not allowed. This meant that if a student with a learning disability needed a modification to take the assessment, it would be granted, but the student's test score would not be valid. However, the judge overseeing the case, based on a report from a court-appointed blue ribbon panel (Elliott, Engelhard, Schrag & Vogel, 2000), found that the list of accommodations was too narrow. Additionally, the list of modifications had been developed based on extant accommodation research but not accommodation research in the context of the state test. Therefore, there was no available research to show that the list of modifications in fact invalidated the constructs of the state's assessment. In the end, the judge ruled that all accommodations (and modifications) be considered valid unless and until research provides evidence that a modification or nonstandard accommodation altered the construct that the test was measuring. (For further discussion, see the Oregon Department of Education website at http://www.ode.state.or.us/. A copy of the blue ribbon panel report is available at http://www.ode.state.or.us/sped/report.pdf.)

Not only has this class-action suit proved to be the nation's landmark case surrounding accommodations, it has made many states and assessment personnel pause to reflect on whether they are next to be called into court for similar issues. The same attorneys, for almost identical allegations, have in fact called the California Department of Education into court, as discussed previously. If a student uses a nonstandard accommodation on California's required SAT9 state assessment, the score gets kicked out of the system and doesn't count in the district's accountability performance index (API). It is just as though the student did not take the assessment at all. Of course, this practice is not unique to California. It is one of the loopholes folks have found to keep test scores up and students with disabilities out.

Teachers have been known to be reluctant, even vehemently opposed, to allowing students accommodations on tests, state or classroom, and on assignments. That reluctance is most often due to lack of understanding or misinformation about the law, the IEP or 504 process, and the purpose and need for accommodations. Furthermore, although IEP teams make accommodation decisions, these teams are not always informed or knowledgeable about how or on what to base these decisions. The trend over the past few years has been for IEP teams to use checklists to guide decisions (see Thurlow, Elliott, &

Ysseldyke, 1998). Another tool that has helped the integrity of accommodation decision making is an IEP page tailored to making these decisions (see Figure 3). By tailoring an IEP to cover assessments and accommodations, we can better ensure that all parties on the IEP team are aware of what assessments are required and what accommodation may be needed for instruction, classroom tests, and district and state assessments.

In LBUSD, the development and use of a new accommodations for assessment page has improved not only the integrity of decision making, but also the appropriate use of accommodations for students. In one year's time the use of accommodations as a whole, including nonstandard accommodations, on the SAT9 dropped by approximately 6 percent. In addition, approximately 1,200 more students took the SAT9 than had taken it the year before. The significance of this statistic is that not only did more students take the required assessment, but more test scores of students with disabilities were included in score reports and in school and district API reports

Although not the focus of this chapter, it would be remiss not to mention the alternate assessment. As mentioned, the use of the new, improved IEP led LBUSD to show incredible assessment participation. The district has developed a standards-based alternate assessment that encompasses several broad domains. It is administered during the same testing window as the state assessment, and it is a secured assessment that is performance based, scored with a rubric, and monitored through inter-rater reliability. We have per-student, classroom, grade-level, domain-area, and building alternate assessment test data. The overall participation and accommodation data for this assessment and the SAT9 are shown in Figure 4. Only 4 percent of students with disabilities (in the third largest urban school district in California) were not tested at all. Some of you may be skeptical about these data; others of you may be eager to know how we as a district accomplished this. Read on.

Figure 3. Long Beach Unified School District IEP Form Example

Student Name ______________________________________
Last   First

IEP Date ______/______/______   Page _____ of______

Supplementary aids, services, and other support required to access general education curriculum:

Timing of Instruction	Scheduling of Instruction	Presentation of Instruction	Response to Instruction	Setting of Instruction	Other
Subject: ___________ Subject: ___________					

XV. **DISTRICT/STATE ASSESSMENT**
Student will participate in the:

☐ SAT9 ☐ Without Accommodations ☐ With Accommodations (see below)

☐ District Assessments ☐ Without Accommodations ☐ With Accommodations (see below)

☐ Alternate Assessment (must use IEP page 9 - Participation Criteria)

SAT9 Participation

STANDARD ACCOMMODATIONS	**All Content Areas**	**Reading (All Grades)**	**Math (All Grades)**	**Language (All Grades)**	**Spelling (Grades 1-8)**	**History (Grades 9-11)**	**Science (Grades 9-11)**
Flexible Setting	☐	☐	☐	☐	☐	☐	☐
Large Print Test	☐	☐	☐	☐	☐	☐	☐
Out of Level Testing (one grade level only)	☐						
Revised Test Directions	☐	☐	☐	☐	☐	☐	☐
NONSTANDARD ACCOMMODATIONS							
Braille Test	☐	☐	☐	☐	☐	☐	☐
Flexible scheduling	☐	☐	☐	☐	☐	☐	☐
Use of Aids and/or Aides to Interpret Test Items	☐	☐	☐	☐	☐	☐	☐
Partial Participation		☐	☐	☐	☐	☐	☐

OTHER ASSESSMENTS

Test	Timing	Scheduling	Presentation	Response	Setting

LONG BEACH UNIFIED SCHOOL DISTRICT Form #IEP8 Distribution: Special Education Office—White; Special Education Teacher—Pink; Parent—Yellow; CUM—Blue

Figure 4. Long Beach Unified School District Graph of Students with Disabilities Participation Rates in 2001 SAT9 and Alternate Assessments

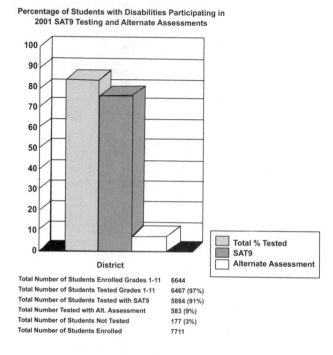

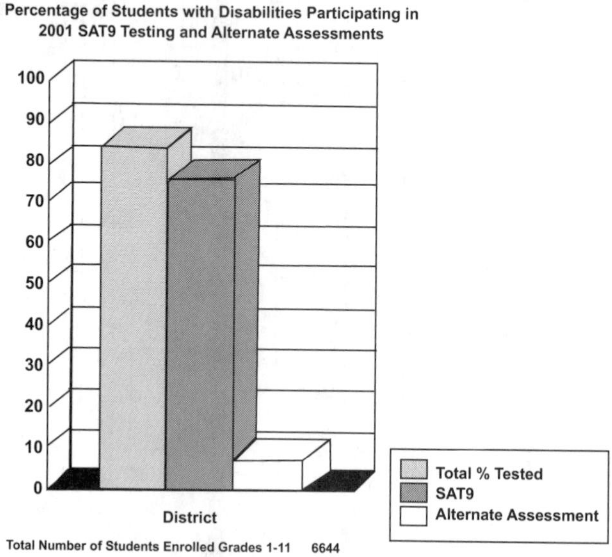

Total Number of Students Enrolled Grades 1-11	6644
Total Number of Students Tested Grades 1-11	6467 (97%)
Total Number of Students Tested with SAT9	5884 (91%)
Total Number Tested with Alt. Assessment	583 (9%)
Total Number of Students Not Tested	177 (3%)
Total Number of Students Enrolled	7711

Where the Rubber Meets the Road: The Use of Data to Drive Reform

As discussed, the spirit and integrity with which IDEA 1997 is implemented begins at the local level. Here's how LBUSD made changes within a two-year assessment cycle. We began by working with our research and student evaluation office to get our hands on district and state assessment data for students with disabilities. These data included participation rates, accommodations used, and test results. What follows is a list of what we did and continue to do with the data on a yearly basis:

- Disaggregate all district and state assessment data for students with disabilities: We disaggregate by type of service provided. For example, students who receive speech and language therapy services only, those who are in self-contained programs, or those receiving resource room services. We also look at the data by disability, individual grade level (such as grade four), and overall grade levels (such as elementary, middle, and high school). And, of course, we can look at data by gender, ethnicity, and the like.

- Disaggregate test results by accommodations used: We look at what accommodations are most requested, how often, at what levels of service delivery, and at what grade levels. We examine the combinations of accommodations requested for assessments and specific subtests. For example, some students are allowed a special location, extended time, and use of a calculator. We look for patterns and trends among grade levels and subtests. (Depending on the type of norm-referenced or criterion-referenced tests your state or district administers, accommodations used will vary widely.)

The usual trend in LBUSD is that there are a few accommodations that are used most frequently, and there is a decrease in use as grade levels go up. For example, high school students often show a drop in accommodation usage. Part of our work has been to find out why. Is it because students do not need them? Don't want them? The IEP team didn't think they were necessary? Didn't know what was allowed or where to write them on the IEP?

Another interesting analysis we do is to select IEPs randomly and look at what accommodations were written in the document, then cross-reference this to what was actually used on the district and state assessments. We also do the opposite, looking at the test accommodations recorded as being used, then cross-referencing them to student IEPs to see if what was actually provided for the test was written in the IEP. Try a similar analysis of your own district's data. You will be amazed at what you find. We were.

We compare the normal curve equivalent or percentile rank by assessment and subtests between general education and special education populations by individual grade level and overall grade levels. We typically find a parallel performance trend, with students in special education achieving at a similar level to each other but below the general education population. This trend may or may not be the same across overall grade levels. We look at individual school profiles, grade level profiles, and so forth to see where the gap is smallest, then dig deep to find out why. It is here we discover what is working to improve student achievement.

We create individual building profiles of student achievement by students who receive only related services, are in a self-contained setting, or are served by resource services (Figure 5). On the same graphic profile we superimpose the general education population scores for the same school. We also create graphic profiles to illustrate and compare the percentages of these student populations that participated in the test. This past year we were able to provide four years of data on one school's profile (Figure 6).

Figure 5. Stanford 9 Reading Subtest scores by student population, 1998-2001

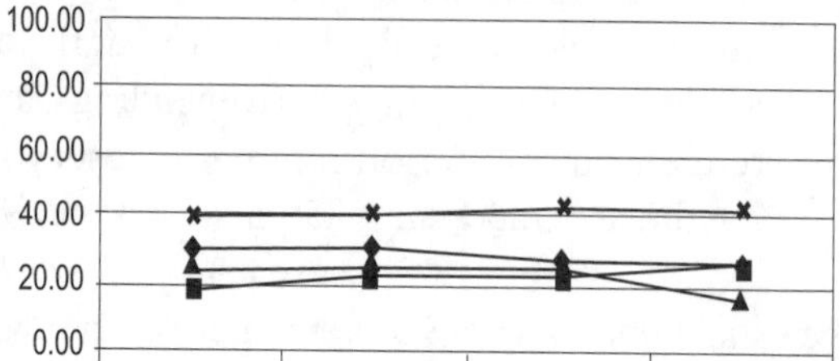

	1998	1999	2000	2001
Related SVCS.	28.94	30.04	27.08	25.59
Resource SVCS.	16.98	20.70	22.87	24.86
Self-contained Class	24.26	24.53	25.51	16.90
General ed.	39.75	40.45	42.98	42.58

Figure 6. Percentage of students taing the Stanford 9 Language Subtest, by population, 1998-2001

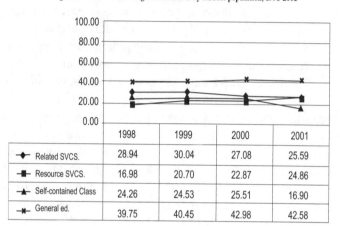

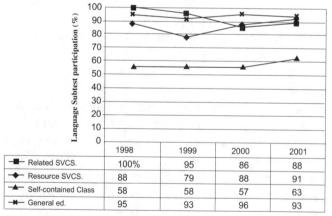

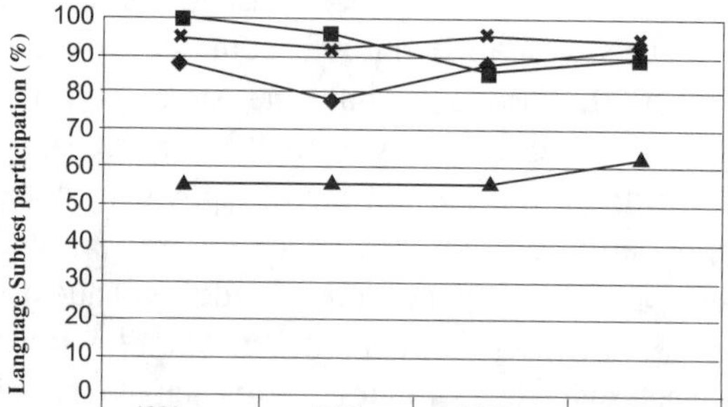

	1998	1999	2000	2001
Related SVCS.	100%	95	86	88
Resource SVCS.	88	79	88	91
Self-contained Class	58	58	57	63
General ed.	95	93	96	93

Then we present these data by school and overall district comparison in a condensed, easy-to-read format to each school principal. When we did this for the first time in LBUSD, we blew folks away. Discussions were rich: "You mean my resource kids outperformed many of my general education kids?" "Look at that, the kids in the self-contained classes outperformed the kids in resource rooms!" "Wow, 'these' kids could really improve my accountability performance index!" By using these data we were able to show our principals through statistics that the best way to raise their site's API scores is to increase the test scores of students in the lowest deciles. Although kids with special needs are not the only ones in this score range, we made our point.

We also present the same information to those who supervise school principals, so that they can focus on the achievement of all students and keep all teachers, including teachers of students with disabilities, on the standards-based instruction path. As discussed earlier, too often teachers of students with disabilities are not supervised as closely as other teachers by site administrators just because of the general lack of knowledge and misunderstandings about teaching students with disabilities. This data-sharing process helps everyone stay focused on what counts—effective instruction.

Administrators and teachers are now more accountable to providing access to the standards and curriculum all students should know. Not only has the participation of students with disabilities in district and state assessments increased, with appropriate use of accommodations where necessary, the quality of IEPs has improved. Through this data-sharing process and other efforts, student IEPs are now evaluated more precisely using progress monitoring and benchmarking—just like the evaluation process used with general education students.

Indeed, implementation issues of IDEA 1997, even six years later, still loom large and at times seem insurmountable. Inclusive assessment and accountability is but one of the important components that educators advocate for all students. Our job as educators is like no other. It often requires a delicate balancing act between compliance and student achievement. However, if we focus only on compliance, that is what we will get. But if we focus on instruction, accountability, and standards-based student achievement, we get it all.

References

Bielinski, J., Thurlow, M., Callendar, S., & Bolt, S. (2001). *On the road to accountability: Reporting outcomes for students with disabilities.* (Technical Rep. 32). Minneapolis, MN: University of Minnesota, National Center on Educational Outcomes.

Elliott, J. (in press). Assessment and accountability of students with disabilities. *CASE in Point.*

Elliott, J., Engelhard, G., Schrag, J., & Vogel, S. (2000). *Students with learning disabilities and the Oregon statewide assessment system.* (Report of the blue ribbon panel for *Advocates for Special Kids [ASK] v. Oregon State Board of Education.*) Portland, OR: Federal District Court.

Elliott, J., & Schrag, J. (2000). *Accommodations: The good, the bad, and the ugly.* Baltimore, MD: International Dyslexia Association.

Elliott, J., Thurlow, M., & Ysseldyke, J. (2000). *Improving test performance of students with disabilities on district and state assessments.* Thousand Oaks, CA: Corwin Press.

Thurlow, M., Elliott, J., & Ysseldyke, J. (1998). *Testing students with disabilities: Practical strategies for complying with district and state requirements.* Thousand Oaks, CA: Corwin Press.

Chapter 14
Assessing Students with Serious Mental Health and Behavioral Problems
Clinical Assessment for Educators

Jo-Ida C. Hansen & Amy L. Conlon

The current intervention trend for many of the mental health and behavioral problems faced by today's youth is an integrative approach that involves the community, families, and schools. These collaborative efforts seek to provide person- and context-protective factors that can serve as sources of adolescent resiliency (Christenson & Sheridan, 2001). The National Association of School Psychologists Position Statement on Home-School Collaboration emphasizes, for example, that "schools can take the lead in providing opportunities for collaborative partnerships to be developed" (NASP, 1999). Clinical assessment for serious mental health and behavioral problems can be an important component in the development of school-based screening programs. The screening programs, in turn, can be useful for identifying students who will benefit from referrals to mental health professionals. Also, techniques such as template matching (Hoier & Cone, 1987), progress monitoring (Shinn, 1997), and the keystone behavior strategy (Nelson & Hayes, 1996) show promise for linking social-emotional and behavioral assessment information to interventions.

The most viable approach to assessment includes direct observation, self-report measures, behavior rating scales, interviews, and record reviews. However, time constraints often preclude the use of multiple measures. Self-report instruments, behavior rating scales, and structured interviews are three approaches that have been shown to provide valid and reliable assessment results (Merrell, 2001).

Advances in the development of self-report instruments for assessing the social-emotional concerns of children and youth have made these instruments the preferred choice in many instances (Merrell, 1999). Self-report measures are especially useful for assessing internalized problems (e.g., depression) that are not easily detected through observation or third-party ratings. One of the best known self-report measures, the Minnesota Multiphasic Personality Inventory for

Adolescents (MMPI-A) is a broadband instrument designed to assess personality domains relevant to various clinical disorders and psychopathologies (Butcher et al., 1992). The MMPI-A is appropriate for students between 14 and 18 years of age. Respondents answer 478 true-false items, and scores are provided on 10 clinical scales (e.g., Depression, Anxiety, Social Introversion) as well as on a number of special content scales. The MMPI-A parallels the adult version of the test in terms of scale interpretation; however, items on the MMPI-A were designed to reflect the background and experiences of adolescents (Wodrich, 1997). Moreover, the MMPI-A includes several content scales developed exclusively for adolescent populations, such as School Problems, Low Aspirations, Alienation, and Conduct Disorder (Hood & Johnson, 1997). Although the information provided on the MMPI-A is not sufficient to offer a formal diagnosis, the profile suggests a set of hypotheses regarding the nature of a student's problems that can be refuted or supported with additional data.

Behavior rating scales, sometimes called third-party instruments, also are widely used to evaluate a range of problems. The raters are typically teachers or parents of the child who rate the frequency and intensity of behaviors they have observed during a specified interval. Behavior rating scales provide a standard format for conducting the evaluations and also provide information for developing norm-referenced scores. Norm referencing allows a comparison between an individual child's scores and those of a reference group, which typically is a national sample of same-age, same-gender youth.

One example of a multiperspective rating system is the Achenbach Scales, which include the Child Behavior Checklist (CBCL; Achenbach, 1991a), the Teacher's Report Form (TRF; Achenbach, 1991b) as well as the Youth Self-Report (YSR; Achenbach, 1991c). Like the MMPI-A, the CBCL is a general purpose or broadband assessment that evaluates a range of problems and competencies. The CBCL, which is appropriate for ages 2 years to 18 years, is completed by a parent. Problem areas are clustered into internalizing (e.g., anxious/depressed) and externalizing (e.g., aggressive) behaviors; and competence items assess adjustment with respect to activities, school, and social domains (Kronenberger & Meyer, 2001). The CBCL offers a comprehensive description of student emotional, social, and behavioral adjustment but is not designed for diagnosis. Moreover, proper use of the instrument requires a thorough understanding of its structure and properties (Wodrich, 1997). The problem items on the TRF parallel those on the CBCL; however, the competence items on the TRF differ from those on the CBCL (Kronenberger & Meyer, 2001). For students who exhibit serious emotional or behavioral disturbances, the TRF might serve as a good screening device for psychopathology. The instrument is less useful for screening normal social behaviors because items tend to be fairly clinical in nature (Merrell, 2000). The final instrument in the Achenbach system is the YSR, which can be used with students ages 11 to 18. Most of the YSR items are identical to the items on the CBCL (but worded in the first person). The components of the Achenbach Scales collectively provide information about students' functioning and adjustment across multiple situations and from multiple perspectives, which might be especially useful in identifying target behaviors (i.e., school-based or home-based behavior) for intervention (Kronenberger & Meyer, 2001).

Another broadband, multiperspective rating scale is the Symptom Inventories-4. This set of checklists was designed to reflect diagnostic criteria for major behavioral disorders of childhood and adolescence as laid out in the *Diagnostic and Statistical Manual of Mental Disorders, Fourth Edition* (DSM-IV), which is the primary diagnostic system used by mental health professionals. Parents and teachers complete the checklists, which have been developed for three age groups: the Early Childhood Inventories (ECI) for children ages 3 to 6 (Sprafkin & Gadow, 1996); the Child Symptom Inventory (CSI) for ages 5 to 12 (Gadow & Sprafkin, 1997b); and the Adolescent Symptom Inventory (ASI) for ages 13 to 18 (Gadow & Sprafkin, 1997a). Because these inventories do not take into account duration of symptoms, time of onset, or exclusionary criteria, they are not sufficient for assigning a diagnosis. Nonetheless, the inventories are unique in the breadth of disorders covered and the direct link between items and DSM-IV criteria (Kronenberger & Meyer, 2001).

Structured and semistructured interviews are another approach for obtaining information about students' functioning in a broad range of domains. These interviews include an organized set of questions geared toward assessing behaviors and feelings, and are typically based on a specific diagnostic classification system, such as the DSM-IV. Detailed information about the nature of problems in various domains is collected through these interviews, including the history, frequency, duration, intensity, antecedents, consequences, and past treatment of the problem. Additionally, questions address school functioning, relationships with family and peers, and developmental history (Kalfus, 1995). The Diagnostic Interview Schedule for Children and Adolescents (DICS; Reich, Welner, Herjanic, & MHS Staff, 1997) and the Diagnostic

Interview Schedule for Children (DISC-R; Shaffer et al., 1993) are two widely used structured interviews. These interviews, which yield information on duration, onset, and severity of 185 symptoms, are highly structured in that the wording and order of questions as well as the coding of responses are specified (Mezzich, Bukstein, & Grim, 1995). The Child Assessment Schedule (CAS; Hodges, 1987) and the Kiddie Schedule for Affective Disorders and Schizophrenia for School-Aged Children (K-SADS; Puig-Antich, Chambers, & Tabrizi, 1983) are semistructured interviews that include open-ended as well as yes-no questions. These less structured approaches require the interviewer to make judgments about the presence or absence of symptoms and thus require more clinical skill to administer than highly structured approaches, such as the DICS and DISC. Structured and semistructured interviews are rarely used in clinical practice due in part to the length of time required for administration (one to four hours, typically). Their utility in schools may be further limited by the questionable validity of self-reports for children under age 12 (Kronenberger & Meyer, 2001).

In addition to their use in broadband assessment, self-report measures, behavior rating scales, and interviews can also be used in conjunction with narrowband assessment to provide more specific information to detect disorders. Clinical assessment frequently is used to evaluate young people for attention and concentration problems, eating disorders, suicidal ideation, schizophrenia, and post-traumatic stress disorder (PTSD). Assessment techniques for each of these disorders are discussed in this chapter.

Attention and Concentration Problems

Attention deficit/hyperactivity disorder (ADHD) has been diagnosed in about 3 to 5 percent of all school-age children (Daw, 2001). Despite debate about the potential overuse of the ADHD diagnosis, it is clear that students experiencing the attention and concentration problems characteristic of ADHD encounter significant difficulties academically, socially, and emotionally. The central features of ADHD are inattentiveness, impulsivity, and physical overactivity. It is also common for children with ADHD symptoms to exhibit conduct problems and antisocial behavior, such as aggression and oppositional behavior (Kazdin, 1994).

A number of factors complicate the diagnosis of ADHD, including the ambiguity of many ADHD criteria and a belief on the part of parents and teachers that they can recognize ADHD symptoms without a thorough assessment (Wodrich, 1997). A comprehensive assessment strategy is vital to accurate diagnosis and should include interviews with primary caregivers, examination of school records and past treatment, and a complete psychological evaluation in which information is collected from multiple perspectives. A medical evaluation is also recommended to rule out physical conditions that may be mimicking ADHD symptoms. Assessing for problems that frequently co-occur with ADHD, such as conduct disorder, learning disabilities, substance use, and low self-esteem, should be part of the assessment strategy as well (Evans, Vallano, & Pelham, 1995; Tripp & Sutherland, 1999). Moreover, an awareness of developmentally normal behaviors that may be similar to ADHD symptoms, such as excessive energy, is important in ensuring that a child is properly diagnosed (Tripp & Sutherland, 1999). Including broadband measures (e.g., CBCL; Behavior Assessment System for Children, BASC; Reynolds & Kamphaus, 1992) in the assessment process is also important because symptoms such as discouragement, poor concentration, and irritability, associated with other disorders, tend to be similar to ADHD symptoms (Wodrich, 1997).

A number of ADHD rating scales and checklists are useful for structuring the evaluation of symptoms and provide a means for collecting information from multiple sources. These assessment tools typically lay out the ADHD symptoms that are described in the DSM-IV and ask the rater to indicate the frequency with which the symptoms occur (Kronenberger & Meyer, 2001). The transparency of items on these types of scales, however, make them vulnerable to manipulation by individuals hoping for a specific diagnostic outcome (Wodrich, 1997). There is evidence that unintentional distortion of ratings may also occur because parents have been shown to use only the upper ends of scales, and teachers' ratings are often distorted for overly aggressive students (Tripp & Sutherland, 1999). Nonetheless, although ADHD rating scales should never be used in isolation to make diagnostic decisions, they may serve as one component in a comprehensive assessment strategy.

The ADHD Rating Scale-IV (ADHDRS-IV; DuPaul, Power, Anastopoulos, & Reid, 1998) is a brief and easy-to-use inventory that has separate forms for parents and for teachers (Merrell, 2000). The scale is based on DSM-IV criteria for ADHD and provides age- and sex-stratified normative data that enable scores to be converted to percentiles (Kronenberger & Meyer, 2001). Similarly, the ADHD Symptoms Rating Scale (ADHD-SRS; Holland, Gimple, & Merrell,

2000) is completed by teachers or parents and evaluates ADHD symptoms as defined in the DSM-IV. The ADHD-SRS is relatively brief (56 items) and easy to use, thus making it ideal for initial assessment of students and for progress tracking (Merrell, 2000). The home and school versions of the Attention Deficit Disorders Evaluation Scale (ADDES; McCarney, 1995) describe typical ADHD behaviors, also based on DSM-IV criteria. A benefit to using the ADDES is the companion manual that offers suggestions for interventions depending on the pattern of symptoms observed (Kronenberger & Meyer, 2001). A self-report measure useful for gathering information on adolescents' and young adults' self-perceptions of ADHD symptoms is the Brown Attention Deficit Disorder Scales (BADDS; Brown, 1996).

In contrast to the global rating scales described previously, the Home Situations Questionnaire (HSQ; Barkely, 1981) and the School Situations Questionnaire (SSQ; Barkely, 1981) describe situation-specific ADHD behaviors and ask parents or teachers to rate whether a child exhibits the problem behavior and to rate the severity of the problem in specific situations. Scores on the HSQ and SSQ indicate the pervasiveness, severity, and location of the symptoms. Compared to global rating scales, these situation-specific measures might be easier for teachers and parents to complete because ADHD symptoms are often observed only in certain settings.

Conners' Continuous Performance Test (CCPT; Conners, 1995) and Test of Variables of Attention (TOVA; Leark, Depuy, Greenberg, Corman, & Kindschi, 1996) are sets of computer-based tasks used to assess attention, impulsivity, and distractibility in children and adolescents. These assessment techniques require a child to respond to a stimulus that flashes on the screen by, for example, pushing a specific button. Responses are then scored based on accuracy, speed, and consistency, from which conclusions about ADHD symptoms are drawn. Generally, scores on these types of tests are moderately related to scores on symptom checklists and other cognitive measures of attention, distractibility, and impulsivity (Kronenberger & Meyer, 2001). However, some researchers have found only minimal associations between CCPT/TOVA approaches and other ADHD measures, leading to questions about the reliability, validity, and theoretical bases of CCPT and TOVA techniques (Evans et al., 1995).

Eating Disorders

Concerns about physical appearance, especially weight and body size, have become increasingly common among young people. High levels of dissatisfaction with body weight and size have been noted in adolescent girls in particular; however, these concerns are observed in grade school children and among boys as well. Anorexia nervosa and bulimia nervosa are two clinical disorders that might emerge when body dissatisfaction becomes extreme. The characteristic symptom of anorexia nervosa is a relentless drive for thinness that results in dangerously low body weight, typically achieved by limiting food intake and exercising excessively. In addition, individuals with anorexia nervosa have a distorted view of their own bodies such that they see their emaciated bodies as fat. Bulimia nervosa is characterized by consumption of large quantities of food in short time periods followed by purging behaviors that may include excessive exercise, vomiting, or abuse of laxatives and diuretics.

Assessment of eating disorders is a multistep process that should include an evaluation of eating behaviors and symptoms as well as collection of background information such as family constellation and dynamics. Given the potentially life-threatening nature of these disorders, assessment should also include a medical examination to rule out physiological contributors and to ensure that the individual's health is not in peril (Woodside, 1995).

The Eating Disorder Inventory-2 (EDI-2; Garner, 1991) is a 91-item self-report measure that assesses common behavioral and psychological symptoms of anorexia and bulimia. Adolescents with anorexia nervosa typically have elevated scores on all eight scales of the EDI-2, and the pattern of score elevations is useful in identifying the particular constellation of behaviors that characterizes the disordered eating (e.g., food restriction, exercise, or binging and purging behaviors; Kalfus, 1995).

Another self-report measure of disordered eating is the Eating Attitudes Test (EAT; Garner & Garfinkle, 1979), a 40-item measure that provides information on three general domains of eating behavior. The brevity of the EAT relative to the EDI-2 might be advantageous for educators and clinicians concerned about time efficiency. However, the cognitive and emotional elements of anorexia and bulimia are better covered on the EDI-2. Shorter versions of the EAT have been developed for use with preadolescent children, ages 3 and up; however, the appropriateness of the adult-level content items on these shortened scales has been questioned (Kronenberger & Meyer, 2001).

Symptoms associated with bulimia nervosa are the focus of the Bulimia Test (BULIT; Smith & Thelen, 1984). This 36-item scale assesses symptoms across five domains—binging, feelings, vomiting, food, and weight (Kalfus, 1995). Although the BULIT has been shown to discriminate effectively between individuals with bulimia and individuals not diagnosed with disordered eating, scores on the test tend to be related to generalized psychological distress, which should be taken into account when interpreting the results.

Suicidal Ideation

Depression can exert moderate to severe effects on overall functioning and is one of the most persistent mental health problems over an entire lifespan. Many significant changes in mood that occur during adolescence persist into adulthood, making adolescence an important developmental stage for understanding and identifying depression problems. There is also a high degree of co-occurrence of depression with other symptoms and disorders, such as attention deficit disorders, eating disorders, and violence. Related to depression, there has been a dramatic increase in the suicide rate among teenagers; it is one of the leading causes of death among adolescents and children (James & Gilliland, 2001). Some estimates suggest that about 10 percent of all 9th and 10th graders have attempted suicide (Shaffer, Vieland, & Garland, 1990).

Although suicidal ideation can exist in the absence of clinical depression, depressed youngsters are at higher risk than their nondepressed peers for having thoughts about and attempting suicide. Broadband instruments such as the MMPI-A or the Symptom Checklist-90-Revised (SCL-90-R; Derogatis, 1994), or narrowband measures such as the Children's Depression Inventory (CDI; Kovacs, 1992), the Reynolds Adolescent Depression Scale (RADS; Reynolds, 1987), or the Reynolds Child Depression Scale (RCDS; Reynolds, 1989) can be used for school-based screening of depression and to provide an opening for assessment of suicidal ideation. Students exhibiting depressive symptoms should be routinely evaluated for suicide risk, and several structured measures exist to help in this evaluation. For example, the Inventory of Suicide-30 (ISO-30; King & Kowalchuk, 1994) is a 30-item self-report measure for use with 13- to 18-year-olds. Comparing total raw scores to cutoff scores offers a rough idea of a student's risk of orientation toward suicide. Scores on critical items that are especially indicative of high suicide risk are highlighted.

Schizophrenia

The detection of schizophrenia in children and adolescents is difficult because the typical time of onset for the disorder is early adulthood. Although precursors to the behaviors seen in adults with schizophrenia may be present at an earlier age, they might manifest in children and adolescents differently than in adults. For instance, the hallucinations and delusions that are characteristic of adult schizophrenia might be less elaborate or bizarre in children and adolescents. Generally, children and adolescents with schizophrenia have been described as appearing physically and emotionally immature and exhibiting awkward body movements, ritualistic behavior, and tangential and peculiar patterns of speaking. Irritability, anxiety, and depression are also common among young people with schizophrenia (Keshavan, Vaulx-Smith, & Anderson, 1995).

Because of the complexity and range of symptoms associated with schizophrenia, projective tests and broadband assessment instruments, such as the MMPI-A, CSI/ASI, or BASC, are necessary. The Kiddie Formal Thought Disorder Rating Scale (K-FTDS; Caplan, Guthrie, Fish, Tanguay, & David-Lando, 1989) may also be part of the assessment strategy. This observer rating system requires coding a child's responses to a game called the Kiddie Formal Thought Disorder Story Game in terms of four patterns of disordered thinking—illogical thinking, loose association, incoherence, and poverty of speech. The procedure is time consuming and requires training to learn the coding system (Kronenberger & Meyer, 2001).

Post-Traumatic Stress Disorder

The diagnostic category of post-traumatic stress disorder was intended to capture the impact of trauma and violence during times of war. However, similar symptoms are now recognized in victims of other violent acts, such as rape, family violence, child abuse, and robbery, or in victims of natural disasters. Across different forms of trauma, the core PTSD experiences of avoidance, intrusion, and physiological arousal are the same (Everett & Gallop, 2001). Like adults, children and adolescents who have experienced traumatic life events may exhibit anxiety symptoms in response to the trauma. If time permits, a comprehensive assessment of PTSD should be multimodal and include gathering information on the student's symptoms, coping mechanisms, beliefs, and strengths and weaknesses.

Development of instruments to assess trauma and PTSD in children is a relatively recent phenomenon. The Trauma Symptom Checklist for Children (TSCC; Biere, 1996) is an example of an assessment instrument designed specifically for evaluating post-traumatic reactions. The TSCC is a 54-item self-report measure developed for children and adolescents ages 8 to 16 who have experienced traumatic events. The TSCC can enable quick evaluation of those children who are at risk and who may require follow-up care. The TSCC has six clinical scales that yield information on symptoms across six domains anxiety, depression, anger, post-traumatic stress, dissociation, and sexual concerns and two validity scales, under-response and hyper-response. Normative data are based on 3,000 inner city urban and suburban children and include nonclinical and clinical samples.

Conclusion

Schools are increasingly involved in issues related to the mental health of students. Educators and teachers are involved in implementing guidance programs, peer counseling, after-school and community outreach programs, and in coordinating efforts with police, city and county government, and other agencies. Often schools are called on to develop wide-ranging screening, prevention, and intervention programs. Assessment for severe mental health and behavioral problems is an important ingredient in school-based screening programs that identify students who are candidates for referral to school counselors, school psychologists, and other mental health professionals. Assessment results can also be used to guide development of prevention and intervention programs.

References

Achenbach, T. M. (1991a). *Manual for the Child Behavior Checklist/ 4–18 and 1991 Profile.* Burlington, VT: University of Vermont, Department of Psychiatry.

Achenbach, T. M. (1991b). *Manual for the Teacher's Report Form and 1991 profile.* Burlington, VT: University of Vermont, Department of Psychiatry.

Achenbach, T. M. (1991c). *Manual for the Youth Self-Report and 1991 Profile.* Burlington, VT: University of Vermont, Department of Psychiatry.

Achenbach, T. M. (1992). *Manual for the Child Behavior Checklist/2–3 and 1992 Profile.* Burlington, VT: University of Vermont, Department of Psychiatry.

Barkely, R. A. (1981). *Hyperactive children: A handbook for diagnosis and treatment.* New York: Guilford.

Biere, J. N. (1996). *Trauma Symptom Checklist for Children professional manual.* Odessa, FL: Psychological Assessment Resources.

Brown, T. E. (1996). *Brown Attention Deficit Disorder Scales.* San Antonio, TX: The Psychological Corporation.

Butcher, J. N., Williams, C. L., Graham, J. R., Tellegen, A., Ben-Porath, J. S., & Kaemmer, B. (1992). *MMPI-A: Manual for administration, scoring, and interpretation.* Minneapolis, MN: University of Minnesota.

Caplan, R., Guthrie, D., Fish, B., Tanguay, P. E., & David-Lando, G. (1989). The Kiddie Formal Thought Disorder Scale (K-FTDS): Clinical assessment, reliability, and validity. *Journal of the American Academy of Child Psychiatry, 28,* 408–416.

Christenson, S. L., & Sheridan, S. M. (2001). *Schools and families.* New York: Guilford Press.

Conners, C. K. (1995). *Conners' Continuous Performance Test Computer Program 3.0 user's manual.* North Tonawanda, NY: Multi-Health Systems.

Daw, J. (2001, June). The Ritalin debate. *Monitor on Psychology,* 64–65.

Derogatis, L. R. (1994). *SCL-90-R administration, scoring, and procedures manual* (3rd ed.). Minneapolis, MN: National Computer Systems.

DuPaul, G. J., Power, T. J., Anastopoulos, A. D., & Reid, R. (1998). *ADHD Rating Scale-IV: Checklists, norms, and clinical interpretation.* New York: Guilford Press.

Evans, S., Vallano, G., & Pelham, W. E. (1995). Attention-deficit hyperactivity disorder. In V. B. Van Hasselt & M. Hersen (Eds.),*Handbook of adolescent psychopathology: A guide to diagnosis and treatment* (pp. 589–617). New York: Lexington Books.

Everett, B., & Gallop, R. (2001). *The link between childhood trauma and mental illness.* Thousand Oaks, CA: Sage.

Gadow, K. D., & Sprafkin, J. (1997a). *Adolescent Symptom Inventory-4 screening manual.* Stony Brook, NY: Checkmate Plus.

Gadow, K. D., & Sprafkin, J. (1997b). *Child Symptom Inventory-4 norms manual.* Stony Brook, NY: Checkmate Plus.

Garner, D. M. (1991). *The Eating Disorder Inventory-2.* Odessa, FL: Psychological Assessment Resources.

Garner, D. M., & Garfinkle, P. E. (1979). The Eating Attitudes Test: An index of the symptoms of anorexia nervosa. *Psychological Medicine, 9,* 273–279.

Hodges, K. K. (1987). Assessing children with a clinical interview: The Child Assessment Schedule. In R. J. Prinz (Ed.), *Advances in behavioral assessment of children and families.* Greenwich, CT: JAI Press.

Hoier, T. S., & Cone, J. D. (1987). Target selection of social skills for children: The template-matching procedure. *Behavior Modification, 11,* 137–164.

Holland, M. L., Gimple, G. A., & Merrell, K. W. (2000). *ADHD Symptoms Rating Scale.* Wilmington, DE: Wide Range.

Hood, A. B., & Johnson, R. W. (1997). *Assessment in counseling: A guide to the use of psychological assessment procedures* (2nd ed.). Alexandria, VA: American Counseling Association.

James, R. K., & Gilliland, B. E. (2001). *Crisis intervention strategies* (4th ed.). Belmont, CA: Brooks/Cole.

Kalfus, G. R. (1995). Behavioral assessment in adolescents. In V. B. Van Hasselt & M. Hersen (Eds.), *Handbook of adolescent psychopathology: A guide to diagnosis and treatment* (pp. 243–264). New York: Lexington Books.

Kazdin, A. E. (1994). Psychotherapy for children and adolescents. In A. E. Bergin & S. L. Garfield (Eds.), *Handbook of psychotherapy and behavior change* (4th ed.) (pp. 543–594). New York: John Wiley & Sons.

Keshavan, M. S., Vaulx-Smith, P., & Anderson, S. (1995). Schizophrenia. In V. B. Van Hasselt & M. Hersen (Eds.), *Handbook of adolescent psychopathology: A guide to diagnosis and treatment* (pp. 465–496). New York: Lexington Books.

King, J. D., & Kowalchuk, B. (1994). *Inventory of Suicide-30 (ISO-30).* Minneapolis, MN: National Computer Systems.

Kovacs, M. (1992). *Children's Depression Inventory (CDI) manual.* North Tonawanda, NY: Multi-Health Systems.

Kronenberger, W. G., & Meyer, R. G. (2001). *The child clinician's handbook* (2nd ed.). Boston: Allyn and Bacon.

Leark, R. A., Depuy, T. R., Greenberg, L. M., Corman, C. L., & Kindschi, C. L. (1996). *T.O.V.A. Test of Variables of Attention Professional Manual, Version 7.0.* Los Alamitos, CA: Universal Attention Disorders.

McCarney, S. B. (1995). *Attention Deficit Disorders Evaluation Scale—School Version.* Columbia, MO: Hawthorne Educational Services.

Merrell, K. W. (1999). *Behavioral, social, and emotional assessment of children and adolescents.* Mahwah, NJ: Erlbaum.

Merrell, K. W. (2000). Informant-report: Rating scale measures. In E. S. Shapiro & T. R. Kratochwill (Eds.), *Conducting school-based assessments of child and adolescent behavior* (pp. 203–234). New York: The Guilford Press.

Merrell, K. W. (2001). *Helping students overcome depression and anxiety.* New York: Guilford Press.

Mezzich, A., Bukstein, O. G., & Grim, M. R. (1995). Epidemiology and adolescent diagnosis. In V. B. Van Hasselt & M. Hersen (Eds.), *Handbook of adolescent psychopathology: A guide to diagnosis and treatment* (pp. 265–294). New York: Lexington Books.

NASP [National Association of School Psychologists]. (1999). *National Association of School Psychologists position statement on home-school collaboration: Establishing partnerships to enhance educational outcomes* (rev.). Retrieved January 22, 2003, from www/nasponline.org/information/pospaper_hsc.html.

Nelson, R. O., & Hayes, S. C. (1996). *Conceptual foundations of behavioral assessment.* New York: Guilford Press.

Puig-Antich, J., Chambers, W., & Tabrizi, M. A. (1983). The clinical assessment of current depressive episodes in children and adolescents: Interviews with parents and children. In D. Cantwell & G. Carlson (Eds.), *Childhood depression* (pp. 157–159). New York: Spectrum.

Reich, W., Welner, Z., Herjanic, B., & MHS Staff. (1997). *Diagnostic Interview for Children and Adolescents Computer Program (DICS-IV).* North Tonawanda, NY: Multi-Health Systems.

Reynolds, C. R., & Kamphaus, R. W. (1992). *Behavior Assessment System for Children manual.* Circle Pines, MN: American Guidance Service.

Reynolds, W. M. (1987). *Assessment of depression in adolescents: Manual for the Reynolds Adolescent Depression Scale (RADS).* Odessa, FL: Psychology Assessment Resources.

Reynolds, W. M. (1989). *Reynolds Child Depression Scale: Professional manual.* Odessa, FL: Psychology Assessment Resources.

Shaffer, D., Schwab-Stone, M., Fisher, P., Cohen, P., Piacentini, J., Davies, M., Conners, C. K., & Regier, D. (1993). The Diagnostic Interview Schedule for Children Revised Version (DISC-R): Preparation, field testing, inter-rater reliability, and acceptability. *Journal of the American Academy of Child and Adolescent Psychiatry, 32,* 643–650.

Shaffer, D., Vieland, V., & Garland, A. (1990) Adolescent suicide attempters: Response to suicide prevention programs. *Journal of the American Medical Association, 64,* 3151–3155.

Shinn, M. R. (1997). *Advanced applications of curriculum based measurement.* New York: Guilford Press.

Smith, M. C., & Thelen, M. H. (1984). Development and validation of a test for bulimia. *Journal of Consulting and Clinical Psychology, 52,* 863–872.

Sprafkin, J., & Gadow, K. D. (1996). *Early Childhood Inventories manual.* Stony Brook, NY: Checkmate Plus.

Tripp, G., & Sutherland, D. M. (1999). Counseling boys with attention deficit/hyperactivity disorder. In A. M. Horne & M. S. Kiselica (Eds.), *Handbook of counseling boys and adolescent males* (pp. 293–312). Thousand Oaks, CA: Sage Publications.

Wodrich, D. L. (1997). *Children's psychological testing* (3rd ed.). Baltimore, MD: Paul H. Brookes.

Woodside, D. B. (1995). Anorexia nervosa and bulimia nervosa. In V. B. Van Hasselt & M. Hersen (Eds.), *Handbook of adolescent psychopathology: A guide to diagnosis and treatment* (pp. 407–434). New York: Lexington Books.

Chapter 15
Broadband and Narrowband Measures of Mental and Behavioral Health
Counseling Assessment for Educators

Amy L. Conlon & Jo-Ida C. Hansen

Assessment tools from the counseling arena can be useful in educational settings for (a) developing effective instructional strategies and learning environments, (b) identifying students who would benefit from referral to a mental health professional, and (c) promoting students' growth and well-being by fostering self-awareness and identity development (Drummond, 1996). The assessment process will be most useful to students when a multifaceted approach is taken that includes naturalistic observation, interviews, valid and reliable self-report instruments, and informant reports, such as from teachers, parents, and peers (Eckert, Dunn, Codding, & Guiney, 2000). Assessment data should be placed within the context of a student's developmental phase and integrated with knowledge of the student's background (e.g., educational history, racial and ethnic identity, social history; Kronenberger & Meyer, 2001). This chapter focuses on structured assessment instruments that may play a role in this multifaceted assessment process.

Assessment instruments vary in the scope of behavioral and emotional functioning they cover. *Broadband* instruments provide information on a wide range of psychological, behavioral, and social domains that may have relevance to multiple problems or disorders. This type of broad-based knowledge can be useful regardless of the specific issue or problem facing a student (Kronenberger & Meyer, 2001). Personality inventories, symptom checklists, self-concept scales, and behavior rating scales are examples of broadband instruments. These tools can help identify students who would benefit from special accommodations or who require referral to an outside mental health professional. Many of these instruments also highlight areas of competency, which can facilitate the development of educational interventions that build upon students' assets and strengths.

In contrast to broadband instruments that provide information on a student's functioning in multiple domains, *narrowband* instruments provide more detailed information about a student's functioning within a particular domain (e.g., social skills) or with respect to a specific problem (e.g., depression; Eckert et al., 2000). Combining broadband and narrowband approaches can be especially effective in offering both a general picture of a student's current level of functioning and specific information on any area in which a student appears to be having particular difficulty. Eckert et al. (2000) suggested that this type of approach "results in a comprehensive assessment of potential behavior problems that concludes with a detailed examination of specific emotional or behavioral functioning" (p. 151). The remainder of this chapter provides examples of specific broadband and narrowband instruments that are commonly used in the context of counseling assessment.

Self-Report

Self-report instruments require test takers to respond to items that reflect on their behaviors, feelings, and attitudes. These types of tests can provide useful information on students' internal processes that might not be evident to an outside observer. Some students might not have the necessary self-awareness or insight to describe their inner experiences accurately, however, thus limiting the validity of the results. Preadolescent students in particular might respond in socially desirable ways in their efforts to provide the "correct" answer. Lack of motivation as well as reading and comprehension difficulty may further limit the accuracy of self-report data from students (Kronenberger & Meyer, 2001).

The Personality Inventory for Youth (PIY; Lachar & Gruber, 1995) is a 270-item self-report inventory designed for students in grades 4 through 12. This broadband personality instrument provides information on a student's level of functioning, relative to a norm group, in nine dimensions: cognitive impairment, impulsivity and distractibility, delinquency, family dysfunction, reality distortion, somatic concerns, psychological discomfort, social withdrawal, and social skills deficits. Its companion instrument, the Personality Inventory for Children (PIC; Wirt, Lachar, Klinedinst, & Seat, 1977), is appropriate for children ages 3 to 16 and is completed by the parent. A strength of both the PIY and PIC is their focus on typical developmental problems as well as disturbed behaviors. Both instruments are also well researched and have large norm groups upon which scores are based (Wodrich, 1997).

Broadband and Narrowband

The Millon Adolescent Personality Inventory (MAPI; Millon & Davis, 1993), another self-report personality instrument, was designed to assess domains relevant to normal developmental processes. The inventory requires at least a sixth-grade reading level and provides scores on 24 scales representing opposing personality styles. An overall index of adjustment is also provided. The scales cover three broad domains of functioning motivating goals, cognitive style, and interpersonal behavior (Hood … Johnson, 1997).

The Symptom Checklist-90-Revised (SCL-90-R; Derogatis, 1994) is a self-report instrument that focuses on specific symptoms rather than on personality styles. The instrument is appropriate for students older than 13, and it requires respondents to rate 90 items addressing the severity with which they have experienced a range of mental health problems. Nine areas of psychological symptoms are covered: somatization, obsessive-compulsive behaviors, interpersonal sensitivity, depression, anxiety, hostility, phobic anxiety, paranoid ideation, and psychoticism. The SCL-90-R also provides a global severity index of overall symptom severity (Kronenberger & Meyer, 2001).

Several broad measures of self-concept and self-esteem are useful for assessing students' self-views. Self-esteem is an important component of emotional functioning that relates to both clinically significant disorders (e.g., depression, social anxiety, eating disorders) and overall student adjustment. The Piers-Harris Children's Self-Concept Scale (PHCSCS; Piers, 1984) is an 80-item measure that assesses self-concept in the domains of behavior, intellectual/school status, physical appearance, anxiety, popularity, and happiness/satisfaction. A total scale score that reflects global self-concept is also provided. Concerns have been raised about the outdated norm sample of the PHCSCS, however, suggesting the need for cautious interpretation of these scores (Eckert et al., 2000; Kalfus, 1995).

The Multidimensional Self-Concept Scale (MSCS; Bracken, 1992) has an adequate norm sample and might be viewed as easier to interpret than the PHCSCS. The six subscales of the MSCS (Affect, Academic, Competence, Family, Physical, Social) can be administered and interpreted separately. Like the PHCSCS, the MSCS provides a global index of self-concept (Eckert et al., 2000). There is a special version of the Coopersmith Self-Esteem Inventories (SEI; Coopersmith, 1981) designed specifically for use in schools. The School Form is appropriate for students ages 8 to 15 and yields information on overall self-esteem as well as self-esteem with respect to peers, parents, school, and personal interests. The Behavior Academic Self-Esteem (BASE) rating scales (Coopersmith & Gilbert, 1982) is used in conjunction with the Coopersmith self-report inventories. Teachers complete the BASE, which was designed to serve as a check on student self-reports (Hood & Johnson, 1997).

Multiperspective Rating Systems

A number of test developers have designed assessment systems intended to facilitate information gathering from multiple sources. These systems typically include a combination of checklists and rating scales that are completed by teachers and parents as well as self-report inventories to which students respond. Obtaining information on a student's functioning from multiple perspectives offers a comprehensive view of the student's current adjustment level; however, the use of these assessment systems can be complicated, and integrating the information often requires clinical skill (Wodrich, 1997).

An example of a multiperspective rating system is Conners' Rating Scales-Revised (Conners, 1997), which collects information from parents (Conners' Parent Rating Scale-Revised, CPRS-R), teachers (Conners' Teacher Rating Scale-Revised, CTRS-R), and students (Conners-Wells' Adolescent Self-Report Scale, CASS). The CPRS-R and the CTRS-R ask parents and teachers to rate the severity of behavior problems in children and adolescents ages 3 to 17. Items assess a variety of problem domains, including anxiety, shyness, perfectionism, and social difficulties. The scales also provide information on the extent to which a student exhibits the symptoms of attention deficit/hyperactivity disorder, which can be useful for screening students for attention and concentration problems. For students ages 12 to 17, the CASS can augment information obtained from parents and teachers by providing students' perspectives on family problems, emotional difficulties, conduct problems, cognitive problems, anger control problems, and hyperactivity (Kronenberger & Meyer, 2001).

Another comprehensive assessment system that gathers data from multiple perspectives is the Behavior Assessment System for Children (BASC; Reynolds & Kamphaus, 1992). The Parent Rating Scale (BASC-PRS) comes in forms for three age groups—preschool (ages 4 and 5), child (ages 6 to 11), and adolescent (ages 12 to 18). Based on the previous six months, parents rate the extent to which their child exhibited behaviors relevant to internalizing problems, externalizing problems, school difficulties, and adaptive skills. An overall index of behavioral symptoms is also provided. The Teacher Rating Scale

(BASC-TRS) elicits the same information as the parent scales with the addition of two scales that assess learning problems and study skills.

A third component of the BASC, the Self-Report of Personality (SRP), can be used with children and adolescents ages 8 to 18. This self-report inventory yields information on how students view their own level of functioning in terms of clinical maladjustment, school maladjustment, personal maladjustment, and emotional symptoms (Kronenberger & Meyer, 2001). The scope of clinical disorders assessed by the SRP is fairly limited, especially in the domain of externalized problems such as aggression; however, school-based practitioners are likely to find the school maladjustment items especially helpful (Eckert et al., 2000).

In addition to the three scales, the BASC includes structured approaches for behavioral observation (Structured Observation System, SOS) and developmental history collection (Structured Developmental History), which have enjoyed widespread use in school settings because of their focus on school-relevant problems and competencies and their developmentally appropriate items (Kronenberger & Meyer, 2001). The SOS is especially useful in making decisions about enrolling students in special programs because it offers a systematic approach for quantifying classroom behaviors (Wodrich, 1997). Although the BASC has been described as "impressive" in terms of both the construction of the scales and the research base supporting their validity, the extensive length of the rating scales might preclude its use for routine screening (Merrell, 2000).

Projective Tests

Projective tests are another class of broadband personality measures that have enjoyed popularity among clinicians working with children and adolescents. Examples of projective tests include the Rorschach Technique (Klopfer, 1962); storytelling approaches, such as the Thematic Apperception Test (Stein, 1955) and Roberts Apperception Test for Children (Roberts, 1994); and various drawing techniques, for example, Kinetic Family Drawings (Burns & Kaufman, 1972). Respondents are assumed to project their feelings, thoughts, needs, conflicts, and attitudes onto ambiguous stimuli, and these responses are believed to be representative of daily behavior and overall adjustment.

Compared with pencil-and-paper objective tests, projective approaches have been described as less threatening and more engaging for children. The great amount of training and clinical skill required to administer and interpret projective tests precludes their use in many school settings, however (Wodrich, 1997). Additional limitations of projective approaches are the often subjective manner in which the tests are interpreted and the fact that responses are affected by transient state factors such as hunger, mood, and frustration (Kronenberger & Meyer, 2001).

Assessing Relationship and Social Skills

Children and adolescents face many important developmental tasks in their relationships and other social interactions. As children develop, their peer groups typically grow as they increasingly seek from friends the support they previously obtained from family members. Moreover, changes in peer groups due to a family move or changes in familial relationships due to divorce are common experiences among children and adolescents. There is evidence that the relationships and social interactions experienced in childhood and adolescence have implications for later psychological adjustment. For example, young people who experience social isolation are at higher risk for dropping out of school, engaging in criminal behavior, and experiencing a wide range of clinically significant emotional and behavioral problems. Deficits in social skills similarly appear to be associated with conduct problems, depression, and anxiety (Hansen, Giacoletti, & Nangle, 1995).

A variety of assessment tools are available for formally evaluating students' social skills. Information garnered from these instruments can be useful in identifying at-risk children and developing interventions to bolster social competence in students. The Social Skills Rating System-Student Form (SSRS-S; Gersham & Elliott, 1990) asks students to evaluate themselves in five domains of social functioning: assertion, cooperation, empathy, interfering behaviors, and self-control. Students are also asked about the frequency and importance of various social behaviors, which can help identify target behaviors for interventions (Eckert et al., 2000). Parent and teacher forms of the SSRS also are available, facilitating the collection of information from multiple perspectives (Merrell, 2000). Teacher and student perspectives are captured in the Matson Evaluation of Social Skills with Youngsters (MESSY; Matson, Rotatori, & Helsel, 1983). Teachers respond to items that rate students' inappropriate assertiveness, impulsivity, and appropriate social skills. The self-report form assesses students' perspectives on their appropriate social skills, inappropriate assertiveness, overconfidence, impulsivity, jealousy, and withdrawal behaviors (Kalfus, 1995).

Teacher ratings of students' social competence can be gathered using the Walker-McConnell Scales of Social Competence and School Adjustment (Walker & McConnell, 1995a, 1995b) and the School Social Behavior Scales (SSBS; Merrell, 1993). Both instruments can be used with students from kindergarten through 12th grade and are relatively brief and easy to administer and score. Because they both focus solely on social competence, additional assessment tools should be used if other problem behaviors within the social domain are suspected (Merrell, 2000).

Assessing Anxiety

Many of the anxieties and fears that emerge in childhood and adolescence are part of normal developmental processes that dissipate with age and have no long-term consequences in adulthood. A challenge in assessing anxiety in young people, then, is determining whether symptoms are developmentally appropriate or warrant additional evaluation and formal intervention (Kazdin, 1994). Anxiety problems most frequently observed in children and adolescents include social anxiety, generalized anxiety, separation anxiety, specific phobias, panic, school refusal behavior, and test anxiety. Obsessive-compulsive behavior and post-traumatic stress disorder also may occur in children and adolescents. Symptoms of anxiety manifest as subjective cognitions (e.g., persistent worries), overt behaviors (e.g., avoidance/withdrawal), and physiological reactivity (e.g., increased heart rate); thus, the most effective assessment strategies examine symptoms across these three domains (Kearney & Silverman, 1995).

Broadband instruments that provide information relevant to anxiety symptoms include the BASC, PIY, Child Behavior Checklist (CBCL; Achenbach, 1991), and Minnesota Multiphasic Personality Inventory-Adolescent (MMPI-A; Butcher et al.,1992; Kronenberger & Meyer, 2001).

The Multidimensional Anxiety Scale for Children (MASC; March, 1997) is an example of a self-report inventory that covers multiple domains of symptoms. The 39 items assess physical symptoms, harm avoidance behavior, social anxiety, and separation fears/panic (Kronenberger & Meyer, 2001). A separate form, the MASC-10, assesses symptoms of generalized anxiety. The MASC is useful for providing information on a wide range of anxiety symptoms and can help differentiate between generalized and specific anxiety disorders, which might prove useful in identifying students who need outside referrals and for targeting behaviors for intervention (Eckert et al., 2000).

The Revised Children's Manifest Anxiety Scale (RCMAS; Reynolds & Richmond, 1978) also provides information on anxiety across several domains, including worry/oversensitivity symptoms, physiological symptoms, and concentration-related symptoms. Although the instrument has adequate research supporting its reliability and validity, the overlap of some items with symptoms of depression has been cited as a limitation of the RCMAS (Kronenberger & Meyer, 2001).

The State-Trait Anxiety Inventory for Children (STAIC; Spielberger, Edwards, Lushene, Montouri, & Platzek, 1973) differentiates between transitory (state) anxiety and more enduring generalized (trait) anxiety. The two 20-item subscales have been shown to discriminate effectively between children suffering from anxiety disorders and children diagnosed with clinically significant depression; however, the scales do not differentiate among various types of anxiety disorders. Utility of the STAIC with very young children might be limited because they may not be able accurately to distinguish transitory from stable anxiety (Kronenberger & Meyer, 2001).

Assessing Depression

Children and adolescents who are suffering from clinically significant depression are characterized by pervasive sadness, limited interest in activities, diminished energy, and feelings of worthlessness. Changes in appetite, weight, and sleep patterns are also common (Kazdin, 1994). Depression greatly affects the social and emotional functioning of children and adolescents and has been shown to increase risk for adult psychopathology (Reynolds, 1995). Children whose depression goes untreated are more likely to experience future adjustment problems, such as dropping out of school, unemployment, substance use, and criminal behavior. In addition, students experiencing clinically significant levels of depression are at higher risk for suicide, a leading cause of death among adolescents.

Assessment of depression can be complicated because it is not always easy to distinguish between clinically significant depressive symptoms and the volatile and labile moods and emotions that are normative characteristics of the adolescent developmental stage. Thus, an understanding of developmental aspects of children's and adolescents' moods is necessary to interpret measures of depression accurately (Caldwell, 1999).

Depression has been described as a prototypical internalizing disorder because the core symptoms are known only to the person experiencing them and thus are not observable by others. Therefore, self-report measures of depression are popular, and they have the added benefits of being easy to administer and appropriate for group administration, which makes them ideal for school settings. A diagnosis of depression cannot be made from these self-report inventories alone, but they provide an index of symptom severity and are good tools for identifying students who would benefit from further evaluation (Reynolds, 1995).

The drawbacks of self-report measures include the potential for students to misinterpret their symptoms or to have difficulty discerning whether symptoms are due to depression or other life events. Furthermore, because most children and adolescents have had limited life experiences, they may lack the context necessary to evaluate subjectively the severity of their symptoms. There is evidence that adolescents' moods are more heavily influenced by environmental factors than adults' moods are, which may further limit the accuracy of self-reports (Caldwell, 1999). Despite these limitations, self-report measures are viewed by some clinicians as more accurate than measures based on the observations of parents, especially in light of adolescents' reluctance to disclose feelings to their parents. Research comparing parent and child reports of depressive symptoms has typically found low levels of agreement (Reynolds, 1995).

The Children's Depression Inventory (CDI; Kovacs, 1992) is one of the most widely used measures of depression in young people (Eckert et al., 2000; Reynolds, 1995). The inventory, which is appropriate for ages 6 through 17, includes 27 items that assess cognitive, affective, behavioral, and social aspects of depression. The CDI is considered a downward extension of the Beck Depression Inventory II (BDI-II; Beck, Steer, & Brown, 1996), which is a popular self-report measure used with adolescents and adults. The materials accompanying the CDI provide cutoff scores designed to help practitioners identify children at particular risk for clinical depression. The norm sample upon which these cutoff scores are based has been criticized, however, so these scores should be used conservatively. Evidence that the CDI does not effectively discriminate between children suffering from depression and those experiencing other clinically significant problems (most notably anxiety), suggests that it might be best viewed as a general measure of overall distress as opposed to a specific measure of depressive symptomatology (Eckert et al., 2000; Kronenberger & Meyer, 2001).

Two instruments that may be especially useful for school-based screening of depression are the Reynolds Child Depression Scale (RCDS), for grades 3 to 6 (Reynolds, 1989) and the Reynolds Adolescent Depression Scale (RADS), for grades 7 to 12 (Reynolds, 1987). Both instruments are based on large norm samples, and a large body of research supports their validity and reliability (Kronenberger & Meyer, 2001; Reynolds, 1995). The content items make the RCDS and the RADS appropriate for diagnostic purposes, and a global severity index provides information on the intensity of the depressive symptoms (Eckert et al., 2000).

In addition to the narrowband measures described above, a number of broadband instruments reviewed in the previous section also provide information that can assist in identifying depressed students. For instance, the MMPI-A, CBCL, and BASC all include subscales reflecting depressive symptomatology (Reynolds, 1995). Structured interviews that assess a range of mental health issues, such as the Diagnostic Interview for Children and Adolescents (DICS; Reich, Welner, Herjanic, & MHS staff, 1997) and the Child Assessment Schedule (CAS; Hodges, 1987), may also be useful because depression in young people often coexists with other behavioral and emotional problems (Caldwell, 1999).

Assessing Conduct Problems

Conduct problems, or conduct disorders (CDs), are characterized by a persistent pattern of antisocial behavior that is significant enough to impair daily functioning across numerous life domains (Borduin, Henggeler, & Manley, 1995). The assessment of conduct problems should include collecting information from multiple perspectives, using multiple methods, and examining behavior across a wide range of settings (e.g., in school, at home, with peers). Moreover, because children and adolescents are likely to misbehave or exhibit disruptive behaviors as they negotiate the developmental tasks of growing up, it is important to distinguish a persistent pattern of disruptive behavior that occurs in multiple situations before attempting to diagnose a CD. There is not a single assessment tool that is sufficient to establish the existence of CDs; however, several self-report and other instruments are available that could play a role in the assessment process.

Broadband and Narrowband

The Eyberg Child Behavior Inventory (ECBI; Eyberg & Ross, 1978) is a rating scale that parents complete by indicating whether their child exhibits any of 36 behaviors commonly reported by parents of children with CDs. Parents rate each behavior in terms of whether the problem exists and the frequency of the problem. Appropriate for children and adolescents ages 2 to 17, the ECBI is considered unidimensional and suggests that the existence of 11 or more of the problems indicates clinically significant conduct problems (Kalfus, 1995; Kronenberger & Meyer, 2001). A simple and quick means of identifying behavior problems is provided by the original Ontario Child Health Study (OCHS) scales, for ages 12 to 16 (Boyle et al., 1993). Separate parent report, teacher report, and self-report forms are used, each of which asks about 34 behavior problems associated with CDs, hyperactivity, and emotional disturbances. The OCHS scales can be administered quickly in a school setting and are a simple screening method for conduct problems (Kronenberger & Meyer, 2001). The New York Teacher Rating Scale (NYTRS; Miller et al., 1995) is another screening instrument that educators and school-based practitioners may find useful for identifying students with clinically significant conduct problems. This 36-item teacher report assesses oppositional behaviors, peer rejection, aggression, and rule breaking in students grades 1 through 10 (Kronenberger & Meyer, 2001).

Social attribution and problem-solving measures can also be helpful in identifying children with conduct problems, because low levels of social problem-solving ability have been shown to relate to conduct disorders among children. These types of assessment tools typically evaluate how children approach solving problems related to social situations. For example, the Means End Problem Solving Procedure (MEPS; Platt & Spivak, 1975) provides children with the beginning and an end of a story and asks them to provide the middle portion of the story. The task requires children to specify in behavioral terms how the goals attained at the end of the story were reached. Responses are coded based on relevance of behavior to goal achievement, awareness of obstacles, and appropriateness of sequencing and passage of time. The responses of children diagnosed with a CD have been shown to contain fewer relevant means and fewer obstacles in pursuit of social goals (Kronenberger & Meyer, 2001).

Anger and aggression inventories are additional tools for assessing conduct problems in children and adolescents because conduct problems are sometimes secondary to anger control problems. Children diagnosed with conduct disorder typically report more anger and less control over their anger, and tend to describe more aggressive reactions to anger-provoking situations. Examples of anger and aggression inventories include the Buss-Durkee Hostility Inventory (BDHI), for adolescents and adults (Buss & Durkee, 1957); the Novaco Anger Inventory (NAI), for adolescents and adults (Novaco, 1975); the Children's Anger Response Checklist (CARC), for children and adolescents (Feindler, Adler, Brooks, & Bhumitra, 1993); and the State-Trait Anger Expression Inventory (STAXI), for adolescents (Spielberger, 1988).

Conclusion

Childhood and adolescence are marked by exciting developmental milestones as well as an array of challenges. Educators and professionals working in educational institutions are well positioned to promote students' growth through these important developmental stages and to help them overcome challenges that may be creating difficulties in school, at home, and with peers. Assessment tools from the counseling arena can play an important role in these processes. The most effective assessment strategy incorporates information from a variety of sources (e.g., child, parent, teacher) and utilizes a variety of approaches (e.g., interview, naturalistic observation, self-reports, teacher and parent reports). Furthermore, to obtain a comprehensive picture of a student's current functioning, it is desirable to combine broadband assessment instruments that cover an array of domains with problem-specific narrowband instruments. Broadband personality inventories can alert educators to particular problem areas and highlight areas of strength and competency. Narrowband instruments assessing depression, anxiety, social skills, self-esteem, self-concept, and conduct problems have particular relevance to educational settings because they highlight problems that might be interfering with a student's performance in school, in classroom behavior, and in peer relationships. A growing recognition of the impact of these problems on young people has led to the development of a wide array of valid and reliable assessment instruments that can play an important role in helping students succeed.

References

Achenbach, T. M. (1991). *Manual for the Child Behavior Checklist/4–18 and 1991 Profile.* Burlington, VT: University of Vermont, Department of Psychiatry.

Achenbach, T. M. (1992). *Manual for the Child Behavior Checklist/2–3 and 1992 profile.* Burlington, VT: University of Vermont, Department of Psychiatry.

Beck, A. T., Steer, R. A., & Brown, G. K. (1996). *BDI-II, Beck Depression Inventory: Manual.*San Antonio, TX: Psychological Corporation.

Borduin, C. M., Henggeler, S. W., & Manley, C. M. (1995). Conduct and oppositional disorders. In V. B. Van Hasselt & M. Hersen (Eds.), *Handbook of adolescent psychopathology: A guide to diagnosis and treatment* (pp. 349–382). New York: Lexington Books.

Boyle, M. H., Offord, D. R., Racine, Y., Sanfors, M., Szatmari, P., & Fleming, J. E. (1993). Evaluation of the original Ontario Child Health Study scales. *Canadian Journal of Psychiatry, 38,* 397–405.

Bracken, B. A. (1992). *Multidimensional Self-Concept Scale: Examiner's manual.* Austin, TX: PRO-ED.

Burns, R. C., & Kaufman, S. H. (1972). *Actions, styles and symbols in Kinetic Family Drawings (K-F-D): An interpretive manual.* New York: Brunner/Mazel.

Buss, A. H., & Durkee, A. (1957). An inventory for assessing different kinds of hostility. *Journal of Consulting Psychology, 21,* 343–348.

Butcher, J. N., Williams, C. L., Graham, J. R., Tellegen, A., Ben-Porath, J. S., & Kaemmer, B. (1992). *MMPI-A: Manual for administration, scoring, and interpretation.* Minneapolis, MN: University of Minnesota.

Caldwell, C. (1999). Counseling depressed boys. In A. M. Horne & M. S. Kiselica (Eds.), *Handbook of counseling boys and adolescent males* (pp. 279–292). Thousand Oaks, CA: Sage Publications.

Conners, C. K. (1997). *Conners' Rating Scales-Revised technical manual.* North Tonawanda, NY: Multi-Health Systems.

Coopersmith, S. (1981). *Self-Esteem Inventories (SEI).* Palo Alto, CA: Consulting Psychologists Press.

Coopersmith, S., & Gilbert, R. (1982). *Professional manual: Behavior Academic Self-Esteem (BASE), a rating scale.* Palo Alto, CA: Consulting Psychologists Press.

Derogatis, L. R. (1994). *SCL-90-R administration, scoring, and procedures manual—third edition.* Minneapolis, MN: National Computer Systems.

Drummond, R. J. (1996). *Appraisal procedures for counselors and helping professionals.* (3rd ed.). Englewood Cliffs, NJ: Merrill.

Eckert, T. L., Dunn, E. K., Codding, R. S., & Guiney, K. M. (2000). Self-report: Rating scale measures. In E. S. Shapiro & T. R. Kratochwill (Eds.), *Conducting school-based assessments of child and adolescent behavior* (pp. 150–169). New York: Guilford Press.

Eyberg, S. M., & Ross, A. W. (1978). Assessment of child behavior problems: The validation of a new inventory. *Journal of Clinical Child Psychology, 7,* 113–116.

Feindler, E. L., Adler, N., Brooks, D., & Bhumitra, E. (1993). The development and validation of the Children's Anger Response Checklist (CARC). In L. Vandecreek (Ed.), *Innovations in clinical practice* (Vol. 12, pp. 337–362). Sarasota, FL: Professional Resources Press.

Gersham, F. M., & Elliott, S. N. (1990). *The Social Skills Rating System.* Circle Pines, MN: American Guidance Service.

Hansen, D. J., Giacoletti, A. M., & Nangle, D. W. (1995). Social interactions and adjustment. In V. B. Van Hasselt & M. Hersen (Eds.), *Handbook of adolescent psychopathology: A guide to diagnosis and treatment* (pp. 102–129). New York: Lexington Books.

Hodges, K. K. (1987). Assessing children with a clinical interview: The Child Assessment Schedule. In R. J. Prinz (Ed.). *Advances in behavioral assessment of children and families.* Greenwich, CT: JAI Press.

Hood, A. B., & Johnson, R. W. (1997). *Assessment in counseling: A guide to the use of psychological assessment procedures* (2nd ed.). Alexandria, VA: American Counseling Association.

Kalfus, G. R. (1995). Behavioral assessment in adolescents. In V. B. Van Hasselt & M. Hersen (Eds.), *Handbook of adolescent psychopathology: A guide to diagnosis and treatment* (pp. 243–264). New York: Lexington Books.

Kazdin, A. E. (1994). Psychotherapy for children and adolescents. In A. E. Bergin & S. L. Garfield (Eds.), *Handbook of psychotherapy and behavior change* (4th ed., pp. 543–594). New York: John Wiley & Sons.

Kearney, C. A., & Silverman, W. K. (1995). Anxiety disorders. In V. B. Van Hasselt & M. Hersen (Eds.), *Handbook of adolescent psychopathology: A guide to diagnosis and treatment* (pp. 435–464). New York: Lexington Books.

Klopfer, Bruno. (1962). *The Rorschach Technique: An introductory manual.* New York: Harcourt, Brace and World.

Kovacs, M. (1992). *Children's Depression Inventory (CDI) manual.* North Tonawanda, NY: Multi-Health Systems.

Kronenberger, W. G., & Meyer, R. G. (2001). *The child clinician's handbook* (2nd ed.). Boston: Allyn and Bacon.

Lachar, D., & Gruber, C. P. (1995). *Personality Inventory for Youth (PIY) manual.* Los Angeles: Western Psychological Services.

March, J. (1997). *Multidimensional Anxiety Scale for Children technical manual.* North Tonawanda, NY: Multi-Health Systems.

Matson, J. L., Rotatori, A. F., & Helsel, W. J. (1983). Development of a rating scale to measure social skills in children: The Matson Evaluation of Social Skills with Youngsters (MESSY). *Behavior Research and Therapy, 21,* 335–340.

Merrell, K. W. (1993). *School Social Behavior Scales.* Austin, TX: PRO-ED.

Merrell, K. W. (2000). Informant-report: Rating scale measures. In E. S. Shapiro & T. R. Kratochwill (Eds.), *Conducting school-based assessments of child and adolescent behavior* (pp. 203–234). New York: Guilford Press.

Miller, L. S., Klein, R. G., Piacentini, J., Abikoff, H., Shah, M. R., Samilor, A., & Guardino, M. (1995). The New York Teacher Rating Scale for disruptive and antisocial behavior. *Journal of the American Academy of Child and Adolescent Psychiatry, 34,* 359–370.

Millon, T., & Davis, R. D. (1993). The Millon Adolescent Personality Inventory and the Millon Adolescent Clinical Inventory. *Journal of Counseling and Development, 71,* 570–574.

Novaco, R. (1975). *Anger control: The development and evaluation of an experimental treatment.* Lexington, MA: Lexington Books.

Piers, E. V. (1984). *Piers-Harris Children's Self-Concept Scale Revised manual 1984.* Los Angeles: Western Psychological Services.

Platt, N. J., & Spivak, G. (1975). *Manual for the Means End Problem Solving Procedure (MEPS): A measure of interpersonal cognitive problem solving skill.* Unpublished manuscript.

Reich, W., Welner, Z., Herjanic, B., & MHS Staff. (1997). *Diagnostic Interview for Children and Adolescents computer program (DICS-IV).* North Tonawanda, NY: Multi-Health Systems.

Reynolds, C. R., & Kamphaus, R. W. (1992).*Behavior Assessment System for Children manual.* Circle Pines, MN: American Guidance Service.

Reynolds, C. R., & Richmond, B. O. (1978). What I think and feel: A revised measure of children's manifest anxiety. *Journal of Abnormal Child Psychology, 6,* 271–280.

Reynolds, W. M. (1987). *Assessment of depression in adolescents: Manual for the Reynolds Adolescent Depression Scale (RADS).* Odessa, FL: Psychology Assessment Resources.

Reynolds, W. M. (1989). *Reynolds Child Depression Scale: Professional manual.* Odessa, FL: Psychology Assessment Resources.

Reynolds, W. M. (1995). Depression. In V. B. Van Hasselt & M. Hersen (Eds.), *Handbook of adolescent psychopathology: A guide to diagnosis and treatment* (pp. 297–348). New York: Lexington Books.

Roberts, G. E. (1994). *Interpretive handbook for the Roberts Apperception Test for Children.* Los Angeles: Western Psychological Services.

Spielberger, C. D. (1988). *Manual for the State-Trait Anger Expression Inventory (STAXI).* Odessa, FL: Psychological Assessment Resources.

Spielberger, C. D., Edwards, C. D., Lushene, R. E., Montouri, J., & Platzek, D. (1973). *Preliminary manual for the State-Trait Anxiety Inventory for Children.* Palo Alto, CA: Consulting Psychologists Press.

Stein, M. I. (1955). *The Thematic Apperception Test: An introductory manual for its clinical use with adults.* Cambridge: MA: Addison-Wesley.

Walker, H. M., & McConnell, S. R. (1995a). *Walker-McConnell Scale of Social Competence and School Adjustment: Adolescent version.* San Diego, CA: Singular Publishing Group.

Walker, H. M., & McConnell, S. R. (1995b). *Walker-McConnell Scale of Social Competence and School Adjustment: Elementary version.* San Diego, CA: Singular Publishing Group.

Wirt, R. D., Lachar, D., Klinedinst, J. K., & Seat, P. D. (1977). *Multidimensional description of personality: A manual for the Personality Inventory for Children.* Los Angeles: Western Psychological Services.

Wodrich, D. L. (1997). *Children's psychological testing* (3rd ed.). Baltimore, MD: Paul H. Brookes.

Chapter 16
Assessment of Family Issues
A Guide for Educators

Craig S. Cashwell & Randolph H. Watts Jr.

This chapter provides an overview of the family assessment process for educators who work in school settings. Although school counselors and other school mental health professionals will most likely implement the formal assessment procedures illustrated in this chapter, all school personnel need to consider family issues that may occasion academic, behavioral, and emotional problems among students. A thorough assessment of a student enables school-based professionals to develop appropriate remediation and intervention strategies. Assessment can help with the identification of a problem or problems, the generation of alternative ways to view the problems, and the process of deciding among interventions (Hood & Johnson, 1991). The following vignettes exemplify family assessment issues.

The Withdrawn First-Grade Student

Jack is a quiet first grader. He does not seem to have many friends in his class. Although he works well independently, he gets frustrated when working in a group with other children. Recently, he became so frustrated in a group that he started crying and ran over to the teacher and grabbed her leg. At other times, he has affectionately referred to the teacher as "Mommy." He wears the same dirty clothes to school almost every day.

The Dieting Middle School Student

Lucy seemed to be a successful and happy student until recently. Although she has always been active in gymnastics, she has become more active in recent months. She talks often about gymnastics competitions and losing weight. She is increasingly distracted in class, often

> fidgeting or looking uncomfortably around the room. She eats almost nothing at lunch, claiming that she is on a new diet. She looks thin and pale. She appears to be in a bad mood most of the time.

The Sullen High School Student

> Jimmy, a junior, seems to have become even more dark and sullen in the past few months. Although he has never put much effort into his schoolwork, his grades have dropped significantly this quarter. He looks tired, with drooping bags under his eyes. He sometimes smells of tobacco. He seems angry and has even gotten into a few fistfights with people he claimed were his friends. His classmates have started to call him "the beast" behind his back. He does not speak in class or even make eye contact with his teachers. He seems to hurry from class intentionally to avoid a conversation with anyone. He grumbles about how no one understands him.

What is going on with each of these children? Is Jack simply a quiet child, or are there neglect issues at home? Is Lucy stressed out and a little overzealous in her diet and fitness program or does she have an eating disorder? Is her family pressuring her to succeed in gymnastics? Is Jimmy going through typical teenage angst, or is he developing a substance abuse problem, and at what level are family members aware of his problems? It is impossible to tell from the preceding descriptions the nature of each child's distress. It is clear, however, that adult attention is warranted and more information is needed.

Assessment of Systemic Issues

When considering familial influences on a student's development and functioning, the assessment process must be multimethod and multimodal. *Multimethod* assessments make use of a variety of assessment techniques, including behavioral observations of the student (and, on occasion, of family interactions); interviews with the student, teachers, and parents; and formal standardized assessment instruments. The term *multimodal* refers to assessing the cognitive, behavioral, and affective domains and the interplay among the three. To conduct an accurate assessment that is multimodal (i.e., assesses thoughts, behaviors, and feelings), it is necessary to collect information in a variety of ways (i.e., conduct a multimethod assessment). Although the student's age may dictate what assessment methods are applicable, the central idea is to avoid overgeneralizing from any one source of information and making misattributions because of limited information. For example, a student in elementary grades may produce a drawing that appears to be sexually graphic. Although this is cause for concern and follow-up, it is important to supplement this piece of "data" with other information, such as a child interview, behavioral observations in the classroom, teacher interviews, and if appropriate, parent interviews.

Assessment is a continual process, and the process typically begins with informal procedures such as observations and interviews before moving on to more formal methods of assessment, such as standardized tests. For clarity, informal and formal assessment procedures are addressed separately in this discussion, though it is important to keep in mind that the two are not artificially separated in reality; that is, informal and formal assessment procedures complement one another and together provide more comprehensive assessment. Information from a standardized test may provide additional data and be integrated with the results of interviews and behavioral observations.

Informal Assessment Process

There are a variety of methods of collecting information on family functioning without using standardized tests. The primary types of informal assessment are interviews and observations of the student and the family.

Student Interviews

When school personnel begin to consider that family functioning may be affecting a student's academic or behavioral performance, the assessment process often begins with a student interview. Clearly, the interviewer must keep in mind the developmental level of the child. A question such as, "How are things going at home?" may produce a useful response from a high school student, but will likely be unhelpful with a student in elementary grades: Responses such as "good" or "fine" are common at this age.

When collecting family information in any form, particularly through interviewing, it is important to consider that family rules may exist against talking about familial problems. Whether this rule is overt (i.e., parents tell the student not to talk about the problem) or covert (i.e., not talking about problems is modeled in the family system), these rules are powerful influences in the student's life. There are two practical implications here. First, it is necessary to build rapport and trust with the student. Often this process includes a period of supporting the student in *not* talking about something, for example, "That's a very difficult thing to talk about. You don't have to talk about that right now if you don't want to." Avoiding the power struggle that often follows when a student is told he or she must disclose personal information may increase trust levels and occasion important disclosures from the student. Second, it is important to watch for subtle nonverbal cues that the student is not being forthright and to listen for what the student is not saying, or how he or she is changing topics away from systemic issues. Decisions about when and if to confront these inconsistencies depend on the level of rapport with the student and perceptions of the student's readiness to discuss the issues further. Because we often do not know when students are ready to make a disclosure, a helpful statement might be "I think there is something about your family that you want to tell me, but it's hard to talk about. Whenever you are ready to talk about it, I would like to hear about it and help if I can." Such a statement treats the student with respect and avoids the types of power struggles that may influence the student to withdraw and avoid further disclosures.

A final caveat about student interviews is warranted. The maxim in family assessment may well be, "What you get depends on whom you ask." Child and parent reports of family functioning often are discrepant, with adolescents commonly reporting greater problems in their families than do parents. When conducting child interviews, it is important to remember the potential for bias in self-reporting and that you are getting only one side of the story. This fact underscores the importance of multimethod assessment.

Genograms

A genogram is a multipurpose assessment tool that may be used either with a student individually or within a family session. Considering how varied and complex family structures can be, a genogram may be particularly helpful in organizing family information. A genogram may help a younger student (who is perhaps functioning at a concrete operational level) to present information about her or his family. In addition to being a useful assessment technique for the professional educator to gain information, the process of co-constructing a genogram often gives students new insights.

Although the process of developing a genogram may be modified to fit the needs of each student, there are common steps and symbols in developing a genogram, a development that occurs in three stages. In the first stage, a family tree is developed that illustrates a student's family structure and relevant information that the student is able to provide. The specificity of this content depends on, among other things, the age of the student. In the second stage, the student provides a detailed description of each person in the genogram. In the third stage, the student discusses the quality of each dyadic relationship. Tailored to the issues and needs of each student, genograms may be used to gather focused information about various aspects of family functioning, such as attachments, emotional expression, gender roles, and culture (DeMaria, Weeks, & Hof, 1999).

Behavioral Observations

Behavioral observations of the student often contribute valuable information. For example, it is often helpful to observe targeted behaviors in the classroom. Observations may not be subject to the biases of self-report information. Further, behavioral observations are an alternative method of collecting information about young students who may not be able to provide useful information in an interview. One important decision is to determine who will make the behavioral observations. Teachers who are trained in the assessment process may observe unobtrusively. Other school personnel, who can focus solely on targeted behaviors of particular students without the responsibility of teaching other students, may provide more focused observations; however, obtrusive observation, such as the school counselor coming into the classroom, may change the environment enough to alter a student's behavior. When such observations are conducted, it is important to follow them up with a teacher interview to see how the behavior was consistent with or different from that shown in typical classroom periods.

Behavioral observations often provide information about the function or purpose of the targeted behavior (the most common purposes of behavior being attention seeking, escape or avoidance, and tangible rewards). Behavioral observations may provide information about what the child needs from her or his environment and how parents may be interacting with the child. Such information informs the efforts of school personnel to advocate for the student by consulting with parents. Consider the following scenario:

> David, a second-grade student whose parents divorced about three months ago, begins having frequent temper tantrums in one class. A classroom observation and subsequent teacher interviews by school counselors reveal that the student is able to avoid certain aspects of schoolwork by having tantrums and being sent to the principal's office. A consultation with his mother (the custodial parent) indicates that this is a common pattern at home as well; she often chooses to let him out of his responsibilities at home when he throws tantrums because it is easier to do so.
>
> The counselor realizes that the teacher and mother are both inadvertently reinforcing the tantrums by letting David out of his responsibilities. Working together, the counselor, teacher, and mother develop a strategy to reinforce David for asking verbally for what he wants (rather than throwing tantrums) and not to allow him out of his responsibilities. The counselor also works to educate the teacher and mother about the likelihood of an *extinction burst* (an initial increase in the frequency and intensity of a behavior when its reinforcer is removed) so that they will be prepared for the behavior to worsen initially and will not abandon the plan.

Family Interviews

An optimal assessment technique involves bringing in all members of the immediate family and interviewing them together. Such an interview provides a wealth of information because the facilitator may collect information based not only on what people say, but also, more important, on how they interact. Information such as who answers for the family, who talks to whom, who talks about whom, and how the problem is viewed by different family members may reveal important information about family functioning, including hierarchies, power issues, and family rules.

Family interviews should not be confused with parent interviews. In a parent interview, a parent is invited to consult with school personnel, usually about the child's behavioral or academic difficulties. Parent report is an important and clearly viable source of information. The distinction between the type of information gained in a family interview and that gained from a parent interview is one of content versus process. Although a parent may provide additional content information, a family interview potentially provides process information about family functioning, information that may not be reported verbally by any individual member of the family because of a lack of conscious awareness of the dynamic.

One vital technique in conducting family interviews is that of circular questioning. *Circular questioning* is used to assess the perceptions of each family member about the functioning of the family system. O'Brian and Bruggen (1985) categorized circular questions as relationship oriented ("When you say you are not going to bed at night, what does your mother do? What does your father do?"), rank oriented ("Who does more disciplining of you, your mother or your father?"), or time oriented ("How was John different before you and your husband divorced?"). A final category addresses a person who does not respond to questions that are asked. Other family members may be asked to provide this information (e.g., "If Samantha had answered my last question honestly, what would she have said?"). Circular questioning is a powerful technique to assess family interactions, help the family learn about perceptions of other family members, and stimulate discussion as family members engage in the process of either agreeing with or correcting statements made about them (Brock & Barnard, 1999).

Family Task Interview

One alternative to a traditional family interview is a *family task interview* (Kinston, Loader, & Miller, 1985). The family is provided a series of structured tasks to complete. The tasks are either observed by an unobtrusive observer or videotaped (with consent) for review. The primary advantages of the family task interview are that families reveal more information about themselves through the completion of these tasks than they do through self-report in an interview (Kinston et al., 1985) and that alliances within the family are not distorted by the involvement of another person, such as a teacher or counselor (Fredman & Sherman, 1987). The family task interview begins by welcoming the family and issuing simple instructions. The family then completes the following seven tasks within a specified amount of time:

Plan together an activity that must take at least an hour (four minutes).

Get the box of blocks and build a tower (four minutes).

Discuss likes and dislikes of each member (four minutes).

Sort a deck of cards according to a pattern (four minutes).

Complete the following story: A family is at home. One

member is missing and late returning. The phone rings, and the family is asked to come to the hospital immediately (nine minutes).

Parents choose a well-known saying, decide what it means, then explain it to the children (nine minutes).

Discuss the task interview process (five minutes).

Family functioning on the tasks is then rated on a seven-point Likert-type scale in the areas of affective status, communication, boundaries, alliances, adaptability and stability, and family competence.

Family Dynamics

Regardless of the type of informal assessment process you select, consider a number of important family dynamics: rules, roles, boundaries, communication patterns, family affect, and flexibility. *Rules* refers to both the overt (e.g., for curfew) and covert (e.g., modeling of emotions that are or are not expressed) processes by which families govern themselves. *Roles* refers to the parts played by each family member. Healthy families tend to be highly conscious of each role, and there is some fluidity and flexibility in roles. Common examples of roles typically considered unhealthy are the *parentified child* (i.e., the child has caretaking and other adult responsibilities) and the *spousified child* (i.e., a child is a primary or sole source of emotional support for a parent). *Boundaries* are invisible barriers that determine amounts and type of contact both within and outside the family. These boundaries may be physical, emotional, spiritual, or sexual and exist on a continuum from disengaged to enmeshed, with healthy families considered to exist somewhere between these extremes. *Communication patterns* are often indicative of power issues in the family or needs for education about healthy communication patterns. *Autonomy* refers to such dimensions as clarity of expression, balance of authority and responsibility, and level of invasiveness. *Family affect* refers to such dimensions as range of feelings, general mood and tone of family interactions, presence of empathy toward others in the family, and presence of irresolvable conflict. Finally, *flexibility* (or adaptability) refers to the ability of family members to adapt as the needs of the family change. Examples of flexibility include modifying family rules as children get older and modifying family functioning when a child leaves home.

Formal Assessment Process

At times, it may be more effective to use standardized measures to provide information about family functioning. When administering paper-and-pencil measures to students, parents, or teachers, remember that this information is self-report and, as such, is subject to the same biases inherent to any self-report. This is a significant issue particularly when dealing with family functioning because many people hold myths about their family, that is, they believe the family is functioning differently than it is actually functioning. For this reason, data gained from standardized self-report measures should be integrated with other information about the student available from interviews and observations.

Although a thorough review of assessment instruments is beyond the scope of this chapter, there are three instruments that are brief and well researched and have reading levels generally appropriate for middle school or older students.

Family Adaptability and Cohesion Evaluation Scales III (FACES III). FACES III (Olson, Portner, & Lavee, 1985) was developed to measure the family constructs of cohesion (closeness) and adaptability (flexibility), two important constructs in the family counseling literature. A substantial volume of research considers relationships among these two aspects of family functioning and a variety of behavioral and academic outcomes. Family descriptions made by various family members correlate weakly with one another (Fredman & Sherman, 1987), and these discrepancies often become a focal point in the counseling process.

Family Strengths Scale. Olson, Larsen, and McCubbin (1992) developed an instrument that measures aspects of sound family functioning rather than focusing on problems. This instrument measures two dimensions of family functioning: family pride (including trust and loyalty) and family accord. Besides looking at overall scores, responses to individual items can serve to stimulate discussion (Fredman & Sherman, 1987).

Parent-Adolescent Communication Scale (PAC). Developed by Barnes and Olson (1992) as an adjunct to the FACES instrument, the PAC measures two dimensions of family communication (open family communication and problem family communication). One unusual aspect of the PAC is that a separate form exists for communication with each parent, allowing for potential differences in these relationships to emerge through the assessment process.

Guidelines for Working with Troubled Students

Whenever school personnel work with students who may have family problems that contribute to academic, behavioral, and emotional problems, they should keep in mind the following guidelines: Consult a school mental health professional, consider legal issues, understand school procedures, and make an appropriate referral when necessary.

Consult a School Mental Health Professional

Consultation with a school mental health professional typically involves sharing observations of the child's behavior and relevant parts of conversations with the child and her or his parents or guardians. It is most helpful to be objective and share concrete information rather than sharing personal feelings about the child or guessing at a diagnosis. The mental health professional will determine the best way to proceed. In most cases, the next step is to gather more information, that is, to start the assessment process discussed throughout this chapter. Although the school-based mental health professional often will coordinate the collection of assessment information, teachers are typically involved in the data collection process.

Consider Legal Issues

The law most relevant to assessment is the Family Education Rights and Privacy Act (PL 93–380). This law, also known as the Buckley Amendment, gives parents the opportunity to see all information affecting the evaluation, placement, or programming of their children (Drummond, 1992). Parents or legal guardians have a right to see all written assessment information collected. Accordingly, it is important that student records include only factual, objective assessment information.

Understand School Procedures

Policies and procedures vary from school to school and are explicated more fully and in more detail in some schools than in others. It is extremely important to understand the procedures at your school before beginning any assessments and to clarify anything that is unclear about the policies and procedures regarding the student assessment process.

Policies and procedures commonly govern the practice of obtaining parental consent for assessment and circumstances that warrant referral to a mental health professional within the school, such as a school counselor, or to a mental health professional outside of the school when the needs of the student exceed the resources of the school (e.g., if the student needs extended intensive counseling or the student's problems are beyond the expertise of school personnel).

Make a Referral

When a student's needs exceed the capacity of the classroom teacher to meet them or extend outside of her or his expertise, a referral to a school mental health professional may be warranted. This person will be trained to collect information about family functioning systematically and to make informed decisions about the mental health needs of the student and her or his family. Similarly, when the needs of the student and her or his family are greater than can be met within the school setting, a referral for services outside of the school may be needed (Schmidt, 1999).

Whenever a referral of any type is made, it is important to communicate with the child what is happening. Although this is true for students of all ages, failure to discuss this with older students often has more serious negative consequences because the student may feel lied to or betrayed in some way. A typical pattern would be for the teacher to tell the child, in a caring manner, that he or she is concerned. For example, a teacher could say, "Lucy, I am concerned about your dieting. It seems that you have lost a lot of weight, and I am afraid that it is unhealthy. I have mentioned to Ms. Garcia, the school counselor, that I am concerned. I have asked her to talk with you. You might need some help and she is a very helpful person." Although this type of statement will most likely meet with some resistance from the child, being truthful and straightforward with the child will be beneficial in the long run.

Making contact with parents to obtain consent for assessment or to solicit participation in the assessment process should also be done in a spirit of care and concern. For example, the school counselor might say, "Ms. Rosa, this is Janette Smith, the school counselor at Jack's school. I am calling about Jack. He seems to be having some difficulties at school. He seems to get frustrated and cries in class quite a bit. I wonder if you would meet with me to develop a plan to help him." The goal here is to develop an allied, rather than adversarial, relationship with the parents. It is all too easy to fall into the unhelpful trap of advocating for the child and becoming adversarial toward a parent or guardian.

Conclusions

Our goal in developing this chapter has been to discuss the assessment process and provide an overview of techniques that may be used to assess family functioning in an educational setting. The assessment of family issues in an educational setting is a difficult and complex task. Yet it is only through understanding the functioning of a student's family that many academic, emotional, and behavioral problems can be fully understood and appropriate interventions developed.

References

Barnes, H., & Olson, D. (1992). Parent-adolescent communication. In D. Olson, H. McCubbin, H. Barnes, A. Larsen, M. Muxen, & M. Wilson (Eds.), *Family inventories* (2nd ed., pp. 29–44). St. Paul, MN: Family Social Science, University of Minnesota.

Brock, G. W., & Barnard, C. P. (1999). *Procedures in marriage and family therapy* (3rd ed.). Boston: Allyn and Bacon.

DeMaria, R., Weeks, G., & Hof, L. (1999). *Focused genograms.* Philadelphia, PA: Brunner/Mazel.

Drummond, R. J. (1992). *Appraisal procedures for counselors and helping professionals* (2nd ed.). New York: Merrill.

Fredman, N., & Sherman, R. (1987). *Handbook of measurements for marriage and family therapy.* New York: Brunner/Mazel.

Hood, A. B., & Johnson, R. W. (1991). *Assessment in counseling: A guide to the use of psychological assessment procedures.* Alexandria, VA: American Association for Counseling and Development.

Kinston, W., Loader, P., & Miller, L. (1985). *Clinical assessment of family health.* London: Hospital for Sick Children, Family Studies Group.

O'Brian, C., & Bruggen, P. (1985). Our personal and professional lives: Learning positive connotation and circular questions. *Family Process, 24,* 311–322.

Olson, D., Larsen, A., & McCubbin, H. (1992). Family strengths. In D. Olson, H. McCubbin, H. Barnes, A. Larsen, M. Muxen, & M. Wilson (Eds.), *Family inventories* (2nd ed., pp. 56–70). St. Paul, MN: Family Social Science, University of Minnesota.

Olson, D. H., Portner, J., & Lavee, Y. (1985). FACES III: Family Adaptability and Cohesion Evaluation Scales. In D. Olson, H. McCubbin, H. Barnes, A. Larsen, M. Muxen, & M. Wilson (Eds.), *Family inventories* (rev. ed.). St. Paul, MN: Family Social Science, University of Minnesota.

Schmidt, J. J. (1999). *Counseling in schools: Essential services and comprehensive programs* (3rd ed.). Boston: Allyn and Bacon.

Chapter 17
SUBSTANCE-Q
A Practical Clinical Interview for Detecting Alcohol and Other Drug Abuse

Gerald A. Juhnke & William Bryce Hagedorn

This chapter describes the SUBSTANCE-Q, an atheoretical assessment scale designed for use as a clinical interview with students who potentially abuse alcohol and other drugs (AODs; Juhnke & Scholl, 1997). The scale is founded upon a clustering effect of 10 literature-identified risk factors that commonly occur among AOD abusing students. When these risk factors are assessed in sequence, the first letter of each risk factor corresponds with the acronym SUBSTANCE-Q. Thus, the acronym serves as a reminder of each of the 10 risk factors that warrant assessment. Following the established "S" through "Q" sequence ensures a thorough student substance abuse assessment. Each high-risk factor is indicated below with a brief summary suggesting the reason for its inclusion.

The 10 SUBSTANCE-Q Risk Factors

Substance Abusing Family Member. Students whose parents and siblings are AOD abusing are at greater risk for abusing AODs themselves (Biederman, Faraone, Monuteaux, & Feighner, 2000; Duncan, Duncan, & Hops, 1996). This seems especially true when AOD abusing parents and older siblings are respected and revered, and when these AOD abusing family members are noted as being important role models (Adlaf & Giesbrecht, 1996). Furthermore, when students are living with AOD abusing family members, psychoactive substances are often readily available within the home, and parents appear to be less concerned about students using AODs or becoming addicted. This may occur because AOD abusing family members don't perceive they have experienced significant negative consequences related to their AOD abuse and don't perceive themselves as being addicted (Kandel, Griesler, Lee, Davies, & Schaffran, 2001).

Undersocialization. This factor refers to students who report few significant friends or limited interactions with significant others. Often these students will present with poor interpersonal skills or reported alienation feelings (Sandhu, 2000). It is unknown whether their AOD abusing behaviors have stunted their social development or interpersonal skills, whether these students initially had limited desire to interact socially, or whether a combination of these factors influences their undersocialization (Brook & Whiteman, 1997). No matter the genesis, undersocialized students are at increased risk for AOD abuse and should be evaluated and referred whenever undersocialization is noted as a symptom of presenting psychopathology (e.g., undersocialization resulting from depression) or promoting AOD abuse (e.g., self-medicating due to undersocialization).

Behavioral Problems. There is a high correlation between deviant and AOD abusing behaviors (Dawkins, 1997; SAMHSA, 2001, Oct. 12). For example, some students may have been formally charged with criminal behaviors such as prostitution, driving while under the influence (DUI), selling AODs, or shoplifting (SAMHSA, 2001, Dec. 14). Still others may present as highly impulsive and sensation seeking (Palmgreen, Donohew, Lorch, Hoyle, & Stephenson, 2001).

Stressful Life Events. AOD abuse is also correlated with reported stressful life events (Biederman et al., 2000). Specifically, many AOD abusing students report using psychoactive substances to reduce anxiety related to stressful life events (Hoffman & Su, 1997). Some of these students may be predisposed to anxiety and, therefore, experience stressful events more acutely than do nonabusing students. It is also possible, however, that AOD abuse brings about stressful life events as well (Weinrich & Hardin, 1997). For example, AOD abusing students may experience stressful life events resulting from behaviors while under the influence, or their stressful life events may be related to dysfunctional interpersonal relationship dynamics that are exacerbated by AOD abusing behaviors.

Tobacco Use. There is a correlation between tobacco use and AOD abuse (Golub, Labouvie, & Johnson, 2000). A sizeable percentage of students who present with AOD abuse concerns also use tobacco. Thus, students using tobacco should be assessed for potential AOD abuse.

Academic Problems. Although there is a misperception by some that all AOD abusing students experience academic problems, this is simply not true. Many AOD abusing students are intelligent and do well scholastically. There are indicators, however, suggesting that a significant percentage of AOD abusing students do experience academic difficulty (Dozier & Barnes, 1997; Register, Williams, & Grimes, 2001). Academic problems may result from significant absenteeism or interpersonal difficulties with peers and authority figures such as teachers. Those experiencing academic difficulties may turn to AODs to reduce the stresses of failure.

Negative Affect. For this scale, negative affect consists of two or more of the following: (a) lethargy, (b) lack of ambition, (c) pessimism, (d) low self-esteem, or (e) a low need for achievement. When combined with other risk factors, negative affect may signal increased probability for AOD use (Hofler & Lieb, 1999; Sutherland & Shepherd, 2001). Any student presenting negative affect, however, warrants immediate assessment to rule out potentially life-threatening behaviors.

Cohort Substance Abuse. Data suggest an increased probability that students will abuse AODs when their close friends and peers are abusing the same substances (NCADI, 2001; Olds & Thombs, 2001). Whenever students note that their close friends and peers are AOD abusing, further inquiry is warranted.

Endorsement of Substance Abuse. This risk factor is especially noteworthy. Students who indicate that they are AOD abusing automatically warrant treatment. Often students initially coming into treatment or being mandated into treatment will indicate they abuse AODs (AAP, 2001). Their statements should be believed, and appropriate treatment intervention should be established.

Quit in Past or Attempted to Quit. This risk factor is related to students who indicate that they have quit or attempted to quit abusing AODs. Often these students will indicate many attempts to discontinue AOD abuse altogether or will indicate they have attempted to decrease their AOD abuse (Stanton & McClelland, 1996).

Once the SUBSTANCE-Q risk factors have been assessed, a score can then be determined. The following intervention strategies, which correspond to each student's score, will aid in the treatment of the affected student.

Scoring and Intervention Guidelines

For each of the SUBSTANCE-Q risk factors, students receive a score between 0 (complete absence of the risk factor) and 10 (significant manifestation of the risk factor). Proposed intervention guidelines are based upon behavioral scoring anchors (Table 1) and total number of points received (Table 2). This total number can range between 0 and 100. The purpose of this clinical interview scale is to ensure a thorough addiction assessment and to augment counselors' clinical judgment when they perceive that students may be AOD abusing. Therefore, the instrument is used only when students are perceived as possibly having an AOD abuse–related concern. Besides the relation to AOD abuse risk factors, the scale's numerical score is correlated to general clinical guidelines that suggest minimal intervention standards. These general guidelines should be adjusted according to the student's specific needs and voiced concerns.

Low SUBSTANCE-Q Scores

The responses of students perceived as AOD abusing who score between 0 and 15 may very well be suspect. Such low scores may indicate students are attempting to present themselves in a favorable manner and are not admitting their AOD abuse concerns or related experiences. Such low scores suggest students are denying the presence of AOD abusing behaviors and experiences commonly acknowledged by AOD addicted students. The primary issue with such low scores is the incongruence between the counselor's initial perceptions related to the student's suspected AOD abuse and the student's low score. Consulting with one's clinical supervisor and professional peers can help clarify whether the counselor's original concerns were likely

TABLE 1. The SUBSTANCE-Q Clinical Interview

Substance Abusing Family Members/Significant Others
Under socialized
Behavioral Problems
Stressful Life Events
Tobacco Use
Academic Problems
Negative Affect
Cohort Substance Abuse
Endorses Substance Abuse
Quit In the Past or Previously Attempted Quits

SUBSTANCE-Q

TABLE 2. SUBSTANCE-Q Clinical Interview Behavioral Scoring Anchors

Substance Abusing Family Member/Significant Others

0	No Substance Abusing Family Members
5	At least one respected family member abusing substances on a regular_basis
10	At least one respected family member abusing substances who has had substance-related negative effects (e.g., job termination, DUI charges, etc.) resulting from frequent and regular substance abuse

Under socialized

0	Good social skills and significant support from others
5	Limited social skills or limited support
10	Poor social skills or very limited support

Behavioral Problems

0	No deviant, criminal, or antisocial behaviors noted
5	Unconventional attitudes or minor rebellion toward authority figures or minor law infractions
10	Recent or recurrent criminal behaviors or high sensation seeking or animosity toward authority figures.

Stressful Life Events

0	Stressful life events denied and student appears to be experiencing a life free from major stressors
5	Some noteworthy stressful life events are noted. These stressors are reported at times as being difficult but are neither insurmountable or thoroughly overwhelming
10	Noteworthy stressful life events are noted and the student reports that the stressors are often perceived as overwhelming

Tobacco Use

0	Student denies smoking tobacco
5	Student reports occasionally smoking tobacco cigarettes or cigars, but reports smoking less than one pack of tobacco cigarettes each week and less than three tobacco cigars per week.
10	Student reports smoking at least one pack of tobacco cigarettes or one tobacco cigar per day

Academic Problems

0	No academic problems noted
5	Decline in academic relations or performance or attendance resulting from substance abuse or substance-related behaviors, or in jeopardy of being dismissed, suspended, or failed due tsubstance abuse or substance-related behaviors
10	Academic course failure resulting from substance abuse or substance-related_behaviors or performance or attendance problems resulting from substance abuse or substance-related behaviors

Negative Affect

0	No lethargy or lack of ambition or pessimism or low self-esteem or low need for achievement noted.
5	Moderate amounts of any of the aforementioned noted
10	Significant amounts of any of the aforementioned noted

Cohort Substance Abuse

0	No close friends or peers are reported as abusing AODs
5	Infrequent AOD abuse by close friend(s)
10	Frequent AOD abuse by close friend(s)

Endorses Substance Abuse

0	Student denies AOD abuse
5	Student reports infrequent AOD abuse
10	Student reports frequent AOD abuse

Quit In the Past or Previously Attempted Quits

0	No previous attempts or thoughts of discontinuing alcohol use
5	No previous attempts or thoughts of discontinuing drug use other than alcohol which costs less than $10 per week, or one or fewer attempts to discontinue AOD use
10	Does not perceive a need to discontinue drug use of more than $10 per week, or more than one attempt to discontinue AOD use.

TABLE 3. SUBSTANCE-Q Clinical Interview Scores with General Clinical Guidelines

Scores	General Clinical Guidelines
0 to 15	Consult clinical supervisor to clarify whether initial AOD concerns regarding the student were likely unfounded. If concerns were unfounded and no basis for questioning the veracity of the student's responses exist, disseminate information indicating how student can access counselors if needed in the future and provide a single follow-up telephone call in 10 to 14 days to reassess possible needs. Oppositely, should the student's responses be suspect, additional assessment via significant other clinical interviews and AOD speciality assessments (e.g., the Substance Abuse Subtle Screening Inventory-Adolescent) are warranted.
16 to 39	If responses do not appear suspect, participation in counseling should be encouraged to address AOD abuse or other voiced concerns. If responses appear suspect, additional assessment via significant other clinical interviews and AOD specialty assessments is warranted.
40 to 59	Counseling and 12-step participation should be advocated. The local 24-hour helpline and relevant support group (e.g., Al-Ateen) telephone numbers should be provided. Student must agree to a "no suicide" and a "no harm" contract. Additional assessment is necessary to determine types, frequency, and amounts of AODs used – especially AODs used within the current year. Rule out the need for detoxification.

60 to 100	Counseling and 12-step participation are required. In addition to providing local helpline and 12-step support group numbers, and requiring the student to agree to a no suicide and no harm contract, detoxification and a restricted environment must be ruled out. Additionally, further assessment is required. Specifically such assessment should note types of AODs used, as well as the frequency of use and amounts typically taken.

If the counselor's original concerns seem unfounded, he or she should inform students about how to access counseling services in the future should the students need help. A single follow-up telephone call within the next 10 to 14 days to reassess the situation and remind students of available services is also suggested. On the other hand, should a student's responses appear suspect, additional assessment is clearly warranted, and depending on the outcome of these assessments, relevant intervention should be conducted to ensure clinically appropriate treatment.

The presence of certain risk factors, even by themselves, warrant further assessment and intervention. For example, it is logical that students who endorse AOD abuse should receive addiction treatment recommendations. Those who report stressful life events, academic problems, or negative affect should be referred for counseling.

Low to Moderate SUBSTANCE-Q Score

Scores between 16 and 39 suggest substance abuse. Additional assessment is warranted if responses appear suspect or if counselors are uncertain whether DSM-IV-TR abuse or dependence criteria are fulfilled. Recommendations for follow-up counseling are a means to address presenting AOD abuse symptoms or other voiced concerns. Follow-up visits are indicated to monitor the students' immediate conditions and to ensure that appropriate services are made available should a change in their conditions warrant more intensive interventions. Giving students a business card with both the local 24-hour crisis and local support group telephone numbers printed on the front and 35 cents taped to the back can provide students with the means to obtain help should they need it.

Moderate to High SUBSTANCE-Q Scores

Those scoring between 40 and 59 points are experiencing a moderate to high number of AOD abuse risk factors and likely warrant addiction treatment. Further assessment related to the types of AODs used, onset of AOD use, frequency of use, and money typically spent each week on AOD abusing behaviors will be helpful. These students should be encouraged to investigate and participate in a relevant 12-step support group (e.g., Alateen). Given the frequency of suicide and violence among AOD abusing students (Dawkins, 1997; Tanskanen, 2000), students scoring in this range should sign a no suicide and no harm contract. This contract has students promise counselors and significant others (e.g., friends, family members, etc.) that they will call the 24-hour crisis hotline should they feel overwhelmed, depressed, or like hurting themselves or others.

Certainly, such contracts hold no legal recourse, and they can't inhibit students from dangerous behaviors (Barnett, 1994). They do, however, provide counselors with robust information and delineate a plan that students and their families and friends can follow. For example, should a student refuse to enter into a no suicide contract, it is clinically appropriate to assess the student for immediate danger and to hospitalize him or her if necessary. In other words, if any students refuse to agree to a no suicide contract, it suggests that those students are entertaining suicidal ideation and may have a plan to harm themselves. Thus, further assessment is warranted and protective measures must be enacted to protect these students from self-harm.

High SUBSTANCE-Q Scores

Scores of 60 or greater suggest significant AOD abuse, as well as possible environmental and emotional stressors. These students are at significant risk for substance abuse or dependence and likely warrant direct intervention. Depending on the amount and frequency of noted AOD abuse, students whose scores fall at the extreme end of this AOD risk continuum warrant possible referral for detoxification. Participation in a 12-step support group should be required, concomitant with addiction counseling. As indicated for moderate to high responses, the student should sign a no suicide and no harm contract and be provided a 24-hour crisis hotline number.

Clearly counselors should recognize that the presence of any single 10-point factor does not mean students are substance abusing or dependent. As noted, however, a clustering of high-risk factors, as noted above, suggests increased risk of substance abuse or dependence. Again, high scores on single factors such as academic problems, behavioral problems, or stressful life events may not by themselves indicate substance abuse or dependence, but they may suggest the need for general counseling services.

SUBSTANCE-Q

Conclusion

School counselors have multiple responsibilities to the students and families they serve, and students and families desire prompt and effective counseling services. The ability to assess student AOD abuse immediately without having to refer can be a significant asset to counselors and students alike. The SUBSTANCE-Q can be easily implemented with students during typical face-to-face clinical assessments and provides school counselors the opportunity to learn about potential student concerns and problems without requiring standardized written testing instruments. As this chapter has noted, in administering and scoring the SUBSTANCE-Q, obtained scores link directly to practical counseling recommendations and guidelines.

Based upon our experiences, we believe the SUBSTANCE-Q allows school counselors an opportunity to quickly establish the basic rapport necessary in assessing the AOD treatment needs of students. Additionally, the student interview enables counselors immediately to assess and implement standardized counseling recommendations that encourage student follow-up and continuity of care. Finally, the use of the SUBSTANCE-Q clinical interview ensures that the counselor asks fundamental questions regarding student AOD abuse and concerns. Therefore, school counselors can intervene before a student engages in more potentially dangerous and lethal AOD abuse behaviors.

References

AAP [American Academy of Pediatrics]. (2001). Improving substance abuse prevention, assessment, and treatment financing for children and adolescents. *Pediatrics, 108*(4), 1025–1030.

Adlaf, E., & Giesbrecht, N. (1996). The substance use–delinquency nexus. *Addiction, 91*(4), 504–507.

Barnett, C. (1994). Symbolic safeguard. *Nursing, 24*(10), 72.

Biederman, J., Faraone, S. V., Monuteaux, M. C., & Feighner, J. A. (2000). Patterns of alcohol and drug use in adolescents can be predicted by parental substance use disorders. *Pediatrics, 106*(4), 792–798.

Brook, J. S., & Whiteman, M. (1997). Drug use and delinquency: Shared and unshared risk factors in African American and Puerto Rican adolescents. *Journal of Genetic Psychology, 158*(1), 25–40.

Dawkins, M. P. (1997). Drug use and violent crime among adolescents. *Adolescence, 32*(126), 395–406.

Dozier, A. L., & Barnes, M. J. (1997). Ethnicity, drug user status and academic performance. *Adolescence, 32*(128), 825–838.

Duncan, T. E., Duncan, S. C., & Hops, H. (1996). The role of parents and older siblings in predicting adolescent substance use: Modeling development via structural equation latent growth methodology. *Journal of Family Psychology, 10*(2), 158–172.

Golub, A., Labouvie, E., & Johnson, B. D. (2000). Response reliability and the study of adolescent substance use progression. *Journal of Drug Issues, 30*(1), 103–119.

Hoffman, J. P., & Su, S. S. (1997). The conditional effects of stress on delinquency and drug use: A strain theory assessment of sex differences. *Journal of Research in Crime & Delinquency, 34*(1), 46–79.

Hofler, M., & Lieb, R. (1999). Covariates of cannabis use progression in a representative population sample of adolescents: A prospective examination of vulnerability and risk factors. *Addiction, 94*(11), 1679–1695.

Juhnke, G. A., & Scholl, M. B. (1997, April 5). *SUBSTANCE-Q: A substance abuse assessment scale.* Presented at the 1997 American Counseling Association World Conference, Orlando, FL.

Kandel, D. B., Griesler, P. C., Lee, G., Davies, M., & Schaffran, C. (2001). *Parental influences on adolescent marijuana use and the baby boom generation: Findings from the 1979–1996 National Household Surveys on Drug Abuse.* Substance Abuse and Mental Health Services Administration, Office of Applied Studies, Analytic Series: A-13, DHHS Publication No. (SMA) 01–3531, Rockville, MD: U.S. Department of Health and Human Services.

Miller, F. G., & Lazowski, L. E. (2001). *The adolescent SASSI-A2 manual: Identifying substance user disorders.* Springville, IN: SASSI Institute.

NCADI [National Clearinghouse for Alcohol and Drug Information]. (2001, Nov. 2). *Youth tobacco surveillance: United States, 2000.* CDC/MMWR Surveillance Summaries. Retrieved February 3, 2003 from www.cdc.gov/mmwr/preview/mmwrhtml/ss5004a1.htm.

Olds, R. S., & Thombs, D. L. (2001). The relationship of adolescent perceptions of peer norms and parent involvement to cigarette and alcohol use. *Journal of School Health, 71*(6), 223–229.

Palmgreen, P., Donohew, L., Lorch, E. P., Hoyle, R. H., & Stephenson, M. T. (2001). Television campaigns and adolescent marijuana use: Tests of sensation seeking targeting. *American Journal of Public Health, 91*(2), 292–297.

Register, C. A., Williams, D. R., & Grimes, P. W. (2001). Adolescent drug use and educational attainment. *Education Economics, 9*(1), 1–18.

SAMHSA [Substance Abuse and Mental Health Services Administration]. (2001, Oct. 12). Youth violence linked to substance use. *The NHSDA Report.* Retrieved from www.samhsa.gov/oas/facts/Violence.htm

SAMHSA [Substance Abuse and Mental Health Services Administration]. (2001, Dec. 14). Alcohol use.

The NHSDA Report. Retrieved from www.samhsa.gov/oas/2k2/alcNS/alcNS.htm.

Sandhu, D. S. (2000). Alienated students: Counseling strategies to curb school violence. *Professional School Counseling, 4*(2), 81–86.

Stanton, W. R., & McClelland, M. (1996). Prevalence, reliability and bias of adolescents' reports of smoking and quitting. *Addiction, 91*(11), 1705–1715.

Sutherland, I., & Shepherd, J. P. (2001). Social dimensions of adolescent substance use. *Addiction, 96*(3), 445–459.

Tanskanen, A. (2000). Joint heavy use of alcohol, cigarettes and coffee and the risk of suicide. *Addiction, 95*(11), 1699–1705.

Weinrich, S., & Hardin, S. (1997). Social support and psychological correlates of high school students who use illicit drugs in response to stress. *American Journal of Health Studies, 13*(1), 17–27.

Chapter 18
Overcoming Test Anxiety
Giving Students the Ability to Show What They Know
Brian Goonan

Tests and evaluations are a nearly unavoidable part of our world. Entrance exams, aptitude tests, driver's license tests, classroom exams, and, in particular, grades are just a few examples of the assessments used throughout our society to make comparisons among individuals. Most people are not concerned about the use of grades to identify areas in need of improvement. When these grades are used to determine who will be permitted access to resources such as higher education, greater opportunities, and financial assistance, however, testing becomes a concern. It is understandable that some people experience test anxiety when faced with this determination and the seeming message that test scores impart regarding an individual's worthiness.

We are tested throughout life. As early as preschool, some schools require entrance evaluations to determine if a child is appropriate for a given program. Parents, teachers, and administrators complain of the overemphasis placed on standardized test scores to evaluate a school's worthiness for funding. This dismay over the emphasis on test scores trickles down to students. In Texas, some educators feel that too much of the curriculum is focused on preparing students to pass the TAAS (Texas Assessment of Academic Skills), one of a long line of group-administered aptitude tests. Even elementary school students feel the pressure and come to regard the TAAS as another four letter word. Given our society's emphasis on getting ahead and the function that tests have come to serve in measuring the ability to succeed, it is not surprising that many individuals have come to see tests as feared objects that threaten their well-being.

There is significant variability in the reporting of test anxiety, with some studies citing test anxiety as affecting as much as 34 percent to 41 percent of third- through sixth-grade children (Beidel, 1991; Turner, Beidel, Hughes, & Turner, 1993). Even if we accept conservative estimates, which range around 20 percent, one out of five students in upper elementary school is likely somehow hindered in his or her ability to show what he or she knows. In reviewing the literature on the impact of anxiety on aptitude, Ball points out that "less than 10 percent of the aptitude variance is accounted for by anxiety, and probably no more than 5 percent on the average. This is nevertheless worth being concerned about: Smoking accounts for only about 3 percent of the variance associated with longevity and people feel this is important" (Ball, 1995, p.110).

Doesn't Everyone Worry About Taking a Test?

Test anxiety is more than normal worry about a test; it is a specific anxiety disorder that involves excessive amounts of concern, worry, and fear about negative evaluation during or in anticipation of performance or evaluative situations. Diagnostically, test anxiety meets the criteria for classification as a specific form of social phobia as defined by the DSM-IV (American Psychiatric Association, 1994). Individuals with test anxiety are excessively concerned with embarrassment or consequences from poor performance; seek to avoid performance or evaluative situations, or endure those situations with intense distress; and have disruptions to their normal routine or academic functioning as a result of the distress or avoidance behaviors.

Students experience test anxiety as difficulty thinking clearly, and in some cases seeming inability to do so. This mental blanking may lift once the exam is over. Before and during the test, individuals may experience physical sensations such as a racing heartbeat, upset stomach (e.g., "butterflies"), muscle tension, perspiration (e.g., sweaty palms), and headache. Irritability and restlessness may also occur. During the exam the student may misread questions, experience difficulty understanding the nature of the questions asked, and have trouble organizing his or her thoughts. Although some educators and researchers suggest that the low performance of test-anxious students is due to a combination of poor preparation and an individual's awareness of that poor preparation at test time, others would support the contention that individuals who are well prepared but experience high test anxiety have true difficulty in retrieving known information and strategies (Birenbaum & Nasser, 1994).

Liebert and Morris (1967) were perhaps the first to break down test anxiety into the two main components of worry and emotionality. The worry component comprises the cognitive aspects of anxiety, typically considered to be rooted in fears of failure, negative comparisons to peers, and doubts about personal ability. Thoughts such as "I'll never get into college with these grades," "Why is no one else struggling with this exam?" and "Maybe I'm just not as smart as I think I am" are examples of the cognitive worry component. Later researchers have specified test-irrelevant thoughts as at least a subset of the initial worry component (Sarason, 1984). All too often families, peers, schools, and society feed the test-anxious student's concerns by emphasizing the subjective notion of performing to one's potential. Some students come to value their academic acumen as indexed partly by how little they studied; therefore, they under-report the amount of studying required in order to appear as though they earned their grades through intellect more than through preparation.

Liebert and Morris's (1967) second component, emotionality, encompasses the physiological sensations associated with arousal of the autonomic nervous system. Although their initial conceptualization emphasizes the physiological aspects of arousal, the emotionality component in actuality comprises both physiological and affective arousal. Thus, emotionality includes increased muscle tension, perspiration, cold hands, racing heartbeat, and upset stomach, as well as sensations of irritability, depression, and agitation.

Consistent with a commonly held belief that cognitions are more likely to influence emotions and physiology than vice versa, most studies I reviewed found the cognitive component of test anxiety to be more influential than the emotionality component. For example, Morris and Liebert (1970) found worry to be more strongly negatively correlated with examination grades than was emotionality. Similarly, Birenbaum and Nasser (1994) concluded that preoccupation with test-irrelevant thoughts leaves less space for the type of processing necessary for complex tasks.

Origins and Impact of Test Anxiety: A Most Unwanted Guest

In a recent review of the literature, McDonald (2001) concludes that there are no consistent findings regarding gender differences, socioeconomic differences, or race differences in the prevalence of test anxiety. There is also no generally accepted causal pathway for the development of test anxiety. Test anxiety is not a simple matter of students who are test anxious doing poorly, and those who are not test anxious doing well. This is largely because test anxiety is thought to be based on a continuum of impairment rather than as being either present or not present (McDonald, 2001). Additionally, the effects of test anxiety on performance are thought to be multidetermined and complex (Hodapp, Glanzmann, & Laux, 1995). Regardless of its causes, once test anxiety is present, it seems to form a self-sustaining feedback loop. Test anxiety decreases performance on tests (or increases inefficiency of preparation), which negatively affects self-esteem and confidence; this supports a belief in decreased likelihood for success (reinforcing the worry component), which, in turn, further increases test anxiety.

In some cases the very thing we think might improve confidence may actually serve to produce or increase anxiety. For example, Mueller and Dweck (1998) found that 10- to 12-year-olds who are praised for test performance tend to choose tasks that allow them to demonstrate their abilities. These children hold strong beliefs that their test scores represent their intelligence, and they would lie to another child if they received a poor score. Children praised for their effort instead of their performance do not return to the same tasks; rather, they choose tasks that allow opportunities for learning. The idea that praising children for effort rather than achievement enhances learning is consistent with findings that praise for performance also undermines intrinsic motivation (Deci & Ryan, 1985).

The effects of test anxiety take on different forms depending on whether students are high or low achievers, according to Birenbaum and Nasser (1994), who evaluated the qualitative and quantitative aspects of student performance on a math test. They found that highly anxious, high-achieving students made more nonserious errors on complex items than did highly anxious, low-achieving students, who made more serious errors. Birenbaum and Nasser take these results to suggest that individuals with backgrounds of high and low achievement need to be treated differently in terms of intervention. They suggest that the highly anxious, high-achieving student would benefit most from learning test-taking skills, such as practicing effective coping methods for different types of formats. The highly anxious, low-achieving student would benefit most from effective learning strategies. Both groups would benefit from therapies that focus on cognitive coping techniques in the face of stress.

Given that anxiety is based on an individual's perception of lack of success or fear of failure, rather than just his or her innate abilities, intellectually gifted students also are vulnerable to test anxiety (Zeidner & Schleyer, 1999). Gifted students' test anxiety does not affect their academic performance to the level seen with nongifted, test-anxious students; however, relative to their peer group, all test-anxious students have a low academic self-concept. Further, high-achieving and intellectually gifted students often self-select into more competitive environments as their schooling progresses. Therefore, the long-term impact of test anxiety on lowering students' self-concepts and the likely negative impact on their academic success cannot be overlooked.

Test anxiety does not have a direct impact on academic achievement, but it may manifest differently based on many factors, including familial background, level of achievement, motivation, and intellectual giftedness. Sources of support have been shown to play a mediating role in the impact of test anxiety (Orpen, 1996). Interventionists would do well to attend to the various expressions test anxiety may take and to design intervention plans that fit each situation.

Measurement: When Is Anxiety More Than Just the Jitters?

A full review of the measures that are used to assess and identify test anxiety is beyond the scope of this chapter. For those who are interested, Anderson and Sauser (1995) provide a thorough review of the literature and the measures that were available by the mid-1990s. Although Anderson and Sauser recommend the Revised Test Anxiety Scale as "state of the art, as of this writing" (p. 22), the Test Anxiety Inventory (TAI; Spielberger, 1980) appears to be the most widely used instrument according to the test anxiety literature. One limitation of the TAI is that it was designed for and normed on high school and college students. The state-anxiety component of Spielberger and associates' (1973) State-Trait Anxiety Inventory for Children (STAIC) offers one perspective on the younger student's response to situational anxiety. The Revised Children's Manifest Anxiety Scale (RCMAS; Reynolds & Richmond, 2000) also offers a window into the cognitive, affective, and physiological experiences of children who experience anxiety.

One of the drawbacks to all anxiety-specific test instruments is their face validity. In other words, the questions on the inventories are addressing exactly what you would expect. Sample items tend to be worded like "I have difficulties concentrating on tests" or "I feel nervous during major exams." For the student who would like to fake problems in order to garner accommodations (such as extended time on the SAT), it would not be difficult to determine how to respond. Although some would question whether an individual would label himself or herself as "disabled" for the purpose of garnering accommodations, many students feel pressured to get into the top colleges at any cost. Anecdotal data concerning college admissions of students who took the SAT with accommodations for learning disabilities or attentional difficulties do not suggest that the special accommodations indicator affects acceptance if a student's scores are in the appropriate acceptance range.

Under the Americans With Disabilities Act (ADA) and Section 504 of the Rehabilitation Act of 1973, individuals with disabilities are protected from discrimination and are assured services. Test anxiety meets the two criteria for a disability as outlined under ADA and Section 504 (Zuriff, 1997). First, it is diagnosable as a mental disorder under DSM-IV. Second, inherent in the DSM-IV diagnostic criteria are substantial limitations on the individual's major life activities (e.g., situational avoidance, disruptions to normal and academic routines). Zuriff argues that individuals with test anxiety are potentially limited in any life endeavor that requires taking tests, such as for application, credentialing, licensure, or training. Thus, at the secondary school and college levels, individuals who experience test anxiety should be eligible to receive accommodations and modifications in their classes when taking tests and quizzes. To my knowledge, no court cases have directly challenged the diagnosis of test anxiety.

The Educational Testing Service (ETS) allows for testing accommodations if the following criteria for the documentation of a disability are present (see www.ets.org/disability/criteria.html):

1. Current documentation by a qualified professional
2. Comprehensive documentation, including evidence for early impairment; evidence for current impairment; ruling out of alternative diagnoses or explanations; provision of relevant testing; identification of DSM-IV criteria; documentation with a specific diagnosis; and inclusion of an interpretive summary
3. A rationale for each accommodation recommended

The ETS has also indicated that individuals wishing accommodations on standardized tests must also be receiving similar accommodations in their present settings. In other words, students receiving no modifications in their present educational setting cannot suddenly need modifications for a specific standardized test.

It is important to rule out alternative diagnoses. Students affected by learning disabilities, attentional problems, and depression often have difficulties with the process of encoding information during studying, giving them a tenuous grasp of the information before any evaluation takes place. Students with attentional difficulties or depression often experience difficulties concentrating and become internally or externally distracted during exams, for reasons that are not exam-specific. Additionally, the student with depression is at particular risk for the exacerbation of the negative self-concept feedback loop, or cycle, that accompanies test anxiety. Too often learning disabilities, attentional problems, depression, or anxiety go undetected or under-reported, and therefore undertreated.

Interventions: How to Stop the Negative Feedback Loop

Many researchers have evaluated effective interventions for test anxiety across a variety of age groups (Beidel & Turner, 1999; Birenbaum & Nasser, 1994; Hobson & Thompson, 1996; Syncamore & Corey, 1990; Thorne, 2000; Vagg & Papsdorf, 1995; Wilkinson, 1990). Most of these studies emphasize the worry component of the Liebert and Morris (1967) model. Many studies point to the importance of test-irrelevant thoughts, primarily self-directed negative thoughts, as interfering with attention and resources during the test-taking process. Accordingly, most interventions focus on increasing cognitive restructuring. Nevertheless, most practical interventions focus on improving the whole picture of an individual's test-taking behaviors.

Although many researchers would agree that inadequate test preparation does not sufficiently explain the low test scores of students with test anxiety (Ball, 1995), at least some portion of students with test anxiety show a pattern of poor test preparation that does not enhance their academic performance in the face of test anxiety (Birenbaum & Nasser, 1994). If test anxiety makes it difficult to retrieve information, it is logical to focus at least some intervention on putting the information firmly in place before the test anxiety tries to shake it loose. There are many programs and books focusing on productive study habits, and many colleges and universities offer free seminars and services to students to help them learn how to prioritize, organize, and schedule so that they learn best. Increasingly, high schools, middle schools, and even elementary schools are beginning to help their students with organizational and study skills. Planning and organizational skills are particularly important if a student has shown tendencies toward avoidance behaviors and self-defeating behaviors, such as procrastination and not remembering or not completing assignments.

One of the better-known study skill methods is SQ3R. In this method, students are asked first to ***S***urvey the material and ***Q***uestion what they see. This first step moves learning from a passive process of reading and decoding to an active process of information finding. The first R is to ***R***ead the material with the questions in mind. The second R involves ***R***eviewing the information gathered during the reading process and answering the initial questions they posed to themselves. Students are encouraged to divide the task of reading longer chapters into manageable pieces. The third R is to ***R***ecite the information as a means of further internalizing the material. I typically add a fourth R of ***R***ewriting small cues to economize the information.

Besides the benefits of developing a more thorough and accessible grasp of the information to be recalled, adequate preparation also assists with desensitization to the feared stimulus, namely tests. When possible, using old exams and practice tests under simulated test conditions (e.g., taking a timed practice exam in a lecture hall where the test is to be administered, under quiet conditions) would further desensitize the student to the potential impact of test anxiety. Test preparation courses, such as the Princeton Review, that incorporate multiple practice tests given under simulated conditions help in the desensitization process for nationally administered standardized tests. Desensitization has been shown to help reduce test anxiety and improve grades (Gonzales, 1995). Informally structured programs of desensitization are also effective, according to Thorne (2000), who found that the use of extra credit exercises (e.g., pop quizzes) helps reduce test anxiety.

As I have reiterated throughout this chapter, individuals who experience test anxiety suffer most from the negative thoughts and self-perceptions of low academic competence. These students overemphasize the effect of test results on their self-worth, their appearance to peers, and their possibilities for success. Derogatory statements such as "If I can't do well on this test, then I don't deserve to go to college," "I am so stupid; how do people put up with me?" and "This [test] is horrible" are just a sample of comments students with test anxiety make on a routine basis. In the face of this pressure, it is no wonder they are more distracted during tests, have fewer resources from which to draw for confronting challenging tasks, and give up earlier on tests than do individuals who are less test anxious.

Test-anxious students can learn several cognitive behavioral techniques, such as challenging irrational beliefs or thought-stopping combined with self-reinforcing statements, self-instruction, and coping strategies when faced with the sensation of anxiety (Ellis & Grieger, 1977; Meichenbaum, 1972). Although the specifics of each technique differ, the overall goals are similar. The primary goal of cognitive behavioral interventions for anxiety is to help the students recognize irrational or maladaptive thoughts and replace those thoughts with more realistic versions of the initial perception. For example, an irrational thought such as "If I fail this exam, I might as well drop out of school" would be "stopped" and replaced by "I would like to do well on this exam, but if I don't, I will learn from my mistakes and be better prepared for the next exam," or "I studied the best I know how. If I don't do well, that is a signal to get extra assistance." Here, the student reorganizes the unproductive worry—which too often is a distraction during the test taking—into productive concern and establishes a plan of action. Similarly, if the student encounters difficulties with a test, he or she is encouraged to replace negative thoughts such as "Great! Now I know I am going to fail!" with "Hmm. I'm not sure of that answer, so I'll come back to it later." Fletcher and Spielberger (1995) support the notion that both rational emotive behavior therapy and cognitive therapy reduce individuals' ratings of test anxiety.

These individuals experience a positive impact on their self-esteem to the degree that they decrease berating self-statements.

Even under the best of conditions, individuals with test anxiety are likely to experience intermittent bouts of elevated physiological arousal (e.g., butterflies in the stomach). Overt and covert desensitization techniques can alleviate this arousal. Overt desensitization involves experiencing the actual anxiety-provoking situation under controlled situations, such as taking practice exams.

In covert desensitization the student visualizes the feared situation and practices self-soothing techniques, such as deep breathing exercises or progressive muscle relaxation, to counter the physiological effects of the anxiety experience. To practice deep breathing exercises, an individual can either sit up straight or lie down flat so that the chest and abdomen are in a straight line. The individual then places one hand on his or her chest and one hand on his or her abdomen. The focus is on gentle, regular abdominal breathing; the hand on the chest should remain relatively still while the hand on the abdomen rises and falls at a regular rate. Gentle, regular abdominal breathing with a focus on slightly longer exhalations than inhalations helps to decrease the autonomic arousal that accompanies test anxiety. Biofeedback, which focuses on the reduction of physiological arousal, has also been shown to help increase students' GPAs and to help reduce emotionality, especially when combined with cognitive therapy (Vagg & Papsdorf, 1995).

The goal of early preparation, desensitization, relaxation techniques, and other forms of covert and overt practice is not to eliminate anxiety but to reduce it to a manageable level. Most individuals who work in competitive or evaluative situations suggest that moderate amounts of anxiety actually facilitate good performance in academic and athletic endeavors (Ball, 1995; Murphy, 1996; Yerkes & Dodson, 1908). Some degree of anxiety heightens our senses and awareness, thereby heightening our performance. Therefore, one cognitive restructuring technique is to come to view moderate amounts of anxiety as healthy and helpful. Statements such as, "This anxiety lets me know that I would like to do well and that I care about my studies," or "A little anxiety will help me focus and concentrate" help a student to accept some anxiety as a natural part of wanting to rise to the occasion.

Too often individuals who experience test anxiety are not adequately attending to their physiological needs. They reduce their usual amount of sleep and exercise, and do not eat a balanced diet. Compromising a healthy, balanced lifestyle is stressful in and of itself and will only exacerbate an already difficult situation. Sleep allows the mind to recharge and prepare for analysis and integration of more information and strategies. Exercise releases endorphins, which enhance mood, and gives us a well-needed break from hours of study. Additionally, we are likely to continue to process information while exercising. It is not uncommon for an individual to understand a technique or to synthesize information only after he or she is able to step away from the material. Finally, maintaining a balanced diet will help to replenish those vitamins and minerals that stress depletes.

Although many of the previous examples of test-anxiety coping techniques are geared toward older students, programs geared toward children often contain similar components but are altered in presentation to be more developmentally appropriate and enjoyable. For example, the Testbusters program (Beidel & Turner, 1999) emphasizes the SQ3R method and is geared toward fourth- through seventh-grade students. The Rain or Shine approach developed by Hobson and Thompson (1996) for elementary school students uses common art materials to express and explore test anxiety. Students draw raindrops, which represent irrational thoughts that come to them when they are taking tests. Then they draw an umbrella, which represents alternative thoughts that protect them from getting wet during the test. The mark of good child intervention is the level to which the child can learn beneficial skills in a way that is enjoyable. Many of the skills outlined earlier in this chapter are readily adapted to children.

Guiding Principles for Intervention: "No, Really, What Specifically Should I Do?"

As this chapter describes, there are several techniques for and many well-written texts on addressing test anxiety (e.g., Johnson, 1997). Whatever techniques you introduce to students, keep in mind the following general guidelines:

1. Identify the problem. Test anxiety typically comes to light when there is a discrepancy between a student's perceived ability and his or her outcome on tests. Many factors can contribute to an individual not performing to his or her ability. Learning disabilities, attention deficit/hyperactivity disorder, social difficulties, depression, and anxiety are just a few of the elements that can affect performance. Referring the student for a good evaluation, including cognitive, academic, behavioral, and emotional components, is a recommended first step for addressing any perceived discrepancy between ability and performance.
2. Encourage more than adequate preparation. Despite some degree of contradictory evidence in the literature, it is clear that a test-anxious student benefits from having the best possible grasp of the material before taking an exam. By teaching students good study skills (e.g., outlining, SQ3R), good study habits (e.g., clean work area, organized task and materials, effective time management), and a willingness to seek further assistance with difficult information, you give them essential tools to succeed despite test anxiety. To the extent that test anxiety knocks information loose or causes difficulties in retrieving information, the individual with test anxiety will need to have that much firmer a foundation.
3. Use desensitization techniques. Similar to treatments for other anxiety disorders, systematic desensitization and graduated exposure help reduce situation-specific anxiety. Pop quizzes, practice exams under timed conditions, and pressured responses (e.g., a tutor, parent, teacher, or peer intentionally second-guessing a correct response) are examples of ways in which you can provide graduated exposure to an anxiety-provoking situation.
4. Encourage relaxation. Because anxiety has physiological correlates, recommend that test-anxious individuals engage

in visualization, progressive muscle relaxation, or other relaxation techniques to gain greater regulation over the physiological sensations accompanying anxiety. Even with adequate preparation, the student with a history of test anxiety is likely to experience the familiar physiological sensations of a racing heart, cold hands, sweaty palms, and tense muscles, triggering the test anxiety–negative self-concept cycle. Also emphasize that some degree of anxiety is normal and perhaps slightly helpful in a test situation to help test-anxious students to relax.

5. Use the system. There is more than one way to take exams and standardized tests (including the SAT). For students with documented test anxiety or performance anxiety, consider accommodations such as untimed or extended time formats, small-group administration, oral administration, or bulleted essays to help them give a more accurate indication of their knowledge. Decide on accommodations based on a thorough evaluation of an individual's difficulty and techniques that have proved beneficial in the past.

Summary

Though many feel that the use of tests is overstressed in our society, the truth is that tests are inherent in evolution. Darwin's theory of survival of the fittest describes species as evolving from a test of which strain has the most adaptive survival mechanisms to perpetuate a given gene pool. Humans evolved into a separate species based on tool usage, intellect, cunning, and the perpetuation of knowledge. It is only fitting that one of the tests of our species is to determine which individuals have the intellectual and emotional capacity, as well as the behavioral discipline, to succeed.

This chapter outlines the concept of test anxiety and its impact on performance, manners in which to diagnose and provide accommodations for the disability, and many means by which to reduce the impact of test anxiety. Overall, it bears repeating that although the concept of test anxiety is relatively simple, understanding how it affects a given individual is complex and dependent on many factors. Despite its complexity, test anxiety is an important consideration as long as we continue to value performance evaluations as determinants for access to education, resources, and other opportunities (such as employment and licensure). It is therefore incumbent on educational and evaluative institutions to teach individuals effective methods to address their anxiety and to assist them in developing independent means to overcome its effects.

References

American Psychiatric Association. (1994). *Diagnostic and statistical manual of mental disorders* (4th ed.). Washington, DC: Author.

Anderson, S. B., & Sauser, W. I., Jr. (1995). Measurement of test anxiety: An overview. In C. D. Spielberger & P. R. Vagg (Eds.), *Test anxiety: Theory, assessment, and treatment.* Washington, DC: Taylor & Francis.

Ball, S. (1995). Anxiety and test performance. In C. D. Spielberger & P. R. Vagg (Eds.), *Test anxiety: Theory, assessment, and treatment.* Washington, DC: Taylor & Francis.

Beidel, D. C. (1991). Social phobia and overanxious disorder in school age children. *Journal of the American Academy of Child and Adolescent Psychiatry, 30,* 545–552.

Beidel, D. C., & Turner, S. M. (1999). Teaching study skills and test-taking strategies to elementary school students: The Testbusters program. *Behavioral Modification, 23,* 630–646.

Birenbaum, M., & Nasser, F. (1994). On the relationship between test anxiety and test performance. *Measurement and Evaluation in Counseling and Development, 27,* 293–301.

Deci, E. L., & Ryan, R. M. (1985). *Intrinsic motivation and self determination in human behavior.* New York: Plenum Press.

Ellis, A., & Grieger, R. (1977). *Handbook of rational-emotive therapy.* New York: Springer Verlag.

Fletcher, T. M., & Spielberger, C. D. (1995). Comparison of cognitive therapy and rational emotive therapy in the treatment of test anxiety. In C. D. Spielberger & P. R. Vagg (Eds.), *Test anxiety: Theory, assessment, and treatment.* Washington, DC: Taylor & Francis.

Gonzales, H. P. (1995). Systematic desensitization, study skills counseling, and anxiety-coping training in the treatment of test anxiety. In C. D. Spielberger & P. R. Vagg (Eds.), *Test anxiety: Theory, assessment, and treatment.* Washington, DC: Taylor & Francis.

Hembree, R. (1988). Correlates, causes, effects, and treatment of test anxiety. *Review of Educational Research, 58,* 47–77.

Hobson, S. M., & Thompson, C. L. (1996). Test anxiety: Rain or shine! *Elementary School Guidance and Counseling, 30,* 316–318.

Hodapp, V., Glanzmann, P. G., & Laux, L. (1995). Theory and measurement of test anxiety as a situation-specific trait. In C. D. Spielberger & P. R. Vagg (Eds.), *Test anxiety: Theory, assessment, and treatment.* Washington, DC: Taylor & Francis.

Johnson, S. (1997). *Taking the anxiety out of taking tests: A step-by-step guide.* Oakland, CA: New Harbinger.

Liebert, R. M., & Morris, L. W. (1967). Cognitive and emotional components of test anxiety: A distinction and some initial reports. *Psychological Reports, 20,* 975–978.

McDonald, A. S. (2001). The prevalence and effects of test anxiety in school children. *Educational Psychology, 21,* 89–101.

Meichenbaum, D. H. (1972). Cognitive modification of test anxious college students. *Journal of Consulting and Clinical Psychology, 39,* 370–380.

Morris, L. W., & Liebert, R. M. (1970). Relationship of cognitive and emotional components of test anxiety to physiological arousal and academic performance. *Journal of Consulting and Clinical Psychology, 35,* 332–337.

Mueller, C. M., & Dweck, C. S. (1998). Praise for intelligence can undermine children's motivation and performance. *Journal of Personality and Social Psychology, 75,* 33–52.

Murphy, S. (1996). *The achievement zone: An 8-step guide to peak performance in all areas of life.* New York: Berkley Books

Orpen, C. (1996). The interactive effects of social support and test anxiety on student academic performance. *Education, 116,* 464–465.

Reynolds, C. R., & Richmond, B. O. (2000). *Revised Children's Manifest Anxiety Scale.* Los Angeles, CA: Western Psychological Services.

Sarason, I. G. (1984). Stress, anxiety, and cognitive interference: Reactions to tests. *Journal of Personality and Social Psychology, 46,* 929–938.

Spielberger, C. D. (1980). *Test Anxiety Inventory.* Redwood City, CA: Mind Garden.

Spielberger, C. D., Edwards, C. D., Lushene, R. E., Montouri, J., & Platzek, D. (1973). *State-Trait Anxiety Inventory for Children.* Redwood City, CA: Mind Garden.

Syncamore, J. E., and Corey, A. L. (1990). Reducing test anxiety. *Elementary School Guidance and Counseling, 24,* 231–233.

Thorne, B. M. (2000). Extra credit exercise: A painless pop quiz. *Teaching of Psychology, 27,* 204–205.

Turner, B. G., Beidel, D. C., Hughes, S., & Turner, M. W. (1993). Test anxiety in African American school children. *School Psychology Quarterly, 8,* 140–152.

Vagg, P. R., & Papsdorf, J. D. (1995). Cognitive therapy, study skills training, and biofeedback in the treatment of anxiety. In C. D. Spielberger & P. R. Vagg (Eds.), *Test anxiety: Theory, assessment, and treatment.* Washington, DC: Taylor & Francis.

Wilkinson, C. M. (1990). Techniques for overcoming test anxiety. *Elementary School Guidance and Counseling, 24,* 24–27.

Yerkes, R. M., & Dodson, J. D. (1908). The relationship of strength of stimulus to rapidity of habit formation. *Journal of Comparative and Neurological Psychology, 18,* 459–482.

Zeidner, M., & Schleyer, E. J. (1999). Test anxiety in intellectually gifted school students. *Anxiety, Stress, and Coping, 12,* 163–189.

Zuriff, G. E. (1997). Accommodations for test anxiety under ADA? *Journal of the American Academy of Psychiatry and the Law, 25,* 197–206.

Chapter 19
Assessments for Children Ages 3 to 8 Years
Age-Appropriate Systems

Marcy Priess Guddemi

For several decades there has been a loud outcry from the early childhood education community that assessment, especially standardized assessment, is inappropriate during the early years. Position statements on assessment state that standardized assessments are not recommended before grade three and would be best delayed until grade four (see, e.g., NAEYC, 1987; NAEYC & NAECS/SDE, 1995; Shepard, Kagan, & Wurtz, 1998).

Those who work directly with children also have strong concerns about assessment in the early years. Classroom teachers report that children at the end of kindergarten cry when they are unable to answer unfamiliar multiple-choice questions that require pencils and bubble sheets or advanced reading skills. Parents report that even children ages five to eight years develop stress-related symptoms such as stomachaches, headaches, and anxiety during these testing periods. Results of some of these assessments give little helpful information to classroom teachers or to parents. In fact the assessments force the curriculum to become more structured and workbook oriented. Parents and educators worry, and research confirms, that children who are labeled early retain that label throughout their entire school experience (NAEYC, 1987).

As we move through the first decade of the twenty-first century, there is a new public outcry for standards and accountability—even for preschool programs (Bowman, Donovan, & Burns, 2000). Therefore, it is critical to understand that both informal and formal assessments, when developmentally appropriate in design and purpose, are a *good thing* in the early years. This chapter examines ongoing perspectives from various national organizations on the essential role of assessment during the early years and defines an appropriate assessment system for this age group.

Early Childhood Assessment

Assessment during early childhood[1] is different from assessment of older children and adults for several reasons. Most importantly, young children learn differently. Young children learn or construct knowledge in experiential, interactive, concrete, and hands-on ways (Bredekamp & Rosegrant, 1992, 1995). They do not learn through paper-and-pencil activities alone nor have they developed abstract reasoning. Young children must touch and manipulate objects, build and create in many media, listen to and act out stories and everyday roles, talk and sing, and move and play in many ways and in many environments. Therefore, young children need to express learning in ways other than traditional paper-and-pencil assessments.

Assessment is also difficult during these early years because a child's development is rapid, uneven, episodic, and highly influenced by the environment (Shepard, Kagan, & Wurtz, 1998). Each child has his or her own rate of development. A child goes through rapid growth spurts and apparent resting periods of development during the early years. Children develop in four domains physical, cognitive, social, and emotional and not at the same speed or pace in each. No two children are the same. Likewise, no two children have the same familial, cultural, and experiential background. A one-size-fits-all assessment will not meet the needs of most children (Shepard, Kagan, &Wurtz, 1998).

Assessment is difficult during the early years because it takes time to do it properly. Early childhood assessments should be administered primarily one-on-one between a child and the child's teacher or parent (Meisels, 1989). The assessment should also be administered in short segments over a few days or even weeks because a young child's attention span is often very short. Although early childhood educators demand developmentally appropriate assessments for their children, they often complain about how much time it takes to administer the assessments and how much instructional time is lost in the classroom. When quality assessments mirror quality instruction, however, assessment and teaching become almost seamless, complementing and informing each other (Neuman, Copple, & Bredekamp, 2000).

NAEYC Position Statement on Early Childhood Assessment

The 1987 National Association for the Education of Young Children (NAEYC) position statement on assessment expresses the views of tens of thousands of early childhood professionals. The NAEYC led the movement to keep standardized assessments and many other types of assessments out of kindergarten and the primary grades across the country. Upon current review, the points in the statement are still valid. The NAEYC stresses the importance of quality instruments and that not all assessments are bad. Quality assessments meet the guidelines for reliability and validity as established by the *Standards for Educational and Psychological Testing* (AERA, APA, & NCME, 1999). As previously discussed, quality assessments are appropriate for the child's age and stage of development. They rely heavily on demonstration or expression of skills and knowledge—not on paper-and-pencil performance. They should also be individually administered to gain the most accurate and useful information for the teacher.

The NAEYC statement also emphasizes that administrators have an important role to play in using the information generated by assessments. Administrators must be aware of and sensitive to an individual child's uneven rates of development when interpreting information from assessments. Decisions about a child's placement or special resources should never be based on a single test score. The appropriate use of early assessment information is to guide instruction and to determine what a child is ready for next in terms of knowledge and skills.

The NAEYC updated and further refined its position in several subsequent documents. The "Guidelines for Appropriate Curriculum Content and Assessment in Programs Serving Children Ages 3 Through 8" (NAEYC & NAECS/SDE, 1995) and *Reaching Potentials*, Volumes 1 and 2 (Bredekamp & Rosegrant, 1992, 1995) provide specific guidelines and recommendations on content and curriculum goals, standards, and systematic, ongoing assessment using various assessment tools.

National Education Goals Panel on Early Childhood Assessment

The National Education Goals Panel, a government-appointed committee and extension of the Goals 2000 education movement, published national guidelines for early childhood assessment (Shepard, Kagan, & Wurtz, 1998). NEGP states that assessment should

bring about benefits for children;
be tailored to a specific purpose;
be reliable, valid, and fair;

bring about and reflect policies that acknowledge that as the age of child increases, reliability and validity of the assessment increases;
be age-appropriate in both content and methodology;
be linguistically appropriate because all assessments measure language; and
value parents as an important source of assessment information.

In addition, the panel clearly states that assessments should be used for a specific purpose and that the same assessment more than likely cannot serve two purposes. The purposes of assessments are to support learning, to identify special needs, to evaluate a program, to monitor trends, or for high-stakes accountability. The panel recommends that assessment for accountability purposes not be administered until grade three or preferably grade four.

IRA/NAEYC Position Statement on Reading and Writing

NAEYC and the International Reading Association (IRA) developed an important position statement in response to the nation's growing interest in and commitment to literacy. Because these two organizations have at times been at odds over what is appropriate for early childhood education, this document is especially powerful as an expression of their agreement on appropriate practices for learning to read and write. The document provides valuable information about how children develop literacy skills and clarifies for both the early childhood community and the reading community that *developmentally appropriate* means challenging yet achievable goals and that the foundation of reading consists of basic skills that can (and should) be taught. Furthermore, it emphasizes that quality, ongoing diagnostic assessment is essential in determining how to help young children become good readers. "Good assessment is essential to help teachers tailor appropriate instruction to young children and to know when and how much instruction on any particular skill or strategy might be needed" (IRA & NAEYC, 1998, p. 8).

National Research Council

The National Research Council (NRC) is another group that was organized to study literacy but has also provided valuable insight to appropriate assessment for young children. The council was convened by the National Academy of Sciences to study the issue of literacy development in this country. After their extensive and exhaustive review of literacy and reading research, NRC published a sweeping report, *Preventing Reading Difficulties in Young Children* (Burns, Griffin, & Snow, 1998), which set forth guidelines and recommendations not only for literacy development but also for assessment of young children. The document states that it is absolutely essential for teachers to know how to use "ongoing in-class assessments" and how to interpret "norm-referenced and individually referenced assessment outcomes, including both formal and informal in-class assessments and progress-monitoring measures used by specialists" (p. 330).

According to the NRC, quality assessment should be child-friendly and include developmentally appropriate activities. The highest quality assessments actually mirror quality instruction and are based on benchmarks and standards of achievement. In addition, they should be individually and orally administered so that they provide immediate diagnostic information to the teacher. Quality assessments actually benefit the classroom teacher by providing reliable information about each child's initial and ongoing literacy level. Quality assessments provide detailed diagnostic information that will guide planning for instruction and monitoring of individual student progress over time.

A Quality Early Childhood Assessment System

Most organizations and educators agree that assessment for young children should involve several quality assessment tools. When used together, these tools create an assessment *system* to provide information to teachers, parents, and administrators. The following examples of quality early childhood assessment tools could be part of a quality assessment system for young children.

Observations and checklists. A well-defined checklist used by a teacher who has had observation training is critical for a quality assessment system. Observations of child behaviors and skills provide the teacher with a powerful measure of a child's abilities. For example, a child telling a teacher, during an informal conversation, what happened the night before at home, with eyes wide open, a big smile, and rich expressive language provides a truer and deeper measure of oral language skills than does placing the child in a contrived situation to retell a story that may or may not make sense to the child or contain familiar items and settings.

Anecdotal records. Collecting short, factual, narrative descriptions of child behaviors and skills over time is another powerful assessment tool. This type of assessment records what the child can do. Anecdotal records should be as objective as possible and only a few sentences long, for example, "Gina chose the library center today. She pretended to read *Peter Rabbit* to two dolls and Jessica. She turned each page and recited with expression the memorized words on each page. She showed the picture at each page turn."

Running records. This type of assessment is similar to an anecdotal record but much longer. An observer objectively writes in narrative format everything the child does and says for a specific time period (e.g., 30 minutes). Running records are especially helpful in analyzing social skill development or behavioral concerns. Running records can also be narrowly focused, such as a reading running record to determine and document accuracy and miscue strategies of a child reading a specific passage.

Portfolios. A flexible and adaptable collection over time of various concrete work samples showing many dimensions of the child's learning comprises a portfolio. This type of assessment tool is particularly suited for use in the primary grades, when children are developing knowledge and skills in several subject areas and at different rates. This type of assessment also focuses on the child's strengths—what he or she can do.

Home inventories. Valuable information can be collected from surveys or a set of short, open-ended response items completed by the adult at the child's home.

Developmental screenings. A screening is a short set of age- and content-appropriate performance items (15–20 minute administration) that are based on a developmental continuum and linked to typical ages of development. This type of assessment is helpful in identifying major developmental delays. Screenings should not screen out children as "not ready," but rather should be a guide for instruction that reflects where the child *is* ready to begin learning.

Diagnostic assessments. The purpose of a diagnostic assessment is to identify a wide range of particular strengths and weaknesses and to suggest specific remediations. At one time a diagnostic assessment was defined as an assessment to be given after a developmental screening identified a special need. A broader definition now includes a type of informal assessment used by classroom teachers to guide and inform instruction. Diagnostic assessments are considered low stakes and should never be used for accountability.

Standardized assessments. Standardized assessments provide normative and scalable data that can be aggregated and reported to administrators and policymakers. These are direct measures of children's performance, administered under stringent protocols. Typically, standardized assessments are paper-and-pencil in orientation and designed to capture the child's response without administrator subjectivity. Quality standardized tests follow the guidelines of the *Standards for Educational and Psychological Testing* (AERA et al., 1999). For young children, they should also be authentic in content and should mirror classroom instruction. They should be inviting in their use of color and graphics and should also use manipulatives. Screenings and diagnostic assessments may also be standardized in the way the assessment is given. Standardized assessments are used to monitor trends and for program evaluation, and they are usually considered high stakes. Because the younger the child, the less accurate, valid, and reliable the measure, formal standardized assessments should not be used as the sole source of information on which to make high-stakes decisions before grade three, and preferably not until grade four.

Conclusion

Educators of young children should not fear a carefully chosen, quality assessment system. These informal and formal assessments are essential to a sound early childhood program. Quality assessments give teachers valuable information about the child's developing skills and knowledge. They lead teachers to select quality early childhood activities and instruction. Finally, quality assessments help teachers help the children so that no child will be left behind.

Note

1. Early childhood is actually defined as birth through age eight (NAEYC, 1987). This age range is often broken into three groups for discussion: infants and toddlers

(birth through age two), preschoolers (ages three through five), and primary children (ages six through eight). This chapter will not address any of the special needs of infants and toddlers.

References

AERA, APA, & NCME [American Educational Research Association, American Psychological Association, and National Council on Measurement in Education]. (1999). *Standards for educational and psychological testing.* Washington, DC: Author.

Bowman, B., Donovan, S., & Burns, S. (Eds.). (2000). *Eager to learn: Educating our preschoolers.* Washington, DC: National Academy Press.

Bredekamp, S., & Rosegrant, T. (Eds.). (1992). *Reaching potentials: Appropriate curriculum and assessment for young children* (Vol. 1). Washington, DC: NAEYC.

Bredekamp, S., & Rosegrant, T. (Eds.). (1995). Reaching potentials: Tranforming early childhood curriculum and assessment (Vol. 2). Washington, DC: NAEYC.

Burns, S., Griffin, P., & Snow, C. (Eds.). (1998). *Preventing reading difficulties in young children* (Report prepared for the Committee on the Prevention of Reading Difficulties in Young Children, Commission on Behavioral and Social Sciences and Education, National Research Council). Washington, DC: National Academy Press.

Harp, B., and Brewer, A. (2000). Assessing reading and writing in the early years. In D. Strickland & L. Morrow (Eds.), *Beginning reading and writing.* New York: Teachers College Press.

IRA & NAEYC [International Reading Association & National Association for the Education of Young Children]. (1998). *Learning to read and write: Developmentally appropriate practices for young children.* Washington, DC: NAEYC.

McAfee, O., & Leong, D. (1997). *Assessing and guiding young children's development and learning.* Boston: Allyn and Bacon.

Meisels, S. (1989). *Developmental screening in early childhood: A guide.* Washington, DC: NAEYC.

NAEYC. (1987). Position statement on standardized testing of young children 3 through 8 years of age. *Young Children, 43*(3), 42–27.

NAEYC & NAECS/SDE [National Association of Early Childhood Specialists in State Departments of Education]. (1995). Guidelines for appropriate curriculum content and assessment in programs serving children ages 3 through 8. In S. Bredekamp, & T. Rosegrant (Eds.), *Reaching potentials: Transforming early childhood curriculum and assessment* (Vol. 2). Washington, DC: NAEYC.

Neuman, S., Copple, C., & Bredekamp, S. (2000). *Learning to read and write.* Washington, DC: NAEYC.

Shepard, L., Kagan, S., & Wurtz, E. (Eds.). (1998). *Principles and recommendations for early childhood assessments.* Washington, DC: National Education Goals Panel.

Chapter 20
Issues in College Admissions Testing

Julie P. Noble & Wayne J. Camara

College admissions tests provide a standardized and objective measure of student achievement and generalized skills. Unlike high school grades or rank, admissions tests are a common measure for comparing students who have attended different high schools, completed different courses, received different grades in courses taught by different teachers, and had access to different opportunities and experiences both in and out of school. For the past 20 years, however, high school grades and rank have consistently been the most important factors used for making college admissions decisions, according to admissions officers. In comparison, both private and public institutions consistently rank admissions test scores as the second most important factor in admissions decisions (Breland, Maxey, Gernand, Cumming, & Trapani, 2002).

In 1999, 82 percent of all four-year colleges and institutions required an admissions test, and more than 91 percent of non-open institutions required one (College Board, 2001). These numbers have remained consistent over the past decade, irrespective of claims that more institutions are moving away from admissions tests. More than half of two-year institutions also require, recommend, or accept admissions test scores.

Factors in College Admissions Decisions

Many different factors are considered in college admissions decisions. Table 1 contains a comprehensive list of the different factors used in college admissions; many fall outside the arena of admissions testing. High school grades, high school coursework, and high school rank are probably the best known college admissions measures. Letters of recommendation, personal statements by the applicant, extracurricular activities, and community involvement are often considered as well. Developers of admissions tests encourage postsecondary institutions to consider multiple measures in the admissions process. No measure captures all relevant student characteristics. Students and counselors need to identify the specific admissions criteria of individual institutions by requesting the information by mail or visiting the institution's website.

Table 1. Factors in College Admissions Decisions

Cognitive Measures			Noncognitive Measures	Achievements/Experiences	Personal Characteristics	Other
Tests *Aptitude* • SAT I *Achievement* • ACT • SAT-II • GED • TOEFL • State-mandated HS achievement • Basic skills • Locally developed *Other* • Career planning/ placement	HS Grades • Rank • Overall GPA • GPA in specific courses • Grade trajectory	HS Courses • AP/IB • Honors • Carnegie units (UC) • College preparatory • Rigor and distribution	• Positive self-concept* • Realistic self-appraisal* • Understanding of and willingness to deal with racism* • Focus on long-range goals over short-term or immediate goals* • Successful leadership experience* • Demonstrated community service* • Knowledge acquired in a field* • Personality measures *Qualities Present on Application* • Motivation/initiative • Follow-through • Moral and ethical character • Compassion, empathy, and social consciousness • Communication skills • Understanding of interdisciplinary study • Intellectual curiosity • Interest in others	• Letters of recommendation • Resume • Communication with counselors and teachers/ counselor evaluation • Portfolios/auditions • Essay/personal statement • Interview • Academic honors • Special projects or research • Extracurricular activities • Leadership activities • Community service • Art, athletic, music, theater, or science accomplishments • Graded high school papers/ writing sample • Employment • Literacy in another language	*Student Body Considerations* • Racial/minority status • Economic disadvantage • State/country of residence • Health statement/physical exam • Ability to pay/need for financial aid • Religion • Gender • Disability • Age • Full-/part-time status • Declaration of major/ professional diversity • Veteran/military service • Disciplinary record • College transfer credit • Development (fund-raising) prospects *Individual Strengths* • Ability to benefit • Ability to overcome life challenges	*High School Characteristics* • Quality of high school (e.g., number of AP/IB courses, percentage of students attending college, average SAT/ACT scores) • Location of high school *Contextual Factors* • Institutional priorities • Competitiveness of applicant pool(number and quality of applicants) • Early decision cycle *Other* • Legacy/alumni recommendation • Provost's discretion • Nomination by U.S. congressperson (for military academies) • Random selection (lottery for those meeting minimum eligibility requirements)

*From W. Sedlacek, University of Maryland College Park

Characteristics of the ACT Assessment, SAT I, and SAT II

This section provides a general overview of the three undergraduate admissions tests. This information was taken from the websites for these testing programs. For further details, visit their websites at www.act.org/aap and www.collegeboard.com.

The ACT Assessment, SAT I, and SAT II provide information about students' relative strengths and weaknesses, and provide normative information regarding test performance by college-bound students nationally. The interpretation of the scores is not dependent on the schools students attend or the teachers who teach the students. These tests are intended to be one of multiple measures used to identify students' preparedness for college-level work, to augment high school grades and rank information, to award scholarships, or to place students into college courses. They also collect comprehensive information about students' background, educational experiences, and educational plans after high school.

Multiple forms of the SAT I and II and the ACT Assessment are administered each year to college-bound students. To ensure that scores across test forms are equivalent, the forms are *equated.* This process converts raw scores (number correct for the ACT Assessment and raw scores adjusted for guessing for the SAT I and SAT II) on each test form to scale scores, while adjusting for minor differences in difficulty among forms. As a result, for example, a composite score of 20 on the ACT Assessment means the same level of achievement for all students with that score, regardless of the test form students complete. Equating permits test users to compare students' test scores even when students complete different forms of the test within the same year or in different years.

The ACT Assessment

The ACT Assessment includes a battery of achievement tests designed to assess students' critical reasoning and higher-order thinking skills in four core subject areas: English, mathematics, reading, and science. The content of the ACT Assessment is based on the skills and knowledge that are taught in high school college-preparatory programs nationwide and that are necessary for success in the first year of college (ACT, 2000b). The content of the ACT Assessment is determined through national curriculum surveys, panels of prominent national specialists in subject matter and curriculum, and reviews of current state standards, curriculum frameworks, and commonly used textbooks.

ACT follows a multistage developmental and review process designed to ensure sensitivity and fairness of ACT test materials for all examinees, regardless of group (ACT, 2000a).

The ACT Assessment yields four subject area scores, a composite score, and seven subscores:

English (two subscores; 75 items; 45 minutes)
- Usage/Mechanics
- Rhetorical Skills

Mathematics (three subscores; 60 items; 60 minutes)
- Pre-algebra and Elementary Algebra
- Intermediate Algebra and Coordinate Geometry
- Plane Geometry and Trigonometry

Reading (two subscores; 40 items; 35 minutes)
- Arts and Literature
- Social Studies and Natural Sciences

Science Reasoning (40 items; 35 minutes)

The composite score is the arithmetic average of the four subject area scores, rounded to the nearest whole number. Scale scores range from 1 (low) to 36 (high) for each of the four tests and for the composite. The subscale scores range from 1 (low) to 18 (high). Beginning in fall 2004, the ACT Assessment will include an optional writing component. Postsecondary institutions will each decide whether to recommend that prospective students take the ACT Assessment or the ACT Assessment Plus Writing.

SAT I: Reasoning Tests

The SAT I: Reasoning Tests were designed to measure students' academic ability in the areas of verbal and numerical reasoning, both of which are needed to do college-level work. Test developers write the questions for the SAT, sometimes incorporating questions submitted by high school and college teachers from around the country. A test committee made up of high school and college faculty and administrators reviews each test before it is administered.

The test is divided into seven separately timed sections:

Verbal (three sections; 78 items; 75 minutes)
- Analogies
- Sentence Completion
- Critical Reading

Mathematics (three sections; 60 items; 75 minutes):
Arithmetic
Algebra
Geometry

Variable (one section; 30 minutes. This section does not count toward students' scores; it is used to test new questions and make sure scores are comparable.)

The SAT I tests are reported on a scale of 200 (low) to 800 (high). A student's Verbal and Mathematics scale scores are computed by first establishing a raw score, corrected for guessing. Raw scores are converted to scores on the 200-to-800 scale. These are the scores that appear on students' score reports. Students who do not answer any questions on a test automatically receive a score of 200.

The SAT I will be substantially revised in 2005. The Verbal section will be renamed Critical Reading and will be shortened to 70 minutes; the Analogies subsection will be replaced with additional passage-based reading items. The Mathematics section will include additional items from advanced math courses such as Algebra II and will also be shortened to 70 minutes. (Math and Critical Reading sections will each have two 25-minute sections and one 20-minute section.) Essay and multiple-choice subsections will comprise a new Writing section, which will be approximately 50 minutes in length and result in a third score on the 200-to-800 scale. The Variable section will be retained but possibly shortened to result in a total testing time of about 3.5 hours.

SAT II: Subject Tests

The SAT II: Subject Tests are intended to measure students' knowledge and skills in particular subjects and their ability to apply that knowledge. Originally called Achievement Tests, the initial tests were primarily developed to aid in course placement. Over the years highly selective institutions have also used them as a supplement to the SAT I and ACT Assessment for making admissions decisions. Students use them to demonstrate their special preparation for various college programs of study.

There are 22 subject tests in Mathematics, Science (e.g., Chemistry, Biology), Social Sciences, Literature, and Foreign Languages. The content of most tests reflects general trends in high school curriculum. In some instances foreign language tests such as Hebrew, Chinese, or Korean have been developed, even though few high schools offer courses in these languages. In these instances, the SAT II tests are designed to reflect the curriculum of special academic courses that are offered in specialized schools or programs.

All SAT II tests are one-hour, multiple-choice tests, except the Writing test, which has 40 minutes of multiple-choice questions and a 20-minute writing sample section. SAT II scores are corrected for guessing and are reported on the same score scale as the SAT I (200–800). Subscores are provided for listening, usage, and reading sections of some language tests. These subscores are reported on a 20-to-80 scale. The 20-minute writing sample for the SAT II: Writing Test is scored on a 1-to-6 scale; the multiple-choice subscore is reported on the 20-to-80 scale.

ACT Assessment/SAT I Concordance

Most postsecondary institutions accept either ACT or SAT I scores for college admission. Both sets of scores are also used for college scholarships, including determining scholarship eligibility for student athletes planning to enter college. To provide equitable decisions regardless of whether students take the ACT or the SAT I, a *concordance* is needed to identify comparable scores on the two tests. ACT, Inc., the Educational Testing Service (ETS), and the College Board, in collaboration with the Associated Chief Admissions Officers of Public Universities, developed the most recent concordance tables between the ACT and the SAT I tests (Dorans, Lyu, Pommerich, & Houston, 1997). The overall correlation between the sum of the SAT I Verbal and Mathematics tests and the ACT composite score is .92. The concordance tables are based on the ACT Assessment and SAT I scores of students who took both tests between October 1994 and December 1996. These tables include concordances between SAT I Verbal and Mathematics and ACT composite, as well as between SAT I Verbal and Mathematics and ACT Sum (the sum of the scale scores on the four ACT subject area tests). Copies of the concordance tables may be obtained by contacting ACT, Inc., or the College Board. The SAT I Verbal and Mathematics and ACT composite concordance table may also be downloaded from the College Board website: www.collegeboard.com/sat/cbsenior/html/stat00f.html.

Influences on Admissions Test Scores

SAT I, SAT II, and ACT Assessment scores provide straightforward, easily interpreted information about students' readiness to undertake college coursework. In conjunction with other achievement-related and noncognitive information, they are intended to predict students' likely success in college. The SAT II and ACT Assessment tests, being achievement-based tests, are also intended to measure the skills and knowledge students have learned in high school that are necessary for success in college. They are often used to aid in college placement decisions and to predict students' likely success in specific college courses.

Scores and High School Coursework

Students' performance on the ACT Assessment and SAT II depends to a large extent on the courses they take and how well they master their high school coursework (as measured by the grades they earn in these courses). ACT research has shown that students who take college preparatory core courses in high school (four years of English and three years each of mathematics, social studies, and natural sciences) score, on average, about 2.5 scale score units higher than those who do not take core coursework (ACT, 2001). Moreover, students who take upper level mathematics or science courses in high school typically earn higher ACT scores than do students who do not take these courses, regardless of the high school they attend; how they spend their time; their perceptions of self, home, and school; or their family backgrounds (Noble, Davenport, Schiel, & Pommerich, 1999b).

Morgan (1989) found that, on average, students who take more mathematics, natural science, and foreign language courses earn higher SAT I scores. Upper level mathematics, natural science, and foreign language coursework had the strongest relationships with SAT I scores. SAT II results paralleled those for the SAT I: The level of coursework in mathematics, chemistry, biology, French, and Spanish was more closely related to their corresponding subject area test scores than was English coursework.

Differential Performance by Population Subgroups

Average differences in achievement are well documented among racial, ethnic, and gender groups on all kinds of measures of academic achievement and aptitude (e.g., ACT Assessment scores, NAEP scores, SAT scores, Stanford Achievement Test scores, performance assessments). On average, African American, Native American, Mexican American, and Hispanic students attain lower ACT and SAT scores than do Caucasian American students, with differences ranging from about .4 standard deviation units to .9 standard deviation units. Such differences on admissions tests reflect similar differences in other predictors (e.g., high school grades and rank, completion of honors courses) and college performance (freshman GPA, cumulative GPA, college graduation; Camara & Schmidt, 1999). ACT Assessment score differences between gender groups are very small: average ACT composite scores of males and females differ by only 0.04 standard deviation units (ACT, 2001). Gender differences on the SAT I Verbal and Mathematics tests are somewhat larger, with differences of .06 standard deviation units for SAT I Verbal, favoring females, and .31 standard deviation units for SAT I Mathematics, favoring males (College Board, 2001).

Students' high school coursework and grades, education-related factors (e.g., needing help with reading or mathematics, enrollment in a college preparatory curriculum), activities and behaviors, perceptions of self and others, family background, high school attended, and race, ethnicity, and gender explain only 1 to 2 percent of the variance in ACT performance (Noble, Davenport, Schiel, & Pommerich, 1999a). Similar results were found for the SAT I (Everson & Millsap, 2001).

Predicting Freshman GPA

ACT and SAT scores and high school grades and rank used jointly for making college admissions decisions yield more accurate decisions than any used alone. Bridgeman, McCamley-Jenkins, and Ervin (2000) showed an adjusted correlation of .52 between SAT I and freshman grade point average (FGPA), and an increase in the adjusted multiple correlation of .09 from SAT I over using high school GPA alone. In a study of admissions decisions at eight traditional to highly selective institutions, ACT scores alone or high school GPA alone accurately predicted academic success for about three-fourths of the students. (Academic success was defined as completing the first year of college with a C or higher average grade.) By using ACT scores and high school GPA jointly, institutions could accurately predict academic success for about 80 percent of the students (ACT, 1997).

Results from a recent study (Noble & Sawyer, 2002) indicate that ACT composite scores provide differentiation across a broader range of achievement in college than do high school grades. High school GPA was found to be slightly more accurate than the ACT composite score for predicting moderate levels of academic performance in college (e.g., 2.50 or 3.00), but the ACT composite score was more accurate than high school GPA for predicting superior levels of academic performance (e.g., 3.50 or 3.75). Similarly, SAT I correlations are higher when predicting performance in more selective colleges and among higher performing students (Ramist, Lewis, & McCamley-Jenkins, 1993).

Research has demonstrated that admissions tests are useful also in predicting college success. In fact, a meta-analysis of thousands of validation studies has shown that the adjusted correlation between SAT I and FGPA is nearly as high as that between high school GPA and FGPA (Hezlett et al., 2001). Studies have also demonstrated that admissions tests and high school GPA are the best available predictors of college persistence and graduation, although the correlations are lower than those with GPA because many factors unrelated to academic achievement affect these outcomes. Among African American, Hispanic, and Caucasian American students with the same ACT composite score, SAT I score, or high school GPA, African American and Hispanic students achieve lower FGPAs than do Caucasian American students (Noble, in press; Bridgeman et al., 2000). In other words, ACT scores, SAT scores, and high school GPAs overpredict FGPAs of African American and Hispanic students. Moreover, high school GPAs are more likely than ACT scores to overpredict FGPA. The degree of overprediction varies, however, depending on gender. Bridgeman et al. (2000) found that FGPAs of women were slightly underpredicted by SAT I Verbal and Mathematics scores. Sawyer (1985) found a similar result for ACT composite scores. For African American and Hispanic males, SAT scores overpredict FGPA, and for females from these groups, high school grades overpredict FGPA.

ACT composite score, SAT I Verbal and Mathematics score, and high school GPA are somewhat more accurate in predicting FGPAs for African American students than for Caucasian American students (Noble, in press; Bridgeman et al., 2000). In contrast, all three are slightly less accurate for Hispanics than for Caucasian Americans. SAT I scores are more accurate in predicting females' performance in college (Bridgeman et al., 2000; Noble, Crouse, & Schulz, 1996; Sawyer, 1985).

Testing Accommodations for Students with Disabilities

By law, testing companies must provide reasonable accommodations for students with qualifying disabilities, unless the accommodation will alter the intended purposes of the test or result in an undue burden. Moreover, the accommodation must be a reasonable one, but might not always be the preferred accommodation. Individual disabilities are not reported with the scores (Noble, Camara, & Fremer, 2002). Effective in fall 2003, ACT Assessment and SAT I and II score reports of those students testing under extended time conditions will no longer be flagged as testing under nonstandard conditions.

Admissions testing programs provide procedures for counselors and individuals with disabilities to follow in order to obtain accommodations. Counselors and students should refer to the ACT (www.act.org/aap/disab) and ETS (www.ets.org/disability/index.html) websites for detailed information about requesting testing accommodations.

Test Preparation

Nearly a dozen studies have been completed examining the effects of coaching on admissions tests. Results from these studies have been remarkably consistent and demonstrate that commercial coaching courses, on average, produce total gains of 21 to 34 points on a 400–1600 combined Verbal and Mathematics scale for the SAT I. Gains are typically larger for Mathematics than for Verbal sections, and coaching does not appear to benefit any particular group more than other students. Briggs (2001) examined the effects of a range of test preparation activities and found extremely small effects attributable to test preparation. He reports gains of 8 and 14 points on the SAT I Verbal and Mathematics tests, respectively, as a result of formal coaching courses, and gains of 2 to 3 points for each test as a result of software and school courses. Formal coaching courses produced gains of no more than .4 and .6 points for the ACT Mathematics and English tests, and actually resulted in lower scores on the ACT Reading test.

Retesting

About 50 percent of students who take the SAT I take the test more than once. About 11 percent of these students test more than twice. Much of the score gain often viewed as resulting from test preparation actually reflects a student's academic development, maturation, and ease and familiarity with taking a high-stakes test like the ACT Assessment or SAT I. For example, most juniors who retake the SAT I as seniors increase their scores; the average gain is 12 to 13 points on Verbal and Mathematics scales. Juniors who score high on their initial test are less likely to increase their scores as much as lower scoring students do when they retake the test.

About 36 percent of students who took the ACT Assessment in 2000–2001 took the test more than once. The average gain from first to second testing was about one composite score point. However, average score gains decreased over multiple testings (ACT, 1997).

Current Concerns and Future Directions

There has always been some controversy associated with admissions tests. Group differences in performance on admissions tests are often seen as evidence of bias. Differential access to test preparation or rigorous high school courses is viewed as giving some students unfair advantages. These concerns, however, extend to all factors used to make educational decisions, such as the rigor of courses completed, high school GPA, college grades, and extracurricular activities.

There has been increased concern that college entrance requirements are not adequately aligned with high school curriculum standards and state assessments. Some proponents of standards-based reforms have advocated using the same assessments used for K–12 accountability purposes as admissions tests for higher education. These proposals have generally not considered many of the psychometric and operational difficulties associated with such dual use of these assessments. The ACT Assessment is aligned with most high school content standards, as well as with the skills and knowledge required for success in college coursework. The SAT II is related to most high school content standards, and the SAT I is aligned to core skills required for success in college. Although some policymakers continue to advocate increased use of state assessments for college admissions (e.g., Gose & Selingo, 2001; Hebel, 2001), little research has been conducted to examine the efficacy of using such tests for multiple purposes. Several state university systems have implemented policies that guarantee admission to students who attain some rank (e.g., top 4 percent, 10 percent, 20 percent) in their high school class, irrespective of differences in academic achievement across high schools. There also appears to be increased interest in examining additional factors such as motivation, leadership, and ability to benefit that may be useful in predicting college completion and success (e.g., Gose & Selingo, 2001; Selingo, 2001)

Finally, ACT, Inc., and the College Board have continued to conduct research on computer-based testing (CBT). Graduate admissions tests and many licensing tests have already made the transition to CBT platforms for test administration and scoring. The difficulties associated with making this transition with ACT and SAT tests are much greater, given that about 4.5 million admissions tests are administered each year and that students prefer to take these tests in high school where differential access and capabilities to monitor testing exist. Yet it is likely that at some time in the future, both the ACT and SAT may change to new delivery platforms if schools continue to increase their technological capabilities.

References

ACT. (1997). *ACT Assessment technical manual.* Iowa City, IA: Author.

ACT. (2000a). *Fairness report for the ACT Assessment tests, 1999–2000.* Iowa City, IA: Author.

ACT. (2000b). *Interpreting and using test results: Standards for transition information services guide for school administrators.* Iowa City, IA: Author.

ACT. (2001). *ACT Assessment high school profile report.* Iowa City, IA: Author.

Breland, H., Maxey, J., Gernand, R., Cumming, T., & Trapani, C. (2002). *Trends in college admissions 2000: A report of a survey of undergraduate admissions policies, practices, and procedures.* Retrieved from www.airweb.org/images/trendsreport.pdf.

Bridgeman, B., McCamley-Jenkins, L., & Ervin, N. (2000). *Predictions of freshman grade point average from the revised and recentered SAT I: Reasoning Test* (College Board Research Report No. 2000–1). New York: College Entrance Examination Board.

Briggs, D. C. (2001). The effect of admissions test preparation: Evidence from NELS 88. *Chance, 14*(1) 10–18.

Camara, W. J., & Schmidt, A. (1999). *Group differences in standardized testing and social stratification* (College Board Report No. 99–5). New York: College Entrance Examination Board.

College Board. (2000). *Annual survey of colleges 2000–2001 of the College Entrance Examination Board.* New York: Author.

College Board. (2001). *2001 College-bound seniors: A profile of SAT program test takers.* Retrieved October 23, 2001, from www.collegeboard.org/sat/cbsenior/yr2001/pdf/NATL.pdf.

Dorans, N., Lyu, C. F., Pommerich, M., & Houston, W. M. (1997). Concordance between ACT Assessment and recentered SAT I sum scores. *College and University, 73*(2) 24–33.

Everson, H., & Millsap, R. E. (April 2001). *Correlates of performance on the SAT: A multilevel model.* Paper presented at the symposium on Research on Minority Issues in Testing and Assessment, at the annual meeting of the American Educational Association, Seattle, WA.

Gose, B., & Selingo, J. (2001, October 26). The SAT's greatest test. *The Chronicle of Higher Education,* 10.

Hebel, S. (2001, February 9). Universities push to influence state tests for high-school students. *The Chronicle of Higher Education,* 23.

Hezlett, S. A., Kuncel, N. R., Vey, M., Ahart, A., Ones, D., Campbell, J., & Camara, W. (2001). *The effectiveness of the SAT in predicting success early and late in college: A comprehensive meta-analysis.* A paper presented at the annual meeting of the National Council on Measurement in Education in Seattle, WA.

Morgan, R. (1989). *An examination of the relationships of academic coursework with admissions test performance* (College Board Report No. 89–6). New York: College Entrance Examination Board.

Noble, J. (in press). *The effects of using ACT composite scores and/or high school grade averages on college admissions decisions for racial/ethnic groups* (ACT Research Report Series). Iowa City, Iowa: ACT.

Noble, J., Camara, W., & Fremer, J. (2002). Postsecondary admissions testing. In R. Ekstrom & D. Smith (Eds.), *Assessing individuals with disabilities in educational, employment, and counseling settings.* Washington, DC: APA Books.

Noble, J., Crouse, J., & Schulz, M. (1996). *Differential prediction/ impact in course placement for ethnic and gender groups* (ACT Research Report 96–8). Iowa City, Iowa: ACT.

Noble, J., Davenport, M., Schiel, J., & Pommerich. M. (1999b). *Relationships between the noncognitive characteristics, high school course work and grades, and test scores of ACT-tested students* (ACT Research Report 99-4). Iowa City, IA: ACT.

Noble, J., Davenport, M., Schiel, J., & Pommerich, M. (1999a). *High school academic and noncognitive variables related to the ACT scores of racial/ethnic and gender groups* (ACT Research Report 99-6). Iowa City, IA: ACT.

Noble, J., & Sawyer, R. L. (2002). *Predicting different levels of academic success in college using high school GPA and ACT composite score* (ACT Research Report 2002–4). Iowa City, IA: ACT.

Ramist, L., Lewis, C., & McCamley-Jenkins, L. (1993). *Student group differences in predicting college grades: Sex, language and ethnic groups.* (College Board Research Report No. 93–1). New York: College Entrance Examination Board.

Sawyer, R. L. (1985). *Using demographic information in predicting college freshman grades* (ACT Research Report 87). Iowa City, IA: ACT.

Selingo, J. (2001, November 23). Broader admissions criteria near approval at U. of California. *The Chronicle of Higher Education,* 24.

Chapter 21
Assessment and College Course Placement
Matching Students with Appropriate Instruction

Julie P. Noble, Jeff L. Schiel & Richard L. Sawyer

College course placement systems match students with instruction that is appropriate to their academic preparation and other characteristics. For example, students whose scores on a mathematics placement test suggest that their academic skills are not sufficiently developed for them to succeed in a standard freshman mathematics course (e.g., college algebra) might be advised or required to enroll in a lower level mathematics course (e.g., elementary algebra).

At a minimum, course placement involves assessing students' academic skills and providing them with instruction that is appropriate to their skills. Student advising is also an important factor in the course placement process because students' academic success can be considerably affected by their nonacademic characteristics. For example, consider a student who cares for a child, works 40 hours per week, and is taking courses for a particular occupational goal. Another student who has the same placement test scores but has no dependents, is supported by her or his parents, and has no particular occupational goals may be advised to take different courses. College advisers are in the best position to observe these noncognitive characteristics, to interpret them, and to give appropriate advice to students.

Types of Course Placement

Course placement systems in different institutions vary in structure, in the assessments that are used, and in the assignment of course credit. Counselors should encourage students to visit the websites of institutions of interest to obtain detailed information about specific course placement procedures and policies.

Upon entry to college, students might encounter different types of course placement: remedial course placement; advanced, honors or accelerated course placement; credit by examination; or English as a second language (ESL) placement. Remedial course placement is perhaps the most common type and affects a relatively large number of entering college students. It is also the focus of much political debate. As such, remedial course placement is the primary focus of this chapter. After brief discussion of the other three types of placement, we discuss the characteristics of remedial course placement systems, currently debated issues concerning remedial instruction, the types of measures used, and technical issues.

Remedial Course Placement

Identifying and providing appropriate instruction for students who are not academically prepared to take traditional first-year courses in college are particularly important today. Policymakers, the press, and the general public usually label college courses provided to academically underprepared students as remedial. In contrast, educators refer to them as developmental, particularly when the courses are based on developmental theory. Following common practice, we use the term *remedial* in this chapter. Of course, what constitutes remedial, standard, and advanced varies from institution to institution.

According to a survey by the American Association of Community Colleges (AACC; Shults, 2000), two-year colleges typically offer four or more levels of remedial mathematics, two levels of remedial reading, two levels of remedial writing, and one level of remedial science. About 95 percent of two-year institutions offer remedial mathematics, reading, and writing. Less than 50 percent of two-year institutions offer remedial science.

Although most institutions and states do not allow students to obtain degree credit for remedial coursework (McCabe, 2000; Shults, 2000), most two- and four-year colleges allow students to take college-level courses concurrently with remedial coursework (NCES, 1996; Shults, 2000). Policies related to taking degree or certificate courses concurrently with remedial coursework vary from institution to institution, so college-bound students need to obtain pertinent information from their preferred institutions (NCES, 1996).

There is little information available about institutional policies related to students' taking remedial and standard-level coursework in the same subject area at the same time. Anecdotal evidence indicates that this practice typically does not occur with English and mathematics courses; however, students are frequently allowed to take remedial reading courses while taking reading-intensive courses such as history, psychology, and other humanities courses.

Advanced, Accelerated, or Honors Course Placement

Successful Advanced Placement (AP) Examination scores in high school (typically scores of 4 or 5) usually permit students to obtain college course credit in tested subject areas, or to achieve advanced course placement in those subject areas in college (College Board, 2001a; College Entrance Examination Board, 1980). Advanced college courses typically parallel standard-level college courses in subject matter but present these subjects at a higher level. Institutions vary in their use of AP scores for course placement.

Credit by Examination

College-Level Examination Program (CLEP) tests and the Excelsior College Examinations (formerly Regents College Examinations) are used to award college credit for prior learning, as well as for advanced course placement (College Board, 2001b; Excelsior College, 2001). More than 2,900 colleges and universities award credit for satisfactory CLEP scores. See the CLEP website (www.collegeboard.com/clep) or the Excelsior College Examinations website (www.excelsior.edu/exams/xms_indx.htm) for more information.

English as a Second Language (ESL) Course Placement

ESL course placement is intended to guide non-native English speakers into courses to improve their English reading and writing skills. About 50 percent of postsecondary institutions offer ESL courses (NCES, 1996; Shults, 2000). Placement into ESL courses is similar in structure to remedial course placement; however, less than 40 percent of postsecondary institutions consider ESL courses as part of their remedial education program (NCES, 1998).

Current Status of Remedial Education

In 1994, *Education Week* reported that postsecondary remedial instruction had increased from being offered in 81 percent of all four-year institutions in 1985–1986 to 90 percent in 1993–1994, and from 85 percent of all two-year institutions to 93 percent during the same time period. A more recent NCES study (Korb, 1999) reported that 99 percent of two-year institutions, 85 percent of public four-year institutions, and 63 to 68 percent of four-year private for-profit and nonprofit institutions offer remedial programs.

A significant percentage of college students are involved in remedial coursework, according to the standards of the institutions in which they are enrolled. McCabe (2000) found that 41 percent of entering community college students and 29 percent of entering four-year college students are underprepared in at least one of the basic skills areas. This means more than one million underprepared students are entering college and enrolling in remedial programs. According to Saxon and Boylan (as cited in McCabe, 2000), 20 percent of entering students are underprepared in reading, 25 percent are underprepared in writing, and 34 percent are underprepared in mathematics. In 1998, 64 percent of students entering the California state college system failed the entry-level mathematics test, and 43 percent failed the verbal test (Estrich, 1998). All these students were in the top one-third of their graduating classes.

Postsecondary institutions and states are closely scrutinizing the costs and benefits of remedial instruction. Estimates of the cost of providing remedial instruction in the United States range from about one billion dollars—roughly 1 percent of all public expenditures for postsecondary education (Phipps, 1998)—to three or more times this amount (Costrell, 1998). Some authors deplore the consequences of remedial instruction in college. They believe that it corrupts the curriculum, demoralizes faculty, and acquiesces to low standards in high school (Costrell, 1998). Phipps (1998), on the other hand, argues for the social benefits of remedial instruction: increased tax revenues, greater economic productivity, reduced crime rates, and increased quality of civic life.

Two results of this scrutiny are discernable. First, some states have given responsibility for remedial instruction to two-year colleges and have entirely removed remedial course placement from four-year institutions. Second, some institutions have outsourced remedial instruction to private organizations (including for-profit organizations).

Remedial Education: Whose Responsibility?

Some assert that because remedial education is not college-level instruction, four-year institutions should not provide it (Ignash, 1997). In 1998 the City University of New York (CUNY) system proposed that admission to four-year institutions be withdrawn from students who failed to pass the placement tests, and that these students be directed to community colleges (Kirst, 1998). This policy is now in effect. California and Georgia have instituted similar policies (Hebel, 1999; Hoff, 1998).

Assessment and College Course Placement

Outsourcing Remedial Instruction

Recently postsecondary institutions have expressed interest in outsourcing remedial instruction to private agencies. Three outsourcing options are to contract out remedial services to off-campus private providers or to on-campus private providers, or to use faculty to provide remedial services developed by a vendor. Kaplan Educational Centers and Sylvan Learning Centers both provide remedial services; colleges from several states are considering hiring these businesses to provide remedial instruction (Gose, 1997). Current research is inconclusive, however, about the relative merits of outsourcing remedial education over providing it on local campuses (Phipps, 1998).

For college-bound students who are interested in attending particular institutions, the best sources of information about local remedial education policies are institutional websites. Depending on state or institutional policies, some students' first-choice institution may not be an option if they are underprepared in reading, writing, or mathematics.

Other Course Placement Issues

Students and counselors need to be aware of two additional issues related to course placement systems: mandatory versus voluntary course placement, and time limits on remedial coursework. Both have implications for the length of time students take to complete their educational programs.

Mandatory versus voluntary course placement. Some institutions require students to follow placement recommendations for remedial coursework, whereas other institutions allow students some choice in the decision. In the latter situation, students should consult with academic advisers who can provide detailed information about the courses under consideration. Either way, students need to consider the implications on their educational and career plans of taking remedial coursework.

Time limits on remedial coursework. In the interest of reducing the quantity of remedial education programs, states and institutions are moving toward limiting the amount of remedial coursework students can take. According to an AACC survey (Shults, 2000), 23 percent of community colleges use various means to limit the number of remedial courses taken, such as raising tuition after multiple attempts to complete a remedial course successfully.

Measuring Students' Readiness for College-Level Work

Several measures are used to estimate students' readiness for college-level work. Among community colleges, for example, common measures include college admissions tests, high school GPA, commercially developed placement tests, AP Examinations, institutionally developed tests, and state-developed tests (Shults, 2000). Other, more subjective, approaches for identifying students who require remedial coursework include faculty or staff referral, and student self-referral (NCES, 1996).

Placement Test Scores and High School Grades

About 60 percent of postsecondary institutions administer placement tests (either commercially or institutionally developed) to all their entering students (NCES, 1996). Hills, Hirsch, and Subhiyah (1990) describe how the wide use of placement tests is a result, in part, of the measurement quality they can provide. Placement tests are, in many instances, objective measures, and the degree of imprecision (i.e., measurement error) of their scores can be estimated fairly accurately. In addition, test scores can be made equivalent across alternate forms of a test to prevent problems with variability in meaning.

Grades, in comparison, are subjective measures whose degree of imprecision is difficult to estimate. They seem efficient for placement decisions because they directly measure, at least in principle, the types of academic skills necessary for successful performance in college (Hills et al., 1990). Course quality and content vary among high schools, however, and grades can vary in meaning from school to school because of differing curricular frameworks and grade reporting procedures. Moreover, students who eventually decide to attend postsecondary institutions may not take college-preparatory courses in high school and, therefore, may not have the corresponding course grades (Hills et al., 1990).

Using multiple measures to determine students' preparedness for college significantly increases placement accuracy (ACT, 1997; Gordon, 1999; Roueche & Roueche, 1999). For example, test scores and high school grades may be used jointly to identify students who are ready for college-level work.

Computer-Based Placement Testing

Traditionally, placement tests have been administered in paper-and-pencil formats, but computerized administration methods are becoming more common. For example, 63 percent of community colleges report using computerized placement testing (Shults, 2000). Items from a paper-and-pencil placement test may be administered via a computer (*computer-based testing*), or a computer-administered placement test may be tailored during administration according to a student's ability level (*computerized adaptive testing*). Computerized adaptive placement testing has several advantages over paper-and-pencil testing, including reduced testing time (by up to 50 percent), quick reporting of results, increased security of test items, adaptation to a wide range of student abilities, reduced proctoring, and flexibility in testing schedules (Smittle, 1994). Some students, however, may not be familiar with computers, and some institutions may have difficulty acquiring the necessary computer hardware (Shermis, Wolting, & Lombard, 1996).

Testing in High School Versus in College

Placement testing may occur in high school or in college, depending on state and institutional policies. Hills et al. (1990) noted that placement testing in high school appeals to postsecondary institutions because it lessens the demands placed on students during the first few weeks of college. College placement testing, in comparison, appeals to high schools because they avoid testing large numbers of high school students who may not even attend college. (Note that some tests that are used for placement, such as the Texas Academic Skills Program [TASP], are administered either in high school or in college.) To ensure students meet appropriate course placement requirements, they need to refer to information provided by particular postsecondary institutions of interest. Counselors and students can also refer to testing program websites for additional information.

Placement Testing in High School

Several placement test options are available to high school students. For example, students may take the ACT Assessment, AP Examinations, the SAT I, or the SAT II, all of which are used in college course placement programs (Hills et al., 1990; NCES, 1996). Note that a student may take more than one of these tests in high school; for example, he or she could choose to take the ACT Assessment and one or more AP Examinations. For a complete discussion of the ACT Assessment, the SAT I, and the SAT II, see chapter 20 on college admissions testing and see the websites of these programs:

ACT Assessment: http://www.act.org
AP Examinations: http://apcentral.collegeboard.com/program/
SAT I and SAT II: http://www.collegeboard.com/

State-developed tests, such as those in the following list, are also administered in high school and are being considered for use in course placement decisions.

Texas: TASP, www.tasp.nesinc.com/fac_sec1.htm
Kentucky: Commonwealth Accountability Testing System (CATS), www.kentuckyschools.net/KDE Administrative+Resources/Testing+and+Reporting+/CATS/default.htm
California: Golden State Examinations (GSE), www.cde.ca.gov/statetests/gse/index.html

Placement Testing in College

Colleges may use any of several commercially developed placement tests. Institutions sometimes also administer the ACT and the SAT I (and, at some institutions, the SAT II) on campus to enrolled college students. The following are three commonly used commercially developed placement tests:

ACCUPLACER (Internet-delivered, computerized adaptive system): www.collegeboard.com/highered/apr/accu/accu.html
ASSET (two-year college advising, placement, and retention system): www.act.org/asset/
COMPASS (computerized adaptive placement and diagnostic system): www.act.org/compass/index.html

Institutions may also choose to develop their own local placement tests to administer to entering students, particularly if in reviewing commercially developed placement tests, postsecondary faculty and staff decide that the tests do not adequately reflect the content of certain courses. Examples of institutionally developed test types include multiple-choice tests (see, e.g., McFate & Olmstead, 1999), performance measures (see, e.g., Bachman, Lynch, & Mason, 1995), writing samples that supplement multiple-choice placement tests (see, e.g., Galbato & Markus, 1995), and Internet-delivered, computerized adaptive tests (see, e.g., Shermis, Mzumara, Brown, & Lillig, 1997).

Technical Issues

In this section, we discuss three technical issues: How do colleges set their cutoff scores on placement tests? How can post-testing be used to improve students' academic success? How do colleges evaluate their course placement systems?

Cutoff Scores

A cutoff score on a placement test is the minimum score students must achieve in order to be advised or permitted to enroll in a particular course. Students who score lower than the cutoff on the placement test are advised or required to enroll in a lower level (e.g., remedial) course. Cutoff scores can be set in several ways: through expert (faculty) judgment, by using norms, by using predictions of success, or on the advice of the test publisher.

Expert judgment requires review of course prerequisites and the items on the placement test. First, faculty members at the institution using the test must specify in detail the minimum knowledge and skills that students need in order to learn course material. Faculty members then review the placement test to determine which score corresponds to a minimal level of preparation to take the course.

Norms (local or national) indicate how many students score at or below particular score levels. Faculty at an institution may know from past experience that a certain rough percentage of their students are prepared to take a particular course. By matching this percentage to the norms, an institution can determine a cutoff score. An institution may also use norms to allocate students to courses based on available resources, such as faculty members or classrooms that are available.

Prediction methods for setting cutoff scores are based on statistical analyses of the relationship between test scores and grades in a course. A statistical model can be developed that shows, for any score on the placement test, a student's chances of success (i.e., completing the course with a given grade or higher). The model also provides evidence of the *predictive validity* of a test for course placement: Higher scores should correspond to higher chances of success. The model can further be used to estimate accuracy rates for different potential cutoff scores. An *accuracy rate* is the proportion of students for whom a correct placement decision is made (Sawyer, 1996).

Test publishers may recommend cutoff scores for particular types of courses (see, e.g., ACT, 2000). These recommendations are useful when an institution has no previous experience with or data on a test but needs to set a cutoff score. The institution should follow up, as soon as is practicable, with its own validity research to adjust the score recommended by the publisher.

Knowing how a cutoff score was set will give students and their advisers a better understanding of placement test scores and a sound basis for making decisions about which courses to take.

Post-testing

A principal reason for providing remedial instruction is to give students an opportunity to acquire the academic skills they need in order to succeed in higher level courses. Institutions vary in their policies about verifying whether individual students do, in fact, achieve this goal. Some institutions require students to retake the placement test (known as *post-testing*). If students have acquired the necessary knowledge and skills, then the test scores they obtain at the end of the remedial course should exceed the scores they obtained at the beginning of the course. Students may be required to meet or exceed the cutoff scores on their post-tests before they are permitted to enroll in higher level courses.

Before deciding to enroll in a particular institution, students need to ask about the institution's post-testing policy. If post-testing is mandatory, and if meeting or exceeding a cutoff is required, then students will want to know their chances of doing so.

Evaluating Course Placement Systems

Before a course placement system can be designed and implemented at an institution, administrators and faculty must decide to allocate resources to the various components of the system. The resulting decisions are often difficult because the required resources may be substantial and could be allocated to other worthy programs or projects. It is therefore important that institutions evaluate the costs and benefits of their course placement systems.

Administrators and faculty should consider two primary questions when evaluating a system:

Correct identification. Are students placed in the correct courses? The accuracy rate and other predictive validity statistics (see previous discussion about cutoff scores) provide useful information about correct identification.

Effectiveness of low-level courses. Are students who are placed in low-level courses actually benefiting from taking them? There are two general methods for documenting the effectiveness of instruction in low-level courses.

1. Post-testing: Effectiveness of the low-level course can be assessed by the proportion of students whose post-test scores exceed the cutoff, and by the average score gain from initial placement testing to post-testing (Sawyer & Schiel, 2000).
2. Collecting follow-up data on students as they take regular college-level courses: With such data, one can relate students' initial placement test scores to the chances of their eventual success in the college-level courses. By comparing chances of success of students who took a low-level course with those who did not take the low-level course, one can estimate the benefit of taking the low-level course for students with any given placement test score.

Other important considerations when evaluating course placement systems include noncognitive characteristics and the costs and benefits of course placement. Administrative data (e.g., the number of students who are tested, exempted from testing, or who file appeals of placement decisions), or data on student or faculty affective characteristics (e.g., do students believe the advice they have been given is appropriate?) can, when monitored over time, signal changes in how well the system is working. Using standardized survey forms, administrators can also compare their students' opinions to those of students at similar institutions. (A variety of survey forms are available through Evaluation Survey Services: www.act.org/ess/index.html.)

Murtuza and Ketkar (1995) studied a course placement and advising program at an urban university for the program's effect on retention and for its cost-effectiveness. They found that the program was cost-effective (the extra tuition resulting from higher retention rates offset the cost of the program), but their analysis of data from only recent years produced an inconclusive result. They also found that a centralized program (in which staff were hired and assigned to work specifically on course placement and advising) was more cost-effective than a decentralized program (in which these functions were assigned as additional duties to faculty members).

Summary

College course placement, particularly remedial course placement, pervades postsecondary education. State and institutional policies will continue to dictate how and where remedial programs are provided to students, and the standards students are required to meet when enrolling in particular institutions. Counselors of potential college students need to be aware of these issues and their implications for students' postsecondary plans. Depending on the student and his or her level of educational achievement, such policies and standards may dictate the type of institution in which the student *can* enroll (e.g., two- or four-year), and the length of time necessary for the student to complete his or her postsecondary educational goal.

References

ACT. (1997). *ACT Assessment technical manual.* Iowa City, IA: ACT.

ACT. (2000). *ACT Assessment cutoff scores and validity statistics for placement in first-year courses in college.* Iowa City, IA: ACT.

Bachman, L. F., Lynch, B. K., & Mason, M. (1995). Investigating variability in tasks and rater judgments in a performance test of foreign language speaking. *Language Testing, 12*(2), 238–257.

College Board. (2001a). *Advanced Placement Program.* Retrieved from http://apcentral.collegeboard.com/program/

College Board. (2001b). *College-Level Examination Program.* Retrieved October 19, 2001, from www.collegeboard.org/clep/.

College Entrance Examination Board. (1980). *Credit by examination comes of age.* New York: Author.

Costrell, R. M. (1998). Commentary on David W. Breneman and William N. Haarlow's Remedial Education: Costs and Consequences, a paper featured at the Remediation in Higher Education symposium. Retrieved April 12, 1999, from www.edexcellence.net/library/remed.html.

Estrich, S. (1998, May 12). It's not who goes to college: It's who can stay there. *USAToday,* p. 13A.

Excelsior College. (2001). *Excelsior College Examinations.* Retrieved from www.excelsior.edu/exams/xms_indx.htm.

Galbato, L. B., & Markus, M. (1995). A comparison study of three methods of evaluating student writing ability for student placement in introductory English courses. *Journal of Applied Research in the Community Colleges, 2*(2), 153–167.

Gordon, R. J. (1999, January). *Using computer adaptive testing and multiple measures to ensure that students are placed in courses appropriate for their skill levels.* Paper presented at the Third North American Conference on the Learning Paradigm, San Diego, CA. (ERIC Document Reproduction Service No. ED425781)

Gose, B. (1997, September 19). Tutoring companies take over remedial teaching at some colleges. *Chronicle of Higher Education, 44,* A44–A45.

Hebel, S. (1999, April). Georgia strives to raise standards without leaving students behind. *Chronicle of Higher Education, 46,* A34–A36.

Higher education at a glance: Colleges and universities offering remedial instruction and tutoring. (1994, April 13). In Alliance for learning: Enlisting higher education in the quest for better schools [Education Week special report]. *Education Week,* 6.

Hills, J. R., Hirsch, T. M., & Subhiyah, R. G. (1990). *Issues in college placement.* Washington, DC: American Institutes for Research.

Hoff, P. S. (1998). The Cal State trustees remediation policy: Assessment as part of the problem and part of the solution. *Assessment Update, 10,* 2, 5.

Ignash, J. M. (1997). Who should provide postsecondary remedial/ developmental education? *New Directions for Community Colleges, 100,* 5–20.

Kirst, M. (1998, September 9). Bridging the remedial gap. *Education Week,* 76.

Korb, R. (1999). *Postsecondary institutions in the United States: 1997–98.* Washington, DC: National Center for Education Statistics.

McCabe, R. H. (2000). *No one to waste.* Washington, DC: Community College Press.

McFate, C., & Olmstead, J. (1999). Assessing student preparation through placement tests. *Journal of Chemical Education, 76*(4), 562–565.

Murtuza, A., & Ketkar, K. (1995). Evaluating the cost-effectiveness of a freshman studies program on an urban campus. *Journal of the Freshman Year Experience, 7*(1), 7–26.

NCES [National Center for Education Statistics]. (1996). *Remedial education at higher education institutions in fall 1995* (NCES 97–584). Washington, DC: U.S. Department of Education, Office of Educational Research and Improvement.

NCES. (1998). *Profile of undergraduates in U.S. postsecondary education institutions 1995–96.* Washington, DC: U.S. Department of Education, Office of Educational Research and Improvement.

Phipps, R. (1998). *College remediation: What it is, what it costs, what's at stake.* Washington, DC: Institute for Higher Education Policy.

Roueche, J. E., & Roueche, S. D. (1999). *High stakes, high performance: Making remedial education work.* Washington, DC: American Association of Community Colleges.

Sawyer, R. L. (1996). Decision theory models for validating course placement tests. *Journal of Educational Measurement, 33,* 271–290.

Sawyer, R. L., & Schiel, J. L. (2000). *Posttesting students to assess the effectiveness of remedial instruction in college.* (ACT Research Report No. 2000–7). Iowa City, IA: ACT.

Shermis, M. D., Mzumara, H., Brown, M., & Lillig, C. (1997). *Computerized adaptive testing through the world wide web.* Indianapolis, IN: Indiana University Purdue University. (ERIC Document Reproduction Service No. ED414536)

Shermis, M. D., Wolting, M., & Lombard, D. (1996). Computerized adaptive testing for reading placement and diagnostic assessment. *Journal of Developmental Education, 20*(2), 18–24.

Shults, C. (2000). *Remedial education: Practices and policies in community colleges* (Research Brief AACC-RB-00–2). Washington, DC: American Association of Community Colleges.

Smittle, P. (1994). Computerized adaptive testing: Revolutionizing academic assessment. *Community College Journal, 65,* 32–38.

Willingham, W. W. (1974). *College placement and exemption.* New York: College Entrance Examination Board.

Chapter 22
Test Consumers in the Military
Use of the Military Career Exploration Program in Schools

Janice H. Laurence

The military is not just a job—it's hundreds of jobs, with plenty of positions to boot. In terms of providing education, training, and employment, the military is unparalleled. The army, navy, marine corps, and air force enlist about 200,000 new recruits and commission more than 16,000 officers annually for active duty. These newcomers top off an incumbent strength of almost 1.4 million active members. Although most of the almost 900,000 selected reservists have had active duty experience, well more than 50,000 come in fresh from civilian life (Department of Defense, 2000).

Besides the traditional combat and seamanship roles, the enlisted military workforce comprises technicians, clerks, administrative associates, mechanics, computer specialists, high-tech equipment operators and repair specialists, health care specialists, and a host of other positions. Table 1 shows the occupational distribution of the enlisted ranks as of fiscal year 1999 (Department of Defense, 2000).

Table 1. Occupational Distribution of U.S. Military Enlisted Force (1999)

Department of Defense Occupational Group	Percentage of Enlisted Force
Infantry, gun crews, and seamanship specialists	17.0
Electronic equipment repair specialists	9.4
Communications and intelligence specialists	9.0
Medical and dental specialists	6.9
Other allied specialists	3.0
Functional support and administration	6.0
Electrical/mechanical equipment repair specialists	19.8
Craftspeople	3.5
Service and supply handlers	8.5
Nonoccupational military	6.9

About one in six enlisted members could be classified as a combat job incumbent or a general military employee, whereas one in five serves in a high-tech job in electronic equipment repair, communications and intelligence, or other allied specialist. Even combat jobs have become more technologically complex and relatively less labor intensive over the years—and more manpower has been added behind the combat scenes. Although most military jobs are in the blue collar category (infantry, gun crew, seamanship specialists; electrical and mechanical equipment repair specialists; and craftspeople), white collar positions (electronic equipment repair specialists; communications and intelligence specialists; medical and dental specialists; other technical and allied specialists; and administration) are almost as plentiful.

The most common jobs in the military are in electrical and mechanical equipment repair, with about one in five armed services workers engaged as an aircraft, automobile, and engine mechanic; ordnance mechanic; line installer; or radio, radar, and sonar equipment repair specialist. About one in six military workers is employed in administration as a stock and inventory clerk, shipping and receiving clerk, dispatcher, and the like.

The military services do not cull seasoned civilian workers to fill the ranks. Instead, they recruit novices and train them to perform myriad duties. Evidence shows that entry-level military jobs are more complex and demanding of workers than are civilian jobs (Laurence, 1994). Thus, selection and classification testing (i.e., assessment) is critical to staffing the military.

Military Career Counseling

Given military workforce requirements, is it any wonder that the military is a steadfast consumer—and producer—of career assessments? The military has in fact been a trailblazer with regard to cognitive test development and validation (Eitelberg, Laurence, & Waters, 1984). Numerous psychometricians and educational psychologists dedicate their efforts to maintain, update, advance, and monitor the exemplary cognitive testing program of the Department of Defense (DoD). The Armed Services Vocational Aptitude Battery (ASVAB; DoD, 1999) measures aptitudes in 10 areas (General Science, Arithmetic Reasoning, Word Knowledge, Paragraph Comprehension, Numerical Operations, Coding Speed, Auto and Shop Information, Mathematics Knowledge, Mechanical Comprehension, and Electronics Information). Various combinations of these subtests are used to assess overall cognitive aptitude as well as aptitudes for performing in specific jobs.

The ASVAB contributes to personnel selection and placement decisions and hence is an important component of military personnel readiness. The attention and resources focused on norming and validation with regard to technical training grades, administrative records, supervisory ratings, job knowledge test scores, and hands-on job performance measures are laudable and unparalleled (see, e.g., Bock & Mislevy, 1981; Fairbank et al., 1990; Green & Wigdor, 1991; Green, Wing, & Wigdor, 1988). Indeed, ASVAB results reliably indicate one's standing relative to the U.S. population of youth ages 18 to 23. Time and again, studies have shown that subtest composite scores fairly and validly assess the likelihood of achieving technical proficiency or effectiveness across the wide spectrum of jobs found in the military (most of which have civilian counterparts).

Since 1968, the DoD has offered the ASVAB at no cost to high schools nationwide to promote career exploration and to facilitate recruiting. Known originally as the Student Testing Program (STP), this idea blossomed over the years into the Career Exploration Program (CEP)—a professional and comprehensive career counseling tool for schools and students. Service recruiters receive the names and ASVAB scores of participating students who agree to have this information released. Thus, there are strings attached to CEP participation, but they are not demanding.

Each year, about 900,000 students in more than 14,000 schools take the ASVAB. More than one fourth of high school seniors participate in the CEP at some point during high school (Baker, 2000). The CEP is designed to help students, primarily 11th- and 12th-graders, explore both military and civilian careers through materials that support educational and career counseling. Recruiters can use the results to identify individuals who qualify for military service. Three primary CEP components assess aptitudes, interests, and work values:

1. The 10 ASVAB subtests are combined and scores are reported on three composites: Verbal Ability, Math Ability, and Academic Ability. ASVAB codes highlight similarities between the aptitude levels of test takers and those of incumbents already performing various jobs. Military Career Scores estimate the likelihood that an individual will qualify for enlistment.
2. The Interest-Finder identifies areas of interest to the test taker (Realistic, Investigative, Artistic, Social, Enterprising, and Conventional).

3. OCCU-FIND links ASVAB and Interest-Finder results, along with other information (e.g., educational goals, work values) to 201 occupations organized by interest area.

Detailed test results (and interpretation) are provided to students, with copies for counselors. Besides the support provided by Education Services Specialists (ESS), civilians with an educational or counseling background, and recruiters, materials are available to help school staff, students, and their parents get the most out of the CEP. These include the *Educator and Counselor Guide, Student and Parent Guide, Counselor Manual, Student Workbook, Military Careers, Technical Manual,* and *Recruiter Guide.* (Most of these documents are available for download from the ASVAB website at www.asvabprogram.com.) The ASVAB is also incorporated into many Career Information Delivery Systems (CIDS)—computerized career information systems made available by states, regions, and commercial vendors.

Recruiting

Military recruiting is always challenging. Getting the word out about military career opportunities is therefore a vital service of the CEP. The ASVAB CEP is an effective marketing and recruiting tool. The program is valued by recruiters as a means of obtaining access to schools, making contact with individual students, and identifying those who are qualified for and interested in military service. Up to one fifth of CEP participants subsequently enlist in the military (Laurence & Ramsberger, 1999).

Evidence suggests that the CEP is a positive influence on those who formerly held neutral or negative views regarding military service (Laurence, Wall, Barnes, & Dela Rosa, 1998). CEP participants are more likely to express an interest in joining one of the military services as a result of the information obtained through the CEP. In addition, data suggest that CEP participants are more likely than nonparticipants to view the military as a place where they can obtain money for education, learn a valuable trade or skill, and receive job preparation.

The ASVAB CEP targets non–college-bound youth. Largely because of its vocational emphasis, the CEP has traditionally been more attractive to young people who are not considering postsecondary education, at least not for the immediate future. Given the increasing numbers of students choosing postsecondary educational opportunities, however, it is important for students to recognize the college opportunities afforded by the military, such as the Voluntary Education Program, the Montgomery GI Bill, and the officer track (Asch, Kilburn, & Klerman, 1999). Besides exploring career and other opportunities afforded by the military, college-bound youth can benefit from exposure to the CEP testing process and outcomes.

Career Decisions

Schools that participate in the CEP choose to do so for a number of reasons: the program is free; it is an effective tool for counseling non–college-bound youth; it provides an opportunity for military career exploration; and it is a readily available, well-documented career exploration tool. Further, the CEP is comprehensive and effective in meeting school career counseling needs, has a positive impact on student career exploration, and is at least as good as other programs (Laurence & Ramsberger, 1999). The vocational emphasis of the program as well as the supplementary materials (e.g., *Student Workbook*) and counseling support provided by the military fill a void, especially in economically deprived schools. Although many students are well prepared for the frenetic activities of registering, paying, and convening for the ACT Assessment or the SAT, others, without plans for college or mentors to show them the ropes, might well remain forgotten without the CEP.

The ASVAB alone provides invaluable information for civilian career counseling. Composites from the ASVAB are predictive of high school course grades (Fairbank, Welsh, & Sawin, 1990). ASVAB tests also correlate highly with comparable tests from civilian aptitude and achievement batteries (Department of Defense, 1999). Based on patterns of ASVAB scores, Armstrong, Chalupsky, McLaughlin, and Dalldorf (1988) classified a sample of individuals into their civilian occupations with a statistically significant degree of accuracy. Even more salient is a study that provides direct evidence of the criterion-related validity of the ASVAB for a sample of 11 different civilian occupations (e.g., bus driver, computer operator, word processor, nurse, electronics technician; Holmgren & Dalldorf, 1993). Further, the accepted theory of validity generalization together with the results of a military-civilian occupational crosswalk extend this mound of evidence from military occupations and the congruent findings from selected civilian jobs to additional occupations. In other words, the ASVAB has demonstrated validity for military and civilian jobs. It is technically acceptable to extrapolate these findings to encompass jobs for which performance is validly predicted by measures highly correlated with ASVAB and for jobs that are highly similar to those included in ASVAB validation studies (Department of Defense, 1999). That is, there is sound statistical evidence that test validity is not situation- or job-specific; rather, if validity is established in one job, it holds for similar jobs. Certainly ASVAB validity has been established above and beyond applicable professional testing guidelines and practices.

The DoD has gone beyond investment in the development and administration of the ASVAB, and program evaluation extends beyond its value in recruiting. Systematic evaluation efforts have provided sound evidence that adolescents who participate in this broad-based program show an increase in career development efforts (Baker, in press; Levine, Huberman, & Wall, 1996). The national normative base of 18- to 23-year-olds, most appropriate for enlistment decisions, was supplemented for CEP use with a high school sample of almost 10,000 students in grades 10 through 12. The inclusion of the additional sample of high school students reinforces the utility of the CEP, especially for participants in 10th grade (Department of Defense, 1999).

The CEP is based upon sound psychometric and vocational personality theory (Wall & Baker, 1997). Participants are provided with more than just scores indicating their standing relative to others; the program helps students to identify occupations consistent with their interests, abilities, and values. The program provides practical information regarding the cognitive demands of and typical educational preparation needed for particular jobs, and the degree to which these jobs match one's preferences for certain activities and the values that one is looking to satisfy through one's career (e.g., challenge, creativity, physical activity, independence; Wall, 1994). This comprehensive and integrated program under DoD's aegis promotes knowledge of self, occupational opportunities, and the world of work. It reduces career confusion and facilitates judgments of career attractiveness (Baker, in press).

Some Parting Thoughts on the CEP

With its dual goals of recruiting and career counseling, the CEP does not operate without suspicion or conflict. Those suspicious of military recruiting efforts can rest assured that the program has strong technical underpinnings. Aptitudes, interests, and preferences are indeed linked to civilian, not just military, jobs. Occupations included for exploration in the OCCU-FIND represent "the range of diversity in the world of work" (Wall, 1994, p. 610). Rather than limiting options, the

CEP encourages rather wide and warranted exploration. The accompanying materials highlight occupations within two contiguous cognitive complexity levels, three interest areas, and up to six personal preferences (Wall, Wise, & Baker, 1996). Certainly, an aim of the program is to garner recruiting leads; however, participants may opt not to share their results with military recruiters.

There is conflict with regard to participation because military recruiters would prefer to test only high school seniors—those who have a shot at helping them meet their recruiting objectives. There is no outcry at including juniors, but extending the CEP to sophomores (or freshmen) may be viewed as a waste of precious recruiting resources and detrimental to recruiters' short-term, "put 'em in boots" perspective. Needless to say, from a career counseling perspective, career exploration should begin early—well before the senior year of high school. This conflict does not speak ill of the program. Quite the contrary; it is the effectiveness of the CEP for recruiting and career counseling that is at the conflict's core.

Although the program is already top-notch, improvements are on the horizon. In response to demographic trends and changes in the workplace, DoD is modifying its testing and assessment practices and technical underpinnings. The psychometric properties and functioning of the Interest-Finder are scheduled for a tune-up as are the ASVAB's accompanying materials. What's more, the version of the ASVAB that is used for operational enlistment decisions is expected to have an interest measure folded in before long.

The military offers education, training, and employment to novices to the workforce, our nation's youth. The military continues to be a trailblazer with regard to testing and human resource assessment. No compendium on career counseling would be complete without mentioning the military. This chapter provides merely a condensed snapshot of the CEP and DoD's commitment to career assessment for both military and civilian careers.

References

Armstrong, T. R., Chalupsky, A. B., McLaughlin, D. H., & Dalldorf, M. R. (1988). *Armed Services Vocational Aptitude Battery: Validity for civilian occupations* (AFHRL-TR-88–20). Brooks Air Force Base, TX: Air Force Human Resources Laboratory.

Asch, B. J., Kilburn, M. R., & Klerman, J. A. (1999). *Attracting college-bound youth into the military.* Santa Monica, CA: RAND.

Baker, H. E. (2000, July). *Cross-sectional vs. cohort participation rates.* Paper presented at the meeting of the National Center for Education Statistics (NCES) Summer Data Conference, Washington, DC.

Baker, H. E. (in press). Reducing adolescent career indecision: The ASVAB Career Exploration Program. *Career Development Quarterly.*

Bock, R. D., & Mislevy, R. J. (1981). *The profile of American youth: Data quality analysis of the Armed Services Vocational Aptitude Battery.* Chicago, IL: National Opinion Research Center.

Department of Defense. (1999, December). *Technical manual for the ASVAB 18/19 Career Exploration Program* (DoD 1304.12-LASTP-TS). North Chicago, IL: HQ USMEPCOM.

Department of Defense. (2000, November). *Population representation in the military services: Fiscal year 1999.* Washington, DC: Office of the Assistant Secretary of Defense (Force Management Policy).

Eitelberg, M. J., Laurence, J. H., & Waters, B. K. (1984). *Screening for service: Aptitude and education criteria for military entry.* Washington, DC: Office of the Assistant Secretary of Defense (Manpower, Installations, and Logistics).

Fairbank, B. A., Welsh, J. R., & Sawin, L. L. (1990). *Armed Services Vocational Aptitude Battery (ASVAB): Validity of ASVAB 14 for the prediction of high school course grades* (AFHRL-TR-90–48). Brooks Air Force Base, TX: Air Force Human Resources Laboratory.

Green, B. F., Jr., & Wigdor, A. K. (1991). Measuring job competency. In A. K. Wigdor and B. F. Green Jr. (Eds.), *Performance assessment for the workplace* (Vol. II, pp. 53–74). Washington, DC: National Academy Press.

Green, B. F., Jr., Wing, H., & Wigdor, A. K. (Eds.). (1988). *Linking military enlistment standards to job performance: Report of a workshop.* Washington, DC: National Academy Press.

Holmgren, R. L., & Dalldorf, M. R. (1993, October). *A validation of the ASVAB against supervisors' ratings in civilian occupations.* Palo Alto, CA: American Institutes for Research.

Laurence, J. H. (1994). *The military: Purveyor of fine skills and comportment for a few good men* (EQW Catalog Number WP25). Philadelphia, PA: University of Pennsylvania's Center for the Educational Quality of the Workforce.

Laurence, J. H., & Ramsberger, P. F. (1999, October). *Evaluation of the DoD Armed Services Vocational Aptitude Battery Career Exploration Program* (FR-WATSD-99–46). Alexandria, VA: Human Resources Research Organization.

Laurence, J. H., Wall, J. E., Barnes, J. D., & Dela Rosa, M. (1998). Recruiting effectiveness of the ASVAB Career Exploration Program. *Journal of Military Psychology, 10*(4), 225–238.

Levine, R., Huberman, M., & Wall, J. (1996, July). *ASVAB Career Exploration Program: Impact on student career development* (Technical Report 96–006). Seaside, CA: Defense Manpower Data Center.

Rohrback, M., Barnes, J. D., Laurence, J. H., & Wall, J. (1996, September). *ASVAB Career Exploration Program: Impact on military recruiting* (Technical Report 96–008). Monterey, CA: Defense Manpower Data Center.

Wall, J. E. (1994). An example of assessment's role in career exploration. *Journal of Counseling & Development, 72*(6), 608–613.

Wall, J. E., & Baker, H. E. (1997). The Interest-Finder: Evidence of validity. *Journal of Career Assessment, 5*(2), 255–273.

Wall, J. E., Wise, L., & Baker, H. E. (1996). Development of the Interest-Finder: A new RIASEC-based interest inventory. *Measurement and Evaluation in Counseling and Development, 29,* 134–152.

Section C

Special Topics and Issues In Assessment

Chapter 23
Educational Assessment in a Reform Context

Michael H. Kean

It is difficult to believe that there was a time when the day's news *didn't* contain any mention of educational assessment. Up until the late 1980s, governors, state legislators, members of Congress, journalists, and other pundits knew little and said even less about how U.S. students were measured and educational programs were evaluated. Although educational assessment has played a pivotal role in American education for well more than 50 years, it remained in the background of our nation's policy debates and was considered a technical, if not esoteric, field.

Fast forward to today. Governors' speeches are peppered with remarks about accountability and standardized testing. Members of Congress engage in lengthy and often acrimonious debate over proposals for national testing of elementary and secondary school students. Local journalists routinely report on educational standards and testing. Moreover, the discussions do not end in the political arena. In political polling parlance, testing has become nightly "table talk" over dinner for moms, dads, and their kids.

At the same time (and through no coincidence), assessment is playing greater roles in the current educational environment. Assessment results are a major force in shaping public perceptions about the achievement of our students and the quality of our schools. Educators use assessment results to help improve teaching and learning as well as to evaluate programs and the effectiveness of schools. Educational assessment is also used to generate the data on which policy decisions are made. Because of the important role it performs, assessment is a foundational activity in every school, in every school district, and in every state.

What events and trends led to the transformation of educational assessment into nightly table talk? Why is there now a strong political dimension to educational assessment? Which aspects of assessment should educators and policymakers bear in mind as they go about their work? This chapter will provide answers to all these questions.

The Political Context of Reform

Over the past 20 years, education reforms have generally been of three types: structural, process, or content:

Structural reform refers to changes in the *structure* of education, such as a longer school day or school year, smaller class sizes, magnet schools, charter schools, or a middle school versus junior high school system.

Process reform refers to the *way* in which teachers teach and students learn. Team teaching, reading recovery, and use of educational software are examples of process reform.

Content reform refers to *what* teachers teach. Examples are phonics or whole language approaches to reading, new math, and standards-based curricula.

Testing entered the political realm with the advent of standards-based school reform, which is both a process reform and a content reform. This reform focuses on improving our schools, increasing student achievement, and building accountability for results through a system with three primary components: (a) new (and higher) *standards,* (b) new *assessments* designed to measure those standards, and (c) *consequences* for meeting or not meeting the standards. Politics is part of this process because of its traditional and rightful (but often unpredictable) role as the driver of policy in our national and state democracies.

The standards-based movement emerged in the early 1990s as a response to the call to arms issued by the 1983 release of *A Nation at Risk.* This slim but seminal report from the National Commission on Excellence in Education characterized U.S. schools as wholly inadequate and went so far as to say, "If an unfriendly foreign power had attempted to impose on America the mediocre educational performance that exists today, we might well have viewed it as an act of war" (p. 1). In short order *A Nation at Risk* galvanized policymakers at the federal and state levels. The nation's governors, acting collectively through the National Governors Association, developed and issued *Time for Results* (1986), a report that called for, among other things, greater accountability in our nation's public schools. Out of this period emerged a group of "education governors" who would later make their mark in education on the national scene: Tennessee Governor Lamar Alexander, Arkansas Governor Bill Clinton, South Carolina Governor Richard Riley, and Colorado Governor Roy Romer. Whereas Alexander and Riley would serve as U.S. Secretaries of Education in the 1990s and Romer would lead many national panels on education, Clinton forged a legacy as the nation's most active education president.

By 1989, concern over the nation's schools reached the level where the governors and President George H. Bush convened the first ever National Education Summit, in order to propose solutions. The fall summit, held at the University of Virginia in Charlottesville, culminated in an agreement to set six (later expanded to eight) broad National Education Goals. The goals were developed and released in 1990. At the same time a federal commission—The National Education Goals Panel—was created by Congress to track national and state efforts to reach these goals by the year 2000.

Although the National Education Goals were not reached by 2000, their impact was felt in two ways. First, they focused public attention on the need for increased student achievement. Second, they served as the starting point for the development of new education standards. This development began at both the federal and state levels, though it was action at the federal level that spurred many states to begin developing and setting their own standards.

Federal action came initially in April 1991 in the form of America 2000, the George H. Bush administration's education proposal. America 2000 set forth voluntary national standards in a range of subject areas and proposed a series of national tests. Although America 2000 did not find its way into law by the end of the first Bush administration, the Clinton administration came forward with a similar proposal, called Goals 2000 (signed into law as the Goals 2000: Educate America Act in 1994). America 2000 and Goals 2000 had some distinct differences, but they were alike in their drive for high standards and new assessments to measure student progress.

Goals 2000 became the most pervasive national K–12 education policy in a generation. It provided federal incentives for states to create new systems of accountability by setting their own standards and creating new assessments, which the states did. At the start of the decade only a handful of states had academic standards. By the end of it, close to 50 states had developed standards.

Despite its pervasiveness and its affinity to the America 2000 proposal, Goals 2000 found itself in the mid- to late-1990s under increasing attack from Republicans and conservatives, who felt the federal government had overextended its reach into state and local education policies. Republican critics claimed that while Washington had historically funded K–12 education at low levels (current funding is approximately nine cents on the dollar), it exerted too much authority in local classrooms. This sentiment led to a policy standoff in the fall of 1997 when the Clinton administration watched its proposal for voluntary national tests in reading and mathematics go down to defeat on Capitol Hill.

In early 2001, the administration of President George W. Bush introduced No Child Left Behind as its proposal for the reauthorization of the Elementary and Secondary Education Act (ESEA). The legislation sought greater accountability through annual testing in grades 3 through 8 in reading and mathematics, but left states to set their own standards and choose their own tests. In doing so, Washington not only re-established individual student progress as a central tenet of ESEA, it also found a politically acceptable compromise on assessment. In late December 2001, Congress passed the legislation by a wide bipartisan margin. President Bush signed the act into law soon after.

Federal Policy Issues

Invariably, and sometimes unfortunately, a recurring set of issues continues to evolve around Washington education debates. Like entrenched armies on the Western Front in the First World War, politicians often fight battles over and over on the same ground for years, and no real victor emerges. Typically, education debates in Washington have to do with the federal government's regulatory power and its authority over our nation's decentralized public education system.

Washington's authority. Local and state control of education is a deeply rooted concept in the United States. It remains so today, with the 50 states and tens of thousands of localities providing 91 percent of the funding at the K–12 level. Not a single education bill is debated in Congress today without at least one lawmaker (and usually many more) questioning the authority of Washington to impose educational mandates on the states and the nation's 15,600 school districts. Lawmakers from both sides of the aisle raise the issue, particularly when Congress mandates billion-dollar programs such as the Individuals With Disabilities Act (IDEA) and fails to fully fund them.

The "devolution revolution." With the Republican sweep of Capitol Hill in the November 1994 midterm elections, the devolution revolution was set in motion. The idea is to devolve as much federal authority as possible to the states and localities, where better decisions might be made. Although this devolution is often viewed as a Republican philosophy, many centrist Democrats also favor devolution initiatives. To date, the revolution has been seen most clearly in Congress's massive overhaul of welfare and job training programs. It has also appeared in the education arena, however, where it emerges in debates over block grants, program consolidation, and "ed flex," all of which opt to lift regulations prohibiting the blending of federal dollars from various programs. Whereas Democrats argue that federal education programs and their accompanying dollars should be carefully targeted to specific populations, Republicans counter that regulations should be lifted so that states and local schools can determine how best to use federal monies. There has not been a clear winner in the debate. Although more flexibility has been provided in various laws, many federal programs—rightly or wrongly—remain prescriptive in their aims and targeted populations.

Testing on a national scale. Between 1991 and 2001 Congress has had three major debates over testing: first with America 2000 in 1991, second in 1997 with the Clinton administration's voluntary national test proposal, and again in 2001 with the testing proposal in No Child Left Behind. Each debate has raised concerns over Washington's role in dictating how states should evaluate students.

Opportunity to learn standards. In 1991 congressional critics of America 2000 argued that if Washington was going to require new, higher academic standards, schools should have increased funding so that they could better prepare students to reach those standards. This same argument has emerged in 2001 as Congress debated the reauthorization of the ESEA.

Use of the National Assessment of Educational Progress (NAEP). Congress has often debated the notion of expanding the NAEP to measure individual student progress. Historically, the NAEP mission has been to intermittently sample student performance in various subject areas. Because of that, various attempts to expand NAEP have encountered opposition on Capitol Hill from lawmakers who fear NAEP expansion would lead to a national test.

State Policy Issues

The list of issues at the state level is more extensive than at the federal level because state policymakers, unlike members of Congress, have been closely involved in setting standards and shaping new assessment programs. The list of important issues for these policymakers ranges from the use of multiple measures to legal defensibility to public relations.

Governance. Consideration of major public policy in any state is a complex undertaking involving a number of different policymakers. While many governors play a central role in leading education reform in their states, at least three other individuals or entities—the state commissioner or superintendent of education, the state board of education, and the state legislature—play crucial roles, too. As the "dance of legislation" occurs, each of these individuals and entities contribute to the debate in some way.

The need for the right kind of information. States are in a unique position to use assessments for generating the types of data that policymakers, educators, and parents need to make decisions about their schools and students. State assessments more frequently serve as the "accountability fulcrum." Why? Because most assessment programs at the local school district level are designed primarily to improve teaching and learning, not to collect extensive, reliable data on student performance. Meanwhile, at the national level, the NAEP—an assessment sanctioned and funded by the federal government—generates snapshots of how small samples of students are performing in a given subject at a particular grade level. NAEP cannot expand on this snapshot function without igniting debates on federal versus state and local governance in education. This situation provides the states with the opportunity to generate more relevant statewide data on their students and school systems. Typically, this is accomplished by giving students a standardized, norm-referenced test. This type of test yields a variety of rich, reliable data that can be used for both statewide accountability purposes and to determine individual pupil progress toward meeting state standards.

Sequencing. Successful standards-based reform is based on a sequence where goals are developed first, followed by standards, then new curricula and instructional approaches, and finally assessments.

Standards setting. How standards are developed has been a very important issue for states. Great care must be taken to ensure that educators, policymakers, business leaders, and other key players are involved in creating new standards. Many states have developed both curriculum standards—criteria describing what students should know and be able to achieve—and performance standards—levels of acceptable student performance. Major test publishers work with standards-setting groups in the states to ensure that newly formulated standards can be measured by valid, reliable, and fair assessments.

High-stakes testing. The term *high stakes* refers to the use of assessments for purposes such as promotion and retention of students; graduation or exit exams; and rewards or penalties for schools or educators based upon student performance.

Legal defensibility. Because of the trend toward high-stakes testing, legislators and other state policymakers must ensure that state testing programs can withstand legal challenges. For instance, the number of lawsuits over high school graduation exams is increasing and is likely to continue to do so. Because of that, states must work closely with their assessment contractors to see that the tests used are valid, fair, and reliable.

Multiple measures. No single test can do it all, and no single assessment should serve as the sole evaluation tool in measuring performance. Multiple measures such as additional tests, grades, and teacher-made classroom quizzes—must be used to fully gauge student achievement.

Inclusion. Standards-based education reforms aim to set higher expectations for all students. In doing so, however, great care must be taken to accommodate children with special needs and those whose first language is not English. These children must not be left behind. The very core of standards-based reform is opportunity: the opportunity for *all* children to learn. Legislators, state education departments, curriculum developers, and test and textbook publishers have moved quickly in recent years to ensure that all students have the tools they need to learn and to demonstrate their knowledge and skills.

Report cards. Nearly all states (and many local school districts) now publish and disseminate report cards on individual districts and schools. These report cards serve a valuable function in informing parents and the public about the performance of their local public schools.

Communications and public relations. The standards-based movement represents a very significant change in how our schools go about educating children. Students, entire schools, and in some cases, teachers and administrators, must now meet higher expectations. When they do not, there may be consequences. Students may not be allowed to graduate, schools may face reconstitution with new leadership and teachers, and teachers may face loss of merit pay. Listing these consequences is not meant to cast standards-based reform in a negative light. Reform has generally been successful in bringing to public schools new standards of excellence, innovative curricula, challenging assessments, and new teaching strategies. Unfortunately, not all members of the public see and understand these positive changes. They see only the bad news of the high-stakes era. We now know why. Well into the 1990s, educators, policymakers, and the schools failed to educate the public about standards-based reform. Whereas some key audiences, such as the business community, were brought on board early, many parents still do not understand the need to hold students to higher expectations through new standards and assessments. As a result, a small but shrill cadre of testing critics has created a testing backlash in some communities. Although this backlash is unlikely to do serious harm to the standards-based reform movement, it represents a lesson policymakers should heed: *Always communicate (and keep communicating) the benefit of your reforms to key audiences.* Use public relations strategies to build understanding and support for reform among teachers, parents, students, and the community at large.

A Final Word: The Second Decade

The various federal and state issues outlined here represent the *current* political context that surrounds educational assessment. We are now in the second decade of standards-based education reform. Like any significant public policy change, the reform movement will be modified and refined in coming years. Educators and public policymakers should anticipate the debates that lead to these refinements. Crystal balls are usually murky at best, but we can anticipate the following changes:

The Bush administration's annual testing initiative. The first challenge will be to coalesce local and state testing programs in ways that meet the Bush administration proposal for annual testing of students in mathematics and reading in grades 3 through 8. Great care must be taken to respect state and local educational goals and curricula while establishing annual testing regulations. Any suggestion from Washington regarding the shape or content of assessments could very well lead to resistance or a backlash from governors and state policymakers.

Revised standards. Educational standards are not static. They must evolve based on society's needs to educate and train its children. This means educators and policymakers must continue to research, write, and rewrite state and local standards. In this process public debates will occur over the content of standards and over how high to set standards at particular grades. It will also mean that classroom curricula, teacher training programs, and assessments will undergo constant modifications to reflect these new standards.

The blending of curriculum and assessment. Curriculum developers, educational technologists, and textbook and test publishers are working diligently to bring innovations to the classroom. Over the course of the next 10 to 20 years the greatest advance in standards-based education may be the blending of curriculum and assessment. Test items will be embedded in educational software so students can be measured as they learn. As a result, evaluation will become transparent and less time will be spent on taking formal tests. This development, perhaps more than any other, will silence the critics of assessment and cause the testing backlash to melt away.

An educated public. Despite the failure of the standards-based movement to quickly educate parents about standards, assessments, and high-stakes consequences, new public information campaigns will be designed to reach out to all sectors of the public and to build greater understanding and support.

Teaching oriented to standards. In the same way that the public was left behind in the first decade of the reform, so were many teachers who were not trained to teach to specific state standards. However, new teacher training programs for college students and in-service programs for current teachers are beginning to create a new cadre of educators oriented to standards-based reform.

Finally, if the reform movement is to reach its true potential, the second decade must be one in which no segment of the public is forgotten. Everyone engaged in public education—governors, parents, children, teachers, boards of education, school superintendents, state legislators, publishers, researchers, school administrators, college faculty, teachers' unions, and members of Congress—should have permanent seats at the table of education reform. The creation of public policy requires the firm and active participation of all affected publics. Education reform and assessment will always have its political and policy dimensions, but the inclusion of all publics will provide a firm foundation upon which to build such reforms.

References

National Commission on Excellence in Education (1983, April). *A Nation at Risk*. Washington, DC: U.S. Department of Education.

National Governors Association. (1986). *Time for Results*. Washington, DC: Author.

U.S. Department of Education. (1991). *AMERICA 2000: An Education Strategy*. Washington, DC: Author.

✦U.S. Department of Education. (2001). *No Child Left Behind*. Washington, DC: Author.

✦ Document is included in the Anthology of Assessment Resources CD

Chapter 24
Educational Assessment in an Era of Accountability

Peter Behuniak

Two trends have converged during the past three decades to change the face of public school education in America. First, achievement testing has been greatly expanded in terms of both the quantity of tests available and the number of uses for the information collected from testing. Second, there has been a significant increase in the development of accountability systems for the purpose of fostering educational reform. Although there are many different ways of designing a system of accountability, virtually all approaches employ achievement test results as one, usually a central, component. As a result, the increases in student testing and greater demands for accountability have interacted to make learning and teaching in U.S. public schools at the beginning of the twenty-first century quite different than they were prior to the 1970s.

In this chapter I discuss these developments in three sections. The first section describes some of the key influences and history behind these trends. The second section examines how the widespread adoption of accountability systems is affecting the types of achievement tests being created, the frequency of their use, and the purposes to which their results are applied. The third section focuses on a number of areas related to these trends that are of particular concern to educators. I offer suggestions to illustrate how teachers and others involved in public education can effectively respond in the current environment.

How Did We Get Here?

Once upon a time the term *accountability* was nearly synonymous with *responsibility.* Students were responsible for learning their lessons. Teachers were responsible for presenting important topics in class and helping students as needed. Administrators were responsible for supporting teachers, monitoring their effectiveness, and communicating with parents. Parents had the responsibility of ensuring their children were good students. Similarly, district administrators were accountable to local boards of education, the local boards were accountable to state agencies and the voters, and so on. In short, everyone was accountable to someone.

Of course, not everyone accepted their role, nor were they equally effective even if they did accept it, but at least the system was easy to understand. Everyone was expected to display responsible behavior (e.g., learning, teaching, parenting) to the satisfaction of at least one other individual or group. If someone did not do his or her job, the next link in the chain would do the responsible thing and intercede. At least that was the plan.

This shared system of responsibility does not place a very high demand on achievement testing. Through most of the early and middle years of the twentieth century, achievement tests served primarily to provide teachers with instructional feedback and confirmation of student learning. In some cases, results were shared with parents or summarized for administrative purposes. In other cases, the information remained with the teacher. Testing was all handled in a low-key manner.

This began to change in the 1970s. Legislatures and educational bureaucracies, particularly at the state level, discovered that standardized achievement tests could be pressed into service as instruments of reform. Throughout the country, minimum competency testing (MCT) was introduced to the public schools. This was a new kind of testing in which each student's performance would be judged against a previously established standard (the minimum competency standard) to determine whether adequate learning was occurring. Some MCT programs were designed to focus attention on the teachers by calling for improved teaching strategies when test results were judged to be too low. Other MCT programs held the students responsible by applying sanctions such as the denial of a promotion or a diploma. Some MCT models tried to hold educators, students, and parents responsible. All of these programs, however, demonstrated clearly that the race to high-stakes testing had begun.

This top-down approach of using educational tests as a hammer to force change became a source of concern almost as soon as it was introduced. Jaeger & Tittle (1980) worried in the prologue to their book *Minimum Competency Achievement Testing* that the implementation of MCT programs was moving ahead too quickly without adequate attention to its consequences. In words that now seem prophetic, they wrote, "Comparatively little attention has been directed to such larger issues as the need for minimum competency testing, the problems it seeks to solve, its likely effects on the structure and operation of the schools, and its consequences for those directly involved in elementary and secondary education, as well as for our larger society" (p. vii).

Eventually, after about a decade, the popularity of MCT waned as some of its negative effects were realized, such as narrowed or watered-down curriculum and reduced student motivation. In its place, new testing programs were implemented with higher standards and broader content. Reports such as *A Nation at Risk* (National Commission on Excellence in Education, 1983) fueled national concerns about the effectiveness of U.S. schools. The old model of shared responsibility was gradually replaced with calls for educational reform and more formal systems of accountability. The political lessons learned years earlier dominated the landscape. The country turned its attention to school and district accountability, then to standards-based accountability (Linn, 1998). The tests mandated in the 1980s and 1990s were implemented with even higher stakes, including programs where the allocation of financial and other resources, the security of teachers' jobs, and even the continued existence of specific schools rested on the results of standardized tests. It suddenly became crucial to have high-quality tests in place, given how much was depending upon them. As Paul E. Barton (1999, p. 6) stated, "Improving testing is important because testing has become, over the last 25 years, the approach of first resort of policymakers."

It is worth noting that the expanded role of testing in the public schools cannot be dismissed as merely a political gimmick. The expansion of testing and accountability systems has support that extends well beyond state legislatures and education departments. Rose and Gallup (2001) report that 66 percent of the U.S. public believes that the emphasis on achievement testing in public schools is at the right level or should be increased. Interestingly, this support climbs to 73 percent when the parents of public school students are polled. Three quarters of the public indicated they support President Bush's proposal to hold the public schools accountable for how much students learn. Phelps (1998) considered a large number of surveys and polls and concluded, "The general public, parents, students, and often teachers want more testing, and they want higher-stakes testing. Perhaps they do because they are not looking at testing's problems out of context, in isolation from consideration of the real alternatives to testing, as testing's critics often are. They are considering testing against the alternatives, and they think that some testing, more testing, is better" (p. 16). Although some would take exception to this claim, particularly regarding the support from teachers (see, e.g., Wassermann, 2001), it is evident that the trend toward more testing and more high-stakes testing has widespread support.

Where Are We Now?

The increased use of tests for the purpose of holding schools accountable has caused much debate and discussion. Warnings have been issued, much like the one Jaeger and Tittle sounded more than two decades ago, that point out the many potential negative effects of such high-stakes applications of tests (Popham, 1999; Shepard, 2000). Concerns include a narrowing of the curriculum, corruption of sound teaching strategies, lessening of attention in classrooms on higher-order skills, lowering of student and teacher motivation, and reduction of attention to students' individual needs. Some researchers, however, have offered strategies for dealing with the current environment (Gallagher, 2000; McColskey & McMunn, 2000).

One positive result of the focus on testing for accountability purposes has been a greater effort to produce tests of higher quality. This attention to test design often grew directly from criticism of the shortcomings or limits of available tests. For example, it is much more common today for achievement tests to include varied formats, with students explaining their work and completing extended performance tasks in addition to answering short-answer or selected-response questions. This has improved the capacity of tests to measure a broader and deeper range of student achievement.

The creation of content standards and the design of achievement tests consistent with those standards is another important development in the evolution of high-stakes testing. It was not uncommon 15 or 20 years ago to create and administer an assessment first, then worry about sharing descriptions of what the test measured later. The increased use of tests in high-stakes situations has made this a less frequent occurrence. Attention is now given to aligning the material covered on a test with established content standards and to publicizing those standards well before the first test administration.

Another area of improvement involves the use of technology to enhance how test results are shared and the speed of returning those results to schools. Higher stakes mean higher interest levels in the test results. Many accountability programs now provide customized reports tailored to the test users' needs, web-based access to data, easy-to-use software for examining the results, and a variety of CD- or web-based tutorials to improve educators' understanding of the test results. Though the volume and complexity of tests have generally increased, many programs have succeeded in maintaining or reducing the time between the test administration and the reporting of the results. One of the more promising developments in the past few years has been advances in making computer-based testing suitable for certain uses with large-scale assessments (Bennett, 2001).

Yet, despite all the improvements in test design and implementation, concerns persist regarding the wisdom of depending too much on one or a few assessments. Even educators and assessment specialists who applaud the improvements in the quality of tests voice doubts about whether using them in accountability systems will have a positive effect on schools (Hilliard, 2000). Haertel (1999), for example, acknowledges the benefits of using performance assessments but questions the underlying assumptions of test-centered accountability. He concludes, "Regardless of the value of performance assessments in the classroom, a measurement-driven reform strategy that relies on performance assessment to drive curriculum and instruction seems bound to fail" (p. 666).

The title of this section is posed as a question: "Where are we now?" The answer to this question will be somewhat different for each classroom in America. One of the impediments to a meaningful discussion of high-stakes testing is that the actual effect of a system of testing and accountability on any particular student, teacher, or school depends upon many components of the system in question and how those components interact. In a review of the assessments and accountability systems planned or in place in each of the 50 states, Linn (2001) found them to differ on multiple dimensions, making the evaluation or categorization of the systems difficult. Consider, for example, one component common to many state accountability systems: Students are required to pass a test to earn a high school diploma. Any two states that have such a requirement may differ on the content areas tested, the rigor of the standards, the number of times a student may retake the test, and the accommodations offered to some or all students. In addition, two students attending different schools (or having different teachers in the same school) may receive instruction that varies in its focus on the content covered by the test.

This means that if 1,000 schools operate under a statewide program of testing and accountability, there are potentially 1,000 combinations of factors producing a system of accountability that is unique to each school. If achievement testing is to play a positive role in improving education, all the stakeholders in a given community will need to examine critically the components of the system operating in their own backyard. Some aspects will be found useful and productive. Others may be ineffective or even counterproductive and should be reconsidered. Overall, it is important to realize that there is no one best model and that many local factors may affect the way the system operates.

Issues and Strategies

One of the few principles that virtually every policymaker and stakeholder involved in education agrees on is the central importance of teachers in any reform effort. There is more than a little irony in the fact that an era of mandated testing and stringent accountability systems could have the unintended effect of disenfranchising the very individuals crucial to the public schools' mission. There are, however, strategies and actions that can be useful in ensuring that educators' voices are heard amid all the cries for reform.

The issues and strategies identified in this section focus on basic principles of assessment and instruction and how these elements interact. They are offered to serve dual purposes. First, they highlight key elements of educational assessments that require scrutiny to ensure that sound tests and testing practices are in place. This is a type of watchdog function, and no one is better positioned to fulfill this function than the individuals who regularly administer and proctor the tests, report the test results to students and parents, and interpret the implications of those results. The second purpose is more oriented to professional development. Stated simply, educators who are more knowledgeable about the form and function of the tools of their trade will be in a stronger position to express their views and concerns effectively.

Learn Basic Measurement Principles

Assessments are tools of the profession of education. High-stakes tests, low-stakes tests, selected-response formats, performance assessments, commercially available standardized batteries, and exit exams are all just variations that may be more or less appropriate for any given purpose. In many cases, one test used for a certain purpose will have both positive and negative consequences. It is important that the educators involved in using these tests have a solid fundamental understanding of the measurement principles on which these tests are based.

This does not mean that every teacher must become a measurement expert. Psychometricians and assessment specialists have a productive role to fill in the field of education, just as do specialists in reading, music, or administration. One course taken during an undergraduate teacher training program is probably not sufficient to provide educators with a working knowledge of measurement principles such as reliability, validity, bias, errors of measurement, and test standardization. They can acquire more information about these principles through such activities as continuing education coursework, private study, and in-service professional development. Regardless of an individual educator's disposition toward educational testing in general or toward any specific test, gaining a better understanding of the principles that guide their development will enhance his or her chances of taking full advantage of reasonable test applications and provide a credible basis to support criticism of unwarranted applications.

Know Each Locally Administered Test

If educational tests are to function as effective tools for guiding students' learning, educators must be prepared to select the right tool for the job. The first step in this process is to become familiar with all the tests being used with local students. This includes all assessments in use regardless of whether they are optional, mandated locally, or mandated externally. Increasing familiarity with the assessments in use could begin with background information, such as who developed the test, for which ages or grades it was designed, and whether evidence of technical quality has been provided. Although some educators are not experienced enough to judge the technical merits of a particular assessment, all teachers and administrators are capable of at least verifying that someone with technical skills has reviewed the tests.

Classroom assessments and teacher-made tests should also be considered. These tests are much less formal and usually do not have evidence of technical quality available. This is acceptable because of the low-key way in which they are typically used. They are important to consider, however, because students often spend more time taking many of these brief, informal tests than they do taking the higher-stakes, more formal assessments. It is not necessary for classroom assessments always to measure the same skills that the more formal assessments measure, for a teacher may well wish to use a classroom test to check on students' understanding of skills prerequisite to or otherwise separate from the content represented on other assessments. It is necessary to ensure, however, that the ways in which students are tested on multiple assessments are not inconsistent or contradictory. For example, if students are expected to produce writing samples as part of their assessments, it could be unintentionally confusing to the students if the criteria for grading the essays differ from one test to another (e.g., spelling counts in one test but not in another).

Consider the Purpose of Each Test

The *Standards for Educational and Psychological Testing* (AERA, APA, & NCME, 1999), the primary reference in the field, makes clear that validity depends on the purpose or purposes for which any given test is used. In fact, the very first standard (Standard 1.1) requires that every use to which a test is put be supported by reasonable evidence. In some cases, identifying the intended purpose of an assessment is easy. Any state or federal agency mandating an assessment will specify at least one intended purpose. In these cases, the judgment necessary in each school or classroom has more to do with the appropriateness of the specified purpose for the students involved. For example, consider a statewide minimum competency test intended to identify students who are not proficient in reading in order to have them receive remediation. The appropriateness of the test for students in a limited English proficient class may be questionable even if the test is reasonable for use with most students.

Sometimes an assessment has no compelling purpose. It is surprising how often an assessment that once served a useful role continues to be administered annually or periodically long after it has ceased to fulfill that purpose. An example of this might occur if a district continues to administer in elementary grades a battery of achievement tests that had been instituted years before the state agency established statewide content standards for the same grades and mandated statewide assessments aligned to those standards. The main purpose for the district assessment may no longer apply if the state assessment is filling that role. The judgment in this case turns on whether the district assessment serves any other suitable purpose or whether the students' and teachers' time would better be spent on other activities.

An additional point concerns the need to consider the technical adequacy of a test in relation to its intended use. Teachers can assist in the process of identifying any shortcomings of a test, particularly a high-stakes measure, by carefully considering test results for the students in their classes. Instances in which the results are inconsistent with existing information about the students should be questioned. All tests include error, so not every student will score exactly as other factors might have predicted. At the same time, unusual results for large numbers of students (or extremely unusual results for one or a few students) may indicate a problem in the test design, scoring, or reporting.

Watch for Unintended Consequences

Almost all policymakers and administrators influencing the course of public education intend to improve the quality of teaching and learning through their actions and decisions. Unfortunately, what is intended does not always happen. Sometimes—some people would argue all too often—testing programs produce the type of negative, unintended results discussed earlier. This is the reason teachers need to be vigilant to the problems that may occur when high-stakes tests are implemented.

This vigilance requires determination and effort on the part of educators. It is not easy to maintain a balanced perspective regarding the effects of an accountability program when part of the purpose of that program is directed at you. Yet, it is undeniable that teachers are the professionals best positioned to notice if one or many students are being negatively affected in some way. If several or all teachers in a school begin to share the same observations and concerns, it is worth discussing and, perhaps, attempting to minimize or eliminate the problem.

Rely on Multiple Indicators

Most educators do this instinctively. For these educators, this principle is merely reassurance that it is indeed appropriate and desirable to consider all available evidence about a student when interpreting a test score. Classroom performance, grades, individual learning styles, and other test results are all useful indicators to consider.

The goal should be to bring any newly available test result into the context of all that is known about each student. If the new test scores essentially confirm existing information, a teacher has one more reason to support the instructional choices he or she is making for that student. If the new test results are at odds with some of the existing information, it is appropriate to dig deeper into the reasons for the discrepancy. It is possible that the new results are somehow invalid, perhaps because problems occurred during the test administration, the student misunderstood the directions, the test was developed or scored inappropriately, or for many other reasons. It is also possible, however, that the assessment is revealing an academic weakness or other aspect of the student's understanding that had not previously been noticed.

The role of the teacher in this circumstance is that of a diagnostician, investigating all reasonable possibilities, with help from specialists when necessary, until the discrepant information can be reconciled and a suitable program of instruction determined.

Make Testing a Positive Classroom Experience

When athletes compete, they give their best effort to the activity. If they did not, if they made only a token effort, the event would be meaningless. Tests of student achievement are also intended to be measures of maximum effort. They are intended to monitor how well a student can do when that student does the best he or she can do. If anything interferes with the student demonstrating his or her best work, the resulting test scores will be misleading and invalid. Many teachers make a reasonable effort to motivate students appropriately. Problems can occur, however, if teachers do either too much or too little.

Excessive test preparation is probably the most common example of how a teacher can do too much. It is appropriate to give students advance notice of an upcoming test. It is also reasonable to ensure that students are familiar with the types of questions and tasks that they are likely to encounter on the test. This is the reason large-scale tests usually are preceded by short practice tests, so that the format of the test does not surprise or confuse students. Repeatedly exposing students to practice sessions involving test questions that are similar or identical to the actual questions is neither good instruction nor good test preparation, however. This problem can become even more pronounced if a school or district administrator encourages or demands such activities. Other examples of inappropriate teaching behaviors include creating excessive student anxiety by overselling the importance of the test or coaching students during the actual test administration.

There are many ways in which a teacher can do too little to promote a positive environment. One is through indifference, for example when a teacher fails to announce or discuss the test with students in advance. Even worse is the situation where a teacher is openly critical of the purpose or nature of the assessment with students. Many teachers appear to be surprisingly unaware of the powerful depressive effect their negative comments can have on their students' motivation and results. This does not mean that a teacher cannot be critical of certain aspects of an assessment or accountability system, as the next section discusses. It does mean, however, that teachers should be circumspect in how and when they express their views.

The most positive testing experiences for students occur when teachers and administrators work together to help students place the assessments in a balanced context. Yes, the tests are important and you should do your best work. No, this test score is not the only thing that matters. Yes, you will have a chance to practice a few questions like the ones that will be on the test. No, we will not shut down the school for a month prior to the test just to drill test questions. The key here is to prepare students effectively to demonstrate to the very highest level possible what they know and can do.

Contribute Constructively to Improved Assessment Practices

In some ways, this suggestion is the logical extension of the points made earlier. Take some time to learn about the principles of good testing practices and the specifics of tests to which your students will be exposed. Prepare your students for the assessment but do not overdo it. Make the most of the test results but interpret those results in relation to all other available information. Be on the lookout for unintended negative consequences on the curriculum or the students. In short, become proactive in a balanced way, acknowledging the productive and useful role that assessment can play while working to change problematic aspects of the system.

Large-scale assessments are complex undertakings. Implementing them as part of an accountability system only increases the complexity and the potential for problems. In order for these systems to function in a manner that improves public education, it is essential that all educators, including classroom teachers, contribute their varied perspectives and talents to improve them. They are the tools of our profession. It is our collective responsibility to see that they are used wisely.

References

AERA, APA, & NCME [American Educational Research Association, American Psychological Association, & National Council on Measurement in Education]. (1999). *Standards for educational and psychological testing.* Washington, DC: American Educational Research Association.

Barton, P. E. (1999). *Too much testing of the wrong kind, too little of the right kind in K–12 education.* Princeton, NJ: Educational Testing Service.

✦Bennett, R. E. (2001). How the Internet will help large-scale assessment reinvent itself. *Education Policy Analysis Archives, 9,* 1–24.

Gallagher, C. (2000). A seat at the table: Teachers reclaiming assessment through rethinking accountability. *Phi Delta Kappan,* 81, 502–507.

Haertel, E. H. (1999). Performance assessment and education reform. *Phi Delta Kappan,* 80, 662–666.

Hilliard, A. G. (2000). Excellence in education versus high-stakes standardized testing. *Journal of Teacher Education,* 51, 293–304. (ERIC Document Reproduction Service No. EJ 613877).

Jaeger, R. M., & Tittle, C. K. (1980). *Minimum competency achievement testing.* Berkeley, CA. McCutchan Publishing.

✦Linn, R. L. (1998). *Assessments and accountability* (Technical Report No. 490). Los Angeles: Center for the Study of Evaluation, CRESST/UCLA. (ERIC Document Reproduction Service No. ED 443865).

Linn, R. L. (2001). *The design and evaluation of educational assessment and accountability systems* (Technical Report No. 539). Los Angeles: Center for the Study of Evaluation, CRESST/UCLA.

McColskey, W., & McMunn, N. (2000). Strategies for dealing with high stakes tests. *Phi Delta Kappan,* 82, 115–120.

National Commission on Excellence in Education. (1983, April). *A nation at risk: The imperative for educational reform.* Washington, DC: U.S. Department of Education.

Phelps, R. P. (1998). The demand for standardized student testing. *Educational Measurement: Issues and Practice,* 17, 5–23.

Popham, W. J. (1999). Where large scale assessment is heading and why it shouldn't. *Educational Measurement: Issues and Practice,* 18, 13–17.

Rose, L. C., & Gallup, A. M. (2001). The 33rd annual Phi Delta Kappan/Gallup poll of the public's attitudes toward the public schools. *Phi Delta Kappan,* 83, 41–58.

▼Shepard, L. A. (2000). The role of assessment in a learning culture. *Educational Researcher,* 29, 4–14.

Wasserman, S. (2001). Quantum theory, the uncertainty principle, and the alchemy of standardized testing. *Phi Delta Kappan, 83,* 28–40.

✦ Document is included in the Anthology of Assessment Resources CD
▼ Document is available on a website

Chapter 25
Applications of Professional Ethics in Educational Assessment

Pat Nellor Wickwire

In the schools, the primary clients are the students. Other clients include parents, citizens, the community, and educators—all stakeholders in the processes and the products of schools. Professionals in administrative, instructional, and student services are committed to serving these internal and external clients by providing for offerings and outcomes to advance and enhance learning and the learning experience.

To ensure effective planning, implementation, and evaluation of these provisions for clients, certain principles and guidelines for beliefs and behaviors are adopted. These principles and guidelines are identified as ethical standards and codes of conduct. *Ethical standards* are broad statements of professional norms, whereas *codes of conduct* are focused statements of professional applications. Generally, professional associations develop, adopt, and enforce both codes and standards, and the continuation of an individual's association membership and professional status are dependent upon the observance of these guidelines. Ethical standards and codes of conduct are upheld through honor first, regulation second, and enforcement third.

Cardinal Principles of Professional Ethics

Professionals in the schools are charged with significant responsibilities and rights. As they work with and influence the lives of others, they honor cardinal principles inherent in professional ethics: beneficence, nonmaleficence, autonomy, justice, and fidelity (Kitchener, 1984). *Beneficence* involves contributing positively to the welfare, growth, and development of clients—in other words, seeking and creating benefits and doing good. *Nonmaleficence* refers to avoiding conditions or actions that hurt, hinder, or place clients at risk—in other words, resisting and refraining from nonbenefits, or doing no harm. *Autonomy* involves securing optimal freedom of choice, action, and consequence for clients—in other words, supporting self-determination and not resisting or interfering with decisions. *Justice* involves offering all clients equal access to opportunity—in other words, providing and ensuring respect and dignity and being fair. *Fidelity* involves maintaining loyalty and honoring agreements with clients—in other words, offering and guaranteeing trustworthiness and being faithful.

In their working relationships with clients, therefore, professionals strive to do good, do no harm, support self-determination, be fair, and be faithful. They recognize the possibilities and opportunities inherent in ethical standards and codes of conduct for clients, for the profession, and for themselves. They clarify their worldviews, establish internal and external constructs for engagement, and conduct self-review. They recognize that law supersedes ethics, and in cases where the two differ, attend, inform, and initiate dialogue, and correction to bring them into alignment.

Individual Practitioners and Professional Ethics

Theory and practice in ethics ultimately reside in the individual. In deciding what to think, feel, and do, the individual practitioner views ethical principles and conduct guidelines and their implications for personal beliefs and behaviors, as well as framing and responding to a hierarchy of universal values, societal norms, and individual desires. Organizations, agencies, institutions, and employers may possess and exercise points of view, but the final decision about professional conduct resides within the individual (Van Zandt, 1990). Peer beliefs and behaviors, and institutional encouragement and enforcement, are influential in decision making, but the final decision rests with the individual and his or her capacity, nature, and degree of subscribed obligation.

An individual's ethical thoughts, feelings, and actions may be proactive or reactive, formal or informal, explicit or implicit, reasoned or intuitive, and reflective or responsive. Thought, feeling, and action are internalized and personalized to issues, situations, and critical incidents; based on a progression of awareness, accommodation, and action; and related to sensitivity, motivation, and constancy. Thought, feeling, and action represent affective and cognitive reasoning and judgment; and, ideally, they are consistent, relevant, coherent, authentic, integrated, comprehensive, systematic, intentional, and congruent in terms of values, attitudes, and behaviors. Intuitively and critically, they address what is good and what is evil for humankind (universal values), what is desirable and not desirable for the immediate and expanded environment (societal norms), and what is wanted and not wanted for the self (individual desires). An individual uses them to evaluate the possibility and credibility of neutrality, and to establish priorities and balance of values, attitudes, and behaviors in decisions and actions.

In developing and practicing ethics, the individual makes choices based on a hierarchy of orientations (Kohlberg, 1969, 1972):

Punishment and obedience orientation. Do it because you'll be punished if you don't. Do it because someone tells you to.

Naive instrumental hedonism. Do it because you've learned or habituated to the behavior. Do it because it makes you feel good or rewarded.

Interpersonal concordance. Do it because there is consensus on the activity. Do it because others expect you to.

Law-and-order orientation. Do it because there are laws, mandates, directives, or other structures regulating or enforcing particular expectations.

Social-contract legalistic orientation. Do it because there is agreement. Do it because there are overtones of positive or negative consequences.

Universal ethical principle orientation. Do it because it will benefit others or society. Do it because your conscience tells you it is right and responsible.

The individual who is making choices sometimes faces conflict and indecision. To reach resolution, the individual may take the following steps: (a) identify the problem and his or her relationship to it; (b) apply the current code of ethics; (c) determine the nature and dimensions of the dilemma; (d) generate potential courses of action; (e) consider potential consequences of all options and determine a course of action; (f) evaluate the selected course of action; and (g) implement the course of action (Muratori, 2001). In this process, the individual follows and sets priorities consistent with doing good, doing no harm, supporting self-determination, being fair, and being faithful. The nature and the quality of benefits for clients are the greatest considerations. Perfect resolutions may not exist, and decisions may be difficult.

Nevertheless, the individual cannot disregard responsibility for ethical standards and codes of conduct. Neither can the profession. The price of abdication is too high.

Educational Assessment and Professional Ethics

Educational assessment offers a significant opportunity to contribute to the welfare, growth, and development of the primary clients and stakeholders of the schools—the students—and to support the efforts and contributions of the team made up of the other clients and stakeholders of the schools. The finding of essential information through educational assessment serves to enhance and advance learning and the learning experience.

Educational assessment is accomplished by sampling student learning of a sample of content in a specified domain under given conditions. The demonstration of student learning and the selection of content and conditions are planned and inferred to be representative of the domain for the individuals, groups, programs, systems, and units of systems that participate in the assessment.

A variety of norm-referenced, criterion-referenced, traditional, alternative, formative, summative, literal, and expressive formal and informal assessments, using oral, written, and psychomotor response modes, are applied in the assessment effort. They include standardized tests, standards-based tests, educator-designed tests, tests of proficiency levels with specified criteria, mastery tests, hands-on performance tests, minimum competency tests, constructed-response tests, anecdotal records, rating scales, observations of behavior, sociometrics, benchmark skill and competency tests, self-reports, questionnaires, demonstrations, projects, exhibits, experiments, inventories, card sorts, structured interviews, focused interviews, critical incident reports, and portfolios, among others. Tests may be framed longitudinally or cross-sectionally, and may use various formats to elicit and validate evidence of student learning.

Information gathering through educational assessment is directed toward identifying the current characteristics of students and, with other available information about students, toward identifying viable options for optimizing student learning. Information about factors in the environment and about alternatives for student interaction with the environment is also operative. Generally, educational assessment leads to analysis and diagnosis, planning and prescription, implementation and intervention, and evaluation and recycling. The intent is to identify and create the best possible student learning in the best possible conditions.

Certain steps, typically sequential, occur in educational assessment: (a) selection of the assessment instrument or instruments; (b) preparation for assessment; (c) administration of assessment, with monitoring; (d) scoring and reporting of assessment results; (e) interpretation of assessment results; (f) communication of assessment results; and (g) application of assessment results. Evaluation of assessment processes, products, and outcomes—that is, whether student learning is enhanced and advanced—is ongoing and summative, and changes are made as needs are validated. Throughout, representatives of all clients and stakeholders are involved in a team approach.

In conducting these steps in educational assessment, professionals recognize and reinforce the purpose of schooling as student learning. In assessing the processes, products, and outcomes of learning, they honor the cardinal principles of professional ethics: doing good, doing no harm, supporting self-determination, being fair, and being faithful. They follow ethical standards and codes of conduct, and develop and practice aligned policies, procedures, and behaviors (Bell, 1994a, 1994b). They stress integrity and focus on the key concepts of quality, competency, need, appropriateness, meaningfulness, authenticity, accuracy, clarity, equity of opportunity, and outcomes. They seek to design, implement, and evaluate educational assessment as a value-added component to advance and enhance student learning. For the greatest effectiveness, they follow ethical standards, guidelines, and practices. A brief, selected review of ethics applicable to educational assessment follows.

Selection of Assessments

Establishment of the specific purpose or purposes of educational assessment is primary in the selection of the assessment instrument or instruments. The parameters of why, what, who, when, where, how, and how much are addressed in this initial step. The needed or desired information about student learning, the content domain, the participants, the intended use of results, and the contributions to be made through gaining the assessment information are identified.

A thorough search, review, and evaluation of available and constructible instruments is then conducted. This step involves studying the various assessments' relevance, utility, cost effectiveness, required resources, currency, strengths, and limitations. The professional test user evaluates the documentation provided regarding instrument development and applications, and reviews expert appraisals of the instrument. The professional gains hands-on experience with the instrument and background materials to evaluate function, appearance, nondiscrimination and equity for the participant population, meaningfulness of score reporting, representativeness of the domain sample, item presentation, scoring and reporting capability, comparison groups, anticipated reception by clients and stakeholders, necessary staff and other resource support, and other relevant factors. Throughout the professional is seeking an appropriate and workable fit, with the highest quality and the greatest benefit. A report that includes conclusions and recommendations, the rationale, and the decision-making model is written, disseminated, and acted upon.

Preparation and Administration

Professional preparation is structured, complete, accurate, precise, and geared to the end of ensuring equitable opportunities for students to demonstrate their learning. Student preparation is limited to test-taking skills and to the content domain, and restricted from familiarity with specific assessment items (Bell, 1994a, 1994b).

Complete disclosure to clients and stakeholders is essential before the administration of an assessment. Disclosure includes but is not limited to purpose, applications, consequences, and expected outcomes; scoring and record keeping; availability and access to results; projected dissemination of results; rights and responsibilities; any prohibitions and assurances; and any situational information. Written consent or verification of receipt of disclosure is sometimes required.

Policies and procedures are developed and practiced by all stakeholders. Test administrators receive training in test administration, monitoring of test takers, and enforcement of administration guidelines to ensure uniformity of preparation and administration within prescribed conditions. Students are offered individualized instructions, accommodations, and exclusions only as permissible. Security of instruments is required, with precise accounting.

Scoring and Reporting

In scoring and reporting the results of an assessment, accuracy, clarity, and timeliness are essential. Meaningfulness is enhanced by providing complete information about the scoring process and rationale, types of scores, schedule and format for reporting, and method and understandability of the presentation of results.

It is important to institute quality control measures, and in case of error or contamination of performance, to ensure immediate full correction and communication. Results are released only to those who have the need and the right to know, as well as the capacity and responsibility to apply the results in decision making. Conditions for confidentiality and appeal are established, communicated, and implemented.

Interpretation

In the interpretation of assessment results, the professional makes only those inferences that are valid for the assessment instrument or instruments; the professional also recognizes that these inferences are valid only if all specified standards, guidelines, policies, and procedures have been followed. Those individuals responsible for interpretation must be trained and educated in educational assessment, know the characteristics of the assessment instrument or instruments, understand the meaning of the scores and results, know their relevance to possible and probable applications and consequences, be able to relate their meaning to environmental alternatives, and have the capacity to estimate their weight in establishing implications and making decisions. Only those individuals competent to provide interpretation do so; and they recognize the importance of informed, objective, and timely interpretation. These professionals pay strict attention to standards, guidelines, policies, and procedures; conduct monitoring for quality control; and immediately correct any errors in accuracy and completeness. Those who participated in the assessment, or their parents or guardians, receive written and oral statements about their results. In decision making, multiple sources of information and prescribed steps are used.

Communication

In communicating the results of assessment, it is important to emphasize information relevant to the advancement and enhancement of student learning. Communication of results includes accurate and meaningful descriptions about the purpose of the information gathered about student characteristics, and about the usefulness of the characteristics of the assessment instrument or instruments. The professional couches the results in clear and understandable terms, addresses the validity and reliability of results, relates them to systemic-environmental alternatives, and references possible and probable implications and consequences for students and the other clients and stakeholders of the schools.

Professionals inform test users and test takers about the rights and responsibilities associated with assessment, including confidentiality, privacy, dissemination, and access. They demonstrate competence in technical and communication skills and knowledge, and use a team approach that involves school, home, and community. They reinforce respect and dignity; recognizing that the need and right to know, and the capacity and responsibility to apply assessment results, vary among different audiences of clients and stakeholders. Where necessary, they establish adaptive parameters for communication.

Application

In applying the results of assessment, the welfare, growth, and development of students have pre-eminence. The enhancement and advancement of student learning and the learning experience are paramount. An analysis and diagnosis of each student's demonstrated strengths and limitations leads to planning and prescription, followed by implementation and intervention. Assessment results are always applied in conjunction with information from other sources.

Professionals evaluate any proposed intervention or other action in light of the nature and degree of confidence in the assessment results, that is, whether a student's performance on the assessment instrument or instruments is an appropriate, adequate, and accurate representation of his or her actual learning in the content domain, and whether the results provide sufficient evidence to support making recommendations and taking action. They plan interventions that encompass the individuals and groups, as well as the programs, systems, and units of systems that participated in assessment. Intervention involves administrative, instructional, and student services components as well as students and other clients and stakeholders. The team reviews available alternatives for student-environment interaction and, if appropriate, creates new and modified alternatives for student success, satisfaction, and productivity. This review encompasses the scope and detail of the content domain as well as the delivery of content. Following this review, the team develops appropriate strategies for delivery of the intervention through administrative, instructional, and student services channels. The parameters and the details of application are developed and communicated through a team approach involving school, home, and community.

Evaluation

Evaluation of the effectiveness and efficiency of the processes, products, and outcomes of assessment is a requirement. This process uses formal and informal means as appropriate to conduct all five levels of evaluation: reaction, learning, behavior, results, and output. Professionals conduct both formative evaluation (ongoing and at specified interim checkpoints) and summative evaluation (at the end and with final benchmarks). All steps in assessment are targeted for review and evaluation: selection, preparation, administration, scoring, reporting, interpretation, communication, application, and evaluation.

Next professionals identify evidence of change in student learning and the learning experience, and correlate the magnitude and the direction of change with the resources used in assessment. They take a team approach to recording quality and quality control information, then communicate this information to clients and stakeholders together with recommendations for continuation or modification; decisions about making changes and recycling through the process are made through a team approach.

Resources for Professional Ethics and Educational Assessment

Several resources provide additional information about professional ethics and educational assessment. These include the professional code of the National Council on Measurement and Evaluation (1995), which is designed for members and anyone else involved in assessment. The codes of ethics of the American Counseling Association (1997), American Educational Research Association (1992), American Psychological Association (1992), American School Counselor Association (1998), American Speech-Language-Hearing Association (2001), National Association of School Psychologists (2000), and National Board for Certified Counselors (1997) include designated sections on assessment, measurement, evaluation, and research. The codes of the American Association of School Administrators (1976), National Association of Elementary School Principals (1976), National Association of Secondary School Principals (2001), National Education Association (1975), and National School Boards Association (1999) also include relevant sections.

The *Standards for Educational and Psychological Testing* (AERA, APA, & NCME, 1999) offers thorough and detailed information on ethical practices. Documents from the American Counseling Association and Association for Assessment in Counseling (1989), Eyde et al.

(1993), and the Joint Committee on Testing Practices (2000, 2002) provide additional information. Professional publications include information on concepts and practices in assessment and ethics (see, e.g., Anastasi & Urbina, 1997; Bauernfeind, Wickwire, & Read, 1991; Garfield & Krieshok, 2001; Hymes, Chafin, & Gonder, 1991; Linn, 1993; Lyman, 1997; Westgaard, 1993; and Wiggins, 1993). Compendia of assessment instruments include descriptions as well as cross-sectional and longitudinal documentation (e.g., Impara & Plake, 1998; Keyser & Sweetland, 1984–1994; Murphy, Impara, & Plake, 1999).

Concluding Statement

Current and future challenges are emerging in the exercise of educational assessment. Among the challenges already being discussed and put into operation are efforts in accountability, including high-stakes testing (Congress of the U.S. Office of Technology Assessment, 1992; National Council on Education Standards and Testing, 1992); in technological change, including e-learning, distance education, computer-assisted assessment, computer-adaptive assessment, and media-assisted assessment (Congress of the U.S. Office of Technology Assessment, 1992; Sattem, Reynolds, Gernhardt, & Burdeshaw, 2000; Wall, 2000); and in partnerships for progress, including an emphasis on the assessment of skills and competencies in cooperation with business and industry (Secretary's Commission on Achieving Necessary Skills, 1991). In addressing these and other challenges, opportunities, and possibilities, professionals serve their clients best by thoughtful and thorough adherence to professional ethics. Professionals practice ETHICS: engage empowerment (E), temper tone (T), honor humanity (H), internalize integrity (I), communicate commitment (C), and synthesize standards (S) as they strive to ensure that educational assessment results in value-added benefits for student learning and the learning experience.

References

AERA, APA, & NCME [American Educational Research Association, American Psychological Association, & National Council on Measurement in Education]. (1999). *Standards for educational and psychological testing.* Washington, DC: American Educational Research Association.

American Association of School Administrators. (1976). *Statement of ethics for school administrators.* Arlington, VA: Author.

✦American Counseling Association. (1997). *Code of ethics and standards of practice.* Alexandria, VA: Author.

✦Association for Assessment in Counseling. (2003). *Responsibilities of users of standardized tests.* Available on *Measuring Up: An Anthology of Assessment Resources* [CD]. Also retrievable on-line: http://aac.ncat.edu.

✦American Educational Research Association. (1992). *Ethical standards of the American Educational Research Association.* Washington, DC: Author.

✦American Psychological Association. (1992). *Ethical principles of psychologists and code of conduct.* Washington, DC: Author.

✦American School Counselor Association. (1998). *Ethical standards for school counselors.* Alexandria, VA: Author.

✦American Speech-Language-Hearing Association. (2001). *Code of ethics.* Rockville, MD: Author.

Anastasi, A., & Urbina, S. (1997). *Psychological testing* (7th ed.). Upper Saddle River, NJ: Prentice Hall.

Bauernfeind, R. H., Wickwire, P. N., & Read, R. W. (1991). *Standardized tests: A practical handbook.* DeKalb, IL: VCB Books.

Bell, G. (1994a). *Making appropriate and ethical choices in large-scale assessments: A model policy code* (Report No. RPIC-MAEP-94). Oak Brook, IL: North Central Regional Educational Laboratory. (ERIC Document Reproduction Service No. ED413353)

Bell, G. (1994b). *The test of testing: Making appropriate and ethical choices in assessment* (Report No. RPIC-TT-94). Oak Brook, IL: North Central Regional Educational Laboratory. (ERIC Document Reproduction Service No. ED379337)

✦Congress of the U.S. Office of Technology Assessment. (1992). *Testing in American schools: Asking the right questions* (Report No. OTA-SET-520). Washington, DC: Government Printing Office.

Eyde, L. D., Robertson, G. J., Krug, S. E., Moreland, K. L., Robertson, A. G., Shewan, C. M., et al. (1993). *Responsible test use: Case studies for assessing human behavior.* Washington, DC: American Psychological Association.

Garfield, N. J., & Krieshok, T. S. (2001). Assessment and counseling competencies and responsibilities: A checklist for counselors. In J. T. Kapes & E. A. Whitfield (Eds.), *A counselor's guide to career assessment instruments* (pp. 65–72). Columbus, OH: National Career Development Association.

Hymes, D. L., Chafin, A. E., & Gonder, P. (1991). *The changing face of testing and assessment: Problems and solutions.* Arlington, VA: American Association of School Administrators.

Impara, J. C., & Plake, B. S. (Eds.). (1998). *The thirteenth mental measurements yearbook.* Lincoln, NE: Buros Institute of Mental Measurement, University of Nebraska-Lincoln.

✦Joint Committee on Testing Practices. (2002). *Code of fair testing practices in education: Guidelines and expectations.* Available on *Measuring Up: An Anthology of Assessment Resources* [CD]. Also retrievable on-line: http://aac.ncat.edu.

✦Joint Committee on Testing Practices. (2000). *The rights and responsibilities of test takers.* Washington, DC: American Psychological Association.

Keyser, D. J., & Sweetland, R. C. (Eds.). (1984–1994). *Test critiques* (Vols. 1–10). Austin, TX: Pro-Ed.

Kitchener, K. S. (1984). Intuition, critical evaluation, and ethical principles: The foundation for ethical decisions in counseling psychology. *Counseling Psychologist, 12*(3), 43–55.

Kohlberg, L. (1969). Stage and sequence: The cognitive developmental approach to socialization. In D. Goshen (Ed.), *Handbook of socialization theory and research* (pp. 347–480). Chicago: Rand-McNally.

Kohlberg, L. (1972, Nov.–Dec.). A cognitive development approach to moral education. *The Humanist,* 13–16.

Linn, R. L. (Ed.). (1993). *Educational measurement* (3rd ed.). Phoenix, AZ: Oryx Press.

Lyman, H. B. (1997). *Test scores and what they mean* (6th ed.). Englewood Cliffs, NJ: Prentice Hall.

Muratori, M. M. (2001). An ethical decision-making model. *Counselor Education and Supervision, 41*(1), 50–56.

Murphy, L. L., Impara, J. C., & Plake, B. S. (Eds.). (1999). *Tests in print: An index to tests, test reviews, and the literature on specific tests* (5th ed.). Lincoln, NE: Buros Institute of Mental Measurement, University of Nebraska-Lincoln.

✦National Association of Elementary School Principals. (1976). *Statement of ethics for school administrators.* Alexandria, VA: Author.

✦National Association of School Psychologists. (2000). *Professional conduct manual: Principles for professional ethics and guidelines for the provision of school psychological services.* Bethesda, MD: Author.

National Association of Secondary School Principals. (2001). *Statement of ethics for school administrators.* Reston, VA: Author.

✦National Board for Certified Counselors. (1997). *Code of ethics.* Greensboro, NC: Author.

National Council on Education Standards and Testing. (1992). *Raising standards for American education: A report to Congress, the Secretary of Education, the National Education Goals Panel, and the American people.* Washington, DC: Government Printing Office.

✦National Council on Measurement and Evaluation. (1995). *Code of professional responsibilities in educational measurement.* Washington, DC: Author.

✦National Education Association. (1975). *Code of ethics of the education profession.* Washington, DC: Author.

National School Boards Association. (1999). *Principles and beliefs: Code of ethics for school board members.* Alexandria, VA: Author.

Sattem, L., Reynolds, K., Gernhardt, G. R., & Burdeshaw, J. R. (2000). Cyberspace education and lifelong learning for professionals: Dangerous opportunities. In J. W. Bloom & G. R. Walz (Eds.), *Cybercounseling and cyberlearning: Strategies and resources for the millennium* (pp. 275–290). Alexandria, VA: American Counseling Association and CAPS.

Secretary's Commission on Achieving Necessary Skills. (1991). *What work requires of schools: ASCANS report for America 2000.* Washington, DC: U.S. Department of Labor. (ERIC Document Reproduction Service No. ED332054)

Van Zandt, C. E. (1990). Professionalism: A matter of personal initiative. *Journal of Counseling and Development, 68*(3), 243–245.

Wall, J. E. (2000). Technology-delivered assessment: Power, problems, and promise. In J. W. Bloom & G. R. Walz (Eds.), Cybercounseling and cyberlearning: Strategies and resources for the millennium (pp. 237–251). Alexandria, VA: American Counseling Association and CAPS.

Westgaard, O. (1993). *Good, fair tests: Test design and implementation.* Amherst, MA: HRD Press.

Wiggins, G. P. (1993). *Assessing student performance: Exploring the purpose and limits of testing.* San Francisco: Jossey-Bass.

✦ Document is included in the Anthology of Assessment Resources CD

Chapter 26
Educational Testing Integrity
Why Educators and Students Cheat and How to Prevent It

Gregory J. Cizek

Cheating undermines integrity and fairness at all levels. It leads to weak life performance. It undermines the merit basis of our society. Cheating is an issue that should concern every citizen of this country. (Cole, 1998, p. A-24)

Sound testing practices and the high-quality information that can result are helpful to those who have oversight, responsibility, or interest in American education. From a broader perspective, sound testing programs benefit society at large (Mehrens & Cizek, 2001). To the extent that tests provide high-quality information, they form the basis for making accurate judgments about individual students. Test data also provide the grist for pursuing well-reasoned courses of action in terms of recommendations for improving policies and practices and evaluating reforms.

It is equally true, however, that factors which attenuate the validity of tests or degrade the usefulness of the information they yield represent threats to sound decision making. Those in the field of psychometrics are what might be called "data quality-control specialists" who help to ensure that tests yield the kind of valid and useful information they were designed to produce. One aspect of data quality control is a professional vigilance about threats to the accuracy and dependability of test information.

To a great degree, modern testing theory and practice have evolved to address many of the threats. For example, validity theory has been advanced through the work of Kane (1992), Messick (1989), and others. Generalizability theory (Brennan, 1992) provides sophisticated new ways of examining the dependability of test scores. Computerization has made automated test assembly and administration as common in high-stakes testing contexts as the No. 2 pencil (Luecht, 1998). The degree and breadth of these changes are witnessed by the recent a more extensive and specific list of cheating methods used by test takers. Student cheating is not the only concern, however. Those who are responsible for administering tests can also act in ways that destroy the accuracy of test result interpretation, and examples of educator cheating will be provided later in this chapter.

Why Cheating Is a Problem

Validity is the single greatest concern in any testing situation. The concept refers to the accuracy of the interpretations made about examinees based on their test scores. Phrased in slightly more technical terms, validity is the degree to which evidence supports the inferences made about a person's knowledge, skill, or ability based on his or her observed performance. By definition, inferences are based upon a less-than-ideal amount of information, such as on a sample of a person's knowledge or skill obtained via a test. Because it is generally too costly or impractical to gather more information, inferences must be based on samples of behavior. Consequently, it is necessary to consider the accuracy of inferences based on the available evidence (e.g., test performance); that is, to consider validity. This idea of validity as accuracy of inferences and sufficiency of evidence are central in modern psychometric theory and are the foundation of professionally defensible testing practices. Any factor that attenuates the ability to make accurate inferences from the sample of performance threatens validity and jeopardizes the meaningfulness of conclusions about the test taker. When cheating occurs, inaccurate inferences result.

Guidelines Regarding Cheating

There is an abundance of information to guide test takers and test administrators in how to avoid inappropriate testing practices. For their part, test developers usually produce carefully scripted directions for administering their tests and provide clear guidelines as to which kinds of behaviors on the part of examinees and educators are permissible and which are not. Acceptable and unacceptable behaviors are sometimes formalized in state administrative codes or statutes; one example is found in the State of Ohio Revised Code (see Amended Senate Bill 230, Ohio Revised Code, 3319.151, 1996). Numerous professional organizations have published statements on cheating (see, e.g., National Association of Test Directors, n.d.). Some of the most explicit statements regarding cheating are found in the aforementioned

Standards for Educational and Psychological Testing (AERA et al., 1999). Among other things, the *Standards* indicate that those involved in testing programs should

- protect the security of tests (Standard 11.7);
- inform examinees that it is inappropriate for them to have someone else take the test for them, disclose secure test materials, or engage in any other form of cheating (Standard 8.7);
- ensure that individuals who administer and score tests are proficient in administration procedures and understand the importance of adhering to directions provided by the test developer (Standard 13.10);
- ensure that test preparation activities and materials provided to students will not adversely affect the validity of test score inferences (Standard 13.11); and
- maintain the integrity of test results by eliminating practices designed to raise test scores without improving students' real knowledge, skills, or abilities in the area tested (Standard 15.9).

Despite these admonitions regarding cheating, not all communication about cheating is clear. For example, the same test publisher that produces a test administration manual with explicit guidelines regarding proper test administration and security procedures might also publish test preparation materials that bear a strong resemblance to actual tests. Moreover, guidelines for appropriate administration can vary from test to test, with one publisher permitting a teacher to clarify a test question for a student and another publisher proscribing the same behavior.

Although some ambiguities will always exist regarding whether a particular action constitutes cheating, there has not generally been a dissemination problem regarding what constitutes integrity in testing or cheating on tests. Virtually everyone involved in testing knows how to administer (and take) tests that yield credible, accurate results. Unfortunately, mere knowledge about what constitutes cheating is not enough.

Who Cheats, How Much, and Why?

Test takers cheat. They let others cheat. Test administrators and proctors cheat. Although hard data on the frequency of cheating are difficult to come by, two types of data exist: results of research studies on cheating (most often surveys), and anecdotal reports that arise via newspaper and broadcast media outlets. Both sources of evidence have limitations. Surveys always suffer from some degree of inaccuracy, particularly when the questions center on sensitive or illegal behaviors. Anecdotal reports are sometimes exaggerated or prove to be false. Despite these limitations, reports of cheating are surfacing with increasing regularity, and enough credible evidence has accumulated to conclude that the problem of educators cheating on tests is increasing.

Summarizing several studies, Bellezza & Bellezza (1989) speculate that 5 percent may be a reasonable estimate of the percentage of test takers who engage in cheating on any particular occasion. And, though the frequency of educator cheating is surely small, the previously mentioned accounts of bribes paid to proctors, the far-reaching investigation in New York City schools, and other reports suggest that those who give tests are also engaging in the behavior with increasing frequency.

Examinees' motivations for cheating are easiest to comprehend. They want high grades, a license to practice in their chosen profession, opportunities for advancement, issuance of a credential, or other payoffs. Sometimes examinees allow other test takers to cheat. Davis and colleagues (1992) conducted a study of college students, examining why they would allow others to cheat; the most frequently cited reasons follow:

- Just to do it. I didn't like the teacher, and I knew if I got caught nothing would happen.
- I knew they studied and knew the material, but test taking was really difficult.
- No particular reason. It doesn't bother me because I probably got it wrong and so will they.
- Because they might let me cheat off them some time.
- She was damn good-looking.
- I wouldn't want them to be mad at me.
- I knew they needed to do good in order to pass the class. I felt sorry for them.
- He was bigger than me.

Cheating on the part of those who give tests is only slightly more difficult to understand. Teachers and principals have professional pride at stake and, increasingly, the potential for personal reward or sanction under school accountability systems. Those who direct medical residency programs or oversee education and training organizations have an interest in promoting strong performance on the part of their students. Numerous studies have documented that the majority of high school and college graduates have cheated on tests in their own academic careers. Because so much of that cheating went undetected and unpunished, and because they can easily put themselves in the position of examinees desperate to pass a test, those who give tests may often be tempted to turn a blind eye to cheating.

A Different Way of Thinking about Cheating

The conclusion that cheating has occurred on a test can be made only after a careful examination of evidence. Such an investigation usually begins following what is initially termed a "testing irregularity." When tests are administered, events that are out of the ordinary can occur. Such an event may be within or beyond the control of those administering or those taking tests. Until causal attributions can be confidently asserted, the event cannot be interpreted as cheating. Examples of irregularities could include these:

- a fire alarm that required evacuation of a building during a testing session. Ordinarily, this event would be beyond the control of test administrators, but the event could increase student anxiety, reduce students' ability to attend to test materials on their return to the testing session, or have other consequences. If this occurred, students' performances on the test may not represent their true levels of knowledge, skill, or ability; that is, the students' proficiency levels would be underestimated.
- permitting examinees to have additional time to complete a test beyond the limits prescribed. This event would ordinarily be within the control of test administrators. If this occurred, examinees' performances on the test again may not represent their true levels of knowledge, skill, or ability, though in this case students' proficiency levels would likely be overestimated.
- repeated, sustained glancing by one examinee at the answer sheet of an adjacent examinee.

Two fundamental questions arise when a testing irregularity occurs. One concerns the likelihood of the event. Unusual occurrences are not infrequent, but some events are less likely than others. The less likely an event is to occur, the more our curiosity is piqued. The rarer an event is—such as winning a super lottery or being struck by lightning—the greater our interest in the event usually is.

The second question centers on explanations for unusual events. For example, airplane crashes are rare; an intense interest in understanding the cause of that rare occurrence can linger for months, even years following the event. Our interest is particularly keen in understanding what role, if any, human intervention may have played in the event. Purely random events occur all the time, and they can be readily accepted as such. For example, in a fair lottery, numbers are selected randomly and those who do not hold the winning number can (usually) accept the randomness of that event. On the other hand, it would not be tolerable if human intervention or manipulation of the lottery tilted the process in favor of certain numbers or gave a priori advantage to certain individuals. This type of human intervention changes our characterization (and acceptance) of the process from random to fraudulent.

The responsibilities of those who administer tests are particularly germane to this point. When we suspect that testing irregularities may have occurred as a result of human intervention—through negligence; deviation from prescribed testing practices; or intentional manipulation of circumstances, testing conditions, or results—then our sense of ethical behavior and fairness is violated as are, in many cases, legal or administrative guidelines. At minimum, a first step in addressing the problem of cheating is to establish and ensure broad familiarity with a set of procedures for observing and documenting irregularities.

Assessing the Possibility of Cheating

There are two general categories of methods for investigating and evaluating the potential that cheating has occurred: judgmental and statistical. As the label suggests, judgmental methods rely more heavily on subjective human interpretations. For example, a student might enlist the aid of a confederate to take the SAT in his or her place. Human judgment is involved in detecting and responding to this irregularity when the proctors for the examination scrutinize photo identification before permitting examinees to take the test. Judgment is also involved in comparing handwriting samples from the student with those of the confederate to make a determination of whose handwriting appears on the test materials.

Statistical methods can be used to estimate the likelihood of events such as anomalous or unusual test results. Some events have very small probabilities associated with them. For example, according to gambling experts, the first-year National Hockey League team the Columbus Blue Jackets was estimated to have only a 1 in 500 chance ($p = .002$) of winning the 2002 Stanley Cup. Those odds are actually fairly good in comparison to the chance of being struck by lightning (1 in 709,260, or $p = .00000141$); the chance of dying from a lightning strike are even less, estimated at 1 in 2,794,493, or $p = 000000358$. Worse yet are the odds of correctly picking 6 numbers out of 49 in a lottery (1 in 14,000,000, or $p = .000000071$).

All the p values mentioned in the preceding paragraph represent extremely small probabilities. In fact, the examples illustrate occurrences that could be considered nearly impossible. But at what threshold should we consider an event as being so unlikely to have occurred by chance that we are compelled to consider other potential causes? In the social sciences, the standard probability level associated with statistical significance (that is, the p value at which scientists come to conclusions or make decisions about human behavior) is $p < .05$.

Of course, highly unlikely events *can* occur, but we ordinarily become suspicious when they do, and we are led to conclude that simple chance should be ruled out as a plausible explanation. If the Blue Jackets were to win the Stanley Cup, such an upset would likely lead to calls for an investigation to rule out any irregularities in that sporting contest. Similarly, unusual results can occur on tests. For example, two examinees seated next to each other during a 200-item multiple-choice licensure examination may each answer the same 146 items correctly. Further, they may choose the same incorrect options for the 54 items they answered incorrectly. Statistical methods for detecting cheating on tests answer the simple question, How likely is it that these examinees would, by chance alone, have produced the same response patterns? If the answer to that question suggests that the events were not very likely due simply to chance, then investigations into plausible alternative explanations begins.

It is important to note, however, that statistical methods do not obviate the need for human judgment. Even once test results are shown to be highly unlikely, human rationality must be invoked to come to any conclusions about whether alternative causes represent more plausible explanations for the results; that is, there still exists a need to make subjective interpretations about whether the unlikely events represent cheating.

Triggers for Investigations of Testing Irregularities

It is not enough to ascertain that a testing irregularity was an improbable event, because improbable events do occur. The probability of obtaining a score of 20 out of 20 through blind guessing on a test comprised of true-false items would be p = .000000954—a nearly impossible event. However, other factors would ordinarily alter our interpretation of that probability. For example, if an examinee used his or her knowledge of the content being tested to make informed answer choices or educated guesses, then the probability of scoring 20 out of 20 would be substantially increased. Further, if the test were an easy one, and the examinee highly knowledgeable, then the probability of obtaining a score of 20 out of 20 could approach p = 1.0. Thus, to evaluate the probability of an occurrence, we must bring ancillary information to bear.

One increasingly essential source of supplemental information is referred to as a *trigger.* In large testing programs such as the SAT, for example, many people obtain highly unusual scores (e.g., a total score of 1600). Such performance would not arouse suspicions of irregularity if that student had taken the test previously and obtained a 1560, had a high school GPA of 4.0, was class valedictorian at a college preparatory school, and the like. On the other hand, such performance would arouse suspicion if, for example, the examinee's previous score had been a 470, if a fellow student reported that the examinee had access to the SAT test questions in advance, or if a test proctor observed the examinee copying from a nearby test taker of extremely high ability. Each of these situations involves what is called a trigger: additional information that suggests further investigation of the irregularity is warranted.

In cases where cheating is suspected, statistical evaluations of test results are usually not appropriate in the absence of a trigger. The presence of a trigger, however, necessarily changes our interpretation of the likelihood that results were obtained fairly. Suppose, for example, the 20-item true-false test described earlier involved simple multiplication facts. It would be highly unlikely for a three-year-old to obtain a raw score of 20. Statistical estimates of the probability of the event would be very small, but the small probability would not necessarily lead to an allegation that the result was improper. If, however, an observer during the test reported that she saw the child's parent whispering in the child's ear immediately prior to the child answering each question, that information—a trigger—would suggest that the unusually unlikely event be regarded with a heightened level of suspicion and that other plausible explanations for the child's amazing performance should be investigated. Common triggers for conducting statistical investigations of alleged cheating include such things as observations by a proctor of unusual examinee behavior during an examination, anonymous tips that a student had unauthorized prior access to a test, and reports by one teacher that another teacher gave students extra time to complete a state-mandated examination.

Of course, triggers usually involve human judgment and, as such, can be fallible. The extensive literature in the field of criminology speaks definitively about the unreliability of eyewitness testimony (see, e.g., Loftus, 1979). An act of inference occurs when a proctor observes one examinee apparently looking at another examinee's answer sheet. Objectively, the behavior can also be interpreted as an examinee innocently averting his or her gaze temporarily to gain relief from intense concentration on the task at hand.

Statistical Tools

A number of statistical tools exist to help detect possible cheating and to provide quantification of the probability that an irregularity can be attributed to chance. Only one commercially available software program exists. The program, called *Scrutiny!*, can be run on a typical personal computer. Unfortunately, *Scrutiny!* has not received strong recommendation in the professional literature (see Bay, 1995; Frary, 1993). Statistical procedures for detecting copying that are technically superior to that used by *Scrutiny!* exist; however, they are not yet commercially available in software packages (see Frary, Tideman, & Watts, 1977; Wollack, 1997). These procedures offer more power to detect true copying while safeguarding against overidentification, and they can be used with relatively small sample sizes.

Although statistical methods may provide a defensible way of producing evidence to support a suspicion of cheating, it is important to restate that statistical analyses should be triggered by some other factor (e.g., observation). None of the statistical approaches should be used as a screening tool to mine data for possible anomalies. A recent court decision involving the Association of Social Work Boards (ASWB) examination program provides an illustration. According to an article in the *ASWB Association News* (Atkinson, 2000), several examinees who had taken the February 1995 administration of the ASWB examination had their scores invalidated and were refused licenses. These actions were the result of analyses of their test scores that "revealed statistical abnormalities" (p. 9). In litigation, it was noted that "there did not appear to be any on-site problems" or reports of irregularities when the test was administered, although an "administrator for the social work board had received a telephone call indicating that certain individuals had copies of the exam prior to its administration" (p. 9). Both the circuit and appeals courts decided in favor of the examinees, noting that there was a lack of evidence to justify the examinees being investigated for possible cheating in the first place. It appears, the telephone call notwithstanding, that no triggering event was found to justify the consideration of statistical evidence.

The Particular Problem of Educator Cheating on Tests

The testing director of a large city school district summarized the problem of educator cheating: "Teachers cheat when they administer standardized tests to students. Not all teachers, not even very many of them; but enough to make cheating a major concern to all of us who use test data for decision making" (Ligon, 1985, p. 1).

One need only search the Internet, look at a national magazine, or skim a newspaper to confirm that many educators are attempting to circumvent the testing, monitoring, and accountability systems. Stories of cheating abound, and the methods are numerous, ranging from subtle coaching to overt manipulation. A *U.S. News and World Report* article described a case in Ohio where one educator is accused of physically moving a student's pencil-holding hand to the correct answer on a multiple-choice question (Kleiner, 2000). A recent *Washington Post* story announced the resignation of a Potomac, Maryland, principal who stepped down amidst charges that she "was sitting in the [class]room, going through test booklets and calling students up to change or elaborate on answers" (Schulte, 2000). A colleague of mine in educational testing tells the story of a principal who would begin the announcements each morning with a greeting via the school public address system: "Good morning, students, and salutations! Do you know what a salutation is? It means 'greeting,' like the greeting you see at the beginning of a letter." Apparently, students learned the meanings of words like *salutation* from the principal's daily announcements; they probably never learned that his choice of such words was not random, but was made with the vocabulary section of the state-mandated, norm-referenced test in hand.

I found out about a particularly blatant form of educator cheating more than a decade ago at an evening reception following a conference for school district superintendents in one Midwestern state. I happened upon a conversation among several superintendents who, with cocktails in hand, were chuckling and winking about how their quality-control procedures for state-mandated student testing involved "prescreening the kids' answer sheets for stray marks." What was so funny, I found out later from one of the superintendents, was that "stray marks includes things like wrong answers." Wink. Apparently, the practice continues. Another recent article describes how 11 school districts in Texas were called to account for an unusually high number of erasures on that state's test (Johnston & Galley, 1999).

Most cheating is probably not this overt. More subtle forms of cheating are undoubtedly more frequent, but they still serve to degrade the meaning of test results and confidence in education systems. More subtle kinds of cheating occur when a teacher prods a student to review his or her answer: "Why don't you take another look at what you wrote down for number 17." Some of those who give tests cheat by proxy, by failing to proctor tests conscientiously, thereby effectively encouraging cheating on the part of students. Cheating also occurs when educators fail to include all students who would be eligible to take a test, as might happen when a teacher reminds certain students who are likely to score poorly on a test that they are permitted to be absent on the day of the test. The *Education Week* article by Johnston & Galley (1999) describes a sophisticated variation of this kind of cheating in which incorrect student identification numbers were apparently purposefully entered on the answer sheets of low-scoring students. This had the effect of kicking those answer sheets out of the scoring process and inflating the school's average performance. Another form of cheating involves affording a student inappropriate or unnecessary testing disability accommodations such as an individual aide, reader, or other assistance not usually a part of the student's educational experience.

Perhaps the most prominent report of educator cheating involved teachers and principals in the New York City school system. Edward Stancik, special commissioner of investigation for the New York City School District, conducted an exhaustive study of cheating. His study found that cheating by 12 educators was "so egregious that their employment must be terminated and they should be barred from future work with the [Board of Education]" (Stancik & Brenner, 1999, p. 63) The report recommended another 40 educators for disciplinary action, 35 of whom engaged in actions judged serious enough to warrant potential termination. Examples of the cheating Stancik identified included a principal who during a test "walked around the room and pointed out [to the students] incorrect choices, saying either 'That's wrong' or 'Do that one over'" (p. 2). According to Stancik's investigation, fourth-grade students at another school reported that their teacher, Teresa Czarnowski, helped them cheat by correcting their answers in advance. Stancik reported, "According to one boy, who is indicative of those we interviewed, after he finished the test on the separate sheet [of scrap paper], he gave it to Czarnowski who checked his choices and marked an X on the scrap next to his wrong answers. Then she returned the paper to the student who corrected his responses and, finally, he transferred his selections to the official bubble form" (p. 11). Overall, the report concluded that there had been "extensive cheating by educators," that the school district had "known about the problem for years," and that "educators were not held fully liable for their misconduct" (p. 60). The public release of the initial report brought greater attention to the problem. According to a follow-up report issued in May 2000 by the investigators' office:

> Almost immediately, our intake unit was busy with new complaints of wrongdoing committed by Board of Education employees during the testing process. Then in February 2000, while we were conducting investigations into those allegations, students took the State English Language Assessment (ELA) examination and reports of suspicious behavior and writing in test booklets again poured into our office. . . . Once again we found proctors who gave answers to students, alerted them to wrong responses, and changed student choices after the exam was turned in. Moreover, this investigation uncovered new methods of misconduct, including prepping children for the third day of the ELA exam by using the actual test material. Finally, our investigations continued to be impeded by delay in the reporting of testing allegations to this office. (Stancik, 2000, p. 1)

The follow-up report named another 10 educators who had engaged in seriously inappropriate behavior during testing in New York City. Many of the educators had cheated so blatantly—for example, by writing answers to test questions on the chalkboard—that immediate termination of employment was recommended.[1]

Research on Educator Cheating

The most common avenue of research does not ask educators directly about whether they engage in what have come to be referred to euphemistically as "inappropriate test administration practices," though a few studies have done so. Usually, educators have been polled regarding their general perceptions of cheating in their schools. One such study asked 3rd-, 6th-, 8th-, and 10th-grade teachers in North Carolina to report how frequently they had witnessed certain inappropriate practices. Overall, 35 percent of the teachers said they had observed cheating, in terms of either personally engaging in inappropriate practices or being aware of unethical actions of others. (The teachers in this study reported that their colleagues engaged in the behaviors from two to ten times more frequently than they had personally.) The behaviors included giving extra time on timed tests, changing answers on students' answer sheets, suggesting answers to students, and directly teaching specific portions of a test. More flagrant examples included the case of students being given dictionaries and thesauruses by teachers for use on a state-mandated writing test. One teacher revealed that she checked students answer sheets "to be sure that her students answered as they had been taught." Other teachers reported more subtle strategies such as "a nod of approval, a smile, and calling attention to a given answer" were effective at enhancing students' performance (Gay, 1990).

A study initiated to investigate suspected cheating in the Chicago Public Schools included a total of 40 schools, 17 "control" schools and 23 "suspect" schools that exhibited irregularities in the performance of their seventh- and eighth-grade students on the Iowa Tests of Basic Skills. Irregularities consisted of unusual patterns of score increases in previous years, unnecessarily large orders of blank answer sheets for the test, and high percentages of erasures on students' answer sheets. The researchers readministered the Iowa Tests under more controlled conditions and found that, even accounting for the reduced level of motivation students would have had on the retesting, "clearly the suspect schools did much worse on the retest than the comparison schools" and concluded that "it's possible that we may have underestimated the extent of cheating at some schools" (Perlman, 1985, pp. 4–5). A study of cheating in the Memphis School District revealed extensive cheating on the California Achievement Test, including one case in which a teacher displayed correctly filled-in answer sheets on the walls of her classroom (Toch & Wagner, 1992).

Educators' Perceptions of Cheating

Perhaps the most troubling stream of research on cheating concerns educators' attitudes toward cheating. Generally, educators appear to be growing increasingly indifferent toward the behavior, and even increasingly to feel that cheating is a justifiable response to externally mandated tests.

Several attempts have been made to investigate educators' perceptions of cheating. In one study, 74 preservice teachers were asked to indicate how appropriate they believed certain behaviors were. Only 1.4 percent thought that either changing answers on a student's answer sheet or giving hints or clues during testing were appropriate, and only 2.7 percent agreed that allowing more time than allotted for a test was acceptable. However, 8.1 percent thought that practicing on actual test items was okay, 23.4 percent believed rephrasing or rewording questions to be acceptable, and 37.6 percent judged practice on an alternate test form to be appropriate (Kher-Durlabhji & Lacina-Gifford, 1992).

The beliefs of preservice teachers appear to translate into actual practices when they enter the classroom. A large sample of third-, fifth-, and sixth-grade teachers in two school districts was asked to describe the extent to which they believed teachers in their schools practiced specific cheating behaviors. On the positive side, a majority of respondents said all but one of the behaviors listed occurred rarely or never (see Table 1). Equally noticeable, however, is that a wide range of behaviors was reported as occurring "frequently" or "often" by, in some cases, 15 percent or more of respondents. A second observation that leaps from Table 1 is the remarkable frequency with which teachers report that they have "no idea how often this occurs" (Shepard & Doughtery, 1991); this response suggests widespread unfamiliarity with other teachers' testing practices or lack of professional collaboration related to assessment.

Though not attempted here (or elsewhere to my knowledge), the costs of cheating probably could be measured in dollars and cents. What cannot be measured are the effects of educator cheating at more fundamental levels. For example, when students learn that their teachers or principals cheat, what is the effect of this kind of role modeling? Whereas fallen professional athletes might be able to say, "Don't look at me as a role model, I am just an athlete doing a job," educators cannot. A significant aspect of their job is the modeling of appropriate social and ethical behavior. In addition, how might educator cheating affect students' attitudes toward tests or their motivation to excel? How might it affect their attitudes toward education, their trust or cynicism with respect to other institutions, or their propensity to cheat in other contexts?

Table 1. Teacher Beliefs About Inappropriate Test Administration Practices

Question: To what extent do you believe these are practiced by teachers in your school?

	Percentage of Respondents				
Behavior	Never	Rarely	Often	Frequently	No Idea
1. Providing hints on correct answers	28.5	20.8	16.9	5.8	28.0
2. Giving students more time than test directions permit	38.0	19.7	15.2	4.4	22.7
3. Reading questions to students that they are supposed to read themselves	38.8	22.2	11.9	2.2	24.9
4. Answering questions about test content	43.2	20.5	8.9	2.8	24.7
5. Changing answers on a studen's answer sheet	58.4	7.8	5.5	0.6	27.7
6. Rephrasing questions during testing	36.3	20.8	16.1	1.9	24.9
7. Not administering the test to students who would have trouble with it	50.7	15.8	7.5	5.8	20.2
8. Encouraging students who would have trouble on the test to be absent on test day	60.1	10.8	5.5	1.9	21.6
9. Practicing items from the test itself	54.6	12.5	8.0	3.3	21.6
10. Giving students answers to test questions	56.8	11.6	6.4	1.9	23.3
11. Giving practice on highly similar passages to those in the test	24.9	15.8	20.5	19.7	19.1

Recommended Strategies for Preventing Cheating

What can be done to deter cheating? Fortunately, many things. As a starting point, bringing the issue of cheating forward as a topic for discussion is likely to increase awareness of the problem by those who give and take tests. It is important to heighten sensitivity about a validity threat heretofore virtually ignored. From the broadest perspective, it may be useful to entirely reconceptualize testing so that successful test performance can be more consistently and directly linked to student effort and effective instruction, and so that unsuccessful performance is accompanied by sufficient diagnostic information about students' strengths and weaknesses. As a result of identifying and addressing students' needs, we advance the perspective that obtaining accurate test results is more beneficial to all concerned than is cheating (Cizek, 1999, chap. 11).

Numerous more pragmatic steps can also be taken. The following list should provide a start. Of the following, some are focused on test givers, others on test takers, and some apply to both.

Get the Word Out

It has been said that we more often stand in need of being reminded than we do of education. Nearly all testing programs provide documentation describing appropriate test administration procedures, state regulations define legal conduct for test administrators, and professional associations have produced documents to guide sound testing practice. Nonetheless, reports of cheating on tests are often accompanied by protestations from the guilty parties that they did not know the behavior was wrong. If only as a reminder and to heighten awareness, every implementation of high-stakes tests should be accompanied by dissemination of clear guidelines regarding permissible and impermissible behaviors. Such reminders should be clearly worded, pilot tested, distributed, and signed by all who handle testing materials, including test site supervisors, proctors, and examinees.

Decrease Reliance on Easily Corruptible Test Formats

Changes in test development practice can reduce the potential for some methods of cheating. For instance, it is more difficult for one student to copy another student's answer to an essay question, case analysis, or other constructed-response format than it is to copy a filled-in bubble response or to obtain the key to a multiple-choice item. Similarly, it is more difficult for an educator to forge or coach a student's answer to an essay question or a science experiment than to alter a filled-in bubble response or provide the key to a multiple-choice item.

It must be recognized, however, that a decreasing reliance on selected-response formats requires tradeoffs in terms of efficiency and scoring costs. It should also be recognized that the use of alternative formats will not completely solve the problem of cheating, for they can also be corrupted. (For an example of how the essay format can be corrupted on a state-mandated examination see Madaus, 1988).

Limit the Amount of Testing

It is probably a truism that limiting the amount of testing will decrease the amount of cheating. As many states continue to expand their pupil proficiency testing programs as a primary mechanism for accountability, opportunities for cheating are expanded. There have been two common, reactionary responses to the predictable increase in cheating. One reaction is the demand that large-scale testing for accountability be abandoned. For example, the September 22, 2000, issue of the *Congressional Quarterly* contained an essay by Monte Neill, the executive director of a group critical of testing, who argued the "pro" position on the question "Should high-stakes tests be abolished in order to reduce cheating?" (Neill, 2000). In the same issue, commentator Alfie Kohn is noted as one of several critics who "have seized on cheating as just another in a long list of reasons to abandon [standardized] tests." According to Kohn, "The real cheating going on in education reform is by those who are cheating students out of an education by turning schools into giant test-prep centers" (quoted in Koch, 2000, p. 759).

The difficulty with these first-blush reactions is that they fail to fully address the core issues. As I have argued elsewhere, the genesis of high-stakes student testing in the 1970s was made inevitable because of poor decision making—or at least the perception of poor decision making—and the resulting search for alternatives (see Cizek, 2001). It was during the tumultuous 1970s that complaints of some business and industry leaders began to receive broad public currency: We are getting high school graduates who have a diploma but can't read or write! As Popham observed at the time, "Minimum competency testing programs . . . have been installed in so many states as a way of halting what is perceived as a continuing devaluation of the high school diploma" (1978, p. 297). The clear public perception was that the gatekeepers were leaving the gates wide open.

Perhaps a widespread misunderstanding of the relationship between self-esteem and achievement was to blame. Understandably, educators wanted all students to achieve and all to have the personal esteem associated with those accomplishments. But assigning higher grades to heighten self-esteem and stimulate accomplishment too often had neither effect. The sense that grades weren't all they were cracked up to be wound its way from business and industry leaders' lips to policymakers' pens.

As the line of reasoning went, if the gatekeepers of the 1970s weren't watching the gates as conscientiously as the public had hoped, then important decisions about students should be remanded to passing one or more common tests. Thus, the obvious error in current calls to return to the past is that such a strategy only puts American education back in a place that caused accountability tests to be introduced in the first place. Moreover, though current tests have been shown to be susceptible to cheating, the solution of returning to measures and procedures that were demonstrably even more easily manipulated is unthinkable.

What should be considered is limiting the amount of testing for accountability. We must remember that there is a distinction between instruction and evaluation. It is obvious that not all tests are done for the purposes of evaluation. Equally true, however, is that not all tests—especially those designed for purposes of decision making—must have instructional value. Once their purpose has been clarified, the scope of mandated accountability tests, the time required for their administration, and the opportunities for cheating can be minimized.

Revise Test Disclosure Laws

States with so-called truth in testing laws or legislation requiring the release of secure test materials following their administration should reconsider the relative benefits of such laws. Despite their good intention, the unforeseen consequence of such laws has been an increase in educators' use of previous versions of tests for classroom practice, resulting in further narrowing of instruction. Additionally, the economic costs of such laws to states have been staggering, because of the need to develop entirely new monitoring instruments one or more times each year.

Audit Test Security Procedures

Those with oversight for testing programs can incorporate operational changes—many of which require only modest changes in current procedures—that can have a cumulative positive effect on reducing cheating. Many of these are not new, and many may already be in place; however, a regular security audit to review procedures is desirable. Common security measures include shrink wrapping, numbering, and bar coding test materials to deter unauthorized access and to permit tracing the path that the materials take. Other simple steps can easily be added, such as delaying delivery of testing materials until just prior to test administration. Once delivered, materials should be maintained securely by a named person responsible for their security. After test administration, similar security procedures should be followed by those responsible for collecting, organizing, and shipping the materials.

Improve Test Administration Conditions

Increased attention must be paid to one of the weakest links in the security chain: proctoring. Too often, the qualifications for supervising or proctoring examinations are only faintly spelled out, the training provided is minimal if any, and no incentives exist to heighten proctors' vigilance or pursuit of instances of cheating. For all testing contexts, proper training must include instruction on methods examinees use to cheat, as well as how to approach a test taker regarding suspicions of inappropriate behavior without unduly disrupting other examinees or inducing anxiety in those who are not cheating. In the context of large-scale testing, training should include effective procedures for documenting on-site testing irregularities.

Use Available Statistical Tools

Finally, recall that statistical detection methods should not be used to screen for statistically unusual response patterns. Nonetheless, research has demonstrated that informing examinees that detection software will be used can dramatically reduce the incidence of cheating. One study by Bellezza and Bellezza (1989) showed a reduction from approximately 5 percent to 1 percent in the incidence of cheating on college-level management course examinations. If a detection program may be used to provide supplemental evidence following a triggering event, it makes sense to inform examinees of this potential use.

Enforce Penalties for Cheating and Change the System of Investigation

In conjunction with limiting opportunities for cheating, procedures for investigating cheating and penalties for educator cheating must be dramatically revised. Many tests are administered behind closed classroom doors with little independent oversight; there are strong disincentives for educational personnel to report cheating; and in most jurisdictions, the responsibility for investigating cheating involves personnel at the school or district level and agencies such as boards of education with an inherent conflict of interest when it comes to ferreting out inappropriately high apparent student achievement.

Revised procedures should include random sampling and oversight of test sites; increased protections for whistle-blowers; more streamlined procedures and stiffer penalties for cheating, including permanent disqualification from teaching within a state and more coordinated sharing of information regarding educators who have had their licenses revoked; and delegation of responsibility for investigating incidents of cheating to an independent authority.

Implement Honor Codes

Because honor codes have been shown to reduce the incidence of cheating in other contexts, their use in licensure and certification testing should be examined. Honor codes require examinees to pledge to abide by a set of standards, including eschewing cheating themselves and obligating themselves to report cheating by others. Requiring examinees to sign such a pledge prior to taking an examination may work in credentialing settings as well.

Summary and Conclusions

Overall, the evidence is in regarding the problem of cheating on tests: Cheating is occurring with increasing frequency. It is fair to conclude that the problem will not disappear. Therefore, it must be addressed in order to ensure the integrity, fairness, and validity of test results. As a beginning step, those who have oversight of testing programs should make themselves aware of the myriad ways cheating can occur, including cheating by examinees and ways test administration staff may aid examinees in cheating. Additionally, those responsible for testing programs and those who oversee or give tests should address how they can help to reduce cheating, and should pursue courses that foster even greater levels of public protection and professional responsibility for the citizens and associations they serve.

Note

1. A response to the Stancik report commissioned by the New York City teachers union called into question his methods and whether some of the accusations of educator cheating were based on credible evidence. The original report and subsequent response in this case highlight the serious nature of cheating allegations, illustrate the ambiguities surrounding the appropriateness of some practices, and recall the need to ensure that adequate guidelines and training regarding cheating are in place.

References

AERA, APA, & NCME [American Educational Research Association, American Psychological Association, & National Council on Measurement in Education]. (1999). *Standards for educational and psychological testing.* Washington, DC: American Educational Research Association.

Atkinson, D. (2000, August). Testimony tests test. *ASWB Association News,* pp. 9, 11.

Bay, M. L. G. (1995, April). *Detection of cheating on multiple-choice examinations.* Paper presented at the annual meeting of the American Educational Research Association, San Francisco, CA.

Bellezza, F. S., & Bellezza, S. F. (1989). Detection of cheating on multiple-choice tests by using error-similarity analysis. *Teaching of Psychology, 16*(3), 151–155.

Brennan, R. L. (1992). Generalizability theory [NCME instructional module]. *Educational Measurement: Issues and Practice, 11*(4), 27–34.

Cizek, G. J. (1999). *Cheating on tests: How to do it, detect it, and prevent it.* Mahwah, NJ: Lawrence Erlbaum Associates.

Cizek, G. J. (2001). Conjectures on the rise and call of standard setting: An introduction to context and practice. In G. J. Cizek (Ed.), *Setting performance standards: Concepts, methods, and perspectives* (pp. 3–17). Mahwah, NJ: Lawrence Erlbaum Associates.

Cole, N. (1998, November 9). Teen cheating hurts all. *USA Today,* A-24.

Davis, S. F., Grover, C. A., Becker, A. H., & McGregor, L. N. (1992). Academic dishonesty: Prevalence, determinants, techniques, and punishments. *Teaching of Psychology, 19*(1), 16–20.

Frary, R. B. (1993). Statistical detection of multiple-choice answer copying: Review and commentary. *Applied Measurement in Education, 6*(2), 153–165.

Frary, R. B., Tideman, T. N., & Watts, T. M. (1977). Indices of cheating on multiple-choice tests. *Journal of Educational Statistics, 2,* 235–256.

Gay, G. H. (1990). Standardized tests: Irregularities in administering of tests affect test results. *Journal of Instructional Psychology, 17*(2), 93–103.

Johnston, R. C., & Galley, M. (1999, April 14). Austin district charged with test tampering. *Education Week,* p. 3.

Kane, M. T. (1992). An argument-based approach to validity. *Psychological Bulletin, 112,* 527–535.

Kher-Durlabhji, N., & Lacina-Gifford, L. J. (1992, April). *Quest for test success: Preservice teachers' views of high stakes tests.* Paper presented at the annual meeting of the Mid-South Educational Research Association, Knoxville, TN. (ERIC Document Reproduction Service No. ED 353 338)

Kleiner, C. (2000, June 12). Test case: Now the principal's cheating. *U.S. News and World Report.*

Koch, K. (2000). Cheating in schools. *Congressional Quarterly, 10*(32), 759.

Ligon, G. (1985, March). *Opportunity knocked out: Reducing cheating by teachers on student tests.* Paper presented at the annual meeting of the American Educational Research Association, Chicago, IL. (ERIC Document Reproduction Service No. ED 263 181).

Loftus, E. (1979). *Eyewitness testimony.* Cambridge, MA: Harvard University Press.

Luecht, R. M. (1998). Testing and measurement issues: Automated test assembly in the era of computerized testing. *CLEAR Exam Review, 9*(2), 19–22.

Madaus, G. F. (1988). The influence of testing on the curriculum. In L. N. Tanner (Ed.), *Critical issues in curriculum: Eighty-seventh yearbook of the National Society for the Study of Education* (pp. 83–121). Chicago: University of Chicago Press.

Mehrens, W. A., & Cizek, G. J. (2001). Standard setting and the public good. In G. J. Cizek (Ed.), *Setting performance standards: Concepts, methods, and perspectives* (pp. 477–485). Mahwah, NJ: Lawrence Erlbaum Associates.

Merx, K. (2000, August 11). Cop test altered in Dearborn. *Detroit News,* A-1.

Messick, S. A. (1989). Validity. In R. L. Linn (Ed.), *Educational measurement* (3rd ed., pp. 13–104). New York: Macmillan.

National Association of Test Directors. (n.d.). *Appendix C: Testing code of ethics for North Carolina testing personnel, teachers, and school administrators.* Retrieved online from www.natd.org/Apndx_c.htm

Neill, M. (2000). Should high-stakes tests be abolished in order to reduce cheating? *Congressional Quarterly, 10*(32), 761.

Payne, P. (2000, August 18). Officials say 52 teachers paid $1,000 to pass competency tests. *[Schenectady, NY] Daily Gazette,* A-7.

Perlman, C. L. (1985, March). *Results of a citywide testing program audit in Chicago.* Paper presented at the annual meeting of the American Educational Research Association, Chicago, IL. (ERIC Document Reproduction Service No. ED 263 212), pp. 4–5.

Popham, W. J. (1978). As always, provocative. *Journal of Educational Measurement, 15,* 297–300.

Schulte, B. (2000, June 1). School allegedly cheated on tests. *Washington Post,* A-1.

Seelye, K. Q. (1998, January 28). 20 charged with helping 13,000 cheat on test for citizenship. *New York Times,* A-1.

Shepard, L. A., & Doughtery, K. C. (1991). *Effects of high-stakes testing on instruction.* Paper presented at the annual meeting of the American Educational Research Association, Chicago, IL. (ERIC Document Reproduction Service No. ED 337 468)

Stancik, E. F. (2000, May 2). Correspondence to Harold O. Levy, Chancellor of New York City Public Schools, pp. 1–2.

Stancik, E. F., & Brenner, R. M. (1999). *Cheating the children: Educator misconduct on standardized tests.* New York: Office of the Special Commissioner of Investigation for the New York City School District.

Sullivan, J. (1997, January 9). 53 charged in brokers' testing fraud. *New York Times,* A-7.

Toch, T., & Wagner, B. (1992, April 27). Schools for scandal. *U.S. News and World Report,* pp. 66–72.

Toy, V. S. (1999, November 23). Drivers' test scheme reveals secret decoder watchbands. *New York Times,* B-2.

Wollack, J. A. (1997). A nominal response model approach for detecting answer copying. *Applied Psychological Measurement, 21,* 307–320.

Chapter 27
Practice Tests and Study Guides
Do They Help? Are They Ethical? What Is Ethical Test Preparation Practice?

Carole L. Perlman

The last decade has seen increasing reliance on standards-based instruction and on assessments that measure students' mastery of instructional standards. Currently, nearly every U.S. state requires at least some K–12 students to participate in state assessments and 27 states use state assessment results for accountability purposes; some state assessments are used to determine which students may be promoted or awarded a diploma (Olson, 2001). The No Child Left Behind Act will require annual reading and mathematics testing for students in grades three through eight, with serious consequences for schools whose students score poorly. Because the stakes can be high for both students and school staff, schools may place considerable emphasis on activities designed to help students perform well on tests. However, as the American Educational Research Association points out in its Position Statement Concerning High-Stakes Testing in PreK–12 Education (2000), high-stakes testing can result in inappropriate methods of test preparation.

What Is Test Preparation?

Within the context of elementary and high school achievement testing, *test preparation* has no single, universally agreed-on definition but instead refers to a number of practices that vary in the degree of specificity with which they address a particular test. Some of the less specific forms of test preparation include teaching general strategies for taking different types of tests, teaching content from the domain being tested, and practicing with items in various formats that measure the domain tested. More test-specific strategies include practice with items in a similar format to those on the test, using state- or district-provided sample items, practice with commercial test preparation materials, practice with parallel forms or old tests, or even practice with items from the actual test—even though that is clearly inappropriate, unethical (Cizek, 2001), and in some places, illegal (Johnston, 1999; Texas Education Code, Chap. 39, Subchap. C, ß101.65; Florida Statutes Title XVI, Chap. 228, ß228.301; the relevant sections of these state statutes may be downloaded from www.tea.state.tx.us/rules/tac/chapter101/ch101c.html and www.flsenate.gov/Statutes/index.cfm?mode=View%20Statutes&SubMenu=1&App_mode=Display_Statute&Search_String=&URL=CH0228/SEC301.HTM).

Does Test Preparation Help?

Some test preparation activities do appear to be beneficial. Mehrens and Kaminski (1989) cite several meta-analyses of test preparation research and conclude that test-wiseness training can improve scores on achievement tests, though not necessarily to a great extent. For example, practice on items similar to those on the real test can be helpful. Research also suggests that familiarizing students with the answer sheet format; encouraging them to do their best, to skip difficult items, and to listen carefully to the test directions; and giving them strategies for dealing with test anxiety *are* helpful. There is little documentation of efficacy for commercial test preparation materials for K–12 achievement tests. Interestingly enough, some commercial test preparation materials offer conflicting advice. For example, on reading tests, some encourage students to read the reading selection before looking at the questions. Others encourage students to read the questions first, which in some instances means that they are encouraging the students *not* to follow the test publisher's directions. This inconsistency can be confusing to students who have been directed to pay careful attention to the test directions. Research also suggests that reading the questions first may actually lower some students' performance (Bishop, 1999; Perlman, Borger, Gonzalez, & Junker 1988).

Those contemplating test preparation programs should remember that there are opportunity costs associated with them. Time spent on test preparation activities often comes at the expense of instruction in the content areas being assessed. The money spent on those materials might also be used in other, more productive, ways.

Effects of Test Preparation on Test Validity

The purpose of achievement testing is to make accurate inferences about what students know and can do with respect to a broad content domain from which the test items constitute a sample of all the questions that could be asked. These inferences may form the basis for evaluating instruction, promoting students, granting merit bonuses to school staff, allocating financial and human resources, providing remedial assistance, or placing students in other special programs. Curiously, test preparation can both improve validity and decrease it.

To the extent that they increase scores without increasing the underlying subject-area knowledge and skills, test preparation activities compromise test validity. Such activities as practice with alternate forms of the test may artificially inflate students' scores, perhaps so much that a student might not receive needed remedial assistance. By providing instruction and practice only on items that mimic actual test items, we risk students not being able to generalize to the broader content area. Shepard (2000) discusses controlled studies suggesting that students who can answer a particular question correctly might not be able to answer the question if it is phrased in a slightly different way. For example, imagine that students have seen subtraction items only in this format:

$$\text{Subtract:}\quad \begin{array}{r} 832 \\ -459 \\ \hline \end{array}$$

We cannot necessarily conclude that a student who responded to this item correctly would perform equally well on the problem when presented in these formats:

$$832 - 459 = ? \qquad \text{or} \qquad \text{Solve for } n\text{: } 832 - 459 = n$$

Certainly, we would want to know whether our students can solve a problem of this nature regardless of how it is presented.

In contrast, learning about the test format and reducing anxiety might improve the validity of the scores (Messick, 1982, cited in Heubert & Hauser, 1999). The National Research Council recommends that "students should receive sufficient preparation for the specific test so their performance will not be adversely affected by unfamiliarity with its format or by ignorance of appropriate test-taking strategies" (Heubert & Hauser, 1999, p. 7).

Ethical Considerations in Test Preparation Practices

It seems clear that some test preparation practices are more defensible than others, but there is less than complete agreement among educators on which are and are not appropriate. Certainly many teachers and principals would not agree with Mehrens and Kaminski's (1989) contention that whereas it is appropriate to briefly teach some general test-taking skills and to give general instruction on all district or state standards, it is unethical to provide practice with parallel forms of the test, to restrict instruction to the content measured by the test, or to assess students only with items similar in format to those on the test. Popham (1991) takes a similar position. School districts routinely encourage school staff to teach what the test measures, however, and many states provide extensive practice tests in order to familiarize students and teachers with test content and format. Is it wrong to use them? What is our responsibility to students' immediate and long-term interests, particularly on high-stakes tests? What kind of behavior should we model for our students? What are our professional responsibilities?

Several publications aim to clarify what practices are ethical and appropriate for professionals involved in testing: the *Standards for Educational and Psychological Testing* (AERA, APA, & NCME, 1999), the *Code of Professional Responsibilities in Educational Measurement* (NCME, 1995), the *Code of Fair Testing Practices in Education* (JCTP, 2002), and the *Rights and Responsibilities of Test Takers* (JCTP, 1998). The purpose of these publications is to foster fair and valid measurement that enables school staff and others to draw correct conclusions about what students know and can do. Thus, these statements provide a basis for evaluating what test preparation practices are appropriate.

Why is it so important to draw the right conclusions? Drawing the wrong conclusions might result in a student not receiving needed help or it might place a student in a course or program for which he or she is not prepared and is unlikely to succeed. It might result in the failure to allocate human and material resources to places where they are most needed. It might result in schools mandating use of inappropriate or ineffective instructional programs. It might provide false information about the course of education reforms and may lead to ill-advised policy decisions.

Some testing opponents might contend that high-stakes testing is so inherently injurious that any attempt to help students get higher scores is acceptable. Popham (1992) rejects that argument as specious, stating that regardless of the quality of the test or the way scores are used, "educators still are responsible for providing test preparation that is both professionally ethical and educationally defensible" (p. 17). Both Cizek (2001) and Popham point out that cheating by school staff sets a bad example for students and conveys the message that cheating is acceptable.

Practice Tests

All four professional guidelines specify that test takers should be informed of the purpose of the test and given general information about the content and format of the test. The *Standards for Educational and Psychological Testing* and the *Code of Fair Testing Practices* state that all test takers should be informed of any test preparation materials that are available, and of test-taking strategies that might be either beneficial or detrimental. According to the *Standards,*

> Test-taking strategies, such as guessing, skipping time-consuming items, or initially skipping and then returning to difficult items as time allows, can influence test scores positively or negatively. Differential use of such strategies by test takers can affect the validity and reliability of test score interpretations. . . . The use of such strategies by all test takers should be encouraged if their effect facilitates performance and discouraged if their effect interferes with performance. (Standard 11.13, p. 116)

An effort should be made to make test preparation materials equally available to all examinees. If calculators, computers, or other equipment is used in testing, test takers should have the opportunity to familiarize themselves with that equipment, unless such practice would compromise the validity of the tests.

The *Standards* and the *Code of Professional Responsibilities in Educational Measurement* direct educators to refrain from engaging in test preparation practices that would lead to invalid scores. The *Code of Professional Responsibilities* enjoins test developers from marketing test preparation materials that "may cause individuals to receive scores that misrepresent their actual levels of attainment." It is the responsibility of those who select tests to "avoid recommending, purchasing, or using test preparation products and services that may cause individuals to receive scores that misrepresent their actual levels of attainment." Those who administer assessments should "avoid actions or conditions that would permit or encourage individuals or groups to receive scores that misrepresent their actual levels of attainment." The language in the *Standards* is similar: "The integrity of test results should be maintained by eliminating practices designed to raise test scores without improving performance on the construct or domain measured by the test." The authors comment that "such practices may include teaching test items in advance, modifying test administration procedures, and discouraging or excluding certain test takers from taking the test. These practices can lead to spuriously high scores that do not reflect performance on the underlying construct or domain of interest" (Standard 15.9, p. 168). The *Standards* further stipulate that "test users have the responsibility to protect the security of tests, to the extent that the test developers enjoin users to do so" (Standard 11.7, p. 115) and the "responsibility to respect test copyrights" (Standard 11.8, p. 115). These standards clearly preclude school staff from duplicating secure test materials and from divulging test items or answers to students.

Finding a Middle Ground

It is necessary to draw a distinction between "teaching the test" and "teaching *to* the test." The former, which is never acceptable, implies disclosing actual test questions ahead of time or providing answers to questions that will appear on the actual test. The latter involves teaching the student the broad content that the test is intended to measure and may include some training in test-taking skills. A number of authors (e.g., Borger et al., 1996; Kilian, 1992; Mehrens & Kaminski, 1989; Perlman, 2000; Popham, 1992; Miyasaka, 2000, cited in Vaughn, 2001) recommend that most test preparation be integrated as seamlessly as possible into regular classroom instruction, rather than becoming a time-consuming add-on that takes the place of instruction in the content being assessed. This is consistent with the advice offered in the National Research Council report *High Stakes: Testing for Tracking, Promotion, and Graduation* (1998):

> The preparation of students plays a key role in appropriate test use. It is not proper to expose students ahead of time to items that will actually be used on their test or to give students the answers to those questions. Test results may also be invalidated by teaching so narrowly to the objectives of a particular test that scores are raised without actually improving the broader set of academic skills that the test is intended to measure. The desirability of "teaching to the test" is affected by test design. For example, it is entirely appropriate to prepare students by covering all the objectives of a test that represents the full range of the intended curriculum. We therefore recommend that test users respect the distinction between genuine remedial education and teaching narrowly to the specific content of a test. At the same time, all students should receive sufficient preparation for the specific test so their performance will not be adversely affected by unfamiliarity

with its format or by ignorance of appropriate test-taking strategies. (pp. 6–7)

This statement suggests that use of sample items is not only acceptable but desirable. Fairness dictates that the sample items be made available to *all* students, especially when the stakes are high. Teachers and students should know what kinds of assessments will be used, and sample items can be an efficient way to communicate that to every student who will be taking the test. In *High Stakes,* the National Research Council recommends that "test users should balance efforts to prepare students for a particular test form against the possibility that excessively narrow preparation will invalidate test outcomes" (p. 280).

Promoting Good Practice

In preparing students to take tests, I recommend following these guidelines:

- Provide all students with the opportunity to learn the subject area to be tested.
- To the extent possible, integrate test preparation with regular classroom instruction throughout the year.
- Assess each student's thinking skills on a daily basis. The majority of standardized test items require students to apply critical thinking skills. The more accustomed students are to doing that, the easier it will be for them to do well on the test. Borger and colleagues (1996) provide suggestions for easy ways to create homework assignments, discussion questions, and classroom assessments that require students to exercise thinking skills. In addition, students should be asked to explain how they arrived at their answers.
- In the classroom, use a variety of assessment formats rather than only the one that appears on the test. Answering open-ended questions in class can be useful preparation for taking multiple-choice tests.
- Allow students to become familiar with the test format and mechanics of test taking, but avoid spending much time on test-taking skills. Often all that is needed is brief practice with the test mechanics. Although it is desirable to familiarize students with the test format, an overemphasis on test-taking strategies may be detrimental in that it reduces the amount of time available for meaningful instruction in

the content areas to be assessed. The best test preparation is solid instruction aimed at increasing students' knowledge of the subject being tested. No amount of instruction in test-taking skills is likely to provide enough help for a student who lacks knowledge of the subject being tested.

- Avoid devoting class time to extensive review of material students have already learned.
- Discuss with students the importance of doing their best on tests.
- Provide explicit written guidelines and training on what constitutes appropriate and inappropriate practices for preparing students for tests and administering tests.
- Select appropriate tests and avoid putting too much weight on any single test.

As Vaughn (2001) points out, "instruction targeted at increasing student content mastery is not only the most ethical approach, but also addresses the overall goal of improving student achievement. . . . The most ethical and appropriate approach to test preparation is, in fact sound instructional practice" (p. 4).

Summary and Conclusion

The increasing use of high-stakes tests has focused attention on test preparation activities. The term *test preparation* can apply to a number of different practices that vary in the degree to which they are defensible. Test preparation activities may either increase test validity or reduce it. Although some test preparation is legitimate, there are concerns that certain test preparation activities may have a negative impact on students' education by causing narrowing of the curriculum and overemphasis on test-taking skills and particular assessment formats. Test preparation is best integrated into regular classroom instruction. Appropriate test preparation can include brief practice of test-taking skills and familiarization with the test format, but much greater emphasis should be placed on teaching students the curriculum standards and thinking skills that the assessments are intended to measure.

References

AERA. (2000). AERA position statement concerning high-stakes testing in preK–12 education. Retrieved from www.aera.net/about/policy/stakes.htm.

AERA, APA, & NCME. (1999). *Standards for educational and psychological testing.* Washington, DC: American Educational Research Association.

Bishop, N. S. (1999). The effects of different test-taking conditions on reading comprehension test performance. Paper presented at the annual meeting of the National Council on Measurement in Education, Montreal.

Borger, J. B., Cano, M., Collins, C. B., Evans, W. J., Perlman, C. L., Qualls, J. W., & Wood, J. A. (1996). *Preparing your elementary students to take standardized tests.* Chicago: Chicago Public Schools. Also available from http://intranet.cps.k12.il.us/Assessments/Preparation/preparation.html.

Cizek, G. J. (2001). Cheating to the test. *Education Next.* Retrieved from www.educationnext.org/2001sp/40.html.

Heubert, J. P., & Hauser, R. (Eds.). (1999). *High stakes: Testing for tracking, promotion, and graduation.* (Report of the Committee on Appropriate Test Use, Board on Testing and Assessment, National Research Council). Washington D.C.: National Academy Press.

JCTP. (1998). *Rights and responsibilities of test takers: Guidelines and expectations.* Washington, DC: American Psychological Association.

✦JCTP. (2002). *Code of fair testing practices in education.* Available on *Measuring Up: An Anthology of Assessment Resources* [CD]. Also retrievable on-line: http://aac.ncat.edu.

Johnston, R. C. (1999, March 17). Texas presses districts in alleged test-tampering cases. Retrieved from www.edweek.org/ew/ew_printstory.cfm?slug=27texas.h18.

Kilian, L. (1992). A school district perspective on appropriate test-preparation practices: A reaction to Popham's proposals. *Educational Measurement: Issues and Practices, 11*(4), 13–15.

Mehrens, W. A., & Kaminski, J. (1989). *Using commercial test preparation materials for improving standardized test scores: Fruitful, fruitless or fraudulent?* Paper presented at the annual meeting of the National Council on Measurement in Education, New Orleans.

✦ NCME. (1995). *Code of professional responsibilities in educational measurement.* Washington, DC: Author. Available from www.natd.org/Code_of_Professional_Responsibilities.html.

Olson, L. (2001). Finding the right mix. *Quality Counts 2001.* Bethesda, MD: *Education Week.*

Perlman, C. L. (2000). *Surreptitious inclusion of good teaching in test preparation activities.* Paper presented at the annual meeting of the American Educational Research Association, New Orleans.

Perlman, C. L., Borger, J., Gonzalez, C., & Junker, L. (1988). *Should they read the questions first? A comparison of two test-taking strategies for elementary students.* Paper presented at the annual meeting of the American Educational Research Association, New Orleans.

Popham, W. J. (1991). Appropriateness of teachers' test-preparation practices, *Educational Measurement: Issues and Practice, 10*(4), 12–15.

Popham, W. J. (1992). The perils of responsibility sharing. *Educational Measurement: Issues and Practices, 11*(4), 16–17.

Shepard, L. (2000, Winter). Why is "teaching the test" a bad thing? *State Education Leader, 18*(1), 6–7.

Vaughn, E. S. (2001, Spring). Ethical and appropriate test preparation. *ERS Spectrum,* 1–6. Retrieved from www.ers.org/spectrum/.

✦ Document is included in the Anthology of Assessment Resources CD

Chapter 28
Test Preparation
What Makes It Effective?
Jeff Rubenstein

As testing has taken on a more significant role in the college admissions process and, more recently, in K–12 education through the increasing popularity of high-stakes testing, so have the urgency of questions surrounding test preparation initiatives, through both private educational ventures and school-sponsored preparation programs. As their popularity increases, no small amount of ink has been spilled and controversy raised about such programs—whether they are fair or not, whether they represent genuine educational enrichment or are somehow "gaming" the system, and whether they are ultimately effective.

Despite the controversy, the debate over the effectiveness of such programs is not a very interesting one. The reason for this is that the question of effectiveness has rarely been posed in an informative way. On the one hand, everyone (even those who are opposed to independent test preparation companies) agrees that test preparation, construed in the broadest sense, works. Where people disagree is on the details: whether a particular course of instruction is effective and exactly what about it is or is not effective. This is to say that the interesting question is not *whether* test preparation works, but *why* and *how* it does: Which aspects in an educational process (whether in school or in a private setting) prepare students adequately for their tests, and how can these best be implemented? This is the intelligent way to pose a question that is worth investigating.

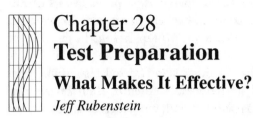

I should make three introductory points about the goals of this chapter before proceeding: First, it is not my intention in this article to propound the virtues of one particular program of test preparation over another; I am writing with as much objectivity as possible given my necessarily interested position in this debate as an employee of Princeton Review. This means that I am keeping the discussion at a relatively general level, without going into specifics of particular programs. Even at this general level, however, there are certain overarching principles of good test preparation that the data show to be effective, and these principles are worth elucidating. Second, for purposes of this article, I use SAT preparation as an example, because this is arguably the most prevalent and best known form of test preparation. In general the principles that apply to SAT preparation also apply, with some modification, to preparation for other standardized tests. Finally, as this anthology is intended for a general audience, I am keeping the discussion as nontechnical as possible, with minimal references. A short guide to further reading can be found at the end of the chapter.

Brief History of the Debate over the Effectiveness of SAT Preparation

The history of this debate can without too much injustice be characterized as one in which the Educational Testing Service (ETS) and the College Board have tried in various ways to discount an obvious fact: that test preparation is, in many cases, extremely effective. Oddly enough, even these critics of test preparation seem to agree that relatively short-term preparation can be quite useful. In fact, ETS internal research has shown that such preparation can be highly effective, and for years the College Board itself proudly displayed a quotation from a student who claimed an increase of 200 points through the use of its products. Nonetheless, these organizations' official position has always been that the gains are small, though somewhat larger for more robust programs (in the range of 40 hours).

When the original studies showing that relatively short-term test preparation could be effective in raising SAT scores were published in the 1970s, ETS and the College Board naturally perceived these findings as a threat to the legitimacy of the SAT. After all, if a few months of preparation could significantly influence scores, then how much "intelligence" could the test be measuring? ETS and the College Board initially responded to such studies by fighting a legal battle against the companies that offered test preparation services. They asked the Federal Trade Commission (FTC) to investigate these companies, accusing them of making false and misleading claims of score improvements.

The ensuing FTC investigation not only failed to indict these programs for fraudulent advertising, but actually provided evidence that these programs were effective: Their report showed that these programs, on average, raised scores by more than 100 points on the SAT combined (Levine, 1979). The FTC went on to state that the ETS was making fraudulent claims in asserting that test preparation was not effective. In fact, Albert Kramer, director of the Bureau of Consumer

Protection, stated that in direct contradiction to what ETS and the College Board were claiming, coaching could be efficacious.

ETS researchers have also published their own studies showing that test preparation is effective. In 1978, one such researcher, Lewis Pike, made a comprehensive study of all available data, both internal and external, on the subject. He reported that the SAT Math section was highly coachable and that the SAT Verbal was also likely so (but the evidence was still insufficient to show this definitively). Shortly after issuing his report, Pike departed from ETS.

The more recent ETS and College Board strategy to discount the effectiveness of test preparation programs has been somewhat more subtle. Recently, they have begun to admit the existence of score improvements while attempting to deny that these improvements were the result of test preparation narrowly defined (which they refer to as "coaching"). This strategy involves two interesting moves that make their studies, although not statistically wrong, certainly misleading. The first move is to throw all kinds of test preparation programs into one category and study them together as if they were comparable. When ETS now does a study on "test preparation," it defines the construct so broadly as to encompass well-researched, 40-hour programs and poorly designed, one- or two-hour after-school preparation sessions. As a result, ETS studies conclude that test preparation does not work. In a way no conclusion could be more obvious; an hour or two of unprofessional preparation is almost certain to be of little use. But the question posed by the study is not very interesting: No useful study can be conducted with constructs that are so broad as to encompass both well-tested, rigorous programs of test preparation and one- or two-hour presentations that call themselves test preparation. If the effectiveness of test preparation is to be studied seriously, such a study will have to be carried out on a specific, well-defined form of test preparation, with rigorous standards as to what this sort of preparation constitutes and what it does not.

The second move made in the more recent studies—after lumping all kinds of test preparation programs together—is to try to separate the parts of any test preparation program that ETS considers "good" preparation (familiarity with question types, general guessing strategies, etc.) from those they consider "bad" preparation (what ETS calls coaching; namely, instruction in test-specific problem-solving skills).

There is more than a little sleight of hand here in the way ETS slices test preparation into "coaching," "preparation," and "enrichment." By removing elements that it now claims are normal and rational kinds of preparatory activities (though the idea that any sort of preparation is a good idea is a very recent discovery on its part), ETS tries to adjust the improvement numbers statistically so as to reduce the perceived net effectiveness of a test preparation program. That is, more recent studies try to chip away at the whole (rather substantial) improvement number by statistically removing the effect of several important elements (such as any genuine educational enrichment and the beneficial effect of timed practice tests). Such studies are misleading because any good preparation program involves many elements, each of which contributes to the effectiveness of the whole program. They are misleading also because ETS has effectively defined test preparation as something that will have no effect: It is committed to the proposition that coaching is ineffective, though genuine enrichment may indeed raise scores. Therefore, if any program does succeed in improving scores, then what that program must be doing is not coaching but rather genuine enrichment. This amazing piece of circular reasoning is what underlies ETS's current view of test preparation programs and its attempt to reduce how effective these programs appear on paper by reclassifying much of the content of such programs under the rubrics of "enrichment" or "preparation."

Given that none of these recent studies—and no proposed study that I am aware of—is going to tell us much of anything interesting about test preparation in general, what can we say of interest about it? In such circumstances, one rational approach is to begin with the evidence closest to hand, then begin to investigate its possible implications. That is, we should start with the following fact: In some cases test preparation, broadly construed, clearly does work well—sometimes extraordinarily so. In other cases, it is less effective. And many cases lie somewhere between the two extremes on this continuum of effectiveness. The proponents and detractors of test preparation all agree on this point (though they may disagree on how much of the effect is due to enrichment or coaching or something else).

The interesting question then becomes, In the cases where test preparation works, *why* does it work? What concrete problems are being addressed by effective test preparation, and how can we systematically address them in the future such that all students have a fair testing experience and are in a position to perform to the best of their abilities?

Areas Where Test Preparation Can Improve Performance

One useful way to begin discussing the reasons why test

preparation is effective is to discuss the problems that unprepared students have when taking standardized tests. There are a great number of such problems, which for our purposes I group into five categories: (a) poor general testing strategies (pacing, question selection, and setting priorities); (b) lack of specific problem-solving skills, which relates to the fact that particular questions on a test instrument are not aligned with a student's learned curriculum; (c) lack of practice with the preceding skills and lack of ability to deal with the psychological difficulties attached to a standardized test; (d) physical exhaustion; and (e) lack of basic skills that were part of a student's learned curriculum. Let us take a closer look at each of these in turn.

Poor Testing Strategies

ETS researcher Franklin Evans (1980) noted in a study that many of his test students, especially minority students, were probably underperforming on his SAT-like tests because they were using inefficient test-taking strategies. What exactly do such strategies constitute?

To formulate a solid test-taking strategy for any particular test requires, at a minimum, (a) understanding how the test is scored, (b) having a timing strategy, and (c) having a question selection and priority setting strategy. Each of these needs to be tailored to the particular characteristics of the test being taken.

Understanding How a Test Is Scored

The particular way a test is scored has a significant influence on the most rational way to approach various aspects of testing. Certain tests have deductions for incorrect answers, which are intended to neutralize the effect of random guessing; other tests do not have such deductions. This distinction makes a large difference when it comes to formulating the most intelligent guessing strategy for a given test instrument. Other tests have essay portions (which may or may not have a specific time frame dedicated to them); students need to know the relative importance of such essays, and how much time they should devote to them relative to the multiple-choice parts of the test.

Further, the newer computer-adapted tests are very particular in their method of scoring and require a much more finely tuned sense of how to achieve the best score. Knowing when it is rational to guess, which parts of the test are worth more or fewer points, and where spending one's time yields the greatest benefit are crucial strategies that are rarely explained in a clear way by the testing companies. A lack of understanding of how a test is scored leads to less-than-optimal pacing and guessing strategies, which may cost a student valuable points.

Timing

Most standardized tests are highly speeded; that is, only a small percentage of test takers are supposed to be able to finish them. How one deals with this fact can make an enormous difference in one's score. Given the short time allowed per question, it is impossible for many students to complete every question on a test. Many students will therefore opt for one of two simple (but often damaging) strategies:

1. Try to rush through the test, responding to every question, even though he or she doesn't have enough time to answer any of them thoroughly. This student spreads himself or herself too thin and may suffer a significant score reduction in consequence.
2. Go through the test at a more moderate pace, starting with the first question and working in order until time runs out. This student might finish questions 1 through 15 or 1 through 20 or 1 through 25, never knowing if there were easier questions later in the test that he or she never even attempted. This may also lead to a significant reduction in score.

Students need to learn how to cope with the highly speeded test environment, how to set priorities in problem solving in order to choose the questions that are most advantageous for them to answer, and how to spend the appropriate amount of time on each question. They also need to learn how best to do this given the particular structure of particular tests: A very different strategy will be warranted depending on how any given test instrument is constructed.

Selecting Questions and Setting Priorities

Those students (the majority) for whom answering every question is counterproductive need a strategy for choosing which questions to answer, and in which order, to make the most beneficial use of their time. Students should usually choose the easier questions to answer first—giving them a better chance of spending their time on problems they will answer correctly—and save the more difficult ones for last (or not answer them at all). Certain tests are constructed with easier questions in identifiable places; other tests do not have an identifiable order of difficulty, which means that students need other tools to help them select and prioritize questions. In either case, part of any good testing strategy is knowing which questions to answer, in what order, and how much time is worth spending on each of them; and a lack of understanding of these points puts students at a significant disadvantage.

Problem-Solving Skills Needed for Questions Not Covered in the Curriculum

Probably the most significant problem with many current tests is the lack of alignment with typical school curricula. That is to say, these tests are in some fashion testing something other than what students are being taught. This is usually not so much a matter of conceptual differences as of application. A particular instrument may test the same basic rules of geometry that students learn in school but test them in a fundamentally different way than students have learned them. This is another kind of misalignment with curriculum, one that has a significant effect on students' ability to show what they know.

A *good* test is a very important tool in the educational process. It helps to inform both teachers and students about how they are doing and gives direction as to how to improve. That is, it gives useful information to answer the question, For any given student, how much has that student learned relative to what should have been learned? The test thereby also indicates what the student has left to learn, and tells student and teacher what particular areas to focus on for improvement.

However, a test can be useful in this way only if the educational objectives are clearly outlined in advance, if the curriculum is well designed around those objectives, and if the test is aligned with that curriculum. Sadly, many tests, including the SAT, are not even remotely curriculum aligned (the SAT, for instance, shows its origins in the world of IQ tests on its face), and this creates a whole series of problems.

To the degree a test tests something other than what is covered in a student's learned curriculum (either by testing concepts that were not covered or by testing them in ways that were not covered) students require some additional preparation to perform up to their abilities. There are three ways in which the tested curriculum effectively goes beyond the learned curriculum, creating difficulties for students who are now being tested on matters for which they might not have been prepared: (a) employing particular question types that have not been covered in a school curriculum, (b) testing concepts that have not been covered in a school curriculum, and (c) testing known concepts in fundamentally different ways than they have ever been presented in a school curriculum.

A good example of the first type is the Quantitative Comparison question type on the SAT. A Quantitative Comparison question looks like this:

Column A	*Column B*
x	x^2

A student is shown two columns of information (occasionally with additional information provided in the center) and is asked to pick a choice based on which of the following obtains:

1. Column A is greater than Column B.
2. Column B is greater than Column A.
3 The two columns are equal.
4. The relationship cannot be determined based on the information given.

For students who have not seen a problem of this type before (and even for those who have), it is not at all obvious what they are being asked to do. In particular, what does choice (4) "The relationship cannot be determined" mean? (In the preceding problem, the answer is in fact [4]. If the variable *x* is 0, then the two columns are each equal to 0; however, if *x* is equal to 2, then the value in column B is greater. Therefore the relationship cannot be determined.)

But, more importantly, even after these directions are explained to a student, is the student any better equipped to solve this sort of problem? Systematic instruction in this sort of problem solving is not part of any school curriculum of which I am aware (and it probably should not be). But if we are to ask students to perform well on this sort of test item, they should be given some sort of systematic instruction in solving it.

Let us move on to a problem of the second type: the testing of known concepts in very strange (and occasionally counterintuitive) ways. Anyone who has looked at an SAT carefully will be struck by the apparent simplicity of the concepts it tests. It is in fact true that the SAT Math section tests concepts from seventh-, eighth-, and ninth-grade mathematics only. How is it possible, then, that some problems on the SAT could seem so difficult? Not because the concepts are difficult, but because the problems present very simple concepts in very odd ways. Here is an example of such a problem, taken from an actual SAT form:

Column A		*Column B*
	$3x + y = 15$	
	$x + 2y = 16$	
$2x - y$		0

This question effectively asks students to establish the value of $2x - y$ given two equations, each of which contains the variables x and y, then to determine whether that value is greater than, equal to, or less than 0. What is curious about this problem (aside from the Quantitative Comparison format) is that it actually works against students who "follow the rules." How? On its face, this question is formatted to look like a simultaneous equation problem. Most students are taught to solve simultaneous equation problems in the following manner: Multiply or divide one equation by a certain factor in order to allow one variable to be removed; solve for a single variable, then solve for the other. That is, do the following:

$$3x + y = 15$$
$$x + 2y = 16$$

In order to make the y variable drop out, we would multiply the first equation by 2, which gives us $6x + 2y = 30$. Now we can subtract one equation from the other:

$$6x + 2y = 30$$
$$- x + 2y = 16$$
$$5x = 14$$

This allows us to solve for x, which yields $\frac{14}{5}$. Now we can use this value for x in either equation to solve for y. Sadly, this is a very messy affair and a very long way to figure out the value of $2x - y$. There is, of course, a shortcut: simply to subtract one equation from the other:

$$3x + y = 15$$
$$- x + 2y = 16$$
$$2x - y = -1$$

Many students, however, will never see this shortcut, primarily because the problem is designed so they will *not* see it if they follow the traditional rules for solving simultaneous equations. That is, students who assume that they should apply the rules they learned in math class will likely do far worse on this problem (and others like it) than students who do not.

This is a perfect illustration of how a student who may be fully competent at a basic skill—such as solving simultaneous equations—will still underperform on the SAT because he or she (even while knowing full well how to solve simultaneous equations) does not understand the particular quirky way that simultaneous equation problems are tested on the SAT.

Now let us turn to the third instance, in which a test actually tests concepts that are not covered in any school curriculum. Here are two more examples, both taken from the SAT:

> If a rectangular piece of paper is cut into exactly three pieces by making two straight cuts, which of the following could be the total number of edges on the three pieces?
> I. 9
> II. 11
> III. 12
> 1. I only
> 2. III only
> 3. I and III only
> 4. II and III only
> 5. I, II, and III

What skill exactly is this question supposed to be testing? Some strange spatial intuition? If one tries to stretch the idea, a case might be made that this falls under "basic geometric intuition or understanding" but that would largely be an after-the-fact rationalization. What this question really tests is whether a student can follow complex directions, experiment with various ways of making two straight cuts in a rectangular piece, and count up the resulting edges.

If you are not yet convinced that the SAT contains questions that are not curriculum aligned, take a look at this final example:

> | 5:05 |
> |---|
>
> The 12-hour digital clock above shows one example of a time at which the number representing the hour is equal to the

number representing the minutes. What is the *least* possible number of minutes from the instant one such "double" reading appears to the instant the next appears?

1. 11
2. 30
3. 49
4. 60
5. 61

Psychological Factors

Although the effect is difficult to quantify, one more factor in poor student performance is undoubtedly psychological. There is an enormous intimidation factor at work in these tests; the more high-stakes the test, the more pressure students feel, and in some cases, the worse they will perform. Add to that the fact that many of these tests are not curriculum aligned, and the result is that students are led to harmful thoughts such as, "This test supposedly only measures seventh-, eighth-, and ninth-grade math; if I can't solve these problems, I must be really stupid." This leads to the perception (which is occasionally correct) that the test questions rely on some bizarre intuition—either students "get it" or they don't—and that there is no relationship between how hard they have worked in school and their performance on the test. Many students who are perfectly adept math students in school but whose testing skills are weak are humiliated by such tests, largely because the tests are not well aligned with their school curriculum.

Most students, in fact, feel that the lack of testing skills that manifests itself in a low test score is an indication of their own lack of ability or a deficiency in themselves as students. The reality may be quite different: Although in certain cases students have simply not learned their lessons, quite often the problem lies in the fact that a question item is not aligned with their school curriculum or that they have never learned the testing strategies required to perform well on a standardized test. This lack of understanding about where their difficulty lies (i.e., that it lies in poor testing skills, not in poor mathematical or linguistic skills) adds to the frustration that many students feel with such tests and to their sense that such tests are unfair. This leads in some cases to a sense of helplessness and a difficulty in preparing seriously to perform well on such instruments.

In the case of minority students, even more significant problems may be at work. Claude Steele, a psychologist at Stanford, has done some interesting work that makes the case that minority test takers, when told that minorities do poorly on a particular test, in fact do worse on that test than when they are told that minorities do equally well as other students on the test. That is, knowing that a test may be biased in fact produces subnormal results for certain groups of people.

Physical Exhaustion

Another reason why students may do poorly on standardized tests comes down to a simple factor of physical and mental exhaustion. Many students are wholly unprepared for the intensity of a testing experience, which demands a great deal of concentration, consistently applied, for quite a long time.

Basic Skills Problems

Finally, students may do poorly on standardized tests because of a genuine lack of the skills that the test is supposed to measure, such as basic mathematical skills. Of course, we have seen that in reality most tests are blunt instruments that measure many factors having nothing to do with basic skills. In many cases, however, a tester will perform poorly due to a genuine lack of certain basic skills.

The Solutions: What Goes Into a Good Test Preparation Program?

If the preceding list (although probably not complete) represents a good number of the factors that cause students to test poorly, then a good test preparation program would be one that addresses a substantial number of these problems, and an ideal program would be one that addresses all of them. That is, at least the following five elements are necessary to a thorough test preparation program:

1. Review of basic skills
2. Instruction in test-specific problem-solving skills, to give students the problem-solving skills they need to tackle non-curriculum-aligned test items
3. Instruction in overall test strategies, to ensure they have a coherent overall strategy (including pacing, question selection, and priority setting)
4. Delivery of full-length practice tests, to allow students to practice the skills learned in (2) and (3), as well as to increase their stamina and desensitize them to the stress

of a testing environment

5. An educational environment specifically targeted toward improving test-taking skills, to show students they are learning a specific task that they have not learned before (and that the lack of these skills is not their fault)

Of course, not every student will need all these elements; however, the more complete the program, the better chance it will have of promoting greater improvement in a greater number of students. Let us briefly consider each element in turn.

Review of Basic Skills

First, there should be a thorough review of those basic skills to be tested on a particular instrument, such as basic mathematical concepts, rules of English grammar, and other skills appropriate to the test in question. Such a review ensures that any gaps or forgotten bits of information get recapitulated in the weeks before testing.

Many students (especially those with well-designed school curricula and well-executed instruction) will gain something but not a tremendous amount from this aspect of the preparation, because they will already have adequate command of all the basic skills tested. The aspects that follow, those that deal with strategies and test-specific skills, are generally the more important factors in a program of test preparation.

Test-Specific Problem-Solving Skills

As we have seen in the preceding example problems from the SAT, any time a particular testing instrument diverges from the school curriculum (i.e., the tested curriculum is not aligned with the taught curriculum) a problem exists. Not only may certain skills be tested that were never taught in school (though these skills ideally would be addressed with supplemental work during the review of basic skills) but, more importantly, basic skills that students have mastered may be tested in ways that students have not mastered. That is, a student may be perfectly adept at a particular skill (e.g., solving simultaneous equations) but have no approach for putting that skill into practice in the particular way that skill is tested.

This mismatch occurs because, as we have seen in the preceding SAT examples, a test may present questions with a very particular sort of logic to them, a logic that students have never been taught and for which they need to learn test-specific problem-solving skills. This means that they need to learn how to put their knowledge into practice given the way that questions are written on that particular instrument.

This is, of course, the reason why test preparation companies (due in part no doubt to their own rhetoric) are accused of merely teaching "tricks"—an accusation that I think is entirely false. Testing companies do indeed teach students how to solve problems in the particular way that they show up on an individual test. These skills are exactly what most students have never learned, and need to learn, to be able to perform to the best of their abilities on such tests. These skills are test-specific (and have little application outside the test itself), but this is not a result of the test preparation companies trying to "game" the system; it is a result of a test that asks questions in a peculiar and nonstandard fashion and therefore requires students to approach problems in a quirky fashion. For instance, a test preparation program might well teach students that when faced with a simultaneous equation problem, they should check to see whether a simple addition or subtraction operation will get them the desired result, instead of assuming that the question should be solved in the traditional way. (More often than not, simultaneous equation problems are structured this way on the SAT.) Students need to learn this test-specific skill in order to be fully prepared for the SAT. What test preparation companies are teaching is in fact genuine enrichment, albeit of a particular sort that is designed to fill the gap between the skills that students are taught and those that are tested on standardized tests. The better the test preparation program, the more it will address these gaps in curriculum alignment.

Overall Testing Strategies

The third element in good test preparation is instruction in test-specific overall testing strategies. For a given instrument, there should be instruction in how it is scored and in the most intelligent approaches to pacing, question selection and priority setting, guessing strategies, and so on, all in light of the particular structure of that test. Optimally, these strategies would be tailored to individual students' skills. Very different strategies will be warranted depending on the particularities of both the test and the student: a higher scoring student as opposed to a lower scoring one, a student taking the SAT as opposed to the ACT, a student strong in math as opposed to one strong in English, a student taking the test under normal time conditions as opposed to one taking it with special accommodations. Each of these factors will contribute to developing an optimal testing strategy for a particular student on a particular test.

Full-Length Practice Tests

The fourth element that adds to the effectiveness of a test preparation program is the administration of practice tests (ideally full-length ones) in the weeks prior to the administration of the actual test. Practice tests are useful for four reasons: to allow students (a) to put their overall testing skills into practice under timed conditions, (b) to learn to apply their newly learned problem-solving skills under pressure, (c) to desensitize themselves somewhat to the high-pressure environment of test day, and (d) to gain the stamina they need to perform with full concentration for the duration of the test. Let us look at each of these factors.

Practice of Generic and Test-Specific Testing Strategies

Once students have learned overall testing strategies: how to choose the ideal number of questions to attempt, how to prioritize and pace themselves through those questions, and so on, they then need an opportunity to put these strategies into practice under actual timed conditions in order to assimilate them fully. Many of these strategies revolve around pacing and timing considerations, so perfecting them requires actual timed practice. Likewise, students need to practice their particular problem-solving skills under actual test conditions, to ensure that they will be able to perform well when the real test day arrives.

Desensitization to the Stress of the Testing Environment

Test anxiety may cause students to fail to test to their ability, especially when they are faced with a high-stakes test (whether or not the test is actually used in such a fashion). Taking several tests under actual test conditions will help students acclimate to that sort of testing environment and make the actual test day less stressful.

Stamina

Although the sheer length of testing time required for many standardized tests probably does not elicit much sympathy, it probably should. Working with full concentration under extreme time pressure for hours on end is not a skill that students are given much room to develop. Students are typically accustomed to 45- or 55-minute examinations in their ordinary courses; the difference between those and a 180-minute (or longer) test is considerable. We should not underestimate the degree to which physical training is an element of test preparation. Many students, whether due to fatigue or inability to concentrate, simply fade away in the final section or sections of a test.

This is why it is important that students take several full-length practice tests in the weeks leading up to the actual test—not wholly unlike training for a marathon or other feat of physical endurance. In the ideal case, they should take the practice test beginning at the same hour and under the same circumstances as the real test (in the case of the SAT, at 9 a.m. on a Saturday).

The qualifier *full-length* is important here. Many tests (such as the SAT) include an extra section that does not count toward a student's score, allowing the testing companies to pretest questions for future test administrations. This section is not identifiable, so students are forced to complete it with the same level of effort as all the other sections. Leaving aside questions about the ethicality of such a practice, it does have a significant effect on the length of the test: In the case of the SAT, it increases testing time from 2.5 to 3 hours. The practice tests prepared by testing companies (usually older versions of the test released in such books as *10 Real SATs* [College Board, 2000]) typically do not include this additional section and therefore do not represent a full-length test. From a purely physical standpoint, training for a 2.5-hour test is significantly different from training for a 3-hour test, which is 20 percent longer. Therefore providing sample tests that are not truly full length does the students a significant disservice in preparing them for test day; they may well end up fading out in the final 30 minutes of the test, which they have not adequately prepared for.

In all the programs I have studied, there has been a significant correlation between score improvement and the number of full-length practice tests administered during the program. The ETS and College Board studies also concur that repeated testing improves students' scores on their testing instruments. However, these studies usually assume that students retake the test months or years later, whereas during a test preparation program a student may take several tests within a four- to six-week period. I am aware of no evidence showing that one or the other method is any more effective in and of itself. I suspect, however, that repeated administrations during a four- to six-week period will facilitate students learning from their mistakes between one administration and the next. In any case, we can say with confidence that the more full-length practice tests offered in a test preparation program—up to four or five separate administrations—the more effective that program will be.

Instruction Oriented Toward the Specific Test

When students take a test such as the SAT that is not well aligned with their school curriculum, they often feel that they are poor students—that there was something they should have learned in school but did not—and that their poor score is therefore their own fault. But we have seen that many of the skills that apply to the SAT are not taught in school—especially SAT-specific testing strategies. Test preparation activities need to be labeled as such, so students understand that what they are now learning is something they were not supposed to have learned until now, and that these skills will have application primarily for the specific test they are to take.

Of course, the greater the misalignment between test and school curricula, the more severe this problem. When a given instrument is not aligned with a specific school curriculum, the test actually poses a social and educational policy problem for schools (and, indeed, for the whole educational establishment). To the degree that such tests are (often inappropriately) used to judge the performance of teachers, schools, and school districts, this creates an incentive for schools to begin doing more test-specific test preparation during the school day, which means diverting time from their standard curriculum. Bear in mind that the whole problem of "teaching to a test" arises *only* when the test is not curriculum aligned. When a test is well aligned with a school's curriculum (both in the concepts taught and in the logic of their presentation), then there is no gap between teaching to a test and teaching *tout court.* They are in that case one and the same.

Conclusion

I have presented the following five components as necessary to a good test preparation program. The more of these elements (and the higher their quality) in a program, the more likely that program will improve test scores:

1. Review of basic skills
2. Instruction in test-specific problem-solving skills
3. Instruction in overall test-taking strategies
4. Full-length practice tests
5. Instructional environment specifically oriented to testing

Does this mean that commercial test preparation is the only or the best option? Not necessarily. Students can get a number, if not all, of these elements in various ways. They may get their basic skills from school and their test-specific problem-solving techniques and practice tests from a book or from an in-school program. Several in-school programs may have several but not all of these elements. The advantage of a professional service is that it delivers all of these elements in a high-quality way.

Of course, this chapter leaves many of the sticky ethical questions unanswered. Should test preparation be necessary? As a practical matter, it probably always will be: To the degree that any test is not quite curriculum aligned, there will be a place for relatively short-term test preparation to fill the gap between the students' learned curriculum and whatever the particular test instrument is testing. Does this make the test unfair? Only if test preparation is not considered an entitlement and not all students have equal access to it. In my personal opinion, this access should be secured equally, and at a national level, in the interests of public education: If we intend to test our students, we should do our best to ensure they have adequate preparation for these tests.

References

College Board. (2000). *10 real SATs.* New York: College Entrance Examination Board.

Evans, F. R. (1980). *A study of the relationships among speed and power aptitude test scores and ethnic identity* (Research Report RR-80–22). Princeton, NJ: Educational Testing Service.

Levine, A. E. (1979). *Effects of coaching on standardized admission examinations: Revised statistical analyses of data gathered by the Boston regional office of the Federal Trade Commission, Bureau of Consumer Protection.* Washington, DC: U.S. Government Printing Office.

Pike, L. W. (1978). *Short-term instruction, testwiseness, and the Scholastic Aptitude Test: A literature review with research recommendations.* New York: College Entrance Examination Board.

Further Reading

College Entrance Examination Board. (1965). *Effects of coaching on Scholastic Aptitude Test scores.* New York: College Entrance Examination Board.

Crouse, J., & Trusheim, D. (1988). *The case against the SAT.* Chicago: University of Chicago Press.

Owen, D. (1985). *None of the above: The myth of scholastic aptitude.* Boston: Houghton Mifflin.

Pike, L. W., & Evans, F. R. (1972). *Effects of special instruction for three kinds of mathematics aptitude items.* New York: College Entrance Examination Board.

Chapter 29
Professional Testing Standards
What Educators Need to Know

Wayne J. Camara

Children are often first exposed to standardized testing in elementary school, and by age 18 assessments may have played a major role in their life decisions, ranging from graduation and promotion to college admission and entry into certain majors or selection into occupations or organizations. Real and perceived misuses of educational tests, errors in test scoring and test use, and incidents of cheating on tests have been widely reported in local and national media (Camara, 1997). As educational tests take on additional importance for students, teachers, and schools, there is appropriate concern about the quality of assessments and the appropriate use of tests and test data.

At times misuse of tests has resulted in legal challenges to state, district, or school assessment practices. In some instances, concerns about testing practices have also resulted in legislation, such as test disclosure laws requiring the release of some test forms in some states. In addition, federal legislation has often included language concerning the types of assessments used and their role in relation to federal funding of educational initiatives. Other federal laws strive to protect certain groups from specific abuses (e.g., the Americans With Disabilities Act of 1990, the Civil Rights Act of 1991). However, the majority of concerns regarding the quality of tests and the appropriate use of tests in education are matters of professional practice and technical, or psychometric, concern. Given this situation, testing standards that represent professionals in educational measurement and psychology have increasing importance in evaluating test use today.

Background

The American Educational Research Association (AERA), the American Psychological Association (APA), and the National Council for Measurement in Education (NCME) completed their fourth collaboration in producing the *Standards for Educational and*

Psychological Testing in 1999. This chapter will provide an overview of the issues addressed in the current standards and their relevance to educators, as well as briefly describe the development of these standards and how they may be used today.

In 1954, APA issued the first set of testing standards, entitled *Technical Recommendations for Psychological Tests and Diagnostic Techniques*. Parallel standards were developed for educational achievement tests in 1955 by the American Educational Research Association and the National Council for Measurement Used in Education (later renamed the National Council for Measurement in Education; Camara and Kraiger, 1996). AERA, APA, and NCME collaborated on joint standards that incorporated educational and psychological testing in 1966; they issued revisions in 1974 and 1985, and completed the current *Standards for Educational and Psychological Testing* in 1999.

The *Standards for Educational and Psychological Testing* (referred to as the *Standards*) is the most widely cited document addressing technical, policy, and operational issues for educational assessment (Camara, 1997). Yet most policymakers and educators with responsibilities for assessment practices may not be familiar with the *Standards* because they are not members of these three associations and because the document is primarily technical in nature and is not likely to be used in introductory testing or measurement courses or workshops that these audiences may frequent. In an effort to address this concern, the Joint Committee on Testing Practices developed the *Code of Fair Testing Practices in Education* (2002). This code attempts to highlight key concepts from the nearly 200-page *Standards* in a four-page brochure that professionals are encouraged to disseminate.

The *Standards* is based on the premise that effective testing and assessment require that all participants in the testing process possess the knowledge, skills, and abilities relevant to their role, as well as awareness of personal and contextual factors that may influence the testing process. "Although the evaluation of the appropriateness of a test or testing application should depend heavily on professional judgment, the *Standards* provides a frame of reference to assure that relevant issues have been addressed" (AERA et al., 1999, p. 2). The term *test* refers to a broad range of instruments and measures, and the standards apply regardless of the specific label applied to the instrument (e.g., assessment, scale, inventory). The only distinction made regards standardization. The authors acknowledge that the *Standards* applies primarily to any standardized measure and only to a lesser degree to nonstandardized methods (e.g., unstructured behavior samples, teacher-made tests).

The *Standards* document contains 15 chapters and 264 standards divided into three major sections: (a) Test Construction, Evaluation, and Documentation, (b) Fairness in Testing, and (c) Testing Applications. The remainder of this chapter describes the major concepts addressed in the three sections and their implications for educators.

Test Construction, Evaluation, and Documentation

This section focuses primarily on the responsibilities of test developers and test users and addresses psychometric issues such as validity, reliability, test development, norms, test administration, scoring, and documentation. The *Standards* defines validity as "the degree to which accumulated evidence and theory support specific interpretations of test scores entailed by proposed uses of a test" (AERA et al., 1999, p. 184). Validity is the most important consideration in developing and evaluating educational assessments. Validation involves accumulating the evidence that provides a scientific basis for the proposed test score interpretations. It is the interpretations of these scores that are evaluated, not the assessment itself. For example, if an achievement test is developed and used for student placement into advanced math courses, evidence supporting the validity of such use is required. One source of evidence may be a finding that performance on the achievement test is related to performance in the subsequent mathematics courses. If a cutoff score or specific performance level is used to make the placement decision, one would want additional evidence that students who perform below the cutoff point are less likely to succeed in the advanced courses than students who perform above that point. When evidence is not adequately compelling, additional measures such as teacher recommendations, student or parent recommendations, and academic performance should be included. In another instance an achievement test may be used to compare the writing skills of eighth graders in a state over a number of years to determine if standards-based reform activities are improving student performance. Because the achievement test is used to make inferences about the comparability of scores for groups of test takers, rather than individual students, different sources of evidence are required. Although more than one source of validity evidence is generally desirable, the quality of evidence is of primary importance. The intended uses of the assessment and the proposed interpretation of scores have implications for test development and evaluation.

The *Standards* notes that a test itself is not validated, but rather the intended use of the test and how test scores will be interpreted are validated. Five sources of evidence that can contribute to a validation strategy are listed: (a) content, (b) relationships between test scores and other variables, such as test-criterion relationships, (c) internal structure of the test, (d) response processes, and (e) consequences of testing.

Test content. Content includes the test items or performance tasks, format and wording of questions, response formats, and instructions for administration and scoring. Evidence based on test content should demonstrate that the test content is aligned to the curriculum taught or the skills required for future success (e.g., placement).

Relationships between test scores and other variables. A typical study examines how accurately test scores predict criterion data at a later time (e.g., admissions testing predicting performance on college coursework), whereas a concurrent study collects predictor and criterion data during a relatively short time frame. Such studies may be used to determine (a) if the relationship between the predictor (e.g., test, grades) and the criterion (or outcome measure; e.g., freshman grades, graduation) differs across subgroups, or (b) the accuracy of a test for admission or placement decisions.

Internal structure of the test. Such evidence examines any relationships among test items or tasks that can provide additional evidence of how test scores may relate to specific aspects of the construct that is to be measured.

Response processes. Evidence based on response processes may be collected by examining the processes that test takers use in responding to test questions or tasks. Often analyses of individual responses can be gathered by questioning test takers about their strategies in responding to a specific question, through examinee responses on computerized assessments, or through experimental studies.

Consequences of testing. Although evidence regarding consequences may influence decisions concerning the use of an assessment or other measure, it will not usually be related to inferences concerning the validity of scores. For example, group differences in performance on an assessment are relevant to a school or institution, yet such differences alone do not necessarily detract from the validity of intended test interpretations.

One of the most important issues for educators in the *Standards* is the discussion about the respective responsibilities of the test developer and test user in accumulating validation evidence relevant to the intended use of the test and the inferences that will be made from test scores. Specifically, the *Standards* states that the test developer should clearly set forth the intended uses for a test, but if a test user wishes to use the test in a way for which sufficient evidence has not been presented, then it is that user's responsibility to provide such evidence. For example, if a test is developed to provide diagnostic information about aggregate groups of students. but a user (e.g., school district, state) decides to use the test to determine student promotion, then it is incumbent on the user to provide evidence to support that new use. If the test is used to classify students into proficiency groups or to assign students to different educational programs or courses, validation evidence for such classifications is required. That is, it is not adequate simply to demonstrate that there is a relationship between the test and some criterion (e.g., grades); rather, evidence supporting the validity of the classification decision is needed. Similarly, the *Standards* notes that when score differences are used to distinguish groups, such as students classified as proficient versus exemplary in an area, the reliability of the data, including the standard errors or confidence intervals for scores, should be reported along with the test score.

This section of the *Standards* also elaborates on procedures for administration, scoring, and interpretation of tests. It addresses issues such as retention of student test scores, errors in testing materials, disruptions in standardized administrations, procedures for challenging test scores, human raters or scores, and the types of documentation that should be provided in a testing program. Finally, a discussion of score reliability and test development issues concerning performance assessments, portfolios, and other educational assessments is provided.

Fairness in Testing

The Fairness in Testing section addresses issues of fairness and bias in testing and includes separate discussions of test takers' rights and responsibilities, the testing of individuals with diverse language backgrounds, and the testing of individuals with disabilities. The *Standards* discusses four different aspects of fairness. The first two relate to ensuring that tests are absent any bias and to the need to treat all examinees in an equitable fashion in the testing process. The third component of fairness is that all subgroups (e.g., based on ethnicity, race, gender, disability) must have equal passing rates or scores. The *Standards* acknowledges that there is broad consensus on the first two aspects, but that the idea that equal outcomes among groups is required for fairness "has been almost entirely repudiated in the professional testing literature" (p. 74). The fourth component of fairness concerns opportunity to learn.

The *Standards* provides a detailed discussion of how item bias and predictive bias could represent major challenges to the technical qualities of a test, and they describe procedures to ensure equal treatment of all students in testing. If some students have not had the opportunity to learn what is assessed in an achievement test, the scores reflect what the test taker knows but also what he or she has not had an opportunity to learn. When students have not had an opportunity to learn all tested information, then any policy about, for example, using the test scores as a basis for withholding a diploma is unfair.

The *Standards* also discusses some of the threats to the validity of inferences made from test scores of students who may not be proficient in the language in which they were tested. The greatest threat may occur when students' language proficiency limits their performance in an area other than language proficiency. Many state tests employ extended reading passages and written responses to demonstrate proficiency in areas such as mathematics, science, or history. To the extent that such assessments rely on language skills, students' scores may not accurately reflect their knowledge in these areas, but may instead reflect a combination of knowledge gaps and poor language proficiencies. The *Standards* describes four types of modifications that are designed to accommodate students with disabilities: (a) presentation format (e.g., large print, cassette), (b) response format (e.g., computer keyboard, aide to record oral responses), (c) extended time, and (d) test setting (e.g., individual administrations). Test users should take steps to ensure that test scores, and the inferences made from them, reflect the intended construct rather than the disabling condition. For example, if a student who needs longer than average time for cognitive processing is required to complete a speeded test, the results may in part reflect the disability. On the other hand, any modifications made should be described in detail and, when feasible, evidence should be provided that the inferences drawn from the results are valid and comparable to inferences based on scores of students who did not receive the accommodation. When testing students with disabilities or limited English proficiency, it is often difficult to demonstrate comparability of scores between those students and other test takers, and professional judgment is required in making inferences from these scores.

Testing Applications

The final section of the *Standards* describes the responsibilities of test users followed by the application of testing in specific settings. Of most relevance to educators are chapters discussing educational testing and assessment and the role of testing in program evaluation and public policy. In this section, a number of important points made earlier in the document are described more fully as they apply to education and public policy:

- Many tests are used for multiple purposes; however, evidence needed to support one use (e.g., program goals) will differ from evidence required for another purpose (e.g., individual student use).
- The higher the stakes associated with a test, the more important it is that test-based inferences be supported with strong technical evidence.
- Performance assessments often require complex procedures and training to increase the accuracy of scorers' judgments, and coverage of content domains is often reduced because each task usually requires more time to complete than do objectively scored items.
- When a test is intended to serve as an indicator of student achievement of curriculum standards, evidence of the extent to which the test samples the range of standards is needed.
- A decision that will have major impact on a student should not be made on the basis of a single test score; other relevant information should be considered in conjunction with the score.
- Individuals who supervise testing should have the necessary education and training to ensure they are familiar with the evidence for the validity and reliability of the test for the uses they intend.
- When schools, districts, states, or other authorities mandate the use of certain tests, those entities are responsible for identifying and monitoring the impact of testing and to minimize potential negative consequences.

- The integrity of test results must be maintained by eliminating practices that could raise scores without improving performance.

Summary

The *Standards* represents an important resource for all educators and policymakers who use and interpret test scores for individual students or groups of students (e.g., in a school, district, state, or nation). First, it represents the consensus of professionals in psychological and educational testing. The standards were developed by a committee composed exclusively of academicians and other researchers who have expertise in testing, measurement, and education, and their purpose is to provide guidance to all professionals who develop, select, or use assessments. Second, it is designed to promote sound and ethical use of tests by providing rigorous standards, some of which may not be feasibly met in many settings, that assist educators in evaluating test quality and appropriate test use. Third, it is based on current scientific knowledge and professional practice. Finally, it provides detailed discussions of several possible conflicts and concerns, ranging from issues that are highly technical and psychometric to those that concern proper administrative procedures or documentation and communications about a testing program. The *Standards* contains an extensive list of organizations and individuals with expertise in testing and education who reviewed, contributed to, and in many instances have endorsed these standards. Given the increased use of educational tests and the role they play in the allocation of resources and accountability in education, it is vital that educators and policymakers concerned with these issues become familiar with the professional and technical requirements related to testing in order to reduce misuse of tests and test results.

References

AERA, APA, & NCME. (1966). *Standards for educational and psychological tests and manuals.* Washington, DC: APA.

AERA, APA, & NCME. (1999). *Standards for educational and psychological testing.* Washington, DC: AERA.

American Educational Research Association & National Council on Measurements Used in Education. (1955). *Technical recommendations for achievement tests.* Washington, DC: Authors.

American Psychological Association. (1954). *Technical recommendations for psychological tests and diagnostic techniques.* Washington, DC: Author.

Camara, W. J. (1997). Use and consequences of assessments in the U.S.A.: Professional, ethical, and legal issues. *European Journal of Psychological Assessment, 13*(2), 140–152.

Camara, W. J., & Kraiger, K. (1996). Organisational infrastructure for selection and assessment in the U.S.A. In M. Smith & V. Sutherland (Eds.), *International review of professional issues in selection and assessment* (Vol. 2, pp. 138–146). Chichester, UK: John Wiley & Sons.

✦Joint Committee on Testing Practices. (2002). *Code of fair testing practices in education.* Available on *Measuring Up: An Anthology of Assessment Resources* [CD]. Also retrievable on-line: http://aac.ncat.edu.

✦ Document is included in the Anthology of Assessment Resources CD

Chapter 30
Training Educators to Develop Good Educational Tests

Patricia Jo McDivitt

In today's educational setting, assessment results weigh heavily in determining what students should know and be able to do. In addition, because assessment scores are often tied to accountability systems that affect both teaching and learning, they influence what is taught in the classroom. "Assessment directly affects learning in that it provides the necessary feedback for effective learning. It indirectly affects learning in that instruction is commonly skewed toward what is assessed; and, obviously, what is taught affects what is learned" (Marzano, Pickering, & McTighe, 1993, p. 11). The changes in the use of assessments underscore the need for educators to understand the role assessment plays in instruction and learning. Teachers, counselors, and assessment professionals are challenged not only to understand the use of assessments and the interpretation of the results, but also to learn more about how assessments are developed. This chapter summarizes the importance of assessment training with an emphasis on the standards-based assessment development process as it relates to recent research in learning and motivation.

Assessment Training Model

Although there are many models for assessment training, this chapter discusses in detail one suggested model. The components of this model are meant to enhance educators' understanding of the link between assessment and classroom teaching and learning. These components reflect recommended steps in the assessment development process:

- defining the purpose of the assessment
- developing content domains and understanding validity
- developing an assessment blueprint
- developing assessment question specifications
- writing and reviewing assessment questions

Defining the Purpose of the Assessment

The first step in assessment development training is to help educators understand the purpose of a particular assessment. Only by fully understanding this purpose can educators use the test scores appropriately. "In the broadest sense, the purpose of an assessment is to gather data to facilitate decision making. But there are many kinds of decisions and many kinds of information that may facilitate such decisions" (Mehrens, 2000, p. 27). Knowing precisely what students will be asked to master is important because different achievement targets require the application of different assessment methods, and there is no single assessment method capable of assessing all the various forms of achievement (Stiggins, 1999). Understanding the purpose of the standardized assessments used in the classroom is a fundamental component of any comprehensive assessment training program. This section summarizes the purpose of the two most common standardized assessments used in today's schools: the norm-referenced assessment and the criterion-referenced, or standards-based, assessment.

Norm-Referenced Assessment

The purpose of many norm-referenced standardized achievement assessments is to measure the academic foundation skills that students need. Therefore, the assessment questions are usually designed to measure a generalized set of objectives that are common across the country for a given content area. The results of this type of assessment allow educators to compare performance of students and to determine relative strengths and weaknesses of students based on the generalized academic foundation skills being measured by the assessment.

Norm-referenced standardized tests are based on national samples of students as the norm group for interpreting relative standing. Because these tests are designed for use in different schools throughout the country, they tend to provide broad coverage of each content area to maximize potential usefulness in as many schools as possible. Thus, educators should closely inspect the objectives and question types to determine how well the test matches the emphasis in the local curriculum (McMillan, 1997).

Criterion-Referenced, or Standards-Based, Assessment

Criterion-referenced assessments typically measure students' mastery of the learning targets as defined by a set of specific curriculum content standards. The use of standards-based assessments in the classroom is a rapidly growing movement within a larger movement of education reform. The use of these assessments calls for a clearer identification of what students should know and be able to do. In 1993 the National Education Goals Panel (1993) published *Promises to Keep: Creating High Standards for American Students.* This report outlines the importance of establishing two types of standards: content and performance. Content standards specify what students should know and be able to do. Performance standards specify the level to which the content standards should be mastered.

Norm-referenced tests provide some criterion-referenced information by indicating the number of questions answered correctly in a given content domain area; however, the norm-referenced tests used in the classroom today typically do not provide information as meaningful as that provided by standards-based assessments because the main purpose of the standardized, norm-referenced test is to compare students. For example, some norm-referenced tests have only three or four questions measuring a particular skill. In addition, norm-referenced tests often do not include questions that are very easy or very difficult because these questions are not typically useful in discriminating among students. The standards-based assessment usually focuses more upon ensuring that the difficulty level of the questions matches the specific learning targets as defined for the core curriculum (McMillan, 1997).

Understanding Performance Levels

In standards-based assessments, performance level descriptors are guidelines for determining what and how much students should know about a given content area at various stages of their formal schooling. Assessment training should include a discussion of performance levels, particularly the need to craft clear descriptors. Writing performance level descriptors requires careful analysis of the curriculum content standards in order to summarize dimensions of performance in a way that is clear and relevant to the standards. McMillan (1997) outlines six steps to follow when summarizing the dimensions of performance:

1. Identify dimensions of excellence.
2. Categorize and prioritize dimensions.

3. Clearly define each dimension.
4. Identify examples.
5. Describe performance continuums.
6. Try out and refine each dimension.

Stiggins (2001) stresses that assessment training must help educators or those developing the assessments to determine where and how evidence of academic proficiency will manifest itself. To identify performance criteria upon which to judge achievement, educators need to analyze the skills students are expected to demonstrate. This requires identifying the important elements that come together to make for sound performance.

Developing Content Domains and Understanding Validity

After determining the purpose of an assessment, educators must learn how to determine what should be assessed. Clear definitions of the purpose and content domains are important for all assessments, whether norm-referenced or criterion-referenced. Clearly defined content domains guide the entire assessment development process and aid in establishing the validity of the assessment. *Validity* refers to the degree to which evidence and theory support the interpretations of test scores entailed by proposed uses of tests (AERA, APA, & NCME, 1999).

As integral parts of assessment training, establishing validity and determining content domains begin with a careful examination of the core skills and standards or learning targets to be measured by the assessment. For many standards-based assessments, the development of content domains first involves an in-depth analysis of the curriculum content standards for a given program. The purpose of this analysis is to give teachers, as well as other educators involved in this process, a full understanding of the fundamental principles underlying what should be taught. Knowing what to ask of and teach students is important because different achievement targets require the application of different assessment methods. In any assessment context, the assessment development process must begin with a clear vision of what it means to succeed in that context. Students are expected to know and understand specific subject matter, some of which they must know outright, and some of which they must be able to retrieve using references as necessary (Stiggins, 1999).

Well-crafted content domains or content domain specifications ensure that assessments measure what they are intended to measure. The following steps are recommended for training educators to develop content domain specifications:

1. Review the purpose of the assessment.
2. Review the purpose for developing content domains.
3. Analyze the curriculum content standards for a given grade level and content area.
4. Determine what is to be assessed.
5. List the learning targets to be assessed.
6. Provide an indication of the relative importance of the content to be assessed.

Without a strong association between the assessment questions and the content domains, the questions will lack meaning and purpose (Osterlind, 1989). The following section illustrates the process used to develop a specific content domain specification.

Example of the Content Domain Specification Process

A group of teachers attend an assessment training workshop. They have reviewed the purpose of the assessment, and they understand the reason for developing content domains. The teachers have been asked to analyze the curriculum content standards for grade eight English language arts. After carefully analyzing the curriculum standards for their program, they determine that three content domains are represented by the curriculum content standards: using resources and following the research process steps, writing effective content and organizing clear paragraphs, and editing and revising paragraphs. The teachers write descriptions of each content domain. The following description is excerpted from one domain:

Subject area. Grade eight English language arts

Content description. Using resources and following the research process steps

Content domain description. Assessment questions in this domain will assess students' ability to understand and identify the steps in the research process, including identifying, collecting, and using sources of information.

Skills measured

Identifies and uses print sources to gather information
Identifies and uses technology to gather information
Identifies and uses media sources to gather

information
Identifies and uses the research process steps

Developing an Assessment Blueprint

After specifying the content domains, the next step in the training process is for educators to learn how to develop or review assessment blueprints. Typically the assessment blueprint will include a list of all standards to be assessed, organized by content domain. This blueprint outlines the number of assessment questions to be developed per learning target. In order for most standards-based assessments to be valid, there must be a close correspondence between the assessment content and the learning targets as specified in the curriculum content standards. Assessment blueprints further define what should be measured and what is important from the content domains. Good assessment blueprints produce reliable and valid assessments. As the *Standards for Educational and Psychological Testing* states:

> Important validity evidence can be obtained from an analysis of the relationship between a test's content and the construct it is intended to measure. . . . Test developers often work from a specification of the content domain. The content specification carefully describes the content in detail, often with a classification of areas of content and types of questions. Evidence based on test content can include logical or empirical analyses of the adequacy with which the test content represents the content domain and of the relevance of the content domain to the proposed interpretation of test scores. Evidence based on content can also come from expert judgments of the relationship between parts of the test and the construct. (AERA, APA & NCME, 1999)

Instructional validity plays an important part in the development of assessment blueprints. *Instructional validity* measures the extent to which an assessment matches what is taught (McMillan, 1997). How closely does the test correspond to what has been covered or should be covered in the classroom? Have students had the opportunity to learn what is being assessed? The process of developing blueprints for various subject areas is often challenging because the nature of learning is qualitatively and quantitatively different across disciplines. For example, teaching and learning mathematics are often tied to a specified instructional sequence. Therefore, what students should know and be able to do is often tied directly to the level and quality of their classroom instruction. Conversely, the learning targets for a grade eight English language arts standards-based assessment might be more generalized and not tied to an instructional sequence. As a result, assessment training must help educators learn how to use their professional judgment and knowledge of the curriculum to make decisions about the importance of different types of learning targets, the content to be assessed, and how much of the assessment should measure each target and content area. The assessment blueprint should provide for a wide coverage of the learning targets (Osterlind, 1989). The following steps are recommended for developing effective assessment blueprints:

1. Review the purpose of the assessment.
2. Review the purpose for developing assessment blueprints.
3. Analyze the curriculum content standards for a given grade level and content area.
4. Determine what is to be assessed and review the content domains.
5. List the learning targets to be assessed.
6. Provide an indication of the relative importance of the content to be assessed.
7. Determine the structure of the assessment, including recommended length, item difficulty, and higher-order thinking skills required.

Developing Assessment Question Specifications

Assessment training involves training educators to develop detailed specifications for writing assessment questions, often called *item specifications.* Item specifications ensure consistency throughout the entire assessment development process. Learning how to write and review item specifications is a crucial component of any comprehensive assessment training program. Through this training educators can begin to see the link between assessment and what is taught in the classroom.

Item specifications are one of the key requirements for a high-quality standards-based assessment. Although there are some similarities between the assessment blueprint and the item specifications, item specifications are usually more specific. They delineate the general characteristics of the questions for each curriculum content standard, and they provide information concerning the procedures for writing and reviewing test questions, including a detailed set of instructions from the assessment developer to the individuals writing the test questions so that the learning standards for a particular program can be translated into good test objectives. For example, when developing an assessment blueprint for English language arts, one standard might read, "Applies standard rules of capitalization." What are the standard rules? Should all be tested? Should standard rules of capitalization be tested using multiple-choice questions or a writing performance assessment only? In developing item specifications or reviewing item specifications for "applies standard rules of capitalization," educators should bring to the task their knowledge of the curriculum and of students to determine exactly what capitalization rules should be included on the assessment at a given grade level and how these rules should be assessed.

Well-crafted item specifications must clearly define the purpose of the assessment and the content to be measured. The following steps are recommended for developing item specifications:

1. Review the purpose of the assessment.
2. Review the purpose for developing assessment blueprints and item specifications.
3. Review the analyses of the curriculum content standards for a given grade level and content area, including what is to be assessed.
4. Review the structure of the assessment.
5. Provide an indication of the relative importance of the content to be assessed.
6. Draft item specifications, including
    - a statement of the content domain
    - a statement of the curriculum standard to be measured
    - directions for how the test questions should be written
    - estimated difficulty of the assessment questions
    - guidelines for determining the cognitive level for learning targets
    - guidelines for how the answer choices should be written
    - any additional guidelines for how a particular learning target should be tested

Writing and Reviewing Assessment Questions

Educators regularly write assessment questions; however, most educators have not received training in how to write or review good test questions. One goal of assessment training is to equip educators with the tools necessary to write and review good test questions. A model training session should include an overview of the basic item writing guidelines, as well as any specific guidelines for a particular program. The assessment blueprint, as well as the item specifications, should also be discussed, along with any general information about basic item writing principles. Educators should then be given the opportunity to write items to measure specific content standards. The training should also include a review of the items written, with suggestions for revision. The following steps are recommended steps for reviewing and writing assessment questions:

1. Review the purpose of the assessment.
2. Review the content domains, the assessment blueprint, and the item specifications.
3. Review guidelines for writing and reviewing good, reliable, and fair test questions.
4. Draft and review items.

Although there are many well-established guidelines for the writing of good, reliable, and fair test questions, the following section focuses on some of the most important guidelines to include in assessment training for educators.

Match the Question to the Content Standard

The first criterion for writing good test questions is that there must be a high degree of congruence between a particular question and the key objective of the test (Osterlind, 1989). How well does the question match its intended objective? The congruence criterion is the assessment writer's or reviewer's primary consideration because it is at the heart of validity. Careful attention to the educational significance of the assessment questions ensures that the assessment mirrors sound instructional practices. Training should include helping educators write questions that measure the specific content objectives. Every question has a purpose, and this purpose should be clearly defined in the question specifications. The standard and the benchmark help to define the nature of the test question.

A major prerequisite for writing and reviewing questions that match the standard is strong knowledge of the content area to be probed by the questions. As an integral part of the training process, teachers should clearly establish the close correspondence between the curriculum content standards and the test questions. The content of each test question must be crafted carefully so that the question measures what is important and what can be successfully taught and learned in the classroom.

Knowledge Specificity

Educators must carefully consider the educational significance of each assessment question. Assessment training should therefore include a discussion of the concept of knowledge specificity. *Knowledge specificity* refers to a continuum of overly specific to overly general questions. Most questions should be written with this continuum in mind (Haladyna, 1999). Questions should not measure simple recall of facts or be classified as "so what" questions. The "so what" question is at the lowest level on the continuum and usually asks for knowledge that has little or no value for assessing a student's progression toward mastery of the learning targets (Frary, 1995).

Item Quality

Potential problems with a test include poorly worded questions, reading or writing demands that require more than a mastery of the material being tested; questions with more than one correct response; incorrect scoring; or racial, ethnic, or gender bias. In addition, the student may experience extreme test anxiety or interpret test questions differently from the author's intent, as well as cheat, guess, or lack motivation. Further, the assessment environment could be uncomfortable, poorly lighted, noisy, or otherwise distracting (Stiggins, 1999). Any of these situations could give rise to inaccurate test results. To prevent problems related to test questions, assessment questions should be well written, following a uniform style. Although there are several published guidelines for writing and reviewing assessment questions, the following list summarizes the major considerations for writing good, reliable, fair test questions.

A good question

- has one and only one clearly correct answer
- is structured around one main idea or problem
- measures the objective or curriculum content standard it is designed to measure
- is at the appropriate level of difficulty
- is simple, direct, and free of ambiguity
- makes use of vocabulary and sentence structure that are appropriate to the grade level of the students being tested
- contains answer choices that that are plausible and reasonable in terms of the requirements of the question, as well as the student's level of knowledge

- contains answer choices that are parallel in grammatical structure and content
- contains answer choices that relate to the question
- reflects good and current teaching and learning practices in the subject area
- is free of bias

A bad question

- provides clues (within a question or within a test form)
- is considered a "trick" or "cute" question
- contains an answer choice that would eliminate another answer choice
- contains vocabulary and idiomatic phrases that could be unfamiliar to students
- asks about trivial information

Levels of Thinking

An important objective of classroom instruction is to help students acquire and use higher-order thinking skills. Assessments, therefore, must include questions that require higher-order as well as lower-order thinking, and educators should be trained to evaluate each question they write in terms of the levels of thinking required to answer the question.

Defining and measuring the levels of higher-order thinking has been a major challenge to educators for many years. Each question in a test measures a specific behavior, and students may respond to questions with a pattern of right and wrong answers, but no one really knows the exact mental processes used in making the correct choices on a test. For any test question, the test taker may appear to be thinking at a higher level, but in actuality, he or she may be remembering identical statements or ideas previously presented. A group of educators may agree that a given question appears to measure one type of behavior, when in fact it may measure an entirely different type of behavior simply because each test taker brings a unique set of experiences to the test (Haladyna, 1999).

Perhaps the best-known source for learning targets and cognitive processing is the *Taxonomy of Educational Objectives* (Bloom, 1956). *Bloom's taxonomy* is probably the most widely used scheme for labeling levels of cognitive processes. Using this taxonomy, assessment questions can be classified into one of three cognition levels: recall, application, and analysis. *Recall* questions are written to measure students' ability to remember isolated facts, concepts, principles, processes, procedures, or theories. When students respond to these questions, the primary cognitive function they use is memory. *Application* questions are written to measure students' ability to provide simple interpretations or limited applications of data or information. Questions written at this level typically require some problem-solving skills. *Analysis* questions are written primarily to measure students' skills in evaluating data and problem solving. Responding to these questions involves application of good judgment and problem-solving skills. Analysis questions involve higher cognitive processes than do the other types of questions (Vacc, Loesch, & Lubik, 2001).

Bloom's taxonomy was developed many years ago, and many educators believe that the taxonomy is no longer adequate for defining levels of cognitive processing. In fact, since the development of Bloom's taxonomy, there have been many changes in the educational and psychological theories that formed the basis for the taxonomy.

Current theories emphasize thinking processes, characterize the learner as an active information processor, and stress domain-specific thinking and learning (McMillan, 1997). For example, the *dimensions of learning* is an instructional framework based on current research and learning theory. Initially, the dimensions of learning framework was designed to help educators plan curriculum and instruction more effectively by using what is known about how students learn. The framework's strong grounding in research and theory, however, makes it a natural partner for assessment (Marzano, Pickering, & McTighe, 1993). Following are the five dimensions of learning:

1. Maintaining positive attitudes and perceptions about learning
2. Acquiring and integrating knowledge
3. Extending and refining knowledge
4. Using knowledge meaningfully

Dimension 5: Developing productive habits of mind

The five dimensions of learning can be used to address current content standards, including acquisition and integration of knowledge, complex thinking standards, and reasoning processes standards (Marzano, Pickering, & McTighe, 1993). Whether or not educators use Bloom's taxonomy or the five dimensions of learning, they must be trained in understanding the precision of the cognitive level definitions adopted for use, and they must be trained to consider carefully the precision with which particular test questions may tap specific levels of mental processing (Osterlind, 1989)

Item Difficulty

Most standards-based assessments used in the classroom today should include test questions that have a range of difficulty so that all students can demonstrate what they know and are able to do. The level of thinking required to answer a particular question is not the same as the difficulty of the question. For example, a question calling for a student to analyze an easy reading passage may be a much easier question than a question that asks a student to demonstrate comprehension of a difficult reading passage. Therefore, a major component of assessment training is to help educators understand item difficulty and that determining the difficulty of a question requires teacher judgment.

Summary

It has often been said that there is a gap between assessment and instruction in the classroom. Often the instruction in the classroom is not geared toward the same objectives as those measured on the assessment, or the assessment may, in fact, fail to provide information about students' strengths and weaknesses as real targets for further instruction. The assessment training model presented in this chapter may serve as a starting point for providing educators with the tools necessary to make the critical connection between instruction and assessment. Through in-depth knowledge of the purpose of the assessment and the assessment development process, instruction can be placed on the same educational continuum as the standards-based assessment.

References

AERA, APA, & NCME. (1999). *Standards for educational and psychological testing.* Washington, DC: AERA.

Bloom, B. S. (Ed.). (1956). *Taxonomy of educational objectives: The classification of educational goals. Handbook 1: Cognitive domain.* New York: David McKay.

Frary, R. B. (1995). More multiple-choice question writing do's and don'ts. *Practical Assessment, Research and Evaluation. 4*(11), 1–4.

Haladyna, T. (1999). *Developing and validating multiple-choice test questions.* Mahwah, NJ: Lawrence Erlbaum.

Marzano, R. J., Pickering, D., & McTighe, J. (1993). *Assessing student outcomes: Performance assessment using the dimensions of learning model.* Aurora, CO: McRel Institute.

McMillan, J. H. (1997). *Classroom assessment: Principles and practice for effective instruction.* Needham Heights, MA: Allyn and Bacon.

Mehrens, W. A. (2000). Selecting a career assessment instrument. In J. T. Kapes & E. A. Whitfield (Eds.), *A counselor's guide to career assessment instruments* (4th ed.). Alexandria, VA: National Career Development Association.

National Education Goals Panel. (1993, November). *Promises to keep: Creating high standards for American students.* (Report on the review of education standards from the Goals 3 and 4 Technical Planning Group to the National Education Goals Panel.) Washington, DC: Author.

Osterlind, S. J. (1989). *Constructing test questions.* Dordrecht, The Netherlands: Kluwer Academic Publishers.

Stiggins, R. (1999). Are you assessment literate? *High School Magazine, 6,* 2–6.

Stiggins, R. (2001). Sound performance assessments in the guidance context. In G. R. Walz & J. C. Bleuer (Eds.), *Assessment issues and challenges for the millennium.* Greensboro, NC: CAPS Publications.

Vacc, N. A., Loesch, L. C., & Lubik, R. E. (2001). Writing multiple-choice test questions. In G. R. Walz & J. C. Bleuer (Eds.), *Assessment issues and challenges for the millennium.* Greensboro, NC: CAPS Publications.

Chapter 31
Assessment Competencies for School Counselors

Patricia B. Elmore & Ruth B. Ekstrom

What assessment and evaluation skills and knowledge should school counselors have? That was the question put to a joint committee of the American School Counselor Association (ASCA) and the Association for Assessment in Counseling (AAC).[1] The goal of the committee was to develop a document describing the assessment and evaluation competencies school counselors need.

There has been some documentation of school counselors' assessment skills and practices. Work behaviors related to assessment are fundamental to the general practice of counseling, according to a survey conducted by Sampson, Vacc, and Loesch (1998). Training in good test use practices is one of three competencies that counselors must have for adult personal and career assessments (Tymofievich & Leroux, 2000). Previous research by Elmore, Ekstrom, Diamond, and Whittaker (1993) found that 67 percent of a group of 423 ASCA members considered testing and assessment an important or very important part of their work. The counselors indicated that they are most often involved in test interpretation and administration. Although the counselors were highly confident in their ability to use test results in counseling, their responses regarding their actual test use practices were problematic. Only 57 percent said they always or almost always read the test manual to find out about any limitations of the test, and less than half (49 percent) said they always or almost always obtain additional information to support or refute test results. Only 36 percent always or almost always take into consideration differences between those being tested and the group(s) on which the test was normed.

Impara and Plake (1995) compared the measurement and assessment competencies of school administrators, counselors, and teachers; they found that in a typical school, the educational professionals who know the most about testing are the counselors. Teachers and principals, especially at the secondary level, rely on counselors as a resource to provide them with test information, to answer measurement-related questions, and to interact with parents on testing issues.

The assessment activities of counselors are affected by their measurement knowledge and training. Elmore, Ekstrom, and Diamond (1993) found that good practices in test selection, test administration, and test interpretation were consistently and significantly associated with having read the *Code of Fair Testing Practices in Education* (JCTP, 2002) or the *Responsibilities of Users of Standardized Tests* (AACD/AMECD, 1989). Good test use practices by counselors seem to derive from their measurement training; therefore, it is important for measurement professionals to develop counselor training programs and materials that will facilitate good test use.

Survey Findings

A subcommittee of the joint ASCA and AAC committee undertook a survey of the assessment activities of a random sample of school counselors. This confirmed that test interpretation and test administration were specific responsibilities for most school counselors. Of the responding school counselors, 91 percent said their work involved interpreting test results and using this information in counseling.

To identify essential assessment skills for school counselors, the subcommittee next conducted a survey of a random sample of ASCA members who indicated "school counselor" as their job setting (N = 600) and a random sample of ASCA members who indicated "counselor educator" as their job setting (N = 200). The survey consisted of a list of 39 assessment activities that were identified from state certification materials. These were assessment training requirements and skill expectations for school counselors. The respondents were asked to indicate how important it is for school counselors to be able to carry out each activity using a three-point scale: (3) essential, (2) desirable, and (1) not necessary.

Of the 179 school counselors who responded, 79 (44 percent) were elementary school counselors, 32 (18 percent) were middle school counselors, 50 (28 percent) were high school counselors, 9 (5 percent) were counseling administrators or supervisors, and the remainder reported other job titles. Most (77 percent) reported earning a degree in school counseling and guidance.

Of the 63 counselor educators responding, 75 percent had received a doctorate. Their degree fields included counselor education (41 percent), school counseling and guidance (37 percent), counseling and school psychology (10 percent), and college student personnel (3 percent), with only 9 percent reporting other fields.

Essential Assessment Skills and Knowledge

Ten skills were rated as essential by 65 percent or more of both the school counselors and the counselor educators. Table 1 shows the percentages of counselors and counselor educators who rated each of the following ten skills as essential.

1. Referring students to other professionals, when appropriate, for additional assessment or appraisal
2. Interpreting scores from tests or assessments and using the information in counseling
3. Communicating and interpreting test or assessment information to students and helping them use it for educational and career planning
4. Making decisions about the types of assessments to use when counseling groups or individual students
5. Communicating and interpreting test or assessment information to parents
6. Reading about and being aware of ethical issues in assessment
7. Communicating and interpreting test or assessment information to teachers, school administrators, and other professionals
8. Making decisions about the types of assessments to use in planning and evaluating counseling programs
9. Synthesizing and integrating testing and nontesting data to make decisions about individuals
10. Reading about and being aware of current issues involving multicultural assessment, the assessment of individuals with disabilities and other special needs, and the assessment of language minorities

Parallels to many of these essential skills can be found in the ASCA *Role Statement* (1990) and the ASCA *Ethical Standards* (1998). For example, even though the school counselor is often seen as the person in a school most knowledgeable about assessment (Impara & Plake, 1995), both counselors and counselor educators stress the importance of referrals to other testing professionals. The *Role Statement* says, "Counselors are aware of their own professional competencies and . . . know when and how to involve other professionals" (p. 5)

Table 1. Assessment Skills Viewed as Essential by Both School Counselors (N=179) and Counselor Educators (N=63)

Skill	School Counselors	Counselor Educators
Refer students to other professionals, when appropriate, for additional assessment/appraisal	84%	89%
Interpret scores from tests/assessments and use the information in counseling	75%	81%
Communicate and interpret test/assessment information to students and help them use it for educational and career planning	73%	87%
Make decisions about the type(s) of assessments to use in counseling groups or individual students	71%	78%
Communicate and interpret test/assessment information to parents	71%	78%
Read about and be aware of ethical issues in assessment	70%	84%
Communicate and interpret test/assessment information to teachers, school administrators, and other professionals	68%	76%
Make decisions about the type(s) of assessments to use in planning and evaluating counseling programs	67%	67%
Synthesize and integrate testing and non-testing data to make decisions about individuals	67%	65%
Read about and be aware of current issues involving multicultural assessment, the assessment of individuals with disabilities and other special needs, and the assessment of language minorities	65%	68%

Less Important Assessment Skills and Knowledge

Four assessment skills were rated as not necessary by 25 percent or more of both the school counselors and the counselor educators. Table 2 shows the percentages of counselors and counselor educators who rating the following four nonessential assessment skills.

1. Scheduling testing or assessments
2. Administering individual standardized tests for diagnostic purposes
3. Conducting nonstandardized testing and assessments
4. Using assessment information to place or group students in classes

Table 2. Assessment Skills Considered Not Necessary by 25% or More of School Counselors (N=179) and Counselor Educators (N=63)

Skill	School Counselors	Counselor Educators
Schedule testing/assessments	30%	54%
Administer individual standardized tests for diagnostic purposes	33%	35%
Conduct non-standardized testing and assessments	31%	29%
Use assessment information to place/group students in classes	29%	29%

Some individuals may be surprised that skills required of or specified for school counselors in some states are considered unnecessary by many of the counselors and counselor educators who responded to this survey. Counselors are often expected to schedule testing sessions for state or locally mandated examinations, but many counselors and counselor educators object, saying that this is primarily a clerical task. While a few states require school counselors to be able to administer tests for diagnostic purposes, in most states this is a task assigned to school psychologists. Grouping of students for instruction is a controversial topic, as is deciding what information should inform the decision if grouping is to occur. There have been increasing pressures to reduce grouping, especially before high school.

Development of the Competencies

The results of the survey provided important information for the joint committee to finalize the *Competencies in Assessment and Evaluation for School Counselors,* which were approved in 1998 by both ASCA and AAC and published in 2001 (Joint Committee of the ASCA & the AAC, 2001).

The preface to the *Competencies* states: "The competencies can be used by counselor and assessment educators as a guide in the development and evaluation of school counselor preparation programs, workshops, in-services, and other continuing-education opportunities. They may also be used by school counselors to evaluate their own professional development and needs for continuing education" (Joint Committee of the ASCA and the AAC, 2001, p. 95). It should be emphasized that these competencies focus on the activities of individual counselors rather than the content of counselor education programs. However, they are consistent with existing Council for Accreditation of Counseling and Related Educational Programs (CACREP, 2001) and National Association of State Directors of Teacher Education and Certification (NASDTEC, 1991) standards.

The following definitions clarify the key terms used in the *Competencies.*

Competencies describes skills or understandings that a school counselor should possess to perform assessment and evaluation activities effectively.

Assessment is the gathering of information for making decisions about individuals, groups, programs, or processes.

Evaluation is the collection and interpretation of information to make judgments about individuals, programs, or processes that lead to decisions and future actions.

School counselors should have all of the nine competencies in the following list. (They should also have the specific skills listed in the *Competencies* document under each competency.)

1. School counselors are skilled in choosing assessment strategies.
2. School counselors can identify, access, and evaluate the most commonly used assessment instruments.

3. School counselors are skilled in the techniques of administration and methods of scoring assessment instruments.
4. School counselors are skilled in interpreting and reporting assessment results.
5. School counselors are skilled in using assessment results in decision making.
6. School counselors are skilled in producing, interpreting, and presenting statistical information about assessment results.
7. School counselors are skilled in conducting and interpreting evaluations of school counseling programs and counseling-related interventions.
8. School counselors are skilled in adapting and using questionnaires, surveys, and other assessments to meet local needs.
9. School counselors know how to engage in professionally responsible assessment and evaluation practices.

There are between three and six specific skills listed under each competency. For example, for Competency 9, the second skill listed is, "They can use professional codes and standards including the *Code of Fair Testing Practices in Education, Code of Professional Responsibilities in Educational Measurement, Responsibilities of Users of Standardized Tests,* and *Standards for Educational and Psychological Testing* to evaluate counseling practices using assessments" (Joint Committee of the ASCA and the AAC, 2001, p. 99). Together the skills constitute a comprehensive statement of what school counselors should know and be trained to do.

Conclusion

In 1998 a joint committee of ASCA and AAC outlined the assessment competencies recommended for school counselors. These nine recommended competency areas were based in part on surveys of school counselors and counselor educators regarding what they felt were essential and nonessential skills for practice in a school setting. Among the skills universally considered important were making decisions about which assessments to use, synthesizing results for use in treatment, and communicating and interpreting test results to parents and school personnel. In addition, knowing when and how to make referrals and being knowledgeable about ethics and multicultural assessment were essential. Among less important skills were scheduling and administering tests and using that information to group students, perhaps reflecting school counselors' opinion that these expectations were an underutilization of their skill level.

Note

1. Committee members were Patricia Elmore (AAC, Chair 1997–2000), William Schafer (AAC, Chair 1993–1996); Ruth Ekstrom (AAC), Daren Hutchinson (ASCA), Marjorie Mastie (AAC), Kathy O'Rourke (ASCA), Thomas Trotter (ASCA), and Barbara Webster (ASCA).

References

AACD/AMECD [American Association for Counseling and Development/Association for Measurement and Evaluation in Counseling and Development]. (1989). *Responsibilities of users of standardized tests.* Alexandria, VA: Author.

AERA, APA, & NCME [American Educational Research Association, American Psychological Association, & National Council on Measurement in Education]. (1999). *Standards for educational and psychological testing.* Washington, DC: American Educational Research Association.

ASCA [American School Counselor Association]. (1990). *Role statement.* Alexandria, VA: Author.

✦ASCA. (1998). *Ethical standards.* Alexandria, VA: Author.

ASCA & AAC [American School Counselor Association & Association for Assessment in Counseling]. (1998). *Competencies in assessment and evaluation for school counselors.* Alexandria, VA: Author.

CACREP [Council for Accreditation of Counseling and Related Educational Programs]. (2001). *CACREP accreditation standards and procedures manual.* Alexandria, VA: Author.

Elmore, P. B., Ekstrom, R. B., & Diamond, E. E. (1993). Counselors' test use practices: Indicators of the adequacy of measurement training. *Measurement and Evaluation in Counseling and Development, 26,* 116–124.

Elmore, P. B., Ekstrom, R. B., Diamond, E. E., & Whittaker, S. (1993). School counselors' test use patterns and practices. *School Counselor, 41* (2), 73–80.

Impara, J. C., & Plake, B. S. (1995). Comparing counselors', school administrators', and teachers' knowledge in student assessment. *Measurement and Evaluation in Counseling and Development, 28,* 78–87.

Joint Committee of the ASCA and the AAC. (2001). Competencies in assessment and evaluation for school counselors. In G. R. Walz & J. C. Bleuer (Eds.), *Assessment issues and challenges for the millennium* (pp. 95–100). Greensboro, NC: ERIC Counseling and Student Services Clearinghouse.

✦JCTP [Joint Committee on Testing Practices]. (2002). *Code of fair testing practices in education.* Available on *Measuring Up: An Anthology of Assessment Resources* [CD]. Also retrievable on-line: http://aac.ncat.edu.

NASDTEC [National Association of State Directors of Teacher Education and Certification]. (1991). *Manual on certification and preparation of educational personnel in the United States.* Dubuque, IA: Kendall/Hunt Publishing.

✦NCME. (1995). *Code of professional responsibilities in educational measurement.* Washington, DC: Author.

Sampson, J. P., Jr., Vacc, N. A., & Loesch, L. C. (1998). The practice of career counseling by specialists and counselors in general practice. *Career Development Quarterly, 46,* 404–415.

Tymofievich, M., & Leroux, J. A. (2000). Counselors' competencies in using assessments. *Measurement and Evaluation in Counseling and Development, 33,* 50–59.

✦ Document is included in the Anthology of Assessment Resources CD

Chapter 32
Test User Qualifications
Who Can Use What Tests?

Thomas Warren Clawson & Wendi K. Schweiger

Many individuals working in education-related professions have a variety of needs for educational and psychological test results regarding their students or clients. This chapter addresses school counselors' use of tests in educational settings and the right to test as a competency-based issue. Although the subject appears on the surface not to be controversial, a history of debate exists as to which professionals should administer various tests.

Staffing, local norms, and state and local rules often dictate what is usually a hierarchy of test use within school systems. School counselors tend to administer achievement tests and career inventories. They also may administer group intelligence tests and, in some locations, individual intelligence tests. School counselors are trained to interpret test results to students, parents, and other educators. All modern counselor education programs require a variety of courses that qualify school counselors to administer, score, and interpret tests. Master's degree programs prepare school counselors to use test results for diagnosis, treatment formulation, educational planning or remediation, and consultation with stakeholders.

In terms of diagnostic use of tests school counselors most frequently use educational and intelligence test results for diagnosis of educational problems. Even though diagnosis is often thought to be a medical or strictly psychological term, in many cases school counselors certainly make psychological diagnoses based upon the integration of test data. School district policies generally ask school counselors to refer students with serious psychological disorders for more specialized treatment. Even if psychological diagnosis is not frequent, however, school counselors sometimes have serious cases in which they must give informed referrals based on interpretation of some psychological tests. The need to refer is more often due to the multiple roles that a school counselor performs and the time these many roles take than to a lack of training or ability to work with these students.

Once the school counselor has made a diagnosis or identified a problem, this information is typically used to create an action plan for remediation or other supportive measures. Usually, the student, parents, teachers, and other educational support personnel work as a team to determine and implement the plan.

Ethical Issues in Test Administration

Training is one of the most important considerations whenever counselors or other professionals use tests to gain insight into a diagnosis and formulate a treatment plan. For all professions involved in testing, the professional body or organization charged with regulating that profession should mandate specific requirements of study to prepare members to use tests as part of their practice. In addition, it is imperative that codes of ethics address the concept that professionals do not practice beyond their scope of training, and those codes should also include test-specific conditions of ethical practice. For counselors, an example can be found in the 2001 Standards of the Council for the Accreditation of Counseling and Related Educational Programs (CACREP, 2001) which delineates coursework that constitutes appropriate training in testing for counselors:

> 7. ASSESSMENT – studies that provide an understanding of individual and group approaches to assessment and evaluation, including all of the following: . . .
>   b. basic concepts of standardized and nonstandardized testing and other assessment techniques including norm-referenced and criterion-referenced assessment, environmental assessment, performance assessment, individual and group test and inventory methods, behavioral observations, and computer-managed and computer-assisted methods. (pp. 9–10)

The 2001 CACREP standards also directly address the expected requirements for school counselors regarding preparation for testing:

> C. KNOWLEDGE AND SKILL REQUIREMENTS FOR SCHOOL COUNSELORS
> 1. Program Development, Implementation, and Evaluation:
>   a. use, management, analysis, and presentation of data from school-based information (e.g., standardized testing, grades,

enrollment, attendance, retention, placement), surveys, interviews, focus groups, and needs assessments to improve student outcomes. (p. 30)

In addition, the National Board for Certified Counselors (NBCC, 1997) addresses testing ethics:

Section C: Measurement and Evaluation:
1. Because many types of assessment techniques exist, certified counselors must recognize the limits of their competence and perform only those assessment functions for which they have received appropriate training or supervision.
2. Certified counselors who utilize assessment instruments to assist them with diagnoses must have appropriate training and skills in educational psychological measurement, validation criteria, test research, and guidelines for test development and use. (p. 5)

In February 1996, the Fair Access Coalition for Testing (FACT) was formed to protect the public and the rights of test professionals to use tests based on the level of competency to administer and interpret the tests each professional chooses. FACT operates under the assumption that training and proven competency, rather than professional degree held, should determine whether a testing professional has the right to administer and interpret a psychological test. The mission of FACT is "to protect fair access to psychological and educational tests by properly trained professionals to better serve the public" (FACT, 2000, website home page).

In January 2002, the National Fair Access Coalition on Testing (FACT, 2002) released a document for public review that is intended for all professionals and is meant to be used as a model for future sections of codes of ethics that address testing. The current FACT Model Code of Ethics is as follows (available from www.fairaccess.org/code_of_ethics.htm):

TEST SELECTION
1) In choosing a particular test, the assessment professional (hereafter "test user") is responsible for reviewing test manuals or materials to ascertain the test's applicability in measuring a certain trait or construct. The manual should

fully describe the development of the test, the rationale, and data pertaining to item selection and test construction. The manual should explicitly state the purposes and applications for which the test is intended, and provide adequate reliability and validity data about the test. The manual should furthermore identify the qualifications to properly administer and interpret the test.

2) In selecting a particular combination of tests, the test user needs to document and justify the logic of the choice(s).
3) Test users avoid using outdated or obsolete tests, and strive to remain current regarding test publication and revision.
4) Tests selected for individual testing must be appropriate for that individual, i.e., appropriate norms exist for variables such as age, gender, ethnicity, and race. The test form must fit the client. If the test must be used in the absence of available information regarding the above sub samples, the limitations of generalizability should be duly noted.

TEST USER QUALIFICATIONS

1) Test users employ only those tests for which they are competent by training, education, or experience. In familiarizing themselves with new tests, test users thoroughly read the manual and pertinent materials, and attend workshops, supervision, or other forms of training.
2) Test users must be able to document appropriate education, training, and experience in areas of assessment they perform.
3) Professionals who supervise others should ensure that their trainees have sufficient knowledge and experience before utilizing the tests for clinical purposes.
4) Supervisors ensure that their supervisees have had adequate training in interpretation before entrusting them to evaluate the test results in a semi-autonomous fashion.

TEST ADMINISTRATION

1) Tests should only be employed in appropriate professional settings or as recommended by instructors or supervisors for training purposes. It is best to avoid giving tests to relatives, close friends, or business associates in that doing so constructs a dual professional/personal relationship, which is to be avoided.

2) Test users make every effort to provide necessary information to the client prior to the testing session. The client should be informed of the length of time required, any special requirements as to their medications (or not taking them), the cost involved, and, in a medical situation, the need for any preauthorization from a third party payer.
3) The test user provides the test taker with appropriate information regarding the reasons for assessment, the approximate length of time required, and to whom the report will be distributed. Issues of confidentiality must be addressed, and the client given the opportunity to ask questions of the examiner prior to beginning the procedure.
4) Care is taken to provide an appropriate assessment environment in regard to temperature, privacy, comfort, and freedom from distractions. Any deviations should be recorded in any written documentation pertaining to the evaluation.
5) Information is solicited regarding any possible impairment such as problems with visual or auditory acuity, limitations of hand/eye coordination, illness, or other factors. If the disabilities cannot be accommodated effectively, the test should not be administered at that time. The test taker may need to be referred to an assessment professional who specializes in evaluation of individuals with that particular disorder. Alternatively, if testing is accomplished with the instruments at hand, limitations of the applicability of the test results should be clearly noted in the test report.
6) Test users familiarize themselves with instructions for administration of a test and follow them carefully in order to insure accurate and valid results. Failure to follow the instructions for administration will result in decreased accuracy of estimates for the trait or behavior being measured. Any deviations from the instructions for test administration should be documented.

TEST INTERPRETATION

1) Interpretation of test or test battery results should be based on multiple sources of convergent data and an understanding of the tests' foundations and limits. If tests of a similar nature are used in a test battery, test users should address any known correlational data.

2) Test users do not make conclusions unless test results (not just history) are present to justify those conclusions. If such evidence is lacking, test users should not make diagnostic or prognostic statements.
3) Interpretation of test results should take into account any qualitative influences on test taking behavior, such as health, energy, motivation, and the like. Description and analysis of alternative explanations should be provided with the interpretations.
4) Test users do not make firm conclusions in the absence of published information establishing a satisfactory degree of test validity, particularly predictive validity. Test users should not imply that a relationship exists between test results, prescribed interventions, and desired outcomes unless empirical evidence for that relationship exists.
5) Multicultural factors must be considered in test selection, interpretation, diagnosis, as well as the formulation of prognosis and treatment recommendations.
6) Test users avoid biased or incorrect interpretation by assuring that the test norms match the population taking the test.
7) Test users who have the responsibility for making decisions about clients or policies based on test results should have a thorough understanding of applicable assessment and therapeutic theory, methodology, and research.
8) Test users should accurately report results regardless of any individuals or groups who may have a vested interest in decisions influenced by test interpretation.

TEST REPORTING

1) Test users write reports in a clear fashion, avoiding jargon or clinical terms that are likely to confuse the lay reader.
2) Test users strive to provide test results in as positive and nonjudgmental manner as possible.
3) Mindful that one's report reflects on the reputation of oneself and one's profession, reports are carefully proofread so as to be free of spelling, style, and grammatical errors as much as is possible.
4) Clients are clearly informed as to who will be allowed to review the report and, in the absence of a valid court order, must sign appropriate releases of information permitting

such release. The test user must not release the report or findings in the absence of the aforementioned releases or order.

5) Test users are responsible for ensuring the confidentiality and security of test reports, test data, test materials, and any transmission of data or reports, whether electronic or by mail. Clients should be informed of how their test data is securely stored.
6) Test users must offer the client the opportunity to receive feedback about the test results and interpretations, and the sources of error and limitation for such data.
7) The test user trains his or her staff to protect the security of test reports in the context of producing, preparing, storing, retrieving, and transmitting them.

COMPUTERIZED OR WEBSITE TESTING

1) When using computerized tests, the test user makes sure that he or she has the appropriate documentation necessary to choose the right test for the purpose.
2) The test user explains to the client the limits of reliability and validity posed by a computerized interpretation format.
3) Any provision of computerized test results to the client is accompanied by a professional interpretation of the results.
4) A professional offering computerized testing through a website must provide appropriate encryption and firewall protection to insure confidentiality of results. Limits of applicability should be provided and explained. Clear explanations regarding the purpose of the test and requirements for taking the test are presented.
5) Test users are responsible for evaluating the quality of computer software that scores and interprets test data. The test user should obtain information regarding validity of computerized test interpretation and review it carefully before utilizing such an approach. Computerized interpretation services should be able to demonstrate that their programs are based on sufficient and appropriate research to establish the validity of the programs and procedures used in arriving at interpretations. Any limitations in applicability should be noted in the report or feedback session.

In the most comprehensive review of testing language within professional codes of ethics, Vacc, Juhnke, and Nilsen (2001) discuss the thoroughness of community mental health service providers' handling of the issue. In this article, the authors compare the codes of ethics of 13 professional organizations and find that some professional codes of ethics clearly address testing more thoroughly than others. The point of their article is that all professions should clearly address the issue of testing as a proactive and constructive way to monitor the use of tests by their professionals.

Levels of Tests

Many test publishing companies use a three-level system to categorize psychological tests, using designations developed by the American Psychological Association in the 1950s. The historical basis for this designation emanates from an early attempt to delineate need for training, not restriction of access. The APA has not promulgated the three-letter classification rubric in decades, yet test publishers, having no better ideas for quality control, continue to use these designations. Most note training standards for their tests and allow individual professionals who do not meet the classification rubric to document the nature of their training and their qualifications in order to buy instruments for use.

School counselors probably administer the highest volume of tests in schools. The majority of their testing duties involve large group testing with level A or level B tests. Level A tests comprise group educational, vocational, or intelligence tests, and structurally simple individual tests. In general, level A instruments require little training to administer, score, or interpret. Level B instruments are more complicated to use and generally are more sophisticated in development and philosophical basis. Accurate interpretation of these tests often requires not only theoretical background but also some knowledge of psychometric principles.

Counselors and any other professionals using level C instruments should be able to prove thorough knowledge, training, and practice in administration. These tests require the most sophisticated level of training. Controversy is ongoing regarding the use of level C tests by professionals other than doctoral-level psychologists, but no professional guidelines prohibit any well-trained professional from using these tests. Doctoral-level psychologists and school psychologists (with entry degree at the specialist level) have little problem meeting all criteria for approval to purchase level C tests. This is generally also the case for all master's level professions such as counseling psychologists, speech and hearing specialists, social workers, educational diagnosticians, and special education teachers.

The Association of Test Publishers, a well-organized and venerable group of more than 200 test publishing companies, has no statement regarding the levels of tests. As a member of FACT, they do however endorse the FACT principle of training, not profession, as the key indicator of access to test use.

Conclusion

School counselors first entered the testing arena en force when the space race created a national urgency to classify students' potential to compete in scientific fields. Group testing, often of hundreds of students at one time, was the norm, and interpretation generally related to explaining normative results or passing scores on to administrators. This introduction to the testing world was inauspicious in technique, but the sheer volume of millions of administrations caught the attention of testing companies. School counselors and administrators became the "buyers" in an industry that was expanding exponentially.

Perhaps the volume of level A tests and their administration by counselors was in the end detrimental to current users' rights. Being associated with one class of test that was important to U.S. schools left counselors little time to use or train in the higher level tests. Therefore, the realm of level C tests was simply not a relevant area for many testing professionals other than psychologists. When master's level professional training became more clinical in nature, these newly trained professionals began breaching the turf of level C testing. Further, at the same time that many professions were beginning to use level C tests, the general acceptance and use of psychological tests increased. Simply put, there was so much testing in the 1970s that psychologists could not possibly meet the demand, and master's level professionals were hired for testing positions. Insurance companies began to rely on quantitative test results for making reimbursement decisions. Before long, psychologists' almost sole command of the domain of testing had eroded. Today, school counselors enjoy more freedom to use tests and test results for their practice. This brings with it greater responsibility for appropriate training and use. Meanwhile, however, who should use what tests continues to be debated in state legislatures across the United States.

References

CACREP [Council for the Accreditation of Counseling and Related Educational Programs]. (2001). *The 2001 standards.* Retrieved February 8, 2003, from www.counseling.org/cacrep/2001standards700.htm.

FACT [Fair Access Coalition for Testing]. (2002). *FACT model code of ethics.* Retrieved February 8, 2003, from www.fairaccess.org/code_of_ethics.htm.

✦NBCC [National Board for Certified Counselors]. (1997). *NBCC's code of ethics.* Retrieved February 8, 2003, from www.nbcc.org/pdfs/ethics/NBCC-CodeofEthics.pdf.

Vacc, N. A., Juhnke, G. A., & Nilsen, K. A. (2001). Community mental health service providers' codes of ethics and the Standards for Educational and Psychological Testing. *Journal of Counseling and Development, 79,* 217–224.

✦ Document is included in the Anthology of Assessment Resources CD

Chapter 33
Assessment for Learning:
Classroom Assessment to Improve Student Achievement and Well-Being

Judith A. Arter

We educators need to rethink the role of student assessment in effective schools by considering questions such as: What uses of assessment maximize student achievement? How can we best use assessment in the service of student learning and well-being? Do external standardized, high-stakes tests serve us best to maximize the achievement and well-being of the greatest number of students, or is there a better alternative?

We do not normally place the phrases "student assessment" and "student achievement and well-being" in the same sentence. That is because of our own personal experiences with assessment and testing when we were growing up. What feelings do you associate with assessment? Most people associate feelings of anxiety, fear, and nervousness with the idea of assessment, not feelings of eager anticipation, confidence, and well-being. Does assessment have to be like this? Does that kind of assessment environment really maximize learning? Research shows that if we refocus our student assessment efforts away from exclusive concern with large-scale, high-stakes accountability tests, and toward ensuring that every educator has the ability to implement high-quality, student-involved classroom assessment, we can develop far more powerful and nurturing assessment systems. The result will be systems that

- are located where the learning occurs—in the classroom
- are under the control of teachers and students
- empower students to self-assess and self-correct their responses
- leave students looking forward to assessment as a source of information and confirmation, rather than dreading assessment as a source of judgment or control

In other words, we need assessment that not only provides good information to the most important decision makers—teachers and students—but can also be used to improve the very student achievement being assessed. In this view, assessment will serve us best if we refocus from an almost obsessive emphasis on assessment *of* learning to assessment *for* learning.

Here is how Terry Crooks, a researcher from New Zealand, defines the difference. Assessment *for* learning is roughly the same as *formative assessment*—assessment intended to promote further student learning. Because the intent of this use of assessment is to create more learning, it occurs almost exclusively in the classroom. The phrase "assessment for learning" has become increasingly popular internationally because it better describes this essential use of assessment: in the United Kingdom (e.g., Assessment Reform Group, 1999; Wiliam & Lee, 2001), New Zealand (Crooks, 2001), and the United States (e.g., Shepard, 2000).

Assessment *of* learning, on the other hand, is roughly equivalent to *summative assessment*—assessment intended to summarize student attainment at a particular time. For example, high-stakes, standardized accountability assessments are assessments of learning, as is grading in the classroom. Thus, assessment of learning occurs both in the classroom and through external assessment systems.

We educators are used to thinking about assessment as the measurer of change—as assessment of learning, the index of what students have learned through our various educational innovations. We restructure the school day or put computers in every classroom, for example, then use assessments to see if that made a difference in terms of student achievement. But the concept of classroom assessment for learning presents assessment as the change itself—a direct precipitator of learning, a way to significantly alter the relationships between teachers and students in ways that promote student learning to higher standards. Because improvement in classroom assessment is a change, it is implemented through the change process just as any other change in practice. This has implications for professional development of teachers, leadership, resource allocation, and policy.

Please note that I am not rejecting assessment of learning. It is not that assessment of learning is inappropriate. I just believe it is insufficient to help us reach our goals for student learning. Simply put, we must have a better balance between large-scale and classroom assessment—between assessment of learning and assessment for learning.

This chapter (a) describes in more detail classroom assessment for learning, providing a concrete example and contrasting it with assessment of learning; (b) reviews research demonstrating how enhancing educators' skills in the area of classroom assessment for learning improves student learning; (c) describes what educators need to know and be able to do in order to effectively implement classroom assessment for learning; (d) discusses the most productive way to gain these skills; and (e) outlines the risks of not attending to classroom assessment.

Assessment for Learning

Assessment for learning—formative assessment—is not a new idea to us educators. During the past several years, however, I have seen new dimensions that take its power to a new level. There has been an explosion of concrete practices and good ideas linked to sound research. (See the sources in the reference list marked with an asterisk.)

Formative assessment is more than testing frequently, although gaining information regularly is important. Formative assessment also involves adjusting teaching to take account of these ongoing assessment results. Yet formative assessment is even more than using information to plan next steps. Here is where the new dimensions come in. Formative assessment is most powerful when students are involved in their own assessment and goal setting.

We involve students in assessment for learning whenever we do things like these:

Help students understand the learning targets they are to reach. What do we want students to know and be able to do at the end of each lesson? Unit? Term? Do students know what we want? After all, which students are more likely to be successful: those who understand the learning targets they are to reach or those who do not? Educators have lots of ways to make learning targets clear to students; examples are using rubrics and scoring guides, stating targets in student-friendly language (e.g., Clarke, 2001, pp. 144–148), and engaging students in determining ways they can tell when they have reached some specified target. (Note: This requires that we, their teachers, also have a clear vision of the learning targets we want our students to reach.)

Engage students in self-assessment. Once students understand the nature of the learning targets they are to reach, they are in a position to begin to evaluate where they are with respect to these targets.

Help students see their own improvement with respect to the learning targets. This happens, for example, with portfolios, where students collect samples of work over time and analyze them for growth.

Give students opportunities to express their understanding. This happens, for example, during dialogue with the teacher or in student-involved parent-teacher conferences where students present the evidence of their own learning (see, e.g., Austin, 1994; Davies & Stiggins, 1996).

Encourage students to set goals and determine the next steps required to move closer to the target.

Such student involvement tends to give students a feeling of control over the conditions of their own success. Research has shown that this control is conducive to learning and results in higher student intrinsic motivation (Caine and Caine, 1997; Jensen, 1998). We all know that one cannot expect positive results from just saying to students, "Now you're going to take control of your own learning through self-assessment and goal setting. So do it." We have to teach students how to do these things.

Royce Sadler (1989, p. 119, as restated in Crooks, 2001, p. 2) discusses what it takes to involve students in their own assessment. First, students must appreciate what high-quality work is. Second, they must have the evaluative skill necessary to compare with some objectivity the quality of what they are producing in relation to the high standard. And, finally, students must have a store of tactics to draw upon to modify their own work. A concrete example of how to accomplish these conditions is the use of rubrics, scoring guides, and performance criteria as instructional tools. Figure 1 outlines strategies for using scoring guides in this manner. Compare the ideas in Figure 1 to the list of requirements described by Sadler. It can be done!

Figure 1. Using Scoring Guides as Instructional Tools
by Judith A. Arter and Jan Chappuis, Assessment Training Institute

What You Need

- A scoring guide (also called a rubric or set of performance criteria) that accurately and completely describes the nature or quality of an important skill, performance, or product you want students to master (e.g., mathematics problem solving, writing, group discussion, oral presentations, science lab reports, literature analysis, critical thinking). A good selection can be found in Arter and McTighe (2001). The scoring guide must be student-friendly and written in language students can understand.
- Anonymous samples of strong and weak student work for the skill or product being taught.

What You Do

1. Teach students the language of quality, the concepts behind strong performance. This step reinforces and validates what students already know, adds to their conceptual understanding of what characteristics contribute to quality work, and ties the terms students use to describe quality to a more formal structure.
    - Ask students to brainstorm characteristics of good-quality work.
    - Show students anonymous samples of low-quality and high-quality work and ask them to expand their list of characteristics based on their examination of these samples.
    - Ask students if they would like to see what teachers think. (They always want to.) Pass out copies of the scoring guide and have them analyze how the features in the scoring guide match with the characteristics they gave.
2. Read (or view), score, and discuss strong and weak sample products or performances. Ask students to use the scoring guide to rate these anonymous samples and justify their rating using wording from the rubric. This process reinforces their ability both to notice what features are important in high-quality work and to use a common vocabulary to describe those features.
3. Use the scoring guide to practice and rehearse making revisions to improve the quality of the work. It is not enough

to ask students merely to judge work and justify their judgments. They also need to understand how to revise work to make it better. Here are various options for doing this:

- Ask students to brainstorm advice for the author on how to improve his or her work. Then ask students (in pairs) to revise the work following their own advice.
- Ask students to write a letter to the creator of the sample, suggesting what she or he could do to make the sample stronger in the dimension of quality under consideration.
- Ask students to rate a product or performance of theirs that they are currently working on, and to revise it to improve the dimension under consideration.

4. Share examples of strong and weak products or performances from life beyond school. Have students analyze these samples for quality using the scoring guide.
5. Model creating the product or performance yourself. Model the messy underside of producing quality work: the initial concepts, how you think through decisions along the way, and what you do when you get stuck. Perhaps ask students to analyze your work for quality and suggest improvements. Revise your work using their advice.
6. Encourage students to share what they know. People consolidate their understanding when they practice describing and articulating criteria for quality. For example, ask students to use the language of the scoring guide to write self-reflections, letters to parents, and papers describing the process they went through to create their work; to revise the scoring guide to make it appropriate for younger students; to write a description of quality as they now understand it (I used to . . . , but now I. . . .); or to participate in conferences with parents or teachers to share their achievement.
7. Design lessons and activities around the dimensions of the scoring guide. Reorganize what you already teach to correspond directly to each dimension of quality in the scoring guide. Make sure students understand how each lesson relates to the scoring guide. This (in addition to step 3) provides students with work-improvement strategies that are keyed directly to the newly learned dimensions of quality.

Note: The "What You Do" section is adapted from work at Northwest Regional Educational Laboratory, Portland, OR.

For additional detail on the strategies outlined in Figure 1 see Arter and Chappuis, 2001 (on applying these strategies to help students develop mathematics problem-solving proficiency), Arter and McTighe, 2001 (applying the strategies to help students become better writers), and Spandel, 2001 (also applying the strategies to writing instruction). Other concrete ideas and practical help on assessment for learning—things you can begin doing tomorrow—can be found in the reference list at the end of this chapter.

Assessment of Learning

The assessment of learning has a long history in this country (Shepard, 2000; Stiggins, 1999b). We began with implementation of the College Entrance Examination Board in the 1930s, and the SAT college admissions test quickly turned into a school accountability measure. Through the 1950s and 1960s we saw the advent of commercially developed norm-referenced, district-level standardized testing programs for local accountability. In the 1970s statewide testing programs made their debut, in the 1980s, national testing programs, and in the 1990s, international testing programs. "Thus we see layer upon layer of tests, each new test expected to accomplish what the prior layers had not done—spark productive school improvement" (Stiggins, 1999b, p. 192). The billions of dollars we have spent on these large-scale, high-stakes assessments of learning is testimony to our national belief that merely by checking achievement status and reporting it we can accomplish important goals:

- Provide the focus to improve student achievement.
- Give all parties the information they need to improve student achievement.
- Apply the pressure needed to motivate educators and students to work harder to improve student achievement.

There is, however, little evidence that these assessments actually acccomplish any of these goals. For example, they do not give teachers and students the information they need to improve student achievement; the results are useful only to those individuals who can use comparable information across students generated once a year—that is, administrators and the general public. Teachers and students make decisions every few minutes, not once a year, so they have to rely on classroom assessments. Annual testing is of minimal value to teachers.

Another mistaken assumption is that these tests motivate educators and students to work harder so students learn more. Some do, but not all. When faced with what they believe to be unattainable goals or additional public evidence of their failure, some students just give up in hopelessness. Wouldn't it be ironic if the very tests currently being proposed to "leave no child behind"—yearly reading and mathematics tests for all student in grades three through eight—actually were themselves the cause of leaving children behind? Indeed, there is little evidence that large-scale, high-stakes accountability tests have any positive impact on student achievement whatsoever. Robert Linn, a well-known researcher in the area of educational assessment, makes the case strongly: "As someone who has spent his entire career doing research, writing, and thinking about educational testing and assessment issues, I would like to conclude by summarizing a compelling case showing that the major uses of tests for student and school accountability during the past 50 years have improved education and student learning in dramatic ways. Unfortunately, that is not my conclusion" (Linn, 2000, p. 14).

Again, let me emphasize that I am not rejecting assessment of learning entirely, I am only arguing that we need to use it more carefully and to attend more to assessment practices that actually do have a track record of improving student achievement—classroom assessments for learning.

Research on the Impact of Assessment for Learning

Paul Black and Dylan Wiliam (1998) summarized some 250 studies from several countries to answer three questions:

1. Is there evidence that improving formative assessment raises student achievement?
2. Is there evidence of room for improvement?
3. Is there evidence showing how to improve formative assessment?

They reported that "the answer to each of the three questions above is clearly yes" (p. 140). They found that effective use of formative assessment can yield achievement gains of between 0.4 and 0.7 of a standard deviation. This level of improvement translates as follows:

- The typical student in classrooms where formative assessment innovations are taking place would show the same level of achievement as the top 35 percent of students in classrooms where such innovations are not taking place. (A gain from roughly the 50th to the 65th percentile.)

- In a recent international comparison of mathematics achievement, such achievement gains would have raised the standing of a nation in the middle of the pack of 41 countries (where the United States falls) to one of the top five.

The most intriguing of Black and Wiliam's findings, however, was that "improved formative assessment helps low achievers more than other students and so reduces the range of achievement while raising achievement overall" (Black & Wiliam, 1998, p. 141). They further state that the sizes of the effects of improved formative assessment were "larger than most of those found for [other] educational interventions" (p. 141). By way of comparison, a recent article in *Scientific American* (Ehrenberg, Brewer, Gamoran, & Willms, 2001) analyzed the effect of reducing class sizes to fewer than 20 students. In the three best (and largest) studies, reduced class size showed effect sizes that were one half to one third those of improved formative assessment. The authors report that students in smaller classes would gain from 0.05 to 0.2 of a standard deviation. Using the larger number, this would be equivalent to raising achievement from the 50th to at most the 58th percentile.

The upshot of these findings is that if we desire to maximize achievement for all students while decreasing the achievement gap between the highest and lowest achievers, the best solution is to improve formative assessment. "Teachers do not have to choose between teaching well and getting good results" on accountability assessments (Wiliam & Lee, 2001, p. 9). Implementing assessment for learning strategies causes a real improvement in student learning. This improvement is reflected in accountability tests.

Maximizing Formative Assessment

Black and Wiliam also make clear that there is room for improvement in formative assessment as it is commonly practiced. They cite these two specific improvements in formative assessment as being likely to have the biggest impact on student achievement:

- Ensure that classroom assessments yield accurate and important information.
- Give effective feedback.

Let's examine each of these factors in more detail.

Quality of Assessment

Black and Wiliam cite common problems with classroom assessments, such as test questions that emphasize rote and superficial learning and test questions that are poorly written. The heart of the issue, they say, is to make sure that the information generated by classroom assessments is accurate and dependable, so that we can use it to know where students are.

It is not surprising that the accuracy of classroom assessments needs to be improved. Most teachers and administrators have never had the opportunity to learn about assessment. Currently only 14 states require competence in assessment for teacher certification (Stiggins, 1999a), and only 3 states require competence in assessment for principals (Trevisan, 1999). Just think about your own opportunities to learn about assessment. In typical groups of educators only about 5 percent of hands go up in response to the question, How many of you had to take an assessment course to get your certificate? The percentage drops almost to zero when they are asked, How many of you found those courses useful for what you do daily in the classroom? When training programs neglect meaningful assessment competencies, assessment accuracy suffers.

I do not mean to imply that we educators know nothing about assessment. We have had in-service professional development, and we have developed our own expertise through years of experience. On the other hand, in traveling around the country talking to teachers, I have noticed several things. First, although educators are doing some great things with formative assessment, they frequently have trouble articulating why what they are doing is good. In other words, educators tend to have an incomplete understanding of how all the assessment pieces fit with the instructional pieces. Second, educators appear to be doing a lot more assessment of learning, even in the classroom, than assessment for learning. Finally, when they are required to develop assessments, for example assessment systems for accountability (assessment of learning), they become very anxious because of their lack of knowledge.

Although it is not our fault that we do not know as much as we should about assessment, we have a responsibility to learn what we need to know. As Rick Stiggins points out in many of his publications, we are a national faculty untrained in assessment, yet assessment (especially the formative variety) plays an essential role in helping students learn. It is time to do something about this knowledge gap.

Effective Feedback

Feedback is most effective when it is descriptive, is focused on the important learning targets emphasized in the instruction, and includes advice on what the student can do to improve the quality of the work. Maximum benefits occur when students are involved in their own assessment in the ways described previously. Before you start feeling nervous about how much time descriptive feedback will take, I want to relate the results of one research study. Caroline Gipps (2000) compared the effectiveness of different types of feedback to students (nonspecific versus specific) and of the source of the feedback (teachers versus students themselves). Nonspecific feedback (e.g., "you did great," "you need to work on this") made no difference in student achievement. Specific feedback from teachers had a big effect on student achievement (but the teachers were exhausted). Luckily, the largest effect on student achievement came from students giving themselves specific feedback. The moral is that once students have the skills of self-assessment, teachers can save a lot of time by not having to be the sole source of wisdom.

What Educators Need to Know and Be Able to Do

Black and Wiliam's research provides a good outline of what educators need to know and be able to do by way of assessment in order to maximize achievement for the maximum number of students: use accurate assessment, give specific feedback, and involve students. Stiggins (2001) organizes these topics into the structure shown in Figure 2. The structure provides an outline of both the things educators need to know and be able to do, and standards for high-quality classroom assessments. A useful and practical treatment of all five of these standards of quality can be found in the textbook by Stiggins (2001) and the accompanying workbook by Arter and Busick (2001).

Standard 1: What to Assess

First of all, we need to be crystal clear about what achievement targets we want our students to reach. I have already mentioned several times the importance of being crystal clear on learning targets as a prerequisite for formative assessment. Only with achievement targets clearly in mind can we craft instruction and assessment to help students meet those targets. Only with clear achievement targets can we involve students in their own assessment. Moreover these targets have to be appropriate and important.

Figure 2. Five Standards of Quality Assessment

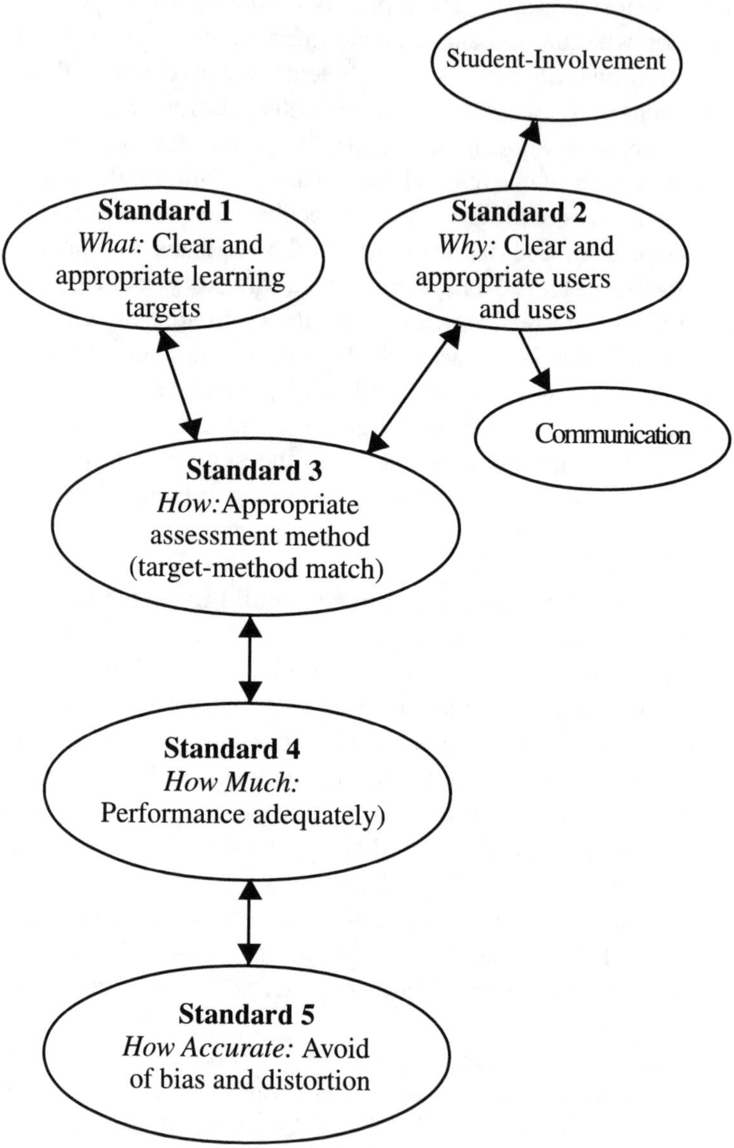

Where do clear and appropriate learning targets come from? They come from research journals; personal content expertise; and several years of effort by states, provinces, and professional organizations that have drafted content standards, or statements of what students need to know and be able to do. With respect to the last, extensive work has been done on tracking standards through grade levels. You may have discovered, however, that these standards and benchmarks usually need additional clarity for use in the classroom. Stiggins (2001, pp. 78–81) provides a very useful way to deconstruct standards into prerequisites that can be more easily integrated into classroom instruction.

Clear targets are also necessary in order to develop accurate, high-quality classroom assessments. Different achievement targets (e.g., mastery of content knowledge, reasoning proficiency, performance skills, and product creation proficiencies) require different types of assessment. The first question to answer is, What do I want to assess? Only with that answer in mind can one determine how best to assess it.

Standard 2: Why Assess

For what purposes are we using assessment? What do we want to accomplish with each classroom assessment? Is the purpose to assign a grade (summative assessment)? Is it to improve learning through student involvement (formative assessment)? Is it to communicate to others the status of student achievement (summative assessment)? Is it to plan the next instructional step (formative assessment)? Is it to provide information to policymakers for accountability (summative assessment)?

These different uses imply different users of the assessment process and its results: parents, students, teachers, and politicians. No single assessment can satisfy the needs of all these people. An accurate and useful assessment is designed with users and uses in mind. For example, parents' need for a summary of their child's learning achievement implies different assessment action than does the need for diagnostic information to plan instruction. Two aspects of users and uses are sufficiently important to be singled out in Figure 2:

Good communication. Different users in different contexts need different information about student achievement in different forms and at different times to do their jobs. Educators need to know who needs classroom assessment information and how to present that information in such a manner that it is clearly understood and can be acted on. A specific example is feedback to students for the goal of improving learning; for maximum effectiveness such feedback needs to be descriptive, to focus on the learning targets, and to include suggestions on how to improve.

Student involvement. Because students are the most important users of assessment materials and results, they merit a special bubble all their own. We need to understand the relationship between assessment and student motivation. We need to know how to bring students into the process of assessment, thus turning assessment into a powerful instructional intervention.

Standard 3: How to Assess

Whereas the first two standards relate to all three issues of accuracy, feedback, and student involvement, standards 3 through 5 relate primarily to accuracy: how much we can rely on the information garnered from classroom assessments. Specifically, standard 3 relates to understanding assessment methods. Educators need to know how to use the full range of assessment options, including selected response, essay, performance, and personal communication assessment formats. We need to know not only how to write good questions, tasks, and scoring guides, but also when best to use each assessment option. Table 1 provides guidelines for when to use each method.

Standard 4: How Often to Assess

Educators sometimes feel nervous when the concept of sampling arises because it seems highly technical. But sampling is a matter of common sense. It's important to know just how much evidence we need to collect to make a confident conclusion about student achievement. Too much is a waste of time, too little does not provide enough information for good planning. For example, one sample of writing is not enough to determine how well a student writes. One would probably need to sample writing for various audiences and purposes to really know how well students write. Educators do not need to use fancy models of sampling. All they need is a good understanding of the content they are teaching and an awareness that they need to sample all aspects of it.

Table 1. Guidelines for Matching Achievement Targets With Assessment Methods

Achievement Target	Selected Response Short Answer	Essay (Extended Written Response)	Performance Assessment	Personal Communication
Knowledge and Understanding	Strong match for assessing elements of knowledge.	Strong match for tapping understanding of relationships among elements of knowledge.	Depends on the nature of the knowledge to be assessed. Generally not a good match.	Strong match for assessing elements of knowledge and relationships among elements.
Reasoning Proficiency	Can assess some patterns of reasoning in isolation, e.g., main idea, what's most likely to happen next. Other patterns of reasoning, e.g., critical thinking, requires another method.	Strong match. Written descriptions of solutions to complex problem can provide a window into reasoning proficiency.	Strong match. Watching students solve certain problems or examining some products can lead to inferences about reasoning proficiency.	Strong match. One can ask students to "think aloud" or ask follow-up questions to probe reasoning.
Performance Skills	Not a good match. Selected response can be used to assess knowledge about how to do something, but to see if students can actually do it requires a performance assessment.		Strong match	Strong match when the skill to be assessed involves oral communication, e.g., foreign language or oral presentation.
Ability to Create Products	Not a good match. Although selected-response formats can be used to assess knowledge about how to create a product, seeing whether students can actually create it requires a performance assessment.	Strong match if the product involves writing, e.g., a term paper or a poem.	Strong match. One can assess attributes of the product itself.	Not a good match. Can get at knowledge about attributes of quality products but not product quality itself.
Dispositions (Affective Domain)	Strong match. There are lots of published	Strong match.	Possible match. One might be able to infer dispositions from behavior and products.	Strong match. Can talk with students about their attitudes.

Adapted from Stiggins, R. J. (2001). Student-involved classroom assessment (3rd ed.). Upper Saddle River, NJ: Merrill/Prentice Hall, p. 93. Available from the Assessment Training Institute, www.assessmentinst.com.

Standard 5: How Accurately to Assess

This is another topic that tends to put educators on the brink. But, again, the answer is a matter of common sense. Lots of things can be wrong with an assessment, leading to an inaccurate picture of student achievement. We all know this. If any topic was covered in preservice courses on assessment, this was it. Unclear targets and poor matching of targets to assessment methods are two sources of distortion on a test. Other things can be wrong as well: too much writing on a reading test, questions that are not fair to all students, assessment conditions that are not optimal, assessment methods that are not matched to student learning styles, and more. We do not need to understand all the statistical procedures related to test bias, we just need to be aware of the potential sources of bias that can creep into our assessments so that we can do our best to avoid them.

Learning More about Classroom Assessment for Learning

Assessment for learning changes the nature of interactions between teachers and students and constitutes a refinement of instructional practice. If we ask ourselves what features of professional development have helped us the most in changing practice, most educators would probably cite some subset of the following:

Clear goals. The practices to be learned are clearly framed—we are able to see where we are headed.

Pacing. Learning begins at our current individual levels of understanding and proceeds at a comfortable rate.

Usefulness. The new information or skills we learn quickly deliver benefits in student motivation and learning, saving us time or increasing our confidence.

Practice. We have the opportunity to practice the new ideas or skills in a low-risk environment where it feels safe to stretch.

Collaboration. We have opportunities to work with others to deepen and refine our understanding and application.

Flexibility and efficiency. Learning occurs in a way that fits easily into our diverse and busy schedules.

Long term. We have an extended time to learn and practice.

Not surprisingly, these are the features generally cited in the professional development literature as resulting in real change (Arter, 2001; DuFour & Eaker, 1998). Now consider the professional development options at your disposal: workshops, individual study, and group study. Which options, or combination of options in what proportion, are most likely to provide a beneficial environment for professional development? The evidence suggests that a heavy reliance on individual and group study with limited use of workshops works best. Here is why:

Workshops by themselves can provide small doses of information in an effective and efficient fashion. Experts can sift through the information that participants need to know and can offer motivational sessions that energize an audience so that they want to learn more. But workshops cannot provide the practice with feedback necessary to implement new ideas in the classroom. Individual study by itself allows the learner to tailor information gathering to personal needs, practice with ideas in an applied setting, and proceed at his or her own pace. But individual study can be inefficient and does not allow for practicing with feedback, bouncing ideas off others, or receiving support during the learning process. Learning teams provide structure for learning about a complex topic, flexibility in structure and pacing, colleagues for group learning, and a support system for practice.

Workshops, individual study, and learning teams are all viable options under certain circumstances. There is considerable agreement, however, that learning teams are the essential element in the mix. Arter and Busick (2001) offer advice on how to set up and conduct professional development learning teams for classroom assessment for learning.

Risks of Not Attending to Classroom Assessment

I have spent considerable ink extolling the potential benefits of refining classroom assessment practices: increases in student achievement and motivation, time savings for teachers, and increases in teacher confidence, to name a few. But I would be remiss if I didn't remind educators of the potential risks of *not* attending to the refinement of classroom assessment.

Classroom Assessment Accuracy

I have already mentioned one potentially huge risk—the risk of inaccurately measuring students. Just think of all the important decisions that teachers, parents, counselors, and students make on the basis of classroom assessment information. For example, students use their classroom assessment performance to make decisions such as these: What should I study? What am I good at? Is it worth trying? Am I capable of learning? Do I like school? Who should my friends be? Is going to college in the picture? What will I be capable of doing in life? Parents make decisions like these: How is my child doing? Is he or she college material? Will I let my child see his or her friends this weekend? Will I support the next bond levy? Teachers make these decisions: What should I teach next? Which students need extra help? Which students should be referred to special programs? How effective is my instruction?Are students working up to their ability? Where are my students performing with respect to state standards?

What would be the impact of making decisions such as these based on inaccurate information? I'm not saying that current classroom assessment information is necessarily inaccurate. I am simply saying that, based on years and years of research on the accuracy of classroom assessments in general, we are currently taking chances that it is. Are we willing to continue taking that risk, or is it time to refine our practice?

Student Motivation

Another risk involves student motivation. No educator wakes up in the morning and says, "Today I think I'll hurt kids." But the truth is that we have considerable power over student motivation, and in no area do we wield this power more decisively than in assessment. Most of the researchers and practitioners cited in the reference list emphasize the need for basing assessment practices on the recognition that assessment profoundly influences students' motivation and self-esteem, both of which are crucial factors in learning (Black and Wiliam, 1998). Students will not learn if they believe they are unable to learn. Students will not learn if they do not want to learn. Assessment has a large impact on students' decisions about how much they want and are able to learn.

Previous practices in both large-scale and classroom assessment can have inadvertent and unanticipated negative side effects on student motivation. Just remember your reaction to the question, What feelings did you associate with assessment when you were growing up? How many students have gotten the inadvertent message through assessment that they are incapable of achieving, so they might as well give up? How many students build unproductive defensive reactions to school because of the inadvertent but consistent message that they are failures?

According to many authors (e.g., Jensen, 1998; Caine & Caine, 1997), humans have an innate desire to learn; we are born with intrinsic motivation. Learning is required for survival. The brain seeks information, integrates it with other information, interprets it, remembers it, and brings it to bear at the appropriate times. These researchers list the following things as tending to snuff out intrinsic motivation:

- coercion
- intimidation
- rewards and punishments
- negative competitive relationships; comparing one student to another
- infrequent or vague feedback
- limits on personal control
- responsibility without authority

Things that tend to increase intrinsic motivation are these:

- providing a sense of control and choice
- increasing frequency and specificity of feedback
- providing challenge without threat
- encouraging self-assessment

The challenge for us educators is how we can craft the assessment process so it builds student motivation and self-confidence rather than squashes it. Which set of features better describes our traditional methods of large-scale and classroom assessments? Which set better describes assessment for learning? Shepard (2000) documents that assessment has lagged behind instruction in terms of incorporating recent research on how humans learn and what motivates us. It is time to bring assessment into the twenty-first century.

Conclusion

A colleague of mine was teaching a class on portfolios. A special education teacher in this class wanted to try having her students self-assess and track the progress of their writing skills. She was nervous that her students' self-concept would be damaged if they realized how low their performance was, but she tried anyway. She had her students keep selected samples of writing in a folder, learn to assess it accurately using a scoring guide called the "Six Traits + One of Writing" (Spandel, 2001), and describe their progress at the end. She reported that her students scored themselves very low on the scoring guide at first, mostly giving themselves 1s. By the end of the year, their self-assessments were higher, mostly 2s. She also reported that, far from being discouraged, her students were very excited because for the first time in their lives they felt they had control over the conditions of their success—they knew that they had made progress and they knew why.

Assessment for learning can result in assessments that have the following features (Rick Stiggins, personal communication):

- encourage rather than discourage
- build confidence rather than anxiety
- bring hope rather than hopelessness
- offer success rather than frustration
- trigger smiles rather than tears

Stiggins also poses the following question. Answer this question well and you are building the assessment environment stressed in this chapter: What assessments might you conduct next week that your students wouldn't want to miss?

References

The references marked with a star (★) offer practical guidance on implementing assessment for learning

Arter, J. (2001). Learning teams for classroom assessment literacy. *NASSP Bulletin, 85*(621), 53–65.

★Arter, J., & Busick, K. (2001). *Practice with student-involved classroom assessment.* Portland, OR: Assessment Training Institute (www.assessmentinst.com).

★Arter, J., & Chappuis, J. (2001). *Student-involved performance assessment* [Interactive professional development video]. Portland, OR: Assessment Training Institute (www.assessmentinst.com).

★Arter, J., & McTighe, J. (2001). *Scoring rubrics in the classroom.* Thousand Oaks, CA: Corwin Press. Assessment Reform Group. (1999). Assessment for learning: Beyond the black box. Cambridge: University of Cambridge, School of Education.

★Austin, T. (1994). *Changing the view—student led parent conferences.* Portsmouth, NH: Heinemann.

Black, P., & Wiliam, D. (1998, October). Inside the black box: Raising standards through classroom assessment. *Phi Delta Kappan,* 139–148.

Caine, R. N., & Caine, G. (1997). *Education on the edge of possibility.* Alexandria, VA: Association for Supervision and Curriculum Development.

★Clarke, S. (2001). *Unlocking formative assessment.* London: Hodder & Stoughton.

Crooks, T. (2001). *The validity of formative assessments.* Paper presented at the annual meeting of the British Educational Research Association, Leeds, England.

★Davies, A., Cameron, C., Politano, C., & Gregory, K. (1992). *Together is better.* Winnipeg: Peguis.

★Davies, A., & Stiggins, R. (1996). *Student-involved conferences* [Interactive professional development video]. Portland, OR: Assessment Training Institute (www.assessmentinst.com).

DuFour, R., & Eaker, R. (1998). *Professional learning communities at work.* Bloomington, IN: National Educational Service.

Ehrenberg, R., Brewer, D., Gamoran, A., and Willms, J. D. (2001). Does class size matter? *Scientific American, 285*(5), 78–85.

Gipps, C. (2000). *Classroom assessment and feedback strategies of "expert" elementary teachers.* Paper presented at the annual meeting of the American Educational Research Association, New Orleans.

Jensen, E. (1998). *Teaching with the brain in mind,* Alexandria, VA: Association for Supervision and Curriculum Development.

✦Linn, R. (2000). Assessments and accountability, *Educational Researcher, 29*(2), 4–16.

Sadler, R. (1989). Formative assessment and the design of instructional systems. *Instructional Science, 18:* 99–144.

Shepard, L. (2000). The role of assessment in a learning culture. *Educational Researcher, 29*(7), 4–14.

★Sizoo, B. (2001). *Teaching powerful writing.* New York: Scholastic.

★Spandel, Vicki. (2001). *Creating writers.* New York: Longman.

Stiggins, R. J. (1999a). Evaluating classroom assessment training in teacher education programs. *Educational Measurement: Issues and Practice, 18*(1), 23–27.

Stiggins, R. J. (1999b, November). Assessment, student confidence, and school success. *Phi Delta Kappan,* 191–198.

★Stiggins, R. J. (2001). *Student-involved classroom assessment* (3rd ed.). Upper Saddle River, NJ: Merrill/Prentice Hall.

Trevisan, M. (1999). Administrator certification requirements in student assessment competence. *Applied Measurement in Education, 12*(1): 1–11.

Wiliam, D., & Lee, C. (2001). *Teachers developing assessment for learning: Impact on student achievement.* Paper presented at the annual meeting of the British Educational Research Association, Leeds, England.

✦ Document is included in the Anthology of Assessment Resources CD

Chapter 34
Maybe We Learned All We Really Needed to Know in Kindergarten
But How Could Anybody Be Sure Until We Took the Test?

Samuel E. Krug

Let me begin by offering apologies to Robert Fulghum, whose poignant essay I in no way mean to disparage with the title of this chapter. I absolutely agree with him that many lessons first encountered in kindergarten are among life's most significant. I mean only to ask how we know these lessons have been learned. Exposure to the curriculum does not in itself guarantee learning.

Instruction and Testing: The Learning Loop

The problem with measuring learning is that it is an internal process that cannot be directly observed. Kids don't come with indicator lights on their forehead that glow when learning has taken place, although things would certainly be much easier for teachers (and parents) if they did.

By defining learning as a relatively permanent change in behavior, psychology emphasizes the external consequences of the internal process and thereby provides a basis for measuring it. That is, we infer that learning has taken place from measured changes in observable behavior. Put a book in front of most kindergarten students and they are unlikely to be able to tell what it contains other than the pictures. Put that book in front of the same students a few years later and they will be able to retell the story, analyze the characters, and relate the book's contents to situations beyond the story. The book hasn't changed, of course, but the students have. They have learned to read.

That is a test in itself, of course, but a fairly gross one that is most likely insensitive to the many changes that occur in the course of learning to read. Tests—typically cognitive achievement tests—are instruments for providing a more sensitive analysis of the learning sequence and of the instruction guiding it. In addition to an overall score, standardized tests usually provide a variety of subscores that help the teacher identify where a student might be encountering the greatest difficulties. By reviewing mathematics subscores, for example, a teacher might understand better whether a student's inability to answer multiple-step problems lies in lack of understanding of the basic concepts involved or in weak computational skills. Testing, therefore, is not some sort of an optional add-on to education but is an integral part of the learning process, part of the instruction-test-instruction feedback loop by which students demonstrate knowledge and skill acquisition.

Do Standardized Tests Duplicate What Teachers Are Already Doing?

Why do we need standardized tests? Don't students demonstrate their understanding and skills in numerous ways already? Don't teachers already give a lot of tests that are subsequently reflected in students' grades? This seemed to be the case when we were in school. Aren't standardized tests just duplicating what teachers are already doing at a cost of valuable instructional time?

Teacher-made tests do serve a valuable purpose. Many, perhaps most, are scored and returned in a short time and thus provide rapid feedback to both the teacher and student about how well learning is proceeding. Teachers can tell whether students have understood the material, what amount of repetition is necessary, and how quickly they can move on to other concepts and skills. Because of this formative function, teacher-made tests usually focus on a relatively narrow spectrum of content. That is, they are more likely to focus on content learned over the course of a unit or a chapter than over a year or more of instruction. Teacher tests undoubtedly also serve an important motivational function—and motivation is a critical element of learning—as students try to demonstrate that they have done what the teacher and their parents have asked: They have learned the material.

Classroom tests also have limitations. Perhaps most importantly, they rarely provide insight into performance outside the classroom for the simple reason that no one outside the classroom takes them. Thus they provide a limited range of normative information. Discovering that *nobody* in the classroom knows the answers to *any* of the questions on the test would likely lead a teacher to revisit the subject matter of the test, perhaps trying a different approach to the subject. Finding out that everybody *outside* the classroom knows the answers to *all* the questions would lend a certain urgency to those efforts.

Norms are important because a person is often judged normatively, and the judgments carry important consequences. The Olympic motto *citius, altius, fortius* (swifter, higher, stronger) is normative and, for better or worse, serves as a motto for life in general when resources are limited. Several people may be qualified for a job, for example, but only one, the best qualified, will get the job. Colleges and universities often receive more qualified applications than they can accept. Consequently, knowing where someone is in relationship to everyone else at a time when something can most easily be done about it—the school years—is important.

One challenge teachers face is that they must focus so intently on what goes on inside their classrooms that they don't have the luxury of exploring fully what goes on outside their classrooms. That is to say, their norms are often narrow, limited by necessity to just a few dozen students each year, usually from the same school.

These classroom norms probably reflect community norms pretty well. In days when communities were fairly narrow and isolated, the norms served very well. But the communities we live in today are no longer narrow or isolated, and our schools necessarily must prepare students for much larger communities. Increasingly, the large rather than small communities of which we are members define learning goals and expectations for student performance. Standardized tests that measure the shared learning goals of our larger communities augment the information teachers gain from more localized and focused tests of instructional goals.

Testing and the Standards Movement

Although normative information is valuable, it is not sufficient. Measuring learning against significant criteria others will employ to evaluate performance is critical.

Several years ago I was asked by a school superintendent to help an elementary school's teachers and administrators prepare for a site visit by the state education agency's accreditation team. The new accreditation model emphasized the importance of data in support of the school's assertion that its students' needs were being met. In the process of reviewing the kinds of evidence the school had accumulated, the teachers pointed to a student evaluation form that instructors filled out at the end of the year as guidance for next year's teacher. This seemed to me a sensible item to introduce at the accreditation visit as it appeared to be useful information for maintaining continuity of instruction as students moved from grade to grade.

After a few minutes of discussion about the form, however, we dropped it from further consideration. It became clear in those moments of discussion that there was no shared understanding of what the information meant. Three teachers at the table explained how they filled out the form and were surprised to discover that they each did it differently. Each applied a different set of standards in completing the form, standards so personal that others were unlikely to interpret the information correctly.

Meeting the standards of the classroom teacher is, of course, critical; however, we need to know that these students also have the skills that society needs to maintain and that they need in order to advance, that they have sufficient knowledge of government, for example, to make them fully participating citizens or that they are sufficiently scientifically and technologically literate to cope with a complex civilization. And the verdict of many important stakeholders in our society is that many—too many—students don't have these skills.

This has directed national attention toward the definition of standards that describe what students are supposed to know and be able to do as a consequence of their education. The standards reflect societal expectations or goals for learning, but they typically also incorporate minimum benchmarks for performance. In Illinois, for example, one of seventeen learning standards for mathematics (see www.isbe.state.il.us/ils/math/mag8.html) states that students will be able to "use algebraic concepts and procedures to represent and solve problems." For students in early elementary grades, this is taken to mean that they will "find the unknown numbers in whole-number addition, subtraction, multiplication, and division situations." For students in late elementary grades this is taken to mean that they will "solve linear equations involving whole numbers." And for 11th- and 12th-grade students this is taken to mean that they will be able to "formulate and solve nonlinear equations and systems, including problems involving inverse variation and exponential and logarithmic growth and decay."

Over the past several years most states have undertaken the development of learning standards in one form or another. A number of broader efforts to develop similar learning standards at a national level have occurred as well. In some areas (e.g., mathematics) significant consistencies in such standards exist across states. In other areas (e.g., social studies) there are important differences among state standards. Such standards are usually developed by educators and the community in a deliberative process to identify a set of agreed-upon expectations or learning outcomes. As the community broadens, the process becomes more complex.

Nevertheless, once such standards are adopted, the question naturally follows as to how well students are performing in relation to them. This is not a normative function but an evaluative function, and the kinds of tests and items that provide the best normative analysis of student performance are not necessarily the kinds of tests that provide the best evaluative analysis.

As a consequence many, perhaps most, states have undertaken programs to develop criterion-referenced tests that are aligned with their own curriculum standards. In many cases, classroom teachers and curriculum experts from the area are involved in every phase of test development: specifications development, item writing, review, and test assembly. The results of these efforts more often than not evaluate what is thought—at least by public consensus—to represent important ideas and concepts and to do so in psychometrically sophisticated ways.

Tests that teachers construct for use in their own classrooms differ in important ways from these kinds of instruments. Classroom tests are more likely to be narrow in focus, and content is most likely to be covered in a lesson, a unit, or perhaps a semester's learning. These tests are primarily intended to be formative evaluations that provide both the teacher and student with information to guide the instructional process.

In contrast, the content of the state-level test is far more likely to focus on cumulative learning. That is, a state science test administered in the seventh grade doesn't usually assess a specific seventh-grade curriculum but instead assesses things about science that students should have learned in their first seven years of instruction. State-developed criterion-referenced tests are intended to provide summative evaluations for public accountability purposes.

Are the Tests Measuring Real Learning?

One of the criticisms frequently hurled at standardized tests is that they simply measure recall of isolated facts, not true understanding and analysis. The multiple-choice format that remains dominant for most standardized tests is a frequent target for critics who decry its simplistic format.

I offer one suggestion in response to such criticism: Take a close look at the test items and student performance on those items. There is no doubt that some questions that make their way into standardized tests could be improved. Many more enter the test via a process that tends to ensure that surviving items address important issues in important ways.

The reading tests of a generation past, for example, presented students with short, disconnected paragraphs about unusual, often uninteresting topics and asked a narrow range of questions, often factual, about the paragraphs' content. Contemporary reading tests, in contrast, present students with extended texts usually drawn from high-quality contemporary or classic literature. They use informational texts drawn from the kinds of material students are likely to encounter in regular classroom instruction. The questions address complex issues like motivation and character development. They require students to go beyond the text and apply related knowledge to answer questions suggested by the text. "What color was the dragon?" is far less likely to be found in most current reading tests than "What is most likely to happen to the main character when the story ends?"

Contemporary mathematics tests frequently require students to solve multistep problems in order to select the correct answer. Incorrect understanding of the steps to take toward the solution is reflected in incorrect selections.

In social studies, it is not unusual to present elementary students with historically significant political cartoons or archival documents and ask a series of questions that require understanding, analysis, and careful interpretation of the material. Consider this example taken from a fourth-grade Illinois social studies test (Illinois State Board of Education, 2001). Questions that follow the picture ask students what the coins in the bank stand for (rights of Americans) and what the axes stand for (attacks on freedom).

The standardized tests of generations past often relied exclusively on multiple-choice items, which emerged as the format of choice during the 1920s. It was attractive to a psychology heavily influenced by behaviorism and the principles of scientific management. In contrast, contemporary tests increasingly rely on constructed-response items that require students to write essays that might take the form of a few sentences summarizing the key concepts of a reading passage. Whereas older "English" tests might have asked students to identify grammatical or stylistic errors in material presented to them through a multiple-choice format, contemporary tests are more likely to ask students to write a two- to three-page essay on presented material. In some cases newer forms of assessment extend to a portfolio of student work accumulated and evaluated over an extended period, although the cost of portfolio assessment has significantly limited its use in large testing programs.

Other Myths About Tests

Despite the facts that testing itself is an integral part of the learning process, that standardized tests supply valuable normative information, and that standards-based tests provide the only credible evidence of whether societally established learning outcomes have been achieved, many still object to what is viewed as an overemphasis on testing in our nation's schools.

The charge is sometimes made that tests narrow the curriculum. This concern usually arises when testing programs of consequence are introduced and teachers begin teaching to the content of those specific tests. This would be a significant criticism if there were, for example, a set of 40 math problems, 20 vocabulary words, 45 historic dates, 20 science facts, or one story that, once taught, would guarantee success on the test. As I have argued earlier, however, most contemporary tests don't rely on simple recall of isolated facts. Students face much more challenging content, content that, quite frankly, deserves to be taught.

In addition, test content changes continually in most testing programs of consequence. Items given one year are unlikely to reappear the next. The item pools for most professionally developed tests are typically extensive. A strategy of teaching students to answer a limited set of test questions, unethical on the surface, would also turn out to be poor strategy in the long run.

Sometimes "teaching to the test" is interpreted as focusing on specific strategies for answering multiple-choice questions. Other times "teaching to the test" is interpreted as teaching students a formulaic writing style that will ensure high scores by graders. With regard to the former, I would argue that there are at least some strategies involved in answering multiple-choice items that are important life skills, such as carefully considering what the question is asking, evaluating each option before responding, and eliminating the least likely answer to reduce the number of choices when uncertain about a decision. I use those skills every day. I think other people do too. I often think that much of life is a multiple-choice test.

With regard to teaching formulaic writing, the charge extends to the supposition that formulaic writing devalues creativity. Don't get me wrong: I like creativity. But I know that life involves a lot of formulaic writing, so it's not a bad thing to understand how to write in this way. If you disagree, try to get published in a behavioral science research journal an article that deviates too far from the abstract-introduction-method-results-discussion format of the *Publication Manual of the American Psychological Association.* Much correspondence required in business follows standard forms as well. So formulas aren't all that bad. They are certainly better than no writing or writing in which it is impossible to detect an orderly presentation of ideas.

The charge is sometimes made that testing takes time that would otherwise be used for teaching and instruction. The usual targets of the criticism are the large state accountability programs, and the implication is that these ponderous programs consume hundreds of hours of valuable instruction time. These programs don't involve hundreds of hours of testing time; at least I haven't encountered one yet that did. In Illinois, for example, the state programs make the greatest demand on student time in 11th grade, when the Prairie State Achievement Test requires about seven and a half hours spread over two days. Almost half of that time is devoted to taking a college entrance examination that the majority of the students would have taken anyway. At other grades, state testing requires no more than five or six hours. Across the nine months students attend school, that doesn't seem unreasonably burdensome.

The charge is sometimes made that testing instills competitiveness. Are we to believe that people were not competitive before educational testing was invented? At the time this chapter was written, the 19th winter Olympic games had just ended at Salt Lake. Talk about competition. Competition is a fact of human nature engendered by the economic reality that resources are limited. Testing may be an unwelcome reminder of that economic reality, but it is not the cause of competition.

A related charge is sometimes made that testing demoralizes students. It is human nature to feel bad when we do poorly. But to blame the test is very much like killing the messenger. The federal education legislation that requires states to conduct assessments of all students in their public schools also requires the reporting of student results in discrete performance categories. One or more of these categories is usually undesirable. Nevertheless, the intent of that legislation is to establish clear goals for improvement and document adequate yearly progress toward moving students out of undesirable categories.

Although it would be preferable to be reinforcing rather than demoralizing and to give out only good news, if the reality is otherwise, then you can't always give good news. During the mid-twentieth century there was substantial belief in the efficacy of our system of public instruction. For most of the first half of that century the public schools of our great cities were some of the best of that system. Although we awoke in 1984 to find that we were a nation at risk, the system did not fail overnight. To a large extent, the current test culture is a consequence of too much good news—undocumented news—for too long. The public requires some assurance that 1984 and the decades of indifference that preceded 1984 won't happen again, and tests provide some measure of that assurance.

The charge is sometimes made that we are testing students too early, that students in the early grades are too young to be other than dismayed by tests. Most state accountability programs require testing for the first time at third grade or later. The No Child Left Behind Act of 2001 requires annual testing of students, but only from third through eighth grades. The problem for me is not testing too early but too late. By the third grade, some of the most significant learning students encounter has or should have taken place. Students in the first two or three years of elementary school, for example, learn how to read. After that they will, for the most part, read to learn, but only if the lessons of the first critical year or two are learned. If not, they will play catch-up for most of the rest of their academic careers, often unsuccessfully. If the first time we are aware that students are being left behind is at the end of third grade, some crucial opportunities have already vanished and can only be made up with considerable effort.

The charge is sometimes made that so much testing of students amounts to little more than weighing the pig over and over. That is, there is little value in testing repeatedly because the action itself does nothing to increase achievement. The criticism misses the essential point that obtaining a measurement is not the purpose. Instead the purpose of taking the measurement is to act on the information it provides.

There are many who agree that public education is in a critical state, that too many students are being denied the quality of instruction to which they are entitled, and that our society is unlikely to continue advancing without significant intervention. In the eyes of these people tests provide the continual monitoring needed to ensure that the student continues to make progress.

The charge is sometimes made that tests have become the ultimate criterion for obtaining diplomas or other valued credentials. That is, the stakes associated with the tests are just too high. At the high school level, the number of states that have introduced a testing requirement for granting a degree has increased in the last few years. But as Cizek (2001) correctly observed, the testing requirement is not an ultimate criterion, just the latest one. There were already a number of criteria in place that students had to satisfy to receive a diploma. These requirements addressed the number of credit hours students must accumulate, completion of specific course requirements (e.g., consumer education, physical education, government), and attendance requirements. The test requirement is one that must be met in addition to these others, but failure to comply with the others denies a diploma just as quickly as a poor score on the test does. Moreover, diploma tests can be attempted more than once, so if a student has trouble with one administration he or she has other opportunities.

The introduction of a testing requirement is little more than what has been done for many years in the area of professional certification and licensure. A person may spend years in medical school or law school and meet the moral character requirements for practice, but absent a passing score on the licensure test, this person will not practice in the profession. Rather than demeaning the four years of instruction that lead to graduation, it seems more likely that the introduction of a testing requirement into the process will result in increased perceived value of the credential as it seems to have done for many professions.

On the other hand, the charge is almost never made that tests are not used enough, but I think that is often the case, at least with respect to their results. More often than not, institutions (e.g., state departments, districts, schools) spend far more time and effort administering test programs than they do studying their results.

Despite the various criticisms that have been directed toward educational testing, there appears to be strong public support for it. If there were not, it would have been far more difficult to achieve passage of the No Child Left Behind Act of 2001, which mandates testing in every grade. The passage of that legislation, and the failure of the previous administration's legislation, which proposed testing all students at just two grades suggest that support has actually increased in the last few years.

This support most likely arises from a pervasive belief that standardized tests are ultimately among the fairest and most accurate indicators of the condition of educational achievement available to us. The classroom tests that teachers administer and the grades they derive from them serve an important function, but they don't always give as clear a picture of performance beyond the classroom as we require.

Despite the many objections, the fact remains that standardized testing itself is an integral part of the learning process, that these tests supply valuable normative information, and that criterion-referenced tests provide the credible evidence of whether societally established learning outcomes—including all we are supposed to have learned in kindergarten—have been achieved.

References

Cizek, G. J. (2001). More unintended consequences of high-stakes testing. *Educational Measurement: Issues and Practice, 20*(4), 19–27.

Illinois State Board of Education. (2001). *Illinois Standards Achievement Test sample social science materials.* Springfield: Author.

Chapter 35
Performance Assessment
Designing Appropriate Performance Tasks and Scoring Rubrics
Carole L. Perlman

A performance assessment consists of two parts, a task and a set of scoring criteria or a scoring rubric. Unlike a multiple-choice or true-false test in which a student is asked to choose one of the responses provided, a performance assessment requires a student to generate his or her own response. For example, a performance assessment in writing would require a student actually to write something, rather than simply to answer some multiple-choice questions about grammar or punctuation. The assessment task may be a product, performance, or extended written response, ideally one that requires the student to employ critical thinking skills. Some examples of performance-assessment tasks are oral presentations, essays, works of art, science fair projects, research projects, musical performances, open-ended math problems, and analyses or interpretations of literature. Performance assessments are well suited for measuring complex learning outcomes such as critical thinking, communication, and problem-solving skills that may not lend themselves well to a multiple-choice or other forced-response format.

Because a performance assessment does not have an answer key of the type that a multiple-choice test does, scoring a performance assessment necessarily involves making some subjective judgments about the quality of a student's work. A good set of scoring guidelines or rubrics provides a way to make fair and sound judgments by setting forth a uniform set of precisely defined criteria or guidelines for judging student work.

Selecting Tasks for Performance Assessments

The best performance-assessment tasks are interesting, worthwhile activities that relate to your instructional outcomes and allow your students to demonstrate what they know and can do. Some ideas for performance-assessment tasks in a variety of subjects can be found at http://intranet.cps.k12.il.us/Assessments/Ideas_and_Rubrics/ideas_and_rubrics.html. A very good resource for science performance assessments is Performance Assessment Links in Science (http://www.pals.sri.com). Two excellent sources of information on developing and using performance assessments are Stiggins (1997) and Arter and McTighe (2001). The ERIC Clearinghouse on Assessment and Evaluation at http://www.ericae.net has links to many publications on performance assessment.

As you decide what tasks to use, consider the following criteria, which I have adapted from Herman, Aschbacher, and Winters (1992):

Does the task truly match the outcomes or standards you are trying to measure? This is a must. The task should not require knowledge and skills that are irrelevant to the outcome. For example, if you are trying to measure speaking skills, asking the students to summarize orally a difficult science article would penalize those students who are poor readers or who lack the scientific background to understand the article. In that case, you would not know whether you were measuring speaking or (in this case) extraneous reading and science skills. Sometimes it is possible to enable students to perform successfully despite gaps in prior factual knowledge by giving them access to textbooks or reference materials.

Does the task require the students to use critical thinking skills? Is recall all that the task assesses, or must the student analyze, draw inferences or conclusions, critically evaluate, synthesize, create, or compare? In general, when you are assigning a performance task, students should not have received specific instruction in its solution. If students know the solution you may be measuring simply rote memory. For example, suppose an instructional outcome deals with analyzing an author's point of view, and you devote a class discussion to an analysis of the authors' points of view in two editorials. If you then ask the students to write an essay analyzing the authors' positions in those editorials, you are essentially measuring students' recall of the class discussion, rather than their ability to analyze point of view. A better assessment would be to ask the students to analyze editorials that have not been discussed in class, in order to see how well they can generalize their knowledge and skills to a novel piece of writing.

Is the task a worthwhile use of instructional time? Performance assessments may be time-consuming, so it stands to reason that that the time should be well spent. Instead of being an add-on to regular instruction, the assessment should be part of it.

Does the assessment use engaging tasks with real-world application? The task should capture students' interest enough to ensure that they are willing to try their best. Does the task represent something important that students will need to do in school and in the future? Many students are more motivated to do a task when they see that it has some meaning or connection to life outside the classroom.

Are the tasks fair and free from bias? Is the task an equally good measure for students of different genders, races, cultures, and socioeconomic groups represented in your school population? Will all students have equivalent resources—at home or at school—with which to complete the task? Have all students received equal opportunity to learn what is being measured?

Is the task clearly defined? Are the instructions for teachers and students clear? Do students know exactly what is expected of them?

Is the task feasible? Can students reasonably be expected to complete the task successfully? Will you and your students have enough time, space, materials, and other resources? Does the task require knowledge and skills that you have taught or are able to teach?

Will the task be credible? Will students, parents, and your colleagues view the task as being a meaningful, challenging, and appropriate measure?

Understanding Scoring Rubrics

A scoring rubric has several components, each of which contributes to its usefulness. These components include the following:

- one or more dimensions on which performance is rated
- definitions and examples that illustrate the attribute or attributes being measured
- a rating scale for each dimension

Ideally, the rubric should be accompanied by examples of student work that illustrate each level of the rating scale. The rubric should organize and clarify the scoring criteria well enough that two raters who apply the rubric to a student's work will generally arrive at the same score. The degree of agreement between the scores assigned by two independent scorers is a measure of the reliability of an assessment. This type of consistency is especially important if assessment results are to be aggregated across classrooms, schools, or districts.

Analytical Versus Holistic Rating

A rubric with two or more separate scales—for example, a science lab rubric divided into sections related to hypothesis, procedures, results, and conclusion—is called an *analytical rubric.* A scoring rubric that uses only a single scale yields a global or *holistic,* rating. In a holistic rating system, the overall quality of a student's response might, for example, be judged excellent, proficient, marginal, or unsatisfactory. Holistic scoring is often more efficient, but analytical scoring systems generally provide more detailed information that may be more useful in planning and improving instruction and communicating with students.

Whether you choose and analytical or holistic rubric, you must clearly label and define each point on the scale. There is no best number of scale points, although it is generally advisable to avoid scales with more than six or seven points. With very long scales, it is often difficult to differentiate adequately between adjacent points (e.g., on a 100-point scale, it would be difficult to explain why you assigned a score of 81 rather than 80 or 82). Different scorers are also less likely to agree on ratings when very long scales are used. Extremely short scales, on the other hand, make it difficult to identify small differences between students. A short scale may be adequate for some purposes, however, such as when you simply want to divide students into two or three groups, based on whether they have failed to attain, attained, or exceeded the standard for an outcome.

A good rule of thumb is to have as many scale points as can be well defined and can adequately cover the range from very poor to excellent performance. If you decide to use an analytical rubric, you may wish to add or average the scores from each scale to get a total score. If you feel that some scales are more important than others (and assuming that the scales are of equal length), you may give them more weight by multiplying those scores by a number greater than one. For example, in the case of a science lab write-up, if you felt that the results section scale was twice as important as all the others, you would multiply the score on that scale by two before you added up the scale scores to get a total score.

Specific Versus General Rubrics

Scoring rubrics may be specific to a particular assignment or may be general enough to apply to many different assignments. Usually general rubrics prove to be more useful, because they need not be constantly adapted to particular assignments and they provide an enduring vision of quality work that can guide both students and teachers. Some states and districts have adopted a set of standard scoring rubrics; in that case, it is advisable to use those rubrics for classroom assessments whenever possible to avoid the potential for confusion when two or more different rubrics are used to score similar assignments.

A rubric can be a powerful communication tool. When shared among teachers, students, and parents, the rubric informs everyone about what characteristics of student work are most highly valued. It provides a means for you and your colleagues to clarify your vision of excellence and convey that vision to your students and their parents. It can also provide a rationale for assigning grades to subjectively scored assessments. Sharing the rubric with students is only fair and is necessary if we expect them to do their best possible work. An additional benefit of sharing the rubric is that students are empowered to critically evaluate their own work.

In order for a rubric to be effective in communicating what we expect of our students, students and parents must be able to understand it. This may require restating all or part of the rubric to eliminate educational jargon and explain the criteria in a way that is appropriate for the students' developmental level. (For example, "The story has a beginning, middle, and end" is clearer and more helpful to students than "Observes story structure conventions.")

Selecting a Scoring Rubric

Teachers interested in using rubrics to assess performance-based tasks have three options: use an existing rubric as is, adapt or combine rubrics to suit a specific purpose, or create a rubric from scratch. One online source of rubrics is the Chicago Public Schools' rubrics bank (Perlman, 1994) at http://intranet.cps.k12.il.us/Assessments/Ideas_and_Rubrics/Rubric_Bank/rubric_bank.html. Some state departments of education have rubrics and scored examples of student work available on their websites. Links to state education agencies may be found at the Council of Chief State School Officers website: http://www.ccsso.org.

If you are considering using an existing rubric, ask yourself these questions:

- Does the rubric relate to the outcome(s) being measured? Does it address anything extraneous?
- Does the rubric cover important dimensions of student performance?
- Do the criteria reflect current conceptions of excellence in the field?
- Are the categories or scales well defined?
- Is there a clear basis for assigning scores at each scale point?
- Can different scorers apply the rubric consistently?
- Can students and parents understand the rubric?
- Is the rubric developmentally appropriate?
- Is the rubric applicable to a variety of tasks?
- Is the rubric fair and free from bias?
- Is the rubric useful, feasible, manageable, and practical?

In order to have an existing rubric better suit your task and objectives, you might make the following adaptations:

- Reword parts of the rubric.
- Drop or change one or more scales of an analytical rubric.
- Omit criteria that are irrelevant to the outcome you are measuring.
- Mix and match scales from different rubrics.
- Change the rubric for use at a different grade level.
- Add a "no response" category at the bottom of the scale.
- Divide a holistic rubric into several scales.

If adopting or adapting an existing rubric does not work for your purposes, here are some steps to follow in developing your own scoring rubric:

1. With your colleagues, make a preliminary decision on the dimensions of the performance or product to be assessed. The dimensions you choose may be guided by national curriculum frameworks, publications of professional organizations, sample scoring rubrics (if available), or experts in the relevant subject area. Alternatively, you and your colleagues may brainstorm a list of as many key attributes of the product or performance to be rated as you can. In brainstorming, consider what you look for when you grade assignments of this nature and which elements of this product or performance you emphasize during teaching.

2. Look at some actual examples of student work to see if you have omitted any important dimensions. Try sorting examples of actual student work into three piles: the best, the poorest, and those in between. With your colleagues try to articulate what makes the good assignments good.
3. Refine and consolidate your list of attributes as needed. Try to cluster your tentative list of dimensions into a few categories or scales. Alternatively, you may wish to develop a single, holistic scale. There is no absolute number of dimensions you should generate, but there should be no more than you can reasonably expect to rate. The dimensions you use also should be related to the learning outcomes you are assessing.
4. Write a definition of each dimension. You may use your brainstormed list to describe exactly what each dimension encompasses.
5. Develop a continuum (i.e., scale) for describing the range of products or performances on each dimension. Using actual examples of student work to guide you will make this process much easier. For each dimension, ask yourself what characterizes the best possible performance of the task. This description will serve as the anchor for that dimension by defining the highest score point on your rating scale. Next describe in words the worst possible product or performance. This will serve as a description of the lowest point on your rating scale. Then describe characteristics of products or performances that fall at intermediate points of the rating scale for each dimension. Often these points will describe some major or minor flaws that preclude a higher rating.
6. Alternatively, instead of generating a set of rating scales, you may choose to develop a holistic scale or a checklist on which you can record the presence or absence of the attributes of a high- quality product or performance.
7. Evaluate your rubric using the questions listed previously.
8. Pilot test your rubric or checklist on actual samples of student work to see whether it is practical to use and whether you and your colleagues generally agree on what scores you would assign to a given piece of work.
9. Revise the rubric and pilot test it again. It is unusual to generate a perfect the first time. Ask yourself these

questions: Did the scale have too many or too few points? How could the definitions of the score points be made more explicit?

10. Share the final rubric with your students and their parents. Training students to use the rubric to score their own work can be a powerful instructional tool. Sharing the rubric with parents will help them understand what you expect from their children and clarify what constitutes excellent work.

Some Considerations in Using Performance Assessments

Performance assessments have advantages and disadvantages. On the plus side, they can provide rich learning experiences; they can simulate real-world problem solving; they can encourage students to critically evaluate their own work; they can provide teachers with insights into their students' cognitive processes; they can foster good instruction; and they can be an excellent measure of students' abilities to synthesize, evaluate, and solve problems. Learning to use a scoring rubric can be an excellent staff development experience for teachers. Finally, some instructional outcomes simply do not lend themselves well to other assessment formats. What are the downsides? Performance assessments can be expensive and time-consuming to administer and score, particularly when they are part of districtwide or statewide assessment. Assessment results are generalizable to the extent available evidence shows that scores on one assessment predict how well students perform on another assessment of the same outcome; a good result on one performance task may not generalize well to similar tasks. The subjectivity inherent in scoring a performance assessment may make some people uncomfortable, although a well-constructed rubric coupled with effective rater training and monitoring can go a long way toward addressing those concerns. Finally, certain kinds of knowledge and skills are more efficiently assessed using other assessment formats, such as multiple-choice tests.

An assessment is reliable if it yields results that are accurate and stable. In order for a performance assessment to be reliable, it must be administered and scored in a consistent way for all students who take the assessment. Once you decide on a rubric, the best way to promote reliable scoring is to have well-trained scorers who thoroughly understand the rubric and who periodically all score the same samples of student work to ensure that they are maintaining consistent scoring.

Another way to increase reliability is to adhere carefully to the rubric as you score student work. Not only will this increase reliability and validity, but it is only fair that the agreed-upon rubric that you have shared with students and parents is what you actually use to rate student work. Nonetheless, human beings making subjective judgments may unintentionally rate students based on things that are not in the rubric at all. Therefore, the conscientious scorer will frequently monitor his or her thinking to prevent extraneous factors from creeping into the assessment process.

Summary

Performance assessments can provide an effective means of measuring abilities that are difficult or impossible to measure with a multiple-choice test, such as ability to communicate, solve problems, and employ critical thinking skills. Performance assessments consist of a task—for example, a project, extended written response, oral presentation—and a set of scoring guidelines, or a rubric. Both performance tasks and rubrics must be chosen carefully. A good assessment task is aligned with the standards being measured, requires the student to exercise critical thinking skills, is fair, and is a worthwhile use of instructional time. A well-defined scoring rubric is essential for reliable measurement and to provide students with a clear vision of what constitutes excellent work. Educators may design their own performance-assessment tasks and rubrics, or they may use or adapt tasks and rubrics created by their state or district educational systems. The Internet is a good source of sample performance-assessment tasks and rubrics.

Portions of this chapter were adapted from C. L. Perlman (2002), An introduction to performance assessment scoring rubrics, in C. Boston (Ed.), *Understanding scoring rubrics: A guide for teachers,* College Park, MD: ERIC Clearinghouse on Assessment and Evaluation, and from C. L. Perlman (1994), *The CPS performance assessment idea book,* Chicago, IL: Chicago Public Schools.

References

Arter, J., & McTighe, J. (2001). *Scoring rubrics in the classroom: Using performance criteria for assessing and improving student performance.* Thousand Oaks, CA: Corwin.

✦Herman, J., Aschbacher, P., & Winters, L. (1992). *A practical guide to alternative assessment.* Alexandria, VA: Association for Supervision and Curriculum Development.

Perlman, C. L. (1994). *The CPS performance assessment idea book.* Chicago, IL: Chicago Public Schools.

Stiggins, R. J. (2001). *Student-centered classroom assessment* (3rd ed.). Upper Saddle River, NJ: Merrill.

✦ Document is included in the Anthology of Assessment Resources CD

Chapter 36
Beyond Assessment to Best Grading Practice
Practical Guidelines

Laurie A. Carlson

Developing meaningful and equitable grading practices is a daily challenge for K–12 educators and administrators. Part of the difficulty in understanding the complicated mechanisms behind grading lies in the confusion surrounding terminology (Speck, 1998). Assessment and grading are related but not exactly the same. For the purposes of this chapter, *assessment* refers to the objective process of evaluation and involves specific tools such as tests and portfolios. *Grading practice,* on the other hand, represents the sometimes subjective, but accepted, process of assigning value to student performance on the assessment tools (Speck, 1998). *Grade reporting* involves disseminating the resulting information about student performance to the student, parents, administrators, and other appropriate parties. In this chapter, grading *practice* refers to the combination of grading practice and grade reporting.

Grading practice serves several functions, including informing parents about their child's progress, informing potential employers, aiding in educational and career planning, and guiding administrative decisions such as graduation, promotion, and honors (Gredler, 1999; Hendrickson & Gable, 1997). An educator may be very knowledgeable and savvy regarding assessment procedures but experience difficulty in translating assessments into appropriate grading practice. Norm-referenced, self-referenced, and criterion-referenced assessments represent the three possible frameworks for grading practice; however, criterion-referenced assessment emerges as the most widely accepted practice (Gredler, 1999). This chapter covers five topics related to criterion-referenced grading practice: (a) the imperative relationship between grading practice and learning objectives; (b) the use of grading practice as a learning tool for students as well as an evaluative tool; (c) validity in classroom grading practice, including the importance of using a variety of evaluative measures; (d) creativity in classroom grading practice, including alternative assessment and constructivist approaches such as portfolios and field projects; and (e) tough issues in the assessment and grading of cooperative learning activities and performances by students with special abilities.

Learning Objectives: The Grading Foundation

Learning standards and learning objectives are often used interchangeably but are subtly different terms. In general, *learning standards* are broad statements of essential knowledge, and *learning objectives* represent specific learning goals for students in a particular learning environment. Meaningful learning objectives based upon accepted learning standards are pivotal to standards-based evaluation and serve as benchmarks for evaluating student performance in a criterion-referenced grading strategy (Colby, 1999; Gredler, 1999; Marzano, 1999; Speck, 1998). Educators must carefully consider the quality of learning objectives because they play such a critical role in grading. Several characteristics are central to the utility of quality learning objectives in grading practice: Learning objectives must be (a) directly related to content, (b) written in clear language that students can understand, and (c) clearly measurable. Learning objectives that demonstrate these characteristics are pivotal to the difference between meaningful and inappropriate teaching strategies and evaluation. When learning standards form the basis for evaluation, the entire system becomes more learner-centered (Colby, 1999).

Grading That Enhances Student Learning

Students may learn important knowledge and skills not only during didactic instruction but also through authentic assessment procedures designed around learning objectives (Moorcroft, Desmarais, Hogan, & Berkowitz, 2000; Smith, Smith, & DeLisi, 2001; Travis, 1996). It seems that what distinguishes evaluative tools that enhance learning from those that do not is the importance of the evaluation to the student. It would be erroneous to suggest that all students value the same experiences; therefore, it is important to consider strategies for increasing the meaning that students will ascribe to an evaluative tool. When students are asked to become an active part of grading strategies, those strategies may become more meaningful, may actually enhance learning, and subsequently may better represent student achievement (Benson, 2000; Rafferty, Leinenbach, & Helms, 1999). One method of increasing student ownership of grading practice is to negotiate learning contracts with students (Stix, 1997). Constructivist educational strategy provides a philosophical foundation for classroom practice that increases students' responsibility for their own performance and speaks directly to the issue of increasing students' ownership of their own educational experience.

Constructivism, founded on the principle of learning through experience, assesses student achievement as learning emerges from ongoing study (Ediger, 2000). In a constructivist environment, students essentially "construct" their own learning experiences. Constructivist classrooms often provide a framework for grading practices that engage students in establishing their own learning objectives and evaluation methods. Common characteristics of constructivist grading practice include student choice regarding tasks to be completed, student self-evaluation, and teacher relinquishment of control (Anderson, 1998). The use of constructivist learning policies in a traditional educational environment poses some unique challenges, which educators must be aware of before implementation to avoid failure. Anderson (1998) identifies challenges in (a) possible modification of existing instructional strategies, (b) implementation of both formative and summative evaluation, (c) instructor guidance during student development of rubrics, and (d) balance among instructor, peer, and self-evaluation.

Validity Through Variety

It is common knowledge among professionals in the test development field that a greater number of items often increases the content validity of an instrument. Likewise, in empirical research limited sample size significantly decreases validity in hypothesis testing. So it is in classroom grading practice. The number and variety of assessment measures employed affect the validity of a student's grade. Take, for example, a seventh grader who struggles with severe test anxiety. It is highly unlikely that a social studies grade determined solely on unit and comprehensive multiple-choice exams will adequately measure what that student has learned in the course. Similarly, a student with motor delay would be unfairly disadvantaged in a physical education class that assigns a pass-fail grade solely on the student's ability to perform during the Presidential Physical Fitness routine. A wide variety of assessment protocols exists, including traditional exams, creative projects, written or narrative works, group assignments, portfolios, and naturalistic assessment techniques. All these protocols present unique advantages and disadvantages, and it is the educator's responsibility to explore and understand the characteristics of each before implementing any of them.

Variety Requires Creativity

Beyond the need for teachers to have an empirical and professional understanding of available protocols, true variety in assessment calls for a noteworthy level of creativity. One common mistake educators make regarding this issue is underuse of the creative energy of students themselves. Even very young students have the ability to conceptualize and express appropriate strategies for performance evaluation (Rafferty et al., 1999).

Several new paradigms in assessment—including alternative assessment, authentic assessment, performance assessment, portfolio assessment, and natural classroom assessment—have recently come to the forefront of the literature and add a creative spark to grading practices (Kohn, 1999; Moorcroft et al., 2000; Smith et al., 2001). Although such strategies hold considerable promise, they also pose unique challenges, including the needs for adequate educator training and clear communication with parents and students (Anderson, 1998; Benson, 2000; Kohn, 1999). One resource to help educators communicate with parents and explain to them assessment tools that enhance learning is *But Are They Learning? A Commonsense Parents' Guide to Assessment and Grading in Schools* by Richard Stiggins and Tanis Knight (1997).

Portfolio Assessment

Portfolio assessment is growing rapidly as a viable tool in the evaluation of student performance (Lustig, 1996; Moorcroft et al., 2000; Rafferty et al., 1999; Spence & Theriot, 1999; Wolfe, 1999). Recent advances in technology and student record-keeping have contributed to this increased viability. Some of the same considerations inherent in traditional grading should be in place for portfolio assessment. First, it is important that the student see a clear connection between portfolio requirements and learning objectives. Second, portfolios that represent work completed over a substantial period and that serve a future purpose are generally better received by students and tend to produce more student effort. Third, when students are involved in making decisions regarding the appearance and content of portfolios, the quality of finished portfolios tends to increase. Finally, for portfolios to be generally accepted as an appropriate evaluative tool, parents, students, and administrators need to understand the purpose and unique value of this type of assessment (Lustig, 1996; Spence & Theriot, 1999). Implementing portfolio assessment as one strategy in an overall grading policy can be time-consuming and costly. It is therefore imperative that the classroom teacher invest the energy up front to build a strong support network for portfolio use.

Exhibitions and Field Projects

Science has much to teach other disciplines regarding meaningful performance evaluation through public exhibitions. Many young people who rush through daily homework assignments will spend an extensive amount of time doing experiments and creating exhibits for science fairs. All at some level we all crave recognition and encouragement for the work we do, and students at all developmental levels are no exception. Further, the ability to represent completed work appropriately and effectively is a necessary life skill that students may learn through such an experience. Field experiences and exhibitions, like portfolios (Ediger, 2000), represent constructivist grading practices that present all the advantages and challenges discussed earlier. In general, exhibitions and field experiences provide opportunities for students to learn through the completion of the task itself and to encounter a great degree of flexibility and autonomy in producing a final product.

Tackling the Tough Evaluation Issues

Effective grading practice relies on equitable and appropriate evaluation. Evaluation becomes especially difficult in the face of cooperative learning activities and students with special needs. Alternative assessment often takes the form of collaborative activities and projects. There is little disagreement in the literature that collaborative projects and activities present advantages related to more engaged learning in a social context and acquisition of transferable life skills such as communication, responsibility, leadership, problem solving, and delegation of tasks (Butcher, Stefani, & Tario, 1995; Cheng & Warren, 2000; Pitt, 2000). On the other hand, educators at both the K–12 and university levels have become painfully aware of the possible grading nightmares associated with group projects.

Cheng and Warren (2000) note a common student complaint that assigning one blanket grade to everyone in the group is unfair, and indeed in many cases it is. Educators are notorious for believing the best about students and for relying on students' motivation and individual sense of responsibility to ensure equal participation in collaborative projects. This may lead to assigning blanket grades that reward noncontributors to the same degree as students who assumed the bulk of responsibility for the project (Butcher et al., 1995). One solution to this issue is involving students in evaluating the contributions of their peers. A variety of issues concerning standards and confidentiality surface in peer assessment, but a number of good resources are available in the literature to inform best practice. One recent resource is an article by Cheng and Warren (2000) that outlines a rather straightforward approach to peer assessment of individual contributions to a group project. Another possible solution to assessment of group projects involves the application of games theory (Pitt, 2000). Whatever strategy an educator employs, it is imperative to be able to articulate clearly to students, administrators, and parents the rationale and procedure for grading, as well as the advantages and disadvantages of the strategy.

Closely related to the issues present in the evaluation of group projects are issues related to the evaluation of performances by students who are either gifted or have special needs. The movement from pullout learning environments to inclusive education pushes this issue to the forefront of the grading discussion. Traditionally, educators' response has been to implement dual grading standards based upon individualized education plans (IEPs) and other criteria, but such a strategy is appropriate only when those procedures do not put any students at an unfair advantage or disadvantage (Hendrickson & Gable, 1997). This leads back to the question, What, then, is the appropriate strategy when grading students with differing abilities? Part of the solution resides in the earlier discussions related to letting students themselves take responsibility for grading criteria and policies. This active student participation would ideally be present throughout the entire process—from decisions regarding the characteristics of the activity to its evaluation. Active participation appears to hold the greatest promise for implementation of a grading policy that meets the needs of all students, from the gifted to the academically challenged (Buckner, 1997; Rafferty et al., 1999).

Conclusion

Appropriate and equitable grading practice is not a simple matter. It requires a great deal of knowledge, skill, and understanding on the part of educators. In spite of a small politically driven cohort calling for the abandonment of all grading policy within public education, grading still stands as the premiere method of informing students, parents, educators, administrators, and community stakeholders regarding an individual student's acquisition of essential skills and knowledge. It is at the base of accountability for public education. Because of its importance in the educational system, K–12 educators and administrators must invest the requisite time and energy to fully understand grading policy and to implement best practice. As outlined in this chapter, best practice is reflected in authentic student assessment that is directly related to learning objectives, expresses variety and creativity, and involves constructivist principles such as deep student involvement throughout the entire process.

References

Anderson, R. S. (1998). Why talk about different ways to grade? The shift from traditional assessment to alternative assessment. *New Directions for Teaching and Learning, 74,* 5–16.

Benson, S. H. (2000). Make mine an A. *Educational Leadership, 57,* 30–32.

Buckner, C. (1997). *Meeting the needs of gifted students in the inclusion classroom* (ERIC Clearinghouse No. EC305733). Salt Lake City, UT: Annual Convention of the Council for Exceptional Children. (ERIC Document Reproduction Service No. ED409687)

Butcher, A. C., Stefani, L. A. J., & Tario, V. N. (1995). Analysis of peer-, self- and staff-assessment in group project work. *Assessment in Education, 2,* 165–185.

Cheng, W., & Warren, M. (2000). Making a difference: Using peers to assess individual students' contributions to a group project. *Teaching in Higher Education, 5,* 243–256.

Colby, S. A. (1999). Grading in a standards-based system. *Educational Leadership, 56,* 52–55.

Ediger, M. (2000). *Assessment of student achievement and the curriculum* (Clearinghouse No. TM032110; ERIC Document Reproduction Service No. ED447202)

Gredler, M. E. (1999). *Classroom assessment and learning.* New York: Longman.

Hendrickson, J., & Gable, R. A. (1997). Collaborative assessment of students with diverse needs: Equitable, accountable, and effective grading. *Preventing School Failure, 41,* 159–163.

Kohn, A. (1999). From degrading to de-grading. *High School Magazine, 6,* 38–43.

Lustig, K. (1996). Portfolio assessment: A handbook for middle level teachers (Report No. ISSBN-1–56090–111-X). Columbus, OH: National Middle School Association. (ERIC Document Reproduction Service No. ED404326)

Marzano, R. J. (1999). Building curriculum and assessment around standards. *High School Magazine, 6,* 14–19.

Moorcroft, T. A., Desmarais, K. H., Hogan, K., & Berkowitz, A. R. (2000). Authentic assessment in the informal setting: How it can work for you. *Journal of Environmental Education, 31,* 20–24.

Pitt, M. J. (2000). The application of games theory to group project assessment. *Teaching in Higher Education, 5,* 233–241.

Rafferty, C. D., Leinenbach, M., & Helms, L. (1999, March). Leveling the playing field through active engagement. *Middle School Journal,* 51–56.

Smith, J. K., Smith, L. F., & DeLisi, R. (2001). Natural classroom assessment: Designing seamless instruction & assessment. In T. R. Guskey & R. J. Marzano (Eds.), *Experts in assessment.* Thousand Oaks, CA: Corwin Press.

Speck, B. W. (1998). Unveiling some of the mystery of professional judgment in classroom assessment. *New Directions for Teaching and Learning, 74,* 17–31.

Spence, S. L., & Theriot, B. (1999). Portfolios in progress: Reevaluating assessment. *Research and Teaching in Developmental Education, 15,* 27–34.

Stiggins, R., & Knight, T. (1997). *But are they learning? A commonsense parents' guide to assessment and grading in schools* (Report No. ISSBN-0–9655101–1-5). Portland, OR: Assessment Training Institute. (ERIC Document Reproduction Service No. ED420685)

Stix, A. (1997). *Empowering students through negotiable contracting* (Clearinghouse No. TM027247). Paper presented at the National Middle School Initiative Conference, Long Island, NY. (ERIC Document Reproduction Service No. ED411274)

Travis, J. E. (1996). Meaningful assessment. *Clearing House, 69,* 308–312.

Wolfe, E. W. (1999). How can administrators facilitate portfolio implementation? Teachers reveal some ways principals can provide real support for implementing student portfolios. *High School Magazine, 6,* 29–33.

Chapter 37
Program Evaluation and Outcomes Assessment
Documenting the Worth of Educational Programs

Bradley T. Erford & Cheryl Moore-Thomas

The impetus for the call for school reform and accountability may be found in the 1983 report *A Nation at Risk* (Angelo & Cross, 1993; Finn & Kanstroom, 2001). National concerns regarding quality education make program evaluation and outcomes assessment more important than ever. Traditionally, however, educators have failed to hold their programs and services accountable, or to provide evidence that selected activities were achieving intended results (Lombana, 1985).

Some argue that the educational process is so complex that obtaining a true measure of its services and results is difficult at best. Others note that school staffs are so busy meeting the needs of students that they shift the time that should be spent on evaluation to instruction and programming. Others suggest educational practitioners lack understanding of the methodology and procedures of accountability studies. Whatever the reason, the result is a lack of accountability that threatens the success of students and the future of some educational institutions. Each reason contributes to avoidance of professional and ethical obligations to ensure that educational programs are of high quality and are effective in meeting students' needs. Without accountability, education service providers and the greater education community may be regarded as suspect.

Stone and Bradley (1994) suggest six purposes of evaluation: (a) to measure the effectiveness of a total program and its activities; (b) to collect data that will help determine what program modifications are needed; (c) to determine the level of program acceptance by and support from stakeholders; (d) to obtain information that can be used to inform the public; (e) to collect data that add to staff evaluation; and (f) to analyze the program budget and compare expenditures to future program needs. In general, then, program evaluation and outcomes assessment work to document and determine the worth of the entire school program.

The purpose of this chapter is to give educators the basic tools needed to design and conduct individualized, effective outcomes assessment and program evaluation that will aim to document and determine the worth of specific educational programs.

The Assessment Loop

The evaluation of a comprehensive educational program is at least two tiered. Gysbers and Henderson (2000) describe two key elements: program evaluation (process), and results (outcomes) evaluation. "Program evaluation is the process of systematically determining the quality of a school program and how the program can be improved" (Sanders, 1992, p. 3). Program evaluation can also be thought of as a process analogous to the measurement concept of content validity (Gysbers & Henderson, 2000). *Content validity* is determined by a systematic examination of a test's, or in this case program's, content. In the context of educational program evaluation, an important guiding question emerges: Does the school have a written, comprehensive program that is fully implemented and aligned with district, state, or national standards? *Outcomes evaluation,* on the other hand, attempts to answer the following question: Does the educational program in fact produce the intended outcomes (Terenzini, 1989)?

Practical guidelines are essential to conducting effective program evaluations and outcomes assessment (Atkinson, Furlong, & Janoff, 1979; Fairchild, 1986; Krumboltz, 1974). It is most practical to connect program concerns to only one or two clearly articulated and defined questions. This practice may help to ensure focused and manageable assessment.

There is much confusion regarding what program evaluation and outcomes assessment are and are not. Undoubtedly, the assessment process is systematic, ongoing, and cyclical. The program evaluation and outcomes assessment processes start small and build upon what is found to work. Successful methods and goals of individual programs are determined and replicated so that over time necessary program refinements work to build a comprehensive educational program that impressively meets an institution's mission. The assessment loop presented in Figure 1 provides a way to visually conceptualize program evaluation and the ways in which outcome studies can be used to improve educational programs.

Figure 1. Program Evaluation Cycle

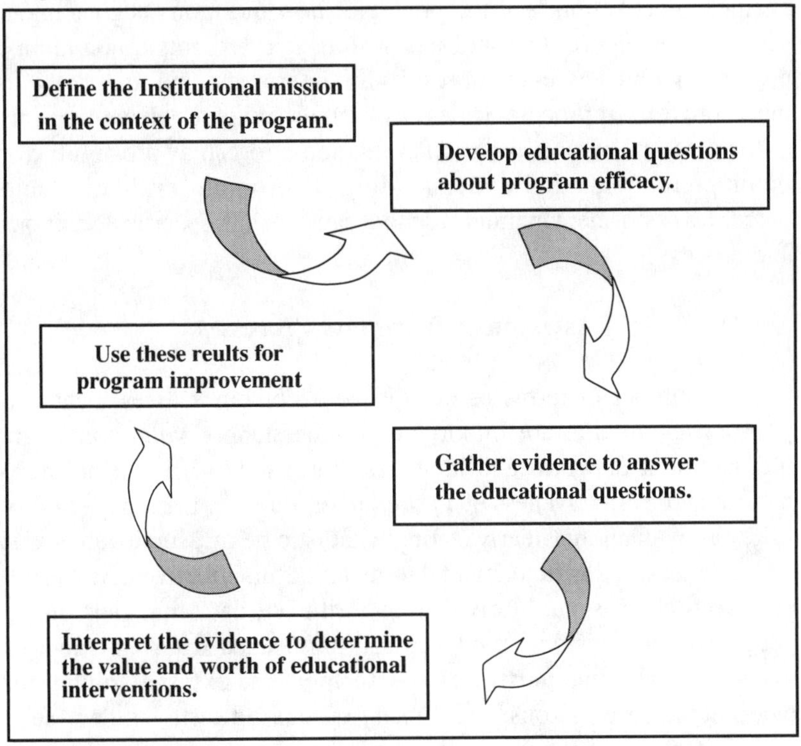

Many educators view assessment as a discrete component of education; however, assessment is actually an integrated part of a continual process for program improvement. Assessment procedures begin with an institution's mission. The mission ideally permeates every aspect of the educational institution. A school's mission should be evident in its structure, decision-making processes, interpersonal interactions, programmatic regularities, and behavioral regularities. The institutional mission provides the basis from which meaningful, institution-specific assessment questions will arise. These assessment questions lead to the determination of what evidence must be collected. Evidence can provide crucial information about program evaluation and program results (i.e., outcomes).

Evidence is typically derived from standardized or informal measures, student performances, or student products. Once a school has gathered evidence, it must interpret the data, then draw conclusions regarding the educational program's worth, strengths, weaknesses, and outcomes. A school should use these interpretations and conclusions to change the entire program or to improve parts of the program.

As assessment information is used to prompt programmatic changes, goal setting and the posing of new questions begins again. The loop in Figure 1 should never stop. It represents a continuous process in which assessment results are interpreted and fed back into the improvement process. Unless assessment involves all components of the assessment loop, program evaluation efforts may prove futile or incomplete. With this understanding of program evaluation and outcomes assessment in mind, a school can consider specific definitions and processes.

Assessment Terms and Processes

A number of terms associated with outcomes assessment and program evaluation are important to understand. *Evaluation* is the measurement of worth and indicates that a judgment will be made regarding the effectiveness of a program (Cronbach, 1983). Specificity is key to evaluation. Clearly stating what is to be measured and how it is to be measured is fundamental to meaningful, effective assessment.

Evidence is qualitative or quantitative data that help make judgments or decisions. Evidence can be gleaned from a number of sources, including portfolios, performances, external judges or examiners, observations, local tests, purchased tests, student self-assessments, surveys, interviews, focus groups, and student work. Some of this evidence may already be routinely collected by a school or district and may thus provide a readily accessible source of data about program effectiveness. Which evidence source to use, however, is determined by the specific question to be answered. Evidence selection should be made carefully. If measures are used, they must be reliable and valid. Sometimes ineffective program outcomes stem exclusively from poor or inappropriate measurement choices rather than program deficits.

Formative evaluation is evaluative feedback that occurs during the implementation of a program. *Summative evaluation* is feedback collected at a specified endpoint in an evaluation process (Worthen, Sanders, & Fitzpatrick, 1997). Formative evaluation allows for midcourse corrective action. Although summative evaluation is more widely used, formative evaluation is an advantageous endeavor when the time, dollar, and human cost of educational programming is considered.

A *stakeholder* is anyone involved or interested in, or potentially benefiting from, a program (Sanders, 1992; Worthen et al., 1997). Students, parents, teachers, school counselors, administrators, community leaders, college faculty, and local employers, among others, are potential educational stakeholders. Inclusion of a variety of relevant stakeholders is important to the assessment process.

Reporting Assessment Results

Reporting assessment findings is also important to effective program evaluation and outcomes assessment. The school leadership team—including administrators, teachers, professional school counselors, staff members, parents, and other appropriate stakeholders—should write and be involved in every step of the reporting process. Although a comprehensive report may be helpful for analysis purposes, a one- to two-page executive summary should also be prepared for release to system administrators and the general school community. As general guidelines for report writing, Heppner, Kivlighan and Wampold (1992) suggest, "(1) be informative, (2) be forthright, (3) do not overstate or exaggerate, (4) be logical and organized, (5) have some style, (6) write and rewrite, and (7) when all else fails, just write!" (p. 376). Although they may have intended the last guideline to be humorous, it is important to note that results must be documented, interpreted, and reported for accountability to occur.

Case Study

The following case integrates, in a practical way, the key concepts of outcome assessment and program evaluation presented in this chapter. Beall Middle School is in a suburban middle-class community. Over the past 10 years, the student population of Beall has changed to match the changing demographics of the surrounding community. Beall's current 600-student enrollment is 31 percent minority. Beall enjoys a 98 percent daily attendance rate. Three percent of the students receive free or reduced-cost lunch.

The slogan of Beall Middle School is "Success for Every Student." The staff has embraced the middle school philosophy to deliver a comprehensive, stable program that provides educational opportunity for all students. The leadership team at Beall has been closely monitoring test results. Over the past four years Beall's standardized test scores have fallen significantly. In light of this finding, the leadership team posed several educational questions, including Is the current instructional program enabling all students to meet the school's mission of success? From the initial question, the school counselor posed a related discipline-specific question aligned with the school's mission, the district guidelines, and the *National Standards for School Counseling Programs*. The counselor asked, Are all students acquiring "the attitudes, knowledge, and skills that contribute to effective learning in school and across the life span?" (Campbell & Dahir, 1997, p. 20). The school leadership team felt that the discipline-specific question was on target and focused enough to guide meaningful assessment and evaluation.

Having identified their educational question, the counseling department and leadership team determined that surveys would provide an appropriate source of evidence to answer the school's question. The department then developed student, staff, and parent surveys based on the school district's guidance and counseling curriculum and the competencies of the academic development standard of the

National Standards for School Counseling Programs (Campbell & Dahir, 1997). To help ensure validity, central office guidance and counseling staff, a college school counseling faculty partner, and parent and student focus groups reviewed the surveys. Distributed, completed, and tallied over the next two months, the surveys yielded important data.

The results seemed to suggest that significant percentages of the students and parents wanted more help with time-management skills. The teacher surveys seemed to suggest that students needed more help identifying attitudes and behaviors that lead to successful learning. The counseling department and leadership team wrote a brief, user-friendly report of the data to be shared at leadership, staff, and PTA meetings. Using these data, the counseling department, in collaboration with the instructional team leaders and chairs of the academic departments, redesigned the second semester comprehensive guidance and counseling plan to include emphasis on these areas. A key component of the redesigned plan called for formative evaluation and midcourse correction that would be jointly monitored by the school counselors, administrators, and representatives of the leadership team. Evidence to be examined for formative evaluation included students' third quarter work-study skill grades, educational management team notes and strategies developed and implemented during the third quarter, and a student assessment built into the third quarter schoolwide guidance lessons on time management. All stakeholders were confident that this assessment loop, with its inherent level of accountability, would more effectively monitor and guide Beall Middle School to its intended goal of success for every student.

Summary

The Beall Middle School case suggests that program evaluation and outcomes assessment are important tools for effective service delivery in every area of a school program. As calls for increased accountability in education rise, educators, school counselors, other school staff members, and other educational stakeholders will be well advised to implement ongoing, cyclical program evaluation and outcomes assessment processes.

References

Angelo, T., & Cross, K. (1993). *Classroom assessment techniques: A handbook for college teachers* (2nd ed.). San Francisco, CA: Jossey-Bass.

Atkinson, D. R., Furlong, M., & Janoff, D. S. (1979). A four-component model for proactive accountability in school counseling. *School Counselor, 26,* 222–228.

Campbell, C., & Dahir, C. (1997). *The national standards for school counseling programs.* Alexandria, VA: American School Counselor Association.

Cronbach, L. J. (1983). Course improvement through evaluation. In C. F. Madaus, M. Scriven, & D. L. Stufflebeam (Eds.), *Evaluation models* (pp. 101–116). Boston: Kluwer-Nijhoff.

Fairchild, T. N. (1986). Time analysis: Accountability tool for school counselors. *School Counselor, 34,* 36–43.

Finn, C., & Kanstroom, M. (2001). State academic standards. *Brookings Papers on Education Policy, 2001*(1), 131–179.

Gysbers, N. C., & Henderson, P. (2000). Developing and managing your school counseling program (3rd ed.). Alexandria, VA: American Counseling Association.

Heppner, P. P., Kivlighan, D. M., Jr., & Wampold, B. E. (1992). *Research design in counseling.* Pacific Grove, CA: Brooks-Cole.

Krumboltz, J. D. (1974). An accountability model for counselors. *Personnel and Guidance Journal, 52,* 639–646.

Lombana, J. H. (1985). Guidance accountability: A new look at an old problem. *School Counselor, 32,* 340–346.

Sanders, J. (1992). *Evaluating school programs: An educator's guide.* Newbury Park, CA: Corwin Press, Inc. (ERIC Document Reproduction Services No. ED 423166)

Stone, L. A., & Bradley, F. O. (1994). *Foundations of elementary and middle school counseling.* White Plains, NY: Longman.

Terenzini, P. (1989). Assessment with open eyes. *Journal of Higher Education, 60*(6), 644–664.

Worthen, B. B., Sanders, J. R., & Fitzpatrick, J. L. (1997). *Program evaluation: Alternative approaches and practical guidelines* (2nd ed.). New York: Longman.

Chapter 38
Interpreting the Meaning of Test Results
The Consultant's Role

Donna M. Gibson

Good assessment is key to providing effective intervention, and thoughtful interpretation of assessment results is an important part of the intervention. Unfortunately, those involved in administering and interpreting test results do not generally have this attitude. Often, they consider test interpretation at the last minute of the assessment process, and the receivers of this information come away from the process feeling confused and dazed. Not surprisingly, the interpreter of those results often feels the same.

Considering the importance of accountability in our society, it would seem that the meaning of assessment should have a stronger emphasis. Moreover, counselors, psychologists, teachers, and administrators are called often not only to interpret the meaning of test results, but to extrapolate that meaning into decisions affecting the lives of individuals, couples, and groups of children and adults. Why then has there not been a stronger emphasis on test interpretation?

One answer is that the focus of assessment consultation has been on the statistical meaning of test results; however, people on the receiving end of such a consultation can verify that the statistical meaning is only a small portion of the true meaning of the results. The recipients of the consultation determine the true meaning of the results. Therefore, this consultation process should include a plan on how to assess the needs of the service recipient during the meeting.

This chapter focuses on the consultant and service recipient in the test interpretation process, including ways to help all participants in this process. In addition, case examples illustrate the salient points of consultation designed to explain the full meaning of test results.

Consultation Process

Why call the test interpretation process a consultation process?

Why not call it simply a meeting where test results are provided to the interested parties? Too simplistic, yes, but do we make this process seem too complex by calling it a formal consultation? Not necessarily. When the consultant perceives test interpretation as a consultation process, it encourages him or her to prepare for addressing the many dimensions and questions that arise during this process. The consultant's actions and demeanor communicate to the service recipient or clients receiving the results the importance of this consultation.

According to Dougherty (1995), there are four stages of consultation: entry, diagnosis, implementation, and disengagement. Because many of these stages are completed in a limited period of time, it may be difficult to conceptualize all the steps in this process and how they contribute to test interpretation.

Several steps can take place during the entry stage of consultation, but the focus should be on exploring the needs of the organization (Dougherty, 1995). Counselors, psychologists, teachers, and administrators usually take this for granted. School counselors and psychologists, who are designated as the professionals that provide test interpretation, understand that they are part of the school system organization and have obligations to multiple clients: not only the administration but also teachers, students, and parents. Hence, unlike in some other settings, these consultants are part of the organization and often have a full understanding of the concerns regarding the assessment recipient. Additionally, when the consultants are also helping professionals, they have to identify with whom they will be consulting during the process. For example, in a school setting, the direct service recipient may be the student, but school administrators, teachers, other helping professionals, and parents or guardians are the primary recipients of the consultation.

The second stage of consultation, diagnosis, consists of gathering information, defining the problem, setting goals, and generating possible interventions (Dougherty, 1995). When the consultant is also a helping professional, this stage is particularly important because it begins when collecting assessment information but continues not only throughout the meeting where the test results are reported but also into the intervention process. This stage involves defining the problem and gathering information during face-to-face contacts with the service recipient and possibly others. Due to time constraints, much of this takes place during the meeting where test results are given. Consider the following scenario:

> Ms. Daniels, the school counselor, met with a fourth-grade student's mother to discuss the student's test results. During the meeting, the mother reported that her husband had recently been diagnosed with cancer and couldn't work. She also reported that she and her husband were very concerned about their daughter's academic work.

Through this meeting Ms. Daniels not only learned new information about the family, but also assessed some of the mother's anxiety and possibly the student's. She discovered that the student's problem may not be purely academic but may also be related to anxiety about the father's illness and nonworking status.

Depending upon the information gathered during this stage, the consultant may need to modify his or her initial plans regarding presentation of test results, recommended interventions, and goal setting for the consultation meeting. For example, the goal may change from focusing on the test results to addressing the service recipient and family's immediate concerns (in this case, the mother's and student's anxiety).

The third stage is implementation of the intervention, which means that the interventions need to have been selected and procedures for implementation and evaluation determined. Therefore, the consultant needs to formulate recommendations about possible interventions after reviewing the test results and before the consultation meeting. The crucial step in this phase of consultation is to co-create the interventions with the service recipient, which is similar to how counselors normally work with their clients throughout the counseling process. In some settings, however, the service recipient may not be involved with the test interpretation due to age, maturity, or developmental level; the setting also often dictates who is involved in the consultation. Within school systems, for example, students below a certain grade are not involved.

The purpose of co-creating interventions is for all the co-creators to "buy in" to the intervention and hold partial responsibility for implementing it. The effort and personal investment that all parties make in the intervention ensures an emotional investment in the welfare of the service recipient. Working as a team, the consultant and service recipient do not want to fail, and they do not want to fail the other stakeholders in the intervention. Monitoring the intervention requires that the intervention team also co-create steps for evaluation and assign each person responsibilities for specific components of the evaluation.

The fourth and final step is disengagement from the consultation process, during which the consultant self-evaluates the consultation process. The consultant could ask himself or herself: Did I present the information clearly? Did we (consultant, service recipient, and other clients) clearly identify the problem? Did we address the problem? Did we identify and acknowledge emotions? Did the service recipient or clients appear confused by the information I provided? Did I provide appropriate written material? Did we establish appropriate intervention plans and steps for implementation? Is it clear who has responsibility for implementation and evaluation? Were any questions left unanswered?

After answering these questions, the consultant determines which ones need follow-up. If any questions were left unanswered, it is not too late to answer them. It is also not too late to modify or eliminate interventions if necessary. Furthermore, if the consultant will not have the role of monitoring the interventions, he or she may need to refer this activity to another professional.

The exact nature of the stages in the consultation process depend on the people involved and what the consultant's role is. The experiences and emotions of the service recipient, his or her family, and the helping professionals involved often affect the meaning of the results.

Recipients of Test Interpretation

After conceptualizing test interpretation as consultation, the consultant must consider the recipients of the information. First there are developmental issues to consider (Lyman, 1998). What is the developmental level of the service recipient? How will this person (and other key recipients) react intellectually? Second, there are power issues. How much power will the service recipient have in helping co-create, implement, and evaluate interventions? Will he or she need to enlist others to help? Third, there are emotional considerations. How do the service recipient and other clients feel about the testing process? How will they react emotionally to this information? How will they integrate this information into their lives? The consultant needs to consider all these issues in some form during the process of test interpretation, but they present themselves differently depending upon who the service recipient and clients are. Consequently, the consultant needs to handle them differently depending on the setting and situation.

Client and Consultation Recipient Are the Same Person

When the consultation recipient is the actual client or student who took the tests, the consultant needs to consider this person's needs when reviewing test results. Depending upon the client's level of understanding, it may not be important to present detailed information about psychometric properties of the test, but the consultant is still responsible for reviewing this information prior to meeting with the client. Reviewing and understanding the test results are essential components of preparation for test interpretation (Hood and Johnson, 1997). The client, however, may be more interested in knowing what the test results will mean for him or her in the future or, conversely, in knowing details of the psychometric properties rather than how the results may affect his or her life. Consider the following case example:

> Denise, a 21-year-old college senior, had majored in business administration with an emphasis in marketing. During the fall semester of her senior year, Denise volunteered to take a battery of five career inventories. Up until the fourth session, Denise had appeared very interested in the results and had asked many questions about the statistical meaning of the scores. The fourth inventory assessed her values. As she and the counselor explored her values and how they affected her career decisions, Denise revealed that her values were not consistent with her business administration major. At the beginning of the next session, Denise asked to discuss the values inventory further instead of moving on to the scheduled inventory. After much discussion, the counselor realized that Denise was feeling very anxious about the meaning of these results. The counselor verified this with Denise, who confirmed that she felt trapped in her major, being close to graduation, and feared disappointing her parents if she changed her major or career path.

This case illustrates the necessity of the consultant following the service recipient's lead in test interpretation when that person is also the client. Denise was primarily interested in the statistical meaning of the inventories until another meaning presented itself during the discussion of her values. This deeper meaning was accompanied by feelings of anxiety, which the counselor needed to address, putting interpretation of the fifth inventory on hold in the meantime. This change of plans shows respect for Denise and allows her to regroup emotionally so she can co-create interventions for her future.

The Client's Parent or Guardian Is the Consultation Recipient

When a parent or guardian is the primary audience of the consultation, it is always advantageous for the consultant to contact that person prior to the test interpretation meeting. This contact allows the consultant to assess the parent or guardian's developmental level, goals, and possible expectations for the test results, and hence to anticipate the individual's likely emotional and intellectual reactions to the results. Additionally, the consultant can begin to assess the power level of the parent or guardian and how helpful he or she will be in co-creating and implementing interventions.

The consultant may find it useful to develop hypotheses about the parent's or guardian's reaction to the results. These hypotheses allow the consultant to plan an outline for the meeting, prepare answers to anticipated questions, and provide written materials appropriate to the issues of concern.

Emotional considerations often outweigh intellectual considerations when parents are the primary recipient of the consultation. These parents are often feeling anxious about their child's health or performance, so empathizing with the parent's feelings regarding the testing process and test interpretation meeting is particularly important. Acknowledging these feelings may help parents to hear and understand the test results. The statistical results of the test are only a small portion of the meaning for parents. The results may force parents to modify or relinquish the hopes and dreams they have had for their child up to that point. Consider the following case example:

> Anthony, a three-year-old, recently received a multidisciplinary evaluation. The psychologist on the team scheduled a time to meet with Anthony's parents to discuss the evaluation results. Because Anthony's parents had been present throughout the evaluation, the psychologist was able to gauge their anxiety about Anthony's behavior and inability to talk. During the evaluation and the test interpretation meeting, Anthony's parents acknowledged that his behavior was not normal, but Anthony was their first child and they had no prior experience with other children his age. The psychologist knew that Anthony had received a diagnosis of severe autism, and she was prepared

> for the parents to feel confused, defensive, and angry on hearing this diagnosis. After discussing the scores and giving the diagnosis to Anthony's parents, she asked how they felt about the information. Surprisingly, they reported feeling relieved finally to know what is wrong and that there were interventions that could help their son. The information had given them hope.

Preparing only for the worst-case reactions does not allow the consultant to prepare for the positive surprises that may occur during consultation with parents. In this case, the parents' dream of a normal child had already faded and left a void until the diagnosis of autism was made. With a firm diagnosis, these parents were mentally available to co-create and implement highly effective interventions for their son. Had the psychologist focused only on preparing to support the parents' emotional response to the diagnosis, she would not have prepared adequately to move forward to intervention planning.

Teachers and Other Professionals Are the Consultation Recipients

When teachers are the consultation recipients, the consultant generally must address two issues: clarifying the problem and responding to the teacher's emotions. Clarifying the problem usually occurs throughout the consultation process after test results have shown that the student has a behavioral or academic problem. However, this process also involves obtaining the teacher's perspective on the issue, including the nature of the relationship between the student and the teacher. The consultant should consider the following questions: Is the student's problem related strictly to factors within the student—such as a learning disability or attention deficit/hyperactivity disorder—or are these internal factors interacting with the teacher-student relationship to exacerbate the problem? Does this teacher view this student positively or negatively? The consultant can collect this information by asking specific questions about the teacher's view of the student and how he or she feels about the student's academic or emotional behavior.

The second issue to address involves the emotions the teacher brings to this process, that is, the feelings that are centered on the teacher not on the student. Much like parents, teachers may feel a good deal of responsibility for the student's progress. If the student is not progressing, the teacher may feel that he or she is failing the student as a teacher and as a responsible adult. The same may be true of other professionals working with a student or other client. These individuals have been given a responsibility for helping and teaching that student or client, but that help has not allowed the person to be successful. Thus, the teachers or other professionals may feel anxious or insecure about their performance, feeling that they have failed not only the student or client but themselves. The consultant needs to assess these feelings and acknowledge them in an appropriate way for the intervention process to proceed effectively. Consider the following case example:

> Ms. Parker, a third-grade teacher, met with the school counselor regarding the test results of her student, Mark. Mark had a troubled past, with a history of sexual abuse, attention deficit/hyperactivity disorder, and learning problems. The test results indicated that Mark had a severe learning disability in reading and written language. The counselor recommended that Mark receive special education but stay in Ms. Parker's class for nonacademic subjects. Ms. Parker strongly objected to this arrangement, becoming extremely agitated in asserting that Mark should remain in a special education class for the entire day. In attempting to calm her, the school counselor observed that this was Ms. Parker's second year of teaching since graduating from college. Ms. Parker acknowledged this and remarked that she was still learning about teaching and may not be the best person to help Mark. The counselor affirmed that Ms. Parker is a dedicated teacher and offered to support her in implementing classroom interventions.

In this case, Ms. Parker's agitation appeared to be linked to her anxiety about being a new teacher and possibly failing this student. To alleviate Ms. Parker's apprehension, the school counselor encouraged her to participate in co-creating interventions during the consultation and followed up by providing a lot of support during implementation. The school counselor, acting as consultant in this case, continued meeting with Ms. Parker to monitor the interventions and assist with necessary modifications as well as to assess her confidence level.

Unfortunately, clients, parents, teachers, and other professionals may show anxiety and apprehension during the test consultation in a variety of ways, including agitation, defensiveness, anger, or sadness (Lyman, 1998). It is crucial that the consultant act on these emotions rather than reacting to them. The consultant is responsible for uncovering the true meaning of those emotions in order to help both the consultation and service recipients appropriately.

Interpreting the Meaning

Conclusion

During test interpretation, the consultant plays a vital role in providing appropriate and lasting help to the service recipients and clients in this process. As a school psychologist and counselor, I engaged in this role frequently with students, teachers, parents, school administrators, and other helping professionals. Consequently, I realized that test results were not the magical ingredients in those meetings. The magic was within the people I consulted with as well as in helping myself and them understand the true meaning of the results for their lives. For consultants, finding and working with this meaning is the true challenge.

References

Dougherty, A. M. (1995). *Consultation: Practice and perspectives in school and community settings* (2nd ed.). Pacific Grove, CA: Brooks/ Cole.

Hood, A. B., & Johnson, R. W. (1997). *Assessment in counseling: A guide to the use of psychological assessment procedures* (2nd ed.). Alexandria, VA: American Counseling Association.

Lyman, H. B. (1998). *Test scores and what they mean* (6th ed.). Boston: Allyn and Bacon.

Chapter 39
Testing FAQ
How to Answer Questions Parents Frequently Ask About Testing

Bradley T. Erford & Cheryl Moore-Thomas

Educational accountability demands that students take tests. Parents and guardians, being committed to their children's academic success, often ask teachers and other educators questions about tests and testing procedures. This chapter provides practical, straightforward responses to many of the questions parents and guardians ask about testing.

The Purpose of Testing

What is the purpose of the tests my child is taking? Can tests determine how well my child is doing in school?

All of us have taken tests. More than ever, school-age children are being required to take many different kinds of tests. Much of the testing in today's schools may be attributed to national concern for accountability in public education resulting from Goals 2000: Educate America Act. Goals 2000 provides a framework for educational reform by improving the quality of learning and teaching in the classroom, and assisting in the development of quality assessment measures. Testing is essential to the very purpose of education (Coffman & Lindquist, 1980).

In general, the main purpose of testing is to benefit students. Tests help educators and parents identify student strengths and areas needing improvement. Educators can use information from tests to plan lessons and design curriculum that meet the needs of all students. Tests can also help evaluate and improve schools or entire school systems. Thus, testing information is crucial for educational accountability (Educational Testing Service, 1999; Eissenberg & Rudner, 1988).

Classroom tests are probably the most common type of tests students take. These tests are often teacher-made and cover a specific body of knowledge. Classroom tests may be short and clear-cut, like weekly spelling tests, or they may be fairly involved, like unit tests in social studies or science or even high school final exams. Classroom tests are given to help educators, parents, and guardians assess what students have learned.

Students may also take standardized tests. Standardized tests are used to help measure student ability or achievement. Standardized ability tests measure students' capacity to learn, whereas standardized achievement tests measure what students have learned about a particular subject. Classroom teachers do not create standardized tests. Commercial test publishers develop most of these tests, which are administered in the same way for all test takers. This standardization is what makes these tests a powerful tool in assessment. Standardization enables comparisons to be made among individuals and schools.

There are two basic kinds of standardized tests: norm-referenced and criterion-referenced. *Norm-referenced* tests compare students' performance to that of their peers, while *criterion-referenced* tests compare or measure students' performance against particular standards. On norm-referenced tests, students' scores are compared to the scores of the original group of students who took the test, called a *norm group.* Norm-referenced tests may answer questions such as, "How does my child's understanding of word meanings compare to that of her peers?"

Student performance on criterion-referenced tests is measured against a specific set of skills or objectives or against an established criterion for passing or mastery. Criterion-referenced tests may answer the questions, "Does my child know the meaning of the word 'periodic'?" or "Does my child know how to add two-digit numbers with regrouping?"

Testing is an important part of the education process. Used appropriately, tests can help educators, parents, guardians, students, and other stakeholders make critical decisions about educational programming and services. Tests alone, however, do not give the complete picture of any student's knowledge or ability. They give a single snapshot of student performance, a single piece of the assessment process (Bagin, 1989; Coffman & Lindquist, 1980; McMillan, 2000; Salvia & Ysseldyke, 2001).

The Content of Tests

Who decides what questions go on the tests? Shouldn't the teacher have a role in question selection?

Test authors and publishers decide test questions; however, test authors rely on content specialists who review applicable national, state, and local standards and curricula (including textbooks) to determine what comprises the domain of knowledge to be tested and to select information that is important for students to know. This ensures a test has *content validity* (Salvia & Ysseldyke, 2001). Many content specialists are current or former teachers.

On standardized tests designed in cooperation with local school systems or state departments of education, selected classroom teachers often have a role in selecting learning objectives that guide question selection. Teachers even submit questions for consideration. Thus, although teachers may not select the actual questions, they often help prioritize the content that guides question selection. In this way, content specialists and teachers work together to help determine what content is assessed, but teachers do not know the specific questions that appear on a test, which may give their students an unfair advantage should teachers "teach to the test" (Anastasi & Urbina, 1997).

Were all the questions on the test covered in class or in the textbook? How can teachers know what to cover to prepare students for the test without teaching to the test?

Curriculum standards provide learning outcomes and objectives that guide classroom instruction. Test content is also guided by these learning objectives, which are operationalized through the test questions (Popham, 2000). School systems should choose standardized tests that have substantial overlap between the test content and school curriculum. If a school system chooses a test that has only a 75 percent overlap between test content and learning objectives, their students will fare worse than students in a school system with a 100 percent overlap not because the former school system has inferior teachers or students, but because about 25 percent of what the test measures is *not taught.* When a curriculum and the test are in total alignment, the burden falls on the teacher to cover all curricular content in an efficient manner. Failure to do so will lead to lower student performance.

Teaching to the test is a problem only if the teacher has advance warning of specific questions that will appear on a test. If a teacher knows that certain content is always emphasized on a particular test, it is appropriate to emphasize that content area in instruction. Likewise, if certain content is regularly de-emphasized on a test, less attention to that content in the classroom may be warranted. It is incumbent on the school system and test publisher to ensure that standards, curriculum, and assessment are well aligned and that all objectives are assessed in the correct proportion. This way appropriate textbooks and classroom activities can be determined.

The Protection of Test Content

Why can't I get a copy of standardized test questions to help my child study ahead of time, like we do for spelling or math?

Test content is protected for a variety of reasons (Anastasi & Urbina, 1997; Cohen & Swerdlik, 1999; Kaplan & Saccuzzo, 2001; Salvia & Ysseldyke, 2001; Thorndike, 1997). Most standardized tests must be administered, scored, and interpreted by individuals with specialized education, training, and experience. Among other things, these individuals must be able to select an appropriate test, administer and score the test accurately, and interpret the score. Test content must be protected because the results will not yield a valid estimate of current abilities if the person taking the test knows the questions and answers beforehand. Standardized tests differ from classroom spelling or math tests in this regard because the content domain on a spelling or math test is usually revealed and studied in close proximity to the test. Studying for a classroom test is generally easy and the test result is compared to a grading criterion (i.e., A, B, C, and so on). On a norm-referenced test, the content is revealed over a period of several semesters or years and preparing for it is therefore much more difficult. In addition, the student's score is compared with those of the same age or grade rather than with a grading criterion.

Finally, results of standardized tests are usually less obvious or understandable than those of teacher-made tests; effectively communicating the results to parents and teachers requires specialized training. Effective communication of results and what to expect during testing helps dispel anxiety, maximize performance, and familiarize the student with the testing procedures.

Preparing for Tests

How can I help my child prepare for tests?

Tests can cause anxiety in students. This anxiety can be diminished if parents, guardians, and educators help prepare students for tests. Most importantly, parents, guardians, and educators should let students know that test taking is a normal part of the educational process. Whether students are preparing to take classroom tests or standardized tests, students should view tests as an important but regular school activity. Students are also well served by knowing what material is being covered on a test and why it is important. Teachers usually help students by providing review materials or study suggestions for classroom tests. Coaching materials are available for some standardized tests. Although coaching materials such as test preparation courses may improve students' test scores, these methods often do not appreciably improve students' mastery of the domain of information being assessed.

Students' performance may also be enhanced if they are familiar with test-taking procedures (Educational Testing Service, 1999). Test-taking procedures include understanding test response format (e.g., multiple choice, essay, true-false), test length, and test directions. Although it is appropriate for students to be familiar with test-taking procedures, it is not appropriate for them to prepare for tests by practicing with the actual test or practicing on a published parallel form of the test (Mehrens, 1989). Students should also be aware of factors that may affect their scores. For example, some tests penalize students for guessing or not answering all questions. Other tests require that students demonstrate their preliminary calculations or show their work in other ways to earn top scores.

Perhaps the best way to prepare students for tests is to consistently monitor their progress, assist them in developing strong study habits, and ensure they approach each testing situation well rested and well fed (Bond, 1996).

The Meaning of Scores

What do all the scores on my child's testing report mean? What are percentile ranks, stanines, and grade equivalents?

Simply put, norm-referenced, standardized scores are all based on the properties of a normal (bell-shaped) curve. In this way, there is consistency in the transformation of scores as long as distributions are normal and standardization samples are similar in constitution (Cohen & Swerdlik, 1999; Thorndike, 1997). Figure 1 illustrates this similarity in score transformation. Notice that a deviation IQ of 100 ($M = 100$, $SD = 15$) will always be equivalent to a percentile rank of 50, T-score of 50, scaled score of 10, and stanine of 5. Likewise, a deviation IQ of 130 will always be equivalent to a percentile rank of 98, T-score of 70, scaled score of 16, and stanine of 9. Table 1 provides many transformations for the standardized scores commonly used in education.

Figure 1. Score Transformation Based on Normal Curve

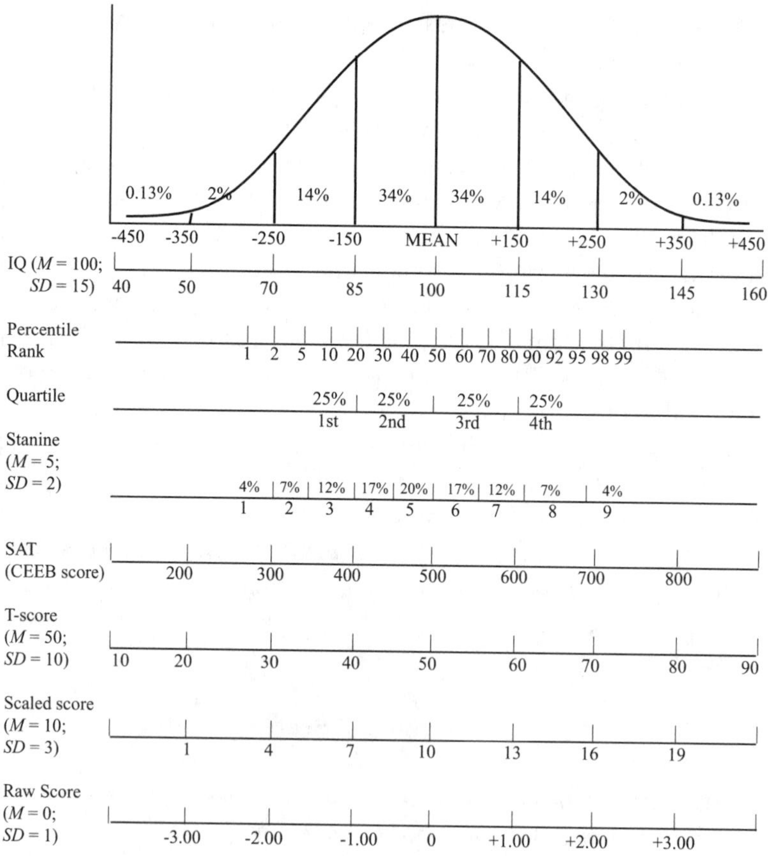

Table 1. Correspondences Among Deviation IQ, Stanine, Percentile Rank, Scaled Score, and Interpretive Range

	Deviation IQ	Stanine	Percentile Rank	Scaled Score	Interpretive Range
Mean	100	5	---	10	—
Standard	15	2	—	3	—
	55	1	<1	1	MD
	56	1	<1	1	MD
	57	1	<1	1	MD
	58	1	<1	2	MD
	59	1	<1	2	MD
	60	1	<1	2	MD
	61	1	1	2	MD
	62	1	1	2	MD
	63	1	1	3	MD
	64	1	1	3	MD
	65	1	1	3	MD
	66	1	1	3	MD
	67	1	1	3	MD
	68	1	2	4	MD
	69	1	2	4	MD
	70	1	2	4	B
	71	1	3	4	B
	72	1	3	4	B
	73	2	4	5	B
	74	2	4	5	B
	75	2	5	5	B
	76	2	5	5	B
	77	2	6	5	B

	78	2	*7*	*6*	*B*
	79	2	*8*	*6*	*B*
	80	2	*9*	*6*	*LA*
	81	2	10	6	LA
	82	3	12	6	LA
	83	3	13	7	LA
	84	3	14	7	LA
	85	3	16	7	LA
	86	3	18	7	LA
	87	3	19	7	LA
	88	3	21	8	LA
	89	4	23	8	LA
	90	4	25	8	A
	91	4	27	8	A
	92	4	30	8	A
	93	4	32	9	A
	94	4	34	9	A
	95	5	37	9	A
	96	5	40	9	A
	97	5	42	9	A
	98	5	45	10	A
	99	5	48	10	A
	100	5	50	10	A
	101	5	53	10	A
	102	5	55	10	A
	103	5	58	11	A
	104	6	61	11	A
	105	6	63	11	A
	106	6	66	11	A
	107	6	68	11	A

	108	6	70	12	A
	109	6	73	12	A
	110	6	75	12	HA
	111	7	77	12	HA
	112	7	79	12	HA
	113	7	81	13	HA
	114	7	83	13	HA
	115	7	84	13	HA
	116	7	86	13	HA
	117	7	87	13	HA
	118	8	89	14	HA
	119	8	90	14	HA
	120	8	91	14	S
	121	8	92	14	S
	122	8	93	14	S
	123	8	94	15	S
	124	8	95	15	S
	125	8	95	15	S
	126	9	96	15	S
	127	9	96	15	S
	128	9	97	16	S
	129	9	97	16	S
	130	9	98	16	VS
	131	9	98	16	VS
	132	9	98	16	VS
	133	9	99	17	VS
	134	9	99	17	VS
	135	9	99	17	VS
	136	9	99	17	VS
	137	9	99	17	VS

	138	9	99	18	VS
	139	9	99+	18	VS
	140	9	99+	18	VS
	141	9	99+	18	VS
	142	9	99+	18	VS
	143	9	99+	19	VS
	144	9	99+	19	VS

MD = Mildly Deficient B = Borderline LA = Low Average A= Average
HA= High Average S = Superior VS = Very Superior

It is essential to understand the scores commonly used when reporting student standardized test scores. *Percentile ranks,* which are probably the easiest score for parents and teachers to understand, are simply an indication of where a student's performance falls compared with other students of the same age or grade comprising the norm group. To explain percentile ranks, it is helpful to visualize a lineup of 100 students of the same age or grade, with the first student in the line being the least proficient and the 100th student being the most proficient. If a student scored at the 72nd percentile rank, her score would be interpreted as follows: "Susan's math calculation score exceeded the performance of 72 percent of other students in her grade (or of her age)."

Stanines (short for "standard nines") are standard score ranges dividing the distribution into nine parts. Table 1 provides stanine equivalents associated with percentile ranks. For Susan's percentile rank of 72, her math calculation performance would have fallen into the 6th stanine. It is difficult to describe to parents how stanines are derived, and therefore stanines should be used sparingly.

Grade equivalents (GEs) are computed by determining the average raw scores obtained by students in each grade at different times during the year. Erford, Vitali, Haas, and Boykin (1995, pp. 28–29) summarize the use of grade equivalents as follows:

> Despite their popular appeal, GEs are frequently misinterpreted and most often not helpful in getting teachers and parents to understand the child's performance. This is true for several reasons. First, if a child in grade 2.0 obtains a math GE of 4.0, this does not mean he/she should be immediately placed in the fourth grade curriculum. His/

> her GE does indicate that he/she will probably be a good math student in his/her second grade class . . . Second, curriculums vary in degrees of acceleration provided. . . . Some third grade curriculums are dealing with second grade concepts, while others are accelerated to the point that fourth and fifth grade content is covered to a substantial degree . . . Finally, . . . GEs should not be viewed as a performance criterion . . . a GE of 3.9 is commensurate with the average performance of an ending third grader. Thus, it would be an unrealistic expectation for all students to achieve a GE of 3.9 or higher at the conclusion of the third grade year.

An *interpretive range* is an easily understood verbal descriptor of a student's performance. Table 2 shows interpretive ranges for comparable standard scores and percentile ranks. Using the previous example of Susan, her math calculation percentile rank of 72 falls in the Average range.

Table 2. Equivalence of Standard Scores (*M* = 100; *SD* = 15), Percentile Ranks, and Interpretive Ranges

Standard Score	Percentile Rank	Interpretive Range
130+	98+	Very Superior (VS)
120–129	90–97	Superior (S)
110–119	75–89	High Average (HA)
90–109	25–73	Average (A)
80–89	10–23	Low Average (LA)
70–79	2–8	Borderline (B)
55–69	< 2	Mildly Deficient (MD)

How are tests scored? Is it possible to score essay exams accurately?

Many objective standardized tests in mass testing programs are scored using high-speed scanners and computer programs. If the students fill out the forms correctly and the publisher's answers are keyed correctly, this scoring system is virtually error-free because objective questions (i.e., multiple choice, true-false, coded) maximize interscorer reliability. *Interscorer reliability* refers to the consistency of agreement among multiple scorers of the same set of scores. Because no scorer judgment is required on multiple-choice questions, consistency is nearly always 100 percent, except in instances of miskeyed responses or errors due to inattention. The advantage of computer scoring is that errors due to inattention are eliminated (Salvia & Ysseldyke, 2001).

On most tests with objective-type questions, only one answer for each item is correct and the number of correct items for a student on a given subtest is summed to give a raw score. This raw score is then converted, using the appropriate norm for the child's age or grade, to a standardized score and percentile rank to indicate the student's performance in relation to his or her peers.

Essay or constructed-response exams are somewhat more complicated, as interscorer reliability can become more of a factor. Under most circumstances, a scoring rubric must be constructed and sample responses, or exemplars, developed (Popham, 2000). Most constructed-response tests must be hand-scored by a qualified examiner, and in many instances, more than one examiner. Having two or more examiners score the response provides an extra check, which boosts confidence that the score has been consistently derived. Still, interscorer reliability for constructed-response tests necessarily introduces unwanted error—usually between 5 and 20 percent, opposed to the nearly 0 percent error rate for machine-scored multiple choice tests. Such a high rate of error lowers confidence in the results and makes reporting of individual scores problematic, as most experts agree that reliabilities must have less than 10 percent measurement error to yield reliable individual results for diagnostic decision-making purposes (Salvia & Ysseldyke, 2001). In sum, objective scoring rubrics are essential to minimizing scorer subjectivity, thus leading to reliable and accurate scoring of essay exams.

How do test developers know what the national average is? How do I know how my child did in comparison to his classmates? Does it matter whether my child is compared to others his own age or in his own grade?

National norms are constructed by testing a representative sample of students from throughout the country. The sample is usually stratified in accordance with the most recent U.S. census to ensure that students in the sample are represented in proportion similar to their occurrence in the general U.S. population (Anastasi & Urbina, 1997). Samples are generally stratified to ensure representation based on sex, race, socioeconomic level (as determined by family income, parent education, or occupation), residence (urban, suburban, or rural), and geographic area of the country. The norm represents an average score for all students of a given age or grade level. Generally, it matters only slightly which norm is used, an age norm or a grade norm; however, if the child is much older or younger than the average child in the grade, the differences in derived scores may have varying consequences. For example, a student who is very young for his or her grade, being less mature than the other students in the class, may not fare as well as the older students. These variations generally become less pronounced as students become older and abilities, rather than maturity, become more important.

On a norm-referenced test the derived scores will determine whether a comparison is being made among students with like characteristics. For example, if a percentile rank or stanine is reported, a comparison to age-mates or grade-mates is being made. If the test is criterion-referenced, as are many school performance tests, the comparison is made with a given standard of mastery (i.e., pass/fail, mastery/emerging/nonmastery), rather than age-mates or grade-mates (Thorndike, 1997).

Are these tests realistic measures of my child's knowledge in a particular subject area? How do these tests help identify my child's strengths and weaknesses? My child gets a single score or grade on all his other school tests, so why do they put bars on the student results graph to give a range of scores rather than a single score?

If students are motivated to perform to the best of their abilities, the test questions accurately measure the domain of knowledge, and testing conditions do not interfere with test performance, then the assessment most likely will accurately depict student performance in a given subject or ability area (Salvia & Ysseldyke, 2001). Most standardized tests provide a score for several subject areas, and this helps determine whether a student displays significant strengths or weaknesses in the areas assessed.

Tests measure strengths and weaknesses in two ways: interpersonal and intrapersonal. Interpersonal strengths and weaknesses are determined by comparing how a student performed compared to age- or grade-mates who took the same test. For interpersonal strengths and weaknesses, a cutoff score is determined and used for decision-making purposes. For example, students performing below the 25th percentile rank may be categorized "at risk" or in need of remedial services. Thus, any score at or below the 25th percentile rank would be considered an interpersonal weakness.

Intrapersonal strengths and weaknesses compare a child's

performance in one skill area on a test to the same child's performance in all other skill areas, to see where particular talents or difficulties lie. To determine intrapersonal weaknesses, an overall average is sometimes provided, or the test scores can be averaged manually. Percentile ranks cannot be averaged because they are not equal-interval units of measurement (Anastasi & Urbina, 1997). Percentile ranks must be converted to standardized scores to be averaged, then converted back to percentile ranks. Significant deviations (strengths if the deviations are above the mean, weaknesses if the deviations are below the mean) can then be determined. A significant deviation is often determined to be one standard deviation (or a given number of standard score points) above or below the average test performance.

The bars on a summary graph are derived from a statistical concept known as *standard error of measurement* (SEM). SEM is based on a test's reliability; the more reliable a test, the smaller the bar, the less reliable the test the larger the bar (Thorndike, 1997). If a test is perfectly reliable, the bar comprises the single score the student obtained on the test. SEM is essential when considering a student's score because, contrary to popular opinion, the score a student receives on a test is usually not the "true" score because no test is perfectly reliable. Thus, it is best to consider that a student's true score falls within a range of scores, as determined by the SEM, or the bar on the graph.

Furthermore, scores can be reported at different levels of confidence (Cohen & Swerdlik, 1999). For example, if a score is reported at a 68 percent level of confidence, then given 100 alternate-form administrations of the test, the student's true score likely falls within the given range 68 times. Thus, if the child's deviation IQ score was 93 and the SEM equals 5 standard score points, with a 68 percent level of confidence, the student's true IQ is likely to fall within the IQ range of 88 to 98 (or 93 ± 5) on 68 of 100 administrations of the IQ test. Although the 68 percent level of confidence is the range most commonly reported for scores, using this level of confidence means the student's score will fall *outside* the given range on about one of every three administrations—that is, the range will be wrong 32 percent of the time. Therefore, it is better to use two SEMs to report scores at the 95 percent level of confidence. Such a range (83–103, or 93 ± 10) means the student's true score will fall outside the given range only about one time in 20, giving far more confidence in the results and in the subsequent decisions.

What does it mean when scores are very different in different areas?

This is generally an indication that the student displays relative intrapersonal strengths and weaknesses. The weaknesses often require remediation, either through additional instruction, tutoring, remedial academic services, or special education services.

Does this test reflect my child's true performance or can outside conditions, like illness or anxiety, affect the test scores?

External conditions, such as noises and illness, as well as internal factors, such as anxiety or motivation, can affect test scores for certain children. On the other hand, many children are resilient and capable of maintaining focus and attention under conditions others would find distracting. Some testing conditions have been shown to adversely affect student performance, including poor lighting, insufficient workspace, uncomfortable seating, interruptions during timed tests, and the demeanor of the examiner (Anastasi & Urbina, 1997). Even the type of response format (e.g., marking an answer on the page versus coloring in an answer bubble) can affect scores for students in grades four or lower. Illness can certainly affect performance, although the effects are child-specific.

Anxiety is a different matter. The Yerkes-Dodson law (Schafer, 1996) indicates that moderate anxiety actually maximizes student performance. Low anxiety tends to result in low performance because it usually reflects low motivation. High anxiety often leads to low performance because the student feels overwhelmed. Indeed, test anxiety (test phobia, test fright) is a common, treatable condition that may lower student performance in up to 10 percent of the school-age population.

Using Test Results

How will these tests affect my child's instruction or the school's curriculum? How will test results determine the amount of assistance my child gets or the quality of the school?

Schools and school systems differ markedly in how they use standardized test results to change curriculum and instructional practices, or to make decisions about individual student placement or services. In general, what happens as a result of student scores depends on the purpose of the test. If the purpose is to assess the effectiveness of the instruction or curriculum, the effects on individual students may be minimal, and the effects on the instructors or the curriculum may be substantial. If the curriculum is being assessed, student performance is an indicator of how closely aligned the school's curriculum and the test are with national, state, or local standards, as well as how effective the instruction is in implementing the curriculum. Because of the factor of alignment, it is important not to conclude immediately that low test scores are the result of poor teaching.

If an individual student scores well on tests, educators often use this information to provide a more challenging curriculum, such as through advanced, honors, or gifted programs. If the student performs poorly, educators often use this information to provide more academic support, such as through tutoring, remedial academic services, or special education services.

The Consequences of Testing

How much emphasis do tests like the SAT or ACT Assessment have on college admissions decisions? Can the scores determine what kind of college or job my child is prepared for?

Scores on tests such as the SAT or ACT Assessment are given different emphases by different universities. Although most institutions of higher learning require students to take an entrance exam, institutions are placing increasingly less emphasis on test scores. It is important to note that tests like the SAT were designed to predict college success, primarily during the freshman year, and they do this quite well. In general, the exclusive, competitive universities require high test scores, as well as high grade point averages, class ranks, and so on. Scores on college entrance exams have little to do with the kind of job the student may attain in the future.

In general, competitive colleges put more emphasis on test scores because test scores are objective, level the playing field, and predict college success. Thus, entrance exams act as an excellent method of screening students to move a pool of candidates to the next level. It is at this next level that letters of recommendation, extracurricular activities, and GPA become essential.

Releasing Test Results

Who sees my child's test results?

The Family Educational Rights and Privacy Act of 1974 ensures that parents and guardians have the opportunity to review, challenge, and correct their children's school records. The right to review test scores included in a child's cumulative or permanent school record is guaranteed by this act. To facilitate the dissemination of test information, school systems often send copies of test scores directly to parents and guardians as soon as the scores become available.

Besides parents and guardians, all persons with a legitimate educational interest in a particular child have access to test scores (Salvia & Ysseldyke, 2001). This may include all teachers and educational specialists who work with the child, school administrators, and other school officials. Parents have the right to request a list of all people who have access to their child's test information.

The Family Educational Rights and Privacy Act also aims to control dissemination of student information. Under the stipulations of the law, test information cannot be released without the parent or guardian's consent (or the child's consent if he or she is 18 years or older) to anyone other than those who have a legitimate educational interest in the child. For example, parent or guardian's consent must be given before test results can be released to social service agencies, law enforcement, or insurance companies. If a subpoena is issued, however, the parent or guardian's consent is not required for the release of test information.

Fair Testing

Are the tests my child takes fair?

Tests should give all students an equal opportunity to demonstrate their ability and knowledge (Childs, 1990). If a test seems not to provide equal opportunity, issues of bias must be considered. Discussions about test bias usually arise around issues of ethnicity, race, and gender. Tests are considered to be biased if individuals of the same ability but different demographic characteristics obtain different scores. Test bias is a complex issue. It may be attributed to representation or lack of representation of diverse populations in assessment materials; test administration procedures; students' knowledge of the nature of assessment; wording of test items; linguistic backgrounds; test format; or even stereotypes, attitudes, and values (Childs, 1990; Coffman & Lindquist, 1980; McMillan, 2000; Salvia & Ysseldyke, 2001).

Developers work hard to eliminate bias in tests, but no test is perfect. Although true bias must be uncovered through statistical analysis, parents and guardians can work with educators to monitor and reduce potential test bias by ensuring that all teachers and students involved in the testing understand and follow the test administration procedures; by eliminating test items or material that may be offensive to individuals of a particular ethnicity, race, or gender; and by eliminating references in a test to things or ideas that may be unfamiliar to individuals of a particular race, ethnicity, or gender.

Although issues of test bias are extremely important and complex, a more important issue may be the fair use of tests. Unfortunately, even unbiased tests can be used in unfair ways that either help or hinder particular groups of students (Childs, 1990). Perhaps the best way for educators, parents, and guardians to address the issue of fairness in testing is to ensure that a variety of tests are wisely used as components of a multifaceted assessment program (ERIC Clearinghouse on Urban Education, 2001; Garcia, 1986).

Special Accommodations

How are tests modified to meet the needs of students with special needs or different learning styles?

The primary purpose of testing is to benefit students (Salvia & Ysseldyke, 2001). To fulfill this aim, tests must be accessible and appropriate for all students. Public Law 94–142 directs schools and school systems to ensure that when a test is given to a child with a disability, the test results reflect the skills the test is supposed to measure, not the child's disability. If a test is designed to measure reading comprehension, for example, it should measure a child's ability to understand what he or she reads, not whether the child may have a visual impairment. Of course, if a test is designed to measure a child's disability, it should in fact do that.

The legal call for accurate and accessible assessment brings to light the need for test accommodations. A test accommodation "involves adapting or modifying measures to enable students with disabilities to participate in assessment" (Salvia & Ysseldyke, 2001, p. 180). Throughout the country, there is great variation in the kinds of test accommodations made. Some frequently used test accommodations include modification in the test format (e.g., large print edition of the test, Braille edition of the test), modification in the response format (e.g., respond orally, respond using a computer), modification in the ways in which the test can be taken (e.g., in a small setting, alone), and modification in the timing of the test (e.g., extended time, over several sessions). Test accommodations may also include the use of technology. Recent court decisions in some states allow students with learning disabilities to use electronic spell checking and dictation machines on tests (Ediger, 2001).

A list of appropriate test accommodations could be endless. As research on learning styles and disabilities continues to grow and educational technology continues to advance, more specific questions about legitimate test accommodations will arise. What is more important than a list of acceptable accommodations, therefore, may be an understanding of the purpose of testing and the specific needs of an individual. When facing difficult questions about test accommodations, parents, guardians, and educators may best serve students by holding fast to the spirit of laws such as Public Law 94–142, which ensure appropriate and accessible education for all students.

References

Anastasi, A., & Urbina, S. (1997). *Psychological testing* (7th ed.). Upper Saddle River, NJ: Prentice Hall.

Bagin, C. B. (1989). Talking to your high school students about standardized tests. *Practical Assessment, Research & Evaluation, 1*(4). Retrieved from http://ericae.net/pare/getvn.asp?v=1&n=4.

Bond, L. A. (1996). Norm- and criterion-referenced testing. *Practical Assessment, Research & Evaluation, 5*(2). Retrieved from http://ericae.net/pare/getvn.asp?v=5&n=2.

Childs, R. A. (1990). Gender bias and fairness. *Practical Assessment, Research & Evaluation, 2*(3). Retrieved from http://ericae.net/pare/getvn.asp?v=2&n=3.

Coffman, W. E., & Lindquist, E. F. (1980). The testing of educational achievement in children. *Journal of Negro Education, 49*(3), 312–325.

Cohen, R. J., & Swerdlik, M. E. (1999). *Psychological testing and assessment: An introduction to tests and measurement* (4th ed.). Mountain View, CA: Mayfield Publishing.

Ediger, M. (2001). *Taking tests: More time for the handicapped?* (ERIC Document Reproduction Service No. ED 455 276)

Educational Testing Service. (1999). *What every parent should know about testing.* Retrieved from http://www.ets.org/pta2.html.

Eissenberg, T. E., & Rudner, L. M. (1988). Explaining test results to parents. *Practical Assessment, Research & Evaluation, 1*(1). Retrieved from http://ericae.net/pare/getvn.asp?v=1&n=1.

Erford, B. T., Vitali, G., Haas, R., & Boykin, R. R. (1995). *Essential Skill Screener (ESS): At-risk identification.* East Aurora, NY: Slosson.

ERIC Clearinghouse on Urban Education. (2001). *Gender differences in educational achievement within racial and ethnic groups* (Report No. EDO-UD-01–3). Washington, DC: Office of Educational Research and Improvement. (ERIC Document Reproduction Service No. ED 455 341)

Garcia, P. A. (1986). The impact of national testing on ethnic minorities: With proposed solutions. *Journal of Negro Education, 55*(3), 347–357.

Kaplan, R. M., & Saccuzzo, D. P. (2001). *Psychological testing: Principles, applications and issues* (5th ed.). Belmont, CA: Wadsworth.

McMillan, J. H. (2000). Fundamental assessment principles for teachers and school administrators. *Practical Assessment, Research & Evaluation, 7*(18). Retrieved from http://ericae.net/pare/getvn.asp?v=7&n=18.

Mehrens, W. A. (1989). Preparing students to take standardized achievement tests. *Practical Assessment, Research & Evaluation, 1*(11). Retrieved from http://ericae.net/pare/getvn.asp?v=1&n=11.

Popham, W. J. (2000). *Modern educational measurement: Practical guidelines for educational leaders* (3rd ed.). Needham, MA: Pearson Educational Company.

Salvia, J., & Ysseldyke, J. (2001). *Assessment* (8th ed.). Boston, MA: Houghton Mifflin.

Schafer, W. (1996). *Stress management for wellness* (3rd ed.). Fort Worth, TX: Harcourt Brace.

Thorndike, R. L. (1997). *Measurement and evaluation in psychology and education* (6th ed.). Upper Saddle River, NJ: Merrill/Prentice Hall.

Chapter 40
Steps in the Right Direction
Reporting Assessment Results to Students, Parents, School Board Members, and the Media

Edward Roeber

Using test results to improve instruction is vital to improving our education system, but equally important is to report results to other stakeholders. These stakeholders include the students who took the test, their parents or guardians, other parents in the school or district, the local school board, and the public at large (Frechtling & Myerberg, 1983). Effective reporting is essential if the data have been and will be used to improve student learning (Gucwa & Mastie, 1989; Roeber & Carr, 1983, Roeber & Mastie, 1999).

The purpose of this chapter is to describe some ways in which educators can report assessment results to various audiences so that they build public confidence and support, strengthen the parent's role in schooling, and help students learn about the challenging standards being assessed.

Reporting Assessment Results to Students

This section addresses reporting assessment results to students: why the results should be reported, how the reporting should be handled, and the resources that are available for this process.

Why Results Should Be Reported to Students

Students want to know how they did on the assessment. In fact, letting them know how well they did, as well as how they will be helped to improve, can go a long way toward motivating them to take the assessment seriously and give it their best effort, particularly if they are informed of the teacher's intentions to use the results in advance of taking the test. Experienced teachers know that the feedback they provide to students can help motivate students to work hard. If they respond to each piece of student work—every homework assignment, every quiz, every paper, and every test—promptly and thoroughly, students will tend to give their work their best effort.

Another advantage of providing feedback to students is that it increases the likelihood that the student will remain actively engaged in learning. If they know which standards and skills they have achieved and which they still need to improve, they are more likely to work on the skills they lack. When this feedback is communicated to them as part of a goal-setting process in which the student plays a role, the student is even more likely to take ownership of the problem and participate in the solution to it.

How Results Should Be Reported to Students

A two-step process is recommended for reporting large-scale assessment results to students. First, the teacher should provide an overview of the assessment results to all students in the class. Then, the teacher should provide interpretation and goal-setting sessions for students individually.

During the group interpretation process, the teacher should

- remind students of the large-scale assessment they took
- explain the purposes for taking that test
- inform students that the results have been returned
- explain the general types of uses to which the district, school, and classroom results will be put
- describe how the teacher will assist students and parents in interpreting and understanding the results
- explain how to read the individual report of results (if reports of results are distributed to students in the group setting)

In the subsequent individual follow-up sessions, teachers should help students understand the significance of how well they performed on the test and how the information will be used to plan instruction for the immediate future. The teacher should adhere to the following guidelines for each session:

- Focus on the standards and skills the student has or has not met or learned, not on the number of items answered correctly or whether the student passed or failed the test.
- Encourage and reinforce both achievement and effort shown.
- Discourage comparisons among students, emphasizing instead the need for each individual to achieve the standards and skills assessed.

Steps

- Develop a plan of action to address the educational needs of the student.
- Discuss how the student can participate in planning and carrying out the plan to address these needs.

In most settings, these meetings will result in a specific but informal agreement about the steps to take to assist each student. In some cases, however, the teacher and student will need to create formal agreements about what services will be provided and the manner in which these services will be provided. This agreement should include a description of responsibilities, schedules, and signatures.

This two-step process, using both a group report and individual student follow-up sessions, will work in most settings. For example, at the elementary level, the classroom teacher should be able to carry out both types of meetings. At the secondary level, it may be advisable for a school counselor or principal to conduct the group meeting, perhaps as an assembly. Classroom teachers, school counselors, or both might hold the individual student meetings, depending on whether the likely plan will include remedial instruction in existing classes, or the student will be asked to enroll in different or additional courses in the subject area assessed (particularly if the student is not taking a class in the area assessed).

Resources to Use in the Reporting Process

A variety of materials and resources are available for teachers and counselors to use during one or both of the steps in reporting the results of large-scale assessments to students. The following materials are useful in planning the group report:

- the explanatory materials returned with the large-scale assessment results, particularly for the individual student report (it may be helpful to duplicate for the students the section of these materials that explains how to read and report the results)
- information on the district and school plans for using the assessment results for instructional review and improvement
- information on how and when parents will receive the individual student results
- information on who will hold the individual student sessions and when they will be held, with a schedule for students to use when signing up for their individual sessions

The following materials may be helpful for conducting the individual student sessions:

- descriptions of the standards and skills assessed
- a sample copy of the test, if use of the test is permitted during interpretive sessions following testing (in some secure testing programs, this is not permitted)
- the student's individual report of the assessment results (a copy for both the teacher and the student)
- written plans for helping the student learn the skills assessed

Summary

No one at school or in the home can work to improve the performance of a student on the standards and skills measured by the large-scale assessment program unless the individual student actively participates in planning the learning activities. In order for that to occur, students must learn specifically how they did, the significance of their performance, and how they can improve. The large-scale assessment program can provide one important source of information, as can other types of information about the student. Specific feedback on performance is a vital part of the process of improving student performance.

Reporting Assessment Results to Parents and Guardians

The emphasis of this section is on reporting assessment results to parents and guardians, both those of students who were assessed and of students who attend the same school as the students assessed. This section addresses why and how the results should be reported to parents, who should report the results, the resources available to assist in reporting, and strategies for accurate and efficient reporting. (Throughout, I use *parent* to signify the parent, guardian, or other designated caregiver of the student.)

Why Results Should Be Reported to Parents

All parents want to know how well the students in their child's school performed, what the school will be doing to improve instruction, and, for the parents of the students who were assessed, what the school will do to help their child do better (Barber, 1992). Are their children exceeding, meeting, or failing to meet the performance standards set for the assessments? The standards and skills measured by the assessment program are often the most critical to the academic success of students, a fact that many parents already know. The assessment results will give parents one indication of how well students are meeting these standards. Sharing results with parents is an excellent way of telling them how well their children are learning the most important skills schools are trying to teach.

Parental concern and involvement are crucial in helping students learn. Research has shown that parental involvement in academic achievement is a critical factor in promoting better student performance (Coleman, 1983). Sharing results with parents can enable cooperative planning by teachers, parents, and students to improve student performance.

Parents also want to know how the school and the school district are doing. In many states, freedom of information acts require that existing information about public schools, such as school and school district test summaries, be made available or be released to the public. Wise educators realize that large-scale assessment programs generate considerable public interest. These educators plan for the release of the results through formal public presentations as well as written reports sent home to parents or included with school newsletters. Formal public presentations reach those parents who do not visit the school yet are interested in how well the school is performing.

How Results Should Be Reported

By taking steps to report test results directly to parents, rather than relying on the news media, schools have a unique opportunity to tell their own story—including what will be done with the results—and perhaps reduce the opportunity for misinterpretation or misrepresentation of the results. The importance of developing an accurate initial school interpretation of the results cannot be overemphasized. A school should share the test results, and the school's interpretation of them, with parents as soon as possible after receiving the information. Being the first party to report to parents the status and progress of student performance is an excellent way to improve public relations at the building level.

Schools should plan to report student and school assessment results. Three activities are involved in this planning: (a) staff preparation; (b) review and interpretation of the test results; and (c) development of an action plan. Sharing test results effectively with parents and guardians, which can be considered the fourth step in this planning sequence, requires careful preliminary work. When the meaning of the results has not been determined and plans for use have not been developed, it becomes difficult for staff members to report the results in a meaningful way, without sounding defensive or indifferent about the results. Through careful planning, staff can convey a thoughtful, concerned attitude that parents will appreciate and support.

The school or teacher should emphasize the following items when communicating individual results to parents and guardians:

- the individual results themselves
- the relationship between the assessment results and other student achievement information
- the plan of action proposed for the student
- the parents' or guardians' role in helping implement the plan

The plan should be the one that the teacher and student have developed during the process of examining the results. Each individual student report should emphasize both the strengths and the weaknesses uncovered, the extent to which this report supports or contradicts other information about the student, and how the teacher and parents or guardians can work together to help the student make improvements.

The school or teacher should emphasize the following items when reporting group results:

- the group results themselves
- the relationship of the assessment results to other information about the group's achievement
- the school's proposed plans of action

In developing the official school interpretation, school staff members should

- reach an understanding of what the assessment results mean
- relate the assessment results to other achievement results, to derive a more complete picture of student performance
- relate all performance information to the instructional program that the school is implementing

Who Should Share the Results?

In elementary schools, the classroom teacher typically bears the responsibility of reporting individual student results. At the middle school or high school levels, this responsibility may be carried out by classroom teachers or by guidance counselors, often the latter if the student is not enrolled in a class in the area assessed. The school results are typically reported by the building principal, the counselor, department heads, or others designated to carry out these responsibilities.

Steps

Resources to Use in the Reporting Process

Each assessment program will produce somewhat different resources for reporting assessment results, such as any of the following examples:

- reports of individual student assessment results
- reports for parents of individual student assessment results
- school summaries of assessment results
- materials for explaining and interpreting these reports
- sample or actual test booklets to illustrate the test that students were given

Four Parent Reporting Strategies

There are four different ways in which to report the assessment results to parents. The strategies may be used as is, or be combined or adapted to fit the individual needs of the school or district. Each requires preliminary preparation, including familiarizing oneself with the assessment program, reviewing the reports of results, analyzing and interpreting the results, setting student goals, and developing a plan of action.

<u>Individual Parent-Teacher Conferences</u>

The parent-teacher conference is the most desirable means of reporting individual results to parents. Its single disadvantage is that it reaches only those parents willing to attend and must be supplemented by other means for the remaining parents. Its advantages are many:

- providing for two-way communication between teachers and parents
- personalizing the test results
- personalizing the plan of action
- getting parents actively involved in the education of their children

<u>Individual Student Report Sent Home</u>

If conferences cannot be arranged, the individual student report should be mailed or sent home with the student. A cover letter should explain the assessment program and the assessment report for parents, summarize the student's strengths and weaknesses as indicated by the results, outline any necessary plans for remediation, and encourage the parents to contact the school for further information.

Sending the student report home is far less desirable than holding an in-person conference, but it may be the only open avenue of communication between school and home. Even though it may be necessary to report results in this manner, the school should still provide an individual interpretation of the results and not just send the report home without any interpretation.

Parent Group Meeting

An open meeting for parents enables reporting of the school assessment data to both the parents of students tested and the parents of students who were not involved in the assessment program but who will be or have been.

Teachers or counselors can share individual student assessment results as a follow-up activity after the formal meeting. A school can either mail the parent a copy of the individual assessment results with an invitation to come to the meeting, or distribute the parent copy of individual assessment results to parents at the meeting (with individual parent-teacher conferences following the presentation of the school results at the group meeting).

The group meeting has several advantages:

- It provides parents with a clear understanding of the assessment program, such as why the tests are given, what is assessed, and how the results are reported and used.
- It creates a setting in which to discuss the overall instructional plan and achievement goals of the school.
- It provides a vehicle for putting the assessment results into the larger context of the total school program.
- The individual results and improvement plans can be put into the larger context of school improvement plans.
- The group meeting can involve the entire staff.

A disadvantage is that it reaches only those parents who attend the meeting. The opportunity for two-way communication, however, makes the meeting the most desirable method of sharing the assessment results with parents of the total school population.

Newsletter or Letter to Parents

The school assessment results can be communicated to parents and the school community at large through a prepared article or short written report printed in school newsletters, parent newsletters, or letters to parents. The written document should be clear, concise, and written for the layperson, using a minimum of educational or assessment jargon. It should address the following points:

- an overview of the school results, findings, and recommendations
- factors affecting the school results
- uses of the results at the classroom or school level
- how individual student results will be made available—either from classroom teachers or via the mail
- what the school is doing to improve achievement in the areas of identified weakness

Summary

Reporting individual student and school assessment results to parents offers a unique opportunity to review student progress, set goals, and elicit parent support and participation. Schools should consider the best strategies or combination of strategies for reporting results: through parent-teacher conferences, by sending reports home, through a combination of group and individual meetings, or by using a school newsletter or general letter to parents.

Reporting Assessment Results to the School Board

One of the important audiences for assessment results is the local board of education. As the entity responsible for the education of students, this group has a vital interest in the performance of students on the assessment. School boards expect school administrators to provide them with information in a timely manner and in a format they can easily understand. They have many issues to consider and a great deal of information to absorb in a relatively short period of time. Most board members are laypeople, albeit with considerable interest and experience in education. They need help in understanding the assessment program, its purposes, it uses, and its reports if they are to provide the types of support needed to help schools and students improve. Hence, reporting to the school board is an important step in the overall assessment process.

Why Results Should Be Reported to the School Board

The natural tension that exists between local educators and their school board often makes reporting assessment results to the board an onerous task. The pressures coming from the media and outspoken parents make reporting even more sensitive. Having a prepared, systematic plan for using and reporting the assessment results can help to make reporting a routine activity and remove much of the accompanying anxiety. The ideas presented here are tied to the principle espoused throughout this document that reporting the assessment results, and planning for their use, are two aspects of a single process, not separate and unrelated activities (Caswell & Roeber, 1983a).

It is ideal to initiate reporting of assessment results *before the assessment results are returned to the school district.* Providing background information will help the school board understand the purposes of the assessment program before they focus on the actual assessment scores. Explaining the assessment before reporting the results clarifies for board members that the purpose of the assessment program is not simply to provide box-score comparative data, but to provide a means to help students learn and to assist schools as they fine-tune their instructional programs.

Planning a Reporting Program

An organized plan for reporting assessment results and related information to the local school board and also to district staff and administrators helps to manage staff time efficiently and to minimize surprises. To develop a reporting plan, identify important school events and activities, in advance if possible, then determine potential audiences and possible reporting activities for each event. Assign responsibilities for preparing and giving the reports and provide appropriate schedules.

Three different types of reports should form the basis of the reporting campaign (Roeber, Donovan & Cole, 1980). The first report to the school board should be the background report. This report should be done before the results are available so that the board can focus on the purposes of the assessment program and the uses to which the results will be put. The report should explain the purposes for the assessment program; provide facts about who will be assessed, and when and how they will be assessed; and indicate when the results will become available and how the results will be used (e.g., at the student, classroom, school, and school district levels) and reported (e.g., to parents, students, educators, and the public).

The second report to the school board is the report of assessment results. This is the report that will be the most challenging to prepare. It should contain the district-level scores, the building-level scores, and state and national scores (if available); an interpretation of the scores from the perspective of each school, the district, and the state or nation (if available); information on how these assessment results are similar to other available achievement information and an explanation of any differences; and a description of how the results will be used at the school level and reported at the school and district levels.

The third report to the school board is a follow-up report on the information provided in the first two reports. Either the background report or the results report may contain statements about steps the schools or the district intend to follow after the data are received and reported; it is therefore important to provide periodic follow-up reports to the school board, giving updates on the progress in using the assessment information at the student, classroom, or school levels. This will help ensure that the school board focuses more on the *improvement* purposes of the assessment program and less on the *comparative* uses often made of the assessment information.

The Background Report

The background report provides the opportunity to discuss assessment without any assessment results to distract the board members' attention. The purposes of the assessment program can be described in some detail independent of natural concerns about whether scores are up or down, or better or worse than neighboring districts or the state or nation. In planning the background report, include the following four parts:

Basic facts about the assessment program. Include facts such as the grades at which assessment takes place, the subjects assessed, the nature of the assessments—standards-based, norm-referenced, and so forth—and the types of assessment items used (perhaps with released samples of each item type).

Purposes of the assessment program. Emphasize the purposes of the program at the student, classroom, school, and district levels. Mention any purposes the board members may assume are relevant to the assessment but that are not intended uses of the information.

Uses of the assessment results. Describe how an individual classroom teacher might use the results, as well as how a school improvement team might use the school results, to help board members see that the primary purpose for the program is instructional improvement.

Steps

District reporting plans. Conclude with the district plan for reporting the assessment results to the school board, parents, educators, and news media. Let board members know when additional board reports will be planned. Finally, let the board know how and when parents of the students assessed will receive their children's results.

The Report of Assessment Results

The second of the three reports that each district should make to its board is the report of assessment results. This report is crucial in establishing what meaning the assessment results have for the district, the schools, and the students. This report to the school board often becomes a report to the news media, who may be attending the meeting or may regularly receive written school board reports.

The results report has four basic parts:

1. Review of assessment program information: A review of the information covered in the background report will serve to remind board members of basic information about the assessment program and its primary purposes.
2. Report of district results: This is the meat of the results report and should contain answers to the following questions:
    - How did we do this year?
    - Has performance improved over recent years in each of the areas assessed?
    - If so, why? If not, why not?

    The percentages of students achieving a proficient level or passing the assessment are the easiest numbers to understand. The report of results should focus on these numbers first when answering the questions listed above.

    If additional reporting levels are used (e.g., advanced or novice), or if results are disaggregated or reported by skill area or content standard (or subunits within these), these numbers can also be reported, but they should not have the same prominence in the report as the percentages of students who passed or achieved proficiency. One way to report additional result information is to follow the overall presentation of results with additional sections that focus briefly on these additional data. Alternatively, these data can be used to answer particular questions as they are asked. For example, in responding to the question about improvement, the report might mention that although the percentage of students at the proficient level or above has not changed much, the percentage of students in the bottom performance level (e.g., novice) has declined sharply.

In reporting changes in student performance, it is important to be modest in claims of improvement (what goes up could well go down in the future) and to be open in acknowledging declines in student performance. (It is better to tell the story yourself and provide appropriate explanations than to have board members or the media discover and interpret the declines.) Although the reasons for improvement or decline in scores may not be known, the declines may encourage a more detailed review to determine the causes. If so, the plans for this review should be mentioned in the report.

The report of assessment results should downplay comparisons among districts or among schools within the district because these comparisons can be misleading. Such comparisons too easily get translated into success and failure judgments of the entire school, the school program, and the school faculty, based on only a small piece of the total picture.

3. Implications of the results: Answer the "so what?" questions clearly, concisely, and honestly. School teams should be involved in developing interpretations of the results and could be involved in reporting these interpretations to the school board. They have firsthand knowledge of student capabilities and what students have been taught, and they can describe the implications of the results for individual students (in summary form) and for the school's instructional program.
4. Plans to use the results: This section of the results report can describe each school's plans to use the results, as well as the district plans to coordinate these efforts, particularly across schools. In addition, because the report to the board may also be the first public release of the information to the news media, the district's and schools' plans to release the results to parents and other citizens should be highlighted.

Follow-up Reports

After reporting the results and the plans for using them, it is logical to report back to the school board throughout the year on the progress made in using the results to improve learning opportunities for students. The following suggested topics are useful in these follow-up reports:

- specific areas of need selected as priority for review
- results of the instructional review process
- new instruction or services contemplated as a result of the instructional review
- planned follow-up assessments of students or schools after remediation
- special activities (awards, summer programs, Saturday programs, and so forth) planned as a result of assessment

Multiple follow-up reports may be used to highlight the different activities taking place in different schools, or in schools at different levels. The follow-up reports may be in writing only, or may involve teachers, administrators, parents, or students presenting some aspect of the program.

Summary

Although the model presented here is not the only possible approach to presenting results, it is effective in focusing the attention of school board members on the instructional uses of the assessment program and in avoiding inappropriate uses of the data. Remember: Assessment results are only as good as the uses to which they are put. An effective plan for reporting results to the school board must be accompanied by appropriate efforts to use the results to review and revise curriculum and instruction as needed.

Reporting Assessment Results to the Public

Reporting, or more accurately, *explaining* the results of assessment programs to the public, via the news media, is the focus of this section. The approach presented here emphasizes once again the connection between the assessment result reports and plans for using the results. As was the case with reporting to the school board, reports to the public should include information about how the results will be used to improve instruction. This will not only make the data more meaningful, it will convey the equally important aspect that the school district is actively

Steps

taking steps to improve teaching and learning, thereby building public support for the improvements being sought (Caswell & Roeber, 1983b). Included in this section is information about

- contacting reporters
- formatting data
- organizing the information
- developing the district reporting program

Getting Started

A majority of citizens in most school districts do not have school-age children, so they do not have much direct contact with local educators. Although parents see the schools in action and hear about them in many ways, average citizens form impressions of the schools based largely on what they hear or see in the news media. Because the media help shape public opinion, educators should work closely with representatives of the news media to ensure they provide the public with accurate and complete information about schools.

Keep in mind, too, that there are other ways of reaching the public. District newsletters and school letters sent to all citizens are just two additional means. The focus of this chapter is on reporting to the public, not reporting to the news media, although it does focus on how to work with news media in reporting the results.

Working with news reporters, especially when presenting assessment results from external programs, may seem difficult to do well. With some preplanning and a few basic ideas, however, school personnel can confidently share assessment results with the public through the media (Perlman, 1985). Reporting to the public should include the following steps:

1. Plan for the use of data. Using scores and reporting scores are closely related activities, and both need to be planned for at the beginning of the school year, regardless of when the administration of the assessment and the reporting of results take place. This will help ensure that the important use and reporting activities take place throughout the entire school year, not just when assessment results are received.

   It is easier to report the results when school officials know what they mean and what will be done as a consequence. Early reports will help the news media understand the purpose of the assessment program, how the results are used to benefit students, and why using the scores for comparative purposes is not the most important use of the assessment results. Reporting information about how the results will be used to strengthen the instructional program and address student weaknesses addresses the "so what?" aspect of reporting the results.

2. Determine purpose and goals. At the beginning of the year, determine the purposes for communication of assessment results. Before testing even starts, district personnel need to have a clear understanding of what it is they want to accomplish by reporting results. Some districts are using assessment reporting as a way to begin a yearlong district information program. Reporting assessment results can be an ongoing effort that begin long before the day the results are released.

Successful school communicators begin the reporting process by explaining the purposes and limitations of the assessment program before the results are received. Then they present the results later with other important measures of school district accomplishments, provide follow-up reports on their progress toward implementing the plans outlined in the previous reports, and wrap up the year by evaluating the success of their efforts.

Selecting reporting goals is also helpful. Such goals need not be limited to the assessment program. These assessment reporting goals might include the following ideas:

- making people in the community aware of the proper use of the assessment results
- encouraging teachers and school administrators to use the assessment results
- convincing the public that educators are concerned about student achievement
- convincing people to support the schools, particularly as educators strive to make improvements in them

3. Think ahead. Designing a district reporting program involves addressing a number of important issues:
   - Who needs to know what assessment information?
   - What steps can be taken to ensure that those who need to know get the information?
   - What are the different possible ways to present the information, and which ones work best for each

audience?
- What steps can be taken to ensure that distributed information is complete, covers major points, and is understandable to those who know very little about the proper uses and limitations of the assessment program?
- What additional information is needed during the year?
- Has the communication program accomplished its intended purposes?

Answers to the following questions may help clarify the previous questions:
- What information about assessment do typical members of the public currently possess?
- Are their interpretations of the information accurate?
- What is their attitude toward this and other assessment programs?
- Who else is talking to them about assessment, and what are those voices saying?
- How does the audience feel about the source of the information, such as the test publisher or school district? What is their level of trust?

4. Decide whose job it is to report to the public. It is also helpful to decide who within the school district will have primary responsibility for organizing the communications program and working with the news media. Ideally, one person who has the time to do the planning and preparation activities recommended in this chapter should be responsible for working with the media.

   If the district has a public information director, that person should coordinate coverage of the results of testing just like any other report. This communications person, the assessment director, and the instructional director should work as a team—the public information director arranging for and hosting briefing sessions for reporters; the assessment director interpreting the results and answering questions about the results reports; and the instructional director adding how the students assessed will be helped, how school instructional programs will be reviewed and improved, and how results will be reported to parents. The public information director writes the news release about the results, but the assessment and instructional staff provide the content for the release. In small districts without a person who regularly handles the media, one person will have to handle all reporting tasks. This may be an assistant superintendent, a building principal, a guidance counselor, or perhaps the superintendent.

Developing Contacts

To develop a list of news media persons you wish to release information to, begin by personally contacting each newspaper, radio, and television station in the school district area. This contact should be made long before the first report is to be released. The initial contact at the newspaper will probably be an editor. Ask whether one reporter has been assigned to the "education beat." If not, the contact person may continue to be the editor you first contacted. The contact may also be a news reporter who regularly attends school board meetings.

Remember the radio and television stations that serve your community. Even if the district is just one of many in a station's service area, broadcasters may appreciate a brief report of the assessment results. Direction of the news in a radio or television station usually rests with the news director. In the absence of someone in that position, contact the program director. After establishing contact, ask when it would be convenient to stop by for a visit. If you're too far away to drop in for a visit, ask how and in what format the written report of assessment results should be provided.

If you make a get-acquainted visit, keep it brief. Editors and reporters are usually pressed for time. Ask about deadlines and how copy should be presented to them. Let them know when the assessment results are expected and that you will contact them again when the information is available. Arrange a mutually convenient time for a background session prior to the release of the results. Personal contact will help media representatives accurately report what will be a complex news story.

Later, when the results are released, provide reporters with detailed reports and charts or graphs. The press will cover the main points, and radio and television media will summarize. Don't be disappointed if the media do not carry all of the report. What is said or printed, and how the message is absorbed by readers and listeners, is really more important than the level of detail of the message.

Steps

Don't forget to follow up. Whether the media report is positive or negative, provide the reporter with a reaction to what was said or printed. Try to emphasize the positive aspects of the report; mention, but do not dwell on, the negative aspects. Find out, if necessary, how communication could have been clearer. This type of follow-up leads to better reporting each year. These contacts can help in other reporting activities as well.

The Background Report

If reporters are given assessment results without any advance preparation, their attention may naturally focus on the comparative nature of the results: which district scored the highest or lowest, which school buildings outperformed others, whose results were most surprising, and so forth. That is why many school districts, after making preliminary contact with editors and news reporters, will arrange a session to report background information prior to the actual distribution of assessment results. Such a session, held shortly before assessment results are to be reported, might be held when testing is taking place (a newsworthy event in itself) or a few weeks before the results are released. This session provides the news media with background copy for their advance story on the upcoming release of the test data, and provides an opportunity to focus on the real purposes of the assessment and uses of the results. Reporters should be told the purpose of the assessment, what it measures, the scoring methods, how to read and understand the test reports, keys to interpretation, and how the results will be used by teachers and other district personnel.

The Results Report

School and district personnel will undoubtedly spend many hours analyzing the assessment results and preparing the written reports of results. The written report will usually be several pages long, with graphs and charts attached. When presenting the results to the school board, some of these graphs and charts will be used to convey the results, showing the overall performance of students at each grade assessed, the breakdown of performance in several different ways, and analysis of performance over time, if available. Listening to this extensive presentation, media representatives may ask, "Could you tell me in a sentence or two what the results mean?" The presenter, who may have talked for half an hour or longer, may be taken aback; however, the reporter is not trying to disregard a thorough or complex story, nor show disrespect. He or she may study the report thoroughly before writing the article, but the request to "boil it down" is a request to find a summary that provides a quick and accurate overview of the test results.

Good communicators are prepared to give reporters the basic information they will need in order to develop the "lead," or introductory paragraph for their story. In fact, a well-written press release gives an overview of the salient facts and outcomes at the beginning and then fills in the details. This type of report is different from those we normally write, where we give all the background first, then the big picture: our conclusions. Plans to report individual student results to parents should also be presented to reporters, because if they mention this in their stories, parents are more likely to learn that the assessment results are available to them and request to see the results.

The complete display of the assessment data that has been prepared for the school board should also be distributed to the news media. To assist the news media in focusing on a few pieces of the overall story, however, the written report should emphasize just a few of the graphs and charts that best support the key points of the story. Graphs should be designed to develop the theme of year-to-year comparisons, comparisons of skill areas, and district-to-state comparisons. Discourage reporters from comparing schools or districts to each other because these comparisons are unfair and do not promote the types of school improvement activities that lead to improved student performance.

It may be helpful to brief reporters on the assessment report shortly before its release at either a separate news conference or a school board meeting. This will enable district personnel to review results and answer questions before the actual report is released. It will permit reporters to better understand the results as well.

Follow-up Reports

When follow-up reports are scheduled for presentation to the school board, news releases describing the types of activities that occurred after the assessment results had been analyzed should also be prepared for the news media. These reports are most effective when they feature tangible activities, such as the purchase and use of new instructional materials, the attendance of teachers at professional development events (and how teachers will be using the new skills they have learned), and so forth.

Hints for Working With the Media

In addition to the advice given thus far, the following hints will help educators work successfully with the news media:

- Begin all reporting on assessment with a quick review of the purposes and limitations of the assessment program.
- Make sure the information given will help the reporter or editor understand and interpret the report.
- Use plain English.
- Be very clear about what it is that the school district intends to do with the assessment results. Be direct.
- Don't try to cover up results that aren't as good as you would like them to be. Don't try to diminish their importance. Don't try to blame others for the lower-than-desired performance. The public will view negatively any attempts to avoid accepting the results.
- Give reporters a list of the student performance measures used in the school district and a summary of how well students did on each of these measures.
- Help the media paint a more complete picture of student performance by giving them data they can use to do so. These may include longitudinal comparisons, district test or college entrance test performance, and other measures of students, such as the number gaining entrance to college, the military, or gainful employment. These data help place the assessment results in a broader context.
- At least once a year, carefully evaluate the communications program. Do reporters, parents, and other citizens now understand assessment? Which of the several ways used to try to reach this audience seemed to work the best? Which conveyed the most information most accurately? Did the press refrain from making unfair comparisons this year?
- Don't surprise anyone. Let the school staff, administration, school board, public, and press know ahead of time that the test results are to be released.
- Cover the inside first. Provide a simple but clear interpretation for all insiders—those building administrators who will be carrying the message to their staff members. Prepare the graphs and charts they will need to assist them. Provide the tools teachers will need to assist them in understanding and using the test data.

- Practice audience identification. Ask yourself four simple questions when you start to plan for the release of testing information: Who needs to know this? When should the identified audiences first hear the information? What's the best way to get this information to each audience? What will each audience be most interested in?

Help the Media Interpret to the Public

Develop a positive working relationship with the news media who will have the job of digesting and reporting your results to the public. Help them as needed to understand and develop an interpretation of the results.

Start with a simple explanation. When you begin the public disclosure of the results, explain the purpose of the assessment program, what the media can and can't reveal about schools, and how the information will be used.

Sum up what the results mean. Make it a point to compare this year's district results with last year's, as long as the programs are comparable. If they aren't, make sure to point this out, including simple explanations of how they are different. See if you can relate these assessment results to other tests given in your school district. Explain in simple terms what the large-scale or national comparisons mean and what they don't mean. Try comparing your district results to what you thought your district should achieve. Be cautious, however, when comparing results within your district or across districts.

Tell what will be done with the results. Indicate the district's plan to work on the weak areas found in the report, as well as to develop the strengths discovered. Explain what administrators, teachers, and others plan to do with the results.

Take the testing story to targeted groups.
Don't expect the news media to do the entire job of public reporting. There are important audiences to reach in other ways, such as through in-person presentations, special written reports, or meetings. After test results have been reported, make a special effort to communicate the results to community opinion leaders in these ways.

Summary

The importance of quickly and accurately reporting results cannot be overemphasized. The strategies suggested in this chapter emphasize the need to preplan a comprehensive reporting campaign that uses the media to reach many important audiences, particularly through the background report and the results report. Although this is not the only approach to reporting you can use, it helps to focus attention on the instructional uses of assessment programs. This in turn may help avoid the use of assessment programs as the sole external evaluation of school systems, which is a misuse of the assessment information. This comprehensive reporting approach can also help ensure that the results are used to improve student learning, the most frequently cited purpose for assessment programs.

References

Barber, B. (1992, Spring). Policies for reporting test results to parents. *Educational Measurement: Issues and Practices, 11*(1), 15–20.

Caswell, M. S., & Roeber, E. (1983a). *Reporting test results to the board.* Lansing, MI: Michigan Department of Education.

Caswell, M. S., & Roeber, E. (1983b). *Reporting test results to the public.* Lansing, MI: Michigan Department of Education.

Coleman, G. J. (1983). *Reporting test results to parents.* Lansing, MI: Michigan Department of Education.

Frechtling, J. A., & Myerberg, N. J. (1983, December). *Reporting test scores to different audiences.* Princeton, NJ: ERIC Clearinghouse on Tests, Measurement, and Evaluation.

Gucwa, B., & Mastie, M. (1989). *Pencils down: A guide to using and reporting testing results.* Lansing, MI: Michigan Department of Education.

Perlman, C. L. (1985, April). *Reporting test results to the public: Exploring the doughnut.* Paper presented at the 1985 National Council on Measurement in Education Annual Meeting.

Roeber, E., & Carr, R. (1983). *Using and reporting test results: Steps in the right direction.* Lansing, MI: Michigan Department of Education.

Roeber, E., Donovan, D., & Cole, R. (1980, December). Telling the statewide testing story . . . and living to tell it again. *Phi Delta Kappan, 62*(4), 273–274.

Roeber, E. D., & Mastie, M. (1999). *Steps in the right direction: A guide to using and reporting assessment results.* Dover, NH: Measured Progress.

Chapter 41
Facilitating Career Development
Assessment and Interpretation Practices

Thomas F. Harrington & Richard W. Feller

As academic assessment drives education reform, the National Commission on the High School Senior Year (2001) has advocated making K–12 and postsecondary curriculum and assessment seamless, raising achievement for all students, and providing rigorous curriculum alternatives. Career assessments play a key role in shaping the career decisions of students and stimulating a seamless transition for the 63 percent of high school graduates who currently continue on to postsecondary education (Jamieson, Curry, & Martinez, 2001). As Herr (2001) suggests, "Assessment, including career assessment, is being expected to perform roles and functions that are unprecedented in its history" (p. 15). Beyond trained school counselors, few educators learn about the opportunities provided through career assessment, however. Recognizing the strong relationship between academic achievement and career options, we review in this chapter the major career assessments, their unique purposes, some technical considerations, and the types of scores used. We suggest ways to enhance interpretation of career assessments using high-speed computers, Internet storage capacity and accessibility, and the ability to provide vicarious experiences through multimedia.

Current career development programs succeed to the degree that they align with an institution's educational mission. Strong programs are accountable for competency attainment in self-knowledge, career and educational exploration, career planning, and self-advocacy. Career assessments are heavily used as specific interventions and as tools to evaluate program outcomes. In addition, cognitive measures of abilities, aptitudes, and achievements provide important information useful in course and program selection. Still, the most frequently used tool for career planning and counseling remains the interest inventory.

Theory as Guide

A Counselor's Guide to Career Assessment Instruments, fourth edition (Kapes & Whitfield, 2001) presents the most recent professional reviews of 56 major career development instruments. Many of the interest inventories covered by the *Counselor's Guide* are based on the Holland model of career development, the most researched theory of career choice (Holland, 1997). There are several advantages to basing an interest inventory on a theoretical construct: It offers the user confidence that he or she is following an appropriate model in working with a client; concepts have been researched; and it broadens the use of interest inventory results because they can be integrated with other concepts covered by the theory.

The Holland model describes people and environments; that is, jobs or academic concentrations of study, with a set of six names: Realistic, Investigative, Artistic, Social, Enterprising, and Conventional. The RIASEC model (an acronym derived from the first letters of the six names), assesses the personality types of each individual and matches the person with corresponding environments requiring similar personality characteristics. Thus, many interest inventories assess an individual on six scales. The first sentence of the definition covers interest, whereas the second sentence describes the associated personality descriptions:

Realistic people enjoy physical activities that involve working and building with their hands, with machinery and mechanical tools, and with plants and animals. They like to see concrete results from their involvement and perceive themselves as physically strong.

Investigative people like science, mathematics, and computers. They tend to enjoy studying and mental activities that involve ideas, thinking, and problem solving.

Artistic people involve themselves in self-expressive activities such as music, dance, acting, design, writing, and entertaining. They perceive themselves as creative, independent, and not needing to follow prescribed rules.

Social people enjoy helping, teaching, and providing service to others. Typically, they are good communicators, have strong verbal skills, and can relate well with others and understand how others feel.

Enterprising people enjoy business activities that involve leading, decision making, persuading, selling, and making money. Many are outgoing, comfortable in dealing with people, and willing to accept the responsibility of making choices that affect others.

Conventional people like structure, are skilled in the use of words and numbers, and frequently are involved in activities such as performing office operations. They are comfortable with following procedures and rules; they accept carrying out other people's directions and policies, and value financial success and status.

Interest inventory results generally are interpreted by matching a person's two or three highest RIASEC interest scale scores with jobs or educational programs that involve the same two or three domains.

For example, if a person's highest interest scores were SIA (Social-Investigative-Artistic), clinical psychology or nursing would be suggested as possible jobs or college majors. Why? Because research has shown that employed clinical psychologists describe themselves as people oriented (social), as working with medically and mentally diagnosed conditions (investigative), and as needing to communicate well to deal with their clients' unique problems (artistic). Employed nurses also describe themselves foremost as skilled in working with people (social) within a medical setting (investigative). They need to be good communicators as they deal with diverse populations and a variety of unique procedures (artistic). Their activities, however, may involve more social and investigative than artistic activities. A good reference to assist in matching people with jobs is the *Dictionary of Holland Occupational Codes,* 3rd ed. (Gottfredson & Holland, 1996).

A Counselor's Guide to Career Assessment Instruments lists these common inventories as being based on the Holland model and having acceptable reliability and validity: the Self-Directed Search (SDS), the Harrington-O'Shea Career Decision-Making System (CDM), the Strong Interest Inventory (SII), the Interest-Finder, and the Career Assessment Inventory (CAI). Both the SII and CAI also use an additional empirical methodology to differentiate the interests of a relatively small number of professional and technical workers, as described later.

Interest Inventory Scale Development

All test development begins with forming an item (question) pool. The recently developed O*NET Interest Profiler (U.S. Department of

Labor, 2000a) is used here to illustrate its developmental process. The authors began by examining older U.S. Department of Labor instruments, which resulted in identifying 532 items that cover the six Holland interest areas. An additional 272 new items were written. Only 500 of the total items, however, met the criterion of a grade 8 reading level, were not outdated, did not have sexist content, and survived statistical analysis after the initial tryout. These items were readministered to 1,123 high school and college students and adults. The final Interest Profiler comprised 180 items based on results of correlations of an item with its proper theoretical scale, gender and race or ethnic comparable endorsement rates, maximum training level and occupational representation, and work content area assignments.

Technical results for this new interest inventory revealed a low percentage of scoring errors in counting scores and a minimal number of people who identified an inaccurate top interest area due to a scoring error. The internal consistency reliabilities ranged from .93 to .96, which are very high, meaning all items in a scale measured the same construct (e.g., Social). Test-retest reliabilities ranged from .81 to .92, meaning people who retook the instrument after a short time received the same results as the first time they took the instrument. However, in what many perceive as the most important criterion for using any test—validity—the O*NET Interest Profiler had difficulties. According to its technical manual, the instrument fails to correspond with the Holland theoretical model upon which it was built, namely "The correlations for the O*NET Interest Profiler suggest a problematic Enterprising scale, because this scale correlates too highly with the Artistic scale and not highly enough with the Social scale . . . comparison to another RIASEC instrument may lead to different conclusions" (U.S. Department of Labor, 2000b, p. 43).

A careful reader might also detect two major concerns of some Interest Profiler users. The instrument was not field tested with middle school children and the instrument's grade 8 reading level can place many users at risk because many high school students may not understand its vocabulary or comprehend the questions or interpretations. Thus, this instrument's value will need to be evaluated over time, especially regarding its use with some school populations.

Types of Scores Provided

Interest inventories use three types of scores to report results: raw scores, percentile scores, and standard scores. Percentile and standard scores are based on comparing a person's results with a norm group whose norm sample is defined in the technical manual for the inventory. To be meaningful to an individual, the results should be derived from a norm group that is similar to the person being assessed.

Raw scores typically are a simple tabulation of a group of items on a scale labeled "like = 1" and "dislike = 0," or perhaps "like = 2," "uncertain = 1," and "dislike = 0." The raw score totals reflect the person's ranking of interests; for example, Conventional 32, Social 25, and Investigative 18. This set of the three highest scores out of the six scales results in a Holland code of CSI, which leads to occupations that involve CSI interests and personality types. Based on interests and personality type, this person might be a local certified public accountant who must follow established tax laws and accounting procedures, be an understanding service provider, and solve financial problems through mathematical calculations. A person with these personality characteristics might prefer structure, enjoy social interactions, and like the mental challenge of problem solving.

Some inventory administrators prefer instruments that use percentiles (such as the Kuder General Interest Survey, Form E, and the Career Occupational Preference System; COPS) because there is a mystique to numbers, and interpretation appears easy. The interpretation that a person's business interests rank at the 85th percentile would mean that they are higher than those of 85 percent of the people who took the inventory, clearly indicating high business interests. Herein lies a problem: Many interest inventory norm groups are not that large, are not based on representatively diverse populations, or are not national in scope. Instruments using percentiles often do not rely on Holland codes for interpretation, but rather use a relatively small number of homogeneous occupations presented as a cluster of careers.

Interest inventories using standard scores frequently rely on a graphic means to report their scores. The SII, CAI, and Campbell Interest and Skill Survey are inventories that use this methodology. Whereas the previous two score types are typically used with groupings of occupations, standard scores are employed with inventories answering the question, How do my interests compare with those employed in a specific occupation, such as speech-language pathologist? Each occupation has a unique scoring key that contains only items that statistically differentiate one occupation from a composite of other occupations.

Standard scores have the same statistical properties, which allow the reporting of one's own results in comparison with those of people employed in a variety of occupations. Most interpretations rely on scores as visual indicators of the degree of one's similarity or dissimilarity to those people employed in an occupation. The presumption is that if one has the same likes and dislikes as those working in an occupation, there is a high probability one will find satisfaction in that occupation.

Beyond Interests

Cognitive assessment also plays an important role in career development. Once individuals identify a preferred program or career area for future study, they next need to explore the specific abilities and levels of the abilities needed for good performance in that area. Therefore, in this section we examine the unique contributions of three types of cognitive measures: ability, aptitude, and achievement tests. On a continuum of generality to specificity, abilities cover the broadest orientation of basic cognitive skills that affect a person's performance in a wide variety of activities. The content of aptitude tests overlaps somewhat with achievement tests; however, aptitude tests have traditionally served to predict future performance in a task. On this continuum, then, achievement tests measure the most narrowly defined attainment of a technical skill or knowledge of factual information. Course grades are another form of achievement measure because they are typically based on a variety of evaluations resulting in a teacher-assigned grade indicating the attainment of defined competencies.

Assessment of Abilities

For more than 25 years, Harrington and O'Shea (2000) have been advocates of self-reporting one's best abilities. These authors have located in the professional and research literature 14 major work-related abilities. They developed an assessment methodology of identifying a person's strongest abilities that has validity demonstrated through research studies. The use of self-reported ability methodology has been widely adopted by career development professionals. In 1996 Harrington and Harrington developed a newer methodology of self-reporting in the Ability Explorer (AE). They combined the self-ratings on 10 micro skills or abilities to identify a total score on a macro ability, which was then compared to one of three national norm groups—middle school students, high school and college students and adults—to obtain percentile scores. The 14 AE macro abilities are artistic, clerical, interpersonal, language, leadership, manual, musical/drama, numerical, organizational, persuasive, scientific, social, spatial, and technical/

mechanical.

These authors advocate the use of self-reports because of their belief in assessing all a person's abilities, given that for some abilities there are no tests. The AE also recognizes the gap that often exists between course grades and a person's own beliefs about his or her performance level in an ability area. Employers have often stated that interpersonal, leadership, organizational, and persuasive abilities are very important in hiring employees. Aptitude tests do not measure these abilities.

Beyond identifying a person's best abilities, a unique feature of the AE is that it provides information on the individual's level of ability development. In fact, the interpretive materials provide information as to how to develop each ability area further. Additionally, the comparison of self-reported abilities with related course performance provides self-efficacy information, which is relevant to one's self-concept. There is high value in comparing one's self-reported ability ratings with occupational information and institutional catalogs that include the desired abilities for success in specific areas.

Aptitudes

The most widely used multiple-aptitude test battery, the Armed Services Vocational Aptitude Battery (ASVAB; Defense Manpower Data Center, 1992), helps a person to identify his or her different abilities. Trained test administrators from the federal government administer the ASVAB in schools at no cost. The test takes about three hours, but a shorter version will soon be available.

Generally offered once a year in high schools, the ASVAB can be completed by students in grades 10, 11, and 12 and in postsecondary education for career planning purposes; 10th graders cannot use their scores for enlistment in the active military, military reserve, or national guard, whereas high school juniors, seniors, and postsecondary students can do so. The ASVAB provides information on a person's learning potential that is useful for predicting performance in school courses. The military services use ASVAB scores to help them determine potential recruits' qualifications for enlistment and to place them in occupational specialties.

The ASVAB is not just for individuals thinking about military careers, however. The results provide information about any student's readiness for advanced academic education. Score results contained in *Exploring Careers: The ASVAB Workbook* (U.S. Department of Defense, 2002) enable a person to match his or her interests, abilities, and personal preferences with more than 200 civilian and military occupations. The purpose is to allow a person to see what career options are most suitable.

The ASVAB norms are a nationally representative sample of men and women, ages 16 to 23, who are attending high school or two-year postsecondary schools. Students receive percentile scores based on their performance as compared to students of the same grade and same sex and of the same grade and opposite sex. The ASVAB subtests are Word Knowledge, Paragraph Comprehension, Arithmetic Reasoning, Mathematics Knowledge, General Science, Auto & Shop Information, Mechanical Comprehension, Electronics Information, Numerical Operations, and Coding Speed. These ten subtests yield three composite scores: Verbal Ability, Math Ability, and Academic Ability.

Reviewers have highlighted as a strength of the ASVAB its use in prediction for more than 50 military training courses with validity coefficients ranging from .36 to .77, with a median of .60. Recent studies show that corrected correlations between ASVAB scores and military job performance range from a low of .23 to a high of .73. Its average predictive validity for courses in high schools and two-year colleges is about .40. ASVAB results are also correlated to success in nonmilitary occupations.

Achievement Tests

Course grades answer two questions: Does an individual have knowledge in a specific academic or technical knowledge area? At what level of proficiency or competency? Achievement tests are another measure of competence. Three types of achievement tests exist: reading tests, statewide assessments of basic skills, and those administered by the College Entrance Examination Board Advanced Placement Program to determine whether a student will receive college credit in a subject taken at the local high school. Each type of test provides valuable information.

Local school districts annually or at specified time periods administer reading tests to all students in order to monitor their development. Poor readers are typically identified as needing additional assistance in this skill area. Minimally these tests provide scores on vocabulary knowledge and reading comprehension, and a total score to determine reading level. Reading level is a critical skill for all other subject areas.

Increasingly states also employ high-stakes testing, which demands that a student attain a preset minimum score on reading/ language and mathematics in order to graduate with a high school diploma. Students take the exam several times during their school life (e.g., in grades 4, 8, and 10), receiving score results typically designated as "needs improvement," "proficient," or "above proficient." This information can indicate how realistic a student's vocational goals may be and serve as feedback for developing a plan beyond a high school education.

Advanced placement tests can be viewed as end-of-course exams, frequently taken in the senior year of high school and administered by a neutral third party, the College Board. Individual colleges and universities determine what level of score they accept in each subject area to grant college credit at their institution. Students and their college advisors use this information to plan a program of studies.

In summary, assessment information is used in a self-discovery and planning process. The first goal is to answer the question, Who am I? Test takers accomplish this by identifying activities that they like and dislike, which generates specific terms that uniquely describe them in personality terms. Toward the end of middle school and during high school, another set of educational goals emerges: career exploration and preparation. Occupational information provides students additional feedback by describing the skills and proficiencies inherent in certain occupations. This information offers students a rationale for selecting and planning their educational programs. Feedback they receive in their courses helps answer questions: Do I really have an interest in this area? and Am I good in performing these activities?

Interpretation Enhancements

The value of a good career assessment instrument is diminished by the absence of an interpretation, whereas a good interpretation can compensate for an average assessment. Interpretation can lead to misunderstanding the results, excite one to explore, leave one feeling beaten, or offer affirmation or confrontation. Done well, it helps identify what one should do next to meet one's goals.

Although career facilitators are intrigued by the potential of technology, some fear that it may replace the human dimension so valued in the counselor-client relationship. The computer, the Internet, and video, now common in most educational settings, will not replace the face-to-face human contact needed within career development, but they can enhance interpretation. Wall (2000) warns that "with technology-delivered assessments, meaningful human contact and intervention to assist with test score interpretation and guidance may be lacking or unavailable. Without a skilled educator or counselor, it may be difficult for a test taker to sort out his or her results and use them in a context of other experiences." (p. 243). Although Internet-based assessments are predominately self-help interventions and cannot ensure enhanced interpretation, most personal computer–based career assessments are designed to include interpretation by a practitioner (Sampson, Lumsden, & Carr 2001). Websites such as http://www.agsnet.com/cdmcareerzone, http://www.thefutureschannel.com, and http://online.onetcenter.org are only three of many sites available to complement a practitioner's interpretation.

DISCOVER, SIGI, and Choices are three highly successful and popular computer-assisted career guidance systems (CAGS) that incorporate assessment modules. Sampson (2000) suggests that test administration, test scoring, and score profile generation complement narrative interpretative report generation and multimedia-based generalized test interpretation as key elements of computer-based assessment. With extensive databases and proper counseling techniques, an exceptional interpretation is possible through the use of a CAGS.

Although video usage in career development has received little attention, Feller (1994) and Feller and Honaker (1997) have conducted counselor evaluations of career development videos using a nine-item quality rating system and recommendations regarding the video's potential of increasing the intended viewer's achievement of the 12 National Career Development Competencies (NOICC, 1989). *The Harrington-O'Shea Career Decision Making System (CDM) Career Video Series: Tour of Your Tomorrow* (Feller & Vasos, 2000) introduces viewers to enthusiastic and authentic workers engaged in real-world experiences corresponding to the CDM interest areas. The overview videotape explains how viewing six tapes related to individual scores can enhance information within the CDM Interpretative Folder, expand career and learning options, provide vicarious experiences for clients, document elements of the "new workplace," and provide nontraditional role models. As Harrington (1997) reports, "The video gives greater meaning to the terms that clients experience on their CDM-R profiles" (p. 220).

Parents must be alerted to a school district's goals for career development and to how and when program objectives are being implemented. Parents and teachers should encourage students to search out additional information about various opportunities and do a reality test of what they have learned from their initial assessments and interpretations. Knowing and accepting that students can change during this development period is an essential principle to complement the use of any career assessment.

Summary

Fortunately, many assessment tools are available to facilitate career development. Whereas interest surveys form the backbone of most programs, feedback gained from ability, aptitude, and achievement assessments is critical. Continued development of enhancements for interpretation will lead to more efficient and effective programs. Improving the facilitation of career development requires maintaining psychometric rigor within all career assessments, maximizing computer speed within CAGS, using the Internet's capacity and reach, and stimulating the vicarious learning possible through video technology. As practitioner interpretation of assessments further integrates these enhancements, students can experience greater academic achievement and gain career development competencies they need to prepare them for a lifetime of career transitions.

References

Defense Manpower Data Center. (1992). *Counselor manual for the Armed Services Vocational Aptitude Battery Forms 18/19.* Washington, DC: Department of Defense.

Feller, R. W. (1994). *650 career videos: Ratings, reviews and descriptions.* Ft. Collins, CO: Colorado State University.

Feller, R. W., & Honaker, S. L. (1997). *Career video reviews 1997: A consumer's guide to career videos.* Ft. Collins, CO: Colorado State University.

Feller, R. W., & Vasos, E. (2000). *The Harrington-O'Shea Career Decision Making System (CDM) career video series: Tour of your tomorrow.* Fort Collins, CO: Valer Productions.

Gottfredson, G. D., & Holland, J. L. (1996). *Dictionary of Holland occupational codes* (3rd ed.). Odessa, FL: Psychological Assessment Resources.

Harrington, T. F. (1997). *Handbook of career planning for students with special needs*. Austin, TX: Pro-Ed.

Harrington, T. F., & Harrington, J. (1996). *Ability Explorer*. Itasca, IL: Riverside Publishing.

Harrington, T. F., & O'Shea, A. J. (2000). *The Harrington-O'Shea career decision making system revised* (CDM-R) *manual*. Circle Pines, MN: American Guidance Service.

Herr, E. L. (2001). Trends and issues in career assessment. In J. Kapes and E. Whitfield (Eds.), *A counselor's guide to career assessment instruments*. Columbus, OH: NCDA.

Holland, J. L. (1997). *Making vocational choices: A theory of vocational personalities and work environments*. Odessa, FL: Psychological Assessment Resources.

Jamieson, A., Curry, A., & Martinez, G. (2001). School enrollment in the United States—Social and economic characteristics of students. Washington, DC: U.S. Census Bureau.

Kapes, J. T., & Whitfield, E. A. (2001). *A counselor's guide to career assessment instruments* (4th ed.). Columbus, OH: NCDA.

National Commission on the High School Senior Year. (2001). *Raising our sights: No high school senior left behind*. Princeton, NJ: Woodrow Wilson National Fellowship Foundation.

NOICC. (1989). *The national career development guidelines*. Washington, DC: Author.

Sampson, J. P. (2000). Using the Internet to enhance testing in counseling. *Journal of Counseling and Development, 78,* 348–356.

Sampson, J. P., Lumsden, J. A., & Carr, D. L. (2001). Computer-assisted career assessment. In J. Kapes and E. Whitfield (Eds.), *A counselor's guide to career assessment instruments*. Columbus, OH: NCDA.

U.S. Department of Defense. (2002). *Exploring careers: The ASVAB workbook*. Washington, DC: Author.

U.S. Department of Labor. (2000a). *O*Net Interest Profiler*. Washington, DC: Author.

U.S. Department of Labor. (2000b). *O*Net user's guide*. Washington, DC: Author.

Wall, J. E. (2000). Technology-delivered assessment: Power, problems, and promise. In J. Bloom and G. R. Walz (Eds.), *Cybercounseling and cyberlearning: Strategies and resources for the millennium*. Alexandria, VA: American Counseling Association.

Chapter 42
Improving Work Life Decisions
O*NET™ Career Exploration Tools
Phil Lewis & David Rivkin

In May 2001 the Occupational Information Network (O*NET), a project of the U.S. Department of Labor (DOL) Employment and Training Administration (ETA), released to the public several O*NET Career Exploration Tools: O*NET Interest Profiler and Computerized Interest Profiler, O*NET Work Importance Locator and Work Importance Profiler, and O*NET Ability Profiler. These tools are designed to help clients learn information about themselves for use in focusing their career search. O*NET Career Exploration Tools assist clients in identifying occupations for which they (a) have basic interests that will be supported by those occupations, (b) place a high value on work outcomes that the occupations will provide, and (c) have (or can learn) the necessary knowledge and skills. The tools were developed for use by the wide variety of clients served by DOL initiatives (e.g., dislocated worker, One Stop System, school to work, veterans' programs, welfare to work, and youth opportunity); program staff providing service to individual clients (e.g., counselors, teachers, intake personnel); and application developers who wish to incorporate the tools into products for specific organizations, businesses, or groups of clients.

Career exploration can help clients make critical work life decisions. O*NET Career Exploration Tools enable clients accurately and reliably to identify their interests, valued work outcomes, and abilities. Emphasis is placed on *whole-person assessment,* which uses different pieces of information about an individual to help that person explore careers and make career decisions, and considers profiles of information rather than relying on a single score (for example, assaying what one's likes and strengths are, as well as where dislikes and areas needing improvement lie). Once clients have gathered information about themselves, they are directed to O*NET occupations linked to the assessment information. Clients can then take advantage of the many systems that use O*NET occupations to discover a variety of information about potential occupations, including descriptions and requirements, related labor market information, job listings, and training opportunities.

This chapter provides a practical overview of relevant information about the O*NET Career Exploration Tools, including a description of the O*NET project, why a new set of tools was needed, an overview of each tool, and a description of the support materials available for each instrument.

The Occupational Information Network Project

O*NET is a comprehensive database system for collecting, organizing, describing, and disseminating information on occupational characteristics and worker attributes. O*NET was conceived of as a conceptual model to replace the outmoded *Dictionary of Occupational Titles* (U.S. Department of Labor, 1991) and to provide information on transferable skills and other occupational requirements for meeting the needs of the twenty-first-century workforce. See Figure 1 for an overview of the O*NET content model. For a detailed description of the development of the content model, see *An Occupational Information System for the 21st Century: The Development of O*NET* (Peterson, Mumford, Borman, Jeanneret, & Fleishman, 1999).

Figure 1.

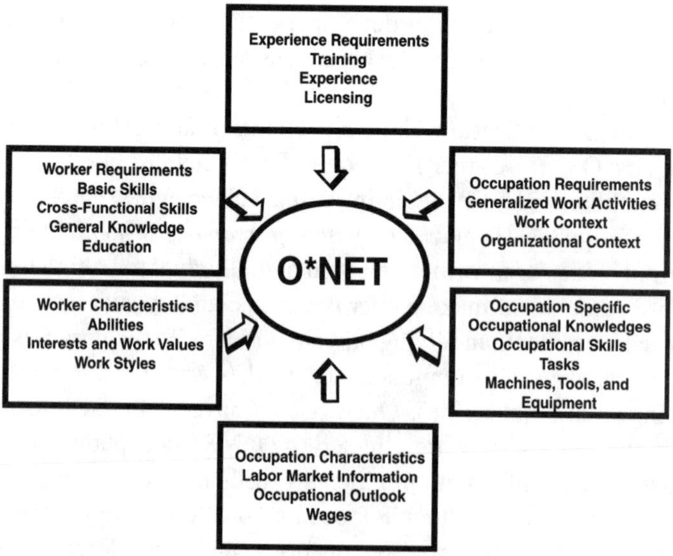

An occupational database was developed containing analysts' ratings of the importance, level, and frequency (where appropriate) of each of the elements in the O*NET content model. The first O*NET database, named O*NET 98, contained analysts' ratings for O*NET Occupational Units (OUs) based on the 1996 Occupational Employment Statistics (OES) program classification system. Both the O*NET and OES programs have now been incorporated in the 2000 edition of the Standard Occupational Classification (SOC) system (Executive Office of the President, Office of Management and Budget, 2000), which led to the release in July 2000 of the O*NET 3.0 database and a web-based accessing application, O*NET OnLine; http://online.onetcenter.org. The new O*NET-SOC classification is compatible with the SOC but provides additional breakouts of certain SOC detailed occupations. For more information on the O*NET-SOC system, see *Transitioning O*NET to the Standard Occupational Classification* (Levine, Nottingham, Paige, & Lewis, 2000) and the introduction to *O*NET Occupational Listings: Database 3.1* (Lewis, Russos, & Frugoli, 2001).

In April 2001 the Office of Management and Budget authorized a new O*NET data collection effort. Four O*NET survey questionnaires—Skills, Knowledge, Generalized Work Activities, and Work Context—are being sent to job incumbents at randomly selected businesses across the country. These job incumbents are being asked to provide ratings for the O*NET elements based on their own work experience. A fifth O*NET survey questionnaire is being used by job analysts to generate data for the elements in the Abilities domain. To facilitate timely and complete responses from incumbent workers, the survey instruments underwent significant improvements from the 1998 versions, including (a) reduction in the reading level and cognitive burden required to complete the surveys, and (b) elimination of items and response scales with poor conceptual and empirical support. These changes to the survey will lead to the development of a database that is more accurate and friendlier for end users. For a detailed discussion of the survey review process, see *Revision of O*NET Data Collection Instruments* (Hubbard et al., 2000). As of 2002, data for approximately 180 occupations are available, and new data updates are being made roughly twice a year beginning in the spring of 2003.

Need for O*NET Career Exploration Tools

For several decades, the DOL has been providing assessment tools for use by employment security agencies and other initiatives. By the mid-1990s the need to update and redesign the available assessment tools was apparent from a variety of sources, including (a) information gathered from a series of informal focus groups conducted by the DOL in 1995 with a number of program and agency representatives, (b) general feedback the department received from counselors and program leaders serving the DOL community, (c) the transition from *Dictionary of Occupational Titles* to O*NET-based occupational information, and (d) advances in computer technology that the educational and vocational fields could use to improve services to clients. The following section describes some of the specific need areas that were identified.

*Current Tools Linked to O*NET Occupations and Information*

Feedback from the DOL community indicated that career exploration tools available for their use were no longer adequate. The materials were outdated and results not easily linked to occupational information. For example, instruments such as the U.S. Employment Services USES Interest Inventory (U.S. Department of Labor, 1981), the Interest Check List (U.S. Department Labor, 1979), and the Job Search Inventory (New York State Job Service, 1985) contained dated language and content that clients found distracting or confusing. A review by the National Research Council indicated that the USES General Aptitude Test Battery (GATB; U.S. Department of Labor, 1970) needed substantial updates (see Hartigan & Wigdor, 1989). In addition, no existing DOL assessment tools for measuring abilities or work values were specifically designed for clients engaged in career exploration. Finally, all existing tools were based on the data, theoretical models, and occupations found within the *Dictionary of Occupational Titles*. As a result, counselors had to use their personal review of results and general knowledge of the world of work to indirectly link client results to occupations. Counselors were looking for an easy way to implement standardized methodology for identifying potential occupations for clients. In addition, assessments were needed that would fit the more current information and theoretical models to be available in the new O*NET database and that would foster additional exploration of occupations in the O*NET system. Finally, there was a need for tools that would be readily available and deliverable via recent advances in computer technologies.

Self-Help Tools

Counselors and program administrators also indicated that they wanted the DOL to initiate more self-help services for their clients. Because of resource constraints, clients were receiving less counselor and one-on-one attention than in the past. Therefore, counselors needed assessment tools that clients could self-administer, self-score, and in some cases, self-interpret. Counselors and program staff wanted tools that could augment or assist clients with their career search, rather than tools that left clients dependent on counselors for all aspects of the assessment process (i.e., administration, scoring, interpretation).

Requests for self-help tools were also motivated by counselors' desire to give clients more control over important work life decisions. As mentioned earlier, in many DOL programs, career exploration was considered to be critical in making successful work life decisions. Tools that allow clients to conduct their search on their own can empower them and give them a strong sense of self-efficacy over their career search.

The availability of personal computers and networked systems also made the development of self-help tools more feasible. Assessments could be computer-scored, allowing for rapid, accurate processing of complex scoring algorithms. Score reports could be generated on a real-time basis and customized based on the individual client's scores.

Whole-Person Assessment

As mentioned previously, whole-person assessment uses a variety of pieces of information, and profiles of information rather than single scores, to help individuals explore careers. Feedback from experts in vocational and educational fields indicated that the reliance on a single score from a single type of vocational assessment did not take into account the complexities or the importance of the decisions that individual clients were making during career exploration. In addition, as described in the previous section, one-on-one counseling sessions during which the counselor would review the client's assessment score and then make broad interpretations and career recommendations were no longer feasible at many DOL program and initiative sites.

Expanding Career Possibilities

Feedback from DOL clients, counselors, and program staff indicated that many of the available assessment tools were too restrictive in the number of career options they generated. After taking an assessment, clients would frequently be presented with two, possibly three occupations to explore. What if they did not like any of the options presented? Students also were found to have need of career information; when students were asked during focus groups what they wanted to do for a living, typical responses were either high-profile occupations seen on television, many of which require advanced degrees (e.g., doctor, lawyer) or were occupations unlikely to have a large number of job openings in the future (e.g., train conductor). What if clients preferred to attend trade school rather than graduate school? What if the three identified occupations for a particular client were all low-growth occupations? Feedback from the field indicated a need to develop tools that would expand career possibilities, rather than narrow them. Clients should learn during career exploration that there are many different types of occupations (more than are portrayed on television) that require a wide range of education, training, and work experience. Career exploration needed to provide clients with lots of options so they would remain engaged and eventually make satisfying career decisions, rather than run into a dead end and become frustrated.

Technical Quality of the O*Net Career Exploration Tools

Many of the assessment tools available to DOL initiatives and programs did not have strong technical underpinnings, lacking adequate research and data on important psychometric characteristics (e.g., reliability, validity). The interpretation materials and client feedback guidelines did not cover all the information recommended by current professional guidelines. During the development of the O*NET Career Exploration Tools, extensive research was conducted examining the accuracy, reliability, and usefulness of the information these tools generated. Steps were taken to ensure that the tools were fair and unbiased for the wide variety of clients that the DOL serves. During development, data were collected across the country from several thousand individuals with a wide range of characteristics (e.g., age, race, gender, education, socioeconomic status). The tools also went through extensive pilot testing and tryouts in many different types of DOL-sponsored initiatives (e.g., school to work, One-Stop Systems, high schools, dislocated worker programs, employment service offices). Lastly, current professional standards and principles served as guidelines for the research to develop each tool, the design of information reported to clients, and the creation of the technical documentation describing each tool. (These included *Standards for Educational and Psychological Testing,* AERA, APA & NCME,1999, and *Principles for the Validation* *and Use of Personnel Selection Procedures,* Society for Industrial and Organizational Psychology, 1987.) For a listing of available development and technical reports associated with the O*NET Career Exploration Tools see the "Bibliography of Materials and Reports" at the end of this chapter or go to www.onetcenter.org

Overview of O*NET Career Exploration Tools

The O*NET Career Exploration Tools were designed using occupational information contained within the O*NET database. The tools serve as a gateway into the O*NET system, allowing clients to identify a subset of the 974 O*NET-SOC occupations that they may want to explore further. Clients can use O*NET OnLine or other applications that contain the O*NET classification or database. Although these tools help clients assess three important pieces of vocational and career information, additional pieces of vocational information are likely to be relevant to their whole-person assessment of themselves and of possible occupations to pursue. The O*NET content model serves as a valuable resource for identifying additional types of occupational information and worker requirements for consideration during clients' career exploration (e.g., occupational skills, knowledges). Other tools assessing similar information as the O*NET Career Exploration Tools are available and can be used effectively to access O*NET information. A brief summary of each O*NET Career Exploration Tool follows, including a description of Job Zones, an important component of the O*NET assessments.

*O*NET Interest Profiler or O*NET Computerized Interest Profiler and Job Zones*

The Interest Profiler and Computerized Interest Profiler measure six vocational interest areas identified in the Holland RIASEC model (Realistic, Investigative, Artistic, Social, Enterprising, and Conventional; Holland, 1985, 1997). The assessment is self-administered via paper and pencil or computer, is self-scored, and includes a self-interpretable score report and occupational listing. It contains 180 work activity items that are representative of the entire world of work, with each RIASEC construct being represented by 30 items. Both versions of the Interest Profiler take between 20 and 30 minutes to complete. Test takers indicate whether they "Like," "Dislike," or are "Unsure" whether they like each activity. The paper-and-pencil version of the instrument enables clients to identify their top interests, which they can then use to locate occupations on the O*NET Interest Profiler Score Report. The computerized version compares the individual's entire RIASEC interest profile (i.e., all six interest areas) to the interest profiles of the occupations in the O*NET database and generates a list of potential occupations for the client.

In addition to receiving interest results, clients taking either version of the Interest Profiler are also asked to select a Job Zone to help them focus their occupational search. The five levels of Job Zones represent the levels of experience, training, and education required for various occupations, with Job Zone 1 requiring the least career preparation and Job Zone 5, the most. O*NET Career Exploration Tool Score Reports present occupational lists sorted first by the variable being measured (e.g., interests, work values, or abilities) then by Job Zone. By allowing clients to select a Job Zone, the O*NET Career Exploration Tools help them focus on whether they have sufficient education and training of the right type for a particular occupation. They can then make decisions about whether they need and are willing to pursue additional education or training.

After taking the Interest Profiler and selecting a Job Zone, clients use that Job Zone with their interest results to identify occupations to explore. On the paper-and-pencil version, clients may, for example, identify the Investigative area as their primary interest area and Job Zone 4 as their desired level of education to identify careers meeting these criteria. (The Computerized Interest Profiler would use the clients' complete six-score interest profile and their selected Job Zone to generate a list of appropriate occupations.) For a description of the development of the Job Zones, see *Stratifying Occupational Units by Specific Vocational Preparation* (Oswald, Campbell, McCloy, Rivkin, & Lewis, 1999).

*O*NET Work Importance Locator and O*NET Work Importance Profiler*

The two versions of this tool measure six important work values (Achievement, Independence, Recognition, Relationships, Support, and Working Conditions) modified from the theory of work adjustment. (In the original theory of work adjustment, the six work values were labeled Achievement, Autonomy, Status, Altruism, Safety, and Comfort; see Dawis & Lofquist, 1984; Dawis, Lofquist, & Weiss, 1968; Lofquist & Dawis, 1969; Weiss, Dawis, England, & Lofquist, 1964.) Both instruments are similar, but whereas the O*NET Work Importance Locator is a paper-and-pencil instrument, the O*NET Work Importance

Profiler is computerized. Each takes approximately 30 to 40 minutes to complete.

The O*NET Work Importance Locator is a self-administered, paper-and-pencil instrument. The test taker is asked to sort 21 work outcomes and need statements into five categories based on their importance to him or her. This sorting exercise results in the identification of two primary work values. The individual can use these work values, with a selected Job Zone, to identify occupations to explore in the Work Importance Locator Score Report. This score report provides lists of O*NET occupations sorted by work value and Job Zone.

The O*NET Work Importance Profiler is computerized. Individuals first rank the importance of 21 need statements, presented in pairs on a series of computer screens. They then rate each of the 21 statements as to whether it represents something they consider important Using the results of the ranking and rating exercises and a selected Job Zone, the computer searches the O*NET database for compatible occupations and generates lists of each individual's most important work values and of occupations that may satisfy these work values.

*O*NET Ability Profiler*

This tool measures nine abilities related to job performance: Verbal, Arithmetic, Computation, Spatial, Form Perception, Clerical Perception, Motor Coordination, Manual Dexterity, and Finger Dexterity. The instrument consists of 11 separate subtests, 6 of which are in paper-and-pencil format (Arithmetic Reasoning, Vocabulary, Three Dimensional Space, Computation, Name Comparison, and Object Matching), and 5 of which are psychomotor in nature (Mark Making, Place, Turn, Assemble, and Disassemble). Vocational counselors may administer the entire test battery, (which takes 2 to $2^1/_2$ hours) or just the paper-and-pencil tests (which takes $1^1/_2$ to 2 hours), depending on a client's needs. The instrument is scored by computer, providing a customized score report for each individual. The report includes the individual's ability profile scores, percentile information, and five lists of O*NET occupations with ability profiles similar to the client's, one for each Job Zone.

*O*NET Career Exploration Tools and Materials*

The various career instruments have a number of associated materials and reports (see the bibliography or go to www.onetcenter.org for a complete list of available materials and reports). Each instrument has a user's guide designed to help workforce development professionals incorporate the instruments into their programs. The guides cover such topics as means of administration, use of score reports, interpretation of results, possible client challenges, and instrument development. More thorough psychometric information about the instruments are provided in detailed development and technical reports. The paper-and-pencil O*NET Interest Profiler and Work Importance Locator have associated score reports, which help each test taker interpret his or her results and link them to lists of occupations provided with the report. These paper-and-pencil instruments also have master lists of occupations, which clients can link to their results. There is also a Combined Interest and Work Values Occupations List that enables clients to search for occupations according to their primary interests and work values. Additionally, for the Ability Profiler, there are separate administration and administrator training manuals, as well as instrument scoring software and scoring software user manuals. These materials in total enable workforce development professionals to take advantage of and successfully implement the O*NET Career Exploration Tools.

Availability and Use of O*NET Career Exploration Tools

The O*NET Career Exploration Tools and materials are available through two sources. They can be purchased through the Government Printing Office, or downloaded free of charge from the O*NET website: www.onetcenter.org. Counselor and client feedback from the field indicate that the tools are easy to use with a wide variety of individuals. Many clients can take the instruments independently and self-interpret the results. Career counselors appreciate the flexibility of the tools, including the ability to select one or several of the tools to collect multiple pieces of information, depending on clients' individual needs. Additionally, the concept of whole-person assessment resonates with both clients and workforce development professionals. Finally, workforce development professionals appreciate the technical quality of the instruments, which allows them to have confidence in the results clients receive and the mechanisms used to link results directly to occupations that they can explore further in O*NET and other systems that incorporate O*NET.

Bibliography of Materials and Reports Associated With O*NET Career Exploration Tools

*O*NET Interest Profiler*

Lewis, P., & Rivkin, D. (1999). *Development of the O*NET Interest Profiler.* Raleigh, NC: National Center for O*NET Development.

Lewis, P., & Rivkin, D. (1999). *O*NET Interest Profiler user's guide.* Raleigh, NC: National Center for O*NET Development.

Rounds, J., Walker, C. M., Day, S. X., Hubert, L., Lewis, P., & Rivkin, D. (1999). *O*NET Interest Profiler: Reliability, validity, and self-scoring.* Raleigh, NC: National Center for O*NET Development.

U.S. Department of Labor. (2000). *Interest Profiler O*NET occupations master list.* Raleigh, NC: National Center for O*NET Development.

U.S. Department of Labor. (2000). *O*NET Interest Profiler.* Raleigh, NC: National Center for O*NET Development.

U.S. Department of Labor. (2000). *O*NET Interest Profiler Score Report.* Raleigh NC: National Center for O*NET Development.

U.S. Department of Labor. (2000). *O*NET occupations combined list: Interests and work values.* Raleigh, NC: National Center for O*NET Development.

*O*NET Computerized Interest Profiler*

Rivkin, D., Lewis, P., & Ramsberger, P. (2000). *O*NET Computerized Interest Profiler user's guide.* Raleigh, NC: National Center for O*NET Development.

Rounds, J., Mazzeo, S. E., Smith, T. J., Hubert, L., Lewis, P., & Rivkin, D. (1999). *O*NET Computerized Interest Profiler: Reliability, validity, and comparability.* Raleigh, NC: National Center for O*NET Development.

U.S. Department of Labor. (2000). *O*NET Computerized Interest Profiler.* Raleigh NC: National Center for O*NET Development.

*O*NET Work Importance Locator*

McCloy, R., Waugh, G., Medsker, G., Wall, J., Rivkin, D., & Lewis, P. (1999). *Development of the O*NET paper-and-pencil Work Importance Locator.* Raleigh, NC: National Center for O*NET Development.

Rivkin, D., Lewis, P., Schlanger, I., & Atkins, S. (1999). *O*NET Work Importance Locator user's guide.* Raleigh, NC: National Center for O*NET Development.

U.S. Department of Labor. (2000). *O*NET Work Importance Locator.* Raleigh, NC: National Center for O*NET Development.

U.S. Department of Labor. (2000). *O*NET Work Importance Locator Score Report.* Raleigh, NC: National Center for O*NET Development.

U.S. Department of Labor. (2000). *Work Importance Locator O*NET occupations master list.* Raleigh, NC: National Center for O*NET Development

*O*NET Work Importance Profiler*

Archambault, C. A. A., Felker, D., & Rivkin, D. (2000). *O*NET Work Importance Profiler user's guide.* Raleigh, NC: National Center for O*NET Development.

McCloy, R., Waugh, G., Medsker, G., Wall, J., Rivkin, D., & Lewis, P. (1999). *Development of the O*NET Computerized Work Importance Profiler.* Raleigh, NC: National Center for O*NET Development.

U.S. Department of Labor. (2000). *O*NET Work Importance Profiler.* Raleigh, NC: National Center for O*NET Development.

*O*NET Ability Profiler*

Gaines, W., & Stroupe, J. (1994). *Implications of deleting the form matching test from the General Aptitude Test Battery.* Raleigh, NC: Southern Assessment Research & Development Center.

Harris, C. D. (2000). *O*NET Ability Profiler user's guide.* Raleigh, NC: National Center for O*NET Development.

Mellon, S. J., Daggett, M., MacManus, V., & Moritsch, B. (1996). Development of GATB Forms E and F. In R. A. McCloy, T. L. Russell, & L. L. Wise (Eds.), *GATB improvement project final report.* Washington, DC: U.S. Department of Labor.

Peterson, N. (1993). *Review of issues associated with speededness of GATB tests.* Washington, DC: Author.

Sager, C., Peterson, N., & Oppler, S. (1994). *An examination of the speededness of the General Aptitude Test Battery power tests.* Washington, DC: Authors.

Segall, D. O., & Monzon, R. I. (1995). *Equating forms E and F of the P & P–GATB.* San Diego, CA: Navy Personnel Research and Development Center.

Silva, J. (1999). *O*NET Ability Profiler scoring program technical manual.* Raleigh, NC: National Center for O*NET Development.

Silva, J., Lewis, P., Rivkin, D., Connel, D., & Koritko, L. (1999). *O*NET Ability Profiler scoring program user's guide.* Raleigh, NC: National Center for O*NET Development.

U.S. Department of Labor. (2000). *O*NET Ability Profiler, Forms 1 and 2.* Raleigh, NC: National Center for O*NET Development.

U.S. Department of Labor. (2000). *O*NET Ability Profiler Score Report.* Raleigh, NC: National Center for O*NET Development.

General Technical Reports

McCloy, R., Campbell, J., Oswald, F., Lewis, P., & Rivkin, D. (1999). *Linking client assessment profiles to O*NET occupational profiles.* Raleigh, NC: National Center for O*NET Development.

McCloy, R., Campbell, J., Oswald, F., Rivkin, D., & Lewis, P. (1999). *Generation and use of occupational ability profiles for exploring O*NET occupational units* (Vols. 1–2). Raleigh, NC: National Center for O*NET Development.

McCloy, R., Waugh, G., Medsker, G., Wall, J., Rivkin, D., & Lewis, P. (1999). *Determining the occupational reinforcer patterns for O*NET occupational units* (Vols. 1–2). Raleigh, NC: National Center for O*NET Development.

Oswald, F., Campbell, J., McCloy, R., Rivkin, D., & Lewis, P. (1999). *Stratifying occupational units by specific vocational preparation.* Raleigh, NC: National Center for O*NET Development.

Rounds, J., Smith, T., Hubert, L., Lewis, P., & Rivkin, D. (1999). *Development of occupational interest profiles for O*NET occupations.* Raleigh, NC: National Center for O*NET Development.

References

AERA, APA, & NCME [American Educational Research Association, American Psychological Association, & National Council on Measurement in Education]. (1999). *Standards for educational and psychological testing.* Washington, DC: American Psychological Association.

Dawis, R. V., & Lofquist, L. H. (1984). *A psychological theory of work adjustment.* Minneapolis, MN: University of Minnesota Press.

Dawis, R. V., Lofquist, L. H., & Weiss, D. J. (1968). A theory of work adjustment: A revision. *Minnesota Studies in Vocational Rehabilitation, 23,* 15.

Executive Office of the President, Office of Management and Budget. (2000). *Standard occupational classification manual.* Washington, DC: Bernan Associates.

Hartigan, J. A., and Wigdor, A. K. (1989). *Fairness in employment testing: Validity generalization, minority issues, and the General Aptitude Test Battery* (National Research Council Committee on the General Aptitude Test Battery report). Washington D.C.: National Academy Press.

Holland, J. L. (1985). *Making vocational choices: A theory of vocational personalities and work environments* (2nd ed.). Englewood Cliffs, NJ: Prentice-Hall.

Holland, J. L. (1997). *Making vocational choices: A theory of vocational personalities and work environments* (3rd ed.). Odessa, FL: Psychological Assessment Resources.

Hubbard, M., McCloy, R., Campbell, J., Nottingham, J., Lewis, P., Rivkin, D., & Levine, J. (2000). *Revision of O*NET data collection instruments.* Raleigh, NC: National Center for O*NET Development.

Levine, J., Nottingham, J., Paige, B., & Lewis, P. (2000). *Transitioning O*NET to the standard occupational classification.* Raleigh, NC: National Center for O*NET Development.

Lewis, P., Russos, H., & Frugoli, P. (2001). *O*NET occupational listings: Database 3.1.* Raleigh, NC: National Center for O*NET Development.

Lofquist, L. H., & Dawis, R. V. (1969). *Adjustment to work.* New York: Appleton Century Crofts.

New York State Job Service. (1985). *The job search inventory.* Albany, NY: Author.

Oswald, F. L., Campbell, J. P., McCloy, R. A., Rivkin, D., & Lewis, P. (1999). *Stratifying occupational units by specific vocational preparation.* Raleigh, NC: National Center for O*NET Development.

Peterson, N., Mumford, M., Borman, W., Jeanneret, P., & Fleishman, E. (1999). *An occupational information system for the 21st century: The development of O*NET.* Washington, DC: American Psychological Association.

Society for Industrial and Organizational Psychology. (1987). *Principles for the validation and use of personnel selection procedures* (3rd ed.) College Park, MD: Author.

U.S. Department of Labor. (1970). *Manual for the USES General Aptitude Test Battery. Section III: Development.* Washington D.C.: U.S. Government Printing Office.

U.S. Department of Labor. (1979). *Interest Check List.* Washington, DC: U.S. Government Printing Office.

U.S. Department of Labor (1981). *USES Interest Inventory.* Washington, DC: U.S. Government Printing Office.

U.S. Department of Labor. (1991). *Dictionary of occupational titles* (rev. 4th ed.). Washington, DC: U.S. Government Printing Office.

Weiss, D. J., Dawis, R. V., England, G. W., & Lofquist, L. H. (1964). Construct validation studies of the Minnesota Importance Questionnaire. *Minnesota Studies in Vocational Rehabilitation, 18,* 1–76.

Chapter 43
Assessment of Workplace Stress
Occupational Stress, Its Consequences, and Common Causes of Teacher Stress

Jo-Ida C. Hansen & Brandon A. Sullivan

There is now overwhelming evidence of what many educators have known for years: Teaching is a highly stressful occupation. In fact, teachers throughout the world deal with a substantial amount of ongoing occupational stress (e.g., Guglielmi & Tatrow, 1998; Kyriacou & Sutcliffe, 1978; Pithers & Soden, 1998; Borg, 1990). As a result, for the past 25 years there has been an active subfield within educational psychology and occupational health psychology focused on what is termed "teacher stress" (see Kyriacou, 2001, for a discussion). The high level of stress associated with teaching has serious implications for the healthy functioning of individual teachers and schools, and entire school systems. Because this stress can take a variety of forms and have many different sources, a comprehensive assessment is an important component of any stress reduction effort.

In this chapter we introduce teachers and other education professionals to the assessment of occupational stress. We begin with a brief discussion of what occupational stress is, an overview of the consequences of prolonged stress, and a review of the common causes of teacher stress. Next, we present methods for reducing occupational stress through organizational and individual initiatives. Finally, we review psychological tests that can be used to assess types and sources of stress within schools.

Occupational Stress and Its Consequences

Teacher stress has been defined as "the experience by a teacher of unpleasant, negative emotions, such as anger, anxiety, tension, frustration, or depression, resulting from some aspect of their work as a teacher" (Kyriacou, 2001, p. 28). This definition probably is close to what most teachers mean when they talk about stress. For purposes of assessment and intervention, however, it is important to distinguish among the components of stress.

Three major components of stress come together to produce the distressing experiences described above. The first is the *stressor,* an event or series of events that occur in the work environment. For example, a group of loud and disruptive students, or rude and disparaging parents, are stressors that teachers may encounter. The second component of stress encompasses the psychological and physiological effects of the stressor on the person. These effects are referred to as *strain* and are what people usually mean when they use the word *stress.* For example, if a teacher's muscles tense and she becomes frustrated and angry when told that class sizes will increase by 10 percent next year, these physical and psychological reactions to the announcement are strain.

Not all stressors inevitably lead to strain, or to the same level of strain, in every person because a third component, called *appraisal,* influences how a person reacts to a stressor. Appraisal involves judgments about the degree of threat a stressor presents and an evaluation of whether sufficient resources are available to cope with the stressor. For example, if a teacher working with unmotivated students sees the situation as a minor irritant and more of a threat to the students' own futures than anything else, this situation is unlikely to lead to a high level of strain. If another teacher in the same situation sees the situation as intolerable and considers his failure to motivate the students as reflective of a personal failure as a teacher, he is likely to perceive the situation as threatening and experience a high level of strain. In other words, how a person interprets an event can influence how stressful it is. Similarly, if a teacher believes that she does not have the energy, skills, or support to deal successfully with the situation, the strain will be greater than if the teacher believes she has access to adequate resources.

Occupational stress can be addressed by removing or changing stressors, reducing or treating the symptoms of strain, modifying appraisals, or a combination of these. Therefore, it is important to separate these components and assess each individually. For example, if a teacher is in distress, it is important to determine (a) what the major stressors in the teacher's environment are, (b) how these stressors are affecting the teacher psychologically and physiologically, and (c) how the teacher is interpreting and understanding the situation, and what resources he believes are available (or lacking). An assessment of these three components of stress illuminates the most likely methods of addressing it. Among these three components, the strain teachers experience is the most important factor influencing individual and organizational health, but removing or reducing the stressors themselves is typically the most effective way of addressing occupational stress.

High levels of prolonged stress are harmful to the health and well-being of individual teachers, their students, and the functioning of the entire school. Individual consequences of excessive occupational stress include a host of debilitating health problems such as heart disease (Theorell & Karasek, 1996) and chronic back pain (Bigos et al., 1991). Stress also may cause psychological problems such as depression (Paykel, 1976) and a very serious condition called burnout (Cordes & Dougherty, 1993). Burnout is a state of extreme physical and psychological exhaustion resulting in negative attitudes toward work and feelings of helplessness and ineffectiveness. Burnout can occur when problems, such as an excessive workload or classroom discipline problems, are unrelenting and the chance of relief is appraised as remote (Pines & Aronson, 1988). One tricky aspect of burnout is that it develops slowly over a long period of time and therefore is difficult to diagnose. Given that burnout is easily overlooked through casual observation and that teachers experience high rates of burnout (Burke & Richardsen, 1996), the assessment of burnout among teachers and educational professionals is particularly important. The Maslach Burnout Inventory (MBI; Maslach, Jackson, & Leiter, 1996) is one useful tool in any such effort.

High levels of stress and burnout also have significant organizational consequences, including poor work performance, low job satisfaction, high levels of tardiness and absenteeism, high rates of turnover, and poor relationships between employees (see Quick, Quick, Nelson, & Hurrell, 1997, chap. 5, for a review). It is hard to imagine that any school characterized by these features would be a good place to work or attend as a student, much less that it would be reaching its potential as an educational institution. Research has shown that interventions can improve such a situation; reducing stress and burnout is likely to improve the experiences of the teachers and students, and increase the success of the school in educating its pupils. In other words, once the types and sources of stress are assessed, action can be taken to reduce and prevent the physical, psychological, and organizational toll stress takes. Assessment can also help to identify patterns of stress throughout a school or school system, as well as differences in the levels and types of stress within a school.

Factors That Cause Stress for Teachers

Although a variety of factors determine how stressful a job is, two factors are particularly important. First is the psychological demands placed on an individual. This includes the amount of time and energy a job requires and can be thought of as the number and types of stressors inherent in doing a job. The Role Overload scale on the Occupational Stress Inventory–Revised (OSI-R; Osipow, 1998), described later in this chapter, is one measure of the level of psychological demands placed on teachers. The second, and perhaps more important, factor is the amount of control a person has over her or his job (Karasek & Theorell, 1990). This includes whether the worker has freedom to determine the work pace, to decide in which order and in what way to accomplish work tasks, and to make other forms of autonomous decisions.

Jobs that are very demanding and provide little control over how the work is done are associated with the highest levels of stress and are called *high-strain jobs.* Work under high-strain conditions is a negative, psychologically draining, and unrewarding experience. In contrast, jobs that are equally demanding but also provide significant control over how the work is done are associated with much lower levels of stress and are perceived by workers as challenging and presenting opportunities for professional growth, rather than as stressful and negative. Jobs of this type are called *active jobs.*

A common example of how a high-demand, low-control situation plays out in teaching is when teachers are expected to prevent disruptions in the classroom and also are expected to accomplish this without support or assistance (see Sutton, 1984). Such a dilemma is called *role conflict* (also measured by the OSI-R) and results from conflicting demands and expectations that cause stress for the person attempting to satisfy them (Van Sell, Brief, & Schuler, 1981).

Providing teachers additional control over their work can often reduce role conflict. Even if job demands remain unchanged, providing increased control can reduce stress and prevent many of the deleterious consequences of prolonged stress. Alternatively, stress can be reduced without an increase in control if the work demands are lowered or if additional people share the demands. In terms of organizational planning and decision making, it is important to realize that increased demands on a teacher that are not accompanied by an increase in control over the work are very likely to result in higher stress levels.

Another common source of teacher stress is *role ambiguity* (see Kyriacou, 2001). Role ambiguity arises when there is a lack of clear expectations, confusing information regarding expectations, or unclear information about how to meet expectations (Van Sell, Brief, & Schuler, 1981). An example of this would be a teacher who is told to cover specific material in class but is not given any help figuring out how best to teach the material. Role ambiguity also results if a teacher is given a classroom but no clear expectations regarding what to teach or how to deal with problems. Role ambiguity is another factor measured by the OSI-R.

Teachers face many other sources of stress that specifically increase demands on their time, energy, and patience, plus other sources that reduce their autonomy and resources. For example, teachers report that common sources of stress include students who lack motivation, discipline issues in the classroom, time pressures, and a heavy workload (see Kyriacou, 2001). Assessing the extent to which these factors are present within a school or school system can help pinpoint sources of stress and predict where future problems may arise.

What Can Be Done to Reduce Stress?

Depending upon the particular sources of stress within a given school or classroom, several approaches can be effective in reducing work-related stress. Formal assessment is an important precursor to intervention because without an accurate and objective understanding of the principal types and sources of stress within a specific school or classroom, it is impossible to design a focused and effective stress reduction program.

One way to reduce teacher stress is through job redesign. *Job redesign* involves making key changes in the work environment or the way work is organized. Identifying and removing (or modifying) specific sources of stress in the classroom and the larger work environment is one direct method of reducing stress. This might mean, for example, decreasing the number or types of demands placed on a teacher or spreading the same demands over additional people. An alternative approach is to increase the amount of control teachers have over their work. This strategy can be effective even if the amount of additional control is limited and even if it is not actually used. One example of this is integrating regular feedback from teachers into organizational decision making. Research has shown that increasing the amount of participation a person has in decision making decreases role conflict and role ambiguity (Jackson, 1983), two major sources of teacher stress. Finally, providing mechanisms that increase social and organizational support for educators is likely to reduce stress by increasing the available coping resources.

Changing the work environment or the work process is typically the most effective method of reducing work-related stress. However, providing support services, such as workshops and counseling, can help teachers cope with existing stressors. Several types of support services have proven effective, including skill-based workshops, career development services, mentoring programs, and personal counseling.

Regardless of the approach used to address occupational stress, the process by which this is done is a key factor in its success. It is important to involve teachers in the assessment process and in discussions of what to do with the results of the assessment. Such participation in and of itself is likely to reduce stress by providing hope of positive change, a sense of connectedness with others, and a feeling of greater control over the work environment. The Job Stress Survey (JSS; Spielberger & Vagg, 1999), described in the next section, is an instrument designed to identify major sources of stress in the workplace.

Inventories to Assess Stress

In this section, we describe three instruments commonly used to assess occupational stress, the Maslach Burnout Inventory, the Occupational Stress Inventory–Revised, and the Job Stress Survey.

Maslach Burnout Inventory

The Maslach Burnout Inventory (Maslach et al., 1996) assesses the three dimensions of burnout that consistently have been identified over a wide range of occupations: emotional exhaustion, depersonalization, and reduced personal accomplishment. The multidimensional theory of burnout (Maslach, 1998) construes the individual stress experience as one that involves the person's concept of both self and others in the context of complex social relations. For example, *emotional exhaustion* is the feeling of being emotionally overextended and represents the basic individual stress dimension of burnout. *Depersonalization* is an excessively detached response to other people and represents the interpersonal dimension of burnout. The self-evaluation dimension of burnout is the feeling of *reduced personal accomplishment* or a decline in feelings of productivity and competence at work.

The original version of the MBI (MBI–Human Services Survey) was developed for use with people in social and human services. The second version of the MBI (MBI–Educators Survey) was recommended for use in educational settings. The most recent version of the MBI (MBI–General Survey) is a generic version with three scales labeled Exhaustion, Cynicism, and Professional Efficacy.

The Emotional Exhaustion scale on the General Survey (MBI-GS) assesses depletion of emotional energy, which is different than mental or physical fatigue. The Cynicism scale reflects an indifference or distant attitude toward work as a way of coping with exhausting demands. The Professional Efficacy scale assesses satisfaction with past and present accomplishments as well as expectations for continued effectiveness at work. A high degree of burnout is represented by a low score on Professional Efficacy and high scores on Exhaustion and Cynicism.

All forms of the MBI take only 5 to 10 minutes to complete and are self-administered. The one-year test-retest reliability coefficients reported in the MBI-GS manual are .67 (Professional Efficacy), .65 (Exhaustion), and .60 (Cynicism). Confirmatory factor analyses, conducted with several samples from various occupations and countries, support the item content of the three scales. Various studies also have shown scores on the Exhaustion and Cynicism scales to be related to mental and physical strain, role conflict, and work overload. Scores on the Professional Efficacy scale are related to job involvement, access to resources, satisfaction, and organizational commitment.

An alternate form of the MBI-GS is the MBI–Educators Survey (MBI-ES) which also has three scales: Emotional Exhaustion, Depersonalization (similar to MBI-GS Cynicism), and Personal Accomplishment (similar to MBI-GS Professional Efficacy). Factor analytic studies have supported these three scales, and Cronbach alphas are reported in the manual as .90 (Emotional Exhaustion), .76 (Depersonalization), and .76 (Personal Accomplishment).

The MBI-ES can be used at district, school, and department levels to detect potential problems. Scores on the subscales, in turn, can be used to guide the development of interventions to improve the organizational climate. MBI-ES scores have been used to identify factors that relate to burnout among educators, including role conflict, participation in decision making, autonomy, role ambiguity, and social support.

Occupational Stress Inventory

The Occupational Stress Inventory–Revised (OSI-R; Osipow, 1998) assesses three dimensions of work adjustment: occupational stresses, psychological strain, and coping resources. Each dimension is measured by several scales. The six scales that comprise the Occupational Roles Questionnaire measure stress-inducing work roles. The four scales of the Personal Strain Questionnaire assess a person's subjective responses to stresses in the workplace. The four scales in the Personal Resources Questionnaire assess a person's coping resources.

The six Occupational Roles scales of the OSI-R are Role Overload (job demands exceed resources), Role Insufficiency (skills are inappropriate to job requirements), Role Ambiguity (lack of clarity of job priorities and evaluation criteria), Role Boundary (conflicting role demands), Responsibility (excessive responsibility for others), and Physical Environment (extreme physical conditions). The four Personal Strain scales measure occupationally induced strain: Vocational Strain (problems with work quality or quantity), Psychological Strain (emotional problems experienced), Interpersonal Strain (disruption in interpersonal relationships), and Physical Strain (physical illness). The four Personal Resources scales measure four sets of coping behaviors widely reported in the literature: Recreation (regular recreational activities), Self-Care (personal activities to reduce stress), Social Support (support from others), and Rational/Cognitive Coping (systematic approach to problem solving).

The manual recommends several uses and applications for the instrument. As a screening device, the OSI-R can be used to identify individuals who are experiencing excessive stress and strain. The information garnered then can be used to help the individual develop strategies for reducing his or her stress. From an organizational perspective, the OSI-R can be used to identify sources of stress in the work environment, leading to an analysis of ways in which the environment or organization might be modified to reduce stress and feelings of strain. Finally, the OSI-R often proves useful in career counseling, especially for individuals who are considering career shifts or changes.

The OSI-R is intended for use with individuals ages 18 or older. The scores are normed on gender-specific samples of adult women and men drawn from a wide variety of work settings. The OSI-R Manual also provides normative data for six occupational groups, including an Executive Group, a Professional Group, and an Administrative Support Group (the last norms are especially appropriate for educators). The 140 items on the instrument are judged to be at the fifth-grade reading level, and the answer sheet is designed to be hand-scored.

The original OSI was published in 1981. In subsequent revisions, items were reworded or replaced to improve their clarity. These modifications have resulted in stronger evidence of reliability and validity for the OSI-R. Two types of reliability estimates are reported in the OSI-R Manual: test-retest and internal consistency (Osipow, 1998). Over a two-week interval the test-retest correlations range from .39 for Self-Care to .71 for Rational/Cognitive Coping. The test-retest coefficients are lower than those typically found for measures of traits, such as personality or interests, and more in line with measures of states such as moods. The internal consistency of the scales ranges from alphas of .70 for Self-Care to .89 for Physical Environment. The OSI-R Manual reports evidence of validity from four different sources: convergent validity studies; item factor analyses; treatment and outcome studies; and studies testing the stress, strain, and coping model.

Job Stress Survey

The Job Stress Survey (Spielberger & Vagg, 1999) assesses specific sources of occupational stress that may contribute to problems in the workplace. The JSS response format emphasizes both the individual worker's perception of the severity of the occupational stressors and the frequency with which the stressor occurs. The 30 generic items of the JSS describe job-related stressor events. Respondents then are asked to rate each event in terms of (a) the amount of adjustment that would be required for the respondent to deal with the event, and (b) the frequency of the stressor event over the past six months. The 30 JSS items were selected from items piloted on samples of police officers, teachers, managerial or professional professionals, and clerical or skilled maintenance workers. The authors of the JSS recommend using it for the identification of significant sources of occupational stress, so they can be modified to reduce or avoid adverse health-related consequences (Vagg & Spielberger, 1999).

The JSS is self-administered, takes about 10 to 15 minutes to complete, and requires a sixth-grade reading level. In addition to Severity and Frequency scores, a Stress Index Score is computed for each of the 30 stressor events (Severity x Frequency = Stress Index), and separate scores are reported for the Job Pressure and Lack of Organizational Support scales. Internal consistency coefficients for the scales range from .87 to .93. The authors suggest that managers can use employees' scores on the JSS to understand the stress experienced in an organization or work group. Individual workers can also use their scores to understand how their level of stress compares to others in the same work group or job (Vagg & Spielberger, 1998).

Summary

Stress in the workplace has reached a critical level. In educational settings, increased workloads, longer working hours, and low salaries all contribute to high levels of employee stress that may lead to absences due to stress-related illness, impairment of coworker relationships, and feelings of hopelessness or disillusionment. Interventions for educators facing burnout and stress include training, individual therapy, and organizational change. Two types of assessment are important prior to developing interventions. The first type measures educators' levels of stress and burnout. The second type measures the work setting to identify environmental factors that contribute to feelings of stress, strain, and burnout. Taken together, assessment of the individual and the organization provides the necessary understanding of the work environment to design an effective stress reduction program.

References

Bigos, S. J., Battie, M. C., Spengler, D. M., Fisher, L. D., Fordyce, W. E., Hansson, T. H., Nachemson, A. L., & Wortley, M. D. (1991). A prospective study of work perceptions and psychosocial factors affecting the report of back injury. *Spine, 16,* 1–6.

Borg, M. G. (1990). Occupational stress in British educational settings: A review. *Educational Psychology, 10,* 103–126.

Burke, R. J., & Richardsen, A. M. (1996). Stress, burnout, and health. In C. Cooper (Ed.), *Handbook of stress, medicine, and health* (pp. 101–117). Boca Raton, FL: CRC Press.

Cordes, C. L., & Dougherty, T. W. (1993). A review and integration of research on job burnout. *Academy of Management Review, 18,* 621–656.

Guglielmi, R. S., & Tatrow, K. (1998). Occupational stress, burnout, and health in teachers: A methodological and theoretical analysis. *Review of Educational Research, 68*(1), 61–99.

Jackson, S. (1983). Participation in decision making as a strategy for reducing job related strain. *Journal of Applied Psychology, 68,* 3–19.

Karasek, R. A., & Theorell, T. (1990). *Healthy work.* New York: Basic Books.

Kyriacou, C. (2001). Teacher stress: Directions for future research. *Educational Review, 53*(1), 27–35.

Kyriacou, C., & Sutcliffe, J. (1978). Teacher stress: Prevalence, sources, and symptoms. *British Journal of Educational Psychology, 48,* 159–167.

Maslach, C. (1998). A multidimensional theory of burnout. In C. L. Cooper (Ed.) *Theories of organizational stress* (pp. 68–85). Oxford: Oxford University Press.

Maslach, C., Jackson, S. F., & Leiter, M. P. (1996). *The Maslach Burnout Inventory* (3rd ed.). Palo Alto, CA: Consulting Psychologists Press.

Osipow, S. (1998). *Occupational Stress Inventory Revised Edition manual.* Odessa, FL: Psychological Assessment Resources.

Paykel, E. S. (1976). Life stress, depression, and attempted suicide. *Journal of Human Stress, 2,* 3–12.

Pines, A., & Aronson, E. (1988). *Career burnout: Causes and cures.* New York: Free Press.

Pithers, R. T., & Soden, R. (1998). Scottish and Australian teacher stress and strain: A comparative study. *British Journal of Educational Psychology, 68,* 269–279.

Quick, J. C., Quick, J. D., Nelson, D. L., & Hurrell, J. J. (1997). *Preventive stress management in organizations.* Washington, DC: American Psychological Association.

Spielberger, C. D., & Vagg, P. R. (1999). *The Job Stress Survey: JSS professional manual.* Odessa, FL: Psychological Assessment Resources.

Sutton, R. I. (1984). Job stress among primary and secondary schoolteachers: Its relationship to ill-being. *Work and Occupations, 11,* 7–28.

Theorell, T., & Karasek, R. A. (1996). Current issues related to psychosocial job strain and cardiovascular disease research. *Journal of Occupational Health Psychology, 1,* 9–26.

Vagg, P. R., & Spielberger, C. D. (1998). Occupational stress: Measuring job pressure and organizational support in the workplace. *Journal of Occupational Health Psychology, 3,* 294–305.

Vagg, P. R., & Spielberger, C. D. (1999). The Job Stress Survey: Assessing perceived severity and frequency of occurrence of generic sources of stress in the workplace. *Journal of Occupational Health Psychology, 4,* 288–292.

Van Sell, M., Brief, A. P., & Schuler, R. S. (1981). Role conflict and role ambiguity: Integration of the literature and directions for future research. *Human Relations, 34*(1), 43–71.

Section D

Musing Philosophical and Looking Toward the Future

Chapter 44
Current Issues in Educational Assessment
The Test Publisher's Role

William G. Harris

As education policymakers have moved to reform K–12 public education, the roles of test publishers in assessment have expanded. In the last two decades these expanded roles have coincided with the movement of assessment to the center of education reform initiatives. In the 1980s, users of assessments largely focused on minimal competency testing. By the 1990s, education policymakers had ratcheted up the expectations. The focus changed to high-stakes accountability in which the assessment served as the leading indicator and, unfortunately, in some instances as the only indicator (Linn, 2000). The drive for improvement in public education has made the roles of test publishers even more demanding while presenting the publishers with new opportunities and challenges.[1]

An educational assessment is a standardized method of gathering data and converting it to information used to evaluate the academic progress of students, the effectiveness of instruction, or the success of educational programs (Cizek, 1997). Ideally, most jurisdictions employ multiple measures for each purpose—such as standardized tests, writing samples, portfolio materials, and teachers' recommendations—to create an educational assessment system for measuring different elements of academic achievement or for evaluating a state or district's overall program performance. For the purpose of this discussion, I define educational assessment specifically as (a) standardized testing used by teachers to identify strengths and weaknesses of students in order to adjust classroom instruction; (b) standardized testing used in making high-stakes decisions such as grade promotion and graduation; or (c) the aggregation of non–student-specific standardized testing data used to make program decisions such as educational funding and school staffing. It is extremely important to identify the type of standardized testing at issue so that a proper context for discussion is available.

Most stakeholders such as education policymakers, educators, and parents embrace the importance of assessment in educational or instructional improvement. Such widespread support begins to waver, however, when the assessments possess high-stakes consequences, which morphs the test into a feature of educational policy. Differences among stakeholders surface on the frequency of testing, its overall weight in academic and programmatic accountability, and its influence on the funding of educational resources. The role of the publishers of all types of tests is first to recognize the legitimacy of the differences and then to campaign energetically for the appropriate and meaningful use of all assessments in an education reform strategy.

Assessments used for high-stakes purposes serve as the gatekeepers of the standards-based accountability reform movement.[2] Standards-based reform refers to the use of state standards for subject matter content (such as mathematics, language arts, or other core subjects in each grade) and to the use of performance levels established by the state for determining if students are performing at acceptable levels of competency (such as "Basic," "Proficient," or "Advanced"). Accountability means that parents, students, educators, and policymakers share the responsibility for improving the academic achievement of students in accordance with specific content and performance standards. Educational assessments are central to the standards-based reform system that stresses the use of measurable outcomes to monitor students' progress. In states that have implemented graduation assessments, however, adverse reactions of parents, teachers, and educators, as well as uncertainty among policymakers, have led to extensions or delays in imposing those graduation requirements.

On top of the academic results, most states and districts have implemented an accountability system for measuring programmatic progress. Some states have even adopted systems for rewarding or sanctioning schools or districts based upon those outcomes. Because of the uncertainties surrounding these accountability measures, many policymakers have delayed implementation of specific rewards or sanctions.[3]

The more that stakeholders depend on educational assessments to direct policy, the more test publishers are placed in the role of securing validity evidence to support high-stakes uses while discouraging the use of any one assessment as a sole determinant in these decisions. Generally accepted professional technical standards emphasize the use of multiple measures especially when the assessment outcomes are tied to high-stakes consequences. In that scenario, test publishers emphasize the value of educational assessments but point to the importance of multiple measures to provide complementary or confirmatory information to aid in the decision-making effort.

A Multifaceted Role

At a strategic level, the roles of educational test publishers are not easily partitioned into discrete functions. The interrelatedness of various roles points to a single role that is multifaceted in its composition. The strategic objectives inherent in the test publishers' multifaceted role are compatible across stakeholder groups. A test publisher's materials may convey the concept of test validity and test fairness differently to education policymakers, educators, and parents. The intent is to assure each of these groups that the inferences drawn from an educational assessment are accurate and that the assessment outcomes do not lead to uneven or unfair treatment of students. Success in managing the test publisher's multifaceted role depends on effective communication of the way a particular assessment functions in the accountability system. As such, the test publisher is strategically compelled to communicate the right information at the right level of understanding to the right stakeholder (e.g., students, parents, educators, policymakers).

A test publisher's multifaceted role is largely molded out of a business necessity, yet this situation creates values and benefits that extend well beyond mere business interests. For instance, a well-designed, professionally developed educational assessment can contribute to understanding the alignment between state content standards and curriculum, to improving the quality of educational diagnostics, to targeting the educational resource needs of low-performing schools, and to monitoring efforts to afford all students the opportunity to learn. When psychometrically supported and appropriately used, the educational assessment adds value to an educational improvement strategy and contributes, both socially and educationally, to the greater good of society.

The broad influence of educational assessments creates for test publishers both opportunities and challenges. As already suggested, some of the opportunities are in educational diagnostics, decision making (e.g., graduation and promotion examinations), classroom instruction, and intervention or remediation strategies. Safeguarding educational assessments from misuse, unreasonable criticism, and misperceptions are among the challenges test publishers face. Another equally important challenge is anticipating and planning for the interplay between assessments and technology.

In its multifaceted role, a test publisher attempts to communicate the appropriate function of assessment in the educational process. The test publisher circumscribes the capabilities of a specific educational assessment as effective when its purpose is well defined and its use does not stray from its intended purpose. Several issues ruffle the neatness of this statement. A particular educational assessment may generate useful information about the performance of an individual student, a group of students, or an educational program. The same assessment may be valid for more than one purpose and in multiple settings. As such, there may be a wide range of appropriate use of some assessments.

Despite stakeholders' heavy reliance on educational assessments, however, assessments are incapable of closing the achievement gap between students from high-performing schools and those from low-performing schools. Assessments offer policymakers and educators guidance on ways to close the gap, but they, as part of standards-based accountability reforms, are powerless to correct long-standing problems of educational indifference. Therefore, it is untenable to burden educational assessments with the task of improving the quality of education without policymakers aggressively addressing factors such as inadequate per-pupil expenditures, unacceptable pupil-teacher ratios, and ill-equipped classroom teachers. When these and related factors (e.g., educational intervention at the prekindergarten level) are addressed with a sustained commitment, the benefits of educational assessment are attainable.

Put differently, a classroom environment that is resource starved and pedagogically shortsighted undermines both learning and the benefits of the educational assessment. Narrowly "teaching to the test" strips the assessment of its value and shortchanges the education of students. On the other hand, when inadequacies in the classroom environment are corrected in concert with the use of a professionally developed assessment, students are given the chance to become better learners, rather than merely better test takers.

In their communicator role, test publishers seek to explain that an accountability system of content and performance standards and assessment is inadequate to sustain long-lasting, meaningful reform. The absence of real changes in the classroom environment, in teacher development, and in technology use marginalizes both the standards and assessment in schools with students who could benefit the most from them. Such tension, if not properly addressed, can only accelerate the erosion of confidence in the reform effort and, perhaps, in the specific educational assessment selected for use in particular states or districts.

A key skill for the test publisher, then, is to perfect the ability to find the appropriate level at which to communicate relevant information to different stakeholder groups. For instance, it is vitally important to explain to teachers the disservice they provide to students when they teach to the test. Such inappropriate test preparation hampers true learning and potentially discolors the usefulness of the test results. Clear, thoughtful, and realistic content standards that encourage the development of a rich, vibrant curriculum are pivotal to any effort to avoid turning the classroom into a test prep shop. As a communicator, the test publisher campaigns continually for stakeholders to use sound testing practices and to integrate the educational assessment into the learning experience of students. As the assessment becomes integrated in learning, it is less likely to be the target of disillusioned stakeholders and testing critics.

Reforming Education and the Educational Assessment

As noted, through legislative reform initiatives that emphasize standards-based accountability, policymakers and educators have fueled the growth of the educational assessment. Such growth has assigned to test publishers a position of influence in the movement to reform the nation's K–12 public education system. The influential role of test publishers and the spiraling rise in testing are events that have evolved over the past two decades.

By the early 1980s, policymakers and educators had sounded the alarm that the nation's education system was performing poorly and that the whole system required a radical overhaul. They assailed the nation's education system as inefficient and ineffective. The inadequacies of a burdened education system produced students of low academic achievement.

In decrying the plight of the education system, policymakers and educators were not alone. Business leaders added their voices to the chorus of critics urging the reinvention of public education. These leaders linked a quality education to the country's future economic security and global competitiveness. They offered mostly anecdotal evidence to support their claims that without a vibrant education system, the business prowess of the United States would suffer increased threats. Such threats from competitive forces were expected to intensify because the nation's education system was fractionated and ill equipped to prepare students to join a technologically demanding workforce. Businesses lamented that often they were forced to provide remedial education to high school graduates or look outside the United States to find employees with the prerequisite skills, training, and education. For these leaders a quality education had become a business imperative.

Despite these needs, meaningful comparisons of student achievement across the 50 states proved elusive. The problem in comparing the 50 state education systems existed in part because each state employed different educational assessment instruments and different testing cycles for different grade levels. With education as primarily the dominion of the state, attempts to equate different commercially published instruments used by states met with only meager success, except for limited situations, such as for assessments used to measure progress among impoverished children. Adding to this complexity was significant state variation in the level of educational expenditures, curriculum content, and standards for measuring student achievement. Cross-state comparisons were fraught with methodological pitfalls, and comparisons of students within the same state were not without limitations due to the use of different local tests by various districts across a state. Even with these methodological barriers, the use of nationally normed, standardized large-scale tests was the best available alternative for measuring the student progress and the success of educational programs.

In 1983, concerns about the nation's education system were confirmed with the release of the National Commission on Excellence in Education's final report, *A Nation at Risk.* That report acknowledged and highlighted deep systemic problems in the nation's education system. It pointed out that the content of school curricula and measurable standards of accountability were woefully inept and needed to be upgraded. The report also called for students to devote more time to learning and for teachers to receive more resources to improve teaching preparation. Although the report has had its critics, it has served, albeit with changes, as a national blueprint for the standards-based education reform movement.

By the 1990s, both a Republican and a Democratic president had reacted to that report by seeking legislation to encourage states to improve their standards-based reform efforts. Initially, after President George H. Bush's education summit of governors and business representatives recommended a series of National Education Goals, he introduced the America 2000 legislation to provide federal money for states to engage in systemic education reform focused on standards and assessments. Picked up, revised, and renamed by President Clinton as Goals 2000, the legislation was enacted into law in 1994 as the Educate America Act with the avowed aim of having states adopt "world-class content standards and break-the-mold assessments to measure them"[4] (p. 8) By 1996, every state had accepted federal funds for these purposes, and to date, nearly every state has developed its own set of content standards; 47 states have adopted some form of assessment system to measure that content.

Criticizing Education Reform and Assessment

The assessment component of the education reform movement has received a disproportionate amount of attention and criticism. Assessment represents only one of the key activities of education reform. Education reform contains two major branches of activities: resource allocation and structural reforms (Grissmer, Flanagan, Kawata, & Williamson, 2000). Resource allocation reforms target factors such as per-pupil expenditures, teachers' salaries, pupil-teacher ratios, and teachers' resources. Structural or standards-based reforms target the development of well-designed, realistic content standards aligned to state curricula, which can then be used to develop assessments. Educational assessments are used to measure directly the effects of standards-based curriculum and to measure indirectly the effects of resource allocations on student achievement and educational programs.

As the standards-based reform movement has charged forward, its reliance on assessment has provoked criticism. The level of resistance to assessment varies among proponents and opponents of reforms. Some proponents of education reforms complain that a standards-based accountability system prematurely places too much emphasis on testing with high-stakes implications. They view the tendency "to rush to test" as outpacing a balanced approached to education reform. Yet there is little disagreement that assessment is fundamental to an effective standards-based accountability system; it seems that testing creates the most concern when it is first introduced. The introduction of large-scale standardized testing is meant to improve education and instruction, not distract from it. This desired use encourages teachers and educators to redesign the curriculum, to establish teacher preparation programs, and to create intervention and remediation programs that reflect clearly defined content standards. These activities are not high stakes because they are not used to make individual student decisions. For state testing proponents, the key drivers are content standards. State assessments used for these purposes provide the classroom teacher, as well as each student's parents, with specific information on student strengths and weaknesses in particular subjects within the state's content standards. Such state standardized assessments have been developed to stimulate a productive learning environment rather than one regimented around test preparation.

In most settings where these state standardized tests are used, except where high school graduation itself is the purpose,[5] many other factors exist from which individual decisions about student placement and promotion are made: grades, portfolios or simple writing samples, teacher recommendations, attendance, extracurricular activities, and the like. It is not appropriate or fair to label these tests as automatically having a high-stakes purpose when the most common use of information is directly by teachers and educators, to guide classroom instruction and intervention or remediation for students.

Using these tests to provide program information is also not a problem. In the most common situation, districts or states will take the aggregated data from their standardized tests, without any identifiable student information, and disaggregate the data. In other words, states and districts are able to determine based on general data how specific subgroups of students (e.g., by race, ethnicity, gender, type of disability, or family income level) are performing against the state content standards. These disaggregated data are used to determine whether the subgroups are "narrowing the gap" with all other students.

Evaluating the Criticism

Some critics insist that too much instructional time and curriculum content is lost to test preparation and test taking. They argue that students are shortchanged because extracurricular activities such as music and art vanish from the curriculum and are replaced with a concentrated effort to teach to the test. They further assert that the growing obsession with accountability and test results narrows the curriculum and stymies creativity. Still, there is nothing intrinsically limiting about using state assessments for instructional purposes.

Other critics assert that the opportunity to learn is grossly uneven for students from low-performing schools and that state standardized assessments further injure them. Students in these schools produce predictably lower scores and their scores are then used to imply that they are less capable than students from high-performing schools. These critics contend that scores on state standardized assessments for students from low-performing schools are difficult to interpret because the gap in instructional resources rivals the gap in achievement scores for high- and low-performing schools. The subpar test scores of students trapped in marginal schools merely subtract from their already low self-esteem. Subsequently, critics are quick to question the instructional purpose of educational assessments. As a remedy they urge greater emphasis on interventions to provide students with greater opportunities to learn (e.g., better facilities, better prepared teachers, smaller class sizes, instructional resources) and less emphasis, at least initially, on test scores. In responding to these critics it is clear that low-performing students stand to gain the most from assessments when teachers use test results to develop and employ strong intervention and remediation strategies. Shortcomings stem from the failure of the state or locality to provide adequate resources, not the use of valid assessments.

Popham (1999a, 2001) insists that typical state standardized assessments are both misnamed and misleading. He opposes the makeup of traditional assessments while embracing the educational assessment engineered to fit his model. Popham (1999b) views state assessments as overly focused on accountability issues and argues that the assessment of instruction is absent in the test design used to construct these state assessments. In the short run, Popham recommends avoiding the use of these assessments to appraise instruction. He offers an all or nothing perspective on existing educational assessment programs. It is unreasonable to ignore the instructional benefits derived from existing state standardized tests. Nevertheless, Popham's recommendation to design state tests capable of measuring both instruction and overall accountability is compelling and is a potentially beneficial refinement.

At another level, Popham (1999a) criticizes state assessments for their inclusion of too many items that measure what students bring to school and not what they learn there. Students from affluent schools come to school with rich and varied life experiences that are captured in the content of many standardized assessment items (Popham,1999b, 2001). In an attempt to advance his perspective, CISA (2001a) has codified Popham's recommendations in a model RFP with nine requirements for states to design tests that promote better teaching and learning. Five leading education groups, including a panel of prominent educators and measurement specialists, endorse this model RFP (CISA, 2001b). Popham's contention that state-specific items developed in conjunction with state educators and teachers are poorly constructed is not well documented. Items developed without regard to measurement principles usually reveal substandard psychometric properties. This is rarely the case for state assessment items. Current standardized state assessments are objective measures of state content standards, which are based on professional norms and psychometric rigor.

The heightened position of assessments in education reform leads to sharpened criticism and intensified calls for alternatives. Testing critics serve as a source of information about the function of assessments in education reform. Publishers are seldom in a position to ignore criticism of testing; instead they try to incorporate criticism, when feasible, into an ongoing test improvement strategy.

Advocating for the Educational Assessment

In advocating the indispensable role of the educational assessment in public education, the test publisher also champions its social value. At one level embracing the social value of high-quality education reform is strategically consistent with business objectives. At another level expressing the social value of the educational assessment and educational improvement is a social responsibility. When the assessment truly meets the demands of the education community and society at large, the business objectives of the test publishers are invariably met.

An educational assessment properly aligned to state standards and the curriculum reveals more than the academic progress of students. The assessment discloses how well and how evenly education reforms are serving all students. The newest federal initiative, NCLB, requires more than the regular assessment of students.[6] Assessment is part of the frontline effort to revamp an education system tattered and frayed in certain respects by providing both longitudinal and cross-sectional data about student progress using each state's own test system. NCLB requires a confirmation by which the state's tests can be generally evaluated. Finally, state measures of "adequate yearly progress" will be reviewed by the U.S. Department of Education and, where appropriate, intervention strategies will be implemented for districts or schools that are not meeting academic improvement expectations.

A wave of recent surveys on educational issues reveals that stakeholders, including parents, describe education in low-income schools as in crisis. These respondents are far less inclined to assign a similar description to high- or middle-income schools (Hart & Teeter, 2001). Schools in low-income areas struggle with overcrowded classrooms, outdated textbooks, ineffective remediation services, too few highly trained teachers, and a host of related school resource issues.

To withdraw the standardized assessment from students in these educationally needy schools would be misguided as well as a disservice to the core meaning of education reform for all students.

All students, teachers, and school administrators need to know how well they measure up to well-defined standards. The social value of professionally developed assessments is in contributing to an intervention and remediation plan that is comprehensive and inclusive. Such a plan does not minimize strong accountability standards or shortchange instruction. Converting score information to a relevant, clearly defined plan for students and programs is the hallmark of a responsible accountability program. To expect anything less from standardized assessments is to emphasize scores at the expense of real reform and an improved educational experience for all students.

The failure to translate state assessment results into educational solutions invites resistance to standardized assessments. To put it more succinctly, generating assessment results without a clear purpose is a misuse of that assessment. The resistance to such misguided actions emerges as complaints of too much testing, boycotts, or initiatives to reduce the influence of the assessment on education reform. Surprisingly, complaints and boycotts of the assessment are less likely to come from stakeholders whose constituents are represented in the low-performing schools. These parents accept, however reluctantly, that the potential benefits derived from the educational assessment outweigh their concerns. Parents in high- and middle-income school areas are more likely to voice discontent about state-mandated content standards, large-scale state assessments, and their supposedly stifling effect on school curriculum.

Recent boycotts and protests of educational assessments in the states of New York, Massachusetts, Arizona, and Illinois further illustrate some parents' growing dissatisfaction (Zernike, 2001). These parents strongly support high standards and demand that their children perform at the higher end of the achievement continuum. They do not, however, endorse standardized assessment as the best way to measure the quality of education. "These kinds of tests reduce content, they reduce imagination, they limit complex curriculum, they add stress and cost money," explains one Scarsdale, New York, parent (Hartocollis, 2001, p. D2). This tremor of discontent is troubling. More importantly, it serves as a signal to test publishers that the success of students on a state assessment does not always equate to unwavering support for testing. Parents contend that state assessments limit the curriculum, curb the use of innovative teaching methods, and suppress creative thinking among students. These are examples of criticism that test publishers need to address. Finding ways to fashion such discontent into benefits of educational assessment adds value to students' academic experiences and increases parental support for large-scale assessment programs.

Besides parents fearing that state assessments adversely affect creativity and learning, there are other reasons stakeholders retreat from assessment. This withdrawal occurs when the assessment is misaligned with the standards and curriculum, and is then improperly linked to high-stakes consequences, such as graduation. In this situation, unreasonably high standards that focus on extremely high performance levels or that are outside the curriculum actually being taught are allowed to shape the development of the state assessment. This scenario illustrates that, even if the content standards and the state assessment are aligned, if actual curriculum and teaching are not tied to the content standards for the result can be disastrous. Because the state test does not fit the educational reality of what teachers are teaching and students are learning, poor test outcomes occur, which inflame students, parents, and educators. The proclivity of disgruntled parents, educators, and in some cases, the media, is to attack the state assessment as inaccurate and poorly designed. Often these stakeholders call for a moratorium on the use of the assessment for high-stakes decisions. Such misalignment problems are generally discovered during the pretesting phase of developing the assessment instrument. Still, test publishers cannot be perceived as providing merely a "plug and play" assessment device without accepting a growing threat from some stakeholders to reduce the involvement of high-stakes assessment in education reform.

Advocating for the importance of standardized assessment is inseparable from the broader activity of advocating for a quality education. A professionally developed assessment instrument is unlikely to survive untarnished in an education system where the other components are not constructed with the same meticulous care. As an advocate, the test publisher's responsibility does not begin and end with the educational assessment. The responsibility of the test publisher extends to proposing refinements to standards, providing insight into ways to create multiple measures that truly complement the assessment, and finding ways to fold salient concerns of parents and teachers into the assessment effort.

Safeguarding Educational Assessments from Threats

The installation of tough standards-based accountability systems with high-stakes assessments as the linchpin of reform holds some risk for test publishers. Testing with high-stakes consequences puts pressure on test validity, security, and other elements of technical quality (Carnevale & Kimmel, 1997). This pressure increases when education policymakers stretch the test purpose beyond its normal limits. For example, the use of test scores to decide bonuses for teachers generally stretches the test beyond its intended purpose. Using test scores alone represents a misuse of the test; administrators have available other factors to use in conjunction with student test scores, including evaluations by supervisors or the principal, review of lesson plans, parent complaints and accolades, teacher attendance, training records, and the like.

The misuses of large-scale standardized high-stakes assessments were a driving force that led the U.S. Department of Education Office for Civil Rights to develop a guide for policymakers and educators entitled *The Use of Tests as Part of High-Stakes Decision-Making for Students: A Resource Guide for Educators and Policy-Makers* (OCR, 2000). The *Resource Guide* informs policymakers and educators about the interplay among large-scale assessments, professional technical test development principles, and federal nondiscrimination laws. The overarching principles of the *Resource Guide* are culled from a report prepared by the National Research Council entitled *High Stakes: Testing for Tracking, Promotion, and Graduation* (Heubert & Hauser, 1999). These principles are that (a) a test be valid for a particular purpose; (b2) a test reflect the knowledge and skills covered in instruction; and (c) scores on a test lead to decisions and to intended and unintended consequences that are educationally beneficial. As this report makes abundantly clear, when stakeholders employ an assessment as the locus of decision making, it is important that they not unwittingly gloss over the implications of the test or the practices that surround its use or misuse.

Some test practices, when compared against the *Standards for Educational and Psychological Testing* (AERA, APA, & NCME, 1999) and the *Code of Fair Testing Practices in Education* (JCTP, 2002), fall short of these generally accepted professional principles. Occasionally, test practices fall short of existing federal constitutional, statutory, and regulatory nondiscrimination principles. These legal principles address assessment issues such as (a) test use that is incompatible with test design and validity evidence; (b) the use of a test score as a sole determinant for making decisions; (c) the opportunity for students to receive quality classroom instruction before taking a high-stakes assessment; (d) the significance of fairness being evident in the assessment system; and (e) the educational rationale for establishing cutoff scores. Legal principles are invoked whenever improper use of the educational assessment is alleged in one of these areas.[7]

Although the analysis of relevant federal court decisions cannot be pursued in this chapter, most of the issues confronting the courts regarding the use of educational assessments for high-stakes purposes are directly relevant to test publishers. The more the assessment results disproportionately affect the educational experience and success of certain groups of students (e.g., minority groups, students with limited English proficiency, or students with disabilities), the more probable the assessment will be embroiled in litigation.[8] The *High Stakes* report (Heubert & Hauser, 1999) stopped short of calling for federal regulation of high-stakes assessments, but it does argue that the two major mechanisms for compelling appropriate test use—voluntary compliance with professional technical standards, such as the *Standards* (AERA, APA, & NCME, 1999), and legal actions—are inadequate. This call for tighter control of the assessment process echoes from groups such as the National Commission on Testing and Public Policy (1990) and preparatory organizations (Katzman & Hodas, 2001).

The OCR *Resource Guide,* more than any other recent document dealing with testing issues, serves as a bridge between the *Standards* and relevant legal standards. It offers practical guidance to stakeholders on appropriate use of assessments for high-stakes decisions and on the legal pitfalls to eschew when using these assessments in accountability systems. Relying on the *Resource Guide* as part of an aggressive preventive outreach program would diminish markedly the need to entertain regulatory remedies for inappropriate test use. Test publishers continue to advocate the benefits of the *Resource Guide,* and have urged the Department of Education to create a substantial outreach program for all stakeholders.

Besides ensuring proper use of large-scale state assessments used in high-stakes decisions, it is important to safeguard their integrity. One of the most common threats to the integrity of assessments is cheating. In May 2001, several Maryland teachers used the actual state sixth-grade mathematics test as practice for their students. Ironically, it was the students themselves who blew the whistle by telling other teachers they had seen the items before. As a result, Maryland had to spend substantial dollars to build a replacement test covering the same content in order to ensure test security and the validity of future test results. Similar threats occur when teachers teach too closely to the test. Test preparation that targets the content too narrowly constitutes cheating. Under this circumstance, the assessment results are less likely to reflect test takers' knowledge and skills than their recall.

Another loss of test security occurs when organizations such as local newspapers seek the release of the questions and answers. As occurred in Arizona, one legal tactic is to demand disclosure of the state assessment items under the state's public records law.[9] A state's public records law directs the disclosure of records that are owned or funded by the state. Without a clear exemption from the public records law, the state's large-scale assessment program may be compelled to release test items that could severely limit the future utility of the tests. Only a few states (i.e., Georgia, New York, and Texas) have designed their state assessments to allow for release of past test items to the public, which requires the state to build disposable assessments. These states release the assessment questions and answers to the public after the completion of the administration cycle in order to allow parents to see the test. This approach is vastly more expensive than development and repeated administration of one test or separate forms of the test over a period of years. In the latter situation, states offer limited inspection of the state assessments on a case-by-case basis, without permitting any copy or transcript of the items to be released. This approach guarantees test security and ensures that the validity of the state test is protected for future use. For most state testing agencies and their test publisher contractors, the disclosure of test items or data under public records laws is inimical to a strong accountability system and to any meaningful effort to use aggregated test results longitudinally to inform educational policy.

As the preceding examples illustrate, a pivotal role for test publishers is to safeguard educational assessments from misuse. This sentrylike role means actively ensuring that each state assessment is aligned with the curriculum and the content standards. Still, a test publisher's effort needs to be much broader than ensuring alignment. As *High Stakes* poignantly concludes, "In the absence of effective services for low-performing students, better tests will not lead to better educational outcomes" (p. 2, executive summary). Safeguarding the state assessment also means that students should be given notice that graduation depends on passing the test; they should be provided with multiple opportunities to complete the high-stakes test successfully;

and they should be given meaningful remediation if they fail the test initially. It is crucial that test publishers change negative perceptions about the use of assessments for high-stakes purposes. Allowing such negative perceptions to persist and gain credibility can only undermine support for the use of assessment and encourage stakeholders to look for less incendiary alternatives.

Ensuring the Future of Educational Assessment

As standards-based curriculum and assessment are woven into the educational fabric, the demand for time-sensitive information will grow rapidly. The informational requirements of stakeholders seem likely to compel test publishers to expand their capabilities and look to technology to meet these and other demands. E-learning, e-testing, and web-based classrooms are a few examples of Internet-related activities that are changing the educational experience. Test publishers are in a position to oversee changes in the way educational assessments are developed, delivered, and used. Multiple-choice, open-ended response, and essay-style items can all share the assessment space with simulation tasks, video, audio, and other innovative item types. Innovative item types will provide a better understanding of how students learn, what they have learned, and how to improve their learning in the future. New learning technologies will advance efforts to improve education.

The delivery of e-testing on the Internet will almost surely compete with the paper-and-pencil test booklet for dominance of mainstream assessment.[10] Web-based platforms are changing the look of adult and postsecondary education. E-learning is making lifelong learning for adults a reality. Information technology certification programs are pioneering the use of innovative item types and enhanced test security. Internet-based test preparatory and tutorial services are advancing instructional technology and influencing learning, especially as they relate to postsecondary admissions testing. Finally, the explosive growth in the use of essay-style items in state assessments for high-stakes decisions is driving the use of advanced computational linguistics techniques to score constructed writing responses. These actions already reveal the tendency of test publishers to seek technological solutions for labor-intensive, time-sensitive tasks in order to meet business and educational objectives; this trend will continue.

Although most of today's K–12 educational assessments are delivered in a paper-and-pencil medium, the signs show clearly that public school systems are migrating to online assessments. Pilot studies of online testing are under way in the states of Oregon, Virginia, and South Dakota (Trotter, 2001a).[11] The speed in which technology is inserted into the educational experience will depend on its cost benefits and on funding.

Test publishers recognize that using a poorly implemented state assessment program for high-stakes decisions erodes public confidence and undermines support for education reforms. Once the NCLB is fully implemented, test publishers expect the demand for various assessments to increase by more than 50 percent (Steinberg & Henriques, 2001). The NCLB mandates testing of all students in mathematics and reading from third through eighth grade, but without any individual student consequences. Although 13 states now offer testing in grades three through eight, only nine of these states have standards-based tests (Olson, 2002). Nevertheless, with roughly 40 percent of 53 million school-age children in these six grades, the additional testing is raising some concerns about test publishers' capacities to handle all assessment needs. Many of the capacity concerns center on the timeliness and accuracy of assessment results for use in individual student decisions (Steinberg & Henriques, 2001). Technology will play a key role in addressing the substantial boost in the number of assessments administered and will be central to test publishers' efforts to provide error-free processing that is responsive to the states' time requirements for scores. Some states use the results of state tests to place students in next year's classes and to help teachers plan for next year's curriculum. In other states, testing occurs earlier in the winter or spring so that scores are received before the end of the school year. Whatever the state's needs, test publishers have always been able to meet them, and the increased role of online assessments will enhance response time and flexibility.

Use of technology to deliver large-scale assessments is not without peril. The mere shifting of the assessment from a paper-and-pencil to an online mode is grossly inadequate to stimulate permanent migration. Adoption of the online medium for assessment depends on its reconceptualization (Bennett, 1998, 1999). The key to revamping traditional assessment is to create new models of how students think and to link these models to new test designs. Such models, using innovative psychometric procedures, explain the ways students apply higher-order thinking and solve problems. Before full-fledged implementation of online testing, we must explore ways in which inequities such as unfamiliarity with or limited access to the online medium may adversely affect some students' performance. The advantage of web-based education, and particularly online assessment, is that it can expand educational opportunities for all students. If it fails to realize such advantages, the use of the online medium for assessments will fall short of its educational and societal expectations.

With standards-based educational accountability comes a never-ending thirst for information from policymakers, educators, parents and even students. This desire for information is difficult to quench without pushing education into the twenty-first century and toward effective use of technology. Landgraf (2001) implores the educational testing community to "harness the power of technology" (p. 14) while urging the U.S. Congress to commission the development and management of Internet-delivered state assessments. The Consortium on Renewing Education (1998) boldly predicts that "new digital technology promises to change the core enterprises of schools teaching and learning profoundly influencing ways in which knowledge and information are discovered, distilled, compiled, stored, accessed, and used" (pp. 53–54). The realization of this prediction is well within reach. The near future of this realization is reason for educational test publishers to become leaders in the technological reform of education. When it comes to technology, test publishers would be wise to take a page out of the lessons learned by businesses over the years technology does not wait for those who are slow to recognize its benefits.

Conclusion

The momentum of testing is unstoppable. Test publishers will continue to play a vital role in the quest to achieve high-standards learning for all students. The role of test publishers will evolve from their present multifaceted role. The publishers' tool, the educational assessment, will provide valuable information about progress toward accountability goals and about the fit among content standards, curriculum, and instruction. Increased demand for test information will come as policymakers ratchet up the expectations for students, teachers, and school systems. Test publishers will have to devote more effort to ensuring appropriate uses of their assessments and to converting test data to better information. The appropriate uses of the assessment will also grow as test publishers introduce more advanced test designs and technical qualities to support the purposes of their assessments.

Still, the pressure of education reform will continue to bear down on educational assessment. The demands placed on assessments used for high-stakes decisions will require the next generation of tests to possess sophisticated reporting capabilities built on innovative cognitive models and item types. When critics assert that the education reform effort is in a "testing frenzy," the discontent stems from testing that interrupts normal instructional activities and drives education policy. The key to addressing this discontent is to redouble publishers' efforts to make assessments as unobtrusive as they can be, similar to the curriculum and classroom instruction. The next generation of educational assessments will merge seamlessly into the educational experience of students.

Standards-based accountability systems raise the bar of academic expectations. At present, this is comparable to raising one side of the bar and ignoring the other side. To truly raise the bar of expectations requires delivering to students high-quality educational assessments, vastly improved teacher training and remedial support services, and a learning environment that fosters student success for all students. Education reform should point to the assessment as the gateway to educational opportunities and better life chances. As former U.S. Secretary of Education Richard Riley stated, "A quality education must be considered a key civil right for the 21st century" (OCR, 2000, p. vi). Test publishers will play a prominent role in achieving quality education for all students, whether through standardized assessments for instructional purposes or through assessments used to make high-stakes decisions.

I gratefully appreciate the critical review and insightful comments of Alan J. Thiemann and Elizabeth M. Fitzgerald. My opinions do not reflect the official position of the Association of Test Publishers.

Notes

1. For purposes of this discussion, I define a test publisher as an entity that develops or publishes education assessments using rigorous, well-accepted professional psychometric procedures. Individually, many test publishers deal with the significant issues presented in this chapter in developing their own products; collectively, they form a specific segment of the test publishing industry that must deal with such issues on a global basis.

2. The significance of this point is not lost on parents who consider education as improving their children's life chances. After grappling with low test scores and high dropout rates, the city of Carson voted to secede from the Los Angeles Unified School District. The leader of the secession movement, Carolyn Harris, said, "the future of our children and our community is at stake" ("City Voting," 2001, p. A16).

3. Although some states have developed rewards and penalties as part of their accountability system, Congress decided to eliminate this form of reinforcement from its initiative. Accordingly, the recent passage of the No Child Left Behind Act (NCLB) of 2001, a reauthorization of the Elementary and Secondary Education Act (ESEA), does not include President Bush's "proposed system of financial rewards and penalties for states based on their progress in improving student achievement" (Robelen, 2002, p. 29).

4. "World-class" refers to national educational standards that reflect a "thinking curriculum" and includes content standards that meetor exceed those of our strongest competitors (National Education Goals Panel, 1993, p. 8).

5. This discussion does not include high school graduation assessments, so-called "exit exams," because the courts have determined that special factors apply to such programs. Generally, states give students ample notice that these assessments must be passed to graduate, the tests are administered not just once but several times during a student's high school experience, and states have put in place remediation efforts to ensure that students who fail an early test have the opportunity to learn the material before being retested.

6. NCLB requires annual testing of students in mathematics and English from third grade through eighth grade. Viewed in the proper perspective, these annual tests are not considered high stakes because there are no high-stakes consequences for individual students based on the tests. They are, in fact, intended to provide parents and teachers with diagnostic information about each student, so that teachers may make changes in instruction and provide appropriate intervention or remediation based on each student's strengths and weaknesses, measured each year. Although data disaggregation by groups without any identification of individual students will occur, such programmatic evaluations are not high stakes, as that term is historically defined. See Heubert & Hauser (1999).

7. After spending more than five years drafting the *Resource Guide,* OCR finally released the document to the public in December 2000. However, it was archived by the Bush administration in January 2001. The Association of Test Publishers, who participated extensively in the drafting process, has met with the Department of Education several times since then to explore creating a public outreach program for all stakeholders using the *Resource Guide*; the reluctance of the department to implement such a program may change now that the NCLB legislation has been enacted.

8. Significantly, the OCR *Resource Guide* makes it clear that test score disparity among groups of students does not alone constitute discrimination under federal law. As then Undersecretary of OCR Norma V. Cantu stated in her "Dear Colleague" letter attached to the guide, "The guarantee under federal law is for equal opportunity, not equal results."

9. The Arizona Court of Appeals recently considered appeals by the state and the Phoenix Newspapers, Inc., seeking to review the decision of the trial court whether items from Arizona's Instrument to Measure Students (AIMS) test for graduation must be released under the state's public records law. The lower court held that certain items the state intends to use as anchor items in future tests did not have to be disclosed but

that the state had no basis to withhold disclosure of other items. Both the state and the Association of Test Publishers, as *amicus curiae,* have contended that because the state had determined to reuse the entire test form again during the period of the assessment program, all items should be protected and should not be released because that would invalidate the test and cause the state to spend additional millions of dollars building new assessments. On November 27, 2001, the Arizona Court of Appeals rendered an opinion that affirmed the decision of the trial court.

10. The proposed federally funded U.S. Open e-Learning Consortium (USOeC) would serve as a state-to-state test item exchange. All participating states would contribute one year's worth of test items to a common clearinghouse. Teachers (and parents) across the nation would have access to the item bank. They would be able to develop online assessment instruments to use as practice tests for students (Trotter, 2001b). These practice assessments would be low stakes, diagnostic, and customized. At first glance this proposed consortium is an exciting way to extend the classroom to the Internet. A potential drawback is that test publishers and test delivery organizations are not engaged at the outset in the development of the digital content (i.e., item bank) or its web-based delivery platform. It is also unclear how the proposed consortium avoids undermining the commercial activities of test publishers that are already offering online practice and diagnostic assessments to school systems.

11. The states of Georgia, Florida, and Pennsylvania are also working with test publishers to develop their online educational assessment capabilities.

References

AERA, APA, & NCME [American Educational Research Association, American Psychological Association, and National Council on Measurement in Education]. (1999). *Standards for educational and psychological testing.* Washington, DC: APA.

Barton, P. E. (1999). *Too much testing of the wrong kind; too little of the right kind in K–12 education.* Princeton, NJ: Educational Testing Service.

Bennett, R. E. (1998). Reinventing assessment: Speculations on the future of large-scale educational testing. Princeton, NJ: Educational Testing Service.

Bennett, R. E. (1999). Using new technology to improve assessment. *Educational Measurement: Issues and Practice, 18,* 5–12.

Carnevale, A. P., & Kimmel, E. W. (1997). *A national test: Balancing policy and technical issues.* Princeton, NJ: Educational Testing Service.

CISA [Commission on Instructionally Supportive Assessment]. (2001a, October). *Building tests to support instruction and accountability: A guide for policymakers.* Retrieved from www.nea.org/accountability/buildingtests.html.

CISA. (2001b, October). *Illustrative language for an RFP to build tests to support instruction and accountability.* Retrieved from www.nea.org/accountability/rfp.html

City voting on leaving Los Angeles School District. (2001, November 2). *New York Times,* p. A16.

Cizek, G. J. (1997). Learning, achievement, and assessment: Constructs at a crossroads. In G. D. Phye (Ed.), *Handbook of classroom assessment.* San Diego: Academic Press.

Cizek, G. J. (2000). Pockets of resistance in the assessment revolution. *Educational Measurement: Issues and Practice, 19,* 16–23.

Consortium on Renewing Education. (1998, November). *20/20 vision: A strategy for doubling America's academic achievement by the year 2020.* Nashville, TN: Peabody Center for Education Policy, Vanderbilt University.

Grissmer, D. W., Flanagan, A., Kawata, J., & Williamson, S. (2000). *Improving student achievement: What state NAEP test scores tell us.* Santa Monica, CA: RAND.

Hart, P. D., & Teeter, R. M. (2001). *A measured response: Americans speak on education reform.* A national public opinion survey conducted for the Educational Testing Service. Princeton, NJ: Educational Testing Service.

Hartocollis, A. (2001, October 31). Scarsdale warned not to boycott state tests. *New York Times,* p. D2.

✦Heubert, J. P., & Hauser, R. (Eds.). (1999). High stakes: Testing for tracking, promotion, and graduation. (Report of the Committee on Appropriate Test Use, Board on Testing and Assessment, National Research Council). Washington D.C.: National Academy Press.

✦JCTP [Joint Committee on Testing Practices]. (2002). *Code of fair testing practices in education.* Available on *Measuring Up: An Anthology of Assessment Resources* [CD]. Also retrievable on-line: http://aac.ncat.edu.

Katzman, J., & Hodas, S. (2001, September 12). A proctor for the testers? *Education Week, 21.* Retrieved from edweek.org/ew/ew_printstory.cfm?slug=02katzman.h21

Landgraf, K. M. (2001, March 8). *Testimony before the Education Reform Subcommittee of the House Committee on Education and the Workforce on Measuring Success: Using assessments and accountability to raise student achievement.* Princeton, NJ: Educational Testing Service.

✦Linn (2000). Assessments and accountability. *Educational Researcher, 29,* 4–16.

National Commission on Excellence in Education. (1983). *A nation at risk.* Washington, DC: U.S. Department of Education.

✦National Commission on Testing and Public Policy. (1990). *From gatekeeper to gateway: transforming testing in America.* Chestnut Hill, MA: Author.

National Education Goals Panel. (1993). *The national education goals report: Building a nation of learners, the national report* (Vol. 1). Washington, DC: Author.

✦OCR [Office of Civil Rights]. (2000). *The use of tests as part of high-stakes decision-making for students: A resource guide for educators and policy-makers.* Washington, DC: Author.

Olson, L. (2002, January 9). Testing systems in most states not ESEA-ready. *Education Week, 21,* 26–27.

Phoenix Newspapers, Inc., v. Lisa Graham Keegan, the Arizona Board of Education, and the Arizona Department of Education. Case No. 1 Ca-CV-00–0284, on appeal from the Maricopa County Superior Court, Case No. CV99–021338 (April 2001).

Popham, W. J. (1999a). Educational quality: Why standardized tests don't measure up. *Educational Leadership, 56,* 8–15.

Popham, W. J. (1999b). Where large scale educational assessment is heading and why it shouldn't. *Educational Measurement: Issues and Practice. 18,* 13–17.

Popham, W. J. (2001, September 19). Standardized achievement tests: Misnamed and misleading. *Education Week, 21,* 46.

Robelen, E. W. (2002, January 9). ESEA to boost federal role in education. *Education Week, 21,* 28–31.

✦Russell, M., & Haney, W. (2000). The gap between testing and technology in schools. *Statements, 1,* 2.

Steinberg, J., & Henriques, D. B. (2001, May 20). Right answer, wrong score: Test flaws take toll. *New York Times,* p. 1.

Trotter, A. (2001a, May 23). Testing computerized exams. *Education Week, 20,* 30–35.

Trotter, A. (2001b, November 7). Online-education consortium created for states. *Education Week, 21,* 26, 32.

Zernike, K. (2001, April 13). In high-scoring Scarsdale, a revolt against state tests. *New York Times,* p. A1.

✦ Document is included in the Anthology of Assessment Resources CD

Chapter 45
Technology, Collaboration, and Better Practice
The Future of Assessment in Education and Counseling

Jo-Ida C. Hansen

The purpose of this chapter is to capture what the future holds for assessment in education and counseling. I will examine only a slice of the exciting times ahead for the field. I trust that many of the other chapter authors in this book have also identified future directions for assessment. I hope my comments are minimally redundant of theirs.

Nature is cyclical. History repeats itself. Fads come and go, then come again. (My university's bookstore is selling tie-dyed t-shirts, and it's not just people older than 40 who are buying them.) Likewise, the popularity of assessment and testing has waxed and waned over the decades. The universe of assessment may be broader now then it was 30 or 40 years ago (e.g., portfolios, performance-based testing, assessment centers, and in-basket exercises are relatively new additions to our available assessment tools) but this decade seems to be moving in the direction of an increasing willingness to employ assessment and testing.

The Impact of Technology

Technology, including technological advances we cannot even imagine, will undoubtedly play a role in the use of assessment and testing by educators and counselors. E-mail, the Internet, the web, computers that are fast and powerful, Palm Pilots, wireless interfaces, and software that accepts voice input will have a profound effect on assessment. Already computerized administration of college admissions achievement tests has essentially replaced paper-and-pencil tests.

Research examining the applicability of computer administration of tests to various populations suggests that this mode of administration is successful (King & Miles, 1995; Reile & Harris-Bowlsbey, 2000). Safeguards can be incorporated to prevent oversights or omissions;

scoring errors are reduced; and feedback can be immediate. As access to computers increases among the general population, computerized testing and Internet-based assessment will become more widespread. Individuals who live in rural areas with limited resources should benefit from this option. Counselors should not automatically assume, however, that all web-based assessments are of high quality. The equivalence of paper-and-pencil and Internet administrations should be established (Sampson, 2000).

Web-based assessment tools are cost-effective and provide results almost immediately. For example, the Child Trauma Academy and the Texas Department of Protective and Regulatory Services are working on the Well-Based Assessment Tool (WBAT), which enables more efficient treatment planning, evaluation, and service delivery for neglected and abused children (Hayes, 2001). The tool assesses various domains of functioning and provides both objective and subjective data. Trained counselors conduct the assessment, and the results are available almost immediately to members of the child's intervention team (e.g., caseworkers and judges).

Advanced programming skills and speedy computers with large memories enable the development of enormous amounts of individualized feedback for test takers. Computer-generated narrative reports were first developed for measures of personality. Instruments such as the MMPI (and MMPI-2) have provided both profile and interpretive reports as feedback for several decades. Interest inventories also have a relatively long history of providing both profiles and interpretive reports (Hansen, 1987). More recent developments include elaborate systems such as ETS's Score Report Plus, which links PSAT/NMSQT assessment with instruction (ETS, 2001). In addition to providing scores, percentiles, ranks, and correct answers, the Score Report Plus includes a section that advises students what they can do to improve their skills. The processes used to generate this information require heavy-duty computing and would not have been technologically feasible 10 years ago.

In the interest measurement arena, the KUDER Career Search Schedule with Person-Match (KCSS), which provides a unique technique for matching an individual's interests to those of a specific person, would not be possible without high-speed, large-memory computers. The KCSS is administered online, takes about 20 minutes to complete, and includes a set of activity preference items; six possible KUDER Career Clusters, representing Holland's six RIASEC types, generated from the 10 homogeneous activity scales of the KUDER;

and 2,000 satisfied employed adults representing 280 of the occupations. The computer sifts through the test taker's interest results and identifies 14 people in the sample of 2,000 who have interests most similar to the test taker's. The report includes a vocational biography for each of the 14 matches as well as suggested steps for continuing career exploration. The inventory is recommended for use with middle school, high school, and community college students to assist them in making educational and career decisions (D. G. Zytowski, personal communication, 2001). An optional package enables students to create an online portfolio that includes the KSA, Super's Work Values Inventory, grades, achievements, and work history. This information can then be used to generate a resume.

Another area in which computers have had, and will continue to have, an impact is on test construction. The emergence of item response theory (IRT) models allows management of item banks to be done automatically. IRT essentially uses responses to items administered at the beginning of a testing session to select items at an appropriate difficulty level for the remainder of the testing session. The IRT approach conserves the number of items required (up to 50 percent), which reduces administration and item development costs as well as test-taking time. Research has shown that IRT methods of test construction can result in shorter tests with better reliability and more precision than conventional achievement tests (Hambleton & Swaminathan, 1985).

The capabilities of computers are leading test developers to expand test batteries to include aspects of abilities that have been difficult to test in the past (e.g., short-term memory, visual-motor coordination, and spatial perception). Furthermore, software can be developed that gives computers the capacity to score open-ended responses. This opens the door for developing computer-based tests of creativity, ideational fluency, and inventiveness.

High-Stakes Testing

Large-scale administrations of achievement tests will be used even more in the future than they are now to make decisions about student progress (e.g., placement, promotion, and graduation). At least 10 states have already developed course exams to be given at the end of specific courses. A passing score is one requirement for passing the course, and the score also figures into decisions to graduate a student (Goetz, Duffy, & Carlson-LeFloch, 2001). In addition to end-of-course exams, about half of U.S. states now require graduation or high school exit exams

(NGA Reports Online, 2002). High-stakes assessments such as these are also being used increasingly in lower grades in efforts to comply with the 2001 No Child Left Behind Act. Assessments start in grade 3 and continue through grade 12, and eventually will be required in reading and language arts, mathematics, and science. In addition to using scores to make promotion, placement, and graduation decisions, high-stakes tests can be designed to assist with diagnosis of student academic strengths and weaknesses. Typically scores on subtests of items are used for this purpose. Performance assessments or portfolios will also be used increasingly as school systems grapple with ways of accommodating students with disabilities and students with limited English proficiency.

Testing Accommodations

According to the U.S. Department of Education, more than 13 percent of children in elementary and middle schools have individualized education plans, and on average 4 to 5 percent of students completing the SAT indicate they have a learning, physical, sensory (e.g., auditory, visual), or psychological (e.g., anxiety disorder, ADHD) disability. Less than 2.5 percent of all tests administered by ETS require accommodations, but the rate is increasing annually, and in 2000–2001 more than 3,000 students received accommodations for testing sessions with the PSAT/NMSQT, SAT I, SAT II, or Advanced Placement Exams (Camara, 2001). Providing accommodations ensures measurement of the intended construct rather than sources of error attributable to the disability, and increases the number of students who can participate in the assessment. As schools try to comply with federal law mandating that all students participate in large-scale assessments, the number and types of accommodations used will increase. Currently, the most frequent accommodations are simply to provide extra time and allow students to be in separate rooms with fewer distractions. In some instances, students are allowed to choose their preferred response format (e.g., in their native language, orally instead of in writing, using typewriters or computers). The way in which a test is administered can also be modified: Braille or large print administrations; translations into native language versions; or oral rather than written administrations are all changes that can be made to enable testing programs to include students for whom standard administration procedures may not result in valid scores.

Mental Health Assessment in the Schools

The traditional separation of children's mental health problems from problems of cognitive development is beginning to give way to a realization that collaborative school environments may best serve the needs of students. Given the number of increasingly complex problems that confront children and young adults, mental health programs located in schools may offer more immediate service and interventions than do community mental health resources. In addition to being able to address mental health problems, schools provide an excellent setting for the delivery of preventive interventions. Preventive interventions include those with a traditional educational focus (such as academic competence) as well as issues of emotional well-being, social skills development, and physical health aimed at helping students before more serious problems develop. School-community-state partnerships are useful in the early stages of implementing and evaluating these programs.

Assessment and testing will be important ingredients in these school-based mental health and prevention programs (see chapters 11 and 12 for descriptions of specific tests for specific uses in school health contexts). Some of the primary purposes of mental health assessment will be (a) to describe current levels of functioning; (b) to aid in differential diagnosis of emotional, behavioral, and cognitive disorders; (c) to monitor treatment and intervention effectiveness; and (d) to manage risk, especially risk related to legal liabilities (Meyer et al., 2001). The usefulness of student assessment will be enhanced when collaborative procedures are used to involve families and others in the student's interpersonal system.

Enhanced assessment and testing training for teachers, administrators, and school counselors will be needed to provide the necessary foundation for understanding personality, cognitive, and behavioral disorders, and psychopathology. Tests can assist counselors in their work with teachers and students, but they are only tools. Ultimately, the counselor must be able to draw inferences from the assessment and test results, and to communicate the results to parents and to educators.

Conclusion

Educational and psychological assessment and testing first began in school settings with measurement of abilities and achievement. This

Technology

purpose remains an important one that is expanding in scope in response to state and federally mandated testing programs. The technology of today and the future will make testing and assessment more available to, and more affordable for, a larger segment of the population. Technological enhancements also will allow schools greater access to a wider variety of instruments.

A greater emphasis on school-community collaboration will reduce the separation of educational and personal counseling, and along with that trend, counselors, teachers, and other educators will use a broader spectrum of instruments to assist them with diagnosis, intervention planning, and outcome assessment. Consequently, educators will need more comprehensive training to prepare them to use testing and assessments responsibly in their work.

Another consequence of the broader use of tests and assessments, as well as new technological innovations, is the need for user guidelines and standards to guide good practice and decision making. For example, the availability of tests on the Internet has many benefits; however, potential problems also accompany this new mode of service delivery. Issues of client confidentiality and privacy, instrument reliability and validity, the ethics of providing adequate interpretation for the client, the consequences of unsupervised test administration, and equitable access for people with limited financial resources will need to be addressed (Sampson & Lumsden, 2000).

The bottom line, then, is that the use of tests and assessment in educational institutions will continue to expand. Enhanced training in the use of tests and assessments for educators, and the development of standards and guidelines, need to go hand in hand with the expanded use to promote ethical and responsible test use.

References

Camara, W. J. (2001, October). Do accommodations improve or hinder psychometric qualities of assessment? *The Score Newsletter,* 4–6.

ETS [Educational Testing Service]. (2001). PSAT/NMSQT‰ Score Report Plus links assessment to learning. *Access, 2,* 6–7.

Goetz, M., Duffy, M., & Carlson-Le Floch, K. (2001). *State assessment and accountability systems: 50 state profiles.* University of Pennsylvania, Consortium for Policy Research in Education website. Retrieved February 22, 2003, from www.cpre.org/Publications/Publications_Accountability.htm

Hambleton, R. K., & Swaminathan, H. (1985). *Item response theory: Principles and applications.* Boston: Kluewer-Nijhoff.

Hansen, J. C. (1987). Computer-assisted interpretation of the Strong Interest Inventory. In J. N. Butcher (Ed.), *A practitioner's guide to computerized psychological assessment.* New York: Basic Books.

Hayes, L. (2001, June). Aided by a "WBAT." *Counseling Today,* 17 & 23.

Helledy, M. S., Zytowski, D. G., & Fouad, N. A. (2001, August). *KUDER Career Search: Consequential validity and test-retest reliability.* Paper presented at the annual meeting of the American Psychological Association, San Francisco, CA.

King, W. C., & Miles, E. W. (1995). A quasi-experimental assessment of the effect of computerizing noncognitive paper-and-pencil measurements: A test of measurement equivalence. *Journal of Applied Psychology, 80,* 643–651.

Meyer, G., Finn, S., Eyde, L., Kay, G., Moreland, K., Dies, R., Eisman, E., Kubiszyn, T., & Reed, G. (2001). Psychological testing and assessment: A review of evidence and issues. *American Psychologist, 56,* 128–165.

NGA [National Governors Association] Reports Online. *Graduation exit exams.* Retrieved February 22, 2003, from www.nga.org/center/divisions/1,1188,C_ISSUE_BRIEF^D_3007,00.html

Reile, D. M., & Harris-Bowlsbey, J. (2000). Using the Internet in career planning and assessment. *Journal of Career Assessment, 8,* 69–84.

Sampson, J. P. (2000). Computer applications. In C. E. Watkins Jr. & V. L. Campbell (Eds.), *Testing and assessment in counseling practice* (2nd ed., pp. 517–544). Hillsdale, NJ: Lawrence Erlbaum Associates.

Sampson, J. P., Jr., & Lumsden, J. A. (2000). Ethical issues in the design and use of Internet-based career assessment. *Journal of Career Assessment, 8,* 21–35.

Chapter 46
The Future of School Testing
A School District Perspective

Linda Elman

Spring state and district testing is wrapping up now, and the test booklets are being counted, sorted, rubber-banded, and carefully placed in boxes to be sent to a far-off scoring center. Teachers and building administrators are emitting great sighs of relief, glad that the "external" testing cycle is ending for this school year, looking forward to getting results back, but mostly happy to be focusing on classroom-based learning again.

So where is the testing program going from here? The passage of the 2001 NCLB is causing major changes in the district testing calendar, and we try to be patient as the state figures out how we will test all students in grades three through eight in reading and mathematics each year using a standards-based assessment. Once the state assessment program is established we will want to re-examine our district assessment plan to ensure that we are assessing what we deem important, in ways that are time- and cost-efficient, and most importantly, we will want to provide information that improves the learning process for our students.

Five years ago in this school district, teachers and building administrators perceived state and district testing as something that *they* made us do. Now, although the testing is still seen as an external imposition that necessitates modifying school and classroom schedules and procedures, the results are highly valued. Teachers and administrators spend many hours analyzing individual and group results, identifying building and grade-level strengths and weaknesses, and planning changes to improve student achievement.

The dilemma now becomes how much testing is reasonable—in terms of time and money, when it should be conducted, and how it should be conducted. For years this district has been doing direct writing assessment at grades that varied from year to year. Over the last two years the testing migrated to the fall of grades 4, 7, and 10, the same grades that are tested each spring on the state-developed standards-based assessment. The writing assessment is given in the first month of school, with scored papers returned about six weeks later. Teachers report that the results add a layer of authority to the scores they give on classroom assessment. Subjecting the papers to an outside authority lent credence to their own evaluation of student work. From a system perspective, as our teachers analyze the externally scored work, they end up recalibrating themselves to the scoring guide.

At the beginning of the year there was some question as to whether the assessment was useful or was intrusive into teachers' instructional time. When the scored papers were returned, teachers made it clear that they wanted to repeat the assessment next fall. But the direct writing assessment is expensive. It costs more than seven dollars per student for scoring, and we question whether in tight times we can continue to support the assessment. Nonetheless, it is clear that when assessment can be used as part of the instructional program, teachers value the information it provides.

One major issue, then, is how we can support more instructionally useful assessment. It is clear that performance-based assessment needs to take place in the classroom and be evaluated by classroom teachers. One of the major implications for future testing is the need to train teachers to design assessments related to identified learning goals and to score them consistently (Stiggins, 2000). For this to happen will require coordinated ongoing efforts on the part of school districts, teachers' associations, principals' associations, state agencies, and institutions of higher education. Many experienced teachers believe that they know how to assess and are reluctant to discuss issues of consistency or even the degree to which their assessments measure the outcomes they really value.

On the other hand, technology may be able to assist with this type of assessment. Project Essay Grade (PEG), Intelligent Essay Assessor (IEA), and E-Rater are online tools designed to use artificial intelligence to score student writing (Rudner & Gagne, 2001). These tools are designed to provide instantaneous feedback to students and teachers on students' writing ability. Although some of these programs provide holistic scores, others provide more extensive trait-based scoring.

For now these systems require that students respond to preselected writing prompts, meaning that these kinds of programs are not open to teachers who want to assign students a content-based essay in literature, social studies, or science; given the rate of improvement in technology as we know it, however, it may not be that far in the future before electronic essay grading is generally available to teachers, allowing them to assign and grade more work. Even more exciting is the possibility that students will be able to submit their essays for electronic scoring, get feedback, and revise their work until they achieve the appropriate level of accomplishment.

Similarly, with voice technology changing at a rapid rate, students may in the not-to-distant future be able to deliver a speech and receive feedback on the content and delivery—though not eye contact—instantaneously. This could improve the consistency and frequency of the evaluation of oral language skills, including speech, drama, and so forth.

But the impact of technology on assessment is not limited to the evaluation of essays or speeches. Technological solutions for testing include the following possibilities:

- online coursework with built-in assessment
- stand-alone systems designed to test one or two students at a time
- networked systems designed to test an entire class at the same time
- Internet-delivered tests, which students take online
- Internet-enabled tests, which students take via network-connected computers, where student data, test items, and scoring information are transmitted online from the testing organization (Olson, 2002)

The possibilities for delivering computerized adaptive tests to students are not new, but as the technological delivery systems become less expensive and easier to use they will make student assessment much more efficient. The benefit of adaptive testing is the ability to get information quickly about a student's level of performance. The testing can quickly focus on a student's achievement level and not waste time giving items that are too easy or too difficult for the student.

Each of these models promises teachers and students almost instantaneous score reporting and feedback. The models also make record-keeping easier by collecting student assessment data into databases that teachers, students, and even parents can potentially access.

So if classroom assessment becomes increasingly efficient, reliable, and standards-based, perhaps there will be less need for standardized district or state assessment. Alternatively, perhaps we will continue to need large-scale assessment to track our progress on our identified learning outcomes. If so, one of the issues we have to deal with is how much time we spend engaged in large-scale assessment. In this district the amount of time spent in district or statewide assessment ranges from no time at 5th and 11th grades to 10 to 12 hours at 4th, 6th, 7th, and 10th grades. These times include only testing time, not the time spent getting students ready for testing or organizing the testing schedule, or the learning time lost, especially in secondary schools, where schedules of students not being tested are disrupted to accommodate the needs of those being tested. Although testing time is not lost time for those being tested, it can have a major impact on other instruction and it can be disruptive to the school program as a whole.

And what about accountability? ESEA calls for improvement of all groups, including all ethnic groups, students with disabilities, disadvantaged students, and students with limited English proficiency. With all the weight of accountability on the state assessments at grades three through eight, there will be major issues regarding test security, ethical test practice, and test inclusion. What about those students for whom our standardized testing is inappropriate? A major thrust in future assessment has to be identifying ways of incorporating results from alternate assessment into the main assessment system.

And then what about students who refuse to participate, or whose parents refuse to include them, in the testing system? Whether they object to the stakes of testing, the time taken by testing, or the limited sample that can be included in a large-scale assessment, parents have been organizing at the grassroots level to oppose large-scale testing and to boycott the tests. The impact has varied across the states, but it does represent a concern that could have major effects on the future of state and district programs.

The future of testing may be exciting—bringing high-quality data into the hands of teachers, students, and their parents so that all students can be well taught and will develop the skills and knowledge they need to be successful workers in the twenty-first century. New testing technology, increased teacher classroom assessment skills, and better record-keeping systems are all trends that will improve the quality of learning for students. On the other hand, heavy accountability requirements and testing that is limited to those constructs that are most easily assessed could have a devastating effect on learning and teaching.

As we wrap up the final boxes, making sure that we can account for each student's test booklets, every teacher's manual, all the alternate assessment forms for students who could not because of disability participate in the regular testing program, we imagine that next year's testing program will look similar to this year's program. But what will it look like in 5 or 10 years?

It is difficult to get outside the realities of today and try to project 5 to 10 years into the future, but why not try? It is 2012, and Mr. Harada's 9- and 10-year-old students are busy with reading and writing activities. Mr. Harada sits down with Yusif to listen as he reads aloud. The tablet Mr. Harada carries is connected via wireless network to the district computer system, and as Yusif picks up his reader, Mr. Harada gets the text of the passage on his tablet. He clicks "start" as he nods at Yusif to begin reading. As Yusif reads, Mr. Harada makes marks on his tablet. At the end he marks "finished" on his tablet and proceeds to discuss the passage with Yusif while making some notes on the child's comprehension. When they are done, Mr. Harada sends his notes to the computer and a report is generated that includes Yusif's reading and error rate, an analysis of reading errors, and a measure of his level of comprehension. With a tap of his stylus, Mr. Harada makes a report appear on his tablet, and he and Yusif discuss the results. Although he is still struggling some, Yusif has made great strides in reading. He identifies some areas that he needs to work on. Mr. Harada identifies some "next tasks" for Yusif and directs him to the classroom library to pull another book off the shelf. Yusif asks if he can take a copy of the report home to his grandmother, and with another tap of the stylus, Mr. Harada rolls a report off the back of his tablet. Mr. Harada can just as easily e-mail a copy of the report from his tablet, but today he knows that Yusif wants to hand the report to his grandmother himself. At any time, however, parents or guardians can check their child's work online and receive a complete report on the child's level of performance, and what next steps the child needs to take.

A few minutes later Mr. Harada sits down at his desktop computer and generates an analysis of his class' performance in reading skills. With this in hand, he takes a few minutes to decide which group of students he is going to pull together next for direct instruction. Between the oral reading assessments he conducts regularly and the assignments that students complete online or on their tablets, Mr. Harada is able to get a pretty complete picture of student progress toward meeting the district grade-level objectives.

Similarly, in the principal's office, or at the district office, an administrator can pull up a report that summarizes reading proficiency in Mr. Harada's class, or among students at the building or district level. Students still participate in the state-required assessments in reading and mathematics at grades three through eight, but these assessments are on their way out. The results of classroom-based assessment have been shown to correlate so highly with the state assessments that the state has concluded that the large-scale assessment is redundant and an unnecessary expense. The money is better spent in training teachers in instruction and integrating assessment into instruction. With new tools coming on line at a rapid pace, all designed to make the assessment process effortless for teachers, keeping teachers and building administrators up to date is a major effort in all states.

At the national level, the National Assessment of Educational Progress (NAEP) is still administered using a matrix-sampling model, but it too has been shown to correlate highly with results reported by individual states based on classroom-level assessments. The president and members of Congress still believe that it is important to have an ongoing measure of student achievement, and NAEP satisfies their perceived need.

At the high school level, demonstration of mastery of essential skills is necessary for a high school diploma. Students begin to collect artifacts of their work at the beginning of ninth grade. As students transmit their work into their electronic portfolios, it is scored and retained. If work is judged not to be of sufficient merit at any time, it is returned to the students with feedback on where the project needs work. All along the way students have the opportunity to submit work and seek feedback, whether it is in math problem solving or reading and writing. At any point teachers can monitor student progress in gathering artifacts, and classes can be grouped or regrouped as needed to assist students in meeting various requirements.

Classrooms look fairly similar to those at the turn of the century, but what is different is the fact that students, being able to receive almost continuous feedback on their work, are motivated to succeed. Their understanding of scoring guides and expectations is simply built into the system, and they are typically able to judge the quality of their own work before either a scoring system or a teacher evaluates it. As teachers are almost totally freed from the drudgery aspect of evaluating student work, they can spend more time evaluating students' strengths and weaknesses, and plan and deliver appropriate instruction to large or small groups, depending on need.

Another major difference is that students are able to progress at their own rates. Although English classes still discuss literature, and foreign language classes continue to build oral communication, much of the skill building occurs within small groups of students. Ongoing assessment provides feedback to all, enabling teachers to focus instruction on those who need it.

The assessment community has not disappeared. Theoreticians are developing the tools to evaluate increasingly complex tasks. They are directing the work on artificial intelligence for evaluating student work, and continually testing the reliability and validity of the models. In addition, they have helped develop security systems that ensure that the student being assessed has actually done the work. Term-paper mills are a thing of the past, because their products won't pass the security system, and if Mom or Dad completes a student's work, that is obvious too. Students are used to the security systems, so it isn't really an issue—besides, the type of feedback they receive is so engaging that the concept of cheating is a foreign one.

Although each state and district has slightly different graduation requirements, students who move from one place to another can transfer their portfolios and have them assessed anew. The feedback they receive makes the process of updating their artifacts for a new system fairly easy.

Rewards for high-performing and punishment for low-performing schools are a thing of the past. Because schools can monitor student progress regularly, and systems are in place at the local and state levels to identify schools where significant numbers of students are not making progress, intervention can happen almost instantaneously. No child is left behind, because there are many resources available to track progress and intervene where needed. State and local SWAT teams can be directed to a site for a short time to work closely with classroom teachers. They can provide training and support for teachers, and provide direct intervention for students when needed. Because the assistance is short, and follow-up can be maintained, teachers welcome the support and assistance.

In 2012 assessment is almost totally embedded in instruction. Because teachers, administrators, and parents can easily monitor results, instruction can be tailored specifically to student needs. Formal large-scale assessments occur on occasion, primarily to ensure that the regularly gathered data are reliable and valid. The focus of teachers, administrators, parents, and students is on learning, and students have become key evaluators of their own achievement. From the outset, students know what they are expected to learn, how that learning will be evaluated, and what they need to do to get there. Teachers can focus on instruction, and administrators are instructional leaders, focused on continual training to help all teachers meet the needs of each of their students.

Back to 2003, the boxes are ready to go. And now we just have to wait patiently for three months until we can get some limited feedback on how well our students are meeting the standards.

References

Olson, A. (2002, April). Technology solutions for testing. *The School Administrator Web Edition.* Retrieved February 22, 2003, from http://www.aasa.org/publications/sa/2002_04/olson.htm.

Rudner, L., & Gagne, P. (2001). *An overview of three approaches to scoring written essays by computer.* College Park, MD: ERIC Clearinghouse on Assessment and Evaluation. (Eric Document Reproduction Service No. ED458290)

Stiggins, R. (2000). *Student involved classroom assessment* (3rd ed.). Upper Saddle River, NJ: Prentice Hall.

Chapter 47
Harnessing the Power of Technology
Testing and Assessment Applications
Janet E. Wall

An explosion! An upheaval! A revolution! Those words are often used to describe the remarkable influence of technology on our lives. In his most recent book, Bill Gates speaks of a "web workstyle" and a "web lifestyle" to describe how technology has permeated all aspects of our lives (Gates, 1999). Education has been a prime beneficiary of technology's power. Projections are that more than seven billion dollars was spent on technology in the 2001–2002 school year (QED, 2001a). Computers used for instruction grew to more than 10 million by the beginning of the 1999–2000 school year (Anderson & Ronnkvist, 1999). According to recent information released by Quality Education Data (QED), 97 percent of U.S. public schools are connected to the Internet, 84 percent of classrooms have Internet access, 74 percent of students use the Internet in school for one or more hours per week, and 90 percent of teachers use the Internet as a teaching resource (QED, 2001b). These numbers will continue to grow. As more technology becomes available, it is being integrated more fully into the mainstream of the educational process (Market Data Retrieval Group, 1998; U.S. Department of Education, 2000). The U.S. Department of Commerce (2002) claims that 90 percent of 5- to 17-year-old children use computers, many of them obtaining information over the Internet. Never before has so much information been available to guide individuals in learning, making decisions, and taking actions. Educators who think this technology is another passing fad are sorely out of step.

One role of counselors and educators is to use assessment in the service of students and clients by monitoring educational progress and ensuring that learning is taking place. Under the right conditions and with proper use, employing technology to foster assessment practices can introduce helpful and productive efficiencies into the educational process. The International Society for Technology in Education (2000) published standards and performance indicators in technology for teachers. The section on assessment and evaluation states that the expectations for educators include these:

- applying technology in assessing student learning of subject matter using a variety of assessment techniques;
- using technology resources to collect and analyze data, interpret results, and communicate findings to improve instructional practice and maximize student learning; and
- applying multiple methods of evaluation to determine appropriate use by students of technology resources for learning, communication, and productivity.

The Collaborative for Technology Standards for School Administrators (2001) advocates that school administrators meet the following standards as they relate to assessment and evaluation:

- use multiple methods to assess and evaluate appropriate uses of technology resources for learning, communication, and productivity;
- use technology to collect and analyze data, interpret results, and communicate findings to improve instructional practice and student learning;
- assess staff knowledge, skills, and performance in employing technology and use the results to facilitate quality professional development and to inform personnel decisions; and
- use technology to assess, evaluate, and manage administrative and operational systems.

Clearly the education profession has high expectations for the use of technology in education, including in testing and assessment. The use of technology as a tool for testing and assessment is the predominant focus of this chapter. To make proper and maximal use of technology tools for assessment, savvy educators will need to

- understand the advantages and pitfalls of technology use, particularly as they relate to the use of assessment tools with clients and students;
- follow the assessment standards and policies of applicable professional associations;
- use the best practices suggested in this chapter to ensure good service to their clientele; and
- stay updated on topics related to assessment and technology.

This chapter provides information to help educators reach those objectives.

Advantages of Assessment Using the Computer and the Internet

The tools of technology offer educators new capabilities and opportunities to add value to their services to students. These include the following.

Accessibility

Increasing numbers of tests are available via the computer and over the Internet. Individuals can take via computer various tests for many purposes, including college entrance, course placement, certification and licensure, career decision making, academic achievement, military selection and classification, personality assessment, and test preparation. Each year the list expands. The locations where computer-based assessments can be taken range from the privacy of one's home to organized computer laboratories in colleges, high schools, and the private sector. Although some decry the disparity in degree of access to technology among certain groups of people, Bill Gates, in his book *The Road Ahead* (1995), suggests that everyone who is "wired" has access to the same information. Therefore, he proposes that virtual equity is more easily achievable than real-world equity. Negroponte (1995) states, in fact, that the social divide between the information rich and the information poor is more generational than socioeconomic or geographical.

Figure 1 shows the trends of public school students' increasing access to computers. In just a few short years, for example, the number of Internet-connected computers dropped from 1 computer per 19.7 students to 1 per 6.8 students.

Figure 1. Nunber of Students per Computer 1998-2001

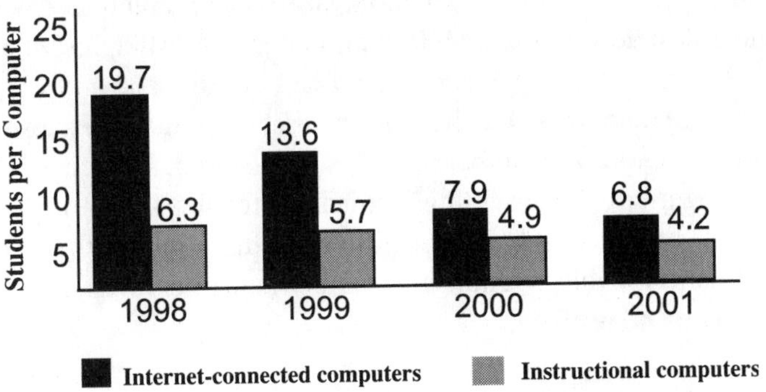

Source: Data taken feom "Technology counts 2002," Education Week special report. May 29, 2002.

Immediate Feedback

The proceedings from the National Summit on Education Technology and Assessment (Lemke, 2000) suggests that "technology-based assessment tools provide educators with real-time data, data sensors, and analyses on which to base better decision-making. Through technology, educators will be able to assess learning in ways never before possible." The potential for obtaining real-time data through immediate test scoring and feedback is a key advantage of technology-delivered assessment and can be a significant motivator for persons taking assessment instruments. Individuals can learn their status on assessments quickly and use that information to take immediate action. For example, the immediate availability of results on a college course placement test can assist both students and educators in registering students for the appropriate level of mathematics class or language program. High school students can acquire immediate information about their performance on academic tests and plan their courses accordingly. Students taking an interest inventory can obtain their results promptly and immediately investigate occupations and job openings that fit their interest profiles.

Embedding Assessment in Instruction

The use of technology in the learning process is increasing. Distance education, spurred initially by universities wishing to reach the adult learner, is becoming more prevalent at the high school level (Bennett, 2001, 2002). As students use technology-based instruction, assessment can be embedded into the learning process at appropriate times. Thereby students can gain a good grasp of what they know and where they might need further assistance. Teachers can receive immediate feedback on students' capabilities and plan instruction to alleviate skill deficiencies. Maintaining records of students' status and progress can become easy and automatic.

Where item banks can be made available to educators, tests based on specific objectives can be created, administered, and scored quickly and efficiently, thus providing immediate feedback to both students and teachers. This timely information gives direction for the next steps in the instructional program at a time when interventions are most appropriate and useful.

Ability to Use New Assessment Theories

The use of computerized adaptive testing, as opposed to computer-assisted testing, allows people to take tests that are targeted accurately to their ability levels (Heubert & Hauser, 1999) basically creating a test reasonably customized to the test taker. Use of technology in combination with the increasingly popular item response theory can determine an individual's performance level using fewer questions than with traditional tests. A RAND Corporation report on web-based testing describes adaptive testing in the following way: "In this type of testing, the examinee responds to an item (or set of items). If the examinee does well on the item(s), then the examinee is asked more difficult items. If the examinee does not answer the item(s) correctly, the examinee is asked easier items. This process continues until the examinee's performance level is determined. Because information about the difficulty of each item is stored in the computer, the examinee's 'score' is affected by the difficulty of the items the examinee is able to answer correctly" (Hamilton, Klein, & Lorie, 2001). The time and money saved by using computerized adaptive testing can be substantial, particularly in large-scale assessment situations or when time is a critical consideration. Attempting to use adaptive testing via paper-and-pencil means would be so burdensome as to be impossible.

Portfolio Assessment

Technology provides one with the capability of placing one's work or educational history in an electronic medium and making that information available to those judging performance or capability. Writing samples, artwork, letters of recommendation, journals, test results, certificates and certifications, verifications of community service, club memberships, project work, and the like can be saved electronically, transported easily (either physically or electronically), and evaluated by others to make decisions related to educational promotion, graduation, job entry, and other purposes. Educators can also observe student progress on various performance requirements and track it over time.

Ability to Assess Higher-Order Skills

Technology permits test developers to use techniques and create situations that are very difficult or impossible to construct in regular paper-and-pencil assessments. Consequently, and with some creativity on the part of the designer, the assessment can reflect more authentic or realistic conditions and may tap into higher-order cognitive skills than a paper-and-pencil instrument can. The use of media, such as audio and video, along with the incorporation of graphics and animation, can enrich the assessment process.

For example, test developers can construct real-world simulations. Test items on computer can simulate events in biology or economics and ask students to take measurements, make observations, analyze results, and propose a theory on how the world works in that subject area. Interactive assessments can present students with new information selected according to their previous decisions, enabling them to test their theory. This interactivity can also yield a more detailed understandings of how individual students approach an assessment situation and can provide insight into their thought process when presented with new information at various stages of the assessment process.

An interactive licensure test in architecture, for example, can simulate the tools an architect would use to create blueprints and engineering drawings, track what tools are selected and how they are used, and determine the design and structural quality of the final product. A technology-delivered foreign language assessment can use audio and video to simulate various situations that would be encountered in the foreign country to assess the students' verbal skills, knowledge of vocabulary, and understanding of the culture and business environment. Having students use the Internet to obtain information on a particular topic then prepare an essay using that information can provide an indication of their information-gathering techniques; abilities to locate, analyze, and synthesize information; and skill in documenting their findings in a well-written and succinct document.

Accommodating People with Disabilities

A powerful use of technology in assessment can be the use of assistive technologies for people with disabilities. Text readers with audio output can help people with visual impairments gain access to testing situations. People with physical impairments can take advantage of voice recognition technology in answering test items, even to the point of dictating long responses to essay questions. Those who experience difficulty with fine motor control can use a touch screen or smart board to respond to assessment items rather than being required to fill out a scannable answer sheet. In fact, computers can be configured with equipment and capabilities that can respond to slight movements of the head or eyes. People who are housebound and unable to travel to a test site can take a test over the Internet from their homes.

Outreach to Others

Technologies such as e-mail, net-meeting, and instant messaging can enable the test taker to reach out to experienced and qualified professionals to obtain further information, test interpretation advice, or discussion of a particular situation or test result. Technologies such as video teleconferencing can enhance assessments through one-on-one interaction between a test administrator and a test taker. This technology can be used to refine assessments when it is important that the test taker be seen and heard. Some applications are able to assess speaking skills, to test foreign language capability by putting a student in touch with persons in foreign countries who can critique language performance, or to determine a person's capabilities through interviews or oral exams. Web cams and video teleconferencing can be powerful tools for test security by providing real-time monitoring of the test administration environment.

Increased Efficiency

To the potential delight of educators, technology-delivered assessment offers efficiencies that can translate into cost savings for schools and districts. Bennett (2001) lists several areas in which electronic media can enhance the testing process. First is the development stage itself. Test items can be written, edited, revised, and managed via technology, reducing the costs of this labor-intensive process. Second, tests do not need to be printed, warehoused, and shipped, thereby saving paper and shipping costs. Third, constructed response items, such as writing samples, can be electronically shipped to scorers, thus eliminating the need to bring scorers to a central location, which accrues travel, food, and housing costs. Additionally, work is under way on automating the scoring process for constructed response items, largely eliminating the need for human readers and scorers. (Thompson, 1999). Fourth, multiple-choice items can be scored immediately, saving the costs of shipping answer sheets and the labor involved in preparing and monitoring the machinery that scores the tests. Last, score reports and interpretations can be sent back to the individual or the school electronically, again saving printing and mailing costs.

Keeping Pace with Curricular Changes and Workforce Needs

In our knowledge-based economy, the skill needs of the workforce are in constant change. The National Governors' Association (2002) believes that what students are being required to learn is outpacing the content found in the usual paper-and-pencil measures. The Web-Based Education Commission (2000, p. 59) echoed this concern when it indicated that "too often today's tests measure yesterday's skills with yesterday's testing technologies—paper and pencil." Simply put, standardized paper-and-pencil measures are not in sync with the content students are required to learn. Further, typical scoring and reporting procedures are not fast enough to inform classroom instruction or state and local policy.

Disadvantages of Computer- and Internet-Based Assessment

Educators need to be alert to the potential problems and limitations of using technology in assessment situations. Some potential disadvantages are listed in the following sections.

Access to Computers

Whereas some assessments are free, others require payment of a fee. People with limited resources, and especially those without computers, who may in fact be in the greatest need of assessment services, may be blocked from using essential assessments due to resource constraints. A recent Department of Commerce study has shown that access to computers and the Internet is highly dependent on income, racial and ethnic group membership, and urban residence (U.S. Department of Commerce, 1999). Figure 2 shows the relationship between income and computer access. Clearly, about 20 percent of the 10- to 17-year-olds in households with gross incomes below $35,000 had access to a computer only at school. A large percentage did not use the Internet.

Test Security

A major concern related to computerized testing and testing over the Internet is the issue of test security. Test items without suitable security can be compromised, resulting in an unfair advantage to test takers who might obtain the questions prior to taking an exam. In addition, there is the potential for individuals taking assessments via the Internet to acquire information from external sources when answering the test questions. Solutions to test security range from using removable hard drives to tracking or prohibiting access to certain universal resource locators (URLs, Internet addresses).

Figure 2. Students' Access to Computers and the Internet by Income Bracket

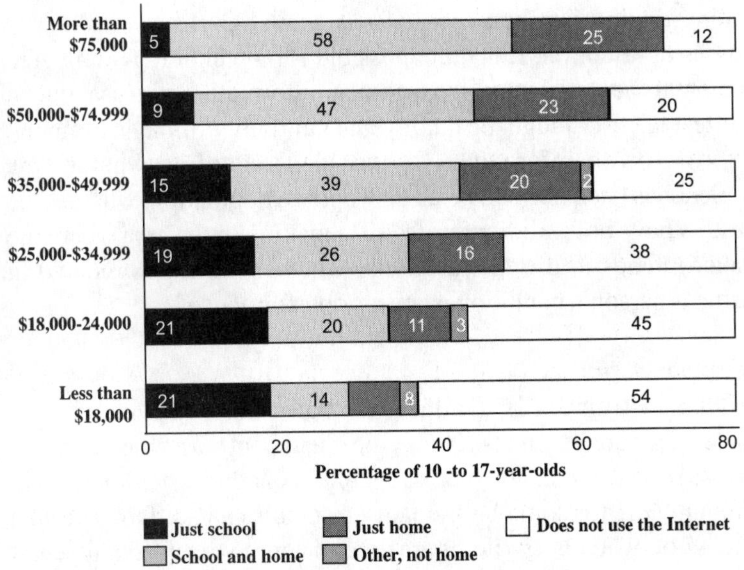

Source: Data from U.S. Department of Commerce (2002). *A Nation online: How Americans are expanding their use of the Internet.* Economics and Statistics Administration, National Telecommunications and Information Administration. Washington, DC: Government Printing Office.

Test Taker Identity

Test administrators need to be sure that the person taking the assessment is representing his or her identity accurately. Special care needs to be taken to ensure that the person answering a licensure test for credentialing, for example, is the actual person who is seeking this certification. Various measures can be taken to reduce the degree of uncertainty. Technological solutions to this problem can range from desktop video teleconferencing or web cams to fingerprint recognition systems, facial recognition techniques, and retinal scans.

Privacy and Confidentiality

As with paper-and-pencil assessments, information about an individual's answers and test scores must be kept confidential and be available only to those individuals who have a need to know. This concern is particularly critical for assessments of a delicate or sensitive nature that are answered over the Internet.

Lack of Information on the Quality of the Instrument

Tests taken on computer or over the Internet may not match the quality of paper-and-pencil assessments. Because taking assessments via the tools of technology is often made to look easy, it may be mistakenly assumed that the test meets professional testing standards. Assuming quality just because a test is available electronically is a dangerous assumption. It is quite possible for a technology-delivered instrument to be deficient in the technical information necessary for a user or test taker to judge the quality and suitability of the instrument. Often little or no information is provided regarding whether the instrument has been normed on an appropriate population, whether the test results have any validity for decision making in the area where the test taker intends to use the results, or whether the test is reliable in assessing a person's condition, status, or performance.

Test Comparability

If an instrument is available in both paper-and-pencil and computer-delivered formats, it may be mistakenly assumed that the two forms produce the same scores regardless of administration format. It is not unusual for some high-quality tests to report different results depending on whether the items are administered via paper and pencil versus computer or Internet. Without the assurance that the test scores are comparable, test takers who take the test in one format may have an advantage over those who take the same test in a different format. For example, several studies have shown that on composition tests where students are required to write responses using paper and pencil, those students who were accustomed to composing on computer received "severely underestimated" scores (Russell & Plati, 2001). Decisions based on inaccurate outcomes may point a student or client in a wrong direction. The discrepancy in results depending on assessment format may occur for any number of reasons including speededness, size of the type, monitor resolution, use of color, comfort with the equipment, or response mode.

Gender, Racial, and Ethnic Bias

That females, persons of color, or individuals of different ethnic backgrounds may be disadvantaged in certain testing situations has been a long-standing concern in paper-and-pencil testing. This problem may be exacerbated with tests delivered via computer or the Internet. If a particular group has disproportionate access to computers and technology, there could be disparity in the test takers' comfort level and familiarity with the use of technology. As a result, test scores could be influenced by both the mode of administration and the content. Recent information, however, suggests that that socioeconomic status—rather than gender, racial, or ethnic status—is the most likely indicator of access to technology (Hamilton et al., 2001). With continuing increases in all students' comfort level with technology, it is becoming less likely that use of technology will influence test scores in a disparate way.

Reporting and Interpretation

Immediate feedback is clearly desirable. Without appropriate interpretation, though, there is danger that the test taker will take actions that are not warranted by the test results. The potential exists for interpretations to appear so definitive and persuasive that test takers fail to understand the degree of error in the scores and the need for caution surrounding further actions and decisions. Conversely, there may be situations in which the feedback is so extensive that the test results are overinterpreted to the point of paralyzing a person from acting, or that they become like a horoscope with little actual value.

Lack of Human Contact

With technology-delivered assessments, meaningful human contact and intervention to assist with test score interpretation and guidance may be lacking or unavailable. Without a skilled educator or counselor, it may be difficult for a test taker to sort out his or her results and use them in the context of other experiences.

Best Practices in Selecting and Using Technology-Delivered Tests and Assessments

Counselors and educators need to be aware of the various issues related to the construction, production, administration, and interpretation of tests delivered via the computer or Internet. Test users should never compromise on the quality of a test administered to a client or student whether the assessment is in a traditional or technology-delivered format. Various agencies and organization have produced policy statements and standards for testing that are applicable to both paper-and-pencil and technology-delivered assessment. Counselors and educators should be cognizant of and familiar with the premises of these documents when considering the use of technology-delivered assessments. A bibliography of relevant standards and policies is provided at the end of this chapter.

The following section identifies best practices in evaluating and using technology-delivered assessments. The guidelines are consistent with professional standards and are categorized into considerations relevant to test administration, test quality, test developer credibility, test interpretation, and access to professionals. Adherence to these guidelines is of vital importance when reviewing, selecting, and using technology-delivered assessment instruments.

Test Administration

1. The test setting should be comfortable, quiet, and conducive to allowing the test taker to maximize performance. The arrangement of the computers should ensure privacy and comfort.
2. Testing equipment should be in good working order and the software or Internet programs operating properly. The condition of equipment should be checked prior to each test administration.
3. A site administrator should be available during testing to troubleshoot any equipment, software, or other technology problems that may occur.
4. Policies and procedures for dealing with a technology failure need to be established, explained to the test taker, and consistently applied. For example, if there is a computer crash or power disruption, are the responses to the completed test items saved or does the test taker begin the assessment over?
5. Test takers should be comfortable and familiar with the test format and use of keyboard, mouse, or other equipment. If there is a question about the test takers' familiarity with the technology, practice exercises should be provided to enable them to become facile with the equipment so they can focus on the assessment rather than the mode of delivery.
6. Test items and answers must be protected from compromise. Security of the equipment and test items is critical to the fairness of current and future test administrations.
7. The identity of the test taker should be verified, particularly in high-stakes testing.
8. Tests must be administered according to the procedures specified by the test developer, particularly in cases where standardization is important.
9. Both test users and test takers need to know whether individual score information is stored and, if so, where and for how long. Periodic purges of individual test results stored locally or centrally may be advantageous in maintaining

privacy. It may be more desirable for an individual test user to save test results on a personal disk rather than on a server, computer network, or local computer.

Test Quality

1. The test content should match the purpose of the testing. Assessment items should cover, at least on the face, the areas that the test taker and user desire.
2. The test developer should provide clear and supportable statements about what the test is intended to measure so that test users can ensure that the constructs of the assessment match their intentions.
3. Evidence should be made available by the test developer and reviewed by the test user to ensure that an assessment is appropriate for a prospective test taker with regard to such factors as age, membership in a subgroup, educational level, disability, and language competence.
4. If the test can be administered in paper-and-pencil and technology-delivered formats, test results should be comparable between the two forms. There should be ample evidence that the test scores are comparable or that necessary and appropriate adjustments are made to scores to ensure comparability.
5. Evidence should be provided regarding the conditions under which the test results have been found reliable. The strength of that reliability should be reported by the test developers and examined by the prospective test user.
6. Test results should only be interpreted in ways that are supported by validity evidence. The test developer should present ample evidence regarding the validity of the assessment for particular uses. Care should to be taken to ensure that the test users or test takers apply and interpret the test results for purposes consistent with the validity evidence. For example, if no evidence is provided that the test result validly predicts a future expectation, performance, or condition, then the test should not be used for this purpose until evidence is obtained to support that premise.
7. Limitations of the test and test results should be clearly specified by the test developer and examined by the test users prior to selection of the testing instrument. No assessment is without limitations.

8. The test user should read published assessment reviews written by qualified persons prior to test selection and use.
9. Before selecting a test, the user should examine the items and technical information to determine their currency. If the standardization data or testing forms are antiquated, the user should carefully consider whether the assessment is appropriate.

Credibility of the Developers

1. The test user (and test taker when appropriate) should determine the identity and professional credibility of the test developer. They should examine the developers' qualifications and determine their adequacy. This may be most important when assessments are published by small companies or individuals without a relevant history of quality work.
2. Test developers should provide information indicating whether they abide by the various testing standards of professional organizations. Professional test developers who pledge adherence to testing standards normally attempt to produce high-quality assessments with sufficient technical and research support. Other individuals or organizations may or may not adhere to the standards of quality generally accepted by the profession. *Caveat emptor!*

Test Interpretation

1. If tests are computer- or Internet-delivered, they should be scored and results returned as quickly as possible, and the results should be accompanied by test interpretations that are comprehensive and accurate, given the limitations of the test.
2. Assessment results should not be over- or under-interpreted. Care should be taken not to develop interpretations or explanations that go beyond what can be supported by the reliability and validity evidence.
3. Test reports should specify appropriate and inappropriate uses of the assessment results.
4. Score reports should include an indication of the degree of accuracy of the results.
5. Score interpretations should specify which interpretations are supported by research and which are based on expert

opinion. Sufficient information should be offered to allow the test taker and test user to weigh the credibility of the expert opinion.

6. Test interpretations should describe the limitations of the test and test results, including common misinterpretations.
7. If scores are used in high-stakes decisions such as graduation, promotion, college entrance, placement, or credentialing, the score report should contain information on how the passing or cutoff scores were set.
8. The score and interpretation report should reveal where further information can be obtained about the test and score interpretation, and how a test taker can verify or challenge the accuracy of the score.
9. Where possible, the score report and interpretation should include and incorporate other information about the individual, such as previous test scores, educational level, and performance indicators. This information should be used to help the test taker gain further insight into the meaning of the test results.

Access to Professionals

1. Because it is unlikely that the technology-delivered assessment will incorporate information on the background and experiences of the test taker, a professional educator or counselor should be available to provide value-added interpretations to the assessment information.
2. Where assessment results may require action on the part of the test taker or interventions to change a situation, human assistance is highly desired and should never be totally replaced by technology.

Staying Current

Given that technology is becoming ubiquitous in our daily lives and is likely to continue becoming increasingly integrated into professional educational and counseling procedures, it is important for professionals to keep tabs on the latest developments in the assessment and technology areas. Information on websites frequently is expanded and updated faster than information in print format. For these reasons, chapter 54 lists Internet resources for finding new and important information related to assessment and its marriage with technology.

Check these websites periodically to gather the latest information.

Summary and Look to the Future

Technology is a tool that can assist educators in locating information about assessment, organizing and maintaining test information, building relationships between and among test results and counseling and education interventions, using alternative assessment techniques, assessing difficult areas via traditional and nontraditional formats, introducing efficiencies into the assessment situation, and reaching audiences that are not normally accessible without the availability of certain technologies. Clearly technology can advance opportunities for individuals and guide them in whatever direction they aspire to go.

This has described the capabilities of technology-delivered assessment and outlined relevant precautions. Various guidelines were provided to assist practitioners in using technology and quality assessments to aid individuals in reaching their goals and aspirations. In addition, the chapter listed suggestions for staying current within the field of assessment, particularly as it relates to technology, and the standards and policies on assessment that have been prepared and endorsed by various professional associations and organizations.

As we look to the future and realize that the impact of technology on our lives has just begun, we see several issues with which we will have to wrestle. Among these issues are personal privacy, security, universal access to technology, and the degree of involvement of human interactions in conjunction with technology and the educational process. Perhaps the most poignant of these issues for educators is that the increasing use of technology would seem to ignore the importance of the human touch, which represents the artistic part of education. It is the combination of science and art that can help individuals understand themselves better, know how their characteristics relate to other information, determine how close they are to a desired goal and what modifications they need to make, reach higher achievement levels, and identify what activities and opportunities are available to fulfill their desires and needs. Qualified educators who make accomplished and proficient use of technology can humanize the educational environment. The power and promise of the future exists in the synergy between the best of both high tech and high touch.

Note: This chapter is a revision and update of "Technology-Delivered Assessment: Power, Problems, and Promise," by Janet E. Wall, which appeared in J. Bloom and G. Walz (Eds.), Cybercounseling and Cyberlearning: Strategies and Resources for the Millennium. Alexandria, VA: American Counseling Association.

References

Anderson, R. E., & Ronnkvist, A. (1999). *Teaching, learning, and computing: 1998 national survey.* (U.S. Department of Education Report No. 2). Washington, DC: Government Printing Office.

✦Bennett, R. E. (2001). How the Internet will help large-scale assessment reinvent itself. *Education Policy Analysis Archives, 9*(5).

✦Bennett, R. E. (2002). Inexorable and inevitable: The continuing story of technology and assessment. *Journal of Technology, Learning, and Assessment, 1*(1). Retrieved from www.jtla.org.

Collaborative for Technology Standards for School Administrators. (2001). *Technology standards for school administrators.* Retrieved from www.ncrtec.org/pd/tssa.

Gates, B. (1995). *The road ahead.* New York: Penguin Group.

Gates, B. (1999). *Business @ the speed of thought.* New York: Warner Books.

Hamilton, L. S., Klein, S. P., & Lorie, W. (2001) *Using web-based testing for large-scale assessment.* Santa Monica: RAND Corporation.

✦Heubert, J. P., & Hauser, R. (Eds.). (1999). High stakes: Testing for tracking, promotion, and graduation. (Report of the Committee on Appropriate Test Use, Board on Testing and Assessment, National Research Council). Washington D.C.: National Academy Press.

International Society for Technology in Education. (2000). *ISTE national educational technology standards (NETS) and performance indicators for teachers.* Eugene, OR: Author.

Lemke, C. (Ed.) (2000). *Summary report for Tahoe 2000: A national summit on education technology and assessment.* Alexandria, VA: National Coalition for Technology in Education and Training.

Market Data Retrieval Group. (1998).*Technology in education*, Shelton, CT: Author.

✦National Governors Association. (2002). *Using electronic assessment to measure student performance.* Washington, DC: Author.

Negroponte, N. (1995). *Being digital.* New York: Alfred A. Knopf.

QED [Quality Education Data]. (2001a). *School market trends: District technology forecast 2001–2002.* Denver, CO: Author.

QED [Quality Education Data]. (2001b). *Internet usage in U.S. public schools: Usage and trends 2001–2002* Denver, CO: Author.

✦Russell, M., & Plati, T., (2001). *Effects of computer versus paper administration of state-mandated writing assessment.* Article No. 10709, Teachers College Record. Retrieved from www.tcrecord.org/ Content.asp?ContentID=10709

Thompson, C. New word order: The attack of the incredible grading machine,*Lingua Franca, 9*(5). Retrieved fromwww.linguafranca.com /9907/nwo.html.

U.S. Department of Commerce. (1999). *Falling through the net: Defining the digital divide.* Washington, DC: Author.

U.S. Department of Commerce. (2002). *A nation online: How Americans are expanding their use of the Internet.* Economics and Statistics Administration, National Telecommunications and Information Administration. Washington, DC: Government Printing Office.

U.S. Department of Education. (2000). *Internet access in U.S. public schools and classrooms: 1994–1999* (NCES 2000–086). Washington DC: Government Printing Office.

Web-Based Education Commission. (2000, Dec.). *The power of the Internet for learning: Moving from promise to practice.* Retrieved from http://interact.hpcnet.org/webcommission/index.htm.

Bibliography of Professional Standards and Policy Statements Related to Technology-Delivered Assessment

AERA, APA, & NCME [American Educational Research Association, American Psychological Association, & National Council on Measurement in Education]. (1999). *Standards for educational and psychological testing.* Washington, DC: National Council on Measurement in Education.

American School Counselors Association and Association for Assessment in Counseling. (1998). *Competencies in assessment and evaluation for school counselors.* Alexandria, VA: Author.

Association for Assessment in Counseling. (2003). *Responsibilities of users of standardized tests.* Alexandria, VA: Author.

Committee on Professional Standards and Committee on Psychological Tests and Assessment. (1985). *Guidelines for computer-based tests and interpretations.* Washington, DC: American Psychological Association.

Dahir, C. A., Shelton, C. B., & Valiga, M. J. (1998). *Vision into action: Implementing the national standards for school counseling programs.* Alexandria, VA: American School Counselor Association.

✦Joint Committee on Testing Practices. (2000). *Rights and responsibilities of test takers: Guidelines and expectations.* Washington DC: American Psychological Association.

✦Joint Committee on Testing Practices. (2002). *Code of fair testing practices in education.* Available on *Measuring Up: An Anthology of Assessment Resources* [CD]. Also retrievable on-line: http://aac.ncat.edu.

✦National Board for Certified Counselors. (1998). *Standards for the ethical practice of webcounseling.* Greensboro, NC: Author.

✦National Career Development Association. (1997). *NCDA guidelines for the use of the Internet for the provision of career information and planning services.* Alexandria, VA: Author.

✦U.S. Department of Labor Employment and Training Administration. (1999). *Testing and assessment: An employer's guide to good practices.* Washington, DC: Author.

✦ Document is included in the Anthology of Assessment Resources CD

Chapter 48
Computerized Adaptive Testing
An Introduction

Stephen G. Sireci

Computers are revolutionizing almost every aspect of our society and testing is no exception. Delivering tests on a computer often improves exam security, testing efficiency, and scoring, and it often allows for measurement of knowledge, skills, and abilities that cannot be measured using traditional assessment formats (Zenisky & Sireci, in press). One of the most widely cited benefits of computer-based testing is the ability to use the computer to tailor the test to specific characteristics of an examinee. In this chapter, I provide a brief overview of this type of adaptive testing, focusing on the issues most relevant to teachers, counselors, and administrators. Readers interested in more comprehensive or technical writings in this area are referred to Drasgow and Olson-Buchanan (1999); Hambleton, Zaal, and Pieters (1991); Mills, Pontenza, and Fremer (2002); Parshall, Spray, & Kalohn (2001); Sands, Waters, & McBride (1997); van der Linden and Glas (2000); and Wainer (2000).

The notion of adaptive testing dates back to the original academic screening tests developed by Binet in 1908. The Binet scales were designed to identify schoolchildren who were not likely to benefit from the typical educational system. Knowing that students who were unable to answer an easy question were unlikely to be able to answer a difficult one, Binet arranged the administration of test items in ascending order of difficulty and used different stopping rules for ending the test session based on a student's patterns of responses. This notion of adapting the test administration to the proficiency[1] level of a student carried over into contemporary intelligence tests that are individually administered (e.g., Stanford-Binet tests, Wechsler scales). Adaptive testing was not logistically feasible in large-scale assessment until the advent of the computer, however.

Computerized adaptive testing is a test administration system that uses the computer to select and deliver test items to examinees. These tests are called *adaptive* because the computer selects the items to be administered to a specific examinee based, in part, on the examinee's proficiency on previous items. Unlike many traditional tests where all examinees take the same form, the computer adapts or tailors the exam to each examinee. This tailoring is done by keeping track of an examinee's performance on each test question and using this information to select the next item to be administered. The criteria for selecting the next item to be administered are complex, but the primary criterion is a desire to match the difficulty of the item to the examinee's current estimated proficiency. Presently, there are numerous examples of computerized adaptive testing programs, including the ACCUPLACER postsecondary placement exams, the Graduate Record Exam, and several licensure and certification exams.

The idea of using the computer to match the difficulty of an item to the proficiency of an examinee was initially proposed by Lord (e.g., Lord, 1980). Lord's idea was to begin a test administration by presenting an item of moderate difficulty. If the examinee answered the question correctly, a slightly more difficult item was administered. If the examinee answered the question incorrectly, a slightly easier question was administered. This iterative process continued until a sufficient number of items had been administered for confident estimation of the examinee's score.

How Computerized Adaptive Testing Works

The adaptive nature of a computerized adaptive test (CAT) stems from the procedure used to select the items to be administered to an examinee. This procedure is often referred to as the *item selection algorithm.* As described previously, a key goal of the algorithm is to match item difficulty to examinee proficiency. Obviously, the proficiency level of an examinee is not known at the time of testing. Therefore, estimates of examinee's proficiency must be used throughout the test session. At the beginning of the test, the proficiency estimate is typically set just below the average of the population of all test takers. (This estimate is usually selected based on extensive pretesting of the examinee population.) A value slightly below the average is used to reduce the chance that the first item on the test will be particularly difficult for an examinee. After each response to an item, the proficiency estimate for the examinee is updated.

The statistical model underlying computerized adaptive testing is item response theory (IRT). IRT posits several mathematical models that characterize items and examinees on a common scale. In IRT, the scale that indicates the difficulty of an item is the same scale that is used to assign scores to examinees. Thus, an item of average difficulty would have the same value on the scale as the value assigned to an examinee of average proficiency. There are several attractive features of IRT, including the ability to provide scores on a common scale for examinees who take different items, which is par for the course in computerized adaptive testing. The details of IRT are beyond the scope of this chapter, but several excellent textbooks on IRT are available (e.g., Hambleton & Swaminathan, 1985; Hambleton, Swaminathan, & Rogers, 1991; Lord, 1980). Suffice it to say that several different types of IRT models are available and all have strengths and weaknesses in particular testing applications.

Using IRT in adaptive testing, an examinee's proficiency estimate is updated each time he or she answers a test item, and a new item is selected based on the updated estimate. When the proficiency estimate is calculated, an estimate of the amount of uncertainty in the estimate (i.e., an estimate of the error of measurement) is also calculated. As progressively more items are administered, the degree of uncertainty diminishes. Figure 1 presents a simplified example of how a traditional CAT works. The horizontal axis in this figure represents the item difficulty/examinee proficiency scale, which is typically denoted using the Greek letter theta (θ).

The vertical axis represents the sequence of test items administered. As one moves from left to right, the items become more difficult. As is evident from the figure, answering an item correctly results in the administration of a more difficult item, and answering an item incorrectly results in the administration of an easier item.

Figure 1. Illustration of a traditional computerized-adaptive test

Arrows pointing to the left indicate the item administered after an incorrect answer and arrows pointing to the right indicate the item administered after a correct answer.

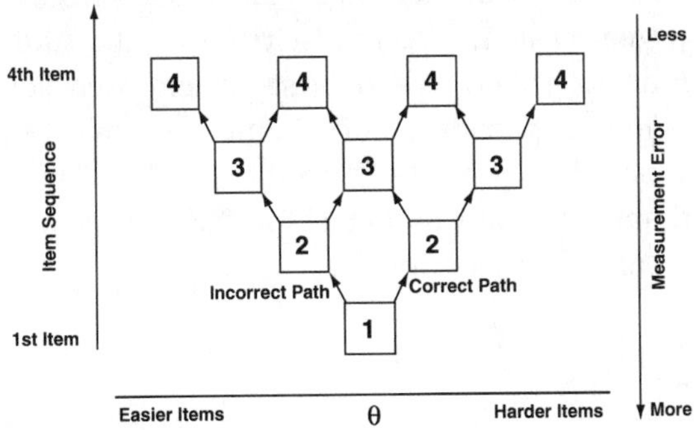

There are several different methods for ending a computerized adaptive testing session. In some situations, fixed-length CATs are used, where all examinees are administered the same number of items, regardless of the measurement error associated with their score. However, many CATs use a variable-length procedure in which the test session ends when some pre-specified level of measurement precision is reached. Test stopping rules for variable-length CATs typically use one of two methods, depending on the testing context. In a norm-referenced context, where no performance standards are set on the test, a minimum standard error criterion is typically used. In this situation, an examinee's test ends when the measurement error associated with her or his score dips below a pre-specified level (Lord, 1980). This criterion ensures that the scores for all examinees meet a minimum standard of reliability. In criterion-referenced testing situations, such as in licensure or certification testing, a test session ends when it is clear that an examinee's proficiency is above or below a specific threshold, such as a passing score (Lewis & Sheehan, 1990). This criterion minimizes measurement error at specific cut scores, which increases the reliability of classification decisions made on the basis of test scores.

In addition to matching item difficulty to examinee proficiency and determining when a test ends, a CAT item selection algorithm also may control several other factors including content representation and item exposure. *Content representation* refers to the ability of the algorithm to ensure that the content specifications of the test are adhered to for each examinee. For example, if the content specifications for a ninth-grade social studies test require that 30 percent of the test items measure history, 25 percent measure geography, 25 percent measure economics, and 20 percent measure sociology, the algorithm can keep track of the content designations of each item to ensure these content specifications are met for all examinees. The algorithm can also keep track of how often an item is administered to make sure that item exposure levels do not get too high. If the same items were administered too often to examinees, knowledge of specific items may be relayed to future test takers, which would inflate their scores. Thus, the item selection algorithm is critically important for ensuring testing efficiency, content validity, and item security.

Benefits of Computerized Adaptive Testing

Many of the benefits of computerized adaptive testing stem from the fact that the administration of the test is computerized. The benefits of computer-administered tests include more flexible test administration schedules, improved test security, instantaneous scoring and score reporting, and inclusion of multimedia in the assessment (e.g., audio, video, and three-dimensional graphics). Given appropriate computerized infrastructures such as secure local area networks for storing items and examinee responses electronically, test security is increased because there are no test booklets that can be lost or stolen before, during, or after test administration. In addition, the computer can keep track of how often an item is administered so that coaching courses and others that try to "beat the test" will not be able to reproduce test questions.

In addition to the practical benefits that arise from computerization of a test, computerized adaptive testing offers improved testing efficiency, which means we can obtain confident estimates of examinees' performance using fewer items than are typically required on nonadaptive tests. This gain in efficiency stems directly from the CAT item selection algorithm, which avoids administering items that are too easy or too difficult for an examinee. Therefore, CATs are often significantly shorter than their paper-and-pencil counterparts—typically about half as long as a parallel nonadaptive test (Wainer, 1993). This reduction in testing time is appreciated by examinees, as well as by teachers and counselors who hate to lose valuable instructional or counseling time.

Another widely cited benefit of computerized adaptive testing is a reduction in test anxiety for many examinees (Gershon & Bergstrom, 1991). In traditional testing, some examinees may freeze when presented with an item that is much too difficult for them to answer. Such examinees may find taking an adaptive test less anxiety-provoking. Recent research suggests, however, that a reduction in test anxiety due to the adaptive nature of the test may apply only to examinees of relatively low proficiency (Wise, 1996).

The benefits of computerized adaptive testing explain its growing prevalence in educational and psychological assessment. Test administrators and examinees like it because it reduces testing time and allows for instantaneous score reporting. Psychometricians and test developers like it because it provides precise scores for examinees using far fewer items than are required using traditional testing formats, which is important in terms of minimizing item exposure and potentially lowering the costs associated with developing new items. Given these benefits, we can expect to see its prevalence increase in the future. There are some problems and limitations with computerized adaptive testing, however, which may restrict its applicability in some situations.

Limitations of Computerized Adaptive Testing

Although there are many positive features of CATs, there are some disadvantages and limitations as well. A disadvantage for many testing agencies is the increased cost of developing and administering a test on a computer. Computer programs must be written to select, administer, and score items; large banks of items must be created to have many items available at all proficiency levels; and computerized testing centers must be leased or acquired to administer the tests. Each of these activities involves substantial investment of money and personnel, which can be daunting in many testing situations.

Another limitation of computerized adaptive testing is the inability to review test forms in advance of test administration. In paper-and-pencil testing, committees of content experts and sensitivity reviewers can evaluate test forms for their appropriateness for all examinees. Such reviews are more difficult in computerized adaptive testing because there is no single form of the exam.

Perhaps the most serious criticism of computerized adaptive testing is that examinees are typically not allowed to skip test questions or go back and review items answered previously. These actions are common in paper-based testing, but because the item selection algorithm in a CAT needs an examinee response to a previous question to select the next question, these behaviors can affect accurate proficiency estimation. In fact, Wainer (1993) pointed out that if examinees are allowed to skip and change answers to questions, they may be able to "trick" the algorithm into administering them the easiest possible set of test questions and subsequently bias their scores upward.

Other limitations of CATs pertain to their reliance on the computer. If schools and other organizations are unable to secure adequate numbers of appropriate computers for test administrations, CATs and other computer-based tests are not an option. In addition, in some situations, examinees' computer proficiency may interact with the construct being measured, such that examinees who are more familiar with computers do better on the test compared with examinees who have equal competence in the subject matter tested but are less familiar with computers (Huff & Sireci, 2001).

Although CATs have their weaknesses, many testing agencies weigh the pros and cons of computerized adaptive and nonadaptive tests and conclude that the strengths of CATs outweigh their limitations. Others seek a compromise between a traditional CAT and a nonadaptive test. These compromises, such as testlet-based testing and computerized multistage testing, are discussed in the next section.

The Future of Computerized Adaptive Testing

Presently, there is increased interest and activity in testing, with most states administering high-stakes tests to students in grades K–12 (Linn, 2000). Recent federal mandates such as the No Child Left Behind legislation and the evaluation requirements for federally funded programs suggest that testing activities will increase substantially over the foreseeable future. Given this increase in testing and a desire to reduce testing time, computerized adaptive testing is likely to become more popular in our schools.

A relatively recent development in the computerized adaptive testing world is the idea of using the computer to administer pre-assembled sets of items, rather than a single item, to an examinee. Wainer and Kiley (1987) introduced the concept of a *testlet* to describe a subset of items, or a "mini-test," that could be used in an adaptive testing environment (Wainer & Lewis, 1990). Examples of testlets include sets of items that are associated with a common reading passage or graphic, or a carefully constructed subset of items that mirrors the overall content specifications for a test. After the examinee completes the testlet, the computer scores the items within it and chooses the next testlet to be administered. Thus, this type of test is adaptive at the testlet level rather than at the item level. This approach allows for better control over exam content and can allow examinees to skip, review, and change answers within a block of test items.

A variation of the testlet CAT model is computerized *multistage testing*. Multistage testing refers to the administration of several testlets in an adaptive, sequential fashion. At the first stage, examinees are administered a *routing test* that determines the difficulty level of the test they will take at the second stage. Their performance on the second stage of the test determines the test they will take at the third stage, and so on. The difference between a testlet CAT and a multistage test is that with the latter the mini-tests administered at each stage can be much larger than a typical testlet, and the number of stages is relatively small, with two or three stages being most common. Both testlet CATs and multistage tests offer a compromise between the traditional nonadaptive format and computerized adaptive testing. Content experts and sensitivity reviewers can review the testlets to evaluate content quality; examinees can skip, review, and change answers to questions within a testlet or stage; and their responses are still used to tailor the remaining portions of the test to their specific proficiency level.

Another potential area in schools where computerized adaptive testing may become particularly beneficial is by tailoring the test to examinee characteristics other than proficiency. For example, information gained from a student's individualized education program could be used to select an appropriate starting point or sets of questions to be administered. The computer could also access different language versions of test directions or test questions for students with limited proficiency in the dominant language used in a school district. The computer could also be used to address test speededness issues by selecting for some students items that require less time to answer. Finally, one other way in which computerized adaptive testing may help teachers and counselors is by providing enhanced information about examinee performance that could be used for diagnostic and instructional purposes. For example, information regarding the amount of time taken to answer an item could be used to assess the strategies examinees used to answer the item.

Conclusion

In this chapter I attempted to provide a basic overview of computerized adaptive testing. This type of testing, or a variant of it, is gaining popularity at a rapid rate and is likely to become more prevalent in educational and psychological testing. I hope that reading this chapter gave you a general understanding of how computerized adaptive testing works and how to explain this type of test to students, parents, and those who make test-selection decisions. For those readers who want to gain a more complete understanding about the specifics of how such tests work, I highly recommend the references provided in the first paragraph of this chapter, most of which are textbooks. Computerized adaptive testing represents the most sophisticated test administration technology that psychometrics currently has to offer. It will remain an attractive testing model for the foreseeable future.

Notes

The author thanks Mary Pitoniak and April Zenisky for their helpful comments on an earlier version of this chapter.

1. In the context of assessment, the term *proficiency* refers to the knowledge, skills, and abilities a student possesses with respect to the construct being measured by the test.

References

Drasgow, F., & Olson-Buchanan, J. B. (Eds.). (1999). *Innovations in computerized assessment.* Mahwah, NJ: Erlbaum.

Gershon, R. C., & Bergstrom, B. (1991, April). *Individual differences in computer adaptive testing: Anxiety, computer literacy, and satisfaction.* Paper presented at the annual meeting of the National Council on Measurement in Education, San Francisco, CA.

Hambleton, R. K., & Swaminathan, H. R. (1985). *Item response theory: Principles and applications.* Hingham, MA: Kluwer.

Hambleton, R. K., Swaminathan, H. R., & Rogers, J. (1991). *Fundamentals of item response theory.* Thousand Oaks, CA: Sage.

Hambleton, R. K., Zaal, J. N, & Pieters, P. (1991). Computerized adaptive testing: Theory, applications, and standards. In R. K. Hambleton & J. N. Zaal (Eds.), *Advances in educational and psychological testing* (pp. 341–366). Norwell, MA: Kluwer.

Huff, K. L., & Sireci, S. G. (2001). Validity issues in computer-based testing. *Educational Measurement: Issues and Practice, 20*(3), 16–25.

Lewis, C., & Sheehan, K. (1990). Using Bayesian decision theory to design a computer mastery test. *Applied Psychological Measurement, 14,* 367–386.

✦Linn, R. L. (2000). Assessments and accountability. *Educational Researcher, 29*(2), 4–16.

Lord, F. M. (1980). *Applications of item response theory to practical testing problems.* Hillsdale, NJ: Erlbaum.

Mills, C. N., Potenza, M. T., & Fremer, J. J. (2002). *Computer-based testing: Building the foundation for future assessments.* Mahwah, NJ: Erlbaum.

Parshall, C., Spray, J. A., & Kalohn, J. C. (2001). *Practical considerations in computer-based testing.* Springer Verlag.

Sands, W. A., Waters, B. K., & McBride, J. R. (Eds.). (1997). *Computerized adaptive testing: From inquiry to operation.* Washington, DC: American Psychological Association.

van der Linden, W. J., & Glas, C. (Eds.). (2000). *Computer-adaptive testing: Theory and practice.* Boston, MA: Kluwer.

Wainer, H. (1993). Some practical considerations when converting a linearly administered test to an adaptive format. *Educational Measurement: Issues and Practice, 12*(1), 15–20.

Wainer, H. (2000). *Computerized-adaptive testing: A primer* (2nd ed.). Mahwah, NJ: Erlbaum.

Wainer, H., & Kiley, G. L. (1987). Item clusters and computerized adaptive testing: A case for testlets. *Journal of Educational Measurement, 24,* 185–201.

Wainer, H., & Lewis, C. (1990). Toward a psychometrics for testlets. *Journal of Educational Measurement, 27,* 1–14.

Wise, S. L. (1996, April). *A critical analysis of the arguments for and against item review in computerized adaptive testing.* Paper presented at the annual meeting of the National Council on Measurement in Education, New York.

Zenisky, A. L., & Sireci, S. G. (in press). Technological innovations in performance assessment for licensure and certification exams. *Applied Measurement in Education.*

✦ Document is included in the Anthology of Assessment Resources CD

Chapter 49
Assessing the Quality of Online Instruction
Integrating Instructional Quality and Web Usability Assessments

Anthony Ciavarelli

A great deal has been written in the educational literature about the use of distance education, given the rapid expansion of the World Wide Web on the Internet. Educators and trainers are enthusiastic about the potential for reaching learners across a medium that allows "anywhere and anytime" teaching. Web-based courses are now available or under development at many academic institutions and through corporate universities. Such online courses allow individuals to complete needed educational or training programs from their desktop computers at a convenient time and place. Online courses are especially desirable for learners who are unable to attend traditional classes on campus because of their remote geographic location or their limited time availability.

Educators are concerned, however, about ensuring the quality of online courses, and many question whether online courses can maintain the same high standards of excellence as traditional classroom instruction. One way to ensure quality control over online instruction is to establish an ongoing instructional quality assessment process. In this chapter I discuss background information and several considerations for assessing the quality of online instruction.

Questions Educators Ask About Online Instruction

Administrators, educators, and students question several key issues of online instructional quality, and some question the feasibility of attaining critical learning objectives outside the traditional classroom and laboratory. Among commonly asked questions are the following:

- Can complex learning objectives associated with problem solving and critical thinking skills be taught online?

- How does one address the issues of socialization and collaboration in learning among students using online instructional formats?
- What makes an online course successful or unsuccessful?
- How can we ensure acceptable quality of online instruction?
- How can we demonstrate that students receiving online instruction have equitable standards, attention, and resources compared to on-campus students?
- What kinds of data should be collected to measure the quality and the effectiveness of online education?

In this chapter I discuss the background and foundation of a proposed conceptual framework for assessing the quality of online instruction. This e-Learning Assessment Framework is presented in the chapter appendix. In this framework, I consider factors related to human learning and motivation, instructional quality standards, best web teaching practices, and web page design and usability guidelines. My premise is that the quality of web-based instruction is a result of all these factors.

The development of high-quality web learning environments requires careful planning and a systematic development process. The development process needs to take into account what we know about human learning capabilities and human motivation to learn. High-quality online instruction also depends on careful application of established principles of instructional design, use of the best web design practices, good human engineering, and adequate provisions for institutional support. The background and formation of this assessment framework is discussed below.

Instructional Design Issues

Instructional design encompasses several issues, including pedagogy, development of instructional systems, theories of human learning, and how web-based instruction must differ from traditional instruction. All these topics are covered in this section.

Pedagogy

The growth of online instruction has raised new interest and much discussion about *pedagogy,* or how best to teach. The term actually comes from Greek roots, *paid* and *agogos,* and in translation means "the art of teaching children." The primary audience for much of our existing online instruction, however, is adults seeking education in a venue that will allow them to continue their employment while working on educational goals part time. Adults have different needs than children. As Knowles (1980) so aptly points out, children have little experience, are able to focus on academics, are subject centered, and are easily motivated by external rewards. Adults, on the other hand, have greater experience levels, tend to be focused on acquiring job skills, are more problem centered, and are self-motivated to learn. A good teacher knows that individual learners have different levels of experience, capabilities, and motivation levels, and takes such factors into consideration in his or her approach to teaching.

I have encountered people involved with online instruction who use *pedagogy* in place of a particular technology or course-delivery method. They might say, for example, that the use of online instructional formats, such as online discussion forums or chat rooms, represent a new pedagogy. In my view, pedagogy refers, or should refer, to the art of effective teaching, not to a specific technology or content-delivery method. Whenever we plan to teach, on the web or in the classroom, we should first address the pedagogical issues of how best to teach our subject to the expected audience. Some questions that every teacher should ask when developing a course are these:

- Who am I trying to teach?
- What content do I need to teach?
- How can I best organize this content?
- What is the best presentation strategy and lesson sequence?
- What is the best way to deliver the content?
- How will I know when I have succeeded in teaching what I intended to teach?

Professional instructional designers typically ask themselves these or similar questions when they apply a systems approach, sometimes referred to as the instructional systems development (ISD) process to course development.

Instructional Systems Development

ISD is a process model that defines steps or tasks that course developers need to complete to ensure that they pay adequate attention to critical components of instruction. The ADDIE model—named after the five critical process steps or phases of analysis, design, development, implementation, and evaluation—is thoroughly described by Hodell (2000) and will not be discussed in any detail here.

The importance of the ADDIE model to assessment is twofold. First, the model has enjoyed considerable success in the training community as a means to standardize instruction and impose quality standards. An ADDIE approach has helped to improve some of the more poorly planned and haphazard training interventions. In traditional classroom education, there has been little acceptance and application of this kind of systematic approach. In contrast, the application of ISD methods to online instruction is receiving much attention, probably because efforts to convert classroom content to web delivery require careful planning, design, and development in order to achieve a seamless integration of course content and teaching strategies with course-delivery technologies.

The ISD model and some activities typically engaged in at each of the development phases are briefly summarized here (based on Hodell, 2000, pp. 12–13):

Analysis. Activities include assessment of student learning needs, data gathering regarding subject matter or content, and organizational and technology implementation issues.

Design. The focus is on specification of learning objectives and performance standards, defining subject matter content, defining the curriculum, designing lesson plans and tests, selecting media, and addressing resource and support needs.

Development. This stage involves production of instructional materials and student and teacher guides, courseware authoring, and software development, according to specifications in the design.

Implementation. Implementation addresses delivery, management, and control of the education and learning process.

Evaluation. Continuous measurement and evaluation of the instructional products and processes takes place in all phases of ISD.

One goal of applying the ADDIE model is to ensure that all critical components of instruction, such as inclusion of learning objectives, appropriate teaching strategies, and relevant assessment methods, are present in any resulting course or curriculum. Most educators know that the mere application of a theory or process cannot guarantee high-quality instruction will result. Educators' opinions vary, however, as to what teachers must do to ensure that learning takes place as intended. Some of the differences in opinion about learning may trace their roots to varying views about human learning. Ultimately, the student who experiences the result of such a process will be the best person to judge the quality of instruction. The perception of quality will be determined by the learner's own goals and expectations and his or her unique experiences taking the course.

Views About Human Learning

There are many views of human learning, but perhaps the most common and relevant are behavioral, cognitive, and constructive learning theories. I briefly compare and contrast each of these viewpoints here.

Behavioral Learning Theory

This approach to teaching humans actually evolved from studies of animal behavior in the psychology laboratory. Early behaviorists (e.g., John Watson, Edward Thorndike, and B. F. Skinner) studied only learning that could be easily observed and measured. As a result their learning approaches tended to focus on tasks and skills that could be objectively defined and taught through hands-on practice with feedback on performance results. Techniques such as defining behaviors to be taught; arranging situations so that the behaviors could be attempted; and providing reinforcement, or feedback about performance, are still used today in many training environments. Such an approach may work well in an application such as training equipment operators to memorize and practice specific operating procedures. But a purely behavioral training method is difficult to apply to teaching complex human problem solving and critical thinking skills (Ford, 2000).

Bell (1985, pp. 36–40) nicely summarized a behavioral approach to education and training:

1. Define learning objectives as measurable outcomes.
2. Define the learning prerequisites or entry skill level.
3. Present instruction in a progressive sequence of least to most difficult.
4. Make connections between current and previous instruction.
5. Present examples, sample problems, and guidance for problem solving.
6. Teach basics, give a variety of examples, give practice with feedback, and test performance at the end of instruction.

7. Provide immediate feedback on results.
8. Provide information about how to correct errors (remedial instruction).
9. Redirect the student's instruction based upon diagnosis of performance problems.

Cognitive Learning Theory

Cognitive theorists recognize that people are different from animals in their thinking abilities, and they are capable of guiding their own learning processes based upon abilities, or cognitive structures, that they establish through a lifetime of learning. Furthermore, cognitive psychologists maintain that humans are both extrinsically and intrinsically motivated to learn. They do not depend solely upon external events to control their learning and motivation to learn. Thus, cognitive learning theorists suggest that educators take advantage of these thinking processes, self-organizing learning strategies, and intrinsic motivation to learn (Ford, 2000; Johnson & Thomas, 1994).

Merrill and his associates developed a theory of instruction based upon cognitive science principles (Merrill, 1983; Merrill, Reigeluth, & Faust, 1979) . This approach to instruction is sometimes called a *prescriptive approach to instruction,* or *prescriptive instructional theory,* because the strategies for delivering and assessing instruction are based upon specific learning objectives and their associated performance requirements. The prescriptive approach to instruction follows a defined process to ensure that certain critical components for producing high-quality instruction are present. The basic components of Merrill's prescriptive instructional design theory, sometimes referred to as *component display theory* or *component design theory* (CDT), are as follows (Ciavarelli, 1988, p. 13):

1. Analyze and classify the task or activities the learner is to perform (as specified in learning objectives).
2. Select the most appropriate teaching strategy based upon the type of learning and subject matter content.
3. Evaluate instructional quality based upon the adequacy and consistency of the key components of instruction across learning objectives, teaching strategies, and assessment methods.

The CDT approach actually borrows heavily from behavioral methods in that it incorporates a systematic process of writing learning objectives as learning outcomes. The instructional presentations are highly structured based upon the particular classification of learning objectives and instructional content. Certain elements of cognitive psychology are added, however, to accommodate concept learning and problem-solving tasks; for example, learning strategies that support the learning encoding process. These cognitive learning strategies include such things as the use of mnemonics, mental rehearsal, and subject matter organizers, highlighting, and isolation of core learning materials to draw the learner's attention to key information. Another fundamental tenet of this approach is to allow some means for the learner to control the learning process.

For example, in some forms of computer-based instruction, learner control is achieved by incorporating learner-selected options or choices (Merrill, 1980). The learner is allowed to select the desired level of difficulty and also can access additional instructional support and help. The instruction typically includes a broad range of subject matter explanations, illustrations, and examples that are helpful in teaching specific concepts and principles. For example, when CDT is used to design a concept lesson, the instructional sequence might go something like this (Ciavarelli, 1988, p. 14):

1. Define the concept and highlight or isolate the key attributes that characterize or typify it.
2. Provide examples and instances that represent the concept. Include both examples and nonexamples (examples that do not represent the concept).
3. Allow the learner to apply the definition of the concept and to list the attributes needed to classify various instances or examples of concept classes.
4. Assess learning by having the student classify new instances or examples as examples or nonexamples of the concept.

Merrill (1994) refined his CDT to provide a broader focus on course structuring and to accommodate the use of expert systems technology (artificial intelligence) in providing advisory tutoring to students taking computer-based or online courses. Using such "expert tutor" technology, the best advice of a teacher can be incorporated into the instruction to guide and advise the student along different learning paths, and to help correct errors and possible misconceptions.

Constructive Learning Theory

Constructive learning theory suggests that students do not just passively receive education; they actively engage in organizing and making sense of the information they receive. In essence, they construct their own knowledge base by integrating new information and experiences with pre-existing (already learned) information. According to constructive learning theorists, learning is best achieved by setting a context in which students can readily understand where new knowledge fits into their own experience and how such knowledge can be used in a real-world setting. The teaching focus is on establishing a learning environment in which the learner is involved in actively constructing knowledge from the ongoing learning experience and in connecting new knowledge to previous experiences (Kerka, 1997).

Teachers play an important role in the learning process by arranging instruction that encourages students to engage in active learning situations and participate in problem-solving activities, sometimes working alone and other times working in groups. The teacher helps to organize problem-centered activities, then guides and encourages inquiry and exploration of possible solutions. Instructional materials, problem-solving situations, and assessments are often set in practical contexts that invite students' interest because the learning experience is directly applicable to real-world environments. This aspect of constructive learning theory is sometimes referred to as *situated learning,* in which knowledge is formed and made more meaningful by establishing an authentic learning situation. (Kerka, 1997).

The most effective learning, then, takes place when learners attempt to understand and make sense of the learning experience and begin to fit their new knowledge into their own unique experience base or conceptual framework. From the constructivist point of view, the most effective learning takes place when teachers allow students to work with engaging, problem-centered instructional materials; when they provide guidance along the way as needed; and when they encourage collaboration among learners.

People learn in social contexts by observing others and by actively participating in conversation and functions with others (Bandura, 1977). The acquisition of language and culture plays a large role in learning higher cognitive skills and in building motivation and strategies for learning how to learn (Vygotsky, 1978).

Bruner (1990), who coined the term *discovery learning,* believes that human learning is inextricably embedded in an individual's culture. Humans learn because they want to make sense of their world and understand its workings. Knowledge about the world, then, is a social construction composed of the information that learners have acquired within a cultural or social framework.

An obvious advantage of web instruction is that one can reach students at a distance, anytime and anywhere. From a constructivist standpoint McManus (2001) points out that another key advantage is that the web represents a vast source of information resources that can be used in an instructional program. Teachers can, in the course of teaching on the web, connect their students with noteworthy institutions of learning, libraries, and museum websites to provide motivation and enhance the educational experience.

The availability of vast web resources invites a constructivist approach to teaching. Spiro, Feltovich, Jacobson, and Coulson (1991) suggest that higher-order learning is not taught very effectively with a behavioral objective approach in which the educator specifies learning outcomes and controls the learning process. From the constructivist view, it should be the learner who sets the learning goals and directs the knowledge acquisition process. Spiro and associates believe that multiple interconnections among knowledge components should be emphasized. In addition, the web provides for a high level of interconnections among knowledge sources (McManus, 2001). The teaching strategy is based upon providing guidance to the student by arranging student-directed web-learning activities that include the use of web resources, and by facilitating collaboration among students via Internet communication modes, such as e-mail and discussion forums or chat rooms.

Web instruction lends itself to constructive forms of instruction through planning engaging learning activities and through planning collaborative learning projects (using communication features). Encouraging collaborative learning and intercommunication among students helps to build a learning community and to offset feelings of isolation that students who take technology-based educational programs may experience. Sandra Kerka (1996) suggests a number of ways to improve online instruction:

> (1) Understand the technologies' strengths and weaknesses; (2) provide technical training and orientation; (3) plan for technical failures and ensure access to technical support; (4) foster learning to learn, self-directed learning, and critical reflection skills; (5) develop information management skills to assist learners in selection and critical assessment options; (6) structure learner-centered activities for both independent and group work that foster interaction. (p. 3)

Constructivism and Authentic Assessment

The constructivist movement places great emphasis on putting the learner in control of the educational process. Going hand in hand with this shift in focus is the movement toward authentic assessment, in which teachers examine students' performance on meaningful intellectual tasks (Wiggins, 1990). Wiggins (1990, p. 1) raises the following key points:

- Traditional classroom exams do not transfer well to the real world, making them poor substitutes for measuring student performance in relation to realistic settings.
- Authentic tests attempt to develop engaging student tasks that simulate realistic tasks such as conducting research, collaborating with other students on a research paper or project, or reporting on current social events or scientific breakthroughs.
- Authentic tests are representative of ill-structured problem domains and are thought better to prepare a student for professional practice and transfer of education to real-life situations.

Authentic testing is often associated with the development of assessment rubrics. A *rubric* is an assessment tool that corresponds as closely as possible to a real-world problem or situation (Moskal, 2000). This form of assessment is considered much more appropriate to enhancing the learning experience than traditional, objectively scored classroom exams.

Recent Ideas in Instructional Design

Sonwalker (2001a) argues that web instruction, with some of its new multimedia enhancements (video, animation, and simulation), requires a new pedagogy. He describes four applicable learning styles: *incidental* (event-driven reactive learning), *inductive* (the introduction of instances or examples of a concept to exemplify a principle being taught), *deductive* (presentation of simulations or graphic or mathematical representations that illustrate trends and drive learners to draw conclusions), and *discovery* (learning within the knowledge domain via self-directed inquiry). Sonwalker suggests multiple modes of presentation to allow for different and wide-ranging learning pathways. A very clever three-dimensional pedagogical learning cube is proposed as a teaching strategy model or conceptual framework.

The cube, similar in appearance to a Rubik's Cube puzzle, depicts an instructional system comprising the teacher, student, learning style, and media type. The model can be used to "organize and sequence multimedia content assets in a pedagogically distinctive learning path that matches the style of the individual learner" (Sonwalker, 2001b, p. 12).

Web Page Design and Usability Guidelines

The part of a computer system (including the Internet and various websites) that the user sees and communicates with is called the *user interface.* The user interface provides the means for the user to interact with the computer. Anyone who has attempted and failed to program a videocassette recorder correctly, or who has accidentally deleted or lost a computer file, knows the frustration of interfaces that are poorly designed for the typical user. Web-based instruction is embedded in a computer system that, if not carefully designed, may result in the same kinds of operational difficulties and consequent user frustration.

Over the years, human factors engineers specializing in human-computer interaction (HCI) and usability engineering have attempted to influence the design of computing systems to make them easier to use. HCI is a discipline concerned with the design, evaluation, and implementation of interactive computing systems. By applying HCI design principles, developers of computer systems have learned to design systems more carefully to ensure that computers are easier to use and less error prone. HCI concerns itself with involving the user in the design process, applying design guidelines to simplify system operation, and providing the user with assistance when needed. An HCI designer works mainly to improve user interface designs. One important part of the human factors method is to conduct usability testing throughout development. Usability refers to a measure of the quality of the user's experience when interacting with the system such as a personal computer, videocassette recorder, or website (Stefanyshyn, 2001). Usability testing is conducted to test the ease of learning and simplicity of operation of the interface by having a sample of intended users try out the system. Usability engineers may observe users operating the system and take note of difficulties, or they may conduct surveys and interviews to obtain data regarding the ease of operation. Based on such information, the usability engineer may redesign the human interface to make it easier to use (Jordan, 1998). One does not have to be an engineer to consider human factors in web page designs for online instruction, however. Some key design questions regarding the human interface are these (Jones, 1989, p. 13):

- How should the function of the system be described and presented to the user?
- How can the design of the user interface help the user to understand and use the system?

  Where am I?
  What can I do here?
  How did I get here?
  Where can I go, and how do I get there?

I would add one more question for the user who becomes totally lost in the system: How do I get out of this mess? The goal of HCI and usability engineering is to design a system that is easy to operate, intuitive, and quickly learned. The following guidelines are used in meeting such design objectives (Jones, 1989, pp. 21–45):

- Maintain consistency in display format, information layout, and position.
- Use landmarks and signposts to show user his or her present (web page) location, the path traversed, and what lies ahead.
- Indicate the present condition or state of the system through operating messages such as "downloading now," "please wait," "estimated time to complete," and the like.
- Indicate the start and completion of each task.
- Give user a way out of a mess. For example, give the user a way to go to the home page and start over.

In summary, the user interface is designed to maintain consistency in information formats and location of content on a web page. The most usable systems pay attention to the target users' needs and abilities. Functional operation and navigation choices are compatible with users' experiences with other similar systems, and the system provides feedback to the user, such as acknowledging inputs, advising the user of processing wait periods, and providing navigational assistance, error alerts, and corresponding recovery methods. The specific application of these principles, and other key design issues and usability methods in creating user-friendly web pages, are covered extensively in Jakob Nielsen's popular book *Designing Web Usability* (2000). The book also contains many examples of good and bad web pages to illustrate design principles.

Institutional Support Issues

Online courses, as I have mentioned, must be carefully planned, designed, and executed. Agencies that govern academic accreditation or set quality standards have considered establishing criteria regarding institutional responsibilities and requirements in online instruction. I have incorporated some of the criteria being considered by the Western Association of Schools and Colleges (WASC) and the National Education Association (NEA) in the e-Learning Assessment Framework in the appendix. By way of summary, an institution planning to offer online courses has to consider where online course offerings fit into its academic mission, as well as to plan for adequate resources and facilities to provide the needed technology, faculty development, and student services support infrastructure. Academic institutions that have a successful campus program and are planning to undertake new programs of distance learning would be wise to follow the example of the British Open University, one of the more prominent and successful distance learning institutions in the world. The ingredients of success for the Open University, as reviewed by Sir John Daniel (2001), are quite revealing: "The Open University is lucky in that it does not have to be satisfied with the assumption of quality. Britain now has a ferocious quality assessment system that sends groups of peers, under state supervision, to judge the quality of teaching of each discipline in each university, against six criteria: (1) curriculum design, content, and organization, (2) teaching, learning, and assessment, (3) student progression and achievement, (4) student support and guidance, (5) learning resources, and (6) quality assurance and enhancement" (p. 3). The current high standing of the British Open University is a consequence of applying these criteria. The quality of its distance learning program is maintained because close attention is given to producing excellent course materials, maintaining close personal academic support for the students, establishing effective logistics (having the right materials at the right place at the right time), and encouraging active faculty research.

Using the e-Learning Assessment Framework

Education and training are all about learning, teaching, and ultimately learner performance as defined by the goals of the institution, the objectives of the course, and the special interests of the student. Assessment should provide an objective and valid means to judge one's educational and training accomplishments as an educator and administrator of learning. Assessment should provide important diagnostic feedback to the student to improve learning, to the teacher to improve the instructional process, and to the institution to improve its curriculum, support services, and infrastructure.

I am in the process of developing an online assessment system, using a web-based questionnaire survey methodology. The e-Learning Assessment Framework in the appendix provides a useful point of departure for specifying measurement dimensions and for constructing survey items. Selecting from the appendix, for example, one might construct a simple checklist to identify important criteria for designing or assessing online courses, as shown in the following examples, one a checklist approach and the other a Likert-scale approach.

Checklist Approach (From Designer's Perspective)

[ ] Course learning objectives are clearly stated.
[ ] The instructor's role is defined.
[ ] Interactivity is consistent with the learning objectives or intent.
[ ] Student collaboration is encouraged when appropriate.

Likert-Scale Approach (From Student's Perspective)

The role of the instructor was clearly defined:

___ strongly disagree ___ disagree ___ neutral
___ agree ___ strongly agree

The course content often included active learning tasks:

___ strongly disagree ___ disagree ___ neutral
___ agree ___ strongly agree

In this manner, a course designer or an instructor can use items in the e-Learning Assessment Framework to build an assessment tool that meets his or her particular interests and requirements. The e-Learning Framework simply provides some assurance that the many dimensions of instructional assessment are considered in the evaluation construction process. The framework incorporates behavioral, cognitive, and constructivist views. It is up to the developer of an assessment instrument to decide on the selections most appropriate to the purpose of the evaluation. Another important point in developing an assessment instrument is to evaluate all components of an instructional system, including the quality and value of the instructional content, the instructor's performance, the instructional strategy used, the presentation method (lecture, seminar, learning activity), the delivery system, the appropriateness and reliability of the technology and media, and the institutional support services.

Appendix A: e-Learning Assessment Framework

Instructional Quality Measure	Suggested Readings
A. Instructional Quality	
1. Learning objectives are consistent with the stated purpose of the course. 2. Learning objectives are clearly stated in terms of performance expected and conditions required (behavior, conditions, standard). 3. Instruction is adequate to meet specified objectives, including a. Content completeness and relevance b.Content organization and information sequencing and structure c. Balance among general facts, concepts, principles, and process steps in applying intended knowledge and skills d. Inclusion of relevant examples, illustrations, and practice exercises 4. Exam content is based on learning objectives. 5. Exam performance requirements are consistent with the learning objectives. 6. Exam items are well constructed (easy to interpret and not ambiguous). 7. Instructions for taking exams are clear, and responses expected on exams are well defined. 8. Learning strategies are selected to enhance learning. 9. Instructional content is presented in the most effective and efficient way, based upon learning strategies selected. 10. Instructional presentations adequately prepare students to perform as specified in learning objectives. 11. Students are given an opportunity to practice and review (with feedback and remedial work if needed) prior to taking an exam. 12. Instruction includes learning activities with authentic and engaging instructional materials and (if applicable) work that requires student interaction and collaboration. 13. Students are given clear instructions and mechanisms for obtaining learning assistance and help from the instructor in understanding course requirements.	Bell, 1985 Johnson & Thomas, 1994 Kerka, 1997 Knowles, 1980 Merrill n.d. Merrill, 1994 Merrill, Reigeluth, & Faust, 1979 Montague, Willis, & Faust, 1980

Appendix B. Web Instruction Best Practices

1. The role of the instructor is well defined. 2. The means of access to the instructor are clearly indicated. 3. Communication methods (e-mail, bulletin board or forum, chat room) are identified. 4. Online help with communication methods is available to students. 5. Multiple varieties of interaction are incorporated (student learning material, student-student interactions, and student-teacher interactions). 6. Media used are appropriate for learning objectives (i.e., media add value to instruction). 7. Student collaboration is encouraged when appropriate. 8. Content engages students in active learning tasks. 9. Internet links are meaningfully related to learning objectives. 10. Internet links are appropriately placed so as not to interrupt the logical flow of instruction. 11. Group activities are used to promote learning. 12. Group activities are used to promote socialization and development of a learning community. 13. Course structure capitalizes on the availability of resources on the Internet. 14. Course structure capitalizes on the communication capabilities of the Internet by encouraging peer collaboration and contact with subject matter experts. 15. Students are provided with a convenient means to interact with faculty and with other students taking the course or instructional program. 16. Students are informed online about how to obtain help with coursework, exams, and assignments 17. Online assessment methods are relevant and fair tests of achievement, based upon learning objectives and course performance expectations. 18. Assessment methods emphasize authenticity in that performance is evaluated using practical (real-world) problem-solving tasks. 19. Feedback on exams and assignments is constructive and timely.	Boettcher & Conrad, 1999 Kerka, 1996 McManus, 2001 Palloff, 1999 Sonwalker, 2001b

Appendix C. Web Design and Usability Guidelines

1. Students are given instructions and guidance on necessary website navigation for the course. 2. Web page navigation links are meaningfully labeled. 3. Information is logically organized into related sets or chunks. 4. Information sets or chunks are logically located on display screen. 5. Information sets or chunks appear consistently in expected display locations. 6. Consistency is maintained in information formats, content layout, and content location on the screen. 7. Logical layout and spacing are used to control display density. 8. Minimum font size is 9 points (10–12 points recommended). 9. Upper- and lower-case letters are used for text. 10. Font size is varied only for emphasis. 11. Use of blue and red colors for text is avoided. 12. Web pages start and end on a coherent topic. 13. Page change function, rather than scroll, is used at the end of a logical segment. 14. Landmarks and signposts are used to show the user his or her present location in instructional sequence or website geography, path traversed, and what lies ahead. 15. A visual sign is used to identify current operating mode, and initial changes in mode are indicated by auditory tone, if multimode functions are accessed. (Applies mainly to simulations and animated demonstrations.) 16. A visual sign or selectable auditory signal, or both, are used to indicate the start and end of a task. 17. The user is given a clearly indicated option to escape from a specific mode, operating condition, unwanted website or page. For example, an option to page back or return to a home page position is always available and clearly indicated. 18. Accommodations are made in display and auditory presentations for students with modest visual and hearing impairments (e.g., selectable font size and text-audio redundancy).	Jones, 1989 Jordan, 1988 Nielsen, 2000 Shneiderman, 1998

Appendix D. Institutional and Support Infrastructure

1. The student is informed about the technology required for taking a course or instructional program. 2. The student is informed about the technical competency required to take a course or a specific instructional program. 3. The student is informed about the institutional requirements, including cost of course or program, course duration, time allowed for completion, any prerequisites or special skills required, and support services available. 4. Instructional materials are kept current through timely updates. 5. Available student services are clearly defined and accessible. 6. The technology delivery system is adequate to support courses offered and student loads. 7. The technology delivery system is as reliable and fail-safe as possible. 8. The student is informed about how to obtain help with technology issues. 9. The student is provided with necessary library and informational resources to meet course objectives. 10. Convenient access is provided for students to obtain assistance with administrative and technology problems.	Daniel, 2001 National Education Association, 2000 WASC, 2000

References

Bandura, A. A. (1977). *Social learning theory.* Englewood Cliffs, NJ: Prentice-Hall.

Bell, M. E. (1985). The role of instructional theories in the evaluation of microcomputer courseware. *Educational Technology, 25,* 36–40.

Boettcher, J. V., & Conrad, R. M. (1999). *Faculty guide for moving teaching and learning to the web.* Tallahassee, FL: Florida State University, League of Innovation in Community Colleges.

Bruner, J. (1990). *In search of mind.* Cambridge, MA: Harvard University Press.

Ciavarelli, A. P. (1988). *Development and validation of instructional strategies for teaching operators of complex man-machine systems.* Unpublished doctoral dissertation, Education Department University of Southern California, Los Angeles.

Daniel, J. (2001). *Open learning and the university of the future.* Retrieved April 2001 from www3.open.ac.uk/vcs-speeches/umbc.htm.

Ford, R. (2000, Fall). Real time learning: The classroom is closed. *Ergonomics in Design,* 17–24.

Hodell, C. (2000). *ISD from the ground up.* Alexandria, VA: American Society for Training and Development.

Johnson, S. D., & Thomas, R. G. (1994, Winter–Spring). Implications of cognitive science for instructional design in technology education. *Journal of Technology Studies, 20*(1), 33–45.

Jones, M. K. (1989). *Human-computer interaction: A design guide.* Englewood Cliffs, N.J.: Educational Technology Publications.

Jordan, P. W., (1998). *An introduction to usability.* London: Taylor-Francis.

Kerka, S. (1996). *Distance learning, the Internet, and the World Wide Web.* Columbus, OH: ERIC Clearinghouse on Adult and Vocational Education. (ERIC Document Reproduction Service No. ED395214)

Kerka, S. (1997). *Constructivism, workplace learning, and vocational education.* Columbus, OH: ERIC Clearinghouse on Adult Career and Vocational Education. (ERIC Document Reproduction Service No. ED407573)

Knowles, M. S. (1980). *The modern practice of adult education: From pedagogy to androgyny* (2nd ed.). New York: Cambridge Books.

McManus, T. F. (2001). *Delivering instruction on the web.* Retrieved December 2001 from www.svsu.edu/~mcmanus/papers/wbi.html.

Merrill, M. D. (n.d.) *Component display theory.* Retrieved December 2001 from http://tip.psychology.org/merrill.html.

Merrill, M. D. (1980). Learner control in computer-based learning. *Computers and Education, 4,* 77–85.

Merrill, M. D. (1983). Component display theory. In C. Reigeluth (Ed.), *Instructional design theories and models.* Hillsdale, NJ: Lawrence Erlbaum Associates.

Merrill, M. D. (1994). *Instructional design theory.* Englewood Cliffs, NJ: Educational Technology Publications.

Merrill, M. D., Reigeluth, C. M., & Faust, G. W. (1979). The instructional quality profile: A curriculum evaluation and design tool. In H. F. O'Neil Jr. (Ed.), *Procedures for instructional systems development.* New York: Academic Press.

Montague, W. E., Willis, J. A., & Faust, G. W. (1980) Instructional quality profile. A formative tool for instructional development. *Performance and Instruction Journal, 22,* 11–14.

Montague, W. E., Willis, J. A., & Wulfeck, W. H., II. (1983). Instructional quality inventory: A formative tool for instructional development.*Performance and Instruction Journal, 22,* 11–14.

Moskal, B. M. (2000). Scoring rubrics part one: What and when. Washington, DC: ERIC Clearinghouse on Assessment and Evaluation. (ERIC Document Reproduction Service No. ED446110)

National Education Association. (2000, April). *Quality on the line: Benchmarks for success in Internet-based distance education.* Washington, DC: Institute for Higher Education Policy, National Education Association.

Nielsen, J. (2000). *Designing web usability.* Indianapolis, IN: New Riders Publishing.

Palloff, R. M. (1999) *Building learning communities in cyberspace.* San Francisco, CA: Jossey-Bass.

Shneiderman, B. (1998). *Designing the user interface* (3rd ed.). Reading, MA: Addison Wesley Longman.

Sonwalker, N. (2001a, November). Changing the interface of education with revolutionary learning technologies: New dimensions in education technology. *Syllabus, 33,* 1–14.

Sonwalker, N. (2001b, December). The sharp end of the cube: Pedagogically driven instructional design for online education. *Syllabus, 33,* 12–16.

Spiro, R. J., Feltovich, P. J., Jacobson, M. J., & Coulson, R. L. (1991). Cognitive flexibility, constructivism, and hypertext: Random access education for advanced knowledge acquisition in ill-structured domains. In T. Duffy and D. Jonassen (Eds.), *Constructivism and the technology of instruction* (pp. 57–75). Hillsdale, NJ: Lawrence Erlbaum Associates.

Stefanyshyn, E. I. (2001). *Principles for web-based instruction.* Unpublished master's thesis, Naval Postgraduate School, Monterey, CA.

Vygotsky, L. S. (1978). *Mind in society: The development of higher psychological processes.* Cambridge, MA: Harvard University.

WASC [Western Association of Schools and Colleges]. (2000, May). *Evaluation of electronically offered degree and certificate programs.* Alameda, CA: Author.

Wiggins, G. (1990). *The case for authentic assessment.* (ERIC Document Reproduction Service No. ED328611). Retrieved December 2001 from http://ericae.net/db/edo/ED328611.htm.

Bibliography of Relevant Articles

Baker, E. L., & Linn, R. L. (1991). *The Center for Research on Evaluation, Standards, and Student Testing (CRESST).* Washington, DC: ERIC Clearinghouse on Assessment and Evaluation. (ERIC Document Reproduction Service No. ED338705)

Bond, L. A. (1996). *Norm- and criterion-referenced testing.* Washington, DC: ERIC Clearinghouse on Assessment and Evaluation. (ERIC Document Reproduction Service No. ED410316)

Brualdi, A. (1998). *Implementing performance assessment in the classroom.* Washington, DC: ERIC Clearinghouse on Assessment and Evaluation. (ERIC Document Reproduction Service No. ED423312)

Elliott, S. N. (1995). *Creating meaningful performance assessments.* Washington, DC: ERIC Clearinghouse on Disabilities and Gifted Education. (ERIC Document Reproduction Service No. ED381985)

Fuchs, L. S. (1995). *Connecting performance assessment to instruction: A comparison of behavioral assessment, mastery learning, and curriculum-based measurement and performance assessment.* Washington, DC: ERIC Clearinghouse on Assessment and Evaluation. (ERIC Document Reproduction Service No. ED381984)

Heaney, B. (1990). *The assessment of educational outcomes.* Washington, DC: ERIC Clearinghouse on Assessment and Evaluation. (ERIC Document Reproduction Service No. ED321834)

Kerka, S. (1996). *Distance learning, the Internet, and the World Wide Web.* Columbus, OH: ERIC Clearinghouse on Adult and Vocational Education. (ERIC Document Reproduction Service No. ED395214)

Kerka, S. (1997). *Constructivism, workplace learning, and vocational education.* Columbus, OH: ERIC Clearinghouse on Adult Career and Vocational Education. (ERIC Document Reproduction Service No. ED407573)

Moskal, B. M. (2000). *Scoring rubrics part one: What and when.* Washington, DC: ERIC Clearinghouse on Assessment and Evaluation. (ERIC Document Reproduction Service No. ED446110)

Moskal, B. M. (2000). *Scoring rubrics part two: How?* Washington, DC: ERIC Clearinghouse on Assessment and Evaluation. (ERIC Document Reproduction Service No. ED446111)

Novak, J. D., Gowin, D. B., & Johansen, G. T. (1983). The use of concept mapping and knowledge mapping with junior high science students. *Science Education, 67,* 625–645.

Plotnick, E. (1997).*Concept mapping: A graphical system for understanding the relationship between concepts.* Washington, DC: ERIC Clearinghouse on Assessment and Evaluation. (ERIC Document Reproduction Service No. ED407938)

Reed, D. S. (2000). *Evaluating technology-based curriculum materials.* Washington, DC: ERIC Clearinghouse on Assessment and Evaluation. (ERIC Document Reproduction Service No. ED449118)

Chapter 50
Needs Assessment
An Ongoing Process for School Improvement

Cheryl Moore-Thomas & Bradley T. Erford

The primary goal of schools may be to provide for the highest possible level of student learning (Angelo & Cross, 1993). Others suggest the aim of schools is simply to provide good-quality education to all students (Lezotte & Bancroft, 1985). Certainly, the first step in meeting the fundamental aim of any educational institution is to understand clearly what the students need. Needs assessment is a tool educators can use to help meet this goal. Needs assessment data suggest the basis for plans, strategies, and practices that may ultimately lead to school improvement (Lezotte & Bancroft, 1985).

Needs assessment accomplishes three main goals. First, it helps educators understand the needs of various stakeholders and subpopulations of a school community. Second, needs assessment helps establish the priorities that guide the development of educational and student support programs. Finally, needs assessment leads to continual quality improvements in educational programs (Cook, 1989). A needs assessment focuses less on present conditions than on how the present condition compares to identified goals and objectives (Wiles & Bondi, 1984).

Frequency of Needs Assessment

Needs assessment should occur on a frequent, rotating basis. Although it may be appealing to conduct just an annual schoolwide needs assessment, such a practice often produces results that end up being obsolete before they are adequately interpreted and used. A continual cycle of program needs assessment, however, allows time for appropriate and timely program change.

National and state standards designate specific components and competencies that should be assessed on a rotating basis. For example, a school can devote years one and two of a needs assessment cycle to conducting assessments and implementing programmatic changes that address curricular and instructional issues (e.g., Year 1: English, social studies, and arts needs assessment; Year 2: mathematics, science, physical education, and health needs assessment). The school can then devote years three and four of the cycle to assessing student support needs such as those related to school counseling and alternative education programming. During years five and six, the school can focus on needs assessment of issues related to school climate and outreach.

A program requiring only fine-tuning may be put on a three-year continual improvement cycle. For ease of interpretation and visual conceptualization, Figure 1 shows this cycle of ongoing improvement. Assessing schoolwide needs is a big job, but it need not be overwhelming. Using a needs assessment cycle permits small increments of programmatic change that aim to improve the educational program continually. Ideally, needs assessment should be thought of as a form of progress assessment. Progress assessment implies ongoing assessment that encourages and allows for change as needed (Terenzini, 1989). Ongoing, appropriate change is fundamental to effective needs assessment.

Figure 1. Needs Assessment Cycle

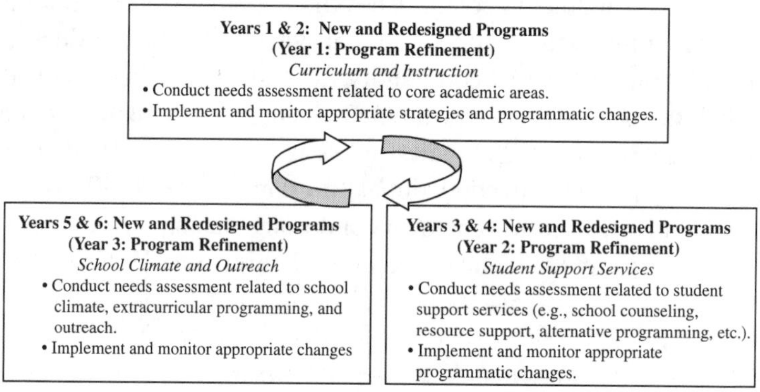

Populations to Be Assessed

Stakeholders can provide useful information about the needs of a school community. Educational stakeholders are individuals who have an interest in the quality of a school's educational program (Sanders, 1992). Teachers, administrators, students, and parents are the primary educational stakeholders. Other stakeholders, such as community leaders, legislators, college and university faculty, and local businesspeople, may also provide valuable information. Unfortunately, it sometimes proves difficult to collect meaningful information from these other stakeholders because of their small numbers. Small sample sizes may lead to questions of validity and statistical significance of the assessment results. For these reasons, teachers, administrators, students, and parents are typically the primary stakeholders surveyed during educational needs assessment. So that the valuable input of non-school-based stakeholders is not lost, however, a school could consider conducting needs assessment with community, business, and other groups through interviews or personal contacts.

Surveys have proved to be an effective needs assessment tool for large primary stakeholder groups such as teachers, administrators, students, and parents. Surveys, however, often present return rate issues. *Return rate* refers to the percentage of surveys returned out of those sent. The higher the return rate, the lower the sampling error. A high return rate may foster greater confidence in the accuracy of the results. Generally, the return rate is increased when those being surveyed are a captive audience. For example, if a "What parents need to know about helping students with homework" needs assessment is conducted and collected at a school's back to school night, the response rate should be very high. On the other hand, if the same needs assessment is sent home to parents, the school staff may receive only 25 to 50 percent of the completed surveys. To maximize the return rate, whenever possible, surveys should be distributed, completed, and collected during a single class session, staff meeting, or parent meeting.

A final consideration in determining populations to be assessed is triangulation. *Triangulation* involves comparing and cross-checking the results of various stakeholder responses so agreement can be reached among groups on the importance of various issues. Triangulation of needs across stakeholder groups is important because it helps guarantee that the school community's needs, and not an individual's agenda, drive the school program. For example, if the school principal considers math programs to be a high priority, but teachers, parents, and students indicate that the math program is equal in priority to implementation of an arts program, the triangulated responses of the teachers, parents, and students can provide compelling evidence to adjust the focus of program change.

Design Issues in Needs Assessment

Efficient needs assessment design is essential to effective assessment. Several different yet efficient methods can be used to determine needs. Stone and Bradley (1994) recommend questionnaires and inventories, records analysis, personal interviews, statistics, classroom visits, use of outside consultants, and systematic evaluation. Although all these methods are important and useful, questionnaires (formal or informal surveys) are most commonly used (Schmidt, 1993). Perhaps what is most important is that regardless of the instrument, the needs assessment use objective methods for data gathering and analysis (Wiles & Bondi, 1984).

Efficient needs assessment questionnaires are one to two pages in length and can be completed in just a few minutes. The content of these needs assessments is topical and focused rather than service-related (e.g., math skills, study skills, or school discipline rather than direct instruction, individual school counseling, or team teaching). Services are ways to meet needs; they are not needs in themselves. Needs assessment topics should also be related to national, state, or local standards to ensure proper program alignment.

The assessment questionnaire should ask for the name of the individual completing the form, unless the form is to be completed anonymously. Although anonymity can increase the return rate and level of disclosure on surveys, requesting the name of the respondent may allow for needed clarification, follow-up, or targeted intervention. A school should carefully consider the value of anonymous versus signed surveys before designing the needs assessment instrument. Surveys used with students should probably ask for grade level, teacher's name, and other relevant information. Parent surveys may ask for the names of the parent's children in case follow-up with the children is required. Figures 2, 3, and 4 are examples of needs assessments for teachers (student conflict resolution skills), students (preparation for college and the world of work), and parents (knowledge of school policy), respectively.

Effective survey response stems are concise and written at an appropriate reading level. Response stems usually lead to a multipoint response scale. Three to five response choices are generally satisfactory. Figure 2, for example, asks about teachers' perceptions of the frequency of situations requiring conflict resolution. The needs assessment uses a five-point scale (i.e., "Rarely," "Sometimes," "Frequently," "Most of the Time," and "Almost Always"). Figure 3 uses a four-point response scale that ranges from "Not Important" to "Very Important." It is generally a good idea not to include response choices that indicate absolutes, such as "never" and "always." Including these response choices may force responses to the center of the distribution, thus truncating the range of results. It is appropriate, however, to use response

Figure 2. Sample Middle School Teacher Needs Assessment of Students' Conflict Resolution Skills

Name: ___________________
Grade you teach: _______ Number of students in your homeroom: _______

Please place an X in the box that corresponds with your response.

Do students in your homeroom class:

	Rarely	**Sometimes**	**Frequently**	**Most of the Time**	**Almost Always**	*About how many of your students need help in this area?*
1. feel safe at school?						
2. complain of being bullied?						
3. feel there are confidential procedures to report violence?						
4. report violence and conflict to staff and administration?						
5. know how to effectively handle conflicts?						
6. effectively use problem-solving strategies to resolve conflicts?						
7. use the violence hotline to report threats?						
8. know how to de-escalate verbal conflicts?						

Thank you for taking time to complete this survey!

Figure 3. Sample Secondary Level Needs Assessment of Career and College Preparation

Student's name: ______________________________

Grade: ______________________________

Rate the following according to its importance to your success in entering college or a career following high school graduation.

	Not Important	Somewhat Important	Important	Very Important	*I need more information on this.* *Yes*	*No*
1. Knowledge of college entrance requirements						
2. Knowledge of employment skills for the profession in which you are interested						
3. Knowledge of how to fill out a college application						
4. Knowledge of how to fill out an employment application						
5. Knowledge of how to finance a college education						
6. Knowledge of starting salaries in particular professions						
7. Knowledge of colleges offering a particular major						
8. Knowledge of companies offering job opportunities in specific professions						
9. Knowledge of how to use media to search for colleges and employers						
10. Knowledge of communication skills necessary for a successful college entrance or employment interview						

Thank you for taking time to complete this survey!

Figure 4. Sample Parent Needs Assessment of School Policy Familiarity

Parent/guardian's name: ______________________________
Child's name: ______________________________
Child's grade: ______________________________

Below is a series of questions. Answer these questions by placing a check mark in the appropriate box.

How familiar are you with the school policy on	**Very Familiar**	**Somewhat Familiar**	**Somewhat Unfamiliar**	**Very Unfamiliar**	Check if you would like to receive more information about this.
1. cheating?					
2. tardiness?					
3. absences?					
4. hallway behavior?					
5. academic requirements to participate in extracurricular activities?					
6. harassment, threats, and fights?					
7. zero tolerance for alcohol and other drugs?					

I believe my child could benefit from a program on these school policies: Yes_______No_______

I believe parents could benefit from a program on these school policies: Yes_______No_______

Thank you for taking time to complete this survey!

choices that indicate slight differences in perception as demonstrated in the response scale of Figure 4.

Notice that a word or two describes each response choice in each of the figures. These descriptors are extremely important. Surveys that include descriptors for the end points of the response scale but provide no descriptors for the center points create reliability concerns. If there are descriptors for the end points of a response scale, but only numbers to designate the center points (e.g., [Never]0 1 2 3 4 5 6 7 8 9 10 [Always]), it will be unclear exactly how each respondent interpreted each response choice.

Another important response component of a needs assessment is frequency count. When possible, the design of the needs assessment should include an indication of how many or which specific students need intervention. Figure 2, for instance, asks teachers to indicate how many of their students need help in the given area. Figure 3 provides frequency information by asking individual students if they need help with a particular skill or topic. Frequency information can help determine implementation strategies. If, for example, the needs assessment results indicate that large numbers of students need help with a specific skill, the school may put into place schoolwide implementation vehicles, such as assemblies, classroom instruction, or schoolwide programs. If the needs assessment results suggest small numbers of students need intervention, services like small-group counseling, workshops, or tutorials may be more appropriate.

Computing Results

Tallying or computing the information from a needs assessment involves counting the number of stakeholders who may benefit from intervention (Myrick, 1997). Assigning a number value to each response category and then averaging all responses for a given item is a straightforward way to compute results. For example, in Figure 2, assume that the response categories are assigned the following values: "Rarely" = 0, "Sometimes" = 1, "Frequently" = 2, "Most of the Time" = 3, and "Almost Always" = 4. For item 6, "Do students in your class effectively use problem-solving strategies to resolve conflicts?" suppose 1 of the 25 teachers polled marked "Rarely," 5 teachers marked "Sometimes," 15 marked "Frequently," 2 marked "Most of the Time," and 2 marked "Almost Always." To compute the average, the first step would be to add the response values. This is done by multiplying the number of respondents in each category by the numeric value of that category: (1 x 0) + (5 x 1) + (15 x 2) + (2 x 3) + (2 x 4) = 49. Next, divide the sum by the total number of respondents: 49/25 = 1.96. The 1.96 average for question 6 of Figure 2 seems to suggest that, on average, teachers believe their students use effective problem-solving strategies "Frequently" to resolve conflicts. It is important to note that this computation assumes a ratio scale. The resulting average is also somewhat nebulous: What does 1.96 really mean? Even with these limitations, the average does offer a reasonable estimate of the frequency of a behavior or importance of an issue in comparison to other needs being assessed on the survey.

Converting Needs to Program Goals and Objectives

If the needs assessment is appropriately designed, translating the results into goals and learning objectives will be straightforward. The first step in the process is to prioritize the needs. Prioritization can be accomplished most easily by using the tallying, computing, and triangulation strategies previously mentioned. Next, the needs must be matched with the goals of the program and the institution, as well as national, state, and local standards. Finally, the goals must be operationalized through the development of learning objectives.

A reasonable goal stemming from the needs assessment in Figure 3 could be "To increase students' knowledge of communication skills needed for successful college entrance or employment interviews." A related objective could be "After completing the English unit on communication, 85 percent of 10th-grade students will be able to state their conversational intent (i.e., name and reason for seeking the interview) in one or two sentences during a 10-minute mock interview." Note that the goal is somewhat vague but the objective points to reasonable, specific actions that are measurable. The objective designates the group targeted for intervention, the desired behavior, measurement criteria, when the expected behavior should occur, and the level of expected performance (Gottfredson, Nettles, & McHugh, 1996). Objectives including these components are effective and lead to meaningful evaluation.

Summary

Effective and efficient needs assessment is crucial to educational programs; it does not involve merely handing out a survey, but also requires careful consideration of a schoolwide assessment cycle, stakeholder involvement, assessment design, results, goals and objectives, and implementation and evaluation strategies. When put into place, the entire needs assessment package begins at and leads back to the primary aim of the institution or educational program. When efficiently and effectively implemented, needs assessment benefits all stakeholders and the overall educational process.

References

Angelo, T., & Cross, K. (1993). *Classroom assessment techniques: A handbook for college teachers* (2nd ed.). San Francisco, CA: Jossey-Bass.

Cook, D. W. (1989). Systematic needs assessment: A primer. *Journal of Counseling and Development, 67,* 462–464.

Gottfredson, G., Nettles, S., & McHugh, B. (1996). *Program development and evaluation for schools and communities.* Ellicot City, MD: Gottfredson Associates, Inc. (ERIC Document Reproduction Services No. ED 429363)

Lezotte, L., & Bancroft, B. (1985). School improvement based on effective schools research: A promising approach for economically disadvantaged and minority students. *Journal of Negro Education, 54*(3), 301–312.

Myrick, R. D. (1997). *Developmental guidance and counseling: A practical approach* (3rd ed.). Minneapolis, MN: Educational Media Corporation.

Sanders, J. (1992). *Evaluating school programs: An educator's guide.* Newbury Park, CA: Corwin Press. (ERIC Document Reproduction Services No. ED 423166)

Schmidt, J. J. (1993). *Counseling in the schools.* Boston: Allyn and Bacon.

Stone, L. A., & Bradley, F. O. (1994). *Foundations of elementary and middle school counseling.* White Plains, NY: Longman.

Terenzini, P. (1989). Assessment with open eyes. *Journal of Higher Education, 60*(6), 644–664.

Wiles, J., & Bondi, J. C. (1984). *Curriculum development: A guide to practice* (2nd ed.). Columbus, OH: Merrill Publishing.

Chapter 51
The National Assessment of Educational Progress
What It Tells Educators

Lauress L. Wise

On October 4, 1957, the Soviet Union launched the first artificial satellite from the Baikonur cosmodrome in Kazakhstan (see www.batnet.com/mfwright/sputnik.html). America's self-image as the world's technological leader was shattered. In the ensuing years, numerous efforts were launched to improve the education of American youth and thus restore our globaal competitiveness. These efforts ranged from "new math" to Project TALENT, an intensive study of 400,000 students in American high schools in 1960. Amid these efforts, Ralph Tyler pursued the sensible notion that we should regularly assess elementary and secondary student achievement so as to measure the progress of education. Planning conferences were held beginning in 1964, and later in the 1960s the National Assessment of Educational Progress (NAEP) was launched (Jones, 1996). A recent review of NAEP by the National Academy of Education (Glaser, Linn, & Bohrnstedt, 1997) begins with the statement, "Since its inception in 1969, the National Assessment of Educational Progress (NAEP) has been the nation's leading indicator of what American students know and can do" (p. 1)

In its beginning, NAEP reported student performance on specific test questions selected to represent subject areas for students at ages 8, 12, and 17. This reporting process has undergone a number of significant changes over the past 30 years, for example, grade cohorts (i.e., grades 4, 8, and 12) have replaced age cohorts in assessments. In the mid-1980s, item response theory (Lord & Novick, 1968) was introduced to provide an overall score scale as a complement to item-by-item results. In response to a book by Alexander and James (1987), an independent governing board was created to oversee the content and administration of the assessment in partnership with the U.S. Department of Education (Vinovskis, 1998). Beginning in 1990, state results were released along with national trend information. The No Child Left Behind Act, passed by Congress in 2001, requires state participation in NAEP. NAEP results will likely be used to audit state measures of yearly educational progress.

Currently three relatively distinct components comprise NAEP. National NAEP reports student achievement for the nation as a whole relative to current content frameworks for each subject area. State NAEP reports results for each participating state on a more limited set of subjects and grades. The long-term-trend NAEP reports student results at the national level based on the content and format of assessment that has been common over the last several decades.

A detailed recounting of the history of NAEP is outside the scope of this chapter. The following sources provide much more detailed information on how NAEP has evolved and what changes may lie ahead:

Alexander and James (1987)
Jones (1996)
Glaser et al. (1997)
Pelligrino, Jones, & Mitchell (1999)

The National Center for Education Statistics within the U.S. Department of Education maintains a website that includes a wide range of information on the current NAEP: http://nces.ed.gov/nationsreportcard/.

The focus of this chapter is on how NAEP, as it exists today, may be useful to educators, in particular four aspects of NAEP that may be of wide interest and use. First, NAEP provides content frameworks for particular subjects that reflect a national consensus on what 4th-, 8th-, and 12th-grade students should know and be able to do. Second, the National Assessment Governing Board (NAGB), which Congress created in 1988 to set NAEP policy, has adopted performance standards for each grade and subject indicating Basic, Proficient, and Advanced mastery of the knowledge and skills specified in each of the content frameworks. Third, NAEP has contributed many innovations to the assessment of student achievement, and questions released by NAEP provide concrete examples of these innovations. Finally, NAEP continues to provide national normative data at the test question level as well as for the overall NAEP reporting scales. This chapter concludes with a discussion of planned or possible enhancements to NAEP that could further increase its usefulness to educators.

National Content Frameworks

NAEP has contributed significantly to the dialogue about what we should be teaching students at the elementary, middle, and high school levels. There is of course a rich tradition of state and local control of schools, yet there is also a growing recognition that students will have to compete in a national, if not international, employment market. Thus while emphases may vary, there is surely a core set of skills that students will need in order to succeed in college, the workplace, avocational pursuits, and civic responsibility. Indeed, business and labor have expended extensive effort to define essential workplace skills through the Labor Secretary's Commission on Acquiring Necessary Skills (SCANS) and later the National Skills Standards Boards. The NAEP content frameworks reflect an important effort to identify essential knowledge and skills for students in all states and local districts.

A national consensus process is used. Several features of the content frameworks developed by NAEP make the frameworks noteworthy. First is the careful consensus process used in developing and adopting these frameworks. The NAGB has contracted with the Council of Chief State School Officers and similar broad-based organizations to manage the development of recommended frameworks. Professional organizations that represent content specialists, such as the National Council of Teachers of Mathematics, have played a leadership role in framework development. The NAGB handles the adoption of content frameworks. NAGB is an independent, bipartisan organization chartered by Congress to manage the content and timing of NAEP assessments. By statute, it includes two governors, two state legislators, two chief state school officers, and a mix of district and school personnel, content specialists, measurement experts, and the general public (Vinovskis, 1998). Before approving the frameworks recommended by a development contractor, NAGB holds hearings at locations throughout the nation to obtain public comment on the proposed frameworks. A subcommittee of NAGB members manages these hearings and processes the input, working with the development contractor on potential changes to accommodate suggestions from the hearings. The entire board must approve final frameworks before they are initiated.

The frameworks are inclusive. If significant consequences for students or schools were attached to scores from NAEP, it would be necessary to limit the content of what is tested to material that is taught in all schools. At the very least, this would mean limiting NAEP content to the intersection of the frameworks adopted by the different states. Because, as of this writing, there are not any direct consequences attached to NAEP scores, this restriction does not apply. In fact, NAEP frameworks tend to be inclusive, encompassing content that is deemed significant by all states and by other sources as well.

The frameworks are forward looking. The NAEP frameworks are not merely a reflection of what is currently taught and are not limited to what is currently included in one or more of the state frameworks. The frameworks attempt to balance what is being taught with expert judgment about what should be taught. In this sense, the frameworks are forward looking and provide a model that many states find useful in updating and revising their own content standards.

What frameworks are available? Table 1 lists the NAEP content frameworks used with recent or pending assessments. In each case, the frameworks specify content for the assessments at the 4th-, 8th-, and 12th-grade levels. A revised framework for mathematics will be used with the 2005 assessment, and a framework for economics is under development. The NAGB website lists updated information: http://nagb.org/. Copies of most of the frameworks can be downloaded from this site. Instructions for ordering printed copies from the NAGB are also available there.

Table 1. NAEP Content Frameworks

Subject	Assessment Years
Mathematics	1996, 2000
Reading	1992–2000
Science	1996, 2000
History	1994, 2001
Geography	1994, 2001
Foreign Language	2003
Writing	1998
Civics	1998
Arts	1997

Student Performance Standards

Since 1990, NAGB has addressed not just what students should know and be able to do as indicated by the content frameworks, but also the level of mastery of each subject that constitutes proficiency. In the beginning, NAEP reported percentages of students answering individual questions correctly. In 1983, the NAEP grant was moved from the Education Commission of the States to the Educational Testing Service (ETS). ETS constructed an overall scale based on item response theory and began reporting yearly means on this scale. The new scale allowed yearly gains to be summarized in terms of a single number rather than reported separately for each test item. Several attempts were made to describe what students knew and could do at various points on the scale for each subject.

Beginning in 1990, the NAGB initiated a process for defining *achievement levels* as regions along the overall reporting scale. Three levels were defined by minimum or cutoff scores: Basic, Proficient, and Advanced. Students who fail to reach the minimum score for the Basic achievement level are considered Below Basic. With these achievement levels, results can be reported in terms of percentages at or above a given level rather than as means on an arbitrary scale. Increases in the percentage of students who are Proficient (or have achieved at least basic mastery) are thought to be more meaningful for the general public and for policy setting than is an increase in the mean on the arbitrary scale.

Details of the achievement-level-setting process are well beyond the scope of this chapter. See NAGB (2000) for a recent discussion of achievement level standards. There has been some controversy about the process and the resulting achievement levels. Panels from the National Academy of Education (Shepard, 1993) and the National Research Council (Pellegrino, Jones et al., 1999) expressed concerns about the process and the resulting achievement level standards. The question is whether experts' judgments about particular students match the way NAEP standards would classify these students. For example, some students scoring 4 or 5 on an Advanced Placement Examination might not be classified as Advanced by the NAEP standards.

The process used to develop and adopt NAEP achievement level standards has evolved considerably over time. NAGB's current review procedures are designed to ensure a reasonable level of consistency across grades and subjects. Over time, the NAEP achievement levels will acquire their own meaning, whether or not they agree with other conceptions of Basic, Proficient, or Advanced performance.

The NAEP achievement levels provide a useful benchmark for state efforts to define proficiency expectations. Estimates of the percentage of students at different achievement levels on state assessments can be compared with corresponding percentages from the NAEP state assessments. Discrepancies will doubtless lead to a political dialogue about the nature of the differences. There is often concern that state standards are too low, with the result that students are insufficiently challenged. Standards that are too high can be equally problematic, although this has been a less common concern. For example, where standards are too high, programs that may be working reasonably well might be abandoned in favor of riskier approaches that promise, but may not deliver, the inappropriately high levels of achievement that the standards require.

For local educators, standards-based reporting may not be important to instruction, at least until NAEP results for individual students or schools are included. Of greater use in shaping curriculum are the descriptions associated with each of the achievement levels. NAGB has established broad policy descriptions for each achievement level. As curriculum frameworks are developed, these policy descriptions are translated to statements about specific knowledge and skills associated with each of the achievement levels. These more detailed achievement level descriptions were originally developed by the standards-setting committees. With the 1996 science assessment, preliminary achievement level descriptions were added to the frameworks, with more explicit attention given to these descriptions in subsequent frameworks.

Sample Assessment Questions

Released NAEP questions and exercises reflect current thinking on how to assess accurately the knowledge and skills described in the content frameworks. A wealth of information about each item adds potential usefulness for educators. Anyone with Internet access can obtain this information from the NAEP questions section of the National Center for Education Statistics (NCES) website (http://nces.ed.gov/nationsreportcard/itmrls/). A list of questions is available for each subject and grade level. An advanced search option enables question selection by content area, ability, question type, or difficulty.

Clicking on a question in the list brings up the text of the question and provides options for viewing the following types of additional information about it:

Performance data provides a graphic indicating the percentage of students answering the item correctly, or for open-ended questions with more than two score levels, the percentage of students at each score level.

Content classification indicates the content and ability categories the item represents and provides a description of these categories.

Scoring guide indicates the correct response option for multiple-choice questions. For open-ended questions that are hand-scored, the scoring rules or rubric is provided.

Student responses shows examples of actual student responses to the essay questions for different score levels.

More data indicates the percentage of students selecting each response option for multiple-choice questions or the percentage at each score level for open-ended questions. Response or score percentages are also disaggregated by gender, race, ethnicity, parents' education, type of school, region of the country, type of location, Title 1 participation, National School Lunch Program eligibility, and NAEP achievement level.

NAEP Question Example

The following example from the NAEP website illustrates the type of information that is available from the NAEP and how it might be used. Reading questions are organized around passages. One of the released passages for the fourth-grade assessment is titled "A Brick to Cuddle Up To." Students are asked to answer nine questions about this passage. The final question asks, "Does the author help you understand what colonial life was like? Use examples from the article to explain why or why not." Selecting this question on the NAEP website will display the full text of the passage, the text of the question, and five blank lines for student responses.

The *performance data* section for this item indicates that 20 percent of students provided responses that were judged as showing "evidence of full comprehension," 29 percent of the responses were judged as showing "evidence of partial or surface comprehension," and 51 percent were judged as showing "evidence of little or no comprehension." We are also told that 0 percent skipped this item.

The *content classification* section tells us that the purpose of this question was "Reading to be informed" and the stance was "Demonstrating a critical stance." A paragraph describing each of these purposes is also provided. Several examples of question types are listed under the critical stance description. This question seems to match the type described as "How useful would this be for ______? Why?" although the question is not specifically tied to this type. A link to the reading framework is also provided in this section.

The *scoring guide* section provides descriptions of the basis for assigning responses to each of the three score levels. Under "Evidence of full comprehension," for example, it states:

> These responses provide an opinion about the author's abilities. In addition, they provide at least one supportive example from the text that demonstrates an objective consideration of the article and/or text-based critical judgment of the author's competence.

The *student responses* section provides examples of responses at each of the three scoring levels.

The *more data* section provides results separately for a wide variety of demographic groups. For example, 23 percent of students in the central region of the country got full credit for their responses while only 17 percent of students in the Southeast and West received full credit. This question appears to be relatively difficult for fourth graders in that among students at the Advanced achievement level, only 35 percent received full credit for their response. The question differentiates clearly between students at the Basic and at the Proficient levels. At the Basic level, 50 percent of the responses received the lowest score, and only 19 percent received full credit. At the Proficient level, 36 percent received the lowest score, and 29 percent received full credit.

Potential Uses of Sample Questions

One obvious use of released NAEP items is to embed them in classroom assessments. The supplemental information provided for each question will enable teachers to score responses, assess the types of questions (by content area or question format) that students can or cannot answer well, and compare classroom results to national outcomes.

Another potential use of the released questions is to provide concrete examples of the different areas of knowledge and skill covered in the content frameworks. This information may be useful to teachers in designing instruction to cover these content areas. The questions might also form the basis of discussions with students about the skills they are expected to master.

Note, however, that some boundaries should be placed on teacher enthusiasm for using these questions. One limitation of the questions is that a small number of questions cannot provide a reliable indication of the consistency of a student's response across a range of stimuli and contexts. It is important not to value responses to a few released NAEP questions to the exclusion of information about students' performance over a substantial period of time.

A second limitation is that schools will vary in the extent to which their curriculum covers or is aligned with different areas of the NAEP content frameworks. An eighth grader's poor performance on algebra and functions questions may reflect the fact that he or she has not yet been taught many of the topics in this area covered by the NAEP assessment. In fact, analyses of student performance on NAEP items may reveal areas where local instruction could be expanded.

National Norms

At the heart of NAEP's design is nationally representative information about what students know and can do in different subjects and grades. Over time, we can see how much student achievement is improving and whether the percentage of students with significantly low levels of achievement is decreasing. We can also monitor trends in performance for specific subgroups of students, such as female achievement in mathematics or Hispanic achievement in reading. We can monitor trends at the state level. In this way, NAEP tells educators whether, as a whole, what we are doing is working.

A significant limitation of the normative information provided by NAEP is that there is currently no accepted way of obtaining NAEP scale scores or achievement level classifications for individual students. The Voluntary National Tests (VNT) proposed by President Clinton in 1997 were developed to assess fourth-grade reading and eighth-grade mathematics achievement relative to NAEP standards (Wise, Hauser, Mitchell, & Feuer, 1999). The tests were designed to be as consistent with NAEP in content and format as possible. Yet a panel commissioned by NAGB to examine methods for linking VNT scores to the NAEP scale expressed significant concerns about potential limitations (Cizek, Kenny, Kolen, & Van der Linden, 1999).

Another limitation of NAEP information is that it provides little diagnostic information about the specifics of what students do not understand or cannot do. NAEP was designed to maximize the accuracy in reporting overall achievement. Student-level assessments are generally more appropriate for diagnostic purposes. Two different committees of the National Academy of Sciences have discussed ways in which richer and more diagnostic information might be provided by NAEP and similar assessments (Pellegrino, Chudowsky, & Glaser, 2001; Pellegrino, Jones et al., 1999).

Until richer diagnostic information is available, educators can fall back on the wealth of normative information available on individual test items as described above. In many cases, released items can be found that demonstrate the specific knowledge and skills covered in particular lessons or curricular units. Comparison of individual student performance on such items with national norms can be useful diagnostic information that complements the summative information provided by overall NAEP results.

Potential Future Developments

NAEP is evolving. The currently proposed schedule for national and state assessments is shown in Table 2. A dramatic change, according to this plan, is that reading and mathematics will be assessed every year at the national or state level, although this assessment will be limited to grades four and eight. Another change is the introduction of a more comprehensive assessment with each introduction of a new or updated framework. New subjects, in particular a foreign language assessment for 12th graders, are also being added.

Pending federal legislation calls for using NAEP results to audit the achievement gains that states report based on their own assessments. The change to yearly assessment of reading and mathematics is designed to support this function, should it be enacted. Legislation establishing NAGB and allowing state reporting was passed by Congress in 1988 (i.e., the Hawkins-Stafford Elementary and Secondary School Improvements Amendments). The Improving America's Schools Act of 1994 further expands the role of NAEP. The No Child Left Behind Act mandated further participation in NAEP by the states and will lead to even greater attention to the state results.

NAEP as it exists today has great value for educators. As described here, the content frameworks, achievement level standards, and normative information are evidence of NAEP's value. Further, NAEP

Table 2. Assessments Scheduled from 1996 through 2012

	Years Assessed	
	National	**State**
Subject	**Year (Grades)**	**Grades 4 & 8**
Reading	1998 (4,8,12), 2000 (4) 2002 (4,8,12), 2003 (4,8) 2005 (4,8,12), 2007 (4,8) 2009 (4,8,12), 2011 (4,8)	1998 2002, 2003 2005, 2007 2009, 2011
Writing	1998 (4,8,12) 2002 (4,8,12) 2007 (8,12) 2011 (4,8,12)	1998* 2002 2007 2011
Mathematics	1996 (4,8,12) 2000 (4,8,12), 2003 (4,8) 2005 (4,8,12), 2007 (4,8) 2009 (4,8,12), 2011 (4,8)	1996 2000, 2003 2005, 2007 2009, 2011
Science	1996 (4,8,12) 2000 (4,8,12) 2005 (4,8,12) 2009 (4,8,12)	2000 2005 2009
U.S. History	2001 (4,8,12) 2010 (4,8,2)	
World History	2006 (12)	
Geography	2001 (4,8,12) 2010 (4,8,12)	
Economics	2006 (12)	
Civics	1998 (4,8,12) 2006 (4,8,12)	
Arts	1997 (8) 2008 (8)	
Foreign Language	2004 (12) 2012 (12)	
Long-Term Trend (Reading and Mathematics)	1996 (Ages 9, 13, 17) 2004 (Ages 9, 13, 17) 2008 (Ages 9, 13, 17) 2012 (Ages 9, 13, 17)	

* Assessed for grade 8 only.

has led to significant developments in the art of assessment, and released NAEP exercises provide useful examples and tools for educators seeking to design their own local assessments. It is ardently hoped that these aspects of NAEP's value will not be diminished as new functions and roles are added in future years.

References

Alexander, L., & James, H. T. (1987). *The nation's report card: Improving the assessment of student achievement.* Washington, DC: National Academy of Education.

Cizek, G. J., Kenny, P. A., Kolen, M. J., & Van der Linden, W. J. (1999). *Final report of the study group investigating the feasibility of linking scores on the proposed Voluntary National Tests and the National Assessment of Educational Progress.* Study commissioned by the National Assessment Governing Board, University of Toledo, OH.

Glaser, R., Linn, R., & Bohrnstedt, G. (1997). *Assessment in transition: Monitoring the nation's educational progress.* Stanford, CA: National Academy of Education.

Jones, L. V. (1996). A history of the National Assessment of Educational Progress and some questions about its future. *Educational Researcher, 25,* 15–22.

Lord, F. M., & Novick, M. R. (1968). *Statistical theories of mental test scores.* Reading, MA: Addison-Wesley.

NAGB [National Assessment Governing Board]. (2000). Student performance standards of the National Assessment of Educational Progress: Affirmation and improvements. Washington, DC: Author.

Pellegrino, J. W., Chudowsky, N., & Glaser, R. (Eds.). (2001). *Knowing what students know: The science and design of educational assessment* (Report of the Committee on the Foundations of Assessment, Board on Testing and Assessment, Commission on Behavioral and Social Sciences and Education, National Research Council). Washington, DC: National Academy Press.

Pellegrino, J. W., Jones, L. R., & Mitchell, K. J. (Eds.). (1999). *Grading the nation's report card: Evaluating NAEP and transforming the assessment of educational progress* (Report of the Committee on the Evaluation of National and State Assessments of Educational Progress, Board on Testing and Assessment, Commission on Behavioral and Social Sciences and Education, National Research Council). Washington, DC: National Academy Press.

Shepard, L. (1993). *Setting performance standards for student achievement.* Stanford, CA: National Academy of Education.

Vinovskis, M. A. (1998). *Overseeing the nation's report card: The creation and evolution of the National Assessment Governing Board (NAGB).* Washington, DC: NAGB.

Wise, L. L., Hauser, R. M., Mitchell, K. J., & Feuer, M. J. (1999). *Evaluation of the Voluntary National Tests: Phase 1.* Washington, DC: National Academy Press.

Womer, F. B. (1970). *What is national assessment?* Ann Arbor, MI: NAEP.

Section E

Resources on Assessment

Chapter 52
The Joint Committee on Testing Practices
Available Publications on Testing

Lara Frumkin

On July 13 through 16, 1984, the American Psychological Association (APA) sponsored a meeting that brought together professional and scientific psychologists as well as members of the test publishing industry. Called to address issues surrounding quality assurance in testing, the meeting attracted the APA Committee on Psychological Tests and Assessment (CPTA), the APA Committee on Professional Standards, 25 test publishers and software developers, and other interested parties. Among the participants, three nonprofit associations surfaced as having the greatest concerns about test quality: the APA, the American Educational Research Association (AERA), and the National Council on Measurement in Education (NCME). During this meeting, a proposal was put forth that a steering committee with representation from these three associations be formed to create an avenue for addressing specific issues related to test quality.

The interim steering committee met in November 1984 at the APA headquarters in Washington, DC. The group, which included representatives from APA, AERA, NCME, and several test publishing companies that had been present at the July 1984 meeting, drafted a mission statement, part of which stated that AERA, APA, and NCME should convene the Consortium on Testing Practices. The purpose of the consortium would be to advance, in the public interest, the quality of testing practices.

The mission statement proposed that the consortium have a three-year initial mandate to address concerns related to the development, administration, and use of standard instruments and methodologies through the development of materials consistent with the *Standards for Educational and Psychological Testing*. The APA Board of Directors met in December 1984 and endorsed the Consortium of Testing Practices mission statement only one month after its drafting by the consortium. The AERA and NCME boards endorsed the mission statement in the spring of 1985. The interim steering committee also established two working groups to prepare statements. One of the statements was conceived to address fair testing practices in education and the other, to address issues of test user qualifications.

On April 4, 1985, AERA, APA, and NCME met with representatives from test publishing companies at the first official meeting of the Consortium on Testing Practices. The purpose of the meeting was to discuss a proposed collaboration to address testing practice issues following the recommendations of the interim steering committee that had met in November 1984. At the November 1984 meeting, the steering committee proposed an organizational structure and the criteria for membership in the Consortium of Testing Practices. Due to various concerns, in April 1985, an amendment was proposed suggesting that the group formed be flexible enough to accommodate a broad purpose but also be responsive to specific interests in testing. The proposal, purpose, and structure of the committee was developed on August 7, 1985, and appears in its original form below:

Proposal

It is proposed the APA, AERA, and NCME convene a Joint Committee on Testing Practices (JCTP). The goal of the JCTP will be to advance, in the public interest, the quality of testing practices.

Purpose and Structure of the JCTP

In keeping with its overall goal, the JCTP will address common concerns relating to the development, administration, and use of standardized instruments and methodologies consistent with the *Standards for Educational and Psychological Testing.* The JCTP will provide opportunities for open exchanges of information and actions to improve testing practices.

The JCTP will be an activity administered by the APA in concert with AERA and NCME. Initial administrative costs will be borne by the organizations. These costs are not anticipated to be substantial in the first six months of activity. Future funding will depend on further definition of the work of the JCTP, the resources available from the three founding organizations, and the income derived from contributions to be sought from other organizations and foundations.

The JCTP will be composed of nine persons: three appointed from among the membership of the three organizations, AERA, APA, and NCME. Each organization will appoint three persons to the JCTP from among its membership. Attention to the need to include persons who can make a professional contribution to the work of the group because they are actively employed in test publishing will be considered. Initial appointments by each organization will be for one, two, or three years with subsequent appointments for three years.

The JCTP will be responsible for appointing work groups to conduct specific projects, for reviewing ongoing projects, for receiving final reports of completed projects, and where relevant, for promoting acceptance of products of working groups.

Initial Working Group Structure

At the time JCTP was formed, the founding organizations also developed a procedure for creating working groups. Any of the three organizations could propose a specific project. For each project, JCTP would develop a plan of action. The plan of action had to include the agenda, time line, budget, and appoint working group members to the project.

Additionally, JCTP must plan for its own and its working group meetings, expected to occur three times a year. The initial funds from the founding organizations were designed to cover all members' travel expenses, unless the member could receive expenses to be paid from outside JCTP. The committee also thought they may, at a later date, apply for funding from private foundations.

Meetings

JCTP currently holds two official meetings per year, one of which is held at the APA convention in August. The second meeting is held at one of the other sponsoring organization's conferences. Every other year the second meeting is held at AERA/NCME. On alternating years the second meeting site rotates among the American Speech-Language-Hearing Association (ASHA), the American Counseling Association

(ACA), the National Association of School Psychologists (NASP), and the National Association of Test Directors (NATD). Approximately every other year, a third meeting is held by JCTP working group members. Those are work-intensive meetings where members meet to work only on specific projects. JCTP does not hold a business meeting or deal with any official committee business at those meetings.

Representation

To become a representative to JCTP, one needs to be appointed from one of the seven sponsoring associations. Criteria for appointment include being knowledgeable in testing, assessment, and measurement principles, as well as being a member of the sponsoring association. Originally, AERA, APA, and NCME agreed to have three representatives from each association sit on JCTP. Since the formation of the committee, this plan has evolved. Currently, APA, ACA, and NCME have two representatives that attend every JCTP meeting. ASHA and AERA have one representative each who attends every meeting. NASP and NATD have two representatives with at least one representative attending each meeting. The representatives' terms vary from two to six years. At any given time, two committee members from different organizations serve as co-chairs. Moreover, because representatives from different associations may work for the same company, the committee is careful never to appoint co-chairs who work for the same company.

Projects

Over its past 17 years of activity, the JCTP has completed several documents it hopes will advance, in the public interest, the quality of testing practices. A brief description of the projects follows.

Code of Fair Testing Practices in Education

The *Code of Fair Testing Practices in Education (Code)* was first developed in 1988 and is currently available in both Spanish and English. The *Code* was developed to document the obligations test developers and users have to the takers of educational tests. It includes information on developing and selecting appropriate tests, interpreting scores, striving for fairness, and informing test takers. The *Code* is disseminated mainly to parents and teachers. In fact, it is written for individuals who are interested in testing but may not have familiarity with complex testing concepts.

In April 2000, a JCTP working group reassessed the usefulness of the *Code*. Given that a new version of the *Standards for Educational and Psychological Testing* had been developed in 1999, they determined that the *Code* should be revised to remain consistent with the *Standards*. The JCTP Code Revision Working Group finalized the revised *Code* in 2002. As of spring 2003, it has been endorsed by several of the seven JCTP sponsoring associations and is awaiting approval from the remainder.

The working group is also planning to launch the *Code* with a press event and to develop supplementary material for it. These materials may include a prepackaged training workshop that anyone familiar with teaching may be able to use to teach schoolteachers about the *Code* and fair educational testing practices. In addition, teachers could pass along the *Code* information to parents. The Code Revision Working Group is planning web-based information to supplement the text of the *Code*. This may include examples of how the *Code* may be used, illustrate some of the points from the *Code*, and clarify points in the *Code*. Supplementary materials will likely not be available until early 2004.

Test User Qualifications: A Data-Based Approach to Promoting Good Test Use

The Test User Qualifications Working Group was formed in 1985 and completed its work in 1988. The initial charge of the working group was to develop a model qualification system that could be used to identify competencies of test users. This model system was to be based on scientific methods and be independent of occupational titles. That is, simply having a doctorate or being a psychologist would not alone satisfy the new model and automatically allow the user to administer tests. Frequently, test user qualifications are determined by the test publisher. When a test is ordered, the publisher sends a form that the prospective user must complete, documenting various pieces of information. After reviewing the information, the publisher ascertains whether the user is qualified to administer a given test and may be sold the instrument.

Soon after the test user qualification project began, it became apparent that the group would need to broaden its purpose beyond developing the model. The working group decided to focus on education of users as well as user qualifications. The group felt it was necessary to inform users and publishers about problems with test use. They saw part of their mission as being to offer guidance to publishers creating qualification policies for the users and purchasers of tests. The working group attempted to identify test user competencies, rather than qualifications (such as PhD or certification or licensure in a particular state). The working group conducted four studies to determine these test user competencies. The first was an analysis of what the job of "test use" constitutes, which was accomplished by identifying the content domain by user qualification. The second study was an evaluation of the key test user behaviors required to administer tests. The third was a taxonomic study identifying the common factors of test misuse. The fourth study involved developing empirically based test purchaser forms.

The working group developed nine principles summarizing their studies:

1. Test user qualification systems should be based on scientific methods and serve as a tool for identifying competencies of test users.
2. Access to psychometric devices should be based on knowledge and behavior of test users, not solely on credentials.
3. The key to a test user model is self-regulation.
4. The model applies to a broad range of professionals who are members of different associations adhering to different ethical principles.
5. Legislation restricting test use is unrealistic and applies primarily to tests used by psychologists while ignoring other practitioners who use tests.
6. Test misuse is more likely a function of lack of information or misinformation than of malfeasance on the test user's part.
7. Education efforts are most likely to be effective in promoting good testing practices.
8. The competency-based model described in the JCTP report is likely to increase the use of tests as an important piece in decision making.
9. By identifying possible test misuse, the model will alert test users to poor testing practices

Responsible Test Use: Case Studies for Assessing Human Behavior

Following the completion of the *Test User Qualifications* JCTP decided to produce what became a 244-page book entitled *Responsible Test Use: Case Studies for Assessing Human Behavior,* published in

1993. By the time this product was being conceived, many JCTP members felt that the most significant problem for the educational and psychological measurement community was the misuse of test data, albeit in most cases unintended misuse. JCTP members wanted to make use of the data they had collected during the Test User Qualifications project to assist their constituents and other test users. JCTP believed that test misuse typically occurred because professionals had not received adequate training on measurement principles. Thus, they designed the book for professional self-study, to supplement materials already being used for professional training.

The working group used an empirical method to evaluate test user competencies. The database developed during the test user qualifications project was applied to address critical incidents, elements, and factors of test misuse. Various common problems with test use were thereby identified. These problems were then used as the basis for soliciting 78 actual cases illustrating proper and improper test use. The cases vary in detail and complexity, offering a broad range of situations and dealing with topics such as professional interpretation of results for individuals and their aggregation for individuals in organizations. The book thus illustrates the numerous ways that test data may be misused. Misusing test data, as the book explains, can lead to errors including misclassification and misdiagnosis. These may result in great harm and cost to the individuals affected, as well as reflecting poorly on the professional misusing the data and the professional organizations of which that person is a member.

The ABCs of School Testing

The ABCs of School Testing project was completed in 1995. It resulted in the development of a videotape and accompanying leader's guide. Intended for individuals who do not have an extensive technical knowledge of testing, the materials are designed so that users can pick and choose the specific information they need to do their jobs. The videotape is designed to assist parents in understanding the multiple uses of testing in schools. A variety of tests and their appropriate use in school settings are described. JCTP hopes that this videotape helps parents to become better consumers of test results and to understand how the test information may be useful to their children.

The leader's guide is a 49-page brochure that complements the videotape. The guide focuses on the following questions:

- Why test?
- What types of tests are there?

- What kinds of test scores are there?
- How can your school select a good standardized test?
- How can you get more information about tests?

Each of the five sections includes instructional objectives, a discussion of some of the topics presented on the videotape, additional information about the testing concepts covered by the videotape, and questions for discussion.

Both the leader's guide and videotape are geared to informing teachers and parents about instructional, administrative, and research uses of test information. Other portions of the leader's guide and videotape have information on classroom versus standardized, achievement versus aptitude, norm-referenced versus criterion-referenced, and objective versus subjective tests, as well as how to choose a good standardized test. The section on types of test scores explains percentiles, standard scores, and grade equivalents.

Rights and Responsibilities of Test Takers: Guidelines and Expectations

In April 2000, JCTP printed its brochure and bookmark entitled *Rights and Responsibilities of Test Takers: Guidelines and Expectations.* This statement was an effort to clarify the expectations that test takers have about the testing process. Additionally it explains the expectations test developers, administrators, and users have of test takers. *Tests,* as used in this document, refer to psychological and educational instruments developed and used by testing professionals and organizations (e.g., schools, industries, clinical and counseling settings), as well as the assessment procedures and devices used for making inferences about people in those settings. The working group that developed this statement hopes that the *Rights and Responsibilities of Test Takers* will help inform and educate everyone involved in testing so that measurements are used as validly and appropriately as possible. The statement was also developed in an effort to inspire improvements in the testing process and to encourage positive and high-quality interactions between testing professionals and test takers.

The working group members clearly explain that the document is not enforceable by law and that the rights and responsibilities listed are not inalienable. Rather, they are a list of reasonable expectations that test users, test takers, and publishers should have of each other. The document comes in two forms, bookmark and 16-page brochure. The former includes the 20 rights and responsibilities (10 each) that follow.

The brochure format includes that same information, along with introductory materials, an explanation of rights and responsibilities, a list of the statement developers, and a reference section. These are the rights and responsibilities:

As a test taker, you have the right to:

1. Be informed of your rights and responsibilities as a test taker.
2. Be treated with courtesy, respect, and impartiality, regardless of your age, disability, ethnicity, gender, national origin, religion, sexual orientation, or other personal characteristics.
3. Be tested with measures that meet professional standards and that are appropriate, given the manner in which the test results will be used.
4. Receive a brief oral or written explanation prior to testing about the purpose(s) for testing, the kind(s) of tests to be used, if the results will be reported to you or to others, and the planned use(s) of the results. If you have a disability, you have the right to inquire and receive information about testing accommodations. If you have difficulty in comprehending the language of the test, you have a right to know in advance of testing whether any accommodations may be available to you.
5. Know in advance of testing when the test will be administered, if and when test results will be available to you, and if there is a fee for testing services that you are expected to pay.
6. Have your test administered and your test results interpreted by appropriately trained individuals who follow professional codes of ethics.
7. Know if a test is optional and learn of the consequences of taking or not taking the test, fully completing the test, or canceling the scores. You may need to ask questions to learn these consequences.
8. Receive a written or oral explanation of your test results within a reasonable amount of time after testing and in commonly understood terms.
9. Have your test results kept confidential to the extent allowed by law.
10. Present concerns about the testing process or your results

and receive information about procedures that will be used to address such concerns.

As a test taker, you have these responsibilities:

1. Read and/or listen to your rights and responsibilities as a test taker.
2. Treat others with courtesy and respect during the testing process.
3. Ask questions prior to testing if you are uncertain about why the test is being given, how it will be given, what you will be asked to do, and what will be done with the results.
4. Read or listen to descriptive information in advance of testing and listen carefully to all test instructions. You should inform an examiner in advance of testing if you wish to receive a testing accommodation or if you have a physical condition or illness that may interfere with your performance on the test. If you have difficulty comprehending the language of the test, it is your responsibility to inform an examiner.
5. Know when and where the test will be given, pay for the test if required, appear on time with any required materials, and be ready to be tested.
6. Follow the test instructions you are given and represent yourself honestly during the testing.
7. Be familiar with and accept the consequences of not taking the test, should you choose not to take the test.
8. Inform appropriate person(s), as specified to you by the organization responsible for testing, if you believe that testing conditions affected your results.
9. Ask about the confidentiality of your test results, if this aspect concerns you.
10. Present concerns about the testing process or results in a timely, respectful way, if you have any.

Assessing Individuals with Disabilities in Educational, Employment, and Counseling Settings

In December 1995 the JCTP began to discuss developing a sourcebook addressing assessment of individuals with disabilities. Members of the working group looking at this issue developed a needs survey. The results of the survey indicated that there was in fact interest in such a sourcebook. The theme of the needs survey results was that the book should be brief, simple, and easy to update.

The working group decided to request information from test publishers and organizations that advocate for or work with individuals with disabilities. Test publishers were requested to respond with relevant information; organizations and individuals working with persons with disabilities were asked for information, articles, and feedback on plans for the sourcebook. Based on these responses, the working group began to determine the contents of the book. The resulting sourcebook, entitled *Assessing Individuals with Disabilities in Educational, Employment, and Counseling Settings,* contains chapters addressing the following areas:

- legal, policy, and psychometric issues
- testing accommodations and score reporting
- assessment of individuals in clinical and counseling settings
- assessment of individuals in educational settings
- assessment of individuals in employment, certification, and licensing
- additional sources of information (including a section on websites addressing disabilities issues in testing)

Published in the spring of 2002, the book is currently available for purchase.

Looking to the Future

Over the past 17 years, the JCTP has developed six products and is working on two more. The committee has grown from three sponsoring associations to seven and has received financial support from a number of test publishers. It has given numerous presentations, and its work has been widely read and cited not only by professionals familiar with measurement issues but also by individuals not well versed in testing principles.

JCTP has recently created its own website (www.apa.org/science/jctpweb.html), which is updated every few months. JCTP actively monitors its bylaws and financial situation to ensure that it remains flexible enough to conduct its business and continue to advance, in the public interest, the quality of testing practices. The Joint Committee on Testing Practices may be contacted at testing@apa.org, 202-336-6000, or Science Directorate, American Psychological Association, 750 First Street, NE, Washington, DC 20002-4242.

Chapter 53
Internet Resources in Educational Assessment
A Webography
Janet E. Wall

Research, policy, and practices in educational assessment are evolving fields of inquiry and practical application. As the profession grows and metamorphoses, new theories are developed and implemented. Practitioners facing new and challenging education reform and accountability issues can benefit from the work of many talented researchers and practitioners. Though the availability of information is a potential boon to practitioners, the plethora of information and advice can make the task of staying on top of the latest research findings and proven practices enormous, even burdensome.

A very good way to keep up to date is to belong to professional associations that focus member expertise on educational assessment. Reading journals, reports, and newsletters are proactive and effective ways for educational practitioners to learn what is best for their particular situation, school, and students. Though staying current with the literature is extremely helpful, educators don't have the time or financial resources to belong to all relevant organizations and to subscribe to all relevant journals. Additionally, by the time they are published, journal articles may represent knowledge gained three or more years ago under already antiquated conditions.

Educators are fortunate in that most professional educational assessment organizations have a substantial presence on the World Wide Web, making reasonably current information relatively easily available. For the most part, reputable websites are kept up to date and offer opportunities to read current and archived articles, reports, newsletters, policy statements, and other materials on educational assessment issues. In addition, access to content-area experts may be available through directly contacting the organization. Most of the time, the statements, policies, briefs, and publications are provided without cost. In some cases, certain documents must be purchased or one is required to be a member of a particular organization to access and download the documents. As a measure of the general accessibility of information, note that all the documents and publications included on the CD that accompanies this book were found and downloaded from the Internet. They were available without cost, and are published with permission.

The web addresses (URLs) listed in this chapter were accurate and active as of the publication of this book. Bear in mind that organizations sometimes change their URLs for a variety of reasons, or on occasion, they may change the architecture and structure of their sites. If one of the addresses is no longer functioning, try locating it using a search engine such as Yahoo, Google, or HotBot.

Most documents available for download from the web are in Microsoft Word or Adobe portable document format (pdf) files. Documents in pdf can be accessed by a version of Adobe Acrobat or by Adobe Reader; the latter may be downloaded without cost from www.adobe.com/products/acrobat/alternate.html

Using an Internet search engine and entering the phrase "educational testing," I identified more than 1.3 million potential sites. After spending many hours reviewing these sites, I selected the following sites as most likely to maintain current and relevant information on assessment issues. I have grouped the sites into four categories: (a) assessment-related professional organizations, (b) test publishers, (c) related organizations, groups, and services, and d) selected federal resources.

Assessment-Related Professional Organizations

Various professional organizations specifically address issues in education and educational research and rely on assessment in a large part of their work. Those most directly supporting the proper use of assessment results in the education community are the following:

American Educational Research Association (AERA). AERA is concerned with promoting the educational process through scholarly inquiry and information dissemination. The more than 22,000 members of AERA are educators; administrators; directors of research, testing, or evaluation in federal, state, and local agencies; counselors; evaluators; graduate students; and behavioral scientists. AERA is a member of the Joint Committee on Testing Practices. Many publications, newsletters, and reports are available via its website: www.aera.net.

American Psychological Association (APA) Science Directorate. The Science Directorate of APA focuses on providing information for APA scientific and academic members. The Science Directorate's mission is to advance psychology as a science by supporting basic and applied psychological research and promoting the needs and interests of research psychologists and academicians. APA is a member of the Joint Committee on Testing Practices, and the committee's website is housed on APA's website. You can reach the APA Science Directorate at www.apa.org/science/.

American Speech-Language-Hearing Association (ASHA). ASHA is the professional, scientific, and credentialing association for speech-language pathologists; audiologists; and speech, language, and hearing scientists. ASHA is a member of the Joint Committee on Testing Practices. Various reports and policy statements on assessment practices relevant to the mission of this association can be found on the site: www.asha.org.

Association for Assessment in Counseling (AAC). An organization of counselors, counselor educators, and other professionals, AAC was created to advance the counseling profession by providing leadership, training, and research in the creation, development, production, and use of assessment and diagnostic techniques. The mission of AAC is to promote and recognize scholarship, professionalism, leadership, and excellence in the development and use of assessment and diagnostic techniques in counseling. Information on assessment issues, test reviews, and other important information can be found on this website: http://aac.ncat.edu

Association of Test Publishers (ATP). ATP is a nonprofit organization representing providers of tests and of assessment tools or services related to assessment, selection, screening, certification, licensing, and educational or clinical uses of tests. The ATP membership comprises the leading publishers and assessment service providers in the modern testing industry. Among ATP's many goals is to promote and preserve the general welfare of testing and its value to society in all its forms and uses, and to encourage programs of education and training. The organization has many statements and publications on assessment available on its site: www.testpublishers.org.

National Association of School Psychologists (NASP). NASP's primary goal is to promote educationally and psychologically healthy environments for all children and youth. The organization accomplishes this mission by implementing effective research-based programs that prevent problems, enhance independence, and promote learning. NASP is a member of the Joint Committee on Testing Practices. Many policy statements, position papers, and responses to frequently asked questions can be found on its site: www.nasponline.org.

National Association of Test Directors (NATD). NATD is an association of professionals who administer assessment programs in K–12 public educational settings. NATD is a member of the Joint Committee on Testing Practices. Various publications, legislative information, and useful links can be found on this site: www.natd.org.

National Council on Measurement in Education (NCME). NCME is devoted to educational assessment issues. Through its many activities, it attempts to advance the science of measurement in the field of education and to improve measurement instruments and applications. NCME is a member of the Joint Committee on Testing Practices. It disseminates information on assessment issues, ethics statements, and a variety of other information through its website: www.ncme.org.

Joint Committee on Testing Practices (JCTP). The JCTP site provides information on the activities of the committee. Available for download from this site are several of the products produced by working groups of this organization (see chapter 52). Many of these products are available without cost, and dissemination is encouraged. This organization has representatives from many of the assessment and assessment-related professional organizations, including ACA, AERA, APA, ASHA, NASP, NATD, and NCME. The address is www.apa.org/science/jctpweb.html.

Test Publishers

Educational assessment has become a profitable business. As states and school districts increase their reliance on tests and assessments to substantiate progress in educational reform and to document accountability, test publishers are benefiting by assisting in the creation of instruments that serve that need. Because the purposes of testing and assessment are varied, many testing companies have been founded and have grown over the years; some of these companies are very large whereas others are small and specialized. Following are the names and URLs of the most prominent testing companies.

The companies will not be described, as it would be impossible to represent completely the various products and services they offer for purchase. Additionally, it is not the purpose of this chapter to promote one testing company over another. The various companies' products and services are best judged on a case-by-case basis and depending on your specific needs. One way to judge the reputability of a testing company is by whether or not it formally subscribes and endorses various ethics and professional assessment standards such as the *Standards for Educational and Psychological Testing* or the *Code of Fair Testing Practices in Education* (information that should be available on the website). Many of the websites also make available various ethics statements, policy papers, primers on testing, and white papers for use by educators and customers. Many of the offerings are highly useful.

ACT, Inc. www.act.org
American Guidance Service Publishing. www.agsnet.com
The Chauncey Group International. www.chauncey.com
The College Board. www.collegeboard.com
Computer Adaptive Technologies, a division of Promissor. www.promissor.com
Consulting Psychologists Press, Inc. www.cpp-db.com
CTB/McGraw-Hill. www.ctb.com
Educational Testing Service. www.ets.org
ETS K–12 Works. www.etsk-12works.com
Harcourt Educational Measurement. www.hemweb.com
Lightspan eduTest Assessment. www.edutest.com
KUDER, a service of National Career Assessment Services, Inc. www.ncasi.com
Measured Progress. www.measuredprogress.org
MetriTech and IPI. www.metritech.com
NCS Pearson. www.ncspearson.com
The Princeton Review. www.princetonreview.com
Psychological Assessment Resources, Inc. www.parinc.com
Riverside Publishing. www.riverpub.com
Thompson Prometric. www.prometric.com

Related Organizations, Groups, and Services

Some education-related organizations are not professional membership organizations or may not have testing and assessment as a primary mission. Others may not be actively involved in assessment issues as a primary mission, yet they have influence over both educational policy and actions that may involve assessments as well as having as members educators who use them. Here are some of these organizations:

American School Counselor Association (ASCA). ASCA is the national organization representing the school counseling profession. The organization provides professional development, enhancement of school counseling programs, and research on effective school counseling practices. This organization has created a number of policy statements and standards for counselor competencies in assessment jointly with the Association for Assessment in Counseling (AAC) and other organizations. www.schoolcounselor.org

American Association of School Administrators (AASA). AASA is an organization of more than 14,000 educational leaders with a mission to support and develop effective school system leaders who are dedicated to the highest quality public education for all children. The four goals of AASA are to improve the condition of children and youth, to prepare schools and school systems for the twenty-first century, to connect schools and communities, and to enhance the quality and effectiveness of school leaders. Several publications on assessment and educational improvement can be obtained from this website: www.aasa.org

American Counseling Association (ACA). ACA represents about 50,000 counselors across the country. ACA is a member of the Joint Committee on Testing Practices. Policy statements and assessment information can be found on this website as can information on the goals and activities of its many divisions, such as AAC: www.counseling.org

Buros Institute of Mental Measurements. This site represents the renowned Buros products and services, including test reviews and searches. This organization is generally considered the most comprehensive source of test information. The reviews of tests can be very useful to individuals who are searching for an instrument with a particular purpose and set of characteristics. www.unl.edu/buros

The Business Roundtable (BRT). This group of business leaders is actively involved in formulating and recommending public policy for the nation. The group sponsors several task forces, each led by a CEO. Among these various task forces are some dealing with education and the workforce, the area most relevant to assessment issues. Various policy statements and recommendations can be obtained from their site: www.brtable.org

The Council of Chief State School Officers (CCSSO). Representing the state superintendents of schools, this organization has many policy statements related to accountability and assessment available on its website: www.ccsso.org

Consortium for Policy Research in Education (CPRE). CPRE is a group of researchers and educators from the University of Pennsylvania, Harvard University, Stanford University, University of Michigan, and University of Wisconsin–Madison. The aim of this consortium is to conduct and disseminate practical research for improving elementary and secondary education. Many documents of interest to educators are available from the CPRE site: www.cpre.org

Education Commission of the States (ECS). This organization works with state educators and legislators to improve educational performance in schools. Statements and policy comments on assessment can be viewed on this site. Accountability issues are of utmost importance to ECS, and related papers are well represented on this website: www.ecs.org

Education Week (EDWeek). Most of the print publication is available online, and it generally contains the latest education news, information on special issues, and special reports. Some of the most useful special reports on national issues can be downloaded from this site. Examples are Quality Counts, a research report discussing important education issues such as quality indicators, technology, and other areas of educational concern. A weekly email update is available by signing up on this site: www.edweek.com

ERIC Clearinghouse on Assessment and Evaluation (ERIC/AE). This clearinghouse is the repository for assessment and testing articles in education. It has a searchable database and supports an online journal on assessment. www.ericae.net

ERIC Clearinghouse on Counseling and Student Services (ERIC/CASS). This clearinghouse solicits, reviews, publishes, and archives digests, reports, policies, and other publications on counseling issues, including assessment and testing. Documents are available via topical searches. Chapter 53 provides information on the full range of ERIC resources for use by educators. http://ericcass.uncg.edu/.

Fair Access Coalition on Testing (FACT). This coalition of organizations focuses on protecting properly trained test professionals (who belong to coalition member organizations) from unreasonable restrictions by regulatory or legislative agencies: www.fairaccess.org/

National Assessment Governing Board (NAGB). This bipartisan organization includes governors, legislators, school officials, and business representatives, among others. NAGB oversees and sets policy for the National Assessment of Educational Progress. www.nagb.org

National Association of State Boards of Education (NASBE). This site has a rich inventory of reports, policy statements, and briefs related to several educational assessment issues. www.nasbe.org

National Board for Certified Counselors (NBCC). NBCC and its affiliates are the credentialing body for counselors. NBCC was created to establish and monitor a national certification system for identifying those counselors who have voluntarily sought and obtained certification, and to maintain a register of those counselors: www.nbcc.org

National Center on Educational Outcomes (NCEO). This group of researchers monitors testing in states and produces reports on the status of various practices in use around the country. Most impressive are the publications related to the assessment of individuals with disabilities. Most of the publications and research reports may be downloaded: www.coled.umn.edu/NCEO

National Center for Research on Evaluation, Standards, and Student Testing (CRESST). CRESST is a partnership of UCLA, the University of Colorado, Stanford University, RAND, the University of Pittsburgh, the University of Southern California, Educational Testing Service, and the University of Cambridge, United Kingdom. CRESST research and publications deal with the assessment of educational quality and issues related to the design and use of assessment systems to serve multiple purposes. A variety of papers, reports and other publications can be accessed through this site. www.cresst.org.

National School Boards Association (NSBA). This site provides policy guidelines on educational accountability, assessment, and reform: www.nsba.org

The **Rand Corporation (RAND).** RAND is a nonprofit, nonpartisan research organization aimed at improving policy decisions through the provision of rigorous and objective research and analysis. A number of their publications are available online: www.rand.org

Teachers College Record (TCRecord). Sponsored by Columbia University, this website provides an enormous number of downloadable publications on education issues, including the topics of testing and assessment. You need to register to gain access to the site, but registration is free. One can also submit articles to the site for peer review and subsequent publication: www.tcrecord.org

Test Locator. The Test Locator can search three ways: With the Test Review Locator you can enter the name of a test and receive references to reviews of the test. The Test Publisher Locator enables you to type in the name of a publisher and locate the contact information on that publisher. Finally, the Test Locator provides access to the ETS test file, which is a database of more than 10,000 published and unpublished tests. The Test Locator can be accessed through any of the three following web sites: http://www.ericae.net/testcol.htm, www.unl.edu/buros, or www.ets.org.

Selected Federal Resources

Board on Testing and Assessment (BOTA). Part of the National Research Council, BOTA advises the federal government on a wide range of issues concerning the science and policy of testing and assessment in education, employment, and the military. Issues addressed by BOTA include the role of assessment in standards-based education reform, the effects of high-stakes testing, the development of professional testing standards and policies to ensure appropriate test use, and the uses of assessment as tools of program evaluation and accountability: www7.nationalacademies.org/bota/

Institute of Education Sciences (IES). Established under the Education Sciences Reform Act of 2002, IES promotes rigorous, evidenced research to advance education. The Institute consists of the National Center for Education Research, the National Center for Education Statistics, and the National Center for Education Evaluation and Regional Assistance. www.ed.gov/offices/IES

National Center for Education Statistics (NCES). This government office oversees the creation and implementation of the nation's large-scale assessment program called the National Assessment of Educational Progress (NAEP). NCES is responsible for implementing the assessment plan, analyzing the results, and reporting them to the general public and policymakers. It is perhaps best known for its Nation's Report Card. NCES also collects, analyzes, and reports on various other data about schools and education: http://nces.ed.gov

National Education Goals Panel (NEGP). NEGP is a bipartisan and intergovernmental body of federal and state officials that assesses and reports on state and national progress toward achieving the National Education Goals. Many publications on standards-based reform and the use of assessment can be obtained from this site: www.negp.gov

Office of Elementary and Secondary Education (OESE). A branch of the U.S. Department of Education, OESE's mission is to promote academic excellence and to enhance educational opportunities and equity for all of America's children and families. It provides technical assistance and support to improve teaching and learning. Statements on the use of assessments in educational reform can be found on this site: www.ed.gov/offices/OESE

U.S. Department of Education (ED). The website of this federal department contains a wealth of information on federal school improvement initiatives. Various statements on school reform, accountability, and assessment are obtainable from their website: www.ed.gov

U.S. Department of Labor (DOL) Employment and Training Administration (ETA). The DOL has pulled together a variety of resources to assist educators and employers in working with and improving the capabilities of the nation's workforce. It has developed several O*NET assessment instruments—the Interest Profiler, Work Importance Profiler, Work Importance Locator, and Abilities Profiler—to assist in these efforts. Several excellent publications on the use of tests related to educational and employability issues can be downloaded from this site: www.doleta.gov.

In addition to the organizations listed here, private companies such as CISCO Systems, Microsoft, and Galton are involved in certification testing. Their sites include information on these assessments. These companies and their activities, though providing valuable contributions, are beyond the scope of this chapter.

The education profession is enriched by the active concern of numerous organizations in outlining and disseminating information, policies, reports, research, and various other documents on assessment issues. Educators can find answers and opinions on many assessment issues, assessment and education legislation, and current research by accessing these sites. Happy hunting!

An Anthology of Assessment Resources

Included with this monograph is an anthology which is the equivalent of approximately 3,000 printed pages. They cover a wide variety of topics identified by the authors and editors as relevant to persons desirous of being knowledgeable about assessment. They are organized by title, topic, and author to assist readers in locating the resources particularly appropriate to their interests.

Most basically, the anthology is intended to supplement and compliment the printed text. It does not duplicate the articles in the printed monograph. Most persons will use it to more fully inform themselves on topics covered in the printed monograph. It is unlikely that anyone will want to go through the CD from beginning to end. Use it whenever you desire to pursue a topic covered in the printed monograph in greater depth.

The files in the CD are in PDF format. This was done to accommodate the wide variety of computer platforms and computer experience of users. It also made it possible to incorporate the wide variety of materials submitted for inclusion in the CD, ranging from website pages to barely decipherable printed materials.

Since many of the topics covered are in materials undergoing constant revision and updating, it behooves the user who wants the latest word on an item to go to the original source from which the CD entry was developed, e.g. websites, professional association papers, etc.

We hope you will find this anthology a useful resource. As you use it, you learn how to navigate it more skillfully. We have devoted countless hours to removing "wrinkles" and making the CD work seamlessly for all users. However, we expect that despite our best efforts, problems may occur. We hope that you will understand that if problems do occur, it is not due to a lack of diligence on our part. It was a first-time experience for us and we are proud of the outcome, but mindful of the challenges that may beset an individual user.

How to use this CD

The *Anthology of Assessment Resources* CD contains the file *start.PDF* and a folder called *Adobe*. To start the CD, double click the file start (*start.PDF*). If Adobe Acrobat Reader is not installed on your computer, open the *Adobe* folder. Find the folder with the operating system for your computer. For the latest version of Adobe Acrobat or if your operating system is not located on the CD, go to http://www.adobe.com/products/acrobat/readstep2.html or for more information on Adobe Acrobat Reader go to http://www.adobe.com/.

Happy searching and use of this unique resource on assessment!

Garry R. Walz
Janet E. Wall